ART AS IMAGE AND IDEA

ART AS

IMAGE AND IDEA

Edmund Burke Feldman

THE UNIVERSITY OF GEORGIA

PRENTICE-HALL, INC.

Englewood Cliffs, New Jersey

ART AS IMAGE AND IDEA, *Edmund Burke Feldman*

Current printing (last digit):
10 9 8 7 6 5 4 3 2 1

PRENTICE-HALL INTERNATIONAL INC., *London*
PRENTICE-HALL OF AUSTRALIA, PTY., LTD., *Sydney*
PRENTICE-HALL OF CANADA, LTD., *Toronto*
PRENTICE-HALL OF INDIA PVT. LTD., *New Delhi*
PRENTICE-HALL OF JAPAN, INC., *Tokyo*

C

PREFACE

This book is meant to stimulate thought and discussion about art as it enters into our private lives and our common existence. At a time when splendid works of art reference and specialized scholarship are readily available, only such a purpose seemed to constitute for me a valid reason for adding to the list of books on the subject. My guiding assumption has been that works of art illuminate life as nothing else can. Therefore I have tried to address myself consistently to the task of showing what light art seems to throw on the recurring features of human affairs as I understand them. This plan has necessitated my dealing with the thematic and utilitarian values of art before taking up formal and technical considerations. Such an approach seemed desirable to gain the interest of the reader or student who wants to know how art speaks to him, what it means, and how it is useful in daily life.

Readers may wish to differ with some of my observations and conclusions or with the way they have been formulated. If so, I shall be pleased they have found the material in this volume stimulating enough to provoke questions, suggestions for modification, or outright dissent. For my part, art is too important and we should care too much about it to be content with bland acceptance or plain indifference to any serious discussion of its uses or merits. As a teacher, I should not regard myself as especially effective if students had little to say or think about following any presentation about art which I had made. Consequently, I hope the commentary in the text will serve as a starting point for further investigation and discussion of the issues raised.

A book that seeks to initiate a kind of humanistic dialogue must necessarily grow out of many such dialogues carried out over the years with teachers, colleagues, and fellow students. I was fortunate as a boy to study with men who liked to talk about art; and so the important aesthetic questions were raised for me through informal conversations long before I realized their significance to the world of learning. Afterwards, through college and university study, I acquired labels for those early questions and categories for their official answers. Now I submit them in the form of a book after they have passed through the crucible of so many anonymous conversations and encounters with art and artists that I cannot honestly say who is responsible for the ideas I mistakenly believe to be my own. But however vague my recollection of the origin of ideas and intellectual influence, I clearly recall those personalities who, as teachers or associates, have contributed to my development in the course of our mutual concerns about the arts: van Dearing Perrine, John R. Grabach, Richard Wedderspoon, Frederick Haucke, Norman Rice, Karl With, Abraham Kaplan, Stanton MacDonald-Wright, Edwin Ziegfeld, and Lyman Bryson.

In the preparation of this book I have been the beneficiary of the labors of many persons who would deserve to be named collaborators were it not for my wish to absolve them of responsibility for inadequacies in the text. Ivan Johnson of Florida State University and William Libby of the Carnegie Institute of Technology were most helpful in the initial planning of the volume. Comments and suggestions by Jerome Hausman of Ohio State University, Harold Schultz of the University of Illinois, Frederick M. Logan of the University of Wisconsin, and Thomas J. Larkin of the University of Michigan have also been valuable during the writing of the text. James M. Guiher, Jr., most patient and amiable of editors, has given his counsel generously and has adhered steadfastly to the highest standards of publishing. And to Ronald Nelson's editorial craftsmanship I owe a considerable debt—for any qualities of logic and readability the text possesses, and for painstaking attention to the details of producing a book so heavily illustrated. Harry Rinehart devised an ingenious design which he has carried out with the consummate good taste an art book deserves but so rarely receives. Also, I am indebted to the Project Planning staff of Prentice-Hall for the extra effort they were called upon to make in the production of this volume. I should like to express my gratitude to Miss June Lange for her typing of the manuscript and to Mrs. A. Louise Meglio for her loyal secretarial support during the entire period of this writing. Finally, my wife and two daughters deserve to be commended for their tolerance and forbearance during these past several years when they had only a part-time husband and father.

TO MY PARENTS

CONTENTS

PART ONE

The Functions of Art, 1

ONE

Personal Functions of Art, 4

Art and Psychological Expression.   Love, Sex, and
Marriage.   Death and Morbidity.   Spiritual Concern.   Aesthetic Expression.

TWO

The Social Functions of Art, 36

Political   and   Ideological   Expression.   Social
Description.   Satire.   Graphic Information.

THREE

The Physical Functions of Art, 70

Architecture: The Dwelling.   Large-Scale Design:
The Community.   The Crafts and Industrial
Design.

PART TWO

The Styles of Art, 135

FOUR

The Style of Objective Accuracy, 138

> The Imitation of Appearances. The Artist as Detached Observer. The Artist as Selective Eye. Variations of the Style. Devices of Objective Accuracy.

FIVE

The Style of Formal Order, 162

> The Transient and the Permanent. Kinds of Formal Order. Conclusion.

SIX

The Style of Emotion, 182

> Romanticism and Emotion. The Role of Distortion. Anxiety and Despair. Joy and Celebration.

SEVEN

The Style of Fantasy, 204

> Myth. Dreams and Hallucinations. Scientific Fantasy. Fantasy and Illusionism.

PART THREE

The Structure of Art, 219

EIGHT

The Visual Elements: Grammar, 222

Line. Shape. Light and Dark. Color. Conclusion.

NINE

Organization of the Elements: Design, 256

Unity. Balance. Rhythm. Proportion. Conclusion.

TEN

Perceiving the Elements: Aesthetics, 278

Empathy. Psychic Distance. Fusion and Funding. Closure and "Good Gestalt." Artistic Perception: Wölfflin's Categories.

P A R T F O U R

The Interaction of Medium and Meaning, 305

E L E V E N

Painting, 308

The Fugitive and the Permanent. Direct and Indirect Techniques. Frottage, Grattage, and Decalcomania. The Picture and the Wall. Beyond Collage: Assemblage, Environments, Happenings. Conclusion.

T W E L V E

Sculpture, 346

Modeling, Carving, and Casting. From Monolith to Open Form. Constructivism. Sculptural Assemblage. Niches, Boxes, and Grottoes. Kinetic Sculpture. The Crafts and Sculpture. Conclusion.

T H I R T E E N

Architecture, 396

The Classic Materials. Modern Materials. The Structural Devices. Constructors and Sculptors.

PART FIVE

The Problems of Art Criticism, 441

FOURTEEN

The Theory of Criticism, 444

The Purposes of Criticism. The Tools of Art
Criticism. Types of Art Criticism. Kinds of
Critical Judgment.

FIFTEEN

The Critical Performance, 468

Description. Formal Analysis. Interpretation.
Judgment.

Bibliography, 499

Index of Names and Works, 502

Index of Subjects, 509

PART ONE THE FUNCTIONS

OF ART

For many of us, the idea that art functions, that it is useful or necessary in the conduct of human affairs, is novel and perhaps, at best, is greeted with skepticism. We have been conditioned to regard art as nonessential, as the product of man's surplus energy and wealth. Moreover, we think of the fine arts, *les beaux arts,* as being *uniquely* useless—impractical and unnecessary for meeting the fundamental requirements of organized living. Nevertheless, the visual arts have existed, in one form or another, throughout human history, and they appear to be thriving at present. How are we to explain their survival, and indeed, their prominence for so long under such varying circumstances and among so many diverse peoples? Do human societies tolerate art and artists because of some blunder in the organization of social life? Or is art practiced and prized because it satisfies vital personal and social needs? Clearly, this book is written in support of the latter premise. I hope to show that the visual arts—painting, sculpture, architecture, industrial design, and the crafts—are everywhere around us, employed in a multitude of useful ways in the lives of all men.

Contemporary art, which is known to many persons in its exotic, experimental, and baffling manifestations, performs essentially the same functions in modern life as did its historic antecedents in earlier epochs. For art continues to satisfy (1) our individual needs for personal expression, (2) our social needs for display, celebration, and communication, and (3) our physical needs for utilitarian structures and objects. However, if it is granted that art *does* provide us with effective advertising designs, for example, as well as soaring airport terminals and handsomely designed table-ware, refrigerators, and typewriters, we are nevertheless curious about how contemporary "extravagances" in paint, concrete, metal, stone, and plastic affect the quality of our lives. We can perhaps accept the illustration for a love story in a ladies' magazine as being necessary to interest readers; and we realize that people who sell products need designers to create packages which can attract and persuade other people to make purchases. But what function is performed, or what significant need is satisfied by paint apparently splashed on a canvas which is then displayed for the amazement and/or edification of honest men? What are we to make of mysterious constructions, designated sculpture, which resemble no man or beast we have ever seen, heard about, or dreamt of in troubled sleep? Is there any reason why our time and energy should be spent in trying to understand the enigmatic work of artists who apparently have not taken the trouble to make their meaning clear? Furthermore, what connection, if any, is there between today's art and the masterworks of the past? Answers to these questions—or attempts to answer them—are what the following pages are about.

CHAPTER ONE

Although man is a social animal who must live in groups and communities in order to survive, he does, of course, have a private and separate individual existence. He can never escape the consciousness of other men and their relation to him, but he also feels that thoughts occur to him uniquely, that there are things he feels or does which are his alone. Inside each of us a multitude of events takes place, and it appears to be our nature to tell others about them if we can. To communicate our ideas and sentiments, we use many kinds of languages. The visual arts constitute one of those languages.

As an instrument of personal expression, art is not solely confined to self-revelation, that is, it does not deal exclusively with the private emotions and details of the artist's intimate life. Art also embodies personal views of public objects and events that are familiar to all of us. Basic human situations like love, death, celebration, and illness constantly recur as the themes of art, but they can be saved from banality by the uniquely personal comment the artist seems to make about them. For example, adolescence is revealed in a new light by the sculpture of Wilhelm Lehmbruck; the expectation of death hovers over every painting by Edvard Munch; and there is an irrepressible love of living in the people painted by Frans Hals. It does not matter whether

PERSONAL FUNCTIONS

OF ART

Hals' subjects were in fact somber or depressed types; when he paints them they appear to be in a cheerful mood. For the robust citizens he portrays, Hals' pictures may serve as signs of prosperity and contentment. For the artist, they are apparently *opportunities* to display his personal outlook: All in all, when the satisfactions of life are weighed against its hazards and frustrations, it is better to live and enjoy the potential for pleasure in each moment.

Perhaps all works of art function to some extent as avenues of personal expression for the artist. That role does not prevent them from serving other purposes, too. As you look at the examples in this volume, however, it should be quite clear that some works are thoroughly devoted to their official purpose. Others cannot avoid being vehicles, primarily, of the artist's personal vision and sensibility. In the modern world, this personal element has been treasured above all others. Consequently, the personal functions of art may seem today to constitute the very essence of art for artist and viewer.

Art and Psychological Expression

Visual images preceded written language as a means of communication. Here, however, we are not primarily interested in art as a vehicle for imparting information, since other languages have evolved as more effective, or more precise, instruments of communication. But we are interested in visual art as a means of *expressing* the psychological dimension of life.

Why is it necessary to distinguish between communication and expression? One reason is that art is not merely a language for translating thoughts and feelings inside of people into conventional signs and symbols outside of them which others might read; that constitutes communication in the sense that a street sign is communication. Art does this, but it also involves finding and forming lines, colors, shapes, and volumes so that they seem to mean something significant to the artist; that constitutes expression in the sense of painting a picture as opposed to lettering a sign. The materials and techniques of art become the artist's mode of expression; they *embody* his meaning since they help create it and give it objective existence. Without art, which is to say, without the use by man of particular materials in particular ways, there would be no possibility of finding objective expression for certain states of feeling and consciousness. Poems or

songs cannot have the same objective meaning as paintings or sculptures about the same subject matter; they embody a different expression, a different set of meanings, because they are made of different materials and employ different techniques. In other words, a painting *of* a tree, like a poem *about* a tree, is an objectification of feelings and states of consciousness somehow stimulated by the tree and given existence by the materials and techniques needed to create the painting or poem. Without words, syntax, rhyme, and rhythm, there would be no poem. Without colors, shapes, textures, and design, there would be no painting.

In *Man Pointing* by the late Alberto Giacometti (1901–66), we see the sculptural expression of loneliness, of the individual who is physically and spiritually remote from other men. In a similar vein is Giacometti's 1962 painting *Large Nude*. The elongation of the figure in both works, the indistinctness of the bodily parts, the attenuation of the forms, and their general lack of corporeality suggest the difficulty we would encounter in attempting to communicate with the individual, to relate to him in some personal fashion. The figure seems surrounded by silence. The discovery of feelings such as these in sculpture, and of the ideas about man they imply, illustrates how art can be the vehicle for an exceedingly intimate kind of expression. Because the sculpture is not of a distinct individual, but rather of a generalized type, we might conclude that the artist is not dealing primarily with the problem of a particular person, but is commenting about a universal problem: Men multiply their media of communication and the number of messages they transmit to each other, but they do not seem to be able, apparently, to *reach* each other; we are all isolated.

The feelings expressed by Giacometti may have more or less universal validity, but they are clearly derived from an individual, psychological appreciation of loneliness and remoteness. The portrait of a specific person, on the other hand, has fewer universal implications; it provides one of the principal artistic opportunities to search and probe the personality of an individual. At the same time, the portrait reveals the values of the artist in his approach to the search, in his choice of subject and treatment. In the portrait of *The Poet Max Hermann-Neisse* (1927), the late George Grosz (1893–1959) presents a penetrating "map" of a man (see p. 8). The artist's linear style and powerful draftsmanship, highly developed in his career as a German newspaper satirist and caricaturist, gives us an almost excessively truthful account of the bones of the skull, the veins of the temple, and the worried wrinkles of the face and forehead. The carefully drawn hands, although folded, present in themselves a portrait of agitation. The total quality of intense brooding is further accentuated by the rumpled clothing, whose folds seem to be in turbulent motion. Any portrait painter possesses the means to ennoble his subject, mini-

ALBERTO GIACOMETTI, *Man Pointing* (1947), left. Collection The Museum of Modern Art, New York, gift of Mrs. John D. Rockefeller, 3rd.

ALBERTO GIACOMETTI, *Large Nude* (1962), right. Courtesy Mr. and Mrs. Arthur J. Kobacker, Steubenville, Ohio.

mize his defects, and to exhibit, in general, the ideal aspects of a person. But Grosz was a trenchant, brutally honest reporter; he also seemed to enjoy dwelling on the fact that man is, after all, a peculiar-looking creature. He was obsessed with the moral ugliness of his country and his civilization and used art to express the far-from-ideal character of everything he saw. Art can embody distaste and aversion, too. Even in a man George Grosz presumably liked (the portrait situation here is intimate), he could not help seeing the frightening countenance of

GEORGE GROSZ, *The Poet Max Hermann-Neisse* (1927), left. Collection The Museum of Modern Art, New York. Purchase.

JUAN GRIS, *Portrait of Max Jacob* (1919), right. Collection The Museum of Modern Art, New York, gift of James Thrall Soby.

sickness, ugliness, and, possibly, cruelty as well.

The *Portrait of Max Jacob* by Juan Gris (1887–1927) shows a subject of about the same age in a similar pose. But here the effect is much more placid and serene. Indeed, the Grosz seems to express the restless Gothic or Germanic temperament while the Gris exhibits the more relaxed and classic qualities of the Mediterranean world. The drawing is excellent in the latter, too, but the artist is unwilling to approach caricature; the gentleness of the sitter is emphasized. The artist does not flatter or idealize his subject; rather, he seems to be making a chart of the convolutions of his face, hands, and body, as if in preparation for the execution of a painting. Nevertheless, a quality of gentle humanity and inner repose emanates from the portrait, a work of high accuracy and delicacy of feeling *and also* of penetrating psychological insight.

The portrait is plainly suited to the expression of personality, but the landscape presents a different psychological problem. Still, in *An April Mood* by Charles Burchfield (1893–), we see the anthropomorphic possibilities of nature when man seeks to project his moods upon her. The trees, stripped of leaves, give Burchfield the opportunity to characterize them as witches or druids or heroic relics, and by exaggerating the menacing character of the dark clouds which frame the brightly illuminated forms in the center of the picture, the artist creates a dramatic, emotionally charged stage. Nature provides theatrical occasions, of course, but only because men see in them the working out of their own private dramas of menace and threat, fear and resistance, deliverance and jubilation. Thus, in this painting, the upraised arms of the trees and shrubs seem to be joined in a weird, natural imitation of primitive human sun-worship.

An intriguing example of art as psychological expression is seen in George Segal's *The Dinner Table*. Mr. Segal (1925–) makes sculptures by placing rags plaster-soaked on the bodies of his models. After the plaster sets, the rags are taken off the model and assembled into a single cast plaster figure. His final forms, therefore, are replicas of living forms without the exaggeration or simplification which would result if the sculpture were carved or modeled. The artist then installs his props to create a "real" environment. Segal seems to find his creative role in the perception and organization of commonplace people in commonplace situations; he does not display sculptural virtuosity. The whiteness of the plaster figures, which are quite naturalistic in all respects except color, is contrasted with the complete realism of the actual materials and objects used as props. This whiteness usually suggests the purity of form and idealization of type which we associate with classical Greek sculpture. Instead, we are presented rather grubby, stolid, ungraceful figures. They are neither ugly nor handsome, strong nor weak; neither friendly, hostile, nor interesting. The artist's theme is *the ordinariness, the banality, the artlessness* of our everyday environment and of many of the people in it. His technique of using plaster-soaked cheesecloths as the actual surfaces of his figures results in a lumpy quality. The forms lack precision and distinctness, and the lack of these qualities is ascribed to the personalities of the people the artist represents. He expresses their lumpiness, indistinctness, colorlessness, and attitude of indifference; he reveals their placid, vegetable-like character.

CHARLES BURCHFIELD, *An April Mood* (1946–55). Collection of the Whitney Museum of American Art, New York, gift of Mr. and Mrs. Lawrence A. Fleischman.

GEORGE SEGAL, *The Dinner Table* (1962). Courtesy Sidney Janis Gallery, New York.

Love as tender eroticism.

AUGUSTE RODIN, *The Kiss* (1886). Courtesy Musée Rodin, © SPADEM 1966 by French Reproduction Rights, Inc.

Love as protective concern.

MARY CASSATT, *La Toilette* (c.1891). Courtesy The Art Institute of Chicago, Robert A. Waller Fund.

Love as the impulse to possess.

ARISTIDE MAILLOL, *Desire* (1904). Collection The Museum of Modern Art, New York.

Love as compassion for living creatures.

PABLO PICASSO, *Shepherd Holding a Lamb* (1944), right. Collection of Mr. and Mrs. R. Sturgis Ingersoll; photo, courtesy Philadelphia Museum of Art.

Love as maternal pride.

JACOB EPSTEIN, *Madonna and Child* (1927). Courtesy The Riverside Church, gift of Miss Sally Ryan.

Love, Sex, and Marriage

In addition to expressing the varieties of personality and the interaction of culture and personality, art also deals with the perennial themes of love and sex, marriage and procreation. The treatment of love varies from the physical embrace of Auguste Rodin's *The Kiss*, to the maternal affection conveyed by Mary Cassatt's painting *La Toilette*, to the motherly pride displayed in Jacob Epstein's *Madonna and Child*. Humane love is expressed by Pablo Picasso's sculpture *Shepherd Holding a Lamb*, and Aristide Maillol proffers a classicized version of erotic attraction in his relief sculpture *Desire*.

The female form is commonly used as a point of departure for the expression of a wide variety of personal feelings about love and sexuality. And the work of a single sculptor, Gaston Lachaise (1882–1935), illustrates two interesting variations on a sexual theme. In the *Standing Woman* of 1912–27, the elegance of the figure's hands and feet is combined with an idealization and exaggeration of the fleshy forms associated with procreation and maternity. The sexual theme is closely related to the maternal, but the eroticism of the whole is tempered by the lightness and terpsichorean agility of the feet and the buoyant grace of the hands. By contrast, the *Standing Woman* executed by the same artist in 1932 reveals a greater exaggeration and stylization of form, with almost athletic emphasis on child-bearing and fecundity. The feet are solidly planted in the earth, and the muscles of the shoulders and

abdomen constitute an aggressive assertion of the female biological role. With less gentleness in the transitions between forms than in the early bronze, the later figure expresses procreative arrogance, and this emphasis diminishes its ability to suggest any of the tender or romantic meanings of love. In *Reclining Nude*, by Amedeo Modigliani (1884–1920), we see, in contrast to the massive fleshiness of Lachaise, a sinuous and elongated version of the female (see p. 12). She is regarded here as an object of pleasure. Her very sleep is an

GASTON LACHAISE, *Standing Woman* (1932), above. Collection The Museum of Modern Art, New York, Mrs. Simon Guggenheim Fund.

GASTON LACHAISE, *Standing Woman* (1912–27), left. Collection of the Whitney Museum of American Art, New York.

expression of satiation, of sexual fulfillment, of the subordination of all functions and meaning to the erotic. Finally, we encounter the ultimate abstraction of the female form and function in *Torse Gerbe* by Jean Arp (1887–1966). In the sculpture of Arp, almost all aspects of personality are denied in favor of a kind of impersonal sexual or biological meaning. He carries abstraction of organic forms as far as one can go without losing contact with what is, biologically and psychologically, human.

Our culture abounds with references to love in marriage, many of them attempts at skeptical humor. A great deal of the humor about conjugal life revolves around the difficulty of sustaining the romantic meanings of love long after the marriage partners have come to know each other so well that they cannot easily hold on to the mystery and illusion which feed romance. Love as romantic transcendence is most popularly expressed in the work of Marc Chagall (1887–   ), as in *Birthday*, which is, with its childlike celebration by a couple, so much in the spirit of our notions of marital obligations: the exchange of gifts on anniversaries; the perpetuation of courtesies and gallantries practiced during courtship; the repeated protestations that romance has not fled. The charm and popularity of Chagall are in good measure traceable to our belief that the substance of marriage consists of just such rituals as the one celebrated in *Birthday*.

A somewhat more cynical view of the marital relation is expressed by Oskar Kokoschka (1886–   ) in *The Tempest*, or *The Wind's Bride*. Here, the pair is seen as swirling in space, before a moonlit mountainscape in the background. Love for them, as for Chagall's couple, has performed the miracle of levitation. But while Chagall's people are magically lifted up, Kokoschka's are *swirled*. Words in both titles for the Kokoschka—"tempest" and "wind"—suggest the *sturm und drang*, the storm and stress, of a Germanic conception of human relations in general and of love in particular. As the bride sleeps, wrapped in tender and trusting emotions, the groom stares starkly and stiffly awake. Although he is physically part of the situation and is also levitated and swirled by the power of romantic love, he remains incapable of suppressing feelings of gloomy foreboding.

Carl Hofer (1878–1955), in *Early Hour*, carries the theme of *The Wind's Bride* one step further to disillusioned domesticity (see p. 14). The crisp, morning light reveals the husband, already awake, dispassionately contemplating the sleeping form of his wife. The dog asleep at the foot of the bed completes the picture of familial routine. The face of the man is not one of anxiety or apprehension as in Kokoschka; rather, its leanness, combined with the man's bald-ness, creates an ironic impression of asceticism, of intellectual resignation to the dilemma of marriage. It is interesting that in both Germanic works on marriage, the wife is shown in contented sleep, while the husband is apprehensively awake in the moonlight or skeptically contemplating the plain truths of domesticity in the clear light of morning. American films, on the contrary, for many years employed in similar situations a convention that the husband sang in the shower or went for an early gallop while his wife blissfully lay abed. The American conception of love and marriage, at least as expressed in films, tended to be similar to the Germanic so far as the bride or

MARC CHAGALL, *Birthday* (1915–23), above. The Solomon R. Guggenheim Museum Collection.

OSKAR KOKOSCHKA, *The Wind's Bride* (1914). Courtesy Kunstmuseum Basel (Art Museum of Basel); photo, Colorphoto Hinz, Basel.

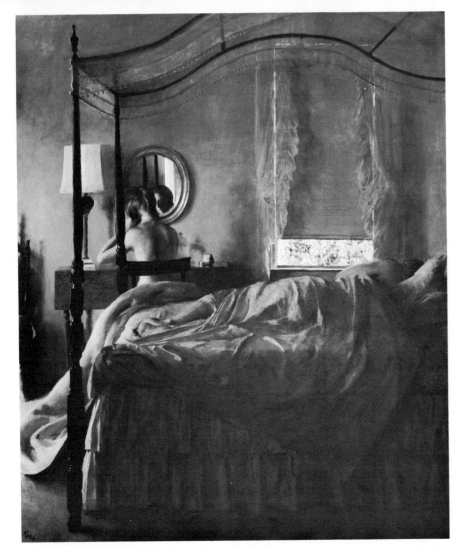

wife was concerned. But the American husband apparently suffered neither qualms nor regrets; neither did he indulge in dark speculation about the fate of his manhood under the constraints of domesticity. In painting, this attitude is expressed by the sophisticated realism of John Koch (1909–) in *Siesta.* Unlike his continental counterpart, the American male, apparently experiences marital love as a casual, uncomplicated episode in the normal routine of everyday life.

Another expression of the marital theme is seen in *Conjugal Life* by Roger de la Fresnaye (1885–1925). Here, in a ness, creates an ironic impression of asceticism, of intellectual resignation to the dilemma of marriage. It is interesting that in both Germanic works on marriage, the wife is shown in contented sleep, while the husband is apprehensively awake in the moonlight or skeptically contemplating the plain truths of domesticity in the clear light of morning. American films, on the contrary, for many years employed in similar situations a convention that the husband sang in the shower or went for an early gallop while his wife blissfully lay abed. The American conception of love and marriage, at least as expressed in films, tended to be similar to the Germanic so far as the bride or

MARC CHAGALL, *Birthday* (1915–23), above. The Solomon R. Guggenheim Museum Collection.

OSKAR KOKOSCHKA, *The Wind's Bride* (1914). Courtesy Kunstmuseum Basel (Art Museum of Basel); photo, Colorphoto Hinz, Basel.

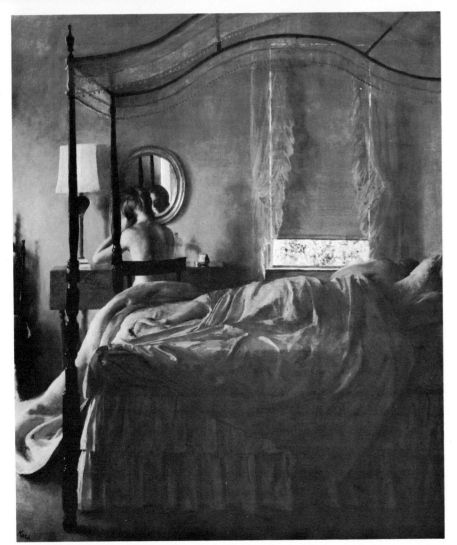

Love as a domestic quandary.

CARL HOFER, *Early Hour* (1935), above left. Courtesy Portland Art Museum, Portland, Oregon.

Love as a proletarian triumph over the requirements of comfort.

BARBARA ADRIAN, *Bed of Stones* (1964), above right. Courtesy Banfer Gallery, Inc.

Love as an extension of upper-class leisure.

JOHN KOCH, *Siesta* (1962), at left. Courtesy Dr. and Mrs. James Semans; photo, Geoffrey Clements.

wife was concerned. But the American husband apparently suffered neither qualms nor regrets; neither did he indulge in dark speculation about the fate of his manhood under the constraints of domesticity. In painting, this attitude is expressed by the sophisticated realism of John Koch (1909–   ) in *Siesta*. Unlike his continental counterpart, the American male, apparently experiences marital love as a casual, uncomplicated episode in the normal routine of everyday life.

Another expression of the marital theme is seen in *Conjugal Life* by Roger de la Fresnaye (1885–1925). Here, in a work by an early follower of Cubism, the process of breaking up the figures and converting them into geometric forms has begun and is most visible in the treatment of the hands and faces. But correspondence to visual reality remains strong, sufficiently strong to resist the depersonalizing effects evident in fully developed analytic cubism. There is about this couple a casual, comradely quality which is accentuated by the matter-of-factness of the woman's being nude while her clothed husband reads the newspaper and enjoys his pipe. Their relationship seems to exhibit a kind of mutual indifference based on the familiarity and comfortable intimacy of the long-established marriage. The composition of the painting strengthens this idea through the manner in which the figures lean on each other, while the principal lines and masses tend to seek the center and to lock the figures into a tight formal structure. There is a slight resemblance between the female figure in this work and the one in *Le Déjeuner sur l'Herbe* by Édouard Manet (1832–83), where we also find a scene of relaxation in which clothed male figures are juxtaposed with the female nude. The Manet painting, executed in 1863, caused a great scandal because of this association and because of the contemporary, as opposed to classical or allegorical, treatment of the subject

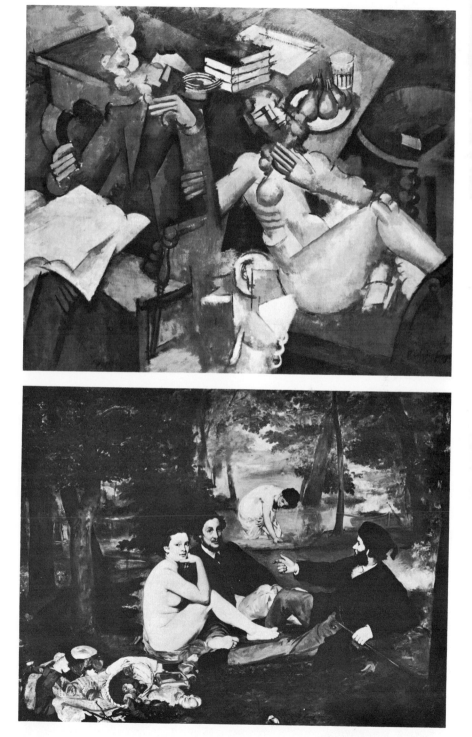

ROGER DE LA FRESNAYE, *Conjugal Life* (1912), top. Collection The Minneapolis Institute of Arts, John R. Van Derlip Fund, 1952.

ÉDOUARD MANET, *Le Déjeuner sur l'Herbe* (1863). Courtesy Musée du Louvre, Cliché des Musées Nationaux.

GEORGE GROSZ, *Couple* (1934). Collection of the Whitney Museum of American Art, New York.

Figure of a Chief, Bena Lulua, Belgian Congo. Copyright 1967 by The Barnes Foundation.

matter. However, the work of la Fresnaye is much less shocking since the subject is *conjugal* life and the cubist style has shifted emphasis from any hint of eroticism to the manner of organizing forms in pictorial space.

Clearly, the many meanings of love find varied expression in contemporary art. If one quality can be said to characterize the modern approach to the subject, it is candor and, with notable exceptions like Chagall, a refusal to sentimentalize romance. On the contrary, a bitter comment on marriage, such as is seen in *Couple* by George Grosz, is probably a more accurate, if exaggerated, expression of contemporary feeling about the institution which St. Paul said was preferable to burning.

In summary, the attitudes which artists express toward women and marriage in their work can serve as an interesting index of values prevailing in their particular cultures. Such works also constitute evidence of the capacity of art to deal with intimate psychological themes in all their variety and subtlety. In Lachaise we found the sexual-reproductive attributes of woman glorified, but at the expense of her femininity and completeness of personality. And in Modigliani we saw frank admiration for the sexual-hedonic qualities of woman: Once again, she was a useful *thing,* but not a person. For Chagall she was a little girl; for Kokoschka and Hofer an enigma, a source of puzzlement; for la Fresnaye a comfortable article to have around the house. These themes and attitudes are not new; they confirm what men have always known—that the holy bond has its problematic aspects. The contemporary artist, however, has been candid enough, or perhaps tactless enough, to say so.

Death and Morbidity

Death has fascinated and frightened man from his earliest records to the present moment. He has never been able to solve to his emotional satisfaction the mystery of how vitality and personality inhabit matter during one instant and depart from it in another. From the paleolithic portrayal of dead animals in the dark recesses of caves to the primitive African sculptures of departed chiefs and ancestors (see *Figure of a Chief* from the Belgian Congo) art has given form to man's attempt to understand, if not to master, the fear and enigma of death. While science advances in its ability to control the causes of death, art expresses the anxiety of contemporary man about the finality of death. Art has always done so. Indeed sculpture, particularly, had its origins in ancient efforts to provide a life-like body for the departed soul to inhabit. The monuments of Egyptian art were, in their principal motivation, enormous, state-supported enterprises aimed at overcoming the anxiety which attends the death of a king who is revered as a god. It might be said that the modern artistic treatment of mortality represents an extension of the anxiety and concern which everyone feels, but which in ancient times was given expression mainly for the benefit of chiefs and kings.

ARTISTIC EXPRESSIONS OF MORTALITY

A lithograph by Käthe Kollwitz (1867–1945), *Death and the Mother*, vividly expresses the almost insane terror which grips a mother whose child is about to be taken. The imagery gains some of its symbolic force from medieval personifications of the devil as the emissary of death. Notwithstanding our emergence from such superstitions, this work is deeply disturbing since it exploits fears which we find difficult to suppress. An impersonal phrase like "infant mortality" is here given powerful emotional content, so that one experiences dread and the impulse to strike out against the death symbol.

A strange portrayal of mortality or of fate occurs in *Death on a Pale Horse* (*The Race Track*) by the American painter Albert Pinkham Ryder (1847–1917). Here the symbol of death carries his conventional attribute, a scythe (to cut down lives), as he rides a white horse around a race track. No one is present to view the sinister race, which curiously involves no competitors. Like other paintings by Ryder, this work looks as if it were dreamed.° Although the figure is unmistakably the spectre of death, the question remains, how does he accomplish his grim task? Perhaps the artist's mythic imagination is at work. The ancients, for example, believed in myths which described the world as being held by a thread, or as

°It *appears* to have been dreamed. Actually, the painting was created in response to the death of a waiter Ryder knew, a man who gambled his savings on a horse race, lost his money, and committed suicide. But we should not let the actual motivation for creating the painting interfere with any reasonable interpretation we can make of the final result. See Chapter Fifteen for a discussion of *interpretation*.

being supported by a brawny god condemmed or tricked into taking it as his burden. Does Ryder's painting mean that death continues to take souls so long as his mysterious figure continues to race around the track with his scythe held aloft? Is the track a symbol of the *orbis terrarum*, the circle of the lands, the world? If so, we have a magical *explanation* of death, a primitive use of cause and effect which operates in dreams and in myth but which our waking minds will not accept. Unlike the Kollwitz, this work is not disturbing: It lacks her vivid realism, and the victims of death are not seen—they are an absent, abstract multitude. If this interpretation of the painting is correct, the rider, the horse, and the track represent the operation of an inevitable process—the universal, necessary passing away of lives con-

KÄTHE KOLLWITZ, *Death and the Mother* (1934). Courtesy Erich Cohn.

ALBERT PINKHAM RYDER, *The Race Track* or *Death on a Pale Horse* (c.1910). Courtesy The Cleveland Museum of Art, purchase from the J. H. Wade Fund.

ical realism is more thoroughgoing than that of Kollwitz, who employed a conventional death symbol. Munch confronts the actual death scene and, in particular, studies its impact upon a child. The child is not too young to understand the full meaning of the event, yet she does not possess adult mechanisms for protecting herself, for softening the blow. The date of this painting is 1899–1900, a time when the confrontation of harsh reality and strong emotion was not encouraged in art, and was avoided, if possible, in life. In Edvard Munch we have a model of the heroic artist who is not afraid to employ his skill to examine reality, using the best available tools of psychological analysis and visual investigation to carry out the task.

The Passion of Sacco and Vanzetti by Ben Shahn (1898–   ) deals with the death by execution of two men convicted of participating in an anarchist bombing. The mourners are represented as "respectable" members of society who have played a role somehow in the miscarriage of justice leading to the execution of the men. The background shows the courthouse and a portrait of a jurist taking the oath. In a scene heavy with irony, lilies, symbols of resurrection, are carried over the open coffins of the dead men, illiterate but not ignorant immigrants who were unfairly tried by a highly prejudiced judge. Shahn reveals Sacco and Vanzetti in death as defenseless, foreign-looking, harmless. Their mourners look guilty and hypocritical. The picture is a work of moral and social indignation: outrage at the society which takes such cruel vengeance, and compassion for the two "little" men caught up in large events which destroyed them. In this

EDVARD MUNCH, *The Dead Mother* (1899–1900). Courtesy Kunsthalle Bremen.

BEN SHAHN, *The Passion of Sacco and Vanzetti* (1931–32), from the Sacco-Vanzetti series of 23 paintings. Collection of the Whitney Museum of American Art, New York, gift of Edith and Milton Lowenthal in memory of Juliana Force.

tingent upon the race of Death around a magic circle.

The Dead Mother by Edvard Munch (1863–1944) is a work of infinite pathos in its feeling, not so much for the mother who is beyond suffering, but for the child who holds her hands to her ears as if to stop the *sound of death*. This is a work whose psychologwork, death is not a mystery nor an adversary to be overcome. Death is understood as the very matter-of-fact, logical consequence of man's mistreatment of man. Our emotions are mainly enlisted against the entire human and social apparatus which kills. But the fact of death itself is treated quite objectively and dispassionately.

In *Girl before a Mirror,* Pablo Picasso (1881–   ) presents some of the morbid anticipations of a young girl as she becomes aware of her impending biological role in womanhood. A kind of X-ray representation of the actual figure on the left and her reflection in the mirror on the right shows the spinal cord and the shapes of internal organs related to reproduction and nurture of the young. The serene and innocent face of the girl is reflected in the mirror by a dark, hollow-eyed visage, surrounded by black and blue moon-shaped crescents. The head on the left is partly surrounded by a bright halo, a sunny nimbus, with a bright yellow passage on the side where a shadow would be expected. This clear-eyed

"sun-face" can be seen as a symbol of unclouded youth and vitality; the "moon-face" in the mirror presents the fearful aspect of death. The girl's arm is shown in motion, reaching across to the mirror and to the apparition which holds the image of her fears. Since the painting is divided vertically into two equal parts, the arm moving across the picture serves to unite the halves compositionally, and, what is more important, psychologically. It is a gesture which represents the end of innocence and a touching expression of sympathy for that other self—the self which may die in the act of bringing life into the world. The painting represents a remarkable achievement of sympathetic imagination and insight on the part of a man into the understandable apprehensions of a girl emerging from adolescence. It should be compared to the more naturalistic treatment of the same theme by Munch in *Puberty,* an equally haunting work, and to the lithograph, *Adolescence,* by the English artist Gerald Brockhurst (1890–   ).

Anticipating her womanly role, a girl confronts a premonition of her own death.

PABLO PICASSO, *Girl before a Mirror* (1932), left. Collection The Museum of Modern Art, New York, gift of Mrs. Simon Guggenheim.

The crisis of adolescence experienced as biological dread.

EDVARD MUNCH, *Puberty* (1895), center. Courtesy Nasjonalgalleriet, Oslo.

The onset of womanhood is discovered in a magical awareness of the body's opulence.

CHARLES BROCKHURST, *Adolescence* (1932), right. Courtesy Collection of Syracuse University.

ARTISTIC EXPRESSIONS OF ILLNESS

Just as the modern expression of love tends to be characterized by candor and a certain skepticism so far as marriage is concerned, the art of our time also confronts illness and disease frankly and courageously. The artist is, of course, interested in pathology, not from a medical standpoint, but as part of the human condition. The artist is not fascinated with the details of morbidity for its own sake, but rather refuses to ignore a whole dimension of experience which helps to define man.

One of the earliest nineteenth-century treatments of mental illness is seen in the *Madwoman* of Théodore Géricault (1791–1824). The artist scrutinizes the woman as carefully as she herself apparently examines some real or imagined threat. She seems to be terrified and deluded at once. But without our knowledge of the subject

and title of the painting, would we not interpret this work as a shrewd study of character, as the portrait of a somewhat suspicious, possibly eccentric French peasant woman? The painting by Géricault should be compared with *The Madwoman* by Chaim Soutine (1894–1943), which was painted in 1920, approximately one hundred years later. Here the artist attempts to convey to the viewer the *experience* of the sick person. She is presented as trembling with fear, and there is no question in our minds that she is mentally ill. Although Géricault maintains his objectivity about the subject, Soutine employs his painterly technique to enter into the life of the subject. The earlier painter is designated a Romantic because his choice of bizarre and emotionally laden subject matter constituted an effort to deal with the intensity of man's inner life by describing his abnormal behavior, his reactions in emergencies, his loss of rational control under stress. Soutine is called an Expressionist because of his subject matter and also because of the distorted, agitated style he uses to render his theme. The Expressionists took the Romantic interest in violent and extreme themes and directed it toward the act of painting itself, which became a record of the convulsions of form. Its imagery reflected the artistic reaction to social injustice and personal struggle. The frightened eyes and tortured hands of Soutine's woman bespeak her illness but also transcend it, as we recognize in her a suffering fellow human.

The Frugal Repast, an etching Picasso executed when he was himself young and very poor, portrays a gaunt, emaciated couple. The man is blind. The drawing emphasizes their almost

THÉODORE GÉRICAULT, *Madwoman* (c.1821), left. Courtesy Musée du Louvre, Cliché des Musées Nationaux.

CHAIM SOUTINE, *The Madwoman* (1920), right. Courtesy The National Museum of Western Art, Tokyo, presented by Mr. Tai Hayashi, 1960.

starving condition and also offers the artist an opportunity to attenuate their hands and bodies, endowing them with a languid as well as skeletal quality. Although the man is afflicted and both are plainly undernourished, the couple seem resigned to their situation, and the artist does not attempt to tax our normal sympathies. They have some food and each other. Neither the handicap of blindness nor the condition of extreme poverty is regarded as a deterrent to enjoying the fullness of life. The etching is a highly civilized tribute to romantic love which does not degenerate into mawkish sentimentality. What appears at first to be a morbid interest in the effect of malnutrition upon lovers becomes a human triumph over serious deprivation. The weakness brought on by hunger is converted into tenderness, as the artist discovers a peculiar kind of amorous beauty in their withered bodies.

Our political and social leaders have lately taken a serious interest in improving the lives of the poor, and consequently the nation as a whole has begun to study the details of social and personal pathology which flow from deprivation, especially when it extends over several generations. But it should not be thought that artists, in works such as *The Frugal Repast*, are attempting to gloss over the reality of poverty, to minimize the need for social and economic measures by appearing to mitigate its consequences. Some artists, to be discussed subsequently, create works designed to *encourage* changes in social life. It is nevertheless an abiding trait of art, as opposed to politics, to reveal the values people can create in any situation or condition in which they happen to find themselves.

PABLO PICASSO, *The Frugal Repast* (1904). Collection The Museum of Modern Art, New York, gift of Abby Aldrich Rockefeller.

Puccini's romantic opera *La Bohème* deals with a theme similar to Picasso's, the composer creating aesthetic values out of the love of a consumptive, dying girl for an impoverished poet. Picasso's etching, made in 1904 when the artist was twenty-two, and presumably as ardent a votary of tragic love as any hero of Puccini, followed by ten years the first performance of *La Bohème* in 1894. Both of these men succeeded in creating works which depend for their emotional effectiveness on the idea of love sustained and carried to intensity

21

because of affliction and *in spite of* the world's opposition.

There is an aesthetic—which is to say, a system of ideas about art—based on the experience of illness and the general decline of vitality. In Géricault and Soutine, we saw this interest as part of a legitimate concern with the total human condition. In Munch, death constituted an omnipresent fact of life, although, in the judgment of some, his total artistic production may have betrayed a somewhat neurotic interest in the onset of mortality. In Shahn's *Passion*, the culmination of a whole series on Sacco and Vanzetti, we encounter death as part of a satiric-ironic statement about injustice. Although the work as a whole belongs to the tradition of social protest, it is also a personal expression of the pathetic death of two simple

men. In Picasso's etching we see the outcome of an aesthetic development in which the signs of affliction or deterioration have acquired artistic, even erotic, significance. In Ivan Albright's *Self Portrait* and Karl Zerbe's *Aging Harlequin*, decline and a certain ugliness associated with senescence (compare Ghirlandaio's *An Old Man and His Grandson*) are recorded in fascinating detail. Zerbe (1903–) endeavors to enlist sympathy for the harlequin and views him in a dignified light despite his ravaged countenance. Albright (1897–) presents himself with familiar personal objects, drinking champagne and contemplating with equanimity the fate which is clearly detailed in his face. This artist portrays aging not so much as a psychological or spiritual condition, but as a stage of life in which the processes of disease and deteriora-

IVAN ALBRIGHT, *Self Portrait* (1935), left. Courtesy The Art Institute of Chicago, lent by Mr. Earle Ludgin.

KARL ZERBE, *Aging Harlequin* (1946), center. Courtesy Dr. and Mrs. Michael Watter.

DOMENICO GHIRLANDAIO, *An Old Man and His Grandson* (c.1480), right. Courtesy Musée du Louvre, Cliché des Musées Nationaux.

tion have grown progressively stronger than the forces of vitality and renewal.

Perhaps the ultimate fascination with deterioration is seen in the work of Hyman Bloom (1913–) and of Alberto Burri (1915–). Bloom, an American painter, reveals in *Corpse of an Elderly Female* a fascination with death and decay unmitigated by any artistic device which might soften its clinical accuracy. Bloom's interest in dissection and in cadavers can be interpreted as a reaction to the slaughter which took place during World War II. Thus, the events of history added to a fascination with the painting of flesh, as exemplified by Rembrandt's *Slaughtered Ox*, possibly account for Bloom's choice of theme. Working abstractly, but with a different clinical emphasis, is the Italian artist Alberto Burri. His *Sacco B.* is made of burlap sacking, stretched and sewn around what appears to be an open wound or incision. Burri, who was a military doctor, creates compositions which seem to be visual variations based on surgical operations, the dramatic focus of which is the opening in the flesh. One can view them as organizations of gauze, burnt wood, burlap, and other materials, but their arrangement seems to have a hidden purpose. When the rents in the sacking are seen as the result of some mysterious surgery, Burri's surfaces become animated with meaning; they are related to disease; wounds and surgery are presented as a kind of primitive handicraft, and a

The clinical ritual of surgery converted into aesthetic drama.

ALBERTO BURRI, *Sacco B.* (1953). Courtesy the artist.

HYMAN BLOOM, *Corpse of an Elderly Female* (1945). Courtesy Swetzoff Gallery; photography by Sandak, Inc., N.Y.C.

REMBRANDT VAN RIJN, *Slaughtered Ox* (c.1655). Courtesy Musée du Louvre, Cliché des Musées Nationaux.

The ritual of surgery portrayed as a triumph of mind over flesh.

THOMAS EAKINS, *The Agnew Clinic* (1889). Courtesy The University of Pennsylvania.

rather disorderly death seems to hover over the whole. It is a far cry from the Thomas Eakins painting of modern surgery in 1889, *The Agnew Clinic,* with its progressive and optimistic presentation of surgical technique.

Although examples could be multiplied, we have seen how one of the personal functions of art—in the modern era as in the past—is the confrontation of death and all its attendant events and feelings. If art does not help us postpone death or the decline of our powers, it *does* help us to face the experience, to see it as part of the gamut of life. Art expresses our fears, curiosities, and aversions about death, and in so doing adds to the interest and variety of life.

Spiritual Concern

We should distinguish between an art of spiritual concern and religious art. Usually, religious art is the expression of collective ideas about man in his relation to divinity. Sometimes it possesses spiritual qualities. But at other times, even when it is successful in its mission, it functions chiefly as education or history or as a kind of visual preaching. Nonreligious art may evince spiritual qualities, as in van Gogh's *The Starry Night* (see p. 26); yet ostensibly religious art may have little spirituality, as in *Christ Preaching at Cookham* by Stanley Spencer (1891–   ). Rouault's works, in contrast, possess spiritual content whether the subject matter is sacred as in *Christ and the Apostles* (see p. 27) or secular as in *Three Clowns.*

What can account for this paradox? Religious art tells a sacred story, or enjoins right behavior, or endeavors to sustain faith. But spiritual art endeavors to be a revelation of the divine in human nature and in the world. That is to say, spiritual art tries to declare the immanence of the divine in the world, often finding it in unexpected places. But it does not come to us with appropriate labels, and its creators may not necessarily think of their work as having a spiritual quality. Furthermore, spiritual art expresses the *questions* an artist may have about man's place in the universe, whereas religious art tends to deal with the *answers* which have been institutionally established. We might define spiritual concern, so far as the present discussion is concerned, as *the personal search for values through art.*

24

For a certain kind of artist, work is an effort to discover meaning in the world through the materials, processes, and stylistic language of art. Particularly in the modern era, the artistic enterprise is identified with search, investigation, and inquiry. In the past, artists, like other men, were more certain about the meanings and purposes of life, hence they tended to concentrate mainly on giving elegant and finished expression to the commonly accepted conceptions of man and existence. But the modern era has witnessed a profound change in the artistic expression of values. The industrial, scientific, and political revolutions of the eighteenth century ultimately caused an almost universal questioning of traditional dogmas and philosophies about the nature of man, the purposes of his existence, his relations to other men, and his relation to the divine. And

although these dogmas and assumptions have been questioned or sometimes abandoned, our era has not been especially successful in providing alternative assumptions which remain tenable even for the period of one lifetime. In other words, the intellectual, spiritual, and artistic activity of our time has been devoted to questioning and searching. Consequently, works of art which deal with personal values are characterized more by the expression of doubt and uncertainty than by conviction and the assumption that artist and public share some orthodoxy.

It is common to contrast the religiously centered art of the Middle Ages with the secular, "religiously indifferent" art of the present era. But this contrast is misleading. One could cite the considerable artistic effort which is expended today in the design of sacred buildings and in the creation

STANLEY SPENCER, *Christ Preaching at Cookham Regatta: Series No. VI: Four Girls Listening* (1958), left. Courtesy Arthur Tooth & Sons, Ltd., London.

GEORGES ROUAULT, *Three Clowns* (1917), right. Collection Mr. and Mrs. Joseph Pulitizer, Jr., St. Louis; photo, Piaget.

LE CORBUSIER, Chapel at Ronchamps (1950–55). Photo, Lucien Hervé.

SEYMOUR LIPTON, *Menorah* (1953). Courtesy the artist and Temple Israel, Tulsa.

VINCENT VAN GOGH, *The Starry Night* (1889). Collection The Museum of Modern Art, New York, acquired through the Lillie P. Bliss Bequest.

Three divergent examples of spirituality in contemporary art.

of the various liturgical art objects employed to enhance and facilitate the conduct of services in houses of worship. It is quite obvious, also, that Le Corbusier's Chapel at Ronchamps and a *Menorah* by Seymour Lipton (1903–) constitute examples of religious art because of their use in worship. But it is less evident that works without plain religious utility and connotation are expressive of the artist's spiritual aspiration and concern.

The Starry Night of Vincent van Gogh (1853–1890) is evidently a picture of a village at night, with particularly prominent cypresses in the foreground and exaggerated concentric and spiral emanations of light from the stars and the moon in the sky. But the flame-like shapes of the trees and the brushwork in the hills and sky tend to animate the entire scene so that everything appears to be alive and in motion. Only the houses and the church are relatively at rest. The artist endows the common features of the landscape with a kind of life they do not normally seem to possess. This sense of the aliveness of all things, not excepting inanimate objects, characterizes van Gogh's work even when he paints a chair or shoes. For him, the distinctions between organic and inorganic, animate and inanimate, or void and mass, do not exist: All of creation exhibits the divine presence. And for those of us who do not possess the spiritual gifts of van Gogh, the experience of his paintings constitutes a glimpse into a hallowed world and an opportunity to share in his "God-intoxicated" perception.

In *Christ and the Apostles* by Georges Rouault (1871–1958), we have a religious subject which also exhibits the distinctive spirituality with which this artist endows all his work. It is noteworthy that there is very little iconographic material in the painting— no conventional symbols or gestures or details of dress which might clearly identify Jesus and his apostles. We have only the downcast countenance of Christ and the vaguely Middle-Eastern head clothing of the disciples. As men, they are characterized by intensity and a certain plainness if not coarseness of feature. They are also crowded together very closely as in the photographs one occasionally sees of very humble people. Rouault's use of heavy, black lines serves not only to bind the composition together and strengthen the impact of the forms, but also to emphasize the sorrowful quality of this close-knit group.

What qualities of the work account for its spiritual character? The first is the similarity, with minor differentiations, of all the men. They are thus able, collectively, to symbolize all men, humanity. Although the Christ figure is the most highly individualized, we view the men as a group rather than as a series of distinct personalities. The second is the lack of refinement of the features, the deliberate avoidance of physical beauty. The result is an emphasis upon the nonmaterial, the nonhedonic. The colors are intense, the features are rough, and the transitions from light to dark are harsh; we are shocked out of our conventional, worldly expectations of harmony of color and elegance of shape and proportion. The third is the passive, accepting expression of the face of Jesus. This not only expresses the ethos of Christianity but also describes the body of humanity as suffering. The fourth is the huddled arrangement of the figures,

GEORGES ROUAULT, *Christ and the Apostles* (1921–28). Courtesy Mr. and Mrs. Jacques Gelman, Mexico City.

as a consequence of which they symbolize the oppressed, frightened, and victimized condition of those who are weak.

These factors, working together, express the wretchedness of the human moral condition. Obviously, they do not describe the power and mastery of man, his technological brilliance, his commercial avidity and materialistic prowess. Certain ideas at the heart of Christianity, such as the virtue of humility and the significance of suffering, are expressed so as to give them universal application. These ideas become descriptions of the spiritual condition of all men. Since the moral status of man, as seen in the work of Rouault, is substantially different from the condition of man as we commonly see him—in the midst of his prosperity, aggressiveness, and competition—we might properly conclude that the artist is attempting to reveal the authentic nature of human nature, what humanity is *really* like as opposed to what man does and seems to be.

Whereas the spirituality of Rouault grows essentially out of one

Recumbent and fallen figures as symbols of resurrection and death.

HENRY MOORE, sculpture for UNESCO headquarters, Paris (1958), left. Photo, UNESCO Volta.

Dying Gaul, Pergamum (c. 225 B.C.), right. Courtesy Musei Capitolini; photo, Oscar Savio.

insight—the moral inadequacy of mankind—we have in the sculptor Henry Moore (1898–) an artist who expresses spiritual affirmation and renewal. His UNESCO sculpture casts humanity in a monumental role. Monumental sculpture is usually employed to celebrate military triumphs, to idolize an emperor-god, a hero, or a general, and to commemorate victories of one sort or another. But Moore, if he celebrates any victory, celebrates the durability of man. The massiveness of the figure creates a powerful sense of stability, and the large forms he has abstracted from the thighs and torso are akin to the shapes of old hills and eroded mountains. The positive forms are punctuated, so to speak, with openings and hollows and surmounted by the head, which seems to symbolize the dominance of intelligence over matter. The openings and deep hollows are not merely "negative shapes" as we sometimes hear them spoken of. They are positively conceived and permit the environment to become a part of the sculpture and to interact with it. Moore's figures are meant to be installed out of doors, preferably in a natural setting, where they can most effectively stand for man and the man-made. Without dramatic devices or theatricality of any sort, this figure suggests resurgence, as if it had once been struck down, penetrated, submerged. The

forms of the sculpture, although taken from nature, have a certain arbitrary quality. Thus, they represent the outcome of human will and intelligence working on the materials provided by art and by life. The image of man here is Promethean; man suffers and is defiant. He is not morally squalid, and although his reclining position can be taken as one of defeat, as in the *Dying Gaul*, he appears prepared for physical and spiritual renewal. Compared with Rouault, Moore seems less theological, less affected by knowledge of the sinfulness and corruptibility of man. Rather, the UNESCO sculpture expresses the forces of human defiance, of an earth creature which slowly rebuilds itself, whether it knows or not that the powers of the universe will strike it down again.

Since spiritual concern in our time is expressed through questioning, uncertainty, and restlessness, it is not surprising that *motion* and *agitation* should be characteristic of some contemporary works. Certainly van Gogh used the motion implied by his patterned brush strokes to express the aliveness of everything he saw. Rouault and Moore, on the contrary, employ stable forms, possibly because the image of man is for them less uncertain. However, in Umberto Boccioni (1882–1916), perhaps the best-known of the Italian Futurists, we see motion described as the essential characteristic of modern man. *Unique Forms of Continuity in Space,* executed in 1913, constituted both the culmination of many studies of the plastic representation of movement and Boccioni's personal adaptation of the lessons of Cubism. It is, of course, an optimistic work and it possesses a gracefulness and embellishment of form which was not evident in the more cerebral works of the French Cubists. This sculpture is perhaps not entirely successful in the expression of spirituality since it surrenders too readily to the desire to create surfaces of fascinating beauty. But the artist did aim at dematerialization; he sought to convey something of the spirit of man by identifying him as a being whose solidity and stability are an illusion—an illusion which, incidentally, this sculpture cannot break down. Hence, notwithstanding the facts that the figure is not enclosed by a single continuous skin and that the movements of muscles and tendons have been permitted to break through the skin, we have a work which remains whole and coherent, which refuses to dissolve at its boundaries and merge with the environment. Thus, despite his obsession with motion and dematerialization, Boccioni preserves the unity and corporeality of man.

A more successful, if also more poignant, expression of the spiritual quandary of modern man is found in the work of Jackson Pollock (1912–56). *Number 1* (1948) shows the typical paint surface of this artist's mature style: tangled skeins of pigment dripped and spattered on the canvas, creating a seemingly infinite labyrinth of pattern and movement. Seeing the work as a whole, one is aware of an over-all

texture as well as a repetition of black, somewhat calligraphic movements overlayed with splashes, unstructured white drippings, and knots and spots of color. Because it is a huge canvas, nine by seventeen feet, one is drawn into details of the maze; only in reproduction, which is to say in reduced size, can one see it whole. The impact of Pollock's work derives from the kinetic power of the paint application and is best experienced directly. Devoid of representational elements, the painting inevitably refers the viewer back to the artist's act of executing it. Its imagery is of paths of motion, at once dancelike and trancelike, more purposive in the blacks, spotted at random with some of the colors, and enmeshed and trapped with the whites. No single movement is fathomable in terms of any intentional origin, departure, journey, and return. We seem to be looking at a multitude of voyages amid various kinds of terrain and conflicting fields of force. The movements are

UMBERTO BOCCIONI, *Unique Forms of Continuity in Space* (1913). Collection The Museum of Modern Art, New York, acquired through the Lillie P. Bliss Bequest.

JACKSON POLLOCK, *Number 1* (1948). Collection The Museum of Modern Art, New York.

attended by the expenditure of considerable energy but seem otherwise to be literally aimless. If the viewer sees beyond the picture as a continuous texture, he cannot fail to be excited by its release of energies and its uniquely repetitious, aimless, restless, antigraceful mode of movement. If he pursues particular passages, he cannot fail to feel himself entrapped, enmeshed. Summoned enthusiastically to a spectacle here or there, the viewer is shunted aside before arriving, cast into mazes and vortices from which he can be extricated only by turning away. The experience of the work, which begins as visually intriguing and exciting, may leave one frustrated and disturbed.

The disturbing features of Pollock's work would not have attracted such wide interest if they did not in themselves constitute so faithful a reproduction of the spiritual landscape of our time. All fields of endeavor and all personal biographies might reveal their similarity to Pollock's "voyages" if we could know the lives and adventures of others from the inside. There is, however, the possibility that the lack of culmination and coherence in Pollock is a feature of some but not *all* interior landscapes. That is, we may from time to time experience illusions, perhaps in dreams, that our own biographies contain small culminations, minor fruitions, and hints of achievement. But such intimations of value in our personal existence combined with the record of social purpose and accomplishment in many public realms of endeavor would not invalidate Pollock's relevance to the spiritual condition of modern man. He remains the painter of our energetic and industrious failures.

Aesthetic Expression

Aesthetic needs and impulses are not the specialized interest of a small group. Everyone seems to be concerned with what is beautiful, pleasing, or appropriate in the visual world. That is, we are interested in beauty wherever it may be found—in people, in nature, and in objects of daily use. Some artists do specialize, however, in making things which are beautiful or aesthetically satisfying *in themselves,* apart from any utility they may have. Objects created to be beautiful or intrinsically pleasing are nevertheless useful because they help to satisfy the aesthetic interests and requirements of modern men. In his earliest days man may have been concerned about colors or shapes only to the extent that they were signs of danger or of opportunity. But since his life depended on how accurately and intelligently he could see, vision was a matter of supreme importance. We still possess remarkable visual equipment and outstanding capacity for interpreting our optical experience. However, the conditions of contemporary life do not demand as much of our perceptual capacities as we are equipped to supply. Hence, some forms of visual art appear to have evolved as a means of engaging our unused perceptual capacity. Perhaps aesthetic pleasure is, in fact, the satisfaction experienced in employing to the full our innate capacities for perception.

An elementary aesthetic pleasure might be called "the thrill of recognition." Obviously, recognition has always played an important role in human survival. Its significant role in all human affairs accounts for the popularity of art which is easily recognized, which provides a multitude of cues to its origin in reality. When we *recognize* something in a work of art, we are in a sense rehearsing our survival technique, sharpening our capacity to distinguish between friend and foe. It is only a short step from the ability to perform such discriminations to the ability to enjoy perception itself, suspending all the while any impulse to fight or flee. Rather, we learn to linger over visual events and thus to maximize our delight in them.

The artist who has done more perhaps than any other to make the art of painting a source of pure visual delight is Georges Braque (1882–1963). An early associate of Picasso in the creation of the intellectual austerities of analytic Cubism, Braque employed the principles of Cubism to paint surfaces of immense sensuous appeal and decorative ingenuity. *The Round Table* shows his mastery with shape and texture and his droll wit in exploiting optical and pictorial conventions. One recognizes the room and the table easily enough, with the top tilted forward to reveal a multitude of ordinary objects: a mandolin, a knife, fruit, a magazine, paper, a pipe, an opened book, and so on. The objects in themselves are unimportant; they have shapes and colors and textures which Braque can rearrange. He can show the

top and side view of an object at the same time; he can paint opaque objects as if they were transparent; he can reverse the expected convergence of lines in perspective; he can exaggerate ornament with white lines, arbitrarily exchange light areas with shadow areas, or paint shadows a lighter and brighter color than the objects which cast them.

GEORGES BRAQUE, *The Round Table* (1929). Courtesy The Phillips Collection, Washington, D.C.

The purpose of these "violations" and surprises is not to create a painting *of* something; rather the painting must *be* something, a kind of organism which lives according to its own law. And that law seems to state that any twisting, slicing, distortion, or reversal of shape, color, and texture is justified if it can increase our delight in looking. The logic of the painting is based on the obligation to please the eye rather than reproduce a set of relatively innocuous objects.

But how does an artist please the eye? Once the logic of reproducing

appearances is abandoned, the possibilities are infinite. The painter becomes a kind of intuitive investigator of the shapes and colors and textures which singly or in combination are somehow appealing. His artistic conscience does not permit him to exploit the associations one has with objects. Any satisfactions one takes in the work must derive from pictorial organization and technique. He tries to arrive at just the right quantity and shape of, say, dark, brown, imitation wood-graining. He surrounds the table shapes with thick and thin white outlines: They flatten out the shape, destroy the illusion of deep space which has been mischievously suggested by shadows cast into the corner of the room. Three-dimensional effects are created and then flattened or penetrated, pressed into two dimensions. The viewer is forced to "read" the painting as if the walls and floor were in the same plane as the table base. There is a certain visual humor or, at least, trickery going on in Braque's painting—humor which, because it is very subtle, does not result in laughter, but which fully challenges our capacity to enjoy ourselves visually.

The development of abstract and nonobjective art has been almost identical to the development of an art of *purely* aesthetic purpose in the modern era. (Aesthetic impulses, of course, operated in the past—usually in the nonutilitarian decoration of useful objects. But we have made sensuous appeal and nonutility in art an end in itself.) As some painting and sculpture has departed (some would say it has been "liberated") from its historical and didactic functions, it has increasingly been devoted to the problems of creating new forms and experiences

JOSÉ DE RIVERA, *Construction "Blue and Black"* (1951), top. Collection of the Whitney Museum of American Art, New York.

ALEXANDER CALDER, *Spring Blossoms* (1965), bottom. Courtesy The Pennsylvania State University Collection.

which would be valid in and of themselves. Thus, in the sculpture of José de Rivera (1904–   ), *Construction "Blue and Black,"* we have a work of mathematical precision and geometric beauty. The sculpture "works" only in an aesthetic frame of reference. Practical objects may, of course, resemble the Rivera sculpture and even derive their design inspiration from it. But we have reached the point where it is not necessary to ask what this work *means* or *symbolizes;* the theme or subject-matter of the sculpture is the formal organization of the thing itself.

Alexander Calder (1898–   ) appears to have invented an entirely new sculptural genre—the mobile— which delights us with the variety of movement of its abstract shapes. His *Spring Blossoms* is a whimsical work, as are so many of his mobiles, in which the slightest movement of air in the room imparts a comic, rollicking motion to the intricately balanced parts. They shift into an infinite number of constellations, arriving at temporary periods of equipoise by wiggling, wriggling routes. Although mobiles do not resemble people or trees, their movement sometimes suggests, for example, the sway of branches or the complex anatomical maneuvers of exotic dancers. But these are only associations of the viewer, stimulated if not encouraged by this truly original and often comic artist. His art is highly intellectual and controlled, even in the latitude it provides for seemingly random motion. Moreover, it is sculpture which "uses" the atmosphere and light of the place in which it is located: The climate of the room collaborates with Calder, helping to carry out his composition.

The *Juggler* by David Hare (1917–   ) is another work in which a playful abstraction of motion is the principal theme. But motion is not intended here, as it was in Boccioni, to be a means of transcending man's physical being in order to reach the spiritual. Rather the balance, grace, and skill of the juggler become an "excuse" to fashion a curious steel "thing." It is very important to understand this recurrent idea in contemporary art: Unlike the arts of tradition in which materials were fashioned so that they might imitate appearances or express ideas about life, the contemporary arts often reverse the relationship. They endeavor to find phenomena in life which seem to suit what can be done with materials. Thus, the juggler provides the theme for a welded steel construction. Our aesthetic pleasure is based on the tension between our idea of a juggler and what has happened to that idea in the course of its embodiment in steel. This latter point demonstrates how important the expectations of the viewer are in the total experience of art. *Your* idea of a juggler contends with the *artist's* idea, which is physically, palpably there to assert its validity. Perhaps you are convinced that David Hare's construction deserves to exist independently, for its own sake. If so, you have probably gone through a process of reconciling your ideas of balance, motion, and skill with the sensations you receive from the steel object before you.

Calder's mobiles show how a new sculptural type, or genre, was developed to give expression to the artist's interest in a particular kind of motion. Hare's sculpture is, very seriously, "a thing" which arouses the idea of a juggler. Neither of these works per-

DAVID HARE, *Juggler* (1950–51). Collection of the Whitney Museum of American Art, New York.

STUART DAVIS, *Report from Rockport* (1940). Collection Mr. and Mrs. Milton Lowenthal.

form any of the world's work, from a practical standpoint. But they do something for us, as viewers: They afford pleasure or delight based on our ability to "follow" the artist as he makes curious comparisons or metaphors connecting and relating ideas, objects, memories, and sensations. Since such works of art answer no practical need, it is necessary that we approach them with a different mental set, a different logic from the one with which we confront the everyday world. We are no longer trying to prove that we can recognize a juggler when we see one; we are rather interested in finding out what special entertainment is to be had in the *difference between* the sculpture and a juggler.

One of the most charming and personal developments of Cubism was created by the late American painter Stuart Davis (1894–1964). In *Report from Rockport*, he uses flat, geometric, wriggling forms to designate the features and qualities of American places

he so enthusiastically enjoyed: street signs, billboards, gas pumps, lettering, the architecture of Main Street, noise, jazz, automobiles. The features of urban life which worry traffic engineers pleased Davis—the profusion and confusion of signs and lights which bedevil motorists; the gasoline gulches which spring up along the sides of every new highway; the dangerous speed of souped-up automobiles; the general lack of over-all design and planning. He was an early and devoted follower of jazz as played in the saloons of Hoboken and Newark; this affinity is echoed in the dynamism and rhythm of his paintings. Davis developed out of the pictorial devices of Cubism a personal style which could convey the impact of our distinctively American chaos in painterly terms. But he was not an illustrator nor a social critic, although he could be satirical. In the main, his paintings accept the disorganization, noise, and commercial blatancy of our environment. He adds to our fund of aesthetic values because he teaches us to see the unique vulgarity of the American highway and the shopping district of Main Street as gloriously funny—confused, disordered, cacophonous, but healthy.

The varieties of aesthetic expression in contemporary art are far too many to discuss with any completeness. There are works which endeavor to appeal to all the senses through the visual; there are whimsical works which themselves contain motion and which act as modulators of light, galaxies of the near-at-hand; there are visual puns and metaphors, objects which, like café performers, impersonate and make fun of their models in life; there are works which celebrate the excitement and energy of places and events we might normally regard as chaotic. Beauty, defined as ideality of form—especially when based on the human figure—is not a common trait of the aesthetic expression of our time. When the figure does appear in art it usually is revealed in unideal or ugly manifestations. We see the figure in paintings of Bacon, Dubuffet, Paolozzi, and deKooning, but it is lonely, awkward, or ungainly. The reasons for this approach to so potent and significant a symbol are complex and beyond the scope of this section. It is fair to say, however, that the aesthetic initiatives of artists and the aesthetic needs of viewers *do* meet in a variety of modes in contemporary art. Never before have the personal functions of art been so variously expressed. Perhaps the requisite attitude toward art in our time is not to deplore the fact that it is so profuse and so hard to understand, but rather to rejoice in the wide array of choices it affords for our every mood and impulse.

CHAPTER TWO

In a sense, all works of art perform a social function, since they are created for an audience. Artists at times may claim that they work only for themselves, but they mean by this that they set their own standards. The artist always hopes, secretly perhaps, that there is a discriminating and perceptive public which will admire and prize his work. Consequently, works of art which have been created in response to the most private and personal impulses nevertheless function in a context which calls for a social response and, hopefully, social acceptance.

There are, however, narrower and more specific meanings for the social function of art than the fact of its being created for the ultimate acceptance of audiences. These meanings have to do with the *character of response* which works of art evoke from various audiences. That is, art performs a social function when (1) it seeks or tends to influence the collective behavior of people; (2) it is created to be seen or used primarily in public situations; and (3) it expresses or describes social or collective aspects of existence as opposed to individual and personal kinds of experience. In all three cases, the individual responds to art with the awareness that he is a member of a group, a group which is in some way characterized or urged to act by the works of art he is witnessing. To take

THE SOCIAL FUNCTIONS

OF ART

an obvious example, the Washington Arch in New York City addresses the individual as a citizen and inheritor of the advantages commonly enjoyed by Americans because of the military and political career of the first President. Although the arch is a memorial to George Washington, one of its chief functions is to characterize everyone who sees it as a member of a society, a nation, which has been affected in significant ways by the life of the person it memorializes. Clearly, a monument demands a wide, social response along with any personal reactions which may be felt. And it speaks to people as Americans; or as descendants of pioneers; or as immigrants; or as bene-

STANFORD WHITE, Washington Square Arch, New York City (1889), above. Photo, H. Rinehart.

A sculptor from western Nigeria participates in the transformation of African society through his employment of a contemporary theme in the context of a traditional ritual of the Yoruba tribe.

SAMUEL LAROYE, Ceremonial Mask (1958), at right. Courtesy Marc and Evelyne Bernheim from Rapho Guillumette.

ficiaries of acts of bravery, wisdom in war, exploration, statecraft, and so on. Monuments and public art in general assume some common denominator in the people for whom they are made to be seen.

Whereas public art very plainly performs a social function, other works less clearly reveal social intent or effect. Nevertheless, many works of art are intended to influence social behavior; the artists may try to make us laugh at the same phenomena, to take certain

kinds of political and social action, or to see our social situation in ways which had not previously been apparent. The visual arts, like the other arts, can function in terms of praise and celebration, anger and protest, social description, satire and ridicule. In other words, art can influence the behavior of people in groups, affecting the way they think or feel and, sometimes, the way they act. Advertising art is a common illustration: Its purpose is to influence purchasing behavior. During a war, through posters, the government attempts to arouse hatred of the enemy, or to stimulate enlistments, or to increase production levels. In peacetime, artists endeavor to affect almost every conceivable kind of group behavior.

Some persons, including artists, regard art which influences social behavior as impure, as "mere" propaganda, as applied sociology, as debased art. And, given certain assumptions about the "appropriate" functions of art, they are right. Nevertheless, artists have always sought to influence collective behavior; hence, we could not present art's complete role in contemporary culture if we ignored its social functions. Furthermore, the history of art appears to demonstrate that artistic excellence is unrelated to the functions which art performs: Excellence is not a simple matter of serving noble purposes. In the final chapters, on art criticism, we shall discuss some of the determinants of artistic excellence as well as the criteria for making judgments about aesthetic value. For now, we are chiefly interested in the connections between art and social affairs.

Political and Ideological Expression

Some artists are interested in the freedom to solve the special problems of style or technique which fascinate them. Others seek the freedom to use style and technique to express their social and political views. This latter group is sometimes inclined to speak about "artistic responsibility." For them, art does not exist merely to entertain and gratify the senses; it must edify. It must play a role in the improvement of our collective existence. So long as there are political wrongs to be righted and unjust or ugly social conditions requiring change, art must participate through visual education and persuasion in the development of popular attitudes which can lead eventually to a better society. This view of artistic responsibility is opposed, of course, by those creative persons who feel they serve society best when they concentrate on the discovery of new form, the creation of new beauty, and the free and honest expression of their personal feelings.

Although the argument about the appropriate social role of the artist is not likely to end soon, it is worth observing that unfettered artistic expression is as likely to result in an art of clear social meaning as in an art of essentially personal, decorative, or aesthetic import. The different kinds of artistic expression in our present period of almost complete creative freedom are more likely based on personality differences among artists than upon varying philosophical views about the proper role of art in society. Artists are, after all, citizens who take an interest, as do other citizens, in the social and political events of their time. Despite stereotypes about the romanticism of artists and their irresponsibility or inability to function adequately in practical affairs, they are as politically and socially mature a group as physicians, businessmen, accountants, or lawyers. But just as some lawyers devote their careers to advising clients on tax matters, property closings, and the merging of corporations, while others may seek public office in order to serve in administrative and legislative roles, so also do some artists create paintings of flowers on tabletops while others portray people amid the struggles and disappointments of life in a complex civilization.

Although Cézanne could generate aesthetic emotion through his paintings of apples, other artists have required themes of more obvious human and social relevance to challenge their creative abilities. Eugène Delacroix (1798–1863) and the Romantics required great historical and political spectacles, as in *Liberty Leading the People*, one of the early monuments of revolutionary art (see p. 40). Earlier, the Greeks adorned public buildings with sculptures depicting the military struggles connected with the mythic founding of their city-states. Although the personal and aesthetic functions of art have always existed, they were never especially prominent in the totality of artistic creativity until the modern era. A career such as Cézanne's, devoted so unswervingly to the mastery of receding planes and the architectonics of pictorial space (see p. 260), is almost inconceivable before the nineteenth century. Consequently, even though contemporary civilization has brought about the cultivation and flourishing of art devoted to highly personal, very technical, or idiosyncratic tendencies, we should not forget the larger historical context: For the most part, art has been brought into being because of public need, social necessity. And even when a society is wealthy and free enough to indulge individual artists in the expression of their private and possibly capricious impulses, we nevertheless have many artists who employ political and ideological themes in their work out of choice, because of their personal interests and preferences.

In this century, Mexico has produced three outstanding painters whose work has been, in the political sense, frankly revolutionary: Diego Rivera (1886–1957), José Clemente Orozco (1883–1949), and David Alfaro Siqueiros (1898–   ). Their paintings, frequently in mural form, deal with themes like the poverty-striken condition of the Mexican masses, the conquest of Mexico by the Spanish invaders, and the exploitation of peasants by avaricious landowners. The paintings range from works of obvious political and ideological content to those in which an intense concern with human suffering is the dominant motive. *Echo of a Scream* by Siqueiros (compare this work with *The Scream* by Munch, p. 195), exhibits the emotional force of a fantastic, almost hallucinatory pictorial device employed to express the idea of poverty and deprivation. The term "echo" in the title and the repetition of the image of the screaming child, together with the anonymous, deserted industrial wasteland which is the setting, tend to generalize and extend the theme of the painting to the entire body of humanity. Presumably the hunger, pain, and abandoned condition of all derelict children is symbolized here. The emotional strategy of such works is to arouse our normal feelings of shock and sympathy. We are forced to confront unpleasant social reality. And although this painting has no specific political content, it does sieze the imagination and enlist our feelings in favor of some kind of action which can relieve suffering.

EUGÈNE DELACROIX, *Liberty Leading the People* (1830). Courtesy Musée du Louvre, Cliché des Musées Nationaux.

A particularly mordant social comment is seen in Orozco's *Gods of the Modern World,* a portion of the fresco mural in the Baker Library at Dartmouth College. An almost completely dissected corpse is shown stretched on a pile of books, where it is attended by a deathly figure in academic costume. Presumably the corpse has just given birth to an infant skeleton, also in academic cap, with the professorial skeleton acting as midwife. In the background stands a collection of dessicated academics wearing their regalia, which survives in universities today from the costumes worn by medieval pedants. This work is an example of exceedingly gruesome humor, especially since it is in the library of a distinguished educational institution. The function of the university as preserver and mediator of ancient knowledge and tradition is presented here as a necrophilic ritual. But it is true that universities have often functioned as midwives at the birth of what the philosopher A. N. Whitehead called

"inert knowledge." At any rate, this portion of the mural illustrates the capacity of the artist to satirize bitterly a respectable institution like education in its very own house; it also reveals that revolutionary impatience and disgust with established convention are characteristic of the satirist when he genuinely detests the subject he ridicules.

Diego Rivera's art has the same ideological commitment as Orozco's but its formal organization is less violent. He is perhaps the best designer and artistically the most sophisticated of the Mexican artistic "troika." Nevertheless, he drives home his political message with simple, unsubtle force. In *Night of the Rich* and *Night of the Poor* we have a morality play: The overindulgence and the corruption of the rich, engrossed in the pursuit of profit and joyless pleasures are contrasted with the huddled, innocent sleep of the poor, some of whom industriously study at night to escape from illiteracy, while middle-class types

DIEGO RIVERA, *Night of the Rich* and *Night of the Poor* (1927–28). Courtesy Instituto Nacional de Bellas Artes, Mexico.

HECTOR POLEO, *The Andean Family* (1944). Courtesy International Business Machines Corp.

in the background evince their disapproval. In these and many similar works we have the stereotyped portrayal of classes and racial groups according to standard Marxist dogma. The ideas are tremendously simplified because they are intended for the instruction of the poor and uneducated. Needless to say, such simplifications lead to a heightening of emotion and a sharpening of ideological points at the expense of social accuracy; that is, the poor are not always virtuous and the rich are not always corrupt. But the principal social and political objective of the mural is here achieved—to endow masses of ignorant people with the consciousness of their belonging to an oppressed class, and further, to arouse their violent antipathy toward

their oppressors. Just as early Christian and Romanesque artists confronted the problem of explaining in simple terms the fundamental concepts of good and evil, sin and expiation, deliverance and damnation, so Mexican revolutionary artists endeavored to explain the meanings of wealth and poverty, oppressors and victims, heroes and traitors, conquest and revolt. It is not surprising that Mexican artists, growing out of a tradition in which the influence of religion upon culture was very potent, should employ the arts in a manner similar to that of the Church, although, ironically, the doctrines of Rivera and his associates are violently hostile to religion.

In another Latin-American work, a social and political message is carried without any overt ideology—*The Andean Family* by Hector Poleo (1918–). The work is in a style of simplified, heightened realism and has the opulent color and clear, distinct forms associated with classicistic art. The figures are taller and physically better proportioned than might be the case of these people in reality. The artist has tried to present them in a very dignified, almost aristocratic manner. Yet they are humble, quiet people, possessed of an almost Grecian athletic grace. Indeed, they are somewhat reminiscent of the Spanish-grandee types Hollywood employs to play the roles of Mexican nobleman and lords of haciendas. Viewing this version of the family, gracefully gathered together on an elevated place among the Andean peaks, one feels remote from the class struggles of the proletarian masses in Rivera and Orozco, although such struggles constitute the ideological context of this work.

ARTISTIC EXPRESSIONS
OF HUMANITARIAN CONCERN

A modern industrial state contends with social and political problems radically different from those experienced in a feudalistic, agrarian society. Problems associated with the modern administration of justice, the operation of democratic politics, and the regulation of a complex economy would seem unreal and remote to people living in a state of peonage. For Americans, the impersonality of government, for example, is a legitimate theme, well-expressed by George Tooker (1920–) in *Government Bureau*. Using repetition of figure and space, like the receding images in parallel mirrors, the artist endows a governmental building with a Surrealist quality, the quality of an orderly, methodical, perfectly credible nightmare. Is this the image of federal, bureaucratic administration which lies behind so many political attacks upon "overcentralization" of power? The Jeffersonian idea of agrarian democracy was suspicious of concentration of power in centers remote from organically functioning local communities. All men in general, and countrymen in particular, seem to dread any contact with government when it is represented by "strangers," especially if they are located in buildings not unlike prisons. But can modern, predominantly urban, mass societies, as opposed to the collection of farming communities of Jefferson's day, function otherwise? Have the architectural forms been developed which can fittingly express the relation of government to people in a democracy? It would appear that modern

banks and office buildings have done a better job of eliminating authoritarian and impersonal qualities in their interiors than have governmental buildings which are, ironically enough, the creation and instrument of the people. What Tooker has done is to dramatize the loneliness and alienation felt by ordinary people when taken out of their living, organic setting and placed by necessity into the sterile, "nightmarish" interior of a typical administrative building.

Isaac Soyer (1907–) in *Employment Agency* presents an aspect of the operation of our economy in human terms. When economists speak of the different kinds of unemployment, of transitional unemployment, of the absorption of new workers by the labor market, of workers with obsolete skills, of displacement due to automation, we tend to ignore what these phrases mean in terms of the individuals affected and of their efforts to cope with an economy which seems at times to

GEORGE TOOKER, *Government Bureau* (1956). Courtesy the artist and The Metropolitan Museum of Art, George H. Hearn Fund, 1956.

ISAAC SOYER, *Employment Agency* (1937). Collection of the Whitney Museum of American Art, New York.

BERTA MARGOULIES, *Mine Disaster* (1942). Collection of the Whitney Museum of American Art, New York.

work against them. Many Americans have been fortunate enough never to experience unemployment. Many others know what it is like to look for non-existent jobs or to find that they are unqualified for the jobs that do exist. But in an economy which receives thousands of new workers each month, which is continuously changed by new technology, and which is variously affected by price, credit, interest, and tax policies, the experience of temporary unemployment, at least, with its psychological as well as economic overtones, is bound to be very widely shared. Soyer views the waiting room of an employment agency as a theater for the performance of a psychological drama, as a revelation of the motivation and anxiety of people who are out of work. Unemployment translates itself, for some, into the feeling of being unwanted by the world, and it is one of the profoundest spiritual experiences of the modern era. As an artist, Soyer offers no economic solution (indeed, economists offer no viable solutions), but deals rather with the objective qualities of the experience itself.

A sculptural work which deals with industrial phenomena in social terms is *Mine Disaster* by Berta Margoulies (1907–). The work is a kind of memorial to the wives of men who are periodically trapped, even today, by some accident in our coal mines far below the earth's surface. Of course, art describes many kinds of tragedy, but the social and psychological implications of mining accidents are stressed here. These women and their families cling to hope mingled with fear because mining accidents are so often fatal, especially if one knows that proper safety precautions have not been taken or that agencies charged with enforcing safety regulations do not always carry out their responsibilities. In this sculpture, as in many other works of social protest, the device of huddling the figures is employed together with psychological analysis of the mixed emotions of hope, suspense, and despair in the faces.

In *McSorley's Bar* (1912), the American painter John Sloan carries on the tradition of vivid reporting and accurate social description which characterized the work of the so-called "Ash Can" School. Outstanding members of this "school" were Robert Henri (1865–1929), Maurice Prendergast (1859–1924), Arthur B. Davies (1862–1928), George Luks (1867–1933), William Glackens (1870–1938), John Sloan (1871–1955), Ernest Lawson (1873–1939), and Everett Shinn (1876–1953). These men organized themselves as "The Eight" in 1908. They were experienced as reporters and illustrators, their services being essential for the illustrated dailies and monthlies which flourished at the time, before the advent and full development of photojournalism. In rebellion against the salon art of Europe, they portrayed working class themes without any hint of condescending or of discovering "picturesque" subjects in hitherto forbidden environments. Henri, who exerted the strongest influence among The Eight, can be regarded as the mediator of the great European painting tradition stemming from Hals, Velázquez, and Manet. Emphasis was on truthful representation, dramatic lighting, spontaneous brushwork, and the capture of transient movement. Social themes, such as a workmen's bar, were not recorded from a particularly ideological or class-conscious point of view. In fact, Sloan was as concerned with paint quality and illumination as with any class or economic issues which might present themselves. His choice of a proletarian subject represented an act of rebellion against the official art of the period, but the painting itself reveals broad human sympathy rather than espousal of a political doctrine.

One of the great works of art that expresses humanitarian concern—one which is also an important historical document—is a photograph by Alfred Stieglitz (1864–1946) *The Steerage*. The picture was taken in 1907 during the height of the massive migration of people from all parts of Europe to the United States. The steerage was

JOHN SLOAN, *McSorley's Bar* (1912). Courtesy The Detroit Institute of Arts.

ALFRED STIEGLITZ, *The Steerage* (1907), left. Courtesy Philadelphia Museum of Art, Stieglitz Collection.

ELIA KAZAN (director), *America, America*, right. Photographs from the motion picture *America, America* © 1964 by Athena Enterprises Corp. Reproduced by courtesy of Warner Bros. Pictures.

A young Greek living in Turkey in 1896 determines to seek liberty in America. He bids his mother goodbye (top), and makes his way to Constantinople (center). There he works as a porter, laboring so diligently toward his goal that he is nicknamed "America, America." At last, crammed into steerage with hundreds of others (bottom), he sails for America.

the most uncomfortable part of the ship, and was hence the cheapest way to cross the ocean for the desperately poor who came to America seeking a new life. An excellent film, *America, America*, written and directed by Elia Kazan, vividly describes the adventures and the final voyage of a Greek immigrant who so idealized life in America that he endured incredible hardship to get passage on one of these ships. The photograph by Steiglitz resembles a medieval cosmological painting in which condemned people wrapped in shrouds come out of some hellish place where they have been confined,

as if in an ocean-going grave, now to greet light and life. Perhaps only men who have been similarly carried in troop transport ships during the great wars have any conception of such voyages—often more than a month of living in crowded holds below decks. But troops traveled on different business. These people came, as did the waves of immigrants before them, to build their lives in some fashion denied them in the "old country."

The German sculptor Ernst Barlach (1870–1938) typifies the artist whose work embodies universal, humanitarian concern although it grows

46

out of particular, national stylistic roots. His sculpture derives in part from the medieval Gothic tradition of wood carving and has an affinity with the socially conscious themes of German Expressionism, although it is not agitated and tempestuous but quietly self-contained. In *Veiled Beggar Woman*, the theme of the begging woman is organized around one emotion—pity; but the individual identity of the woman is concealed by the cloak over her head, so that the main idea of the work is concentrated in the supplication of the hands. The anonymity of the subject helps us to see the sculpture as an example of social expression, specifically an expression of pity for the economic and human conditions which cause anyone to beg.

The most monumental and celebrated work of social and political expression in our time is Picasso's *Guernica*. The painting, which is of mural size, was executed in 1937 to memorialize the frightful bombing of the Basque town of Guernica by Franco's forces during the Spanish Civil War. In it Picasso created the forms and imagery which have influenced an entire generation of artists, when their theme is violence, suffering, war, and chaos. Using black, white, and gray only, the artist tried to fashion a work which would simultaneously express multiple perceptions of a single, calamitous event: newspaper accounts of the bombing; the terror of victims; the symbolic meanings of war; the experience of pain; and the interactions among these episodes as viewed from the standpoint of history. Images such as the fallen statue, the mother and dead child, the burning building, the shrieking horse, and the spectator bull function as actual descriptions of the result of civilian bombing at the same time that they symbolize ideas of

ERNST BARLACH, *Veiled Beggar Woman* (1919). Private Collection, New York. Courtesy Galerie St. Etienne, New York.

PABLO PICASSO, *Guernica* (1937). On extended loan to The Museum of Modern Art, New York, from the artist, M. Picasso.

modern war compared to traditional forms of military violence. In Picasso's major works, there is frequently some reference to classical beauty and order. Here the classical image operates as a symbolic point of reference against which contemporary chaos is portrayed. The drawing style of children is employed to represent the presence and victimization of children as well as to permit the artist to show multiple views of the same phenomenon—for example, the outside of the face and the inside of the mouth. Adult methods of representation and conventional pictorial logic would have limited the multidimensional expression the artist sought. The opened mouth is a recurrent symbol in this work, standing for death, cries of insane fear, and pain. Only the dead child to the left has a

closed mouth. The work is a terrifying document of the devastation of human values.

Picasso's painting was an artist's reaction of shock, his feeling of being wounded. But the bombing of the Spanish town in the 1930's was only an anticipation of the holocausts later suffered by many cities during World War II, culminating in the atom bombing of Hiroshima and Nagasaki. The painting was thus sadly prophetic, but its focus was mainly confined to the individual suffering caused by war. When it was done, its imagery was adequate for the violence of the period, since more sophisticated concepts for thinking about large-scale human carnage—"overkill," for example—did not yet require development. Consequently, while this work of Picasso remains relevant to the contemporary problems of humanity, it exists within the same frame of reference as Goya's *Disasters of War* done in the nineteenth century; it is not equal to the conceptual challenge implied by calculations of the fifty or eighty million casualties which a society might sustain, according to some thinkers, in a first assault by modern weapons of destruction. The *Guernica* of 1937, therefore, may be the last important work of art to deal with war as an enterprise carried on by semi-industrial but not automated methods. It was still possible for Picasso to think of war as a catastrophe which has *individual* consequences. Now, its scale has been so enlarged and its methods so transformed that artists are compelled to use an abstract and dehumanized form-language to cope with modern modes of obliteration (see Adolph Gottlieb, *Blast II*, 1957, p. 238).

War's cruelty in the nineteenth century, before its mechanization in the twentieth century, is felt as a social catastrophe with tragic personal consequences.

FRANCISCO GOYA, *Disasters of War: And They Are Wild Beasts* (c.1810). Courtesy The Metropolitan Museum of Art, Rogers Fund, 1922.

Social Description

One of the social functions of art is performed by works which simply describe facets of life without necessarily implying that there is an urgent problem to be considered. The very act of selecting portions of ordinary existence for artistic treatment helps to focus our attention on the quality of daily life. Unless some dramatic incident takes place, we do not normally pay much attention to conventional places and events. Only when a "frame" is placed around them do we begin to discover their distinctive quality, or flavor, or meaning. This newly discovered value in common experience can lead to several results: It can heighten our insight into daily existence; it can help us compare the quality of contemporary social life with that of other places and periods; it can cause decisions to change, correct, or improve the visual environment; it can lead to a new perception of ourselves as part of, and also apart from, contemporary social reality.

Some works attempt to govern the attitude of the viewer; others can be governed by the viewer's already formed attitudes. The *Pool Parlor* by Jacob Lawrence (1917–) can be seen as a seriocomic portrayal of pool-hall drama, intensified by the almost macabre action of the figures, their flat patterning, and their deadly concentration on the game. The artist has exploited the attitudes commonly associated with Negro ghetto activity by creating mock-sinister silhouettes of their bodies, viewing them from above

through the glaring lights which hover implacably over the pool sharks as they go about their business. If we regard the pool hall as a "bad" place where criminal plots are hatched, then we perceive the painting in humorless, legalistic, or moralistic terms and miss its light, comedic touch, its spoof of the folklore about pool parlors, which is accomplished precisely because the sinister action is exaggerated. In contrast to this quasi-humorous version of pool hall emotion and acrobatics is the dramatic American film *The Hustler*, in which the actors, Paul Newman and Jackie Gleason, portray rival pool "artists" involved in a series of tense contests which express the obsessive character of the game practiced as an

JACOB LAWRENCE, *Pool Parlor* (1942), left. Courtesy The Metropolitan Museum of Art, Arthur H. Hearn Fund, 1942.

ROBERT ROSSEN (director), *The Hustler*, below. Still from The Museum of Modern Art Film Library.

art, together with the heightened emotions of suspense and danger resulting from heavy gambling on that artistry. In the film and in Lawrence's painting, we see how urban patterns of idleness and leisure are given aesthetic form without direct political or ideological emphasis.

The cultural patterns of ethnic groups, particularly of the first and second generations in America, have been the subject of systematic study by sociologists. One of their findings is that while the first American-born generation is anxious to forget or conceal its inherited ethnic practices and rituals because of anxiety to become "acculturated," or Americanized, the next generation, feeling more secure, is often proud of its inheritance and even endeavors to revive the customs of its immigrant forebears. Louis Bosa (1905–   ) is an American painter who has drawn primarily on the customs of immigrant and second-generation Italian-American families as they try to

maintain some of their traditions, to transplant them somehow in their new country. *My Family Reunion* shows one of those old-country "tribal" feasts set in the strange American landscape. Bosa's art relies substantially upon his appreciation of the unique incongruity of Mediterranean customs viewed against the predominately Anglo-Saxon background of American culture. His people are painted to reveal their feelings of awkwardness and also their determination to conserve and perpetuate the ancient festivals and family rituals which make life meaningful for them. This painter is an excellent draftsman and composer, and has a sharp eye for the gesture, the bodily proportion, the clothing choice, and the characteristic trait or expression which reveal the immigrant's personal crisis of adaptation, of holding on and letting go. Now that pizza pies, submarine sandwiches, and minestrone have become part of the mainstream of contemporary American civilization, the rich, symbolic elements of the immigrant subculture celebrated by Louis Bosa may appear increasingly remote, especially to that young third generation so thoroughly absorbed in baseball and the "top ten 'pop' tunes."

Portrayals of the landscape or the cityscape have their social connotations whether or not people are visible in them. We see the signs of human use: care or neglect, abandonment or affection. The environments men build influence their builders at the same time that they reflect human choices and limitations of imagination. In the painting *Landscape Near Chicago*, Aaron Bohrod (1907–   ) offers an ironic comment on that half-way region—neither urban, suburban, nor

LOUIS BOSA, *My Family Reunion* (1950). Collection of the Whitney Museum of American Art, New York, gift of Mr. and Mrs. Alfred Jaretski, Jr.

rural—one sees on the outskirts of large American cities, with its home-made architecture, accumulation of rusting equipment, and evidence of repairs begun but never entirely completed. Bohrod's detailed naturalism is ideally suited to painting the portrait of a house—and, by implication, of its inhabitants, people who occupy the lonely, undefined space between country and city, who cannot quite mold their immediate environment into a convincing imitation of a community. Edward Hopper (1882–   ) paints a related building portrait in *House by the Railroad,* although here it is the faded glory of a Victorian mansion which is portrayed, as opposed to the impoverished, anonymous style of building and living shown in the Bohrod painting. Hopper's house may now be a relic; perhaps it is presently a rooming house whereas once it represented elegant domesticity; but it has its own wilted dignity, conferred by the artist's presentation of the forms as a unified, coherent, sculptural mass, isolated but wearing its dated architectural adornments with a certain forlorn pride.

Two versions of New York's "El," the almost extinct elevated railway, are seen (p. 52) in a watercolor by Dong Kingman (1911–   ), *The 'El' and Snow,* and in *Third Avenue* by Franz Kline (1910–62). Kingman's facility with watercolor is challenged by the enormous variety of surface and material in the city. The artist seems to revel in the structural complexity and labyrinthine spaces and recesses everywhere one looks: He has deliberately selected an intricately built-up, virtually enclosed location, with its tangle of street signs, traffic signals, utility poles, overhead wires, and store-window displays. And in this overwhelmingly man-made situation, nature is modestly represented in the form of snow. Kingman's approach to social description is through the crisp representation of complex layers and levels, directions and labels, of the dense, tight

AARON BOHROD, *Landscape Near Chicago* (1934), left. Collection of the Whitney Museum of American Art, New York.

EDWARD HOPPER, *House by the Railroad* (1925), right. Collection The Museum of Modern Art, New York.

DONG KINGMAN, *The 'El' and Snow* (1946), above left. Collection of the Whitney Museum of American Art, New York.

FRANZ KLINE, *Third Avenue* (1954), above right. Collection Mr. and Mrs. B. H. Friedman.

The subway felt as urban man's experience of the physical and psychological underground.

GEORGE TOOKER, *The Subway* (1950), below. Collection of the Whitney Museum of American Art, New York.

environment in which urban man makes his home. Kline, on the other hand, is much more selective in approach and endeavors to describe less of what is objectively seen and more of what is subjectively felt. For him, the steel structural members of the elevated constitute an opportunity to paint large, black, powerful forms advancing toward the viewer and almost filling up the canvas. The effect upon the viewer is of shapes about to occupy his entire optical field: They loom up and press in upon him and seem capable of blotting out all light. Kline's image is sufficiently abstract and general to suggest any large-scale, structural element in the city. His execution is purposeful and decisive, carrying all the authority of engineering—its formidable, masculine power as well as its aura of menace.

The dramatic imagery of Kline consisted essentially of a struggle between his black *shapes,* representing the structural element, and his white *spaces,* representing the element of light. Each element endeavors to preempt the place of the other in a figure-and-ground contest, with the black asserting its role as figure first, and then yielding to the advancing, expanding white spaces, as the viewer is drawn into the conflict. This struggle to establish a *gestalt,* or pattern, within Kline's canvases is very well suited to the themes of urbanism and social description, since cities are indeed battlegrounds where contending demands for space and light are being fought out. In our cities, as in Kline's painting, the battle remains fluid, with temporary resolutions achieved intermittently, depending on the optical

energy and social intelligence we bring to the contested arena.

The theme of urban struggle is quite explicitly treated in *Battle of Light, Coney Island* By Joseph Stella (1877–1946). In this work, the fascination with movement, which Stella imported from Italian Futurism, is given full scope by the systematic distractions and attention-getting devices of a famous American amusement park. For Stella, flickering neon signs, the amplified voices of barkers, the on-

A Surrealist version of the sense of loneliness and menace which the city's streets can evoke.

LOUIS GUGLIELMI, *Terror in Brooklyn* (1941). Collection of the Whitney Museum of American Art, New York.

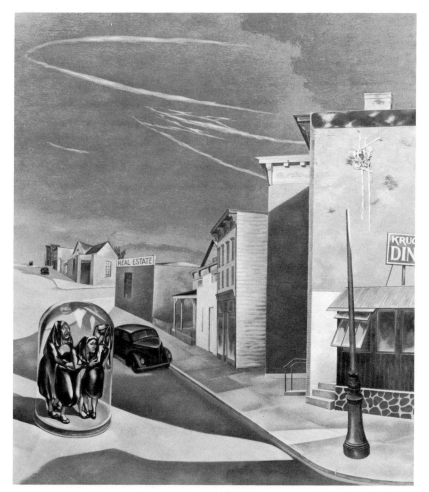

and-off patterns of colored light-bulbs, and an authentically raucous, honky-tonk atmosphere epitomized the distinctive American harmony of sensuous and dynamic forces. This painting might be regarded as symbolizing the affirmation by a European (Stella was born in Italy and came to the United States when he was twenty) of the social achievment of our adolescent civilization: the synthesis of all the kinetic, unsophisticated, "hard-sell" elements of the culture into a glorious explosion of energy, color, and form.

Stella transmuted the cacophonous sounds and flashy illumination of Coney Island into an exciting spectacle of

JOSEPH STELLA, *Battle of Light, Coney Island* (1913). Yale University Art Gallery, Collection Société Anonyme.

brassy exuberance in 1913; in 1936 Mark Tobey (1890–   ) undertook a similar theme in *Broadway*. Tobey was equally fascinated by the light from a thousand signs and by its ability to express the frenetic pursuit of amusement by millions who are drawn like moths to the synthetic jubilee continuously on view in the center of Manhattan. Later, in 1942, Piet Mondrian (1872–1944), the almost monastic Dutch abstractionist, was to succumb to Broadway's glitter with a sparkling canvas, *Broadway Boogie Woogie.* Tobey's tempera painting is "written" in light, a sort of neon script blurring into an incandescent haze in the center of the picture, where the scale grows smaller, the signs and people come closer together, and the motion of men and vehicles more nearly resembles the heat and commitment of battle. But Mondrian, as befits the artist of ultimate abstraction and detachment, views the Great White Way as a musical composition. The restrictions imposed by his rectangular mode of composition do not allow the freedom of description we see in Tobey, nor the spiral, radial compositional devices which Stella employs to suggest expansiveness and intersecting vectors. However, with dozens of little squares and abrupt changes of primary color, Mondrian could convey the flickering, dance-like quality of light and movement in the thoroughfare. Whether or not Mondrian really "knew" the boogie-woogie, which involved a forward movement of the body and arms and then a reversal before the forward inertia was concluded, his painting does express the short bursts of energy, the go-and-stop, the scurry-and-halt, of the Broadway "mell-o-dee."

MARK TOBEY, *Broadway* (1936), left. Courtesy The Metropolitan Museum of Art, Arthur H. Hearn Fund, 1942.

PIET MONDRIAN, *Broadway Boogie Woogie* (1942–43), right. Collection The Museum of Modern Art, New York.

Satire

The social purpose of satire is to ridicule people and institutions so that they will change. As a type of humor, satire is not merely aimed at the feelings of relief and superiority we get from laughter. Satire is aggressive in intent. It makes fun of its object— sometimes bitter, derisive fun. Although laughter is involved, satire is a *serious* art form, serving to puncture pretension, to cut the mighty down to size, to dramatize the gap between official purpose or promise and actual performance.

Just as humor plays an important role in the psychological health of the individual, satire is vital for the healthy functioning of society. The capacity of responsible persons to accept satirical criticism gracefully and without efforts at suppression is probably a good index of their ability to exercise noncoercive leadership. And if our society as a whole cannot accept satirical comment and criticism in its stride, then our institutions and customs are fragile indeed. Often, individuals or groups that have been stung by satire question the legitimacy of the offending material by creating a casuistical distinction between constructive and destructive criticism. Naturally, an offended individual or group will feel itself the victim of destructive criticism. And it is possible to think of satirical material in literary or visual form which appears to have violated commonly accepted ideas of propriety in expressing criticism. But the impulse to suppress disagreement, whether it appears in satirical or other forms, can often be evidence of unwillingness to examine the causes which gave rise to the criticism originally. Certainly the dictatorships of modern times have been notoriously inhospitable to satire directed at themselves, and certainly the right to use humor in social and political criticism is indispensable, part of the very essence of freedom.

Democratic societies, too, go through solemn phases when satire is regarded as negative, uncooperative, and divisive, if not actually subversive. An administration's humorless image of itself may be caused by the personality traits of high officials, variations in their ability to "take it." In this connection, President Truman very aptly observed, "If you can't stand the heat, then get out of the kitchen." Yet is there any special trait of satire which makes its victims more uncomfortable than does conventional criticism, the complaints and comments found in

the usual media of news and information? Furthermore, are there any characteristics of satire in the visual arts which are uniquely painful?

First, to be the object of ridicule is probably more difficult to bear than to be scolded. To be laughed at by a community or by substantial groups in the community is very much like being ostracized. It is an exceedingly severe kind of humiliation. Second, laughter is both a physiological and a psychological phenomenon; it involves the total organism and thus implicates an individual more completely in an act of ridicule. We are likely to remember a satirically comic reference to a public figure long after we have forgotten his specific acts and policies. Many American voters will not forget the damaging visual comparison of Thomas E. Dewey, twice an unsuccessful candidate for President, to the groom on a wedding cake. Finally, the visual forms of satire often use caricature or some other means of exaggerating the physical shortcomings of their targets. Needless to say, we are, for the most part, quite aware of our personal imperfections; to have them magnified and made to symbolize policies and

Capp's professional interest in comic repulsiveness or ugliness was fully echoed by his readers who generously contributed drawings of their candidates for the supreme ugliness accolade.

AL CAPP, Panels from *Li'l Abner,* Ugly Woman Contest (1946). Courtesy Al Capp and United Feature Syndicate.

attitudes which the community finds repulsive is very painful, especially if one's psychic defenses are not strong.

An observation about caricature needs to be made here: Fashioning grotesque images of real or imagined people is a universal practice. All children are intrigued by the creation of fantastic, hideous, incredibly ugly faces. Leonardo da Vinci made many such grotesque heads which he designated "physiognomic studies"; but they were, from a psychological standpoint, similar to the images children and others create—explorations of the frontiers of the human. Such graphic images are comparable to the rich body of spoken and written material which exists for characterizing persons of ordinary appearance as ugly. Adolescents seem to be especially adept at the creation of derisive physical descriptions and comparisons. Further, popular comedians can convulse audiences for hours with minute descriptions of the ugliness of their spouses and other female relatives. In short, fascination with ugliness is widespread; it is perhaps as pervasive as the interest in beauty. The interest may appear to be malicious, but more likely it grows out of anthropological and psychological needs which have little connection with malice. Whether or not caricature is malicious, however, the visual forms of satire (which often employ caricature) *are* intentionally malicious. The malice is not a moral fault, but a kind of civic virtue, since satire serves society by acting as a check on the excesses and misapplications of power. And satire serves culture by acting as a check on the excesses and grossness of current customs and tastes.

Perhaps the greatest political satirist of World War II, if not of the first half of the twentieth century, was the Briton, David Low (1891–1963). His cartoons were in many respects visual counterparts to the speeches of Winston Churchill: He could ridicule the Axis leaders, appeal to the courage of his countrymen when they were taking a terrible beating, express fierce defiance, appeal for help from America, and grieve over the valorous dead. Every editorial cartoonist develops a visual formula for the portrayal of the world's political leaders, a formula which quickly identifies a personality physically and also endows him with traits such as villainy, hypocrisy, courage, or madness. David Low, technically very able, was especially successful in his personality formulations, his characterizations of the dictators. At a time when their military and racial insanity, matched with immense power, had succeeded in bludgeoning and terrifying the civilized world, David Low shrewdly managed to identify Hitler and Mussolini as asses—dangerous, to be sure, but asses nevertheless, and thus hardly supermen. Low's assessment was not complete or entirely accurate (it may have been sound as far as it went), but it served to hearten the hard-pressed Britons; he used satire to reduce the dictators to less-than-invincible size.

The political satirist at his best is shown in Low's cartoon *Rendezvous*, which deals with one of the strange consequences of political expediency— the Russo-German nonaggression pact of 1939. The Russians hoped by the treaty to buy time to rearm against the expected invasion by Germany. And Germany hoped to secure the neutrality

LEONARDO DA VINCI, *Caricature of an Ugly Old Person*, top. Courtesy Biblioteca Ambrosiana.

When satire dwells on the ugly, it has a timeless and universal character; very little separates Al Capp's twentieth century version of ugliness from the vividly repulsive countenance drawn by a Japanese artist twelve hundred years ago.

Caricature (bottom) from the ceiling of Horyu-ji, Nara (eighth century A.D.).

DAVID LOW, *Rendezvous* (1939), left. Reproduced by permission of the London Evening Standard.

DAVID LOW, *The Angels of Peace Descend on Belgium* (1940), right. Reproduced by permission of the London Evening Standard.

of Russia during its planned attack upon Poland, France, and the West. Hence the mortal enemies, soon to be locked in the bitterest struggle of the War, greet each other with feigned and exaggerated gestures of courtesy while addressing each other with their customary rhetoric of insult.

Another powerful satiric thrust is seen in Low's cartoon *The Angels of*

ROBERTO ROSSELLINI (director), *Open City*. Stills from The Museum of Modern Art Film Library.

Peace Descend on Belgium. It deals with the brutality of Heinrich Himmler's Gestapo, or secret police, which followed the German armies into conquered countries, organized the looting, and tortured and murdered potential resistance leaders. Although Italy was a German ally, it too was a victim of the systematic Gestapo methods as the war began to turn against the Axis powers. The great Italian film *Open City*, is a dramatic document of that tragic period. But Low, in this cartoon, is a satirist rather than a tragedian. The symmetry of the figures, their military precision, even their identical dance-like foot positions, serve to symbolize the mechanical, efficient, and highly organized aspects of Gestapo torture. Finally, the silhouettes of great black birds descending upon a city establish symbolic connections with vultures and medieval myths of death.

We expect satire in the graphic arts, especially in news media, but it also occurs, although less frequently, in "serious" painting. Most of the work of the American painter Jack Levine (1915–   ) is satiric in intent, *The Feast of Pure Reason* constituting a typical example. The ironic point here obviously lies in the contrast between the title, which celebrates a rational, totally logical approach to human affairs, and the actualities of decision-making in some communities—the secret meetings and negotiations of corrupt officials, politicians, and merchants. Levine employs realistic caricature, tending to identify moral and civic corruption with physical grossness and ugliness. His people are meant to be detested rather than laughed at, his satire deriving mainly from the sarcasm of the title and the ponderous, bloated qualities of the social types he represents as occupying positions of influence and authority.

Woman, I by Willem de Kooning (1904–) possesses satirical values, although the violent execution of the painting or the shock with which the viewer reacts to the work may momentarily prevent his seeing its elements of burlesque. The artist presents an older woman, heavy-set, wearing a light, flimsy shoe, overexposing her body in a scantily designed dress, and exhibiting a grimacing expression when she would doubtless wish to appear bewitching. The oversized eyes are probably the result of grossly overdone make-up; the horrible mouth expression probably the result of trying to fashion a fascinating smile through ill-fitting dentures. The tiny ankle and the swollen foot attempt to support a massive superstructure and all, together, betray the fierce and pathetic exertions of a "mom" gone beserk. The artist presents *Woman, I,* not merely as a single clini-

JACK LEVINE, *The Feast of Pure Reason* (1937), left. On extended loan to The Museum of Modern Art, New York, from the United States WPA Art Program.

WILLEM DE KOONING, *Woman, I* (1950–52), right. Collection The Museum of Modern Art, New York, purchase.

cal study, but as an authentic portrayal
of the inner and outer condition of a
sizable body of older women in our
culture. The artist is plainly indignant,
enraged to the point where he wants to
make as horrible a contrast as he can
between the woman's pretensions and
the actual results we see. Jack Levine
seemed to dwell more lovingly upon
the bloated surfaces of his people, but
de Kooning barely establishes his forms
before tearing into them with angry,
slashing, painterly attacks.

A work of similar satiric anger is
the etching *The Patroness* by Peggy
Bacon (1895–   ). Here, too, the subject is corpulent and hamhanded; she
is surrounded with furs which are of no
help so far as attractiveness is concerned. Her face is pinched and ugly ·
in contrast to her bodily bulk—a symbol, no doubt, of her minuscule soul
contrasted with her excessive wealth.
The artist means to imply that large
funds rather than sensitivity and connoisseurship enable this gross person to

play the role of patron of art. It is
perhaps a typical if exaggerated expression of the attitude of the artist toward
his patron, a sort of compensatory act
of derision toward the persons on
whom he feels dependent, a malicious
bite of the hand that feeds him.

Satire thrives in art whenever
there is freedom from political or
social repression. As the visual arts
have embraced abstraction, however,
there has been a lessening of artistic
ridicule, of thrusts directed at the old
familiar targets. Art seemingly with-
drew from the social and political
arena after 1946 and devoted itself
more to the analysis of personal emotion and the refinement of the visual
language used to express that emotion.
A similar development has taken place
in literature and in philosophy. Philosophers for some time now have been
concerned with language, that is, with
the analysis of linguistic structures as
vehicles of meaning rather than with
the content of philosophic propositions

Art satirizing art: a semi-abstract sculpture which mischievously pokes fun at the Art Nouveau style.

H. C. WESTERMANN, *Nouveau Rat Trap* (1965). Courtesy Allan Frumkin Gallery; photo, Nathan Rabin.

and systems of thought in the manner of traditional philosophy. Pop art, which may be a fleeting phenomenon, has satiric potential, although it lacks the sharpness and precision of genuine satire. Its target is very broad: all of modern culture. Nevertheless, its stance is mainly a critical one, although it is difficult to say whether some of the "Poppers" deride or celebrate the banalities of popular culture. Still, they are aware of the noise and commotion around us, and are busily engaged in developing artistic weapons to cope with the noxious environment. As yet, the weapons appear to be fragments of the environment itself (which is damning enough), but we may confidently expect that the more gifted among our contemporary artists will find some way of making significant statements about our environment—statements which deserve to be taken seriously as social criticism.

Graphic Information

We are accustomed to think of visual art in terms of objects which are prized and admired. But as we have already seen, visual art also constitutes a language—a language which is useful for a variety of social and institutional purposes. Forms and images can be organized so that they communicate with extraordinary effectiveness, and, in conjuction with verbal language, their explicitness and precision of meaning is maximized. Understandably, our industrial civilization, which has developed mass production and mass distribution to a very high degree, employs the language of visual art extensively in its marketing operations. And graphic design, particularly of posters, books, and other printed matter, is an indispensable tool of the communications industries and the so-called "knowledge explosion." What is today known as advertising design used to be called commercial art. Although such labels are not very important, they call attention to the crucial function of art in conveying information from industry and commerce to the specific social groups upon whom they wish to exert influence.

Advertising design, however, is only a single, although prominent, instance of the social function of art as a communication medium. The purposes of visual communication vary, and consequently the artistic organization of images, forms, words, and subject matter also varies. In general, the professional education of contemporary artist-designers prepares them to create and organize images which can serve a variety of information and communication objectives. That is, the artist who can design an advertisement to promote the sale of an automobile or a lipstick may also be able to design a record album cover, a book jacket, an outdoor poster, or a package label. However, such versatility is not too frequently put into practice by professional designers, who increasingly restrict their efforts to particular communication media and particular kinds of products or information. Also, the arts of information and communication design are so specialized that very few advertisements, packages, posters, or labels are ever the work of a single person. Art which serves commerce and industry is *collective* art, just as almost all phases of industrial engineering, manufacture, and distribution are team enterprises.

Since we have been nurtured on fairly romantic ideas about *individual* artistic creativity, the collective character of modern communication design may be somewhat dismaying. But we should remember that most of the ambitious artistic projects and many of the minor artistic efforts up to the Renaissance were collectively created. Anonymous, collective creation typifies design today as in the medieval period: We seldom know who designed a particular Gothic cathedral, carved its stone sculptures, or executed its stained glass. Likewise, when a modern office building, hotel, or college dormitory is erected, we often cannot be certain of the personal origin of the design in the large architectural firm which carried out the commission. Even when we know who the senior design partners are in a prominent firm—for example, Skidmore, Owings and Merrill—the collaborative, fragmented character of contemporary architectural practice does not permit the identification of a single designer in the same sense that we know Michelangelo created the original design for St. Peter's and Jefferson designed his home at Monticello. But notwithstanding modern and medieval similarities in artistic execution, we are inclined to regard collectively created works less seriously than works done by an individual. This is so because, since the Renaissance, we have believed in "genius," and in the art object as an embodiment and reflection of genius. Even the cinema, a twentieth-century art form illustrating collective creativity to a high degree, was prolific with production "geniuses" during its early Hollywood days. At present, the industry is more sophisticated, and one hears less of a single, guiding genius and more of gifted writers, imaginative directors, and talented actors.

Although the collective or collaborative origin of art devoted to information and communication accounts for its minor status according to some persons, its connection with commerce is another source of detraction. Thus, a poster which is designed to persuade, to sell, is regarded as inferior, *a priori*, to a painting or sculpture which was never soiled by commercial motivation (although the painter usually hopes to sell his pictures). In this period, we have come to believe that works of art created for no particular client and embodying no ideas other than those the artist freely chooses to include, are superior to those commissioned by commerce or industry. Advertising art is especially suspect, as is advertising in general. We are all more or less convinced believers in the motto *caveat emptor*—"let the buyer beware"—because we do not in our hearts entirely trust salesmen, even if our society rewards them munificently. Art which persuades or sells is considered less pure, less idealistic, less *fine* than art which just is. Quite possibly, we expect the arts to perform certain religious and ethical functions exclusively, to appeal to our better natures, to enlighten us and elevate our moral character (which they may do) rather than to remind us of the getting and spending which occupies so much of daily life.

But an appeal to logic should show that artistic excellence is not necessarily related to the social or financial arrangements for bringing it into being. "Who pays the fiddler calls the tune." So far as artists are concerned, this proverb can be understood to mean that art will be paid for by kings and cardinals when they are socially powerful and possess large means, or by merchants and industrialists when they are rich and powerful. The patronage of art and artists responds to social and economic change. As a corollary, the uses and subject matter of art change because of the shifting requirements of the individuals and institutions who commission or patronize art. But artistic excellence is more likely related to the imagination and mastery of the artist (and his client's ability to recognize these traits) than to the moral status of commerce or the ethical level of advertising. Indeed, the history of art offers ample evidence of distinguished works created for relatively trivial purposes—Cellini's salt-cellar, for example. We remember the artist now and prize the object, although many of us do not recall the patron and are not particularly interested in its effectiveness for holding salt.

THE PROBLEMS OF COMMUNICATION

What are the characteristic problems of information design which the artist must solve in carrying out the social function of this art form? First is the matter of arresting the attention of a portion of the public. This is a problem for all effective communication. Its challenge varies from the five-second viewing limitation for an outdoor poster to the fifteen- or twenty-minute perusal of a magazine page. Second, and related to the difficulty of gaining attention, is the over-all psychological and sociological strategy: identifying the particular group which is addressed and knowing its interests and motivations. Third is the problem of characterizing the use and meaning of the product, idea, or service which is to be sold or communicated. How can a complex idea or an intricate product be presented quickly and memorably to a vast public which is under almost continuous visual assault from competing designs and media? Finally, there is the problem of the content and amount of verbal material which may appear as a caption for a poster, as copy within an advertisement, as dialogue on television, or as the sole visual material on a book jacket. It should be stressed that the design and effective presentation of letter forms may constitute a visual problem which is even more significant than the verbal-literary problems of information design. Much of our learning in the realm of values and attitudes takes place under the auspices of nonverbal media. In television, designers must relate their imagery to unseen words or music, material which occupies aural but not optical "space." That is, although we do not employ our ears to see, they must find out how the acuteness of visual perception is affected by the stimulation caused by sound.

These general problems of information design are closely related to technical, possibly more prosaic matters. Processes of reproduction affect artistic rendering which may affect design. The size of the final reproduction will dictate the detail or simplicity of the image and the choice of

SEGUNDO FREIRE, carnival poster (1957), top.

PABLO PICASSO, *Design*, color stencil (1922), bottom. Courtesy The Metropolitan Museum of Art, gift of Paul J. Sachs, 1922.

type face. Some faces are highly legible at a distance or can be read easily when the viewer is rapidly moving. The funds available for the entire communication process govern media resources and affect the decisions of the designer: the use of color, of photographs, or painted illustrations; the amount of white space in a quarter page as opposed to a full page; the particular media used—newspapers, posters, television, or magazines. The quality of paper and printing, too, affects decisions about color and design. These problems are comparable to those faced by an architect who must also contend with cost as well as site and functional factors. His art is to find a solution within the limitations set for him.

Simplicity and logic are the dominant traits which emerge from the successful solution of problems in information design. Visual simplicity implies a bias in favor of bold, abstract forms—forms which are easily visible, quickly identifiable, and capable of rich, symbolic meaning. By logic I mean a sense of connectedness among the elements of the total design: the product or idea; the pictorial or other visual material; and the caption, copy, or other verbal material. It is interesting to observe how often designers have drawn upon the stylistic innovations of contemporary painting in endeavoring to solve their problems of communication, originality, and stimulation of interest. The following illustrations taken from the work of designers throughout the world often demonstrate the dependence of information design on the allegedly useless fine arts. While abstraction has followed its own internal development within painting,

it has been indirectly the most important reason for the effectiveness of modern information and communication design.

SOLUTIONS

The Mexican carnival poster by Segundo Freire shows the unmistakable influence of Picasso's paintings of harlequins and musicians. The poster designer, however, retains only the flat patterning of Cubism and does not go so far as to slice the figure and recompose its elements to the point where his work would require too much intellectual effort of the viewer. We realize that the human figure is less readily truncated and distorted than machinery or nonhuman subject matter, if quick communication is a primary objective. On the other hand, a certain amount of simplification and generalization of the figure is an aid to recognition and identification in advertising; hence, cubist abstraction has been a fertile source of ideas for designers interested in graphic communication. The Italian designer Pino Tovaglia created a bold railroad poster based largely on the painterly style of Fernand Léger. *Three Women* by Fernand Léger does not, of course, contain machinery, but it does reveal the attempt by this follower of Cubism to convert all visual material into mechanical equivalents. It is possible to think of this crisp, powerful, poster design as the result of a series of steps—from Picasso and Braque to Juan Gris, to Fernand Léger, to Tovaglia; an aesthetic equivalent of the baseball trio: Tinker to Evers to Chance.

A cover design for *Fortune* magazine by the late Alvin Lustig (1915–

1955) reveals the influence of another facet of Cubism—collage, the creation of pictorial images and textures by pasting flat material, especially printed matter, on the picture's surface. Picasso and Braque combined the pasted material (*papier collé*) with drawn or painted forms, as in the Picasso collage *Bottle of Suze*, which contains pasted papers, newsprint, wallpaper, and the label from a liquor bottle. Although the original Cubists deliberately used papers whose printed material was unrelated to their aesthetic aims, Lustig has employed the words and type faces of the collage material to reinforce his theme—"the language of advertising." Furthermore, his shapes are those of television masts, billboards, and related display devices. Thus, designers for information and communication try to increase effectiveness by stating their message two or three times simultaneously, and with varied formal devices. The Picasso collage, on the contrary, has no explicit message, but rather communicates an aesthetic effect. Hence, the bottle and its label serve mainly as an "excuse" for organizing a series of forms: The print is not there to be read, but to be experienced as texture and color.

An especially interesting example of what anthropologists call cultural diffusion is seen in a Japanese cosmetics poster by Tsuneji Fujiwara. The faces are remarkably similar to those painted by Amadeo Modigliani, an Italian-born artist who spent most of his working life in France. Modigliani began his career as a sculptor and was especially influenced by African sculpture, as in the example illustrated, translating African forms into the small

PINO TOVAGLIA, railway poster (1957), above left. Courtesy the artist and Ferrovie Nord Milano.

FERNAND LÉGER, *Three Women* (*Le grand déjeuner*) (1921), above right. Collection The Museum of Modern Art, New York, Mrs. Simon Guggenheim Fund.

ALVIN LUSTIG, cover design for *Fortune* magazine (1952), below left. Courtesy Time, Inc.; photography, Sandak, Inc., N.Y.C.

PABLO PICASSO, *Bottle of Suze* (1912–13), below right. Collection Washington University.

mouth, elongated ovoid head, and delicate, stylized arches over the eyes of the women in his paintings. Apparently, the Japanese designer found in Modigliani an ideal of female beauty which would appeal to the audience he was trying to reach. As a result, the feminine ideal which a painter in Paris distilled from African sculpture and his own sensibility and presented in the context of traditional easel painting finds itself utilized in a totally different context—advertising design.

The English artist Ronald Searle places his satirical gifts at the disposal of poster design in a drawing for the United Rum Merchants of London. Using humor to arrest attention has obvious advantages provided the product emerges in a favorable light. From the standpoint of the client, entertaining the public must somehow also induce that public to notice the product, think well of it, and wish to buy it. Solemn people always seem concerned that humor might divert interest from the message or create an unfortunate association of the product with laughter. Consequently, Searle's satirical drawing style needs to be carefully employed. Fortunately, this artist specializes in caricature of distinctively English, mainly Victorian types, and seems to understand the varieties of British mustache as few others do. His view-

point is very much an insider's; hence, the ridiculous situation he portrays can be seen as an acceptable spoof, with its mock consternation, its irreverence for the genteel culture represented by serious musicians, and its ill-concealed disapproval of the sly old gentlemen whose absurd violation of convention can be tolerated if he drinks Lemon Hart Rum. It is worth noting that the abstract approach to poster design can be successfully abandoned in this case because there is a sure grasp of humor and a traditional product addressed to a tradition-oriented public—assets combined with the highly individual, quickly identified style of an artist whose employment by an advertiser itself constitutes an endorsement of the product.

The film illustration by Ted Hanke, *Oil Men Call This a Christmas Tree,* illustrates an intelligent use in industrial advertising of aesthetic discoveries made originally by artists

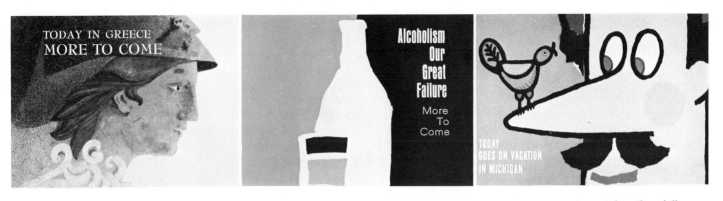

who celebrate the machine: such painters as Léger, Duchamp, and Sheeler, along with a host of contemporary sculptors who weld together discarded metal scraps and machine parts. The painted illustration is obviously based on a photograph of something real, but, so far as the layman is concerned, this combination of valves, pipes, gauges, nuts, and bolts is an impressive mystery, a symbol of technological mastery. The angle of vision is from below, and since there are very few cues to the scale of the construction, we see it almost as a monument. In addition, the strong light-and-dark contrast, with some of the shapes almost in silhouette, simplifies and dramatizes the stark, mechanical forms. Design is thus employed to endow the day-to-day achievements of industry with heroic, monumental qualities. Although contemporary types of monumentality are new, and although we use mass communication and reproduction processes to embody their meanings, the social intent is similar to that of ancient kings and generals who erected heroic statuary, triumphal arches, and obelisks to celebrate their victories and call attention to their power and achievement.

An area of potentially huge influence for graphic design lies in television. Its electronically reproduced announcements and title cards now tend to resemble the imagery employed in magazines and outdoor posters. Still, the poster has not been disdained by a number of masters, including Picasso and Toulouse-Lautrec, both of whom created works for reproduction. (Indeed, Lautrec is responsible for a body of poster work which holds an enduring place in the history of modern art.) The intimacy of the television image permits the medium to deal very frankly with social problems like alcoholism (when its producers possess the courage to undertake controversial or emotion-laden themes) and the skill and insight of the designer can do much to establish a mood of sympathetic candor. Also, the continual improvement of the technical quality of broadcast and received images promises that as time passes fewer and fewer artistic values will be lost in transmission. As color television is perfected, we may confidently look forward to an enormous growth in the commissioning of visual art for TV reproduction, not only for advertising spots, title cards, and animated films, but also as the primary material of regular shows. Today books are published which allow us to examine at leisure works we may or may not have seen in museums; and such publications, being relatively inexpensive, have brought about a revolution in the artistic literacy of the world. However, books have also been published since the invention of movable type with visual material created for the books alone. So, similarly, will television commission works of art specifically for entertainment and educational purposes as the quality of visual reproduction improves.

The genealogy of the forms in the poster by Saul Bass (1920–   ) for Pabco Paint Company would not be difficult to trace to Paul Klee, Jean Arp, and Joan Miró. What is interesting to the student of graphic information is the adaptation by the designer of surrealist imagery to advertise house paint. But some reflection supports the wisdom of the strategy employed here. The manufacturer is attempting to interest housewives in his product, and a key problem to solve is to convince women that house painting is not an arduous, dirty job—not, at least, with this product. Klee did, so to speak, considerable "research" into child-like imagery, while Miró has added to that "research" his own whimsical conceptions of a world inhabited by and perceived through the eyes of children or of persons with child-like mentalities. Both artists succeeded in invading the carefree world of children, where adult notions of responsibility and fear of error have not yet penetrated. The forms which Saul Bass draws upon, in short, tend to express freedom from inhibition, a rollicking, neurosis-free approach to adventure and experience. The timid housewife, afraid lest she undertake a job beyond her powers or make a glorious mess of painting her kitchen, is encouraged to view the operation as a romp, easy enough for a child to accomplish. With these unconscious suggestions present in the imagery, the art of the designer carries the message further through the small photographic illustration of the happily employed *hausfrau*, bottom center, while the outline of the drawing itself is executed in bright, clean color. Thus, although the design is simple enough and easily and quickly perceived, it makes very sophisticated use of modern art history and of unconscious sugges-

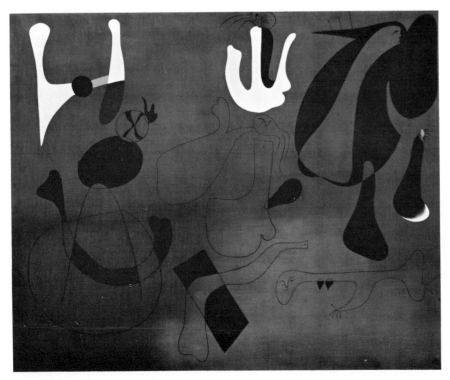

tion to advance the advertiser's objectives.

The foregoing examples have tended to emphasize the dependence of information design on the detached and autonomous fine arts; yet there is no reason why excellence and innovation of a high order cannot occur in graphics. The designer, however, is usually under the pressure of deadlines, not to mention the demands of his various clients and superiors in the organizations where he may work. Hence, the scientific tradition of pure research followed by technological application may be analogous to the artistic situation also. But great corporations in our society *employ* pure scientists to carry on research which they hope will ultimately benefit their enterprises. They and their agencies do *not* find it necessary to employ painters and sculptors whose work they may apply for practical advantage. On the other hand, contemporary support of museums and foundations, patronage of artists, and gifts to institutions which educate artists come largely from corporations and individuals who must feel they benefit aesthetically or practically from the innovations of fine art.

Apparently, relationships among artists, designers, and patrons in our society are quite complex. As yet, most artists live and function in the time-honored tradition of undernourishment or they are employed as designers; but few can flourish in both areas at a high level of performance. Yet the education of artists and of designers is quite similar. Perhaps the future will witness an increase in the professionalism of designers for industry and commerce with a consequent growth in their artistic autonomy. There may also be an associated improvement in the technical competence of fine artists, since it often appears that students with technical virtuosity are largely drawn toward the design professions. We may eventually arrive at a condition like that of the Renaissance, when no line could be drawn between artists and designers since, with very few exceptions, they were the same men.

CHAPTER THREE

Both paintings and buildings can serve as symbols, but only buildings perform a physical function. By the physical function of art, I mean the creation of objects which operate as containers and tools. By "container" we can designate a range of objects from a carton of milk to an office building. Both need to be shaped and constructed primarily according to the requirements of their contents (if people can be thought of as "contents"). Both are used as well as looked at. A tool can be a tablespoon or a locomotive. One is a simple, the other a complex, machine. Both need to be designed so that they operate efficiently. And one aspect of their operation is their visual appearance. Any tool or machine looks like something. The artistic problem is to make it look like what it does, while also making it look "good" to the persons who may use or buy the tool. Thus, the physical function of art or design is connected with the effective operation of objects according to criteria of usefulness and efficiency as well as those of appearance and appeal.

The difference between a painting and a building or a machine is that a painting is used *only* by looking at it, whereas a building or tool is used by doing something *in* it or *with* it, as well as by looking *at* it. It was formerly thought that art affected useful objects by adorning and embellishing them or by creating surfaces or skins which con-

THE PHYSICAL FUNCTIONS

OF ART

cealed their working parts. To some extent, this view survives in erroneous conceptions and applications of industrial or product design. Presumably, all the important problems of function were handled by engineers while artists looked after superficial beauty. But now it is recognized that appearance and function are inextricably linked: Engineers are more consciously aware of aesthetics, and artists are more knowledgeable about operational design. Many useful objects today are totally created by artist-designers because their education in production methods, engineering, and art equips them to exercise substantial responsibility for a product from its conception through its design prototype, manufacture, packaging, and sales promotion. The profession of industrial design—or product design, as some people call it—constitutes a new and fruitful synthesis of art, engineering, and marketing.

During the Renaissance, artists were often architects and engineers simultaneously. But the Industrial Revolution, starting in the eighteenth century, was mainly responsible for the separation of art, as such, from the structural aspects of building and manufacture. Civil, industrial, and mechanical engineering have developed as professions separate from art and architecture during the modern era, and although their resulting specialization has yielded many benefits, one of the disadvantages society has experienced during the past two hundred years or so has been the increased proliferation of ugliness in our large- and small-scale environment. Often engineers have been excellent designers, as in the cases of Paxton, Roebling, Nervi and Maillart (see discussions in Chapter Thirteen on Architecture), but increasing specialization, with its emphasis on a narrowly conceived utility, together with the indifference to aesthetic values of a society excessively oriented toward materialistic goals, accounted for the abundance of trashy design which characterized the early fruits of industrialism and mass production.

Between the eighteenth and the twentieth centuries, the handcrafts survived as obsolescent vestiges of preindustrial modes of making, as status symbols for the few who could resist the inroads of engineer-design, or as focal points of idealism for craftsmen like William Morris, who hoped to reverse the development of industrialization and capitalism through a revival of medieval artisanship. But the crafts have embraced new functions in the twentieth century—functions less related to nostalgia for their role in preindustrial economies, and more relevant to the requirements of men who have passed through the Industrial Revolution and now cope with an Electronic Revolution and its offspring, automation.

In addition to the design of small tools and large machines, private dwellings and great public buildings, art is concerned with the design of the man-made environment. Through the professions of community planning and urban design, art contributes to the harmonious shaping of *all* the parts of the man-made environment *in relation to each other*. Modern societies can no longer afford to have their communities develop on a piecemeal, fragmented, unrelated basis. Too many of the problems of urbanism have their origin in social failure to plan *comprehensively* and in advance of need. Here, as in the case of industrial design, art consists of more than the embellishment of outdoor spaces with parks, plazas, and monuments, although these are certainly elements which reveal the aesthetic concern of the community. But we realize that the best spatial organization of a community grows out of solutions for the functional and visual problems which any inhabited area creates. In a sense, the artistic problems involved in the design of containers or buildings are present on a vastly augmented scale in connection with organizing the masses and voids and functional elements of the huge containers we call communities. However, the process of community planning obviously has more relationship to sociology, law, and politics than does product design.

The physical functions of art, therefore, affect us in our immediate and intimate affairs as well as in our public role as citizens—as people who use and are used by the man-made organisms called communities. In the following sections we shall discuss some of the large and small structures created for practical use as well as for aesthetic and symbolic enrichment of our lives.

Architecture: The Dwelling

Of all the types of building— churches, schools, shops, palaces, castles, skyscrapers, airports, factories, and hockey rinks—the dwelling is the earliest, the closest to our daily lives, and perhaps the best illustration of the varied innovations and philosophies which affect and afflict architecture. Architecture is a social art, and in the dwelling we see its most intimate effect upon that prime social institution, the family. It is worth our while, therefore, to look at some of the principal effects of families on home building and of domestic architecture on families.

If we approach the modern home as a social container, our first observation concerns the implied purposes of its size and design: The home today is intended almost exclusively for the child-rearing family. It does not usually have sufficient room for the permanent residence of grandparents, maiden aunts, bachelor uncles, or assorted other relatives. Nor does it any longer have a parlor, library, pantry, or front porch. Instead, there may be new rooms or spaces—called the game room, patio, family room, car port, recreation room, bar, or solarium—where parents, children, and adolescents can entertain their friends and pursue their hobbies. A second observation is that, compared with the homes of a generation or two ago, there is less privacy, more open planning, and fewer single-purpose spaces in the contemporary dwelling. Partitions are either eliminated, or do not go from floor to ceiling, or do not really separate and insulate spaces and sounds from one another. Third, homes are increasingly built on one level or on split levels, but they seldom have two, three, or four distinct layers, one on top of the other. The one-level, or ranch-type, dwelling promotes mobility and the loss of privacy mentioned above. Fourth, multipurpose rooms reduce the over-all size of the house and cause intensive use of space and heavy wear of equipment. Fifth, but not least important, the mechanical services and labor-saving devices built into the home have absorbed a larger proportion of its total cost, and these have for most people become the principal index of its value—economic, aesthetic, and spiritual. That is, we probably love our dishwashers, rotisseries, air conditioners, automatic ovens, tile bathrooms, and built-in stereo equipment more than any of the amenities or spatial qualities which architectural design can bring to the home.

If these observations are correct, it would appear that Le Corbusier's old dictum about the dwelling—"The house is a machine to be lived in"—is accepted in practice if not in theory. However, what factors have made it possible for the modern dwelling to operate as an efficient machine while retaining some of the warmth and sentimental association of the old idea of home? Obviously, technology is an indispensable factor since it cuts down the space and time needed to perform the arduous tasks connected with food preparation and storage, laundering and house cleaning, heating and cooling, decoration and maintenance. Modern building materials and techniques have enlarged the possibilities open to the designer: light, strong, structural elements, some of them metal and plastic instead of wood; plate glass; new insulation materials, adhesives, and fasteners; strong new surface materials—paints, plastics, metals; prefabricated units, especially for kitchens and bathrooms; and almost universal availability of low-cost electricity (until the 1930's many rural homes had no electric power). Other factors we might cite are the generally increased family incomes which permit us to purchase and operate the often costly tools and appliances needed in the modern home, and the industrialization, to a small extent, of home building. Families purchase more than one home in a lifetime; they change and modernize its equipment frequently; and our current banking practices encourage the financing of new homes or the remodeling of existing homes.

The versatility of technology permits the inexpensive imitation of traditional hand-crafted home furnishings, so that really "modern" appliances and materials are confined to the kitchen and bathroom. Thus, living-rooms and bedrooms can appear untouched by technology and so retain their traditional sentiments and symbolic associations. Glass-fiber drapes, for example, can look like the finest hand-woven Irish linen; pressed-board can imitate any wood grain; industrially manufactured lighting fixtures, floor coverings, furniture, bric-a-brac, knicknacks, and what-nots, and even paintings can fairly well pretend to be handmade, and thus preserve our allegiance to former modes of making and former objects of cherished ownership.

Plate glass may be the single most influential material in affecting the dwelling. Ideal for warm climates, it is also used extensively in temperate and cold climates because we have enthusiastically accepted one of the main tenets of modern domestic architecture: the interpenetration of indoor and outdoor space. The contemporary house is designed so that its outer walls or shell constitute a screen rather than an impenetrable barrier. The one-level dwelling has many openings to the outdoors: Its floor is close to ground level; it may have a patio as part of its integral design; it tries to locate its "lamp and picture window" opposite a vista more inspiring than the neighbor's back yard. The picture window and the patio are so essential to our way of life that even apartment dwellers have them, with a balcony substituting for the patio, although that balcony high above the traffic is rarely used; it is usually an architect's device for breaking up a monotonous exterior facade or a realtor's device for renting apartments. There are, however, technical and structural reasons for the widespread use of glass. (1) The walls of many modern buildings can be penetrated at almost any point because they do not bear weight; they serve as curtains. Post-and-beam construction permits glass walls in homes as the steel frame does in skyscrapers. (2) The loss of heat moving in either direction through glass has been greatly reduced through double paning, while the framing and walls around glass are tight and well-insulated (older homes had no insulation except air space, or sometimes, layers of brick). (3) Modern plate glass is strong and durable, even over relatively large areas. (4) Careful orientation of the house on its site and proper location of the windows can admit the sun to rooms at the time of day when it is most desired. The architect who chooses to cooperate with nature can design eaves, overhangs, or sunbreaks so that the heat of the summer sun is blocked out while the warming winter sun is invited into the house.

Another device for control of interior climate is air-conditioning, which is not only a form of technology but also a symbol of philosophic disagreement in modern architecture. We possess the technology and soon will be wealthy enough to air-condition all interior living space. (If Buckminster Fuller succeeds in throwing domes over our cities, we shall be able to air-condition or weather-condition the urban out-of-doors too. Victor Gruen, an architect and city planner, has already constructed some shopping centers whose outdoor areas are under transparent enclosures and are thoroughly air-conditioned.) Much of modern domestic architecture, especially under the influence of Frank Lloyd Wright, is based on the goal of continuity with nature—using advanced technology to build structures which seem to grow out of their surroundings. But the philosophy of the so-called International Style architects, exemplified best by Walter Gropius, Ludwig Mies van der Rohe, and Marcel Breuer, urges the conception of the dwelling—or, indeed, any building—as an interior

BUCKMINSTER FULLER, proposed Geodesic Dome over New York City. Photo, copyright by Buckminster Fuller.

environment which can be completely controlled by technology. Architects can and have designed buildings without windows, with no modification of their exterior form in response to climate, orientation, or prevailing winds. Since engineering can take care of these problems, the architect presumably devotes his energies to designing beautiful spaces. And where the focus of activity is almost wholly internal—as in a museum, factory, department store, church, gymnasium, or laboratory—such buildings have been very successful. The high-speed elevator, the steel-frame skeleton, and light curtain-wall construction have enabled us to build almost as high as we wish, and to create a uniformly equable atmosphere throughout the structure. But there are some disturbing rumbles: When the technology is not working too well, uncomfortable temperature variations develop; where there are no windows, the inhabitants want to look out; where the air-conditioning works well, the dwellers wish to sense the advent of spring, the odor of gasoline fumes and damp city streets, the sound of automobile horns and the scuttle of pedestrians racing for cover. Such noises and waftings serve the urban office worker as the sound of the neighbor's gasoline lawn mower and the fragrance of burned barbecue serve the suburbanite. At any rate, they are among the real considerations of an art which, according to Vitruvius, the ancient Roman architect and theoretician, must satisfactorily afford firmness, commodity, and *delight* (strength, utility, and beauty).

FRANK LLOYD WRIGHT, Robie House (1909), top.

FRANK LLOYD WRIGHT, Fallingwater (1936), bottom. Photograph by Michael Fedison, courtesy Western Pennsylvania Conservancy.

FRANK LLOYD WRIGHT

The great artist-poet of the dwelling was Frank Lloyd Wright (1869–1959). In a long and controversial career—during which he designed skyscrapers, museums, housing developments, office buildings, shops, factories, college campuses, and hotels—he brought to the art of creating human shelter an original, pioneering, and distinctively American genius. He was independently ahead of European architects in many ways: in his understanding and exploitation of modern technology; in his revolt against the stultifying architectural baggage of the past; and in his aesthetic innovations, that is, his ability to deal with the dwelling as an art object, as something both beautiful to look at and a delight to live in. Wright's forays into social philosophy and community planning have not been as universally praised as his achievement in domestic architecture, although they are worth serious attention and have been provocative of healthy debate. But his houses are his chief monuments, and it is difficult, when we look at a building so sculpturally vital and exciting as the Robie House to realize that it was built as early as 1909.

Perhaps his most widely cited and reproduced house is "Fallingwater," built in 1936 for Edgar Kaufmann at Bear Run, Pennsylvania. It is at once a triumph of architectural romanticism and an example of the brilliant exploitation of technology. Only steel-and-concrete cantilever construction would permit the design of such graceful but massive overhanging slabs, which complement the rugged natural setting with their horizontal rectangular precision. There is an echo of International Style devotion to the unadorned cubical mass, but the over-all conception is romantic. The heavily textured masonry of the vertical masses associates the building with the materials, shapes, and colors of the site, an association which is an axiom of the Wright philosophy of building. Wright did not disdain engineering—indeed, he was one of its most original exponents. But he did not see sound engineering as an end in itself: To him, engineering was a tool to be employed in the light of his guiding concept of what a shelter is, a dwelling organically related to nature.

Wright's ideas about the internal organization of the house still provoke controversy, although many of them have been widely accepted. He held that a massive fireplace and hearth should be the physical and psychological center of the house. He disapproved of basements and attics. Materials like paint, plaster, varnish, and wood trim were to be avoided or reduced to a minimum. Ornament was not to be *applied* to the structural elements but would result from the natural patterns *inherent* in the building materials or growing logically out of the processes of forming and constructing. Cooking and dining facilities should be adjacent to the living room, located in the center of the house, away from the exterior walls. The kitchen or "work-space" should be a tall space behind the fireplace or adjacent to it so that cooking odors can flow up through it rather than into the house. Most of the rooms radiate from the fireplace core so that Wright's houses tend to have a cross-shaped plan. The arms of the cross are thus open to the outdoors on three sides, with horizontal bands of windows or clerestories around them and very wide overhanging eaves which create porch-like spaces underneath.

The interior of Mr. Wright's house, Taliesin East (see p. 78) in Spring Green, Wisconsin, shows the inviting warmth and variety of surface, space, and light which Wright built into his famous prairie houses. Oriental rugs are used to break up the floor space and to define functional areas, while Japanese screens and Chinese figurines are located on ledges set at various heights so that the eye is encouraged to linger and refresh itself. Wright's interiors were sometimes criticized for being too dark. But it would appear that he took care to calculate the modulation of light more than designers who simply flood a room with light, obliging the occupants to install acres of drapery to gain a measure of privacy and control over outside illumination. For instance, the rough ashlar (stone) masonry at Taliesin requires slanting light to set off its texture. And to be intimate, a corner meant for informal conversation needs a modulated, blended light, rather than the inhibiting glare of flood illumination. Of course, this room suggests the cave more than the tent or the metal cage. Perhaps we are drawn inward by our atavistic desires—deep, subconscious feelings of safety and comfort derived from the paleolithic memories of the race. With respect to comfort, the architect was less successful; the furniture, which Mr. Wright insisted on designing himself, seems unintended for the human backbone: Wright's right-angled chairs and sofas refuse to accommodate the compound curves of the garden-variety spine. Cushions and upholstery might mitigate their discommoding effects, but these seating arrangements could never approach the com-

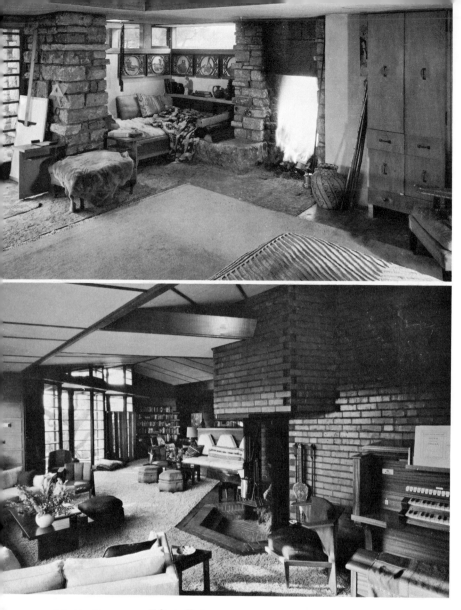

FRANK LLOYD WRIGHT, Taliesin East (1925), top. Photo, Bill Hedrich, Hedrich-Blessing.

FRANK LLOYD WRIGHT, Hanna House (1937) bottom. Courtesy Paul R. Hanna.

of the furniture, and the powerful fireplace projections. Into this complex space, direct sunlight is admitted, but it must pass through tree branches first, then through the small window panes and past the chairs until it reaches the brick fireplace wall and the sunken, stepped-down hearth which makes its own shadow pattern. Thus, we have a marvelously rich and complex orchestration of the textures and colors of materials, with moving, patterned light working on them. It should be stressed that these interior effects are not the result of an unthinking, cluttered architectural design—a mere addiction to broken surfaces. Rather they are the consequence of a fully developed philosophy of shelter combined with the design ability to create the spaces which that philosophy implies.

LUDWIG MIES VAN DER ROHE

Conceivably, the rectilinear austerities of International Style architecture can best be understood against the background of Art Nouveau, a manner of design and decoration which affected all the arts at the turn of the century. The subway, or Métro, station, one of several designed for the city of Paris by Hector Guimard (1867–1942), exhibits most of the typical features of an Art Nouveau structure about the size of a house: the generous use of exposed, ornamental and structural elements of cast iron, the avoidance of right angles, the heavy reliance on a serpentine line, and the location of sinuous curves at every joint and change of direction. This style had a revival, which started slowly after World War II (possibly as a reaction to the economic and aesthetic restraint imposed by wartime restric-

fort or the sculptural elegance of, say, a Hans Wegner chair (see p. 131). It was not as a furniture designer, but as a master of space and light *modulation* that Wright demonstrated his artistry.

The living room of the Paul Hanna House (1937) in Palo Alto, California, has a less cavelike quality than Taliesin and shows how important the pattern of light and cast shadow is in Wright's total conception. There are very few right angles in the room itself, with its gently sloping ceilings, the polygonal shapes tions), and reached its peak in the early 1960's. Perhaps affluence encourages baroque impulses among the leaders of fashion and design. In prosperous times, the doctrine of Mies van der Rohe that "less is more" begins to seem unnecessarily ascetic; we grow interested in a kind of frivolous, lavish elegance. But Art Nouveau was not really elegant or grand in the classical manner (though it may have been exuberant); rather it sought to unite art and nature—nature conceived as a forest grove—through imitating organic forms, especially plant life. Wright, who was an active young architect in 1900, was also interested in the organic, but in a less derivative and more sophisticated manner than Guimard, Horta, Hoffman and the other Central European designers working in this botanical mode. Later, Wright did not have to react against Art Nouveau, whereas Gropius, Breuer, Mies, Neutra, and Le Corbusier may have felt they did. At any rate, the International Style architects, strongly under the influence of the Bauhaus (see pp. 119–123, "The Emergence of Industrial Design"), seemed to have as doctrinaire a devotion

to the right angle as did Art Nouveau adherents to the S-curve. Hence, from the 1920's until about 1942, with the exception of Wright and his followers, avant-garde houses were austere white cubes, devoid of ornament, with extensive glass facades and no-nonsense flat roofs minus eaves. Small wonder that the popular reaction to these buildings was chilly and that, because of severe commercial or industrial versions of the style, it became known irreverently in some quarters as "gas-station moderne."

Of course, in the hands of a master the International Style had authentic elegance, as in the famous Tugendhat house in Czechoslovakia, which was designed in 1930 by Ludwig Mies van der Rohe (1886–   ). Floor-to-ceiling windows, black marble partitions, polished metal columns, silk curtains, and oriental rugs created an atmosphere of restrained splendor, of sensuous appeal within a controlling, intellectual framework. An exterior view of the house conveys no such sumptuous impression: The rear elevation reveals the debt of modern architecture to the asceticism of Mondrian. Mies appears to have been

HECTOR GUIMARD, entrance gate to Paris subway station (Métropolitain) (c. 1900). Collection The Museum of Modern Art, New York, gift of Régie Autonome des Transports Parisiens.

LUDWIG MIES VAN DER ROHE, Tugendhat House (1930), interior and exterior. Courtesy The Museum of Modern Art, New York.

LUDWIG MIES VAN DER ROHE, Farnsworth House (1950), left. Photo, Hedrich-Blessing.

LUDWIG MIES VAN DER ROHE, Crown Hall (1952), right. Courtesy Illinois Institute of Technology.

LUDWIG MIES VAN DER ROHE, floor plan of Farnsworth House, below. Photo, Hedrich-Blessing.

the most craftsmanlike of the International Style designers in that he never abandoned an ideal of *beauty* achieved through well-made and well-proportioned parts, never became addicted to design as mere multiplication of standardized parts: He showed how to achieve a quiet, controlled splendor by attention to detail and without architectural histrionics.

In the Farnsworth House (1950) built in Plano, Illinois, Mies employed a formal vocabulary similar to one he was to use again in his School of Architecture for the Illinois Institute of Technology in 1952. Both structures are approached from a raised platform and both make elegant use of a simple series of slab-like steps as a transition from the plane of the floor. The Farnsworth House consists of two connected rectangular boxes that are raised off the ground; to establish continuity with nature, rather than exploit natural materials in the building itself, he uses large expanses of glass, which afford generous views and produce reflected images. Extreme simplification of form and function is seen

in the use of pristine white posts to support the roof, to separate the large glass panes, and to act as stilts, raising the house off the ground. In the Illinois Tech building, Mies has hung the ceiling from imposing steel girders stretching across the roof to black exterior steel columns which also function visually as satisfying vertical accents. The building is not raised off the ground as in the Farnsworth House, but the platform and two sets of gently ascending steps create the impression that it is. The repeated horizontals of the steps help to balance the vertical rhythm of the columns and the mullions (bars between the windows) and thus endow the structure with a classic dignity and repose.

A Miesian house is essentially *one* large cubical space in which functional space divisions and rooms are achieved by nonstructural partitions and by the location of utilities, closets, kitchens, and so on. For Mies, the real work of architecture lies in the creation of unencumbered interior space which the occupants may subdivide and use as they wish. These internal arrangements are, after all, a matter of private and temporary caprice, a matter of interior decoration. Perhaps Philip Johnson's glass house in New Canaan, Connecticut (1949), expresses this Miesian point of view best, although it represents an obviously limited solution to the problem of shelter for a family. By refusing to be overly concerned about *who* uses his buildings, or *how* they will employ the interior vistas he has created, Mies has been able to concentrate on the design of what is becoming that rarest, most unobtainable commodity in the modern world—pure, unobstructed, undemanding, serene space.

LE CORBUSIER

Le Corbusier (Charles Édouard Jeanneret-Gris, 1887–1965), who began with assumptions similar to those of Mies, moved in a more sculptural direction as his career progressed; increasingly he employed poured-concrete forms and left the steel-glass vocabulary to Mies, Johnson, and their numerous imitators. In 1928, Le Corbusier's Savoye house

exhibited the influence of Cubist painting (he was himself an active abstract artist) and employed forms much as they were to be seen in the contemporaneous architecture of Mies, Gropius, and Breuer. But the house also shows an early use of his stilts, a brilliant structural device which has been widely adopted in apartment houses such as his *Unité d'Habitation* (see p. 82) and in buildings designed by architects throughout the world. These reinforced columns of concrete, which the architect called *pilotis*, exploit the fact that steel-and-concrete construction has permanently freed architecture from the requirements of earth-bound, compression construction (structures in which the building material is *squeezed*, as opposed to tension construction in which the material is *stretched*.) A structure can now be lifted into the air, freeing the space at ground-level for a variety of practical

LE CORBUSIER, *Unité d'Habitation*, Marseilles (1947–52), above. Photo, Lucien Hervé.

FRANK LLOYD WRIGHT, Johnson Wax Administration and Research Center (1938), interior, below. Courtesy Johnson Wax.

LUDWIG MIES VAN DER ROHE, Barcelona chair (1929), top. Courtesy Knoll Associates.

ALVAR AALTO, armchair (1934), center. Courtesy Artek.

LE CORBUSIER, chaise longue frame (1927), bottom. Photo, Lucien Hervé.

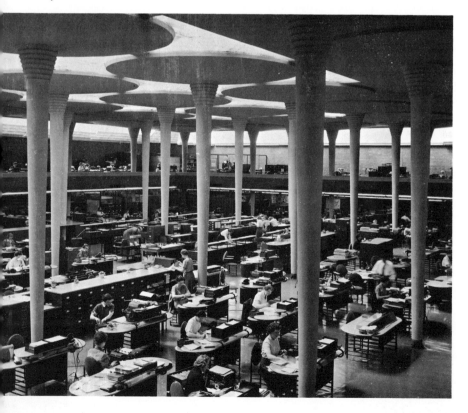

activities. The open area also creates an appealing visual organization, with a strong shadow pattern at the building's base crisply defining the concrete forms above it.

Wright, too, developed his own "mushroom" pillars (something like *pilotis*) in the Johnson Wax building interior (1938), partly as a structural but mainly as a decorative device. Since his houses generally rose from a concrete pad, he employed cantilevered forms to open up ground space and provide an interesting light-and-shade pattern (Sturges House, 1939). But Wright was temperamentally attached to the earth. Le Corbusier and the Bauhaus designers had a better appreciation of the possibilities of suspension engineering; indeed, they developed several classic chairs based on suspension and tension principles. Houses on stilts were used as early as the neolithic riverbank villages of about 12,000 B.C., but it remained for Le Corbusier to create a viable application of the same principle in the twentieth century.

The Villa Shodan, built for an Indian businessman in 1952 by Le Corbusier, shows the development of his style within the directions indicated by the Villa Savoye of 1929. The mastery of poured concrete is now well established, with the textures that are imprinted by the rough wooden formwork serving to overcome any unpleasant, mechanical slickness of surface. We also see the full development of Le Corbusier's invention, the *brise-soleil*, or sunbreak, a device which is especially useful in tropical countries, but is also employed wherever the unobstructed sun would create interior problems of heat and glare. The occupants can look out, yet the exterior rooms are shaded against the steady beating down of the sun, and visually, a delightful articulation of surface, of light and shadow, is achieved. The Brazilian Oscar Niemeyer (1907–   ) has been much influenced by Le Corbusier, and throughout South America there are magnificent public and private buildings of poured concrete in which Niemeyer, and others, employ sunbreaks and pilotis.

It should be realized that the complicated wooden formwork required to build these virtually sculptured concrete structures is more feasible economically in countries which have abundant,

In the interior of the Villa Shodan, Le Corbusier virtually paints with light through the design of the window perforations, much as in his Chapel at Ronchamps.

LE CORBUSIER, Villa Shodan (1952), interior and exterior. Photo, Lucien Hervé.

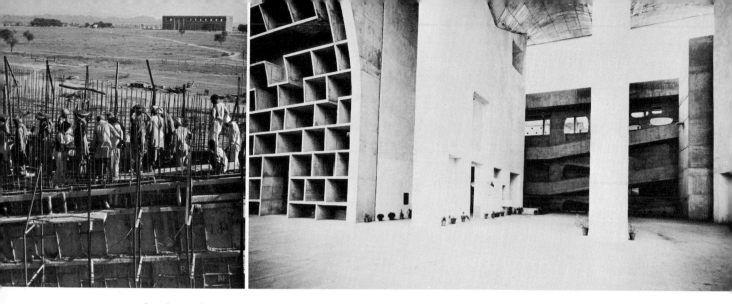

LE CORBUSIER, wooden formwork used in construction at Chandigarh, India, left. Photo, Lucien Hervé.

LE CORBUSIER, High Court Building, Chandigarh, India (1955–56), right. Photo, Lucien Hervé.

OSCAR NIEMEYER, President's residence, Brasília (1960), left.

PAUL RUDOLPH, Art and Architecture Building, Yale University (1963), right. Courtesy Yale University News Bureau.

inexpensive sources of hand labor. Thus, Le Corbusier could employ his structural vocabulary on a vast scale for the creation of an entire national capital city, as at Chandigarh, India. And Niemeyer has been engaged on a project of similar size and scope, the building of a whole new capital, Brasília, in the interior of Brazil. However, when reinforced concrete is employed in industrially advanced countries, especially in the United States where labor costs are high, construction time must be held to a min-

imum, and therefore variations in shape and space tend to be eliminated. A building vocabulary of steel frame, glass wall, and metal panel with some minor masonry trim is more suitable to our economy. And when concrete slab construction *is* used, design restrictions and limitations are so great that the visual results are very much like steel-frame structures. It would be difficult for the nonexpert to look at a row of glass boxes on Madison or Park Avenue in New York City and distinguish the steel-frame from the reinforced-concrete buildings. As for home construction, poured concrete is very rare; since it is quite expensive and mostly reserved for clients who are friendly to experimentation. In the Yale art school designed by Paul Rudolph (1918–), we see a lavish and costly use of poured concrete containing a special aggregate which endows the building's surface with a coarse, rich texture; the texture was heightened by vertical striations imprinted by the formwork, after which the concrete surface was hand-hammered by the workmen. What is especially noteworthy is the courageous commissioning of so daring a structure by Yale's late President Griswold; he could easily have satisfied the practical requirements of the University with the usual glass-steel-and-masonry box.

If Wright was poet of the house, Le Corbusier was poet of the apartment and the multiple dwelling. His *Unités d'Habitation* (apartment houses) have been widely imitated, especially his building at Marseille (1947–52). The influence of his stilts, sunbreaks, roof sculptures, and rough concrete are particularly evident in several buildings by the brilliant Japanese designer Kenzo Tange (1913–)—the Peace Museum at Hiroshima, his own residence, his Tokyo City Hall interior, and his Kurashiki City Hall. Tange's Imabari City Hall (1957) seems derived from the chapel at Ronchamp just as his wall treatment in the Kurashiki City Hall derives from the chapel interior at Ronchamp. However, imitation of forms is one matter, the original conception of shelter another. Le Corbusier thought of an apartment as a drawer sliding into a building skeleton; the whole might be compared to a chest of drawers. He also used

the analogy of a bottle and a bottle rack. In the Marseille building, each apartment is a self-contained unit of two levels which can slide into a stardardized cavity in the "bottle rack," or building skeleton. If mass-production methods were fully extended to housing, these drawers or bottles could be completely fabricated in factories elsewhere, hoisted into place in the building skeleton, and plugged in. At Marseille, the apartments are sound-insulated from each other by lead sheets between the common walls, something modern apartment dwellers would appreciate, as there has been virtually no acoustical privacy in many of our most costly new multiple dwellings. The kitchens are air-conditioned; living rooms are two stories high and give onto a balcony with sunbreak and magnificent view. On every third floor there is a corridor, called an "interior road," which runs the length of the building. The interior roads on floors seven and eight contain an indoor shopping center, with shops for fish, meat, dairy food, fruit and vegetables, and a bakery, liquor store, and drug store. To complete its list of essential services, the *Unité* has a laundry, cleaning service, barber shop, and post office. It has many of the features of a resort hotel, but is intended for *permanent* residents. The building holds three hundred thirty-seven apartments of twenty-three different types, and thus can accommodate large families or unmarried individuals. The seventeenth floor has a kindergarten and nursery; and above it on the roof is a roof-garden, children's swimming pool, gymnasium, running track, solarium, and snack bar. The various roof structures for elevators, ventilation, and other utilities have been designed as playful sculptures, while

KENZO TANGE, Imabari City Hall (1959), above, top.

LE CORBUSIER, Chapel at Ronchamp (1950–55), above, bottom. Photo, Lucien Hervé.

KENZO TANGE, Kurashiki City Hall (1960), below, top.

LE CORBUSIER, interior of Chapel at Ronchamp, below, bottom. Photo, Lucien Hervé.

the machinery for elevators, generators, and air-conditioning is tucked under the first floor above the stilts.

It should be stressed that the Marseille apartments were built by the city and were intended to be working-class dwellings. The occupants formed an association to secure social and cultural benefit for themselves and to administer their affairs in connection with living in the *Unités*. The only comparable social arrangement in the United States would be cooperative apartments, though these are usually occupied by persons of substantial means.

It is clear that Le Corbusier intended to make urban residence a positively satisfying and rich experience, not merely a compromise painfully accepted by people who would rather live elsewhere. In the United States, our population has become increasingly urbanized, but, it seems, increasingly unhappy with urban living. We too have built immense multiple dwellings for persons of all economic levels, but however striking or "modern" these structures may appear to be from the outside, we do not seem to be able to develop satisfying patterns of life within. At least those who can escape to suburbs or small towns continue to do so. What can the reason be for these costly failures? Is it that Le Corbusier's pattern does not work? Or is it inapplicable to the circumstances of American life? Do we design and build badly? Do our huge apartment houses constitute a *new conception* of social living carried out in new architectural terms in response to new conditions of urban life? Or do these structures represent the same, old conceptions of urban life in multiple dwellings which have been given a spurious novelty by applications of the latest steel-glass technology?

THE MODERN DWELLING

Wright, Mies, and Le Corbusier, then, are the three acknowledged geniuses of modern architecture. Their contributions to the design of the dwelling—and indeed, to the design of all structures—have been among the most original and influential features of our civilization. Many gifted designers have appeared among their followers, men who understood, adapted, and refined the language of form, the philosophy of shelter, or the utilization of technology inherited from the masters. But the genius of the "form-givers," as they have been called, consisted of their ability to synthesize or create a new conception of dwelling space based on stubbornly held convictions about the nature of living together under one roof, the requirements of modern life, and the bewildering array of forms, processes, tools, and devices preferred by applied science. That is why these architects are honored above others, although other men have made distinguished contributions to architecture as builders, teachers, designers, engineers, and even as clients.

Today the magazine racks of any drugstore display a staggering number of publications about home building, decorating, and remodeling. Their colored photographs, architectural renderings, and suggestions for decoration are often so glamorous and exciting (and expensive) that the individual is easily overwhelmed and confused. Once we have been liberated from the idea that the form of a house is something traditionally, naturally, and permanently set, like the shape of a tree or the color of snow, we are confronted with a bewildering array of choices even within a narrow economic range. That is, despite our talk about conformity, this civilization offers more options to the individual than any other in history, *provided he is able and willing to exercise intelligent choice.* What are some of the principles or guiding ideas about domestic architecture which can be used by the well-intentioned citizen who feels at once liberated by modern architecture and perplexed by its infinite variety?

(1) A house does not exist in a physical or social vacuum. It is set among other houses to which it must be harmoniously related. It is not primarily a form of self-expression. It is oriented on a specific site to which it should seem to belong and from which it should derive specific advantages. Increasingly, the house does not shut out the environment, but rather chooses deliberately to include parts of the environment within itself—visually through its fenestration, and physically through its patterns of ingress and egress and traffic circulation between the house and grounds.

(2) The real substance of a dwelling is the shape of its space, not its kitchen and bathroom fixtures. Utilities change and can be replaced but the spaces through which we move remain fairly constant, and they are the chief determinants of our psychic satisfaction in the dwelling. Surfaces and surface materials receive more attention than they deserve. Elegant panelling or papering cannot overcome badly shaped space, whereas a poor or unsuitable surface material *can* be changed. Space should be shaped around the requirements of a particular family rather than the supposed requirements of fashion or style. This calls for a certain amount of self-knowledge, a realistic assessment of one's present habits and anticipated needs. Since it is difficult to predict requirements and preferences with much accuracy, flexible or informal space arrangement is best for most people.

(3) The outside of the dwelling is, in part, a membrane which selectively transmits light and heat for the comfort of its occupants and reflects the shape of the interior space. Traditional features of building—cornices, gables, entablatures, pediments, cupolas, and so on—tend to be survivals of obsolete building technologies. Their symbolic-expressive power is far less potent and dramatic than the forms which can be created with modern materials and structural devices. Unfortunately, some modern builders make eclectic use of materials, producing results which are frivolous or ostentatious. They may combine brickwork, stonework, wood, concrete, stucco, glass, marble, mosaic, asbestos, plastic, and metal in vulgar profusion in the same structure. Simplicity of material is a virtue in building, especially when the shape is complex. But the exterior is more than a membrane; it has a *pictorial* relationship to the site. The relationship is harmonious to the extent that indigenous materials and skillful landscaping are employed and the dominant lines and masses of the structure respond to the topography, that is, the shape of the land. (The urban dwelling is usually part of a multi-unit structure and thus does not *directly* confront the problem of relatedness to its environment. Perhaps that is the reason for the heavy emphasis on interior decoration in some apartment dwellings.)

(4) Interior decoration should not mean merely the application of ornament, the embellishment of surfaces, the collection and display of objects, or

the selection of furniture. (Its most professional practitioners prefer the designation interior designer or interior architect.) Since the dwelling interior and its contents are experienced visually as well as used, their arrangement needs to be considered from an aesthetic as well as a practical standpoint. Rules, principles, and guides about the use of color, scale, textures, period styles, fabrics, and so on are easily obtained. They are most needed in apartments, where architectural qualities are generally very limited and where emphasis must be placed upon furniture, color schemes, objets d'art, and lighting. For the private dwelling, built-in storage units often take the place of some pieces of furniture. But for any dwelling, the problems of unity, focus, coherence, articulation, and expressiveness must be solved, unless an architect has designed the house down to the final door-knob.

For most of us, the normal accretions of living, the gifts of well-meaning friends, the hand-me-downs of honored ancestors, combined with our everyday debris, constitute the decorative objects of our interior environment. The possessions we purposely acquire, like furniture and rugs, soon receive a patina of wear which makes them seem to belong with everything else, no matter how incongruous. A merciful psychological mechanism blots out any consciousness we may have of aesthetic or stylistic struggle among our possessions and so we can live amid our clutter in relative equanimity. After some time, the hideous things we own may become positive necessities without which we could not comfortably endure. But at this point in architectural history, one can only observe that despite the best efforts of Mies, man is something of a squirrel, and he will continue to accumulate things he does not need and can find no place to store. The interior designer cannot very well change our squirrelly nature, and so he justifies his role by creating ingenious containers to store or display our possessions; he tries to endow them in the aggregate with unity, pattern, and coherence through arrangement or lighting; or he substitutes new fetish objects for the old ones if we can be persuaded to part with them.

(5) Genuinely satisfactory architectural solutions to the problems of apartment dwelling are not too readily available except in the work of a few architects like Richard Neutra and Le Corbusier. Interior decoration or design is largely a corrective effort, an endeavor to conceal bad design or make undistinguished design interesting. The apartment houses of Mies van der Rohe are magnificent in their totality, but their individual cells appear to be neutral. That is, they do not seem to create the positive excitement to be found in the interior of a Wright house. (Yet there are those who prefer them to the sometimes forced rusticity of Wright.) They require the ministrations of an interior designer. Until original architectural and social thought is applied to the multiple dwelling in the United States, apartment dwelling will be attractive mainly for the accessibility and convenience of other urban attractions and services. Positive delight in one's home is largely the prerogative of the inhabitant of the single, mortgaged, detached dwelling.

CONCLUSION

Since the days when men lived in caves, tents, and huts, domestic dwellings have gone through immense transformations accompanied by equally radical changes in human personality. Now space exploration and scientific fantasy contemplate residence on distant planets in strange or nonexistent atmospheres. In the present era of innovation and experiment, the very idea of a shelter which assumes a hostile environment—a safe inside and an unfriendly outside—may become obsolete. If climate is controlled, our only shelter might be our clothing, and that for privacy, not protection. Perhaps houses will only be storage places for certain private effects while the rest of life is carried on in specially designed structures for particular activities. There may even be distinct structures for the enjoyment of privacy, just as there now are special buildings to which we go for collective dreams—motion picture theaters. The line between the home and the community may substantially disappear. Perhaps families will live in disposable dwellings like the nests which birds build and discard each year. Architecture can accomplish such wonderful (or dreadful) ends now, if we wish. But do we wish? Look about, and see how the ideas of planners, talent of designers, and investments of bankers give form and texture to the architectural fabric of society.

Large-Scale Design: The Community

Everyone seems to be aware of our community problems of crowding, air pollution, traffic snarls, noise, pedestrian danger, visual chaos, and ugliness. We also know that communities are not always and inevitably afflicted by these problems. Communities are built by men, hence men are responsible for the predicament we are in. Only men—not nature or the passage of time—will get us out of our difficulties. What are some of the remedies which have been tried or proposed to make human communities truly livable again? If the community is thought of as a work of art—either well or badly executed—what are the elements of that art?

We know how to design and construct excellent buildings and roadways of all types but we do not seem to be able to put them together so that the results are anything short of lethal. Even if it is granted that the automobile is a deadly weapon and the source of many of our problems, do we not possess the design ingenuity to minimize its destructiveness? Can we build cities and towns which are not completely at the mercy of noxious exhausts and murderous fenders? Is peaceful coexistence possible? Or, stated more positively, since man is a social animal, can we create the physical arrangements which will allow him to enjoy social life?

Architects and planners, engineers and philosophers have thought about these problems and have made proposals ranging from extreme utopianism to modest and cautious reform. We shall examine a few of their ideas. Considering the growth of populations and the physical and aesthetic inadequacy of most communities, the design of cities and towns should be of vital concern to every citizen in a democratic society. If comprehensive ideas and designs exist which can help cure our various civic diseases, it is exceedingly important that

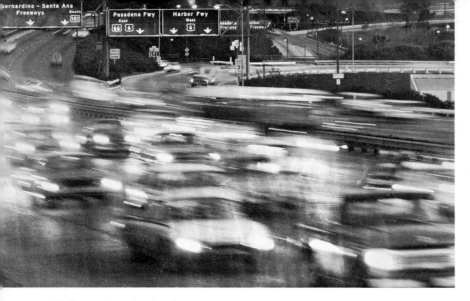

Traffic on Los Angeles freeway.
Courtesy American Airlines.

EBENEZER HOWARD, Garden City plans (1902). From *Garden Cities of Tomorrow*.

citizens know about them, exercise informed judgment about them, and ultimately act to reshape the man-made environment.

EBENEZER HOWARD:
THE GARDEN CITY

In the nineteenth century as today, people left farms in droves and added to the congestion of cities. The countryside was depopulated and the cities teemed. By 1902, Ebenezer Howard, an Englishman without architectural training, realized that the problem was not merely one of reversing the flow of migration: It was necessary to create communities which combined urban and rural features—communities not wholly engaged in industry nor wholly devoted to rural or suburban life. His solution: "Town and country *must be married,* and out of this union will spring a new hope, a new life, a new civilization."° He wrote a book which advanced the concept of the "Garden City," a community of concentric belts of land alternately used for commerce or manufacturing and "green" belts or park land. The greenbelts would insulate the functional areas from each other while providing recreation space and that balance of rural and urban qualities needed for a healthy and aesthetically satisfying existence. He planned to have administrative and recreational buildings at the core of these communities—something like the squares and village greens which give emotional and visual focus to small towns and some city districts.

Land would not be individually owned, but would be held and developed by a common body which would limit the growth of the community to about 30,000, thus preventing speculation and high density of habitation. Beyond this population, it would be necessary to start a new garden city. The outermost belt of the community might be used to grow food for local consumption or be left uncultivated so that it could serve as recreation space and function as a natural defense against absorption by other towns. (Many of today's overpopulated urban districts were once lovely villages which were eventually surrounded and swallowed up.)

Howard hoped his plan would lead to the decentralization of London, an event which never took place. But it

°Ebenezer Howard, *Garden Cities of Tomorrow*, 1902.

was translated into reality in several English and American suburbs. The *word* "greenbelt" has been widely adopted, but rarely have all of Howard's principles been applied in a single community: controlled growth; ownership of land by a common authority; and the systematic segregation rather than the indiscriminate mixing of residential, industrial, recreational, and administrative functions.

It should be stressed that Howard's garden city was to be a balanced community, with the activities of work, recreation, residence, and government contained within it. Today's suburbs or satellite towns are mainly one-function communities: They have been called "dormitory suburbs." Without an industrial base, the community of home-owners, heavily engaged in child-rearing, is hard pressed to finance and maintain good school systems, not to mention other essential services: police and fire protection; street lighting; water supply and sewage disposal; road maintenance. As industries move or are lured into such communities, as the highways to the central city grow more crowded, as commercial and industrial facilities sprawl in unplanned profusion outside their corporate limits, the suburbs lose the advantages of decentralization which their residents presumably left the city to gain. Aside from the moral aspects of suburban parasitism—using and enjoying urban services without contributing to their maintenance and support—there are practical disadvantages in a living arrangement which grows increasingly insupportable from an economic standpoint and is architecturally monotonous. One begins to learn painfully that "no community is an island."

FRANK LLOYD WRIGHT: BROADACRE CITY

Of course, one way to deal with the problems of urbanism is to eliminate cities, to start all over again, in a sense, by reorganizing society into small, almost self-sufficient communities. Or, if cities cannot be dispensed with, and since their problems are too deep-seated to be solved, we can proceed to reform part of society by creating ideal communities outside the megalopolitan monsters. This might be called the Noah's Ark approach to urban redesign. If the ugliness as well as the social disorganization of the city is due to overcrowding, then decentralization—spreading out the population—overcomes the mechanical and space problems of urbanism. Also, it enables men to establish a better relationship to the land and to nature. In his Broadacre City plan of the 1930's, Frank Lloyd Wright proposed a decentralized solution: an acre of land for each person. (The United States population at the time could have been accommodated on the available acreage.) Farmers would have ten acres, but everyone would raise some of his own food, supplementing what full-time farmers could grow. This procedure might be less efficient from the standpoint of agricultural yield per acre, but Wright believed, as did Jefferson, that moral and educational benefits accrue to people who till the soil, at least part of the time.

In a land area of four square miles, fourteen-hundred families or six thousand people could live, produce some food, provide each other with a variety of personal services, and engage in some light manufacturing. Wright believed,

FRANK LLOYD WRIGHT, Broadacre
City plan (1933–40). By permission
of the publisher, Horizon Press,
from *The Living City* by Frank
Lloyd Wright. Copyright 1958.

quite correctly, that the automobile and
helicopter liberate men residentially.
Unlike nineteenth and early twentieth
century workers, we do not have to live
immediately next to where we work.
The telephone enables us to communicate
easily with cities, if we need to; radio
and television broadcast news and entertainment; and motion picture theatres
are everywhere. Thus, we do not have to
live *in* the city to use or enjoy some of
the essential goods and services created
there. (Some of us can live parasitically
off of the city, however.)

But can communities of six thousand create the necessities of modern
civilization? How many people are
associated with a modern university?
Fifteen thousand? Thirty-five thousand?
How many are needed to support a first-
class museum, hospital, theatre, department store, school system, steel plant,
state capitol?

Wright did not plan to dispense
with cities at once, however. Eventually
they would wither away. But the existence of the city was part of his plan
(albeit grudgingly), since some of the
residents of Broadacre would commute
there to work. (Today commuters wonder
whether two or three hours per day of
boring, unproductive travel are suffi-

ciently rewarded by character-building
activities in the suburbs like raising toma-
toes and mowing the lawn.) Still, contemporary suburban life is a caricature of
the Wright idea. He genuinely wished
men to raise their own food, to improve
the land, to be substantially free of money
and its associated evils. Their houses
would be designed by architects like
Wright, who would relate the dwellings
to the shape of the land. The shape of
city lots, which strongly governs the
design and orientation of the houses on
them, is based on the speculator's need
to cut land up into standardized packages which can readily be sold. Wright
believed that the operation of a money
economy distorted the natural and
proper architectural solution to man's
problems of work and shelter. People
would not own land in Broadacre City,
but would hold it so long as they could
make productive use of it. The point
of this idea is that land would not be a
commodity which is traded for profit,
but rather a source of sustenance and
delight for those who can live harmoniously on it.

Americans have traditionally believed that individualism and independence are the possession of men who do
not work for wages. Of course, when
farmers produce so much that they depend on the income received from the
sale of their surpluses, they become enmeshed in the money economy. It is difficult to think of our large-scale farmers
with their subsidies, price-supports, and
scientific assistance from the great land
grant universities, as independent, rugged individualists. That is why Wright
and other utopians wished agriculture
and light manufacture to be a sort of
serious avocation—necessary to sustenance, but not so industrialized that it

became a business. When Mr. Wright was asked, "Can you produce U.S. Steel by decentralized methods?" he replied, "Yes, of course; more effectively, so far as human life is concerned and the benefit it derives from steel . . . .The Garys and the Pittsburghs have served their term. We do not need them now."[*] There speaks the authentic utopian, a sensitive man despite his aggressive tone, who had looked at Pittsburgh (before its rebirth in the 1950's) and decided it would be better to begin again in the uncorrupted countryside.

The principles on which Broadacre City would be organized are best summarized in the following list prepared by Wright himself:[**]

> No private ownership.
> No landlord and tenant.
> No "housing." No subsistence home-
>   steads.
> No traffic problems. No back and forth
>   haul.
> No railroads. No streetcars.
> No grade crossings.
> No poles. No wires in sight.
> No ditches alongside the roads.
> No headlights. No light fixtures.
> No glaring cement roads or walks.
> No tall buildings except as isolated in
>   parks.
> No slum. No scum.
> No public ownership of private needs.

LE CORBUSIER: VILLE RADIEUSE

The garden city is a suburb; the suburb is a tentacle of the city. According to Le Corbusier, it creates more problems than it solves: commuting; expensive installation of utilities from the central

[*] Baker Brownell and Frank Lloyd Wright, *Architecture and Modern Life*, 1937, p. 302.
[**] Frank Lloyd Wright, *The Living City*, Horizon Press, 1958.

city; too many vehicles; costly maintenance. And eventually the garden city is absorbed by the spreading central city. The *Ville Radieuse* or its variants, proposed for several French cities in the 1920's, is a plan for as many as three million people. Unlike Wright the American, who generally detested skyscrapers, which are an American invention, Le Corbusier the Frenchman found them absolutely essential. He would create *vertical* garden cities. The *Ville Radieuse* paradoxically has a higher population density than present cities and yet *more* open space. The explanation lies in its huge but widely separated office buildings and apartment houses. Instead of being clustered to form the well-known canyons of Manhattan, they are open to light and air, surrounded by park areas on all sides, and approached by unimpeded highways on several levels. The highways, subways, and trainways radiate outward from the center of the city, much as do the streets in Washington, D.C. At the outer rings of the city are located large apartment houses of the

LE CORBUSIER, *Ville Radieuse: Voisin* Plan for Paris (1925). Photo, Lucien Hervé.

type at Marseille, fifteen or twenty stories in height, with some individual dwellings situated among them. Industry would be located still further out from the city, but not very far from the apartments where workers live.

The space opened up in the city by high-density skyscrapers could be safely used by pedestrians since the different kinds of transportation would have their own levels. This is an ideal of today's city planners which we cannot seem to reach. Some of our most modern urban redevelopment schemes locate parking garages in the core of the city, thus drawing vehicles into the center city and forcing pedestrians to compete with them for space. Such an arrangement results in so much inconvenience and harassment for people who have come "downtown" to shop or dine that they are increasingly drawn to suburban shopping centers. As a consequence, shops and restaurants in downtown areas, even when abetted by low-cost parking garages, find it increasingly difficult to compete with decentralized shopping centers.

Le Corbusier was reconciled to the existence of the city and of its unique culture. He did not seek to escape but to change the city. And the world seems to have accepted his commitment to high-rise structures but, until recently, was unwilling to carry out the radical surgery in the central part of the city necessary to rationalize the transport systems and admit light, sun, and air to the downtown districts by opening up the space around the skyscrapers. Also, when we tear down decaying urban areas in order to create the space for a new and comprehensive plan, we find ourselves faced with many painful decisions. Must everything go? Tearing down some

areas involves the destruction of our visual history. Can some of the monuments of architecture be retained? Can the architectural "cure" of a city evolve gradually, incorporating the new with the old, or will such gradualism inevitably fail?

It should be pointed out, in fairness, that when an irreplaceable monument is torn down today, it is rarely because of large-scale urban redesign. Rather it is because our major cities do not have adequate legislation to protect these monuments. The pressure to wreck some of the great and expensively constructed buildings of the past comes from real estate and other interests that perceive larger revenues from new structures on the old sites. The cost of operating older hotels, train stations, and private mansions reduces profit margins to the point where it seems economically wise to replace them. Alas, their replacements are too often designed on the basis of maximum utilization of the site, maximum rentable space, and a minimum of architectural amenity. The architectural quality of much urban construction is based on investment considerations for the most part: hence, there is a great deal of tearing down and building of commercial structures in American cities.

In Europe, legislation, as well as a long tradition of profound reverence for artistic monuments, prevents the destruction of great buildings. There, cities seem to grow organically; the continuity of the past with the present is maintained. And when drastic urban surgery is called for, it is usually undertaken to improve the visual organization of space and with full attention to the *total* context of buildings and open areas. War and bombing devastation, of course, make it possible to design and build from scratch. For instance, the opportunity for Le Corbusier's Marseille apartment house grew out of the need for housing following World War II. But a great deal of rebuilding in Europe has taken place since then, hence the architectural crises of urbanism cannot be traced to the War, but rather to the unsuitability of cities, as we knew them, to the conditions of modern life.

However, the *Ville Radieuse* was a plan dating from 1925. It sets ideals of efficiency—the rational use of energy and space—above all others. Order and beauty would result from the intelligent application of "the Modulor" to building and large-scale planning. Stripped of the Gallic enthusiasm with which Le Corbusier promoted the modulor, it is a common-sense set of dimensions and ratios based on the parts and intervals of the human body. These dimensions help a designer plan a chair, ceiling height, or door opening, and multiples of the modulor guide the architect in laying out gardens, parks, and whole cities. Through use of these fundamental ratios, all building and planning is presumably endowed with human scale. There may be some utility in employing a modulor for various design problems. And since human perception *is* guided by a self-image of the body, its size, and operation, a certain harmony can result from the systematic use of a human canon of proportions. But the plastic qualities of Le Corbusier's buildings are more likely based on his artistic intuition and his experience as a painter than on the mechanical application of the modulor system.

So much of architecture or of history depends on the emotional biases of its leading personalities. Le Corbusier,

an active and tremendously productive person as writer, painter, sculptor, architect, and planner, feared boredom. According to him, the detached family dwelling in the suburbs is most efficiently and satisfactorily used for about twenty years, while a family is being raised. Then the children leave, and the parents, alone in a house larger than their needs require or their strength can maintain, are vulnerable to attacks of boredom. This would not happen in the *Ville Radieuse*. Instead of social isolation, there is the companionship of people in one's *Unité d'Habitation*. The residents are of all ages and family conditions, unlike the single age-group environment of some American retirement communities. Apartments are not primarily for life-time residence; one occupies them so long as they meet one's needs. As children leave or one's job changes, one moves to another suitable place. This part of his plan, then, conforms to the increased mobility of populations.

In addition to the human activity around one, in the *Unité* and in the city, there is the visual excitement of sculptural buildings and the sparkling silhouette formed by the skyscrapers which are visible from one's balcony. Le Corbusier admired the skyline of Manhattan, but only at a distance. He deplored the living and working arrangements which it implied: "Our American friends have erected skyscrapers and made them work. They are constructions of an astonishing technique, tangible proofs of present possibilities. But, from the planning point of view, their skyscrapers are tiresome and their towns wretched to live in (though vibrant and meriting the closest attention)." And he went on about single dwellings: "Instead of multiplying innumerable suburban

LE CORBUSIER, Modulor (1947–52). Photo, Lucien Hervé.

houses let us equip ourselves with impeccable dwelling-units (that is, apartment houses) of an appropriate stature."*

An important facet of Le Corbusier's approach to community planning lies in his commitment to mass production of cells or dwelling units in his apartment houses. Most of us accept the benefits of mass production while at the same time we fear it lessens individualism. But Le Corbusier and his followers cite the American automobile as an example of a product which is mass produced and is offered in so many shapes and types and by so many manufacturers that there is a wide range of choice for the individual. Individualism grows out of the way one uses mass-produced goods, not in their rarity, cost, uniqueness, or unavailability to others. To be sure, single dwellings when mass-produced and given superficial variety by the color of roof shingles or details of trim make up dismal, monotonous streets and neighborhoods. Standardization is more acceptable in a large apartment building because (1) there is variation in the types of units or cells; (2) an outsider sees, not the individual apartments but the totality of the building, which can be architecturally impressive; (3) the cells do not need to indulge in architectural pretension to uniqueness; (4) residents do not look out at dwellings identical to their own but instead are in visual contact with the shifting patterns of sky, land, and cityscape.

Perhaps Le Corbusier's contribution to city planning can best be seen in his demonstration that, since urbanism is an inescapable fact of modern life, rational ordering of space can make

urban life highly satisfying, even exciting. Great architecture is possible without atavistic return to the building techniques and living patterns of the past. Reinforced-concrete construction ("reconstituted stone," as he calls it) can be spiritually satisfying, functionally adequate, durable, and reasonable in cost without surrender to the austerities of the steel-and-glass boxes which Wright so disliked. Finally, good design in the community results from artistic sensitivity wedded to a conception of man: his work, recreation, visual satisfaction, feelings about space, and need to move about freely on his own feet. Indeed, if Le Corbusier or any architect can devise ways for men to move on foot freely, safely, and with delight, in communities numbering in the millions, then the notion of individualism will have been greatly strengthened.

Following are some principles of town planning advocated by Le Corbusier:

The *keys* to town planning lie in designing for the four functions: Living, Working, Recreation, Circulation.

The *materials* of town-planning are sunlight, space, greenery, and steel-reinforced concrete.

Enough dwellings should be concentrated in one building to liberate the space around it.

Pedestrian routes and mechanized-transportation routes should be separated.

Distance between home and work must be minimized.

Living quarters should have the best urban sites.

Pedestrian paths should not be obstructed by buildings, which should be elevated on stilts.

Autos, buses, and other vehicles should travel on elevated roadways, beneath which are housed pipes and other utilities now buried below ground; easier repair and maintenance would result.

*Le Corbusier, "Concerning Town Planning," Yale University Press, 1948, p. 118.

Industrial areas must be separated from residential areas by greenery.

Architectural monuments should be safeguarded.

ELEMENTS OF PLANNING: RESIDENTIAL GROUPING

Almost all community plans call for special areas set aside for residential purposes. With the exception of the large apartment houses of Le Corbusier, these residential areas are occupied chiefly by detached, single-family dwellings. They vary greatly in cost, quality of design, size of lot, and orientation on their sites. They may have been built speculatively, by contractors in huge developments, or they may have been built on an individual, custom-made basis. Yet some developments are composed of very costly dwellings while some individually built houses may be relatively inexpensive. Cost and the organization of construction however, do not necessarily govern the patterning

Vällingby, Sweden. Flygfototjänst Oscar Bladh.

of dwellings, roads, and open space in a residential area, although the designer of a large development has the best opportunity to make provisions for comprehensive design.

What are the objectives sought by the grouping of houses, the design and location of roads, and the shaping of open space? The chief reason why most persons choose to buy separate dwellings is to live in a quasi-rural setting, to capture, if possible, the charm of village

New town in Cumbernauld, Scotland (1965), left. Courtesy Planair Photography.

Playground in Cumbernauld, Scotland, right. Copyright Cumbernauld Development Corporation.

life while enjoying the amenities and conveniences of modern suburbanism. Consequently, they hope their houses will blend gracefully with the landscape; afford convenient and safe access on foot to neighbors; provide roads nearby for reaching shops, schools, churches, recreation; and present a varied but unified visual appearance. Of course, these desires are also accompanied by a host of other requirements (some not admirable) concerning: the social status, ethnic origin, age, or income of neighbors; preference in architectural style; desire for privacy or seclusion; and space requirements for gardening, landscaping, outdoor recreation, and so on. At a certain point, the individual has to make compromises, based usually on his available funds; or, a contractor makes the compromises for him in a development already planned and built. Up to the point where it is necessary to compromise, however, what are the desirable features of residential groupings?

Curving roads are best for providing visual interest and variety; they permit more freedom for siting houses on different axes in relation to the road axis. Curved roads also tend to slow down motorists. Of course, a main thoroughfare should never pass through a residential area. Where straight roads are necessary, houses need not be set parallel to the road; all can be given a slight, consistent tilt to create more varied space intervals and to take advantage of the best orientation to sun and view. If every house in a group is independently tilted and sited on its lot, the result can be the creation of chaotic, jarring space areas. Some zoning ordinances attempt to prevent this through rules for uniform set-backs and minimum

distances between houses. Very narrow lots, of course, impose severe design limitations unless they are developed as a group so that the designer can put together adjoining side spaces for maximum visual effect. So far as intersections are concerned the four-corner intersection is usually best avoided, whether curved or straight roads are employed. The simple T-intersection is best. A variety of road types can be employed to connect with larger arteries: the cul-de-sac, dead-end, loop street, the collector road, rectangular grid, and their modifications and combinations. Hopefully, of course, the bulldozer will be used as sparingly as possible, natural contours will be respected, and good trees and interesting stone outcroppings will be permitted to stand. In general, it would be best if houses were sited as well as possible in relation to the land and each other, with a minimum of road introduced to serve the houses. It often appears that houses and lots are located so as to serve the road.

Flat terrain lends itself to any pattern; but it is good design to avoid the obvious, especially the unmodified rectangular grid; an attempt should be made to introduce variety and a semblance of changing vista where nature has not been too generous with trees, rolling landscape, or other sources of visual interest. It has been found in highway design that a good view is enhanced if we approach it by a curved route rather than by a straight line. By this principle, even a fairly commonplace row of houses can be made more attractive if we do not see them all at once, as if they were lined up along a straight railroad track. In addition to the horizontal curve in the road, the vertical curve, the rise and dip of the road, can add interest to individual dwellings and to the group. But the houses must be designed to take advantage of the changing levels of vision from which they will be seen. In general, the best rule to follow is to make certain that the dominant roof lines follow the slope of the land. When houses are close together because of narrow lots, they harmonize best if there is some continuity among their roof lines: They should seem to flow together, and this effect can be further enhanced with landscaping.

Unfortunately, one of the motives for residence in detached houses is a laudable but misunderstood individualism. To avoid the monotony of some mass-produced developments, designers, contractors, and home-owners indulge in orgies of spurious originality in their fencing, lamp-posts, planting, shutters, shingles, siding, mail boxes, garden sculpture, and so on. Horrors are perpetrated in an effort to deny that the houses carry approximately the same price charged by the same contractor, and contain about the same number of door knobs. But outrageous aesthetic efforts usually work against the intent of the home-owners who, to avoid the jarring visual discontinuities of the city, sought out the suburban development in the first place. Villages of the past achieved much of their harmony because there was very little variation in construction methods and building materials in any given area. The farmhouses of a region tended to be alike in construction, but farmers, because of their sensitivity to the land, arrived at a subtle individuality; they seemed to know how to site a house quite well. This had nothing to do with the "rugged individualism" of the yeoman farmer; it had to do with his common sense about wind

direction, tree protection, commanding view, drainage, the flow of water on the surface, and the water table below ground. A knowledge of geology helps, especially if one must dig a well.

Our zoning laws and attitudes about property ownership make it very difficult to achieve the design benefits of clustered houses and pooling of space for common amenities and services. Think of the space wasted in the thousands of developments with small lots where the legal minimum of a ten or twelve foot side yard is just barely maintained! Such amounts of space do very little visually or otherwise. They merely serve to separate. Consider also the space devoted to individual garaging. A variety of architectural services and design benefits would result from thinking of a cluster or group of houses as a single design problem rather than using the atomistic, single dwelling as design unit. Group garaging, fencing, and landscaping alone would vastly increase safe play space for children, reduce the amount and cost of roads and driveways, introduce handsome fencing where desirable (compare the solid, consistent stone walls of farm villages to the changing fences on every 100 feet of frontage in a typical suburban development), and extend the benefits of professional landscape architecture.

Richard Neutra has written very candidly about the problems and illusions of home-ownership which so many dwellers in tract developments inherit. The freedom and independence that home-ownership seems to imply is rarely exercised in any real sense by the time land developers, zoning boards, lending institutions, contractors, building trade unions, and public utilities have organized their various skills, assets, energies, and interests to produce the detached dwelling the citizen buys. Indeed, that citizen is not likely ever to *own* his house.

But it is his to use and pay for. And the detached dwelling, with its design atrocities and the illusions of individualism it confers, may yet constitute a better solution to the problems of shelter than the alternative—undistinguished boxes in urban apartment houses, dwellings increasingly reserved for the very rich or the very poor. Unfortunately, the poetic promise of the domestic dwelling we inherited from Frank Lloyd Wright has not been realized in housing for the millions. Perhaps it never can be. But it would seem that here architecture and community planning are ahead of society. We know how to design better communities than we are permitted to build, better indeed than most citizens realize is possible.

Complex freeway interchange in Los Angeles. Courtesy State of California, Division of Highways.

ELEMENTS OF PLANNING: THE HIGHWAY

Trains and buses are more efficient vehicles of transportation than automobiles. Nevertheless, if we have a choice, we prefer to drive an automobile to the same destination we could reach by bus. Why? There is the sense of freedom and personal control in a car. An auto trip has elements of the unexpected. If modern existence is increasingly mechanized and automated, the motor trip, at least, provides the opportunity to exercise skill and judgment—not merely to arrive at a destination point—but to meet the challenges and overcome the problems of getting there. Doubtless, also, the automobile is felt as an extension of the driver's body: He wants to test it against the rigors of distance, the competition of other drivers, and the demands of "the road." The auto voyage along with the shopping trip is one of the central experiences of twentieth-century man. In the face of transportation alternatives, casualty statistics, and all the obstacles which hinder a painless approach to the highway, motorists surge toward the broad concrete strip like lemmings drawn to the sea.

What draws the motorist in addition to the need to get somewhere is the chance to feel the land moving under his vehicle, to view the changing sky and countryside at 60 m.p.h., and sense the response of the car to the shifting shape of the road. We have to acknowledge the fact that the highway, the parkway, the bridge, and the viaduct constitute art objects, sources of aesthetic experience for the millions.

Highways are man-made, they employ plastic materials, they affect our experience of space, and they are made of shapes and structures which could have been built differently. The aesthetics of driving is partly based on the way our vehicle "handles." It is also based on the opportunities the road provides for the vehicle to work, and for us to see and respond to the spatial expanses hollowed out by the highway. The connection of the driver to the car and of the car to the road is part of a kinaesthetic continuum of amazing complexity and varied occasion for pleasure.

Safety is, of course, a principal objective of the highway designer. But aesthetic considerations are intimately related to safety. The designer knows how far ahead a driver can see at given speeds, as well as his degree of peripheral vision and ability to discriminate objects. He knows how the banking and grading of the road and the transition to and from curves affect comfort and pleasure as well as safety. The architect Richard Neutra has brilliantly discussed the deep-seated human desire for precision—smoothness and regularity of surface and contour.° For the motorist, this need for precision is satisfied in the pleasurable feelings experienced in smooth car maneuvers assisted by the shape of the highway and its access roads. The well-designed highway *leads* the eye of the driver, preparing him for certain operations while affording sufficient variation to avoid monotony. (In addition to the pleasure it affords, variety is desirable because of the dangers due to the hypnotic effects of unvarying highway design.)

The right-of-way of the highway ought to be chosen not only for econ-omy of construction but also to exploit topographic and scenic advantages. Given any particular terrain, the designer should consider how its features are seen, not by a man on foot, but by a motorist. The problem becomes somewhat architectural: controlling and organizing the vision of an individual as he moves through a particular spatial sequence. Designers can go around a hill, over it, or into it with a tunnel, or they can make an open cut through it. Funds will govern the decision to some extent. But as aesthetic considerations apply increasingly, it becomes necessary to employ the techniques of the architect and sculptor as well as those of the engineer. Three-dimensional models should be used in planning much more than is now the practice. Sculptors and painters should be employed as consultants so that qualities of color, shape, and texture will be properly exploited. Cinematic techniques combined with three-dimensional models of proposed highway constructions would immensely increase our knowledge of the psycho-aesthetic factors of highway design. The cost of such studies would be minuscule in relation to the staggering sums we expend for highway engineering and construction. And some of our ugliest blunders might be avoided.

The wide interest in sport cars is partly to be explained as an interest in the aesthetics of driving, and particularly in the psycho-aesthetic values of the machine for its own sake and as an extension of the body. Sport-car enthusiasts often prefer side roads with poor surfaces, bad turns, and no banking to the smoother pleasures of the highway. This preference can be understood as a reaction against the aesthetics of precision, regularity, and predictability. It

°Richard Neutra, *Survival through Design*, Oxford University Press, 1954.

TR-4 sports car on the road. Courtesy Standard-Triumph Motor Company, Inc.

Garden State Parkway south of Raritan River crossing. Courtesy of Garden State Parkway.

also suggests that kinaesthetic needs (muscular, bodily sensations) for some motorists, at least, require satisfaction more urgently than visual needs. There is a very clear connection between the riding properties of the conventional automobile and the ratio of visual to kinaesthetic values in the modern highway: Road design is moving toward an increase in pictorial, plastic, and architectural values. As roads become safer, the driver's reactions fall into a smoother, less erratic pattern: There are surprises but he is prepared for them. His physical awareness of the machine diminishes. By contrast, the aesthetics of speed, surprise, unpredict-

ability, danger, and death are quite understandably associated with romantic figures like James Dean and Jackson Pollock, both of whom died in crashes of cars they were driving. Romanticism thrives on the exaggerated expression of a single emotion, and if the human body and the machine must be joined together in order to express the aesthetic of accelerated motion through unpredictable space, the result is likely to be fatal.

The park-like character of the highway has led some designers to rely too heavily on formal, regularly spaced planting of trees and shrubs. This approach may be acceptable for roads of relatively low speed and where the median strip is narrow. But for the fast, large-scale roads, it has seemed best to preserve the character of the countryside as much as possible, retaining local vegetation, selectively thinning wooded groups, and providing visual definition and accent through the road itself and its auxiliary structures. The design of viaducts, bridges, multi-level interchanges, side slopes, retaining walls, safety railings, embankments, and urban approaches constitute difficult problems if they are regarded as more than questions of engineering. In particular, we are rarely able to bring a highway into or through a city harmoniously: How can major arteries be visually integrated with the various structures and facilities which surround them in the city? What are the best shape and scale relationships for the areas created by the crossing, paralleling, descending, or rising of freeway ramps and strips as they meet local traffic patterns?

And there are other questions. What can be done to minimize the number of signs and directions posted by well-meaning highway departments? Can visual information be given more concisely, in more attractive and professional designs, and sufficiently in advance of need? Can the right-of-way be somehow extended so that billboards will not invade the motorist's privacy nor exploit the passage of citizens on thoroughfares built with public funds? One need not listen to radio and television commercials, but vision is essential to driving, hence billboards cannot be "turned off." Obviously, the best efforts of architects, engineers, and planners will be frustrated if there is no appropriate legislation to protect the visual, structural, and topographic relationships they are learning to create.

Although the automobile is the cause of much civic and social mischief, it is also the parent of the highway and parkway. These, in turn, have been carried to the point where they constitute exceedingly complex and monumental art forms. Given the most expensive and vastly organized expression in America, the modern highway illustrates our resemblance to the ancient Romans, solid builders and great administrators, but not especially sensitive to the nuances of human or aesthetic relationships. Since 1946, Germany and Switzerland have demonstrated on a smaller scale a more advanced and comprehensive idea of the highway as a form of attenuated architecture. The world's greatest democracy has yet to accept the legitimacy of expending public funds for sculpture which might enliven a long and dull stretch of road. The pathos of Edward Hopper's *Gas* tells the story well. But we are learning that with our frontier gone and our natural resources limited, the spoliation of the landscape must cease. A well-designed highway may be the

EDWARD HOPPER, *Gas* (1940). Collection The Museum of Modern Art, New York, Mrs. Simon Guggenheim Fund.

most effective instrument we have for educating the millions to enjoy the countryside and wish to preserve it unravaged.

ELEMENTS OF PLANNING: PLAZAS, MALLS, CIVIC CENTERS

The advent of television has made our public life a living-room experience. Momentous world events are witnessed from the same sofa which used to serve for courtship before automobiles overtook us. Indeed, one of the most tragic events of our time, the death of President Kennedy, was experienced over television by Americans with all the immediacy and sense of personal distress that are felt by members of a single family. For a long time, this fact about political life has been apparent: We cannot, like the free citizens of a Greek polis, or the inhabitants of a small New England town, gather together in a single square to hear issues debated and to transact the public business. But our communications media have only recently become effective and vivid enough to provide an alternative sense of community, since the old forms of physical community appear to have broken down. However, television and radio and the journals and news magazines create only a community of mind and opinion, entertainment, and information. We require physical and palpable symbols of community too—places in the open where we can come together out of the darkness of our TV dens to experience the exhilaration of *being with,* as opposed to *looking at,* or *reading about,* people.

What are the places in the community which now bring large numbers of people together? They are shopping centers, parks, sports arenas, schools and universities, theaters, municipal and civic centers, hospitals and clinics, airports, bus and train terminals, skyscraper groups, hotels and museums, and combinations of these buildings and places. As individual structures, such buildings are designed with fairly clear and definite ideas about the way the interior space they create will be used. Consequently, even the office building of mediocre design works fairly well—as a technical if not an aesthetic entity. But the space *around* the building does *not* work very well, because it has rarely been planned: It is merely left-over space, occupied largely by the avenues and streets required to carry the people to the buildings. Sidewalks and pedestrian space in general are immensely crowded. The noise, jostling, auto fumes, and confusion of even the most distinguished thoroughfares are so disturbing to the pedestrian that he must flee indoors to "hear himself think."

Yet we want to stroll, window-shop, sit on benches, watch the passing parade, and enjoy the visual qualities of structure and open space under varying seasonal and light conditions. These are the traditional and deeply rooted desires of people who congregate in market places, church plazas, parks, and governmental centers. Many Americans visit Europe for these reasons—so that they can browse among outdoor book stalls, shop in open markets, stroll along park lands, explore crooked little streets opening into enclosed squares where there might be a church, some statuary, a fountain, an outdoor restaurant, some children playing, or older people chatting in groups. Imagine that—people carrying on a conversation out of doors! American college students can do so on campus: They may even have some outdoor classes if the weather permits. But after graduation, daily life will be largely an indoor affair.

In 1945 Lewis Mumford wrote about the practice of removing shade trees from commercial areas: "The merchants' notion that the chopping down of shade trees on business thoroughfares is a sign of progress or business efficiency is one of those blind superstitions that cannot be justified by sound business practice."* Largely due to the design ingenuity of Victor Gruen, shopping space has been recovered for pedestrians in centers created by his organization in Minneapolis, Minnesota (the Southdale Shopping Center); Cherry Hill, New Jersey; Rochester, New York (Midtown Plaza); and elsewhere. These shopping plazas or malls may be new, enclosed structures with natural light admitted at the top, generous and often exotic plantings (as at Cherry Hill and Minneapolis), and air-conditioning throughout. Or the mall may be created

*Lewis Mumford, *City Development,* Harcourt, Brace & World, Inc., 1945, p. 121.

VICTOR GRUEN ASSOCIATES, Cherry Hill Shopping Center, left. Courtesy The Rouse Company, Baltimore, Md.

VICTOR GRUEN ASSOCIATES, Midtown Plaza, Rochester, N.Y., right. Courtesy Midtown Holdings Corp.

by the closing off of downtown streets as at Rochester. Converting some of the streets of "center city" to pedestrian use can accomplish a great deal toward reclaiming the city for people: This move does not necessarily require that buildings be torn down; auto traffic can, of course, be rerouted and underground garages can be built. Although expensive, such measures are sometimes undertaken to counter the flow of retail business to outlying shopping areas. But as piecemeal efforts, they are not likely to succeed; they must be accompanied by large-scale redesign of the slums and obsolete structures which usually surround downtown areas.

Rockefeller Center in New York City, begun in 1931, provided the impetus for all subsequent design of public plazas and buildings in the high-density core of a modern metropolis. The Center consists of sixteen buildings occupying fourteen acres of very expensive real-estate in Manhattan; the complex surrounds a pedestrian mall and a sunken plaza which is an ice-skating rink in the winter and an outdoor restaurant in the summer. The buildings, designed collec-

tively by a team of architects under the leadership of Wallace K. Harrison (1895–   ) (who subsequently headed the architectural team which designed the U.N. complex), are massive slabs which in their honesty and boldness represent the first significant departure in New York City from the idea of the skyscraper as a tower, as a sort of over-sized church steeple. This complex of buildings, built on costly land and requiring complex utilities and banks of elevators to service their tenants, embodies a frank if unspectacular solution to the problem of getting a maximum of light into the interior of very tall structures: No office is more than twenty-seven feet from an exterior wall; thus, all have light, fresh air, and a view. The clean plane of the walls of the R.C.A. building is given a pleasing surface texture by the vertical strips of light-colored stone facing; its profile departs only slightly from a perfect rectangle in staggered setbacks located where the elevator shafts end. But the main advantage of the unbroken curtain wall surfaces and the slab-like quality of the structures lies in the sense of enclosure

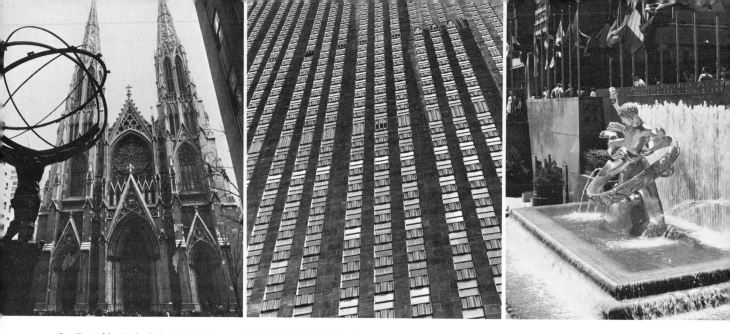

St. Patrick's Cathedral (1858–79), from Rockefeller Center, above, left. Photo, Pan American Airways.

Wall of R.C.A. Building, above, center. Photo, Standard Oil Co. (N.J.).

Rockefeller Center (1931–55), below. Courtesy Rockefeller Center, Inc.; photo, Thomas Airviews.

PAUL MANSHIP, *Prometheus* (1933). Courtesy Rockefeller Center, Inc.

and protection they give to the plaza and mall. The popularity of this site grows out of the feeling it affords the pedestrian of being at the focal center of an energetic and exciting city, indeed of being at the center of civilization itself. The mall, which is quite small, has colorful, carefully tended, and frequently changed flowers and plantings. The sculpture is fairly undistinguished but is enhanced by the elegant setting provided by the fashionable shops which face the mall and the generally chic and cosmopolitan types who stroll in from Fifth Avenue. St. Patrick's Cathedral, with its Gothic stonework across the avenue from one of the buildings in the complex, provides a very satisfying complementary architectural note and appears to be, not diminished, but rather enhanced by its contrast with the scale and structural massiveness of its neighbors. A fountain in the lower plaza, surmounted by a gilded sculpture of Prometheus visible from the entry to the mall, constitutes both a center of visual and ambulatory focus as well as a transition to the unadorned vertical plane of the R.C.A. building. The sense of space in the mall is reminiscent of the experience of moving down the center aisle of a high-naved cathedral (the space is squeezed at the sides and opened up at the top) and then one emerges as if released into the vast, bright opening on each side and overhead at the transept crossing; this promenade corresponds in Rockefeller Center to one's approach to the sunken plaza. Indeed, the outdoor space at the Center is a modified mirror-image of the indoor space at St. Patrick's Cathedral up the avenue.

Built during the heart of the depression by a group with huge resources at its disposal, Rockefeller Center was intended to be a commercial as well as an architectural success. And it has achieved its objectives: It created jobs, it brought a good return to its investors, and it established a model for subsequent efforts. Indeed, the Rockefeller family has been the prime mover behind a huge philanthropic project for housing some of the principal cultural enterprises of New York City in the Lincoln Center for the Performing Arts.

Theaters, opera houses, and office buildings, then, are the magnets which draw people together in great numbers: The art of large-scale design lies not only in attending to the mechanical needs of crowds with efficiency and dispatch—in other words, minimizing confusion, inconvenience, danger, and outright pain—but also in designing inspiring spaces, spaces which make them feel the community was created with human beings in mind. A city is large and frustrating, at once exhilarating and

Lincoln Center for the Performing Arts (1960–66). Photo, H. Rinehart.

depressing. The individual privately lost in its vast and often monotonous routine needs to be publicly reminded of his participation in humanity, that is, of his capacity to experience emotions arising from large-scale, collective effort. Knowing that powerful persons and institutions have assembled vast resources and outstanding designers in order to please and impress him (as well as justify their power) has comforted the ordinary citizen from ancient times to the present. Even when we know full

St. Mark's Square, Venice. Courtesy Foto ENIT, Roma.

well that a building has been endowed or a vast project initiated by men anxious to show they are worthy stewards of the world's wealth, the sense of satisfaction we experience in the presence of great public architecture is undeniable. So passing over, for the moment, the inescapably ambiguous record of power, we honor the Medici of Florence, the Doges of Venice, and the Renaissance popes for the monuments which they caused to be built and which stand after the political acts of their builders have long been forgotten.

The romantic and picturesque imagery associated with artfully photographed industrial structures is not always compatible with an aesthetically satisfying way of life for nearby inhabitants.

The steel mills of Pittsburgh, top left. Photo, Standard Oil Company (N.J.).

Powerhouse of the Watts Bar Dam (1939–42), Tennessee, top right. Courtesy TVA.

Bayway Refinery, Linden, New Jersey, bottom left. Photo, Standard Oil Company (N.J.).

Freight yards, Salt Lake City, bottom right. Union Pacific Railroad Photo.

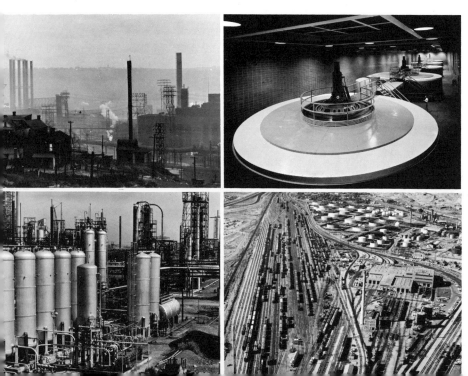

ELEMENTS OF PLANNING: INDUSTRIAL AND COMMERCIAL STRUCTURES

Not many years ago, a factory or warehouse was an ugly place, usually grimy, surrounded by refuse, clutter, and bad odors. Viewing the industrial sprawl from the train window as one crossed the New Jersey meadows, one wondered how workmen ever became accustomed to the sights and sounds once they had overcome their reactions to the stench. The same wonder arose in connection with steel mill towns along the Ohio River, wood pulp mills in the South, the slaughter-houses of Chicago and Kansas City, and the scarred mining towns of Pennsylvania and West Virginia. The active and obsolete remains of these sights still mark the places where we live and work. From the standpoint of aesthetic detachment, they are often romantically picturesque or symbolically impressive: the open-hearth steel mills of Gary, Indiana at night; the oil refineries of Galveston and Bayonne; the railroad marshaling yards of Chicago or New York; the almost deserted textile factories of Utica and New England; the "gas house" area of any large city hard by its abattoirs, and produce wholesalers and fish markets. But these romantic and/or malodorous places are disappearing, mainly because their operation has become uneconomic. They were in the wrong location; they were too costly to maintain; some of them could be automated; or their managements became concerned with their public image. The Victorian notion that industrial manufacture was an inherently ugly process, even though its products were necessary, has given way to the idea that the rationality, order, precision, and planning which are essential for successful industrial enterprise can also be visible in the places and structures where that enterprise is carried on.

A pioneering and individualistic industrial statement was made, once again, by Frank Lloyd Wright in his administration building (1936–39) and research tower (1946–49) for the Johnson Wax Company in Racine, Wisconsin. Some of its features appear dated now, and the structural vocabulary (with the exception of the tower) seems more related to the domestic dwelling than to business activity. But is that a fault? Should we criticize the many contemporary factories and research centers which look like collegiate buildings? Their occupants are probably pleased and companies can thus attract the scientific and technical personnel so essential for the survival of a modern industrial enterprise. The Johnson buildings are also located in the center of the city, where their horizontal lines, small scale, brick surfaces, and sculptural accents are an asset. A globe of the world, given a prominent location in a formal garden-type of setting, is rather trite and somewhat reminiscent of exposition planning. (Planners and designers often succumb to the temptation to erect a massive "symbol," like the trylon and perisphere of the World's Fair of 1939, or the immense globe conceived as the official symbol for the World's Fair of 1964–65. The result is usually too literal, while also being dull as expressive symbol and boring or irrelevant as sculpture.) In the Johnson complex at Racine, the genuinely interesting forms inhere in the structures themselves and in the research tower, which rises dramatically from a seemingly hovering platform.

Its horizontal bands repeat the emphasis of the administration buildings, and its circular roof turrets provide a note of variety for the tower while restating similar forms which appear elsewhere. The floors, or layers, of the tower are cantilevered from a central core which passes through the building and is visible as the turret on the roof. Night illumination reveals the structure very clearly and shows the Wrightian concept of a tower as opposed to the Chicago and New York conceptions of a skyscraper. A high-rise structure resting on a platform is a design device which is increasingly used today, and with conspicuous success, as in Lever House (1952) and the Chase Manhattan building (1961), both designed by Skidmore, Owings, & Merrill (see p. 110). The City University of New York plans to redesign its City College campus with all buildings rising from a common platform which unifies the site, and beneath which a variety of activities can take place.

FRANK LLOYD WRIGHT, Johnson Wax Administration and Research Center (by day and by night). Courtesy Johnson Wax.

SKIDMORE, OWINGS, & MERRILL, North Campus master plan for The City College of New York (1966). Courtesy The City College of New York.

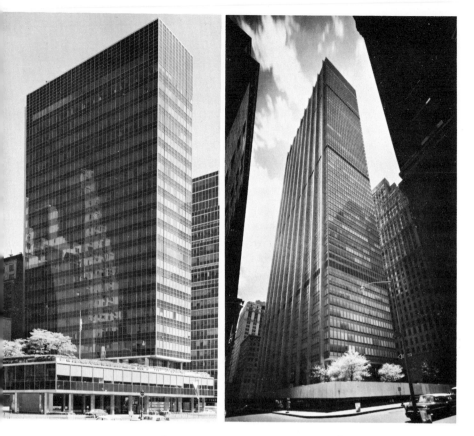

SKIDMORE, OWINGS, & MERRILL, Lever House (1952). Courtesy Lever Brothers Company.

SKIDMORE, OWINGS, & MERRILL, Chase Manhattan Plaza (1961). Courtesy The Chase Manhattan Bank; photo, Sam Falk.

The extent to which modern industrial buildings have departed from the stereotypes of earlier days is seen in Paul Rudolph's Endo Pharmaceutical Center. The building vocabulary employed in Rudolph's Yale School of Art and Architecture is repeated here, confirming the observation above that collegiate and industrial buildings now often look alike. Similarly the Sara Lee bakery plant, designed by A. Epstein & Sons, appears to have been influenced by the architecture building at Illinois Institute of Technology designed by Mies van der Rohe (see p. 80). These stylistic similarities show the interest of industry in seeking a level of architectural quality no less excellent than is sought in university buildings. Also, the distinctiveness of such industrial architecture provides a competitive advantage for firms heavily engaged in retail operations.

The interior of the Administration Building in the General Motors Technical Center, designed by Eliel and Eero Saarinen (1873–1950; 1910–61), shows the elegance and devotion to aesthetic effect which the modern giant corporation seeks for its administrative and research headquarters. The buildings of the center surround a man-made lake one-third of a mile long, hence the distances between them can only be negotiated, appropriately enough, by auto. The buildings are chiefly rectilinear structures, three or four stories high,

PAUL RUDOLPH, Endo Pharmaceutical Center (1964), left, top. Photo, Bruce Cunningham.

EPSTEIN & SONS, Kitchens of Sara Lee Administration Building (1964). Courtesy Kitchens of Sara Lee.

and spread out generously on the vast, flat site. Drama is not sought in sculptural treatment of the exterior as in Rudolph's Endo Center; rather, a serene effect is pursued in the quietly spacious interiors and the lavish, uncluttered areas between the buildings, whose regularity can be viewed without obstruction across the expanse of lake. Plantings soften the straight structural lines and glazed brick walls in primary colors enliven an otherwise sober complex of forms. The Center undoubtedly impresses the viewer with the size and complexity of General Motors, but it would appear to be intended mainly as an ideal work setting: The promotion and sale of General Motors products is accomplished in other ways. A research and development campus is not a place meant to dazzle visitors or its employees, but to create an environment in which they can most effectively function at their jobs. Hence, the total organization of space does not promote the type of aimless strolling, sight-seeing, and visiting we hope to create in urban neighborhoods and plazas. Such informal activity can take place on the walks and verandas around individual buildings, but the focus of this architecture, notwithstanding excellent outdoor sculpture and water displays, is within the buildings, and it should be. Thus, a fine balance is struck between the pleasing but not distracting outdoor organization and the somewhat richer and more active interiors.

Dramatic industrial and commercial structures can be seen in the municipal asphalt plant of Ely Kahn (1884–   ), the St. Louis airport terminal by Minoru Yamasaki (1912–   ) and the North Carolina State Fair Arena by Mathew Nowicki (1910–49) and W. H.

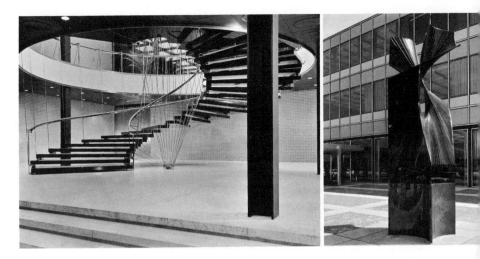

ELIEL and EERO SAARINEN, General Motors Styling Administration Building (1949–56), above left. Courtesy General Motors Corporation; photo, Ezra Stoller.

ANTOINE PEVSNER, *Bird in Flight* (1955–56), above right. Courtesy General Motors Corporation.

E.J. KAHN, Municipal Asphalt Plant, New York City (1944), below, top left. Photo, H. Rinehart.

NOWICKI & DIETRICK, J. S. Dorton Arena, Raleigh, North Carolina (1953), below, top right. Courtesy North Carolina Department of Conservation & Development.

MINORU YAMASAKI, St. Louis airport terminal (1954), below, bottom left. Photo, Bill Hedrich, Hedrich-Blessing.

EERO SAARINEN, TWA Terminal, Kennedy International Airport (1960), below, bottom right. Courtesy TWA; photo, Ezra Stoller.

Pennsylvania Station interior (1906). Courtesy The Pennsylvania Railroad Company.

Dietrick (1905–   ). And the late Eero Saarinen, who collaborated with his father in the design of the classical, somewhat reserved General Motors Center, displayed his theatrical gifts in the TWA terminal at Kennedy International Airport. However, before congratulating ourselves on the drama, versatility, and grandeur of contemporary architecture and planning, we might look at the interior of Pennsylvania Station, designed in 1906 by McKim, Mead and White, the classicizing old firm which based the Waiting Room of the terminal on the Roman Baths of Caracalla. Here in the main concourse of the station we could see drama in unadorned steel structure equal to the best modern work, or even to the Brooklyn Bridge. But we can see it no longer: The venerable landmark has been torn down to make way for a sports arena.

LARGE-SCALE DESIGN: CONCLUSION

The present time is one of frantic urban and regional transformation. The confluence of several forces has brought this about: (1) We realize that many social problems, now at the stage of crisis, partially originate in the physical design of the community; (2) we realize that our society is productive enough, rich enough, to undertake the massive architectural and design measures which are called for; (3) we realize that problems of health, transportation, recreation, commerce, and employment often transcend traditional political units; they embrace regions extending beyond towns, cities, and states; (4) modern technology has provided the tools which make it practical to think in terms of large-scale, comprehensive design; (5) professional specialists—architects, en-

gineers, sociologists, lawyers, administrators, land-use experts—have developed patterns of cooperation and unified action for community and regional design; (6) architectural education has evolved to the point where designers have a more sophisticated idea of comprehensive design than they formerly possessed.

Art contributes to the physical character of the community in a narrow sense through the skills of those who practice the several design professions. In a broad sense, the aim of all who participate in the design of the large-scale environment—artists or not—is to create communities which approach the condition of high art. One persuasive writer on the problems of cities, Jane Jacobs, says quite flatly: "A city cannot be a work of art."[*] She feels that architects and planners perpetrate ghastly urban errors by confusing art with life. But she may base her views on a definition of art as identical with sculpture or painting, both highly personal and individualistic types of expression in modern times. The fact is that some of our poorest architecture is too *im*personal, while industrial design is highly "other-directed" Often it is overinfluenced by what designers and businessmen believe will sell rather than what they know from professional experience to be excellent. The cure for poor design is not "no design," but "better design." Skilled and professional planners or designers know that communities are not merely oversized problems in abstract sculpture. They realize that the random impulses of people—their freedom and partial unpredictability—must be considered in

[*] *The Death and Life of Great American Cities*, Random House, 1961, p. 372.

any total plan. It is true that communities may grow organically and unpredictably and that parts of them are often used for purposes not originally intended. Nevertheless, our knowledge of the inevitability of growth and change should not inhibit deliberate efforts to create order and delight in communities, consistent with the freedom of their inhabitants, and employing the best forms and ideas our feeble intelligence can devise.

The Crafts and Industrial Design

We have already observed that art performs a physical function through the designing and forming of all kinds of tools, implements, and containers. The important principle to stress is that art is not only decorative or symbolic: It is also utilitarian. There are significant differences between objects and utensils made by hand and those which are produced by mechanical-industrial methods. But we should not forget the central idea that, while methods, materials, and processes of making vary, the business of organizing them to satisfy human needs is an artistic problem.

In different historic eras, the individual responsible for the design or production of eating and cooking utensils has been called an artisan, a craftsman, an engineer, or a designer. And, indeed, the family itself often has produced its own food, clothing, shelter, and most of its tools and utensils. The hard-working housewife of American Colonial days may not have regarded herself as a craftsman or designer, but she made her own cloth, cut and sewed clothes for the family, made blankets and rugs, painted and embroidered, and carried out other craft activities we would normally assign to specialists. When we study art, however, we are interested primarily in how a particular art object looks or operates and what it seems to mean. We care only secondarily about the fact that it was created by a colonial housewife or a textile designer, a civil engineer or an architect in the conventional sense. Our interest in the method of making an article or the occupation of its maker derives from our curiosity about the object itself and our effort to understand it.

The water jug made by a potter and the aluminum pitcher mass-produced by machine are similar in shape and function. The art and fingers of the potter formed the clay jug. Forming the aluminum pitcher was a much more complex matter. But that pitcher, resulting from the collaboration of man and machine, has its own distinctive excellence: It too is an "art" object. It will be our task to examine some of the historical, technical, and psychological factors involved in the transition from clay pot to metal pitcher. Our discussion will, in effect, ask the question, "Can men teach machines to create art?"

CHARACTERISTICS OF HANDCRAFT

Usually, a hand-made object has been planned and executed by the same person. This is always true if the maker is what we call an artist-craftsman. But in the cottage and village crafts of many

The crafts tend to perpetuate tradition: we do not expect "originality" in the design of a violin or the pattern of a Persian rug.

Lavere Kerman (Persian) rug. Courtesy A. Beshar & Company, Inc.

preindustrial economies, some division of labor occurs, so that artisans may execute the designs created by others and employ members of the family to carry out minor operations repetitively. Nevertheless, there is a certain unity of control and execution in the hand-made object. The excellent craftsman not only does all the work himself, but also varies and adjusts his design according to the requirements of his client or customer. A tailor or seamstress or shoemaker who sets out to make an article for a patron also undertakes to satisfy the individual in terms of his personal measurements and requirements. Hence, the characteristics of handcraft include unified responsibility for the creation of the object and adjustment of design and execution to the patron's individual needs or caprice. The result of this process inevitably exhibits variation. We can speak of the craft object as "one-of-a-kind," no matter how similar it is, in general, to other objects of its type. The uniqueness of the handcraft object may be based on idiosyncrasies of the craftsman's technique or the special desires of the patron. In any event, that uniqueness is identified by many as being the essence of art. It pleases us to know that we own or are looking at an object which is absolutely singular, which cannot be found elsewhere.

Not all craftsmen create for a particular patron. The great violin makers of Cremona—Stradivarius and Guarnerius—made some violins in advance of orders for them. Here, uniqueness is not based on the individual requirements of a customer so much as on the craftsman's understanding of his art and his drives toward perfection. Modern artist-craftsmen—potters, enamelists, jewelers, glassmakers, furniture-makers, and weavers—also endeavor to operate on this basis. However, their economic situation is precarious because they must compete with mass-produced articles. The Cremona violin makers were not threatened by mass production. They *could* have been threatened by the work of inferior craftsmen, except that violinists are good judges of excellence in violins.

Another feature of handcraft in preindustrial cultures is, paradoxically, its relative sameness. Variations in detail occur because absolute duplication is not possible in hand-made articles. But the people and the craftsmen living within a so-called "folk tradition" do not regard change for its own sake as a value. They change their modes of making, thinking, and behaving very slowly and only because of stimulation from the outside. Peasants and people remote from urban centers of ferment and innovation are inclined to resist novelty. Consequently, craftsmen in these cultures are content to use formulas and patterns in their work which were inherited over the generations. For them, such inherited practices constitute an honored tradition which they must pass on as exactly as possible. Persian rugmaking is a good example. Such traditions in the crafts promote the development of a high degree of technical skill, since the folk craftsman concentrates on mastery of skill more than originality of expression. The problems of design and of content have, in principle, been solved for him. It does not occur to him to change his designs, especially as life itself, in folk cultures, does not change very much. It has a timeless quality which fascinates and charms the visitor, even if the peasant may not think of himself as "charming."

Although the older craft tradition places no premium on change or novelty, it *does* stress the proper use of tools and materials and the importance of durability. "Proper" in this context means employing the "correct"—that is, inherited—technique, and also respecting the working properties of the leather, fiber, wood, metal, or stone being formed. Furthermore, it means producing long-wearing, durable objects, Since the craftsman-customer relationship is a close one, the craftsman cannot easily escape responsibility for what he has made and sold. In the modern setting, responsibility for performance is shared by the manufacturer with a multitude of middlemen. Thus, we derive one of the fundamental meanings of craftsmanship: The patron values the hand-made object because he knows and trusts the craftsman who made it. Modern manufacturers attempt to develop a similar trust and regard for their products among merchants and consumers, but as a rule, the consumer can only depend on performance data and specifications of materials. Claims for workmanship—in a hand-iron or a radio, for example—are not always reliable unless supported by government regulations or by independent testing and evaluation agencies.

One other trait of handcraft as contrasted with machine production may account for the survival of artist-craftsman today, notwithstanding their struggle with the economic facts of life: It is difficult to produce a great many ugly products by hand. There are inferior craftsmen, of course, but they are usually discouraged, weeded-out by the poor reception of their work. Secondly, it is very difficult for any human being to make something badly over and over again. He inevitably improves a little bit. Indeed, the visible results of his efforts to overcome technical deficiencies often seem more attractive than the perfection of the mature and accomplished craftsman. This appeal is based on the relatively modern discovery and admiration for crude, untrained, or primitive artistic effort. We may, for example, prefer the early, unsophisticated pottery of pre-Columbian Mexico to the highly perfected black-figured pottery of classical Greece. In other words, hand-wrought objects of less than perfect technical mastery seem to satisfy human interest and may even arouse admiration for the proficiency they *do* exhibit. But the machine can produce badly designed objects at a fantastic rate. The result improves only if the designer improves. In the meantime, a vast amount of trash can be manufactured. Then, if these products are profitably sold, it may be thought undesirable to change their design. In an industrial civilization, excellence is often defined in terms of mass acceptance, an acceptance which may only reflect the absence of qualitatively superior alternatives.

During almost all of human history, man's utensils and objects of daily use have been made by hand, mostly with the aid of small hand-tools which are virtually extensions of his fingers and senses. Consequently, we have been thoroughly habituated to the visual and tactile characteristics of handcraft. It is doubtful that we shall ever entirely escape our emotional attachment to the properties associated with material which has been worked by hand—not as long as we have our amazingly strong and versatile fingers and opposable thumbs. But civilization as we know it now is grounded on mechanical and automated forms of making. Since 1750, the world has been going through a period of transition, accompanied by conflicts between our old emotional attachments and the new material basis of civilization. Now the conflict is almost over. That is, machine methods of making and machine-made products have been successfully absorbed into the ordinary routines of almost all societies. Those newly emerging nations which still subsist on the basis of a handcraft economy are rushing eagerly—foolishly in some instances°—toward machine-based industrialism. Thus, mechanical-industrial production has become a symbol of national prestige while handcraft is regarded as a quaint survival of colonial dependence. It appears that a certain amount of experience with self-government and with the operation of an industrial economy is needed to confer the breadth of view which perceives a healthy role in modern culture for the crafts along with mechanical production.

THE ORIGIN AND PRINCIPLES OF MASS PRODUCTION

To understand how industrial design functions in modern manufacture and to see the role of the machine as a tool of art, it is first necessary to describe the changes in methods of making brought about by mechanization. It would be a mistake to regard mass production as the result simply of the application of mechanical power to what were formerly handcraft processes.

°Some states on gaining independence almost immediately begin to build skyscrapers and steel plants although they do not have the supporting service facilities for high-rise buildings and could buy steel more cheaply than they can manufacture it.

The first principle of mass production is *duplication*, the second is *accuracy*, the third is *interchangeability*, and the fourth is *specialization*. The art of casting is the oldest method of duplication, one which goes back to neolithic man. From this art, the enormous metal foundries of the present evolved. Today, there are very few manufactured products which do not contain some parts of cast metal or cast plastic. A second neolithic invention, the potter's wheel, led to the wood lathe and then to the metal lathe, which is the basic machine tool of metal-working. Drill presses, milling machines, turret lathes, and grinders are all variants of the lathe, which, with attachments, can perform the essential turning, drilling, milling, and grinding operations of the modern machine shop. Die stamping, another method of duplication, was used by Darius in the fifth century B.C. to manufacture coins. In duplication, then, we have the earliest attempt of man, following emergence from a purely hunting economy, to satisfy his growing physical needs. Casting, turning, and stamping, therefore, are ancient processes of duplication which in more sophisticated forms become prominent in modern mechanized production.

War has always created incentives for technological experiment. The army of Louis XIV numbered 100,000 men and was perhaps the first to be uniformly dressed and equipped. Hence the French textile industry was the earliest to confront large-scale demand for standardized goods. In the Middle Ages, the Venetians were able to set up an assembly line with which they could build a ship a day. Gutenberg's invention of movable type, however, is the method of duplication most familiar to all of us, and perhaps the most far-reaching in its effects. But before Gutenberg, the Chinese practiced a cruder form of duplication in block printing. The entire page of a book was carved in wood and printed, thus requiring several hundred blocks for a book.

Gutenberg's movable type was a kind of interchangeability since his letters could be used over again in different combinations. But the tolerances of accuracy were quite wide and the interchangeable principle was applied only on a two-dimensional surface without moving parts. Great accuracy, however, is required in watch parts, since they are small and moving. A watch cannot be successfully duplicated unless its parts are accurately machined. In 1740, the French developed a machine which could cut a gear blank into a given number of evenly cut teeth. Shortly afterward, James Watt, an instrument maker, was attempting to improve the steam engine already developed by Newcomen. He called on a mechanic, Smeaton, for assistance, but Smeaton could not bore an eighteen-inch engine cylinder with less than three-eighths-inch error. Such workmanship seems incredibly crude to us, since we can work to standards of accuracy which are measurable only by electronic instruments. It is interesting to note that the steam engine, which is *the* great machine, the great source of motive power for the Industrial Revolution, was well understood in principle long before it could be perfected; it required far greater accuracy (that is, better craftsmanship) than was available; and when it was perfected, it helped to bring about the obsolescence of craftsmanship.

By 1776 Watt had found a mechanic named Wilkinson who could bore a cylinder fifty inches in diameter which "did not err the thickness of an old shilling in any part." A degree of accuracy began to be approached which not only improved efficiency of operation but also would permit interchangeability of parts: the stock of spare parts we now take for granted, and the possibility of manufacturing parts in one place and assembling them in another. These developments, in turn, depended on uniform standards of measure—that is, agreement about the meaning of dimensions—something handcraftsmen did not have because they did not need it.

Eli Whitney, inventor of the cotton gin, is often credited with the first experiments with interchangeability, but a Frenchman, le Blanc, preceded him. Jefferson wrote from Paris in 1785 about what he had seen of le Blanc's work:

"An improvement is made here in the construction of muskets which it may be interesting to Congress to know . . . It consists in the making of every part of them so exactly alike, that what belongs to any one, may be used for every other musket in the magazine . . . The advantages of this when arms are out of repair, are evident."

However, le Blanc did not secure the funds for the necessary tooling to complete his experiments. Almost fifteen years later, in 1798, Eli Whitney proposed to manufacture ten to fifteen thousand muskets for the American government, which had no arms for its troops. His proposal stated, "I am persuaded that machinery moved by water, adapted to this business would greatly diminish the labor and greatly facilitate the manufacture of this article." It took Whitney two years to tool up, during which time the government was quite impatient with his meager production since there had been no experience with tooling up for large-scale production. As there was a shortage of skilled gunsmiths, Whitney instituted the division of labor so that each step in his manufacture did not have to be performed by a master craftsman. He also devised special machines and gauges, both to guide semiskilled craftsmen and to lessen visual fatigue.

Specialization in mass production refers not only to workmen but also to machine tools. Although a lathe with proper attachments can perform all the basic machining processes,° it is wasteful of time to change its "set-up" when a new operation needs to be performed. Consequently, individual machine types have been developed to carry out specific operations. The versatility of a machine is wasted if it is employed to perform only one operation for a long period of time. Also, the versatile machine may not function with maximum effectiveness on any single operation. The ideal manufacturing machine, then, is one designed to carry out a single operation or set of operations simultaneously on a particular product. And the ideal factory consists of a series of such machines connected to each other, all electronically guided by instructions from a computer which has been programed by men.

The assembly line is the modern, dramatic manufacturing device which fully employs interchangeability and specialization. It is associated with Henry Ford although, as we have seen, Eli Whitney set up such a system to

manufacture guns in the late eighteenth century. In automobile production, Olds established a forerunner of the assembly line in 1899. At that time, manufacturers assembled automobiles from parts made by other companies. The engine was passed along a line of men, each of whom added parts until finally the springs, axles, wheels, and body were assembled. Spare parts were distributed in bins along the way. Olds produced 7,000 cars a year in this manner, and was the first to apply the progressive system of assembly. Henry Leland, who formed the Cadillac Automobile Company in 1902, applied more exacting standards of accuracy to Olds's engine and was thus able to double its horsepower without increasing its size. His interest in accuracy was indicated by his importing the first set of "Jo" blocks° to this country—but the important concept he introduced was that of the greatest possible accuracy in mass production in order to compete with the quality of European hand-fitted cars. Interchangeability without further tampering and fitting also meant greater service to the consumer.

In 1907 Henry Ford hired Walter Flanders, and together they took apart his old factory and rearranged it for maximum efficiency. As many processes as possible were made automatic by the development of special jigs and fixtures, and several machine operations—on the engine block, for example—were

°The eight basic processes are: turning, boring, drilling, milling, planing, shaping, slotting, and grinding.

°Johansson blocks are metal blocks used as standard machine shop gauges, with an accuracy within four-millionths of an inch. Carl Johansson was a Swedish armory supervisor who developed his blocks in 1890 to settle shop disputes among craftsmen arising from the lack of a fixed standard. The United States government formed the National Bureau of Standards in 1901, although there had been a department of Standard Weights and Measures since 1832.

Ford Motor Company assembly line (early 1900's). Courtesy Ford Motor Company.

performed simultaneously. The point had arrived where Ford could tolerate no hand-fitting because it was associated with inaccuracy and waste of time. (This is an attitude completely contrary to that prevailing in the handcrafts!) Quality and numbers had to be sought by eliminating the possibility of human error. Human error could be reduced or eliminated by making the human contribution as remote as possible from the process of making. Ford may have been influenced by his observation of the dis-assembly process used by meat packers in rolling carcasses along travelling overhead tracks and "deproducing" as they went. Reversing the meat-packing process, he introduced power-driven conveyors and overhead carriers in 1913, and reduced the chassis assembly from fourteen hours to an hour-and-a-half. Subassembly times were also reduced by the same means. And so began the mass-production, assembly-line techniques of modern manufacture. The germ of the idea which le Blanc had and which Eli Whitney applied, could be summarized as follows: The quality of a product can be improved, its price lowered, and much larger numbers produced, if component parts can be made accurately with specialized equipment used by workmen who could not otherwise make the whole product.

Modern manufacturing operations fall into three distinct phases: plant lay-out and tooling; duplication of parts; and assembly of mechanically duplicated units. These phases follow, of course, decisions by management to manufacture a new product or model. The decisions of management are guided by many considerations, including finance, marketing, engineering, research, and also design. The role of design in rela-

tion to research, engineering, and marketing is difficult to describe with precision since it varies with the type of industry and the size of a particular enterprise. Although design or redesign involves enormously costly retooling operations in the automobile industry, it very evidently is a crucial factor in any company's prosperity. However, the building of clay and wooden automobile models following marketing and engineering specifications might more accurately be designated "styling" than designing. Perhaps styling can be defined as that type of design which changes the superficial appearance of a product, largely in response to merchandising pressures. The role of styling in product design and some of the questions of artistic integrity it raises will be discussed below (pp. 123–125).

THE EMERGENCE OF INDUSTRIAL DESIGN

One of the consequences of the Industrial Revolution in the eighteenth century might be called "the replacement of the human hand." Until that time, no important changes in manufacture had taken place since the Bronze Age; tools were more refined, but principles of operation remained the same. Then a series of inventions, largely in the English textile industry, began to supplant the hand. Tools inherited from the Neolithic Age—the axe, the hammer, the spade, the knife, the awl—had been operated by hand, but the new machine tools were set in motion by impersonal forces: water, wind, steam. The long process of depersonalization through manufacture began, culminating in mass production and the conviction that a machine product cannot be a work of art.

Child labor in a textile mill, nineteenth century. Photo, Brown Brothers.

How could the machine tool be humanized? By converting it into "art"—by covering all its exposed surfaces with ornament.

German Rose Engine, (c.1750). British Crown Copyright. Science Museum, London.

The economic principle of preindustrial manufacture was that the craftsman applies his skill and imagination to raw materials which, when formed into a finished product, have more value than they had formerly. After the Industrial Revolution, the workman's contribution ceased to be skill, judgment, and imagination. He offered labor, which became a commodity like wool, leather, metal, or wood. It was the machine tool which accomplished the changes from raw material to finished product with results which were uniform and predictable. And so the craftsman ceased to be an important variable factor in production and now became an anonymous constant factor.

The early social consequences of the Industrial Revolution were, from a human standpoint, disastrous. Human effort having lost its unique value, work was converted into labor, a commodity. Women and children competed to sell their labor with steadily diminishing bargaining power; wages and living conditions grew more wretched. The machines which created more real wealth, and also more jobs, paradoxically brought poverty and lowered standards of living for those who tended them. The population increased, and concentration into crowded urban industrial areas began—a concentration which survives to this day. The hours of work were so long and the struggle to exist so critical that little energy remained for the working man to cultivate leisure or to improve his natural capacities. Thus, the Machine Age, whose technological miracles were hailed in enthusiastic language, brought in its wake poverty, degradation, over-crowded cities, ugly, mass-produced objects, and the brutalization of human beings.

The sordidness of cities, the wretchedness of the working classes, and the deadly monotony of labor resulted in romantic escapism in the arts, their divorcement from life's dismal reality. Sensitive people could not conceive of art as existing in a context which was so ruinous of human resources. And the early products of machine production gave little contrary evidence. Since machine tools were not understood as having distinctive aesthetic possibilities, they were used to imitate hand-wrought ornament, with results totally unsuited to the materials and process used. Craft revivals were attempted in the nineteenth century, notably by William Morris, who was influenced by John Ruskin; but the artistic problems of industrialism were not effectively faced until Walter Gropius established the Bauhaus in the twentieth century.

As early as 1845, however, the Swedish Society of Arts and Crafts (*Svenska Slöjd Foreningen*) was founded to encourage industries to join with artists to pursue excellence in mass-produced objects of daily use. This was well ahead of Morris, who set up his shop in 1861 to produce stained glass, tapestries, wallpaper, printed textiles, tableware, and furniture. But it was not until 1886 that Morris helped found the Arts and Crafts Exhibition Society in England, which encouraged the architects Lethaby, Gimson, and Mackintosh to design furniture. It is to the credit of Morris that he insisted on designers knowing how to *make* the articles they designed, on not confining their work to the drawing board. He perceived a basic flaw in the design of useful objects by engineering draftsmen: They frequently had no first-hand experience or understanding of the working properties of the materials their plans and specifications called for.

As Swedish industrial art developed, the more personalized crafts developed also. There is an important relationship between the individual ceramic craftsman, for example, and the large-scale ceramic industry. The great Gustavsbergs Works in Sweden maintains a studio where outstanding resident ceramists like Wilhelm Kage, Stig Lindberg, and Bernt Friberg, as well as visiting craftsmen, have been given free rein to experiment and develop new types. They are artists working in stoneware and faïence, utilizing the most advanced technical facilities, and endeavoring steadily to improve the regular production of the company. Their personalized ware constitutes the necessary pilot types which may subsequently be mass-produced. Since tooling is an enormously costly process, the value of individual craftsmen associated with a large plant or industry is apparent.

In 1907, the German Craft Union (*Der Deutsche Werkbund*), like the Swedish Association of Arts and Crafts, was founded to serve society with products of better design and workmanship. Its purposes were idealistically announced as "the ennoblement of industrial labor in the cooperation of art, industry, and handcraft, by means of education, propaganda, and concerted action on relevant questions." Its most active figure, Dr. Hermann Muthesius, an architect and educator, encountered considerable opposition in the inertia of most German manufacturers. Still, by 1910, the *Werkbund* had seven hundred and thirty-one members, of whom three hundred and sixty were artists, two hundred and sixty-seven manufacturers or merchants, and ninety-five experts,

museum administrators, and educators. Hence, this organization was an association not merely of artists, but also of whole firms, including the so-called *Künstlerwerkstatten,* or artists' workshops, as well as business men who were not producers themselves. From 1890, German industry had been very eclectic in its production; an obsession with ornament had obscured more fundamental determinants of form. Consequently, the *Werkbund* attempted to promote these simple standards for production: (1) good material, (2) technically perfect workmanship, and (3) practical form and harmony of color. But the competitive situation of manufacturers meant that changes in materials and production methods could not be expected even from members of the association. They realized it would be necessary to educate the public to raise its standards before significant reforms in design or manufacture could develop. Hence, the *Werkbund* joined with an Association for Mercantile Education to sponsor public lectures and forums. In addition, the artists' workshops at Dresden and Paderborn instituted training shops for apprentices in their plants. Finally, to carry out a program of consumer education, the Werkbund subsidized a museum founded by Karl Osthaus—the German Museum for Art in Commerce and Industry.

In 1890, the Belgian architect Henri van der Velde had proclaimed

In Sweden, under the influence of the Svenska Slöjd Foreningen, *design of household products was simplified during the nineteenth century. The florid, scenic plate dates from the 1830's, the less elaborate designs date from the 1890's and show the influence of Art Nouveau.*

Courtesy AB Gustavsbergs Fabriker.

the engineer as the true architect of the times. Technology deserved to be glorified if its engineers were willing to break with older techniques and materials to serve the present with steel and reinforced concrete. Muthesius had correctly formulated the problem and goal of modern manufacture by asserting that mass production and the division of labor *must be made to serve quality.* And the *Werkbund* endeavored to implement this directive. Walter Gropius, an architect associated with Muthesius, realized that the differences between the crafts and machine production were due not so much to the new machine-tools as to differences in where production control lay: in one man in crafts but in a division of labor in industry. He had written a paper on the "Industrial Prefabrication of Homes on a Unified Artistic Basis" which suggested the use of mass-production techniques for building and the possibility of achieving distinguished products through large-scale industrial methods. The net result of these ideas was the opening of the Bauhaus at Weimar in 1919, with Gropius as its director. It was formed by the combination of a trade school with a school of fine arts. As an architect, Gropius shared with Morris a unified, architectural approach to the arts. However, it was the unity not only of the cathedral, but of the home, the factory, and the school. As Gropius said in Britain in 1934: "Our governing conception of the basic unity of all design in its relation to life, which informed all our work, was therefore in diametrical opposition to that of 'art for art's sake' . . . ."

At first, each Bauhaus student had two teachers, one an artist and the other a master craftsman, because no individual instructors could be found who combined the appropriate qualities of both. It was necessary to produce students who had knowledge and experience of the whole of machine production and who could therefore give manufacture the integrated control which it lacked. Accordingly, the Bauhaus set about providing modern artists with a knowledge of science, economics, and craftsmanship. And in this manner, industrial designers as we know them were first trained.

In 1925 the Bauhaus left the somewhat hostile atmosphere of Weimar and reestablished itself at Dessau, where a new faculty, now composed of Bauhaus graduates, combined the technician and artist in the same instructor. The school became an experimental workshop in which models for mass production were continually built, revised, and improved. Some attempt was made to exploit the unique qualities of each type of machine; thus there was a beginning to the creation of a mechanical idiom or style, one which was distinctly different from handcraft forms and could make itself felt in furniture, pottery, textiles, typography, layout, and architecture. And, of particular importance, invidious distinctions were not made among the skills of painters, sculptors, craftsmen, and architects, since the new artists or designers might employ several of these skills in the process of creating an object.

The Bauhaus was driven out of Germany in 1933 when the Nazis came to power, and subsequently one of its younger instructors, Laszlo Moholy-Nagy, established an American branch, the Institute of Design in Chicago, where it was eventually absorbed into the Illinois Institute of Technology. Aside

An example of Bauhaus-inspired design.

MARIANNE BRANDT, teapot (1924). Collection The Museum of Modern Art, New York, Phyllis B. Lambert Fund.

from creating a new profession, Industrial Design, the Bauhaus has permanently influenced the education of artists throughout the world. Most courses in design today are largely derived from the Bauhaus curriculum, although it is a sign of successful assimilation that students and even their instructors may not be aware of the fact.

The Bauhaus *had* to emerge because conventional academies of art had become inadequate. They had begun as places to train artists and craftsmen who would produce the art objects required by a wealthy and elegant aristocracy. But academically trained artists began to lose contact with modern life as the social class for which they produced art disappeared. The academies served to shut off talented students from the realities of industrial production by machines and from social reality itself, inculcating ideals and methods which were obsolete as they were being taught. Consequently, their graduates usually were forced into the poverty, the romantic Bohemianism, and the economic displacement with which artists became identified after the democratic revolutions of Europe and America in the late eighteenth century.

Today, industrial designers, design consultants, package designers, stylists, and designers specializing in certain kinds of products are firmly established in the commercial and industrial world. Manufacturers either employ their own designers on a continuing basis or retain the services of industrial-design firms and free-lance consultants. Almost all professional art schools and many university art departments offer curricula leading to degrees in industrial design, organizing their instruction very much like schools of architecture. No article,

from a can of soup to a locomotive, goes out into the world without the ministrations of a designer. Of course, the spectacular success of the profession may have been achieved for the wrong—that is, commercial—reasons. However, if the services of industrial design are sought primarily to stimulate the sale of products, we cannot deny that a desirable side effect has been the visual improvement of a multitude of large and small objects in our environment. Beyond that, where the able designer has been given free rein, visual improvement has been accompanied by the dividend of better performance.

FORM AND FUNCTION

It was Louis Sullivan, the Chicago architect (1856–1924) and *lieber meister* of Wright, who originated the phrase "Form follows function." Applied to architecture or to manufactured objects, the phrase became an axiom, a first principle, for all modern design. It means that the outer shape and appearance of any designed object follows, or is a result of, its inner operation. From this postulate, we can derive correlaries, as in plane geometry: The object should look like what it is and does, that is, there should be no deceptive appearance—metal should not imitate wood, plastic should not imitate marble, the small cottage should not imitate a temple or fortress. The design of buildings and useful objects before the modern period often began with the outer shell, the façade, and then proceeded to divide and arrange the interior space. The essential problem of design had been to determine which period style to follow in building a library, a house, or a chair. Where the form of an object was functionally determined, ornament was applied to cover its nakedness, so to speak. Thus, architecture and design had become—especially in the late eighteenth and nineteenth centuries—increasingly decorative. Form did *not* follow function: It followed the prevailing taste in period styles and decorative ornament.

Industrial design, beginning with a body of such liberating and idealistic axioms, was able to bring common sense and a distinctive, abstract excellence to machine-made objects. However, as the practice of industrial design evolved, it became subject to a variety of aesthetically irrelevant pressures. Sophisticated and even misleading interpretations of form and function affected design. Does "function" mean only the physical and utilitarian operation of an object? Is there only one "form" possible as the correct solution to a design problem? Are alternative forms equally valid? Doesn't the appearance of an object also need to function by making the object appealing to consumers? If so, the form of an object is not merely the result of satisfying its internal operational requirements; the form of a product, its outward appearance, must enable it to compete successfully with similar products of other manufacturers.

Thus, we arrive at a type of design specialization, a child of industrial design—styling. Manufacturers discovered in the 1930's that the clean, functional lines of industrially designed products stimulated sales. Hence, they employed designers to redesign their traditionally styled merchandise. It was a simple deductive step, then, to conclude that the periodic redesign of a product would increase its saleability *whether or not* any significant changes in its physical functioning had taken

place. In other words, redesign, or styling, created a new value for useful objects: new appearance. New appearance or novelty became for many products as important a factor in their salability as operational or utilitarian factors. A newly styled product had the effect of making older designs seem less valuable and out-of-date, although such products may have been no less useful to their owners. This cycle of design, redesign, and new styling of useful objects, leading to an apparent loss of value in older "models" of the product, has been called *planned obsolescence.*

Normally, we regard a useful object as obsolete if one of two conditions develops: (1) The product wears out, it no longer operates; or (2) the product operates, but a new model does the job better. When a new model of a product appears, newly styled or packaged, the consumer is led to believe that some significant improvements in operation have been made. This may not, in fact, be the case, but consumers will discard the old and buy the new because novelty has become an important value in our culture. Furthermore, the quick obsolescence of useful objects has important economic implications. Industries need to use most of their productive capacity to keep their workers employed. They can operate profitably on less than full production for a time, but, obviously, unemployed workers cannot buy the automobiles, refrigerators, television sets, and other appliances produced by manufacturers if they are not earning wages. Hence, persuading the public to use and discard goods more rapidly is vital to a growing economy. For the same reason, the public is encouraged to buy *more than one* automobile, TV set, table service, or radio. We should own

Through one of its byproducts, styling, industrial design developed unfortunate associations with fashion.

Refrigerator of the early 1930's, in a modern reenactment. Courtesy General Electric Company.

more than one home, keep a boat, build a ski lodge, take more vacations, raise a second family when the first family has grown up. Without doubt, planned obsolescence has contributed to the steady raising of the American standard of living in the course of the general effort to use more of the productive capacity of industry.

However, our standard of living may be defined too exclusively in terms of the *number* of useful objects we own and the *frequency* with which we replace them. Durability, one of the chief traits of handcraft, becomes less prominent in machine production. We also increase each year the number of articles which are made to be used once and discarded. Package designers specialize in the creation of containers, most of which are disposable. Such package designs may be very attractive from an aesthetic standpoint, yet the idea of their disposability somehow violates our emotional associations with art, which is expected to be enduring. A country as wealthy in resources as the United States can afford to employ its design skills in the creation of disposable packages and containers, while other societies, whether from lack of resources or cultural tradition, will stress re-usable containers, durable products, and continuity of style.

The industrial designer has been inescapably drawn into the world of economics and marketing. His training equips him to analyze the purpose and operation of a product and to find the best combination of form and material to suit the product's function. His knowledge of production methods enables him to keep manufacturing costs to a minimum consistent with quality. He is able to consider in his design the problems of packaging, shipment, and display of the product. Unfortunately, the designer is often obliged to fabricate a new "skin" for a product to create a deceptive appearance of uniqueness, in order to arrive at a result which is spuriously "different." Thus, we have come to the question which all artists, architects, and designers must ultimately answer: Should the public or client be served with the solution which the designer deems best according to his professional standards, or does professionalism consist of finding the solution which best satisfies the client's formal, functional, *and* marketing requirements? It would be too easy to answer the question in terms of designers who have integrity and those who do not. The way in which a designer is employed obviously affects the way he practices. Advertisers, too, are faced with the conflict between presenting information effectively and presenting information so as to leave a misleading impression. It would appear that as the worlds of commerce and industry grow more complex, the professions which serve them become more strongly and securely institutionalized. As design professionalism grows, we can look forward hopefully to the time when an increasing number of individual designers and design firms will offer a quality and integrity of service such as one expects from outstanding lawyers and surgeons.

INDUSTRIAL DESIGN: THE CHAIR

Until we sit on it, a chair is a work of abstract sculpture. It is also a complex engineering problem. The habit of sitting in chairs, which we take for granted in the Western world, is carried on in many positions, for different purposes, and with a wide variety of seating

ANTONIO BONET, JUAN KURCHAN, JORGE FERRARIHARDOY, lounge chair (1938). Collection The Museum of Modern Art, New York, Edgar Kaufmann, Jr. Fund.

LUDWIG MIES VAN DER ROHE, Barcelona lounge chair (1929). Collection The Museum of Modern Art, New York, gift of the manufacturer, Knoll Associates, Inc., U.S.A.

apparatus. We expect comfort, support, and stability from our seating equipment. And we should like to get into and out of a chair with a certain amount of dignity; but some chairs make acrobatic demands of middleaged ladies and gentlemen. We want some chairs to be light and portable; others, to be sturdy and resist abuse; some will be placed outdoors and must be weather-resistant. Generally, chairs should not be too bulky, for the contemporary home or apartment cannot afford to invest a great deal of space in a chair which approaches the problem of comfort by assembling mattresses. As sculpture, chairs possess symbolic value: They clearly designate the seat of the ruler, the throne of a king or a bishop, or the inviolable perch on which the master of the house dines, reads his paper, or watches television. Chairs are feminine or masculine, juvenile or adult, alert or lazy, shy or assertive, austere or frivolous, To a crawling child or a kitten, the chairs in a room must constitute a forest of legs. To a mother of small children, chairs may represent a series of nonwashable surfaces in which margarine and jam become too easily embedded.

A total design philosophy is revealed by a chair. The attitude of the designer toward comfort, toward the chair as architecture or decoration, toward exposure or concealment of the structural elements, can be clearly expressed. For example, the famous Barcelona lounge chair by Mies van der Rohe is an eloquent demonstration of his architectural philosophy and style: simplicity of materials and form; careful attention to details, especially at intersections and joints; absence of ornament; and elegance of proportion and scale. Technological innovation is also bril-

liantly in evidence. The cantilever principle (see pp. 421–22) is used in conjunction with the elasticity of metal. The same continuous metal bar serves as curved leg and back support while functioning visually in counterpoint to the metal element which it crosses. Finally, the tufted leather cushions offer bulk, warmth, and color in contrast to the thin and precise metal members. The spacing of the tufts and the webbing, visible at the front end of the seat, create rhythm and pattern through their repetitions so that a certain amount of visual variety and textural change can balance an otherwise austere effect. The chair is unquestionably a masterpiece, likely to endure as an active classic for many years to come. It is all the more remarkable when we consider its date; 1929, and the fact that interiors designed today still specify the Barcelona lounge chair.

The earlier armchair (1926) by Mies is interesting more as a revelation of the designer's thinking than as a completely successful work of art. The cantilever principle is again employed, along with continuity of structural elements—from back to seat to base. The arm-rest helps to strengthen the back support, but its joint at the base is not too satisfactorily accomplished. The chair is obviously influenced by the bent-wood Thonet rocker of 1860, with polished metal tubing employed for its elastic properties as was the bent-wood formerly. But the Barcelona chair is a more original and finished solution to the problem.

Marcel Breuer's tubular-steel-and-canvas chair of 1925 illustrates an early use of polished metal in furniture. The innovation provides great strength and stability with a minimum of weight and bulk. The result is a strong arm chair which is nevertheless portable, visually open, and harmoniously attuned to modern developments in steel-frame architecture and machine technology. Unlike the later Miesian chairs, there is a distinct separation between the supporting structure (two connected metal rectangles) and the seating itself. The seat is hung or suspended from the arms; *it is not in compression.* One sits on and rests against canvas which is stretched between metal tube frames. Thus, the suspension principle is used twice: once in the framing and once in the textile seating. Notice how Mies and Breuer arrive at design solutions by exploiting the inherent properties of materials: the relative resistance of canvas to stretching; the resistance of metal tubing to bending; the capacity of flat metal bars to bend and recover their original position, in short, their elasticity.

The painted wood armchair by Gerrit Rietveld, a Dutch designer, was made in 1917 as an experimental project. It is mainly interesting as a demonstration of the influence of painting upon utilitarian design. Here the rectilinear bias of Mondrian's work is clearly visible. We cannot say there is any innovation in structure or material, with the possible exception of the almost unsupported,

GERRIT RIETVELD, armchair (1917). Collection The Museum of Modern Art, New York, gift of Philip Johnson.

LUDWIG MIES VAN DER ROHE, armchair (1926), top. Collection The Museum of Modern Art, New York, gift of Edgar Kaufmann, Jr.

GEBRUDER THONET, rocking chair (1860), center. Collection The Museum of Modern Art, New York, gift of Café Nicholson.

MARCEL BREUER, armchair (1925), bottom. Collection The Museum of Modern Art, New York, gift of Herbert Bayer.

almost cantilevered arms. Structurally, it is a compression-type of chair, built on post-and-lintel principles (see pp. 418–421). The chief effect sought is that of hovering planes, open structure, and avoidance of curves. Clearly, this project is designed to function primarily in visual terms, since it is the result neither of anatomical analysis of sitting nor of structural analysis of materials. It is important as a reaction to the curvilinear extravagances of Art Nouveau, especially as seen in the furniture of Hector Guimard. Wright also reacted against Art Nouveau, as in the 1904 office chair of metal and oak for his Larkin Building in Buffalo. The curved and shaped seat and the slight tilt of the back-rest represent an unusual concession on the part of Mr. Wright to the generally convex shape of the body, while the visual effect is somewhat more open than is usual in Wright's furniture, which would not be out of place in a Norman keep.

The 1929 armchair by Le Corbusier shows some debt to the similar type by Breuer in 1925, although it contains a few refinements and structural changes. He has abandoned the side

HECTOR GUIMARD, side table (1908). Collection The Museum of Modern Art, New York, gift of Mme. Hector Guimard.

FRANK LLOYD WRIGHT, office armchair on swivel case (1904), top. Collection The Museum of Modern Art, New York, gift of Edgar Kaufmann, Jr.

FRANK LLOYD WRIGHT, armchair (1904), center. Collection The Museum of Modern Art, New York, gift of Frank Lloyd Wright.

LE CORBUSIER, armchair with adjustable back (1929), bottom. Collection The Museum of Modern Art, New York, gift of Thonet Industries, Inc.

rectangular support and reverted to four straight legs, with the front pair ingeniously connected to the back pair through the seat and arms. While the sitter's weight rests on the canvas, it is less clear that the seat frame is suspended. It appears to be conventionally supported in compression at the front. But the back and rear portion of the seat may represent a better suspension design than Breuer's. Le Corbusier's adjustable chaise longue of 1927 is more original, more reminiscent of his architectural use of pilotis. The wooden base lifts the seating structure off the ground and possesses some quality of organic form in contrast to the mechanistic, tubular steel frame. The separate seating and supporting structures permit a variety of reclining positions without using the mechanical equipment employed in contemporary adjustable lounge chairs which are less honest in the expression of their function. Furthermore, Le Corbusier has arrived at a comfortable position for the recliner, one very similar to that afforded by today's "tilt-back" lounge chairs, yet without bulky upholstery and concealed working parts.

Another classic armchair is by the Finnish architect Alvar Aalto. His chair, made in 1934 of bent plywood, carries out in wood the principles explored earlier by Breuer, Mies, and Le Corbusier in metal. Wood is a congenial material to the Scandinavians, and it imparts a warmth which polished, chrome-plated steel may lack. This chair, too, has a clear separation between the structure which supports and the structure which is supported. However, the single continuous bent plane of the seat does not possess the resilience of canvas, nor the suggestion of comfort and luxury of

leather or conventional upholstery. The chair is notable for its clear statement of function, obvious stability, and its exploitation of the elasticity of wood in the seating. The curved and bent plane of the seat actually forms a modified coil spring at the front and rear points where it is anchored to the frame; thus the seat will "give" to the weight of the sitter. Although rather bulky (there is too much wasted volume inside the frame), the seating structure represented perhaps the best solution that could be achieved with bent plywood in 1934, as opposed to modern "molded" plywood chairs.

Bruno Mathsson used laminated plywood and fiber webbing in a 1940 armchair which requires much less floor

LE CORBUSIER, chaise longue (1927). Collection The Museum of Modern Art, New York, gift of Thonet Industries, Inc.

ALVAR AALTO, lounge chair (1934), left. Collection The Museum of Modern Art, New York, gift of Edgar Kaufmann, Jr.

BRUNO MATHSSON, armchair (1940), right. Collection The Museum of Modern Art, New York, Edgar Kaufmann, Jr. Fund.

CHARLES EAMES, dining chair (1946). Collection The Museum of Modern Art, New York, gift of the manufacturer, Herman Miller Furniture Company, U.S.A.

EERO SAARINEN, armchair (1957). Collection The Museum of Modern Art, New York, gift of the manufacturer, Knoll Associates, Inc., U.S.A.

space than Aalto's chair and yet provides equivalent opportunity to recline. The webbing has more resilience than bent plywood, of course, and also affords textural relief. By the shape and location of the seat, Mathsson is able to establish a low center of gravity well within the chair base; hence the seat back can extend well behind the base, unsupported, and without fear of tip-over. The curve in the seat, then, is not merely visual play or the result of conformation to the human posterior. It locates the weight of the sitter in the place where it will add to the stability of the chair.

The molded walnut-plywood chair with metal rod frame by Charles Eames dates from 1946 and has become an American, even a world-wide, classic. Molded-plywood technology was substantially perfected during World War II: British De Havilland Bombers were made of this material. And Eames has solved the problem of making wood comfortable by: (1) imparting to the plane a complex, biomorphic shape; (2) permitting the sitter to change position easily; (3) using open space at the lumbar base of the back to free rather than restrict the sitter; (4) providing support for the back exactly where it is needed; and (5) creating a brilliant system of articulation among the seating elements. Thus, while the elasticity of metal and wood are exploited, a small rubber cushion between the back-rest and its metal support permits further independent lateral movement without strain to the structure. Also, the seat is anchored firmly to the front legs just behind the knees, while the rubber pad further back beneath the seat permits it to "give" and to rotate slightly in response to the weight and movement of the sitter. As a result, a remarkable amount

of comfort is achieved in a mass-produced chair which is light, inexpensive, easily stored, and very durable. As the legs are splayed, the chair increases in stability when it supports weight. The sitter feels he is very securely connected to the chair and is able to maintain an excellent posture while seated and as he gets in or out of the sitting position.

A recent development in furniture design is seen in the armchair by Eero Saarinen. The cast-aluminum pedestal base represents an effort to avoid the "forest of legs" effect created in any furniture-filled room. And the molded plastic seat affords the maximum of continuity among the structural elements. The plastic material, reinforced with Fiberglas, permits the entire shell to perform a load-bearing function at the same time that a sculptural, biomorphic form is achieved. The fabric seat pad could be eliminated if desired, but it helps to add a note of textural and color variety. Such pedestal bases have been hitherto used in commercial settings, as bases for restaurant tables and ice-cream-counter stools. In addition to good stability, they offer room for one's feet, eliminating the uncomfortable leg-straddling we must often endure around a dining table. Although this chair and coordinated furniture dates from 1958, it has not had a huge reception from consumers, despite its practical advantages. Three-legged chairs have not done well either. Perhaps the zoomorphic associations of four-legged chairs remain too precious, as yet, to be surrendered.

Charles Eames has designed a modified pedestal-based lounge chair (1958) which has legs and thus avoids the comparisons with a dental chair which a molded plastic pedestal might suggest. The anodyzed-aluminum frame has a thick-and-thin, sculptural shape which overcomes many of the objections the public had to the tubular-steel-frame furniture of the Bauhaus designers in the 1920's. And the flexible plastic seat and back offer a rich and comfortable textural contrast to the polished metal. The chair is an exciting solution to the problem of carrying the sitter's weight down to the floor. At first the sitter is suspended on the plastic between the metal frame. Then his entire weight is clearly received at two points and transferred to, and concentrated in, the post of the pedestal, from whence it is distributed among the legs. Very rarely do we see a structural function carried out with such clarity and precision. A similar visual effect occurs when we see the huge weight of a bridge truss concentrated at one small pivot on top of

HANS WEGNER, dining chair (1949). Collection The Museum of Modern Art, New York, gift of Georg Jensen, Inc.

the pier which carries the load to earth. This dramatization of the load-transferring function, as carried out by Eames, is very satisfying: An unusual visual gratification is generated as we can almost "see" the weight traveling to points where it is collected, concentrated into a core, distributed to the legs, and then safely dispersed. In the connection between the seat and base, there is a remote analogy to a waiter supporting a tray, its weight carried down via his upturned fingers and thumb, through his wrist and into his arm. Such design is deceptively simple; in fact, the chair is a very sophisticated work: It clearly demonstrates that the materials and techniques of the Machine Age have arrived at the condition of art.

The Scandinavian approach to the chair has been structurally correct but conservative, and very single-minded in its pursuit of simplified sculptural form. The handcraft tradition there is strong, and hand-formed wood is the admired structural material, together with fabric or leather as a covering. Conventionally-sprung upholstery and thick slabs of foam rubber would amount to an admission of failure to the Scandinavian designer. He has studied the anatomy of sitting carefully, shapes his oak, birch, teak, or rosewood lovingly and with precision, and requires only a thin, coarse-textured fabric pad to achieve the firm seating comfort he wants. The famous Hans Wegner dining chair of 1949 in oak and cane is another international classic. Wegner, a Dane, is noted for his careful attention to the arm- and back-rests, to the felicitous matching and flow of wood grains, and to the tactile appeal of his wood surfaces. Another Danish designer, Finn Juhl, exhibits a strong sculptural im-

CHARLES EAMES, lounge chair (1958). Collection The Museum of Modern Art, New York, gift of the manufacturer, Herman Miller Furniture Company, U.S.A.

FINN JUHL, teak armchair (1945).

FINN JUHL, leather-and-teak armchair (1949).

BORGE MOGENSEN, oak-and-leather armchair (1950). Courtesy the artist.

The influence of painters Arp and Miró on contemporary French furniture design.

OLIVIER MOURGUE, chairs (1965). Photos, Roger Gain.

pulse in his chairs, with a beautiful separation between the "bearing" and the "borne" elements. The two rear legs receive the weight at the "elbow" of the arm-rest and use this function as an opportunity to create visual interest in the play of negative shapes—that is, air spaces—in the openings between the wooden members and the curved plane of the chair back. The form language of Finn Juhl's chairs belongs more to the craft tradition (with a strong influence from modern abstract sculpture) than to the machine. A leather-and-teak chair by Juhl (1949) is somewhat more flamboyant and zoomorphic and also reveals the two pronounced tendencies of this designer: clear separation of

supporting and support*ed* elements and a sculptural attention to the play of negative shapes.

A dramatic and unconventional Danish chair is seen in the oak-and-leather armchair (1950) by Borge Mogensen. The wood framing has an aggressively rustic quality, enhanced by wide leather straps and buckles. The unsupported, upward-tilted arms counterbalance the massive, earth-bound triangular support and rearward tilt of the back. The seat element seems to derive from a ladder. In a chair of this sort, the designer has found an almost theatrical solution to the structural problem, but one which is completely honest nevertheless.

We have not examined several varieties of collapsible chairs and stacking stools, nor have we explored thoroughly many interesting new combinations of wood, metal, plastic, fabric, and leather. In general, it is surprising how many of the genuinely fundamental new ideas in chair design go back to the Bauhaus and, more recently, to Eames. Further developments have been essentially refinements based on improved production methods and more sophisticated technology. The great Scandinavians like Mathsson, Ekselius, Wegner, Juhl, and Klimt have grown out of their own folk-craft tradition, and, while aware of the Bauhaus philosophy, have been more attracted by the sensuousness of their materials than by a primarily cerebral approach to form and structure. Alvar Aalto, the Finnish architect, has been something of an exception among the Scandinavians, who, while maintaining their craft tradition, are now moving in more international directions, employing mechanically formed glass, polished metal, and plastics, and attack-

THE MATERIALS AND METHODS OF MANUFACTURE

The size of manufacturing plants (most furniture factories are small)

Technical development and experimentation (the industry is not well organized for this)

Manufacturer's prejudices and vested interests, as well as their insight

Wars, forest fires, taxes, and other natural and unnatural phenomena

CONSUMER NEEDS

Convenience for: moving, cleaning, renovating, shipping, storing

Economy in: initial investment, up-keep

Durability to withstand: pets, time, children, shipping, back-tippers, elements

Comfort of: size, shape, proportion, resilience

Adaptability for: purpose, appearance, comfort

COST

THE MODERN CHAIR AS YOU FIND IT

THE DISTRIBUTION SYSTEM

A demand by retailers for "selling points" instead of problem-solving, resulting in competing models rather than perfection of types

A decorator's nightmare: a client who might like a chair indefinitely because it is well designed

Retailer's conception of "what will sell" (this gets behind the times like anything else)

THE DESIGNER

The designer's expressive needs — his whims, fantasies, and phobias

Schools and museums

The idiom of the times, or the character of contemporary human expression

Critics and competitions

Painters: Miró, Mondrian, Arp

Sculptors: Moore, Noguchi, Calder

Architects: Breuer, Mies van der Rohe, Saarinen

"The Modern Chair As You Find It," adapted from *Everyday Art Quarterly* No. 20, courtesy Walker Art Center, Minneapolis.

ing the problems of mass-produced, inexpensive furniture, lighting, rugs, and tableware.

Where sturdy, inexpensive, easily stacked and transported seating has been required, especially for public uses, designers have been drawn to molded and stamped plastic forms with tubular- or rod-metal legs and supporting elements. Naturally, when cost is a factor, comfort tends to be pursued with molded plastics rather than with more expensive and destructible leather or fabric coverings. But it is interesting to observe that austere new materials like chrome-steel tubing, plastic coverings, and cast-aluminum pedestal bases were introduced for domestic use and were by no means inexpensive. Still, a mass market and lowered unit cost are ideas built into the philosophy of modern product design. Expensive new products are eventually "adapted," "styled," and brought to a large public at lower cost. In the United States, Charles Eames, George Nelson, Henry Dreyfuss, Russel Wright and Raymond Loewy, among others, have brought design of good quality to American consumers at a modest price. Ironically, American production methods and marketing techniques are better able to apply the design philosophy of the Bauhaus than the nations of Europe, where capitalism, in general, has been less creative, more tradition-bound, and, until the Common Market, adjusted mainly to the requirements of national markets.

Today an enormous world market for good design is in process of development. Production facilities are very widely dispersed since they are no longer dependent on local water-power and coal resources to the extent they were in the nineteenth century. Population increases imply that manufactured products do not need to be transported long distances to reach a good market. People in what were remote places are increasingly informed about new developments in consumer goods and have acquired appetites for quality in product design. We are entering a world in which the ownership of vast natural resources and elaborate production facilities will not be the exclusive basis of national eminence. Inexpensive atomic power will permit production to be carried on virtually anywhere. The tools of production will, no doubt, be radically transformed, many of them miniaturized, computerized, and electronically linked. In this not-too-distant future, design will be a crucial element for the capture and retention of markets; the conservation of raw materials; the discovery and satisfaction of subtle and evanescent human requirements; and the employment of men's energies and imagination to make beauty and utility synonymous.

PART TWO THE STYLES

OF ART

The concept of style is indispensable for the study of art, and yet it can be a source of confusion because the word has so many different meanings. Sometimes, style refers to the work of a particular historical period. It may refer to the art of a nation or several nations, or to the art of a region within a country. The growth and development of a single artist's way of working is often called "the evolution of his style." In addition, style can be a certain technical approach to the creation of art. The word "style" is also used as a term of approval, as recognition of a high level of accomplishment. In connection with the design of clothing or the changing appearance of appliances, "style" is equivalent to the latest fad or fashion. All the uses of the word and the concept, however, seem to have a single purpose—the classification or arrangement of a variety of seemingly unrelated works of art into categories which will make them easier to study, talk about, and understand. At the broadest and most general level, therefore, an art style is a grouping or classification of works of art (by time, region, appearance, technique, subject matter, and so on) which makes further study and analysis possible.

As with all scientific classification, the sorting of phenomena into categories is based on traits or qualities which the phenomena have in common. Styles of art, therefore, can be thought of as families. Just as members of a family have certain traits or features which give them what is called a "family resemblance," works of art can also resemble each other. They may have many differences, too, but they have at least *some* common traits which are discernible and hence make classification in a family or style possible. That common, uniting element may be directly visible in a particular use of color, shape, space, line, or texture; or it may be detected in a qualitative relationship among these elements. In other words, style may be discerned, not only in what is visible on the surface of a work of art, but also in the over-all feeling or quality the work seems to exhibit. This over-all, or *pervasive*, quality of a work of art frequently constitutes the basis for its classification within a certain style. But it is not very helpful for students of art if the so-called style qualities are merely identified and classified. We need to know what traits or features of the work help to place it within a style. In other words, we must try to *explain* the connection between the work and the style quality it seems to possess.

The reasons, then, for studying the styles of art, might be summarized as follows:

(1) To acquire useful categories for thinking and talking about the variety of works of art produced during various periods.

(2) To help understand an artist, a period in history, a country, or a region in whose art a certain style seems to predominate.

(3) To help compare intelligently (hence, to judge) works of art which are stylistically related; only works which are stylistically similar can be compared for the purposes of making critical judgments.

(4) To gain some idea of the connection between the artist's manner of working, the visible results, and our reactions to his work as a whole.

After we have some understanding of art styles, we are in a better position to read the so-called "hidden language" of art. An interest in style leads us to look for meanings beneath the subject matter and apparent purpose of a work of art. Just as handwriting, for the trained observer, conveys meanings which are not contained in the words themselves, a knowledge of style reveals much about an artist's way of thinking, about his environment, and about the society and culture in which his work is rooted. Archaeologists use the concept of style to help reconstruct past cultures on the basis of fragments of useful objects they discover. They put pieces of stylistic evidence together like a mosaic, to form an intelligible idea of the culture or civilization as a whole. Similarly, we study the styles of art—both past and present—as evidence for assembling in our own minds an idea of the changing condition of man. We are, in a sense, archaeologists of the artistic image of humanity.

At the present time, art is being created in many styles at once throughout the world. In previous epochs some variation existed, but there was less stylistic variety in any single place and hence less confusion for any given public about the purposes of art, the standards of artists, or the greatness or mediocrity of individual works. But modern styles vary greatly and change rapidly, and it is difficult to see in contemporary art the type of stylistic unity which persisted for long periods during the past. Therefore, instead of searching for a single stylistic common denominator for the art of our time, it might be better to describe the principal tendencies which appear to be operating simultaneously today. These tendencies are also modern versions of styles which have persisted through the entire history of art. Fortunately, the contemporary development of social science and the humanities permits an analysis of style based on our growing knowledge of the interactions among human behavior, personality, and artistic creation. As a result, we have better conceptual tools for the treatment of the diversity of modern styles than was available in the eighteenth century when this subject first began to be studied systematically.

The style of objective accuracy pertains mainly to painting, drawing, and sculpture since these are the arts which often have a close connection with the imitation of visual phenomena. (Architecture and industrial design, however, also produce works which depend for their success on forms of great precision; their dimensions have to be exceedingly accurate because of the processes of forming and fabrication used in construction and manufacture.) This is the style of art which is most familiar to people, whether they have studied art or not. It is also the style which many feel most confident in judging, since they can compare a painting or sculpture with what they believe is its original model in life. For many persons, accuracy, or closeness of resemblance to what is depicted or portrayed, is the principal means of determining the excellence of a work of art.

Other words, such as "realism" or "naturalism" are loosely used to designate the style of objective accuracy. Faithfulness to what is seen is a principal feature of this style, and since most of us have good vision, we feel we can judge an artist's fidelity to his model, or his skill in creating the *illusion* of reality. To create the *illusion* of reality, some artists painstakingly reproduce every detail of a model on the assumption that a convincingly real or accurate work is the sum of carefully observed and ex-

THE STYLE

OF OBJECTIVE ACCURACY

ecuted parts. Sometimes this kind of artistic approach is called "photographic realism." Of course, the invention of photography in the nineteenth century (and its continued perfection in the twentieth century) has made the style of photographic realism almost obsolete. The masters of the past knew how to create the *illusion* of reality without trying to reproduce everything the eye can see. And most artists today see no reason to compete with the camera in the pursuit of realism. Hence, the problem of many contemporary artists is to create the impression of reality through a selective use of the many available visual facts. Clearly, this artistic approach requires more than good eyesight in order to be successful. The simplification or the editing of nature, while creating the illusion of the *presence* of nature, calls for considerable judgment and skill in execution. Also, through his selection of certain details of visual reality, and his omission of others, the artist can create a dominant mood or feeling which the viewer is encouraged to share.

In this chapter we shall discuss the varieties of expression which are possible within the style of objective accuracy. We shall mention some of the ways in which artists create the sense of reality without actually reproducing all the details of an object or place. Also, we shall speculate about why some artists prefer accuracy of representation or the illusion of the presence of nature instead of abstraction or distortion of what the eye sees.

The student of art should learn that, although the style of objective accuracy has been in decline during the modern period, it is nevertheless a powerful means for the expression of ideas and feelings. Our problem is to learn how to distinguish between those works in which the artist slavishly imitates the details of visual reality and those in which he uses objective accuracy to imply much more than is seen. In our effort to investigate this problem, we shall examine the work of some contemporary artists who produce work that is very recognizable in terms of reality but who succeed in using visual facts to convey meanings beyond the visible.

The Imitation of Appearances

Giraffes fighting, Paleolithic cave painting. From the book *The Search for the Tassili Frescoes* by Henri Lhote. Copyright, ©, 1959 by E.P. Dutton & Company, Inc. and Hutchinson & Company, Ltd. Reproduced by permission of the publishers.

Why does a painting or sculpture which looks convincingly like its model in reality fascinate us? Why do artists, modern and traditional, attempt to imitate what the eye can see or what the camera might record? These questions are fundamental since almost everyone assumes that the accurate representation of reality is the basis of art—even art which is subsequently distorted or carried to a degree of abstraction where the original point of departure cannot be visually detected. Also, it is true that the earliest known art, the cave painting of Paleolithic man, is highly representational, beautifully accurate. Children, too, at a fairly early stage of their development, endeavor to represent real objects accurately, although they do not succeed from an adult standpoint. But when they are very young, children are not bothered by requirements of visual logic as adults are; as they grow older, however, children *do* attempt to imitate the appearance of things as accurately as possible. Imitation for them is part of the process of coming to terms with the world in which they must live.

It is very likely that imitating the appearance of reality represents an effort to control reality. At very deep levels of awareness, our desire to paint a head, for example, so that it appears alive and capable of speech, is part of an effort to develop mastery over life. Drawing an object over and over again creates confidence in our ability to control it. Perhaps we think we are less likely to be victims of the seemingly capricious actions of a world we do not understand if we can create images which are accurate and faithful enough to take the place of those portions of the world we must deal with.

For the artist, accurate drawing, painting, modeling, and carving are part of his basic body of skills, part of his development of craftsmanship, part of his training in learning to see and represent with fidelity, in the material he has chosen, the objects of his vision. It is usually through drawing from reality—from the living figure, from nature, and from the man-made world— that artists gain confidence in their powers of observation. It is also through drawing from reality that they often acquire ideas which can later be transformed into more ambitious, imaginative projects, far removed from original studies in observation and imitation of appearances.

For the viewer, a naturalistic work of art may be fascinating because admiration for the artist's skill is aroused. At another level, the viewer is attracted by the successful imitation of appearances on canvas, in bronze or in stone, because he knows that he is really looking at paint, stone, or wood—not at flesh, leaves, sky, cloth, and so on. Many of us enjoy so-called *trompe-l'oeil*, or fool-the-eye, paintings for this reason. There are stories as far back as the Greeks about artists who could paint grapes so faithfully that birds were tempted to pick at them. The conflict between what a work of art looks like and what we know it is, can be fascinating under certain circumstances and aesthetically pleasurable. Indeed, the appeal of a work

executed in a style of objective accuracy always has at its base this fascination caused by the tension between appearance and reality.

Another reason for the interest in imitation of appearances lies in the artistic concern with narration—telling the viewer as clearly as possible what happened. From its beginning, visual art has played a role in the transmission of information. Although photo-journalism has now largely supplanted the artist as a recorder of events, artists nevertheless continue to create works which not only inform the viewer through naturalistic description and representation, but also depend for psychological effectiveness on very accurate rendering of visual details. Andrew Wyeth (1917–   ) is an artist who uses a style of objective accuracy for narrative purposes, to convey the moving, internal drama in the lives of the people, objects, or places he represents. In *Christina's World*, we are aware of the struggle and loneliness in the inner life of a physically

ANDREW WYETH, *Christina's World* (1948). Collection The Museum of Modern Art, New York. Purchase.

handicapped woman. Wyeth's attention to detail helps to establish the moods of harsh reality and pathos which are strongly present in the picture. His style also avoids excessive sentimentality. The tempera medium gives the work a dry, matter-of-fact quality which heightens our awareness of Christina's difficult existence. Wyeth uses accuracy of representation; but location and selection of details are also important. Notice the high horizon and the low position of the figure. This serves to connect her more closely to the ground as we see more of the earth than of the sky. Distances must be tremendous in her groping world; this impression is created by the skilled use of perspective—the small, distant house, the large expanse of field intervening between the figure and the house. It is exceedingly difficult to paint so large an area of relatively unimportant material—grass—and keep it interesting to the viewer. Yet Wyeth succeeds in giving the field a powerful psychological charge because of the tension created between the girl and the house: We view the grass as space which must be painfully traversed. The design of this picture combines with the artist's representational skill to make the work memorable.

There is a tendency in American art and thought to favor accurate, matter-of-fact representations of life. This may grow out of the traditional suspicion with which a frontier society views the customs and culture of the long-established old world: Older civilizations are associated, perhaps wrongly, with the ornamental, the insincere, and the pompous; for example, *American Gothic* (1930) by Grant Wood (1892–1942) is a well-known work which celebrates the homely, simple, unadorned virtues of rural life. The picture and its title are intended, of course, to constitute an ironic comparison with the soaring, complex qualities of Gothic architecture. The pointed-arch window of the wood-frame dwelling in the background is an example of the so-called "carpenter Gothic" style, the American version of the illustrious European style which is carved much more ornately in stone. But the ironic force of the work is based on the accurate and convincing likeness of a farm couple set in an environment of striving for Gothic style and splendor. Their plainness is severe, even pathetic, but authentic too.

An interesting comparison can be made between Grant Wood's solemn couple and the double portrait, *My Parents* (1921), by the German artist Otto Dix (1891–   ). We are confronted here with similar human types, but Dix departs further from naturalism although he creates an overwhelming impression of realism. His enlargement of the hands and emphasis upon wrinkles, which are echoed in the rumpled clothing, convey the stiff and awkward characteristics which Europeans associate with the peasantry. Wood distorted his heads imperceptibly to stress their oval shape and to repeat the shape of the pitchfork. Otto Dix has employed somewhat more distortion and exaggeration. Does his work properly fit into the category of objective accuracy? Probably it does, because the narrative element, the purely reportorial, dominates the painting. The work is primarily responsive to what must have been the visual facts.

Grant Wood painted at a time when there was an attempt by some artists, particularly in the Midwest, to create a distinctive, American style or several regional styles which would reflect

GRANT WOOD, *American Gothic* (1930), left. Courtesy The Art Institute of Chicago, Friends of American Art Collection.

OTTO DIX, *My Parents* (1921), right. Courtesy Otto Dix; photo, Kunstmuseum Basel.

native traditions, attitudes, and subject matter. The effort was in part a reaction against the sense of cultural inferiority which Americans felt in the 1930's (and perhaps still do) toward the artistic traditions and achievements of Europe. However, World War II, the second forceful reminder within twenty-five years of America's intimate involvement in world affairs, effectively ended the attempt to create art along nationalistic or regional patterns. While works of art with a strong local flavor continue to be created, they stand or fall on their artistic excellence and aesthetic expressiveness rather than their regional distinctiveness. Indeed, the communications media and the mass distribution of goods have tended to eliminate many of the pronounced local variations in customs which existed among people as little as thirty years ago. Our myths and traditions today are largely manufactured by television and the films and then almost universally disseminated. Hence, pro-

vincial and regional differences in artistic expression have little foundation for existence.

The similarity in the paintings by Otto Dix and Grant Wood reflects a similarity of outlook in two artists separated by nationality and culture but united by a common interest in fidelity to optical evidence. It appears, therefore, that the style of objective accuracy is based on an artistic or human trait which is more fundamental than nationality or culture. In fact, a tremendous amount of artistic evidence can be gathered to show that the graphic or plastic imitation of appearances is very widespread. It may be a mistake to regard skill in imitation as the only criterion of artistic excellence. But it would be equally mistaken to ignore the large body of art which shows how men of almost all times and places have tried to create, first, actual models of what they see; second, symbolic representations of what they see; and third, credible

143

imitations of visual appearances. In other words, as men become sophisticated, they realize that there is a difference between an actual object and its appearance to an observer. Certain types of artist create, knowingly or otherwise, on the basis of such a difference. In effect, they hope their imitations will succeed in convincing viewers that reality is also present in their art. A type of magical behavior is thus involved in artistic representation. There resides the fascination of the imitation of appearances for artist and viewer alike.

The Artist as Detached Observer

Another characteristic of the style of objective accuracy lies in the frequent concealment by the artist of the technique used to achieve his effects. It is as if he were trying to deny that his pictures are made of paint, or his sculptures modeled in clay or carved from stone. The marks of his tools must not be visible in the final product. The artist wishes to focus the viewer's attention on his subject matter, not on the way the picture was put together. There is a certain artistic modesty implied by this approach, a self-effacement in the interest of heightening the illusion created by the image. Whereas a painter like Soutine was anxious to reveal his brush strokes and the vigor and sureness with which he applied paint, an artist like Charles Sheeler uses a very smooth, thinned-out, impersonal technique which seems highly appropriate to his industrial, machine-made subject matter.

The attitude of the objective artist is one of detachment. He presents himself to his audience as a person who selects, arranges, and represents reality but suppresses his own personality in the process. If we are to learn anything about the artist as a person, it is through his over-all organization and choice of subject matter, not because of his individuality of technique or intensely personal manner of execution. There is something scientific in such an attitude. As we know, the scientist takes many precautions to be sure that his private feelings will not affect the observations and measurements he must make. He hopes other investigators will come to the same conclusions as he has if they examine the same data. The artist interested in accuracy also wishes his results

CHARLES SHEELER, *City Interior* (1936). Courtesy Worcester Art Museum.

to have a validity independent of his personality; the work should appear to be almost anonymous; only the signature reveals the author.

The suppression of the personal in the artist's style is due to his desire to make vision, the act of seeing, the most important part of experiencing his work. In a sense the Impressionists fit this description: They used scientific theories of color and optics; they freely exchanged technical "secrets"; they painted as accurately as possible the object seen quickly in a particular light. For example, in the Rouen Cathedral series of Claude Monet (1840–1926), we have a very single-minded effort to represent the same building under varying light conditions according to a theory of color which was considered more "realistic," that is, based on a firmer scientific foundation than conventional techniques of applying color. It is quite correct to think of Impressionism as a style of objective accuracy since it constituted a disciplined endeavor to use scientific discoveries about color and visual perception to present the object in its atmospheric setting with full fidelity. The genius of Impressionism lay in the realization that the object—a tree, a mountain, a still life—could not be seen nor represented accurately without considering the character of the light and atmosphere around the object and the source and nature of the illumination which enables us to see the object in the first place.

Impressionism evolved, and as its concern with the treatment of light became more intense, the represented object tended to disappear; light itself, as in the earlier paintings of J.M.W. Turner (1775–1851), became the subject. At this point, the term "style of objective

CLAUDE MONET, *Cathedral (in Sunshine)* (1894). Courtesy Musée du Louvre, Cliché des Musées Nationaux.

CLAUDE MONET, *Cathedral (in the Fog)* (1894). Courtesy Musée du Louvre, Cliché des Musées Nationaux.

J. M. W. TURNER, *Steamer in a Snowstorm* (1842). Reproduced by courtesy of the Trustees, The National Gallery, London.

accuracy" could no longer be applied to Impressionism. The artist's fascination with light had become an emotional matter, strong enough to submerge the earlier concern for fidelity to the *object* in its environment. Although late Impressionism still deals with visual phenomena, the form of objects is almost completely dissolved in color: A virtually total abstraction is achieved. This is especially evident in Monet's water lilies (see pp. 328–29)—the forms of nature become inseparable from light and from the brush strokes of pure color. One cannot tell shape from light or from color.

It appears that so long as an artist can deal with reality optically—through his eyes alone—he adheres to the style of objective reality. But when he allows himself to become emotionally involved with his subject, or with some personal feature of technique, he loses his detachment and his status as a "disinterested observer." Of course, this change of attitude and style may be a very logical and desirable development from the standpoint of aesthetic value. The change in the representation of reality, however, is caused by a fundamental change in attitude toward vision and the world on

EDGAR DEGAS, *The Glass of Absinthe* (1876), left. Courtesy Musée du Louvre, Cliché des Musées Nationaux.

HENRI DE TOULOUSE-LAUTREC, *Monsieur Boileau at the Café* (1893), right. Courtesy The Cleveland Museum of Art, Hinman B. Hurlbut Collection.

the part of the artist. He has placed a higher priority on the personal act of seeing than on the objective character of what is seen.

In the work of Edgar Degas (1834–1917), we see a style of supreme fidelity to optical and psychological reality at the same time that an Impressionist palette is employed. In *The Glass of Absinthe*, the artist plays the role of reporter, of detached observer of humanity. The drinkers are shown in clinically honest detail, with no preaching, and very little dramatization of their condition. We can read for ourselves the dull, weary state of the woman and the mean, sodden look of the man. Degas seems to be a disinterested eye: He catches the couple casually, toward the side of the picture, as if he were using a candid camera. As a matter of fact, Degas was interested in the seemingly accidental compositions of photography and designed his pictures to look as if the subject matter had been suddenly discovered. There is no obvious posing, no heroic or pathetic gesturing. As a result, his pictures of ballet dancers, laundresses, women bathing, jockeys, and so on, are exceedingly convincing because we sense an element of candid observation as opposed to the theatrical staging of the painters who preceded him. Later, Henri de Toulouse-Lautrec (1864–1901) would benefit from the compositional audacity and psychological honesty of Degas. His portrait composition *M. Boileau at the Café* (1893) employs the same diagonal treatment of the tables as in the Degas, together with figures spilling out of the upper right-hand edge of the canvas. However, the central figure is more conventionally located than the Degas couple. Also, M. Boileau is hardly a derelict; he is the very solid embodi-

ment of bourgeois comfort and self-satisfaction.

The art of Degas and Lautrec shows how Impressionist color, space representation borrowed from Japanese prints, and pictorial composition influenced by photography do not obscure the fundamental psychological stance of the artist toward the world he observes. Both men were tremendously interested in people; they were passionate observers of behavior; but they refrained from insinuating their own moral judgments. They were *detached observers*. This much we can conclude from their work, without looking into the biographies of the artists. They were, in a sense, the radical empiricists of painting: Meaning, ideas, and knowledge arise from sensation, that is, from data based on observation of the real world. All other considerations must give way to the necessity of seeing clearly what is out there and reporting it—elaborately or concisely—but without distortion of the visual facts.

For the detached observer, distortion is a type of artistic and moral vice. The Philadelphia painter Thomas Eakins (1844–1916) felt that distortion was ugliness, and his entire career as artist and as teacher seemed to be a single-minded and almost fanatical pursuit of the methods which would ensure the sort of accuracy which results from scientific knowledge of what the artist observes. He taught artists anatomy by dissecting cadavers and took an almost perverse delight in portraying the unvarnished facts of operating technique, as in *The Agnew Clinic* (1898) (p. 148). Dr. Agnew was not pleased to be shown with blood on his hands as he lectured, but Eakins was too stubborn a realist to compromise the facts. He had been similarly candid in 1875 when portraying a blood-spattered Dr. Gross and assistants in *The Gross Clinic*. By contrast, Rembrandt's *The Anatomy Lesson of Dr. Tulp* (1632) is a restrained, dignified tribute to the undeviating pursuit of learning in which the medical profession prided itself in the seventeenth century.

THOMAS EAKINS, *The Agnew Clinic* (1898), left above. Courtesy The University of Pennsylvania.

REMBRANDT VAN RIJN, *The Anatomy Lesson of Dr. Tulp* (1632), left below. Courtesy Mauritshuis, The Hague; photo, A. Dingjan.

THOMAS EAKINS, *The Gross Clinic* (1875), below. Courtesy Jefferson Medical College of Philadelphia, photo, Philadelphia Museum of Art.

The Artist as Selective Eye

The artistic concern with accuracy does not always result in photographic realism. Often the illusion of reality is created by elimination of details which the eye might see. At other times, there is a deliberate piling up of detail to create an impression of the complexity of the object. Some artists possess a technique which enables them to accumulate detail; and for some, an obsession with the subject may make it difficult to leave a work: Such an artist will add to it, and embellish it, and enrich its surface. Hence, the result may show the months or years of labor he has put into the execution of the work. Ivan Albright's painting (see p. 150) is the result of years devoted to the amassing of detail. Appropriately enough, Albright was chosen to paint the portrait for the film of Oscar Wilde's *The Picture of Dorian Grey.* As in Wilde's story, Albright's paintings appear to have aged along with their subjects. Often the viewer is encouraged to examine a work of art so arduously produced with greater seriousness than if it seemed very spontaneously created. The visual evidence of long and sustained effort by the artist induces a type of empathy in the viewer: The respect for work, which is part of our heritage, is converted into respect for the painstakingly produced art object. Hence, by choosing to show an abundance of visual facts—more than would be casually noted—the artist can govern, to some extent, the attitude of the viewer.

Among the artists who simplify— who eliminate detail—while maintaining the feeling of objective reality is Edward Hopper. In *Nighthawks,* for example, his picture is divided into quiet, simple, uncomplicated areas. The brushwork is hardly evident; we sense the materials of the place instead: bricks, stone, glass, and of course, the people in the café. The mood of silence, of stillness, of a great city asleep, is accentuated by the small inactive figures, the emptiness of the street, the sharp, crisp shadows thrown by strong artificial light, the dominance of vertical and horizontal lines. Hopper shows just enough of a building or a person to enable the viewer to identify it; he is not a "tricky" or dextrous painter: Each area of his picture seems to have been carefully and patiently pruned of nonessentials, reduced to the minimum needed for recognition. Like Andrew Wyeth, Hopper relies on placement for psychological

EDWARD HOPPER, *Nighthawks* (1942). Courtesy The Art Institute of Chicago, Friends of American Art Collection.

emphasis, upon careful, undramatic execution of each part to create a cumulative effect which has a quiet drama of its own. His painted areas of light or of shadow tend to be flat and uncomplicated; he uses perspective and contrasts of illumination to suggest the solidity, the heaviness, of the objects and places he records.

Ivan Albright, who painted *Into the World There Came a Soul Called Ida*, relies on an accumulation of visual detail to suggest the process of human aging and deterioration. An almost pitiless observer, he brings out the evidences of sagging flesh at the same time that he reveals the woman's pathetic effort to reverse the aging process. But we are also made aware of the artist's compassion for his subject: Her face, which

is plain and homely, is also shown in a tragic light as if she knows as well as we that cosmetics, clothes, and even hope will not restore a youthful appearance, and by implication, the unique enjoyments reserved to youth. Paintings of this sort encourage speculation by the observer—what is sometimes decried as literary association. It is important to remember, however, that in the well-executed work, our speculation is encouraged in a particular direction—a direction which is intended by the design of the art object. In Albright's canvas, the details which reveal so much, combine successfully to create a living organism—*Ida*, who appears very pathetically alive: She is both painted surface and human document. Albright's technique, which is tight and cumulative—suited to the visual exposition of facts—also suggests decay when he chooses; he gives skin a leathery quality to suggest a drying out process accompanied by the accumulation of unwanted flesh.

In the portrait of Elsa Maxwell by René Bouché (1896–   ), we see another work which in its accuracy and careful draftsmanship conveys some of the drama of aging. Mr. Bouché has chosen to view his subject from below her eye level, which, in an elderly and stout person, tends to be unflattering. Indeed, there is a nervous, comic, but also oddly *dignified* quality about this portrait. Whenever a sitter is presented honestly by the artist, without any attempt at beautification or glossing over of unpleasant details, a certain measure of respect is earned by the subject. The lady who exhibits a grossness in her person retains a measure of human dignity through the artist's presentation of her in a hard, uncompromising light,

IVAN ALBRIGHT, *Into the World There Came a Soul Called Ida* (1929–30), left. Collection Mr. and Mrs. Ivan Albright; photo, The Art Institute of Chicago.

RENÉ BOUCHÉ, *Elsa Maxwell* (1958–59), right. Courtesy Alexander Iolas Gallery, New York; photo, The Museum of Modern Art.

from a bad view, and in a slightly un-comfortable pose.

Because of its frankness of observation and execution, Bouché's painting shares some of the journalistic flavor of the work of America's so-called Ash Can School, the group of eight painters who portrayed the unfashionable or seamy side of life during the early part of this century. The Bouché portrait also shares with Impressionism the unusual angle of vision which gives the painting a candid, spontaneous look. And the paint application has some of the movement and energy of the French artist Soutine, although it is not distorted or agitated. If it were, we should classify this picture within the style of emotion. As it is, Bouché stays with the visual facts, which convey a rumpled, stout, old woman approaching her later years with some humor and a certain amount of self-acceptance.

Among sculptors, the contemporary Italian artist Giacomo Manzù (1908–   ) exhibits a refined sort of realism which has roots in the Renaissance yet appeals to modern tastes nourished on distortion and abstraction. *Girl in Chair* (p. 152) is an example of careful observation combined with elimination of detail so subtle that it is difficult to say where the simplification has taken place. The serenity of the figure results partly from the sculptor's ability to convince the viewer that a distinct person has been portrayed at the same time that the basic forms have been stripped of all but their most essential qualities of shape and surface. The figure is simple and restrained; yet it has extraordinary psychological presence. Even the chair has a curious perfection: It falls just short of a sculptor's abstraction (after all, a chair *is* an abstract

object). Instead, its spare open form serves to accent the solidity, the corporeality of the girl's slender body. In choosing a subject who is neither a child nor a woman, Manzù has undertaken a very difficult challenge for an artist working in an objective style: He must manage to imply her inbetween and as yet uncertainly defined form and personality within a format of sound observation. Still, he must not fall into the trap of reproducing dimensions as if for a dressmaker's dummy. His solution appears to result from stressing accuracy in the over-all dimensions of the figure combined with simplification in the modeling of subordinate forms: Thus he approaches but does not quite touch abstraction, while retaining considerable naturalism in the total contour.

Manzù's *Girl* could well be compared with *Young Man Seated* (p. 152) by Wilhelm Lehmbruck (1881–1919). Although the figure of the young man might be understood as conveying a mood of despondency or of fatigue in contrast to the more confident attitude of the girl, it also results from careful observation of the adolescent body together with subtle simplification of surfaces. Lehmbruck, however, goes beyond objective accuracy in his attenuation or elongation of forms. This "stretching" of the normal dimensions presents more vividly to the viewer the idea of rapid growth in youth and the various types of physical unease and psychological tension which accompany such growth. Another reason for Lehmbruck's attenuation of forms may lie in his consciousness of being the inheritor of a Gothic tradition, that is, a tradition of building and carving which stresses tall, narrow solids and voids. At the same time, his Gothi-

GIACOMO MANZÙ, *Girl in Chair* (1955), left. Courtesy The Joseph H. Hirshhorn Collection; photo, The Solomon R. Guggenheim Museum.

WILHELM LEHMBRUCK, *Young Man Seated* (1918), right. Courtesy Wilhelm Lehmbruck Museum.

cism seeks a reconciliation with the classic, Mediterranean tradition of order and repose.

The suppression of detail without the loss of essential traits of form which make objects recognizable cannot take place unless the artist has observed his subject very carefully. He must *know* the subject as well as *see* its surface characteristics; otherwise his work of simplification and elimination will be unsuccessful: The result will be simple and empty rather than simple and significant. Every work of art within the style of objective accuracy represents the end result of a long process of observation and simplification. Even the work of Albright, with its elaboration of detail, represents a synthesis of many perceptions. Albright tells the viewer what he "knows" about

the object by synthesizing many visual facts about it in a single painting. Manzù and Lehmbruck convey what they "know" by eliminating what they consider inessential. But Lehmbruck created new visual "facts" through distortion: To the extent that he distorts, the artist departs from absolute fidelity to the object. Clearly, this departure represents a decision about the priorities which shall be placed on visual fidelity relative to emotional evocation. Art becomes a game played according to rules the artist recognizes: He may change the rules in the interests of a more effective work. One of the satisfactions in the study of art is finding out the rules which the artist appears to recognize and then deciding, if we wish, how well he has played the game.

Variations of the Style

Although many artists feel obliged to render very faithfully what is seen, and often try to suppress personal traits of execution in the process, they nevertheless achieve results which reveal their individual viewpoints. For example, Ben Shahn in his painting *Handball* gives us an exceedingly accurate and matter-of-fact image of city boys caught in somewhat awkward athletic and spectator poses, an image which is quite different in mood and feeling from the equally accurate Wyeth, *Christina's World*. Both pictures show isolated figures. Shahn, like Wyeth, shows a large expanse of relatively uncluttered space in the wall of the handball court. He uses some urban detail around the edges of his canvas to establish his setting, just as Wyeth silhouettes his small houses at the top of his canvas, against the horizon. Shahn also "freezes" the action of his characters as does Wyeth. But note that Shahn deliberately draws his figures so that their clothes seem lumpy and rumpled, their bodies thick, stubby, and ungraceful. Their surroundings are drab and they are trying to find some excitement in a place which appears indifferent if not hostile to outdoor recreation. If the painting of a group of awkward boys has elements of pathos, it is an impersonal, collective pathos. Christina's tragedy is individual and personal because Wyeth has painted her—not as an example of a type—but as a unique personality whom we feel we can know without seeing her face. Wyeth's drawing dwells on the contours of a particular person; Shahn's drawing dwells on the general characteristics of boys raised in a crowded city neighborhood. It is easy to conclude that Shahn is mainly interested here in the problems of people in the aggregate, whereas Wyeth concentrates on the private dramas of individuals.

John Kane (1860–1934), in his *Self Portrait*, shows how a primitive or relatively untrained artist approaches objective accuracy. Stripped to the waist, using a direct front view, he paints his hard, aging body, showing the muscles, veins, bones, and flesh as honestly as his command of technique will allow. He reveals a combination of pride in his strength and pugnacity along with utter

JOHN KANE, *Self Portrait* (1929). Collection The Museum of Modern Art, New York, Abby Aldrich Rockefeller Fund.

BEN SHAHN, *Handball* (1939). Collection The Museum of Modern Art, New York, Abby Aldrich Rockefeller Fund.

honesty about the kind of man he is. Notice that the edges are hard and sharp and that the modeling or shading is achieved with difficulty. The primitive artist usually tries for accuracy by the use of line and multiplication of detail. He rarely can use masses of rich pigment or intense color skillfully since these call for art-school training as a rule. Even if he were interested in concealment or evasion of truth, he usually does not possess the technique to heighten one area and suppress another. Furthermore, it is often a matter of principle with him to be scrupulously candid about what he sees and knows of his subject. Viewers admire so-called primitive art precisely for its sometimes brutal or sometimes naive candor. In a sense, we can only learn the truth about persons and places through seeing them portrayed by an artist who does not care for dressing up reality or who has not received an education in the artistic traditions of representing reality in a prescribed way.

Charles Sheeler (1883–   ) is an artist whose work seems closely related to photography, and he is, indeed, an excellent photographer. However, his paintings of industrial subjects such as Ford's River Rouge plant, of grain elevators, or of machinery as in *Upper Deck*, reveal his interest in the geometric purity of form which an industrial world creates. His pictures are characterized by immaculate whiteness, smoothness, regularity of shape, and absence of clutter or blemish. Although he is regarded as a realistic painter, he actually portrays a world in which noise, dirt, and confusion have been eliminated. In some ways, the atmosphere of his pictures is similar to that of Lyonel Feininger (1871–1956), whose art is classical and orderly but hardly within

CHARLES SHEELER, *Upper Deck* (1929), left. Courtesy of the Fogg Art Museum, Harvard University.

LYONEL FEININGER, *The Steamer "Odin," II* (1927), right. Collection The Museum of Modern Art, New York, acquired through the Lillie P. Bliss Bequest.

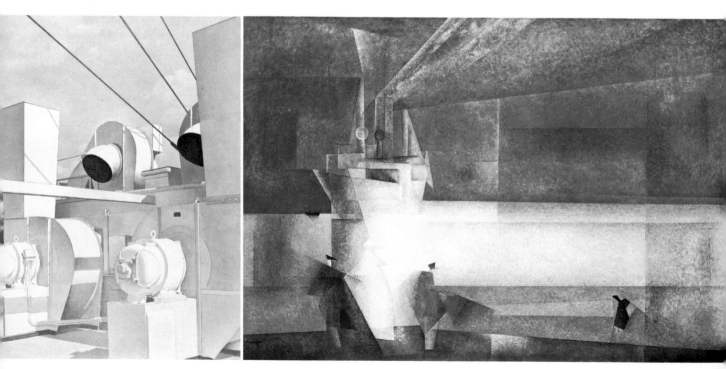

the style of objective accuracy. Sheeler shows how accuracy of representation, if combined with a smooth, almost photographic technique and the suppression of chaotic detail can create a highly convincing result which is nevertheless much idealized. His is an art which helps us to see some of the possibilities of formal beauty where it normally is not thought to exist.

There is a type of realism, sometimes called "magic realism," which falls within the style of objective accuracy but which is not authentically realistic as the public often supposes. An example is *Old Models* by William M. Harnett (1848–92). Such works, which have been widely admired because of their capacity to create convincing illusions, rely on a sort of photographic accuracy. That is, they recreate on canvas the retinal image of arranged objects. Also, the artist's juxtaposition of related still-life material (with an occasional ironic note from the insertion of a jarring object) provides a comfortable set of literary or practical associations. After the viewer has finished with checking the resemblance of the painting to reality, he can enjoy a moment of spurious philosophic contemplation as he recognizes the relatedness of the objects, the beauty of commonplace things, the striving of art to capture reality and its inevitable failure, and the curious little visual thrills one experiences in seeing painted nails driven into painted wood, painted letters written on painted paper, and so on. Even though craftsmanship and accuracy of a high order are required, it must be remembered that such "realism" dares not to present what the artist knows or feels. His selection of detail is governed solely by the invocation of optical criteria,

that is, by asking what elements of the object would be registered on the retina of a viewer with normal vision. Needless to say, comparable effects can be achieved by skilled color photography, and, indeed, in the better women's magazines color plates showing elaborate holiday table settings often achieve similar results. The "magical" element in magic realism consists of the viewer's knowledge that he is examining a man-made object and that skillfully created illusions can *almost* convince him of their reality. But modern illusionism in photography, the cinema, and the electronic media, are technically superior to painted illusionism and have, in addition, been developed into richer and more veritable art forms.

The principal difficulty of nineteenth-century *trompe-l'oeil*, or magic-realist, art lay in its lack of humanistic ambition: It reduced the contribution to art from human personality to a decision about the faithfulness of painted surfaces to retinal images. But man knows, does, and feels more than can be accounted for by consulting the light-sensitive membranes of his eyes. Perhaps Harnett, John Peto, and the other magic realists were, unwittingly, precursors of Surrealism, which also relied on illusionistic portrayal of objects and spaces. Surrealists endeavored to excite emotion in the viewer by unusual juxtapositions of objects. But illusionists like Harnett do not appear to have had a strategy of psychological shock and restructuring of the imagination such as the Surrealists possessed. At most, fool-the-eye painters may have sought to undermine the viewer's reliance on the absolute validity of his optical sense. In this respect, they challenged the strict and occasionally naive empiricism of nineteenth-century

WILLIAM M. HARNETT, *Old Models* (1892). Courtesy Museum of Fine Arts, Boston, Charles Henry Hayden Fund.

American civilization. But mainly, *trompe-l'oeil* engendered a popular confusion between objective accuracy and retinal illusionism. Objective accuracy means, among other things, fidelity to the visual facts. However, it also means fidelity to a *truth* about objects which visual facts reveal. This latter definition, which fits most of the works discussed in the present chapter, makes the creation and study of art vastly more satisfying than a purely illusionistic idea of art. It has not been easy for many persons to understand the difference between art as the creation of illusions and art as visual presentation of what is known about the world. Once the difference is learned, however, art becomes a high road to knowledge that is not easily gained through other studies.

Devices of Objective Accuracy

We have already discussed some of the ways artists arrive at convincing representations of reality. Obviously, accuracy of size and shape relationships—in other words, "correct" drawing and modeling as traditionally understood—are the most common devices. This sort of mastery is not easily acquired, although the impression of accuracy can be fairly well achieved through painstaking attention to dimensions, through assistance from photographs, tracing, photographic projection, use of calipers, and other measuring and reproducing devices. But reliance on mechanical aids may seem to possess an element of dishonesty, although some artists use such devices without becoming excessively dependent on them. In general, the well-trained artist abjures these aids and can usually recognize when they have been used excessively to the detriment of expressive power. Commercial artists and illustrators, of course, freely use whatever mechanical devices they can, because they frequently work under the pressure of time, and because individuality of vision and style may not be their primary objectives. The attempt to draw an object accurately produces numerous variations from what a photograph would show, and yet a viewer can be equally impressed by the "reality" of several drawn versions. It is the drawing "error" due to the artist's age, sex, characteristic touch, attitude, training, and a host of other traits, which create interest and delight in the pursuit of objective accuracy.

In addition to accurate size and shape relationships, the artist's control and handling of illumination assists him in creating realistic images. The amount of light an object or place receives, the shape of shadows, the transition from light to shadow, the portrayal of natural and artificial, direct and reflected light—these the artist learns to observe and control in the various media he uses. Through his mastery of illumination alone he can model objects and spaces illusionistically quite apart from the use of line or contour. In sculpture, although the artist creates the actual forms the viewer will see, the control of light as it falls over the forms is very carefully considered.

Certainly Auguste Rodin (1840–1917) studied light as intently as the Impressionist painters, so that his sur-

AUGUSTE RODIN, *The Burghers of Calais* (1889), left. Photo, H. Rinehart.

AUGUSTE RODIN, head of Eustache de St. Pierre [detail of *The Burghers of Calais*], right. © SPADEM 1966 by French Reproduction Rights, Inc.; photo, Musée Rodin.

faces are sensitively animated and varied at the same time that they describe large, three-dimensional forms in space. He attempted to create an activity of surface in sculpture such as painters were achieving through broken color and the use of short, heavily weighted touches of pigment. His head of Eustache de St. Pierre from *The Burghers of Calais* presents a good example of the sculptural surface which has an almost painterly effect while giving to bronze a soft, flesh-like quality.

Another device of the artist is focus: sharpness or softness, distinctness or vagueness of form and contour. The rather elementary fact about perception—that objects lose distinctness at the periphery of our field of vision—becomes a device for the artist in his control of a viewer's examination of his work. The eye is drawn, of course, to the most distinctly represented form,

other things being equal. As a painted form or object has its edge softened or blurred, we tend to view it as further away or withdrawn from the center of our field of vision. In drawing, forms in the same plane can be made to advance or recede depending on the "lose and find," "hard and soft," "light and dark" characteristics of the contour line. An artist like Léger deliberately uses a line of uniform weight, thickness, and color to prevent his forms from oscillating in space, since he wishes to press all forms forward into the surface plane of the picture. Masters of drawing from Holbein to Picasso, on the other hand, have varied the focal properties of line in order to move forms in and out, forward and back, when they sought objective accuracy.

In sculpture, forms may be sharply raised or softly melted within the same work, thus controlling the attention of

MEDARDO ROSSO, *The Age of Gold* (*L'Età d'Oro*) (1886). Collection Peridot Gallery, New York; photo, Geoffrey Clements.

ERNST BARLACH, *Man Drawing Sword* (1911). Courtesy Cranbrook Art Galleries.

JACOB EPSTEIN, *Head of Joseph Conrad* (1924–25). Courtesy Joseph H. Hirshhorn Collection.

the viewer. For the sculptor, the sharpness of focus, the degree to which a form emerges from sculptural relief into the "full round," becomes a tool of artistic expressiveness. Thus, in *L'Età d'Oro* by Medardo Rosso (1858–1928), we see soft focus used to create a very poetic and romantic impression, as of forms perceived through a haze. Aristide Maillol (1861–1944), the French master, avoided sharply undercut forms so that the unity and repose of the entire work, rather than the realism of any single part, is achieved. Yet Maillol's bronze sculptures seem to possess the weight and warmth of flesh and bone, much as Rodin's do, while using a different surface entirely. Jacob Epstein (1880–1959) produced portraits, executed in clay and cast in bronze, which are very sharply focused to heighten the sense of aliveness of his subjects. In his heads, the modeling is exaggerated—that is, the hollows of the eyes, cheekbones, and lips are deeper than would be the case in life. Also, the rough projections of clay catch the light and bring forms so sharply before our eyes that a powerfully vivid impression is created. It is interesting to compare the agitated surface of the head of Conrad by Epstein with the more melting forms on the equally agitated head of Eustache de St. Pierre by Rodin. Ernst Barlach (1870–1938), working mainly in wood, defines his forms less sharply than Epstein but nevertheless gives to wood the soft and hard properties of flesh, cloth, or bone as the subject requires. At the same time, he maintains our awareness of the material and the process of carving by which the forms were created.

Color is, of course, a powerful instrument, if not the most important one, at the disposal of the artist—especially of the contemporary painter. Many painters try to create form by color alone, and if line or illumination is present in their work in a calculated way, it is managed through the manipulation of pigment solely. For the artist interested in objective accuracy, the use of color is mainly connected with the description of the colors of the objects he represents. The color of these objects varies, of course, depending on the kind, amount, and source of light they receive, and the location of the objects in space. Just as we know that focus grows less distinct as objects recede in space, we also know—at least since Leonardo°— that color becomes less intense as objects recede. Conversely, intense or brightly colored forms appear to be closer to our eyes. Brilliance of color combined with

°Leonardo da Vinci, *The Art of Painting,* Chapter CCXCV—Of the Perspective of Colours: "The principal colors, or those nearest to the eye, should be pure and simple; and the degree of their diminution should be in proportion to their distance. . ." Philosophical Library Edition, p. 172.

sharpness of focus is consequently a powerful means of attracting visual attention and of defining forms so that they appear to be accurate and veritable.

Sometimes an artist uses color arbitrarily but combines it with precise drawing so that a style of accuracy is achieved while abstract elements are present. Even the most "realistic" artists may exaggerate color while they tend to remain faithful to the object in their drawing. It is as if the artistic conscience were willing to permit a certain amount of playfulness with color, but would tolerate no deviations from objective reality so far as drawing is concerned. In Ben Shahn's work, we see color used in a fairly flat, poster-like manner; it is the authority of his line (a widely imitated line, incidentally) which establishes the concreteness and particularity of his people and places. Wyeth's color tends toward grey, although it possesses many subtle variations within its narrow range. It is a mistake to believe that only a painter who uses color riotously is truly a colorist. The commitment to intense color used only in bold contrasts may signify not only the absence of inhibitions about color but also the absence of sensitivity toward color. It is safe to say, however, that one of the most significant features of the modern movement in painting is a transition in the use of color from a purely descriptive function to an independent, expressive function. As a result, many artists feel liberated with respect to their use of color but, as mentioned above, they feel varying degrees of attachment to objectively accurate drawing.

Perspective is the pictorial device (really a body of knowledge and devices) which most laymen know about and which a few have mastered in a rudimentary way. It is closely related to an artist's ability to create the illusion of deep space within his picture frame. The technical features of linear and aerial perspective, the perspective of shadows and reflections, of receding measured forms, of single-point and two-point perspective systems, of the interaction of perspective with color and illumination, are exceedingly complex. Suffice it to say that an understanding of at least the fundamentals of perspective enables the artist to simulate on a flat pictorial surface many of our optical experiences in the presence of nature or reality. Here again, the modern movement has first questioned and then largely abandoned the simulation of deep space in painting. The Surrealists have been the principal artists of the modern movement who have used perspective, and even then principally for the creation of fantastic illusions of infinitely receding space. In the Cubism of Picasso, Braque, and Gris, we see rather amusing and witty combinations of conventional perspective and other illusionistic devices along with arbitrary anti-illusionistic devices. Having learned, since the Renaissance, to "read" pictures in terms of the illusion of deep space, we have been taught by twentieth-century art to see pictures as they actually are: flat surfaces with colored lines and shapes resting upon them.

There are many other devices of illusionism and objective accuracy in art, most of which are combinations of those mentioned above. One, for example, consists of juxtaposing two objects—let us say, a hand and a figure—so that the hand is as large or larger than the full figure. Since we "know" this cannot be objectively true, we "read" the relationship to mean that the hand is very close to our eye while the figure is at a considerable distance. Within the picture, this device creates the illusion of a vast space between the hand and the figure. It is called by the French a *repoussoir,* a set-off or foil. Of course, the device is based on the laws of perspective governing size relationships; and there are many others related to foreshortening, overlapping planes, distortions due to angle of vision, and so on. The illusions possible through play with the laws of perspective have been well explored by E. H. Gombrich.° For our purposes, it is well to know that perspective is an important tool

for simulating optical effects, and it is employed most effectively, as in *Christina's World,* for dramatic and expressive purposes.

It seems likely that artists will always endeavor to master the devices which enable them to create illusions, to work in a style which makes possible the objective treatment of reality. As they grow beyond the student stage, they may abandon some or all of these devices, or they may discover novel combinations and uses of the tools they have acquired. Certainly our principal masters have undergone the discipline of faithfully reporting their visual experience, and this discipline has served them well when they sought "to render the invisible visible." But the mastery of techniques of accurate representation is not undertaken by artists merely in order to discard them later, or to possess the sort of confidence which is based on having endured a difficult discipline. As mentioned above, learning to draw accurately teaches the artist to see, that is, to *understand* what he is looking at. He must learn to distinguish between superficial imitation of surfaces and informed representation of visual phenomena. Similarly, viewers who are not artists can benefit from the artist's struggle to come to terms with visual reality if they learn to compare his rendering of reality with the world as they have come to know it. In the difference between the two lies the important body of meaning which the study of art endeavors to uncover.

° E. H. Gombrich, "How To Read a Painting." *Saturday Evening Post,* July 29, 1961, p. 20f.

CHAPTER FIVE

The style of formal order expresses an artist's preference for balance and stability in his creative work, and, by implication, in the world as a whole. To the extent that Western civilization bears the imprint of classical Greek thought, order has been its constant ideal—order in art, in politics, in religion, in knowledge, and in human behavior. The Greeks sought order through measure, proportion, or ratio—through the mathematical statement of relationships which would, they believed, produce harmony, balance, and beauty. That is why "formal" is combined with "order" in the description of a style whose most illustrious embodiment is Greek art of the fifth century B.C. *Formal order* is balance, harmony, or stability in art created through the methodical application of rules of measure. It is another term for Classicism—a Classicism found in all periods.

The immediate source of proportions for order and beauty was, according to the Greeks, the human body. They made a momentous aesthetic discovery in concluding that what we call "beautiful" is the result of a harmonious relationship among the parts of any whole, and that a mathematical ratio based on the human figure lies behind every visual harmony. The human body is beautiful, they believed, because it is an expression of the intellectual order which can be found in the entire uni-

THE STYLE

OF FORMAL ORDER

verse. The problem of the artist is to apply that universal order or measure to the construction of buildings, the writing of plays, and the fashioning of human images which must be absolutely correct in shape and anatomy and perfect in appearance. These human images were rarely drawn from specific personalities; rather they were "idealized" versions of the human, that is, they embodied a mathematical average of the best proportions encountered in the human category as the Greeks knew it. The Greek painter Zeuxis is supposed to have studied many beautiful women before he painted the portrait of Helen of Troy. Always, in classical art or the style of formal order, there is a rule of

LEONARDO DA VINCI, *Studio del corpo humano.* Courtesy Alinari—Art Reference Bureau.

number or measure applied to the problems of artistic creation. Art is a search for the "right" proportions. Rules are guides in the search.

The most conspicuous modern supporters of the Greek interest in measure are not artists but rather our social and physical scientists. Artists today tend to rely on intuition. But scientists depend on accurate measurement in their empirical and experimental research, followed by statistical formulation of their findings. The scientific pursuit of *truth* or *norms* through measurement of phenomena and abstract formulation of results—statistical analysis and mathematical statement—is comparable to the classical Greek pursuit of harmony through measurement and arithmetic averaging, through the formulation of ratios or proportions—that is, *norms* to which the artistic results should conform.

But Western man has not been unswerving in his devotion to classical ideals of measure, order, and moderation. Periodically he has been caught up in violent convulsions such as our own era has known too frequently. Even the classical Greek passion for formal order gave way to Hellenistic ideals of dynamic movement, tempestuous emotion, and unstable forms. Similarly, today's art has been characterized by chaotic and violent style features as well as by rationality and order. Often, in the career of a single artist—Picasso, for instance—both the style of formal order and that of emotional, spontaneous expression may be present. Apparently, Nietzsche was correct in his analysis of Greek culture into Apollonian and Dionysiac strains: The Apollonian strain is characterized by a *dream* of order and serenity; the Dionysiac strain is characterized by a *frenzy* of movement, an explosion of energy. In the past, one strain or the other may have dominated the artistic scene; today, both exist side by side.

The freedom and openness of modern culture (at least in the West) permits artists the almost totally unhampered expression of their Apollonian or Dionysiac impulses. The style of formal order, therefore, need not be the only artistic expression of a region, group, or nation. Nor does it necessarily represent the official taste of influential persons and institutions in the art world. Rather, it expresses the choice of creative individuals who feel an affinity for stable forms and balanced composition—men who possess a serene vision of the world. In other words, the style results from *personality* factors in the artist rather than *power* factors in the culture. We have to understand Classicism, or order, as a wish (felt by many persons but expressed only by the artist) that the world be governed by reason and logic. Whether the artist admits it or not, his work has the effect of restricting the uninhibited rule of impulse. Through the visual evidence presented in his art, we see how deliberation and measure, calculation and the weighing of alternatives, have managed to overcome the spontaneous expression of feeling. Thus, we see Maillol instead of Rodin, Mondrian instead of de Kooning. We see man *measuring* the visual consequences of his planning and forming and building.

The Transient and the Permanent

If there is a single attitude or trait which characterizes an artist who employs the style of formal order, it is his interest in dealing with what is fixed and permanent, or, at least, relatively unchanging. When such an artist works with a subject we know to be mainly dynamic and variable, he finds some way to stress its quiet or immutable qualities. With the human figure, he will select positions where it tends to be most stable, avoiding the suggestion that it is about to change attitude or location. One of the reasons Rodin's *St. John the Baptist Preaching* (1878) was criticized, at a time when critics preferred Classical art, was the impression the figure creates of walking off its pedestal. Sculpture, it was felt, belongs to architecture and should stand still. Furthermore, the French have always identified their culture very strongly with the classical Greek tradition; a statue which really seems to move would be in the nature of sacrilege. Jacob Epstein's *Madonna and Child,* on the contrary, is a work of formal order because the composition is highly symmetrical, hence balanced and stable: wide at the base (like a triangle resting on its long side) and almost devoid of casual or incidental motion. The suggestion of movement, particularly of movement which would carry the viewer's eye beyond the art object, militates against the idea of permanence. All monuments which are created to express the durability of a person, event, or idea, stress the motionless character of their forms; otherwise, they may amuse or entertain the viewer, but they will not persuade

him to believe the monument has succeeded in arresting the flow of time which governs the majority of mortals— those who are not heroes or kings.

Art instruction in the academic manner was largely biased in favor of formal order. It taught the student to recognize shapes which are relatively fixed and either to avoid the representation of changing shapes or to give changing shapes a permanent and classical quality. (Of course, the very act of drawing or painting from a rigidly posing model has the effect of freezing movement, a practice which permits study but which also appears somewhat unnatural as one carries it out.) The implicit purpose of such instruction was to teach

JACOB EPSTEIN, *Madonna and Child* (1927), left. Courtesy The Riverside Church, gift of Miss Sally Ryan.

AUGUSTE RODIN, *St. John the Baptist Preaching* (1878), right. Collection The Museum of Modern Art, New York, Mrs. Simon Guggenheim Fund.

An example of Miesian mastery of ideal dimensions and proportions.

LUDWIG MIES VAN DER ROHE, Seagram Building (1957). Photo, © Ezra Stroller Associates.

LYONEL FEININGER, *Church of the Minorites* (*II*) (1926), right. Collection Walker Art Center, Minneapolis.

students to create works of art which would seem resistant to all the forces of atrophy and change. It was as if the artist were asked to discover what it is that can survive amid all the things, including ourselves, which must die.

Students of philosophy will recognize as Platonic this academic approach to art instruction and creation, for it is related to Plato's interest in knowing the permanent forms of thought which lie behind the temporary and transient examples of acting and being we commonly see before us. The beautiful is the imitation, not of appearances, but of ideal and unchanging essences. Ideal essences must be known intellectually and mathematically before they can be imitated, hence the artist must know the ideal dimensions and proportions of his subject before he attempts to imitate its form. Such knowledge will cause his work to be a closer approximation of the essential type it endeavors to represent. (It is interesting in this connection that casual conversa-

tion about men and women often begins with a description of their physical dimensions followed by a judgment of their proportions.) More important, however, than the philosophic origin of the attitude expressed in the style of formal order is the fact that artists probably work in this manner because of some inner necessity rather than because of any deliberate philosophic choice. That is, some artists find themselves creating forms which exhibit order and careful structure although they may have set out to work in a very loose, spontaneous fashion. Other artists seem naturally to create forms which are characterized by indistinct shape and transient movement—forms which look as if they are about to expand into the space around and beyond them. The artist who happens to prefer the sort of result he naturally and inevitably achieves is fortunate indeed. Often the chronic unhappiness of creative individuals is due to the conflict they feel between what they like and the only work they are able to produce.

The painting *Church of the Minorites*, II (1926) by Lyonel Feininger is an example of the style of formal order by an artist who was much influenced by Cubism. There is a quality in all of Feininger's work which suggests an effort to give the geometric order of crystalline structures to the visible world. Architectural forms, of course, lend themselves to this treatment, but Feininger used a distinct, sharp-edged, geometric form-language in representing boats, landscapes, and even people. It was Cubism, with its tendency to convert all forms into geometric shapes, which created the breakthrough Feininger exploited in order to express the extraordinarily clear, serene, and restful qualities of the chapel and its setting. The subject and its world are not separated into solids and empty spaces. Instead, the air, the building and the land are treated similarly, as if they were facets of a remarkable gem. In this painting, Feininger created a world of hieratic repose and fixed order; his work implies that our universe has an underlying structure which is also fixed, ordered, and, perhaps, divinely decreed.

It is not difficult to see that the style of formal order, in the hands of certain artists, has religious implications. This is understandable since the great protagonists of the style, the Greeks, had an almost mystical view of mathematics: It possessed a divine beauty for them; art created according to rules of proportion would therefore share the divinity of mathematics. Hence, the implication in Feininger's work that the universe is permanent and orderly is very much like saying that a divine being exists, has created the order which is reflected in the artist's painting, and wishes it to continue. At any rate, Feininger's painting represents one of the ways an artist would make such a statement, since he must use images rather than words to express his view of the universe.

Of course, another artist employing a different style may also express religious feelings, but the content of these feelings is less likely to be concerned with the changeless universe and the order behind it. The style of formal order possesses a certain gravity and dignity by virtue of its emphasis on vertical and horizontal directions, measured intervals, and clarity of articulation. But it cannot cope well with troubled souls, demonic obsession, or the Dionysiac transformation of personality. If an artist is interested in man's effort to unite himself with some transcendent idea or being, for example, his work is more likely to exhibit qualities of turbulence, of encounter and resistance, of endless space and shifting forms rather than contained space and measured forms. The paintings of van Gogh well illustrate this way of expressing a man's mystical emotions—his striving for self-transcendence. He was an artist who did not find the style of formal order congenial since the trees, flowers, objects and people he saw and painted appeared always to be in a state of agitation, always restlessly moving. One might say that his forms were seeking a consummation—a point of rest—which they could not find within his paintings; hence van Gogh's style expresses a certain tension, even anxiety, which is foreign to the serenity of formal order. It is nevertheless a style which deals eloquently with the inner turmoil of certain kinds of religious struggle and aspiration. (See van Gogh's *Starry Night*, p. 26.)

Kinds of Formal Order

Although the style of formal order is characterized in general by stability and permanence, there are also variations within the style—different ways of exhibiting the qualities of formal order. These variations are *intellectual order, biomorphic order,* and *aesthetic order*. Of course, such types are not

PIET MONDRIAN, *Composition with Red, Yellow and Blue* (1921). Collection Haags Gemeentemuseum, The Hague.

GEORGES BRAQUE, *Man with a Guitar* (1911). Collection The Museum of Modern Art, New York, acquired through the Lillie P. Bliss bequest.

absolutely distinct, but one or the other tends to predominate in given works or in the entire production of an artist.

INTELLECTUAL ORDER

Perhaps the best known examples of *intellectual* order are to be found in the work of Piet Mondrian. In his *Composition with Red, Yellow and Blue,* we see a picture which has been created entirely with vertical and horizontal lines, with areas of unvarying color, and with no representational elements whatever. The elimination of curves, of modeling, and of subject matter in the conventional sense obliges us to examine the work solely in terms of the restricted formal vocabulary the artist uses. He has employed only the type of pictorial device which can be completely controlled, which is to say, horizontal and vertical lines of equal thickness, measured rectangular shapes, and only three or four relatively unmixed colors. Yet with this deliberately narrow range of pictorial language, the artist can produce considerable variety—in the shape of the rectangles (their ratios of length to width), in the length of lines considered by themselves, in the apparent "weight" and location of the colored areas, and in the spatial relationships among all these elements. Indeed, it is the interaction among the forms which suggest an intellectual order of mathematical complexity. If a viewer calculates visually how the balance of the total canvas has been achieved, he will see that the work reveals multiple balances or reconciliations of horizontal and vertical movements and of light and heavy shapes—a series of large oppositions and small adjustments. By reducing and refining his pictorial vocabulary, Mondrian

managed to employ the pure activity of the viewer's eye to create impressions of motion, opposition of weight, and assymmetrical balance. The movements of our eyes, which are guided by the design of the canvas, initiate kinaesthetic reactions in our total organism. The elements of the design are *intellectually* interpreted as weight, space, and motion since they do not look like or represent objects which possess mass, volume, and mobility. Hence, the balance we perceive can be regarded as a type of intellectual order—an order based on operations performed by our minds with our kinaesthetic reactions which have, in turn, been excited by the visual material organized by the artist.

One of the earliest twentieth-century forms of intellectual order appeared in Cubism, especially in its stage called Analytical Cubism (1910–12). Braque and Picasso worked together at this time (in close association with Juan Gris and Fernand Léger), and their work is so similar that it often appears that either one of them could have painted any given picture. The similarity suggests that a common *intellectual method* of formal analysis and artistic execution was employed by both painters; consequently, individual variation was subordinated to the requirements of a method of organizing pictures and representing the surfaces and shapes of things. In Braque's *Man with a Guitar* (1911), straight lines, a narrow range of color, and a kind of slicing of the figure into geometric shapes suggest his highly impersonal and unemotional approach to the figure. We learn nothing about the personality, age, occupation, or appearance of the subject. The artist asserts, in effect, that painting pictures is no longer a narrative art. Instead, he presents a rather quiet arrangement of geometric forms which appear to be floating gently in the picture space. The edges of the figure are indistinct; we see that the forms are denser toward the center and loosely distributed around the edges of the subject. No distinction is made between solid and void, hard and soft, skin and cloth. Indeed, it appears that we are dealing with an artistic approach to the nature of matter—the expression of the idea that, fundamentally, all substances have a common structure. The artist appears to be saying that all the variations we see in the visible world are superficial—shells, as it were, underneath which there is an order like the order of mathematics. Here again, the influence of Platonic thought is evident. Also, it is interesting to note that important theoretical developments in mathematics with implications for physics were being made at this time, notably by Einstein.

Cubism offered an analysis of form that artists could use in a wide variety of media and for many expressive purposes. In sculpture, *The Horse* (1914) by Raymond Duchamp-Villon (1876–1918) appears to be an attempt to translate the animal into mechanical equivalents, using the geometric format of Cubism. The painterly language of Cubism was enlarged by the incorporation of forms taken from machines, or, quite possibly, from the working drawings of mechanical engineering. Although there is an attempt to visualize motion here, the poise and stability of classical order predominate. Indeed, as we view the sculpture, we are not so much impressed with the work's motion—actual or potential—as with the sculpture's *analysis* of motion in a

"horse-machine." Consequently, it is the intellectual element, the process of taking apart the animal and reconstructing it along rational-mechanical lines, which characterizes this example of formal order. Compare this work with a mural detail by Orozco, *The Mechanical Horse*, which deals with the same subject in an emotional, nonintellectual style.

The processes of engineering and mechanization have been enormously fascinating to artists, whose reactions as expressed in their work have ranged from enthusiastic approval to contempt to violent revulsion. Classical artists, in general, have tended to see their ideals of rationality, elimination of excess, efficient organization, and mathematical order realized in the machine. Accordingly, they have borrowed the forms developed by mechanical engineering and incorporated them into their work. But as soon as machine-made forms are taken out of their original contexts and exploited in art for qualities of shape, surface, or motion, they begin to function as symbols.

RAYMOND DUCHAMP-VILLON, *The Horse* (1914). Collection The Museum of Modern Art, New York, Van Gogh Purchase Fund.

JOSÉ CLEMENTE OROZCO, *The Mechanical Horse*, mural detail, Hospicio Cabañas, Guadalajara, Mexico (1938–39).

CHARLES DEMUTH, *My Egypt* (1927), left. Collection of the Whitney Museum of American Art, New York.

ROBERT DELAUNAY, *Eiffel Tower* (1914), right. Courtesy The Solomon R. Guggenheim Museum Collection.

PIET MONDRIAN, *Flowering Trees* (1912). Courtesy Nieuwenhuizen Segaar Art Gallery, The Hague.

As symbols, geometric-mechanical forms need not necessarily operate within the style of formal order. In the crisp, Euclidian shapes of *My Egypt* by Charles Demuth (1883–1935), formal order is clearly evident, much as in the work of Charles Sheeler and Lyonel Feininger. But in the *Eiffel Tower* (1914) by Robert Delaunay (1885–1941), the

engineered forms are seen in a state of partial disintegration; instead of resting in classical repose, they appear to be exploding upward before coming down in a final collapse. Therefore, while the choice by an artist of geometric or biomorphic forms may offer a clue to his interests, it is their *organization* which establishes his style. And in the organization of forms, personality factors, such as the artist's characteristic way of feeling and seeing, are more determinative of style than the source in reality from which the forms were derived. Hence, Delaunay's Cubism does not prevent him from feeling and expressing a surging, explosive emotion when he views the Eiffel Tower. Mondrian, on the other hand, could paint living trees and yet endow their organic shapes with the fixed and measured character of plans made by a mechanical draftsman.

In architecture, the buildings of Ludwig Mies van der Rohe are considered classically simple and severely intellectual in conception and appearance. This may be due to the crucial importance which the architect attaches to purity of space and surface in his buildings (as in the Seagram Building, p. 166), achieving his austere effects through restraint in the use of materials, careful attention to joints and change of plane, and a candid revelation of his structural method. There is no effort to use natural materials except in the planned landscaping around the building. There is no suggestion of handcraft or of the contribution of skill from the workmen who erected the structure. The result is a product of design—that is, of thought applied to the problem of using modern, industrial materials fastidiously and with precision.

Mies, like Mondrian, restricted himself to a narrow building vocabulary; he gave up the suggestions and associations of natural materials as Mondrian eventually gave up the associations of curving lines and representational forms. Mies has refused to explore the sculptural possibilities of reinforced concrete in his later work, although the virtuoso effects of the material are increasingly apparent. He has always disdained coarse, irregular textures: Smooth materials, straight lines, clean planes, and regular intervals characterize his building surfaces. But, since he is a consummate classical artist, he introduces just enough variation in surface to avoid monotony.

The architectural style of Mies van der Rohe has been widely imitated, in part because it is admired for its elegance and classical perfection, but also because it fits so logically into a world of industry and technology. It has been equally well used for apartment houses, libraries, academic buildings, office buildings, and research centers. Its flexibility of application combined with an essentially fixed identity also relates the style to man's search for permanent and unvarying forms. Indeed, Mies has stated his interest in creating structures and spaces which could be universally used. His buildings do not vary according to the local climate or the availability of different materials. They do not reflect shifts in function and client or differences in emotional and symbolic meaning. But this lack of variation is not to be regarded as a fault from the standpoint of classical order. Rather, it is intended to illustrate the victory of architecture over the limitations and restrictions of climate, handcraft, provincialism, and literary association. It is the visible evidence of man's effort to create something more durable than style.

BIOMORPHIC ORDER

While some artists achieve the quality of order by using forms derived from mathematics or engineering, others pursue order through the organization of shapes based on the biological world. The term "biomorphic" designates artistic forms which *look as if* they had developed in the same way that all living organisms develop: through the division of cells. An excellent example of biomorphic order is seen in Jean Arp's *Human Concretion*. Whereas other artists regard nature as fundamentally chaotic and therefore indifferent to the order of classical art, this artist sees regularity and formal perfection in natural objects and events. The material

JACOB EPSTEIN, *Mother and Child* (1913), right. Collection The Museum of Modern Art, New York, gift of A. Conger Goodyear.

JEAN ARP, *Human Concretion* (1935). Collection The Museum of Modern Art, New York, gift of the Advisory Committee.

CONSTANTIN BRANCUSI, *Torso of a Young Man* (1924), left, Courtesy The Joseph H. Hirshhorn Collection.

MARCEL GROMAIRE, *Nu bras levé sur fond gris et or* (1957), right. Courtesy Galerie Leandro, Geneva, Suisse.

of the sculpture is stone and yet Arp has given it a soft, flesh-like quality. His title suggests that he was attempting to create simplified abstract forms derived from the human figure while avoiding any features which might identify arms, legs, torso, or head in a specific way. Thus, the connection with the distinctively human is somewhat remote although the identification with the living and the organic is very strong. Nevertheless, these organic shapes exhibit the unmistakably classical qualities of permanence and stability. In *Torso of a Young Man*, a polished brass sculpture by Constantin Brancusi (1876–1957), biological and geometric forms meet in the same work. There is no question of Brancusi's devotion to classical order— that is, to mathematical regularity, stability, and clear articulation. However, he is also determined not to let

his Classicism sever the connection with organic life. He has therefore pressed geometry into the service of the biomorphic. The truncated cylinders which make up the torso stimulate memories of ancient figurative sculptures—the armless or headless gods and goddesses unearthed in Hellenistic ruins. At the same time the long trunk and the distinct joints where the thighs meet the body recall the African sculpture which so obviously influenced Picasso, Marcel Gromaire (born 1892), Modigliani, and others. It is possible to think of Brancusi's work as the result of a process of simplifying and generalizing *from* biological models or as the product of fundamental geometric units combined to suggest biological models. In any case, his work occupies a realm where geometry and living forms successfully meet. He and Arp demonstrate the compatibility of a style of formal order with rounded shapes and swelling curves.

The English sculptor Henry Moore is also a classical artist, but most of his work is less abstract than that of Arp or Brancusi, closer to the identifiably human. His reclining figures and family groups are monuments to vital repose, as in his bronze *Family Group* (1949–54). Moore stresses the roundedness of forms—even the bench on which the figures sit has no sharp angles. Nevertheless, his figures proclaim strength; clearly, biomorphic order need not result in a limp or structurally weak composition. An impression of strength is created because underneath Moore's smooth and rounded surfaces, there is a forceful and virile understanding of skeletal structure, of a supporting system of bones and muscles which completely controls the massive weight of his figures.

It is noteworthy also that Moore puts very small heads on his people, a proportional device which suggests great bulk and stability in the rest of the figure. Although this device produces a monumental effect, it also creates additional problems for the artist because he must control the resultant masses and weights if he is to achieve the effect of classical balance he apparently seeks.

Because Moore has successfully solved the artistic problems of the human and the abstract—of monumentality and control, of rounded form and structural power—we as observers are privileged to see one of the most effectively affirmative artistic statements about man created in the twentieth century. These people, who are a family, and thus confront the struggles and fears which beset all families, appear extraordinarily courageous and very much equal to any challenge—from nature or from society. Perhaps Henry Moore's experience at the time of the bombing of London during World War II, when he made hundreds of drawings of Londoners in subways and other underground shelters, helped to build his attitude of respect for human fortitude under extreme conditions. The attitude may have been even more basic, for Moore's family had been miners for generations and so were accustomed to labor which obliged them to go deep into the earth, to work hard, and to risk their lives daily.

It is important to recognize that a personal style such as Henry Moore's grows out of his technical mastery; but we must also note that it derives from his experience both as a Briton at a particularly challenging time in England's history and as an individual with a particular family history who himself grew up amid harsh conditions of living and

HENRY MOORE, *Family Group* (1945–49). Collection The Museum of Modern Art, New York, A. Conger Goodyear Fund.

working. One of the interesting phenomena of artistic style is that other artists can borrow from or be influenced by Moore's art without themselves having shared Moore's experiences. And as observers, we too can understand his work without having been through the London blitz, without having been so personally and directly threatened by destruction from bombs.

Some of the range of variation in the biomorphic style can be seen in a painting by Joan Miró (1893–   ), *Personnages Rythmiques*. This artist creates playful forms that are based on human figures but almost resemble the seal or walrus. They seem boneless and make no effort to describe visual reality. A crescent stands for the moon in one place, and in another it schematically represents the arms across the torso, at the same time reminding us of a penguin.

The breasts in the lower right portion repeat the same forms directly above, where they are greatly enlarged feet.

A number of absurd comparisons and associations of this kind are present in the work of Miró and they account for his being associated with the Surrealists, although his fantasies tend to be childlike or whimsical rather than shocking. Surrealists as a group deal with fantasy, the absurd, and unconventional or shocking combinations of subject matter. But the form language they use can range widely—from the biomorphic of Miró to the almost photographic of Salvador Dali, to the osseous and geologic of Yves Tanguy, to the architectonic of Giorgio de Chirico. Surrealism, therefore, does not constitute a single style of execution so much as a distinctive way of confronting the viewer with fantastic subject matter. But some artists who have been grouped with the Surrealists—Miró, Chagall, Tanguy, and Paul Delvaux—seem more interested in dreams, trance-like states, and quiet fantasies than in shock or violent grotesquerie.

In Miró we have an artist who enjoys playing with the multiple associations of biological forms. To do so successfully, he must create shapes which can look at once like images of living organisms seen through a microscope and like zoological or human shapes seen with the naked eye. In addition, the general atmosphere of his canvas must be such that common sense or

JOAN MIRÓ, *Personnages Rythmiques* (1934), left. Courtesy Kunstsammlung Nordheim-Westfalen, Dusseldorf.

WILLIAM BAZIOTES, *Pompeii* (1955), right. Collection The Museum of Modern Art, New York, Mrs. Louise Smith Fund.

practical reality does not intrude. Hence, although the result might appear to reflect the thinking of a child, the development of these forms and their juxtaposition call for considerable adult wit and creative imagination. The classical quality of *Personnages Rythmiques* is seen in the predominantly vertical organization of the principal shapes and the clarity and distinctness of each form. Although the shapes seem to have a wriggling motion, they appear to wriggle in an assigned area. Therefore, notwithstanding the movement and playfulness of the forms, there is an over-all sense of control, of fun according to rules devised by the artist.

The late William Baziotes (1912–64) was a painter greatly concerned with the biomorphic, as in his work *Pompeii*. His paintings exhibit an extraordinarily sensitive perception of the quiet vitality to be found or imagined in all things: the rocks in a landscape or the cracks in a plaster wall. In Baziotes' work, as in dreams, inanimate objects acquire biological life. Although Baziotes was a superb colorist who could intrigue the eye with almost imperceptible changes of surface, of modeling, and of edge, the interest of his pictures does not cease with their surfaces: He animated the shapes in *Pompeii* by endowing them with the most subtle and gentle movement—an effect that calls for considerable craftsmanship in control of the pigment and sensitivity to line. Such works speak very quietly but may endure longer than more blatant painterly statements. It is the restraint and control of Baziotes' work which endow it with a classical quality: Thus, we see formal order in the work of an artist who is an abstractionist, who is interested in living

PIER LUIGI NERVI, Little Sports Palace, interior roof detail (1957). Photo, Jan C. Rowan, *Progressive Architecture.*

things, and who animates his surfaces with gently controled movement.

In architecture, biomorphic order has been given a fresh impetus by new materials and construction devices. Collapsible domes whose skins are curved metal hemispheres; shells made of concrete sprayed over inflated balloons; ribbed arena ceilings possessing an almost botanical delicacy and grace; and paraboloid roof structures combined with daring suspension systems—these have liberated designers from their age-long reliance on rectangular and triangular shapes (see Chapter Thirteen, especially pp. 432–433, 437–439). Of course, the dome, which has always expressed biomorphic impulses, is an ancient device going back to the early tumulus, or burial mound. It was never a frivolous form but rather a shape associated with man's wish to be inside a womb-like enclosure: either the artificial earth-mound grave uniting him with an all-embracing mother or the curved ceiling of his church, the dome of the heavens, symbolizing the encircling, benevolent universe. These structures combine formal order with symbolic meanings which are ultimately biological.

FRANK LLOYD WRIGHT, The Solomon R. Guggenheim Museum, interior (1959). Courtesy The Solomon R. Guggenheim Museum Collection.

Frank Lloyd Wright wrote about and practiced what he called an "organic" philosophy of architecture—one in which buildings seemed to assert their kinship with nature through their materials and spaces. But only in the Guggenheim Museum did he base his design quite openly on the structure of a natural object: The building is like an enormous nautilus shell, within which the visitor easily descends a spiral ramp, building serried memories of nonobjective art at a somewhat faster rate than the sea creature fashions its spiral series of chambers, one a year. The principles of growth followed by the nautilus and the museum visitor are the same: Each creature moves on when his physical or imaginative space has been fully occupied.

Wright's biomorphism is followed in other contexts. Just as the gently descending ramps of the Guggenheim ease the aesthetic journey of today's "man on the go," the modern parking garage serves his transformation from motorist to pedestrian by using the same structural devices and architectural forms to create a niche for his gasoline-driven chariot; such a garage is a sort of automotive Guggenheim whose outer covering has been stripped away. The ramps might also be compared to the life journey of the nautilus through its shell, but here as in the Museum, it is a greatly accelerated journey. Nevertheless, the same biomorph suffices. We are presented with the image of a gigantic, concrete sea shell, holding within its labyrinthine recesses thousands of nests for temporarily quiescent gasoline engines.

"Build thee more stately mansions,
　　O my soul,

As the swift seasons roll!
Leave the low-vaulted past!
Let each new temple, nobler than the last,
Shut thee from heaven with a dome
　　more vast,
Till Thou at length are free,
Leaving thine outgrown shell
　　by life's unresting sea!" °

The nautilus image creates a strangely fitting description of biomorphic order and the uses to which it is put by our civilization. The pedestrian emerges from the shell, like a butterfly emerging from its chrysalis: But, to shift the metaphor slightly, the motorist is a moth, governed by lights, whereas the butterfly can wander about freely.

AESTHETIC ORDER

Aesthetic order is the style evident in works which achieve balance and stability mainly through the organization of their sensuous qualities. The artist adjusts the various surface appeals of the work so that we experience what is often called the "beauty" of the work. Aesthetic order does not rely necessarily on accuracy, meaning, or symbolic reference. Rather it depends on the human capacity to enjoy, admire, and prize what is directly and immediately satisfying of itself and for no reason beyond itself. The simplest analogy is our satisfaction in the taste of foods apart from considerations of nourishment or health. Such satisfactions do not occur because they mean something, resemble something, or are particularly useful. They make an appeal to something within us which responds with the emotion of delight. Perhaps there is

°Oliver Wendell Holmes, *The Chambered Nautilus.*

THE STYLE OF FORMAL ORDER   177

some optimal organization of perceptual energies which works of aesthetic order encourage, leading to an experience which is unusually tranquil and serene.

The Breakfast Room by Pierre Bonnard (1867–1947), for example, is a work by a later Impressionist who relied on coloristic invention to orchestrate a symphony of quiet, chromatic delight. Although he benefited from the color experimentation of the Impressionists, Bonnard did not have their scientific motivation. He was more concerned about weaving a tapestry which was partly suggested by the color of the objects before him but more nearly created by his own imagination and facility. The table and the objects on it, the window, the fragmented figure to the left, and the scene through the window are only nominally established. They constitute an opportunity for the artist to create a multitude of variations on yellow, yellow-green, yellow-orange, violet, blue-violet, and so on. Deep space is only casually represented; the drawing is quite perfunctory. Most of the color does not "move" in or out of the picture space; rather it tends to shimmer and coruscate on the surface of the canvas.

It is interesting that painters such as Bonnard do not especially attempt to remind us of the appearance of trees, sky, fruit, and tableware. The material we are chiefly aware of in their work is the material of which the work is made—in this case, oil paint. Bonnard and his great predecessors such as Monet, Renoir, and Degas educated us through our eyes to a delight in pigment and in color quite apart from what it represents.

Georges Braque, the early collaborator of Picasso, developed their common intellectual style into one of aesthetic order—an objective which occupied the greater part of his mature career. *Woman with a Mandolin* shows how the classical qualities of Cubism have been placed at the disposal of aesthetic pleasure. As compared with Bonnard, Braque is the greater designer: He more consciously and precisely establishes his shapes and areas, is also more inventive and varied. He also has a deeper interest in the differing textures of objects and surfaces; Bonnard suppresses all textures in the interest of *one* texture—that created by his paint application. Braque adds sand and in other ways manipulates his pigment so as to increase the variety of surface and tactile appeal of his canvases. He exaggerates the pattern of wallpaper, pressing it forward into the same plane as his figure, thus indicating that the sensuous qualities of the patterned wall are more important than its "correct" location in the picture space. He also

PIERRE BONNARD, *The Breakfast Room* (c.1930–31), left. Collection The Museum of Modern Art, New York.

GEORGES BRAQUE, *Woman with a Mandolin* (1937), right. Collection The Museum of Modern Art, New York, Mrs. Simon Guggenheim Fund.

HENRI MATISSE, *Lady in Blue* (1937). Collection of Mrs. John Wintersteen, President, Philadelphia Museum of Art; photo, Philadelphia Museum of Art.

RICHARD LIPPOLD, *Variation Number 7: Full Moon* (1949–50). Collection The Museum of Modern Art, New York, Mrs. Simon Guggenheim Fund.

gives attention to the music stand almost equal to that given to the silhouette of the figure and mandolin, thus extracting the maximum decorative effect from each object, volume, or space which is present before his eye. Notice that, as in Bonnard, we learn very little about the subject matter of the pictures: It is the opportunity subject matter creates for the artist to manipulate pattern, texture, and color which is important.

Perhaps the most elegant modern master of aesthetic order was Henri Matisse (1869–1954). His personal style was greatly enriched by the study of classical Persian art which, as with much of Near Eastern art, emphasized opulence of color and surface and elaborate decorative effects. In painting such as that of Matisse, Bonnard, or Braque, there is an almost Oriental emphasis on splendor, on subordination of expressive meaning in the interest of richness of aesthetic surface. The *Lady in Blue* by Matisse reveals the painter as a very sophisticated European designer of patterns and decorative forms building on a Persian tradition. The elegance of the artist lies in his ability to find precisely what he needs from the abundance before him: the ornamented furniture, the rich gown, the room interior, the lady casually sitting, a bouquet of flowers to frame her head, and pictures on the wall with somewhat classical evocations. These subject matters are present in highly simplified form; only shape has been taken from their total reality and then reassembled by the artist to create a new reality. The virtue which Matisse possesses pre-eminently is that of subordinating drawing, color, and design to a single pictorial effect which is meant to be pleasurable

as a whole. Hence, in viewing his work, it is very important not to let the eye linger on any part of the picture by itself; one must attempt to see the entire canvas at once, to let it *fill the eye*, and then the effect of the carefully calculated quantities and intensities of color will be felt. Toward the end of his life, illness confined Matisse to bed. But he continued to compose with scissors and colored paper, and in this manner produced some of his most sophisticated works. This fact suggests that the artist did not rely on dexterity or sensitivity of touch, as did Degas, for example. Rather it is his calculation of quantities and shapes of intense color which is critical; likewise his considerable experience with classical drawing enabled him to simplify, to suggest what the viewer needs to know about the subject, and to eliminate what is aesthetically irrelevant. Matisse never felt himself under any obligation to prove that his representational powers were strong; hence he could subordinate representation and objective accuracy to the aesthetic requirements of his pictures.

In sculpture, we may see aesthetic order as a primary consideration in the work of Richard Lippold (1915–   ), such as *Variation Number 7: Full Moon*. In this work, as in others by the same artist, the subject is light or light rays as represented by fine filaments of metal radiating from several centers, forming complex geometric shapes, and seemingly hanging suspended in space. The gold and silver filaments are so light that the movement of air in the room where the work is displayed or the changing light in the room creates delicate, shimmering effects and gentle vibrations which would seem to suggest outer space. However, this construction has no scientific validity: We perceive it chiefly as an aesthetic order. It has its own perfection based on precision, lightness, delicacy, and the ability of the work to trap and distribute light harmoniously throughout its parts.

Another American sculptor, Harry Bertoia (1915–   ), created for the Manufacturers' Trust Company in New York City a metal screen which exploits the aesthetic possibilities of brass, copper, and nickel. Such a work departs from traditional sculpture and more nearly approaches interior design or architecture. It serves, of course, as a partition and also as a fascinating plane against which the normal activities of a bank take place. And because this screen wall has a primarily architectural function to perform, the sculptor has wisely decided to let the aesthetic properties of the materials dominate the space rather than create symbolic forms which would compete for the viewer's attention with the living persons and events before the wall. As a result, there is a mutually enhancing relation involving the room, its people, and the wall itself. Since passers-by and patrons are encouraged to see into the bank, an excellent architectural effect is achieved— the bank presents an image of openness and hospitality: Its personnel and patrons are complemented by the architectural space and the sculptural wall.

The concept of aesthetic order— of an art which appeals primarily to the senses without invoking ideas, symbols, or description—is closely tied to the main objectives of the modern abstract movement. Much of modern painting can be understood as an effort to develop a language which is purely visual, communicating qualities which belong to the world of line, shape, and color alone. Painters and sculptors devoted a large part of their energies during the early twentieth century to pursuing the autonomy enjoyed by composers and architects. Now they have, to a considerable extent, succeeded.

In the work of such artists as Bradley Walker Tomlin, Mark Rothko, Barnett Newman, Adolph Gottlieb, and

HARRY BERTOIA, Screen for Manufacturers Hanover Trust Company (1954), left. Courtesy Manufacturers Hanover Trust Company; photo, © Ezra Stoller.

BRADLEY WALKER TOMLIN, *No. 10* (1952–53), right. Collection Munson - Williams - Proctor Institute, Utica, New York.

Ad Reinhardt, a type of order has been achieved which is essentially in the tradition of Classicism—the Classicism of the Parthenon and J. S. Bach. See, for example, *No. 10* by Tomlin (1899–1953). The painting of these men is totally abstract; its serenity is the product of calculation, simplification, and measurement. It departs from Mediterranean conceptions of order only in the absence of a canon of proportions based on the human figure. Unlike the Greeks, who required that mathematical perfection be embodied in the form of a man, the modern followers of Classicism have put the human image aside. Instead, they rely on contemporary man's highly developed capacity to perceive abstract types of order: the order of ideas, or intellectual order; the order of living forms, or biomorphic order; and the order of sense data, or aesthetic order.

It is true that the pioneer efforts of Wassily Kandinsky (1866–1944) to develop a purely visual and abstract language of painting were expressionistic in appearance. His swirling, amorphous colored areas could hardly be regarded as stable, distinct, or measured approaches to formal order. But since 1912 (when Kandinsky published his book *Concerning the Spiritual in Art*), classical as well as expressionistic developments have taken place in painting. As a result, an Apollonian vision has emerged in abstract painting. It is based on the perception of order in the sense data arising from works of art created expressly to exhibit order. In the eighteenth and nineteenth centuries, discriminating viewers may have been instinctively aware of the order underlying the Neoclassic themes of masters such as David and Ingres. But not until the twentieth century did artists deliberately attempt to paint that underlying order, dispensing with objects and themes, employing only the purest data of visual perception which the art of painting could devise. It is this ambitious endeavor to create a classical style appealing directly to the visual sense which I have called an art of aesthetic order.

Conclusion

Classical styles of art have been closely associated with measurement, calculation, mathematics, and geometry. But the use of geometrical shapes is not necessarily a sign of formal order. The essence of formal order lies not so much in the kinds of shapes and volumes employed, but rather in an implicit attitude toward motion and stability. If forms seem to be at rest, they contribute to the sense of order; if forms appear to be moving, their motion is orderly only if it proceeds in a measured and predictable fashion. These assertions could be made about life as well as art. Parents usually learn to judge the activity of their children by the way they are moving: Certain patterns of movement mean trouble; other patterns are reassuring. Of course, there are some parents for whom almost *any* movement by children signals danger. According to our usual standards, such parents may be neurotic and are likely to raise neurotic children.

Extending this observation to art

history, we find that in certain social and political climates there is a preference for absolute stability in the forms employed by the visual arts. The art of ancient Egypt and of Byzantium, for example, placed a premium on immobility. Should we then conclude that the art of these great civilizations reflected neurotic obsession with order? It is true that both civilizations resisted change and also managed to last as politically distinct empires for at least a thousand years. On the other hand, the sheer durability of a political state may not signify that most of its people are living what we, or they, would regard as the good life. Conceivably, the style of formal order—especially when it is an official and prescribed style—is an instrument of social control, a device for keeping the masses in awe of their rulers. Modern dictatorships have shown a preference for a type of trite Classicism, possibly because they recognize the crucial role of order in Classicism and because they usually justify their absolute rule on the basis of society's need for order and discipline.

If the times have been characterized by a great deal of confusion about standards and by individualistic behavior carried to what some observers may regard as licentious extremes, then a style of formal order—in art, in manners, and in government—will seem attractive. It may even impress men as the only legitimate style. There are occasions in the lives of most persons when stability appears more desirable than anything else. On other occasions, Classicism may strike them as painfully dull. From the standpoint of the health of a culture (assuming cultures can be sick or well), the opportunity for non-formal styles to flourish *along with* formal or classical styles seems essential. But in the modern world, it is not possible to decree the creation of art in *any* style with the certain expectation that the results will exhibit excellence or satisfy existing desires for something different. The underground hunger of Russian and East European young people for American and western European cultural products is a sign of the deadly boredom an official style of dated Classicism creates in that portion of a population which is most alive and hopeful of change. Sooner or later a stylistic reaction emerges—a reaction all the more extreme in its forms and ill-considered in its objectives because it has been so long repressed. The coexistence of divergent styles in free societies, then, appears to be one of the best signs, not only of a healthy culture, but also of properly functioning social and political institutions.

CHAPTER SIX

Many persons recognize that the art of our time should not attempt to compete with the camera: Hand-made imitations of appearances have become obsolete. They also realize that most human beings have emotions and feelings which they cannot or prefer not to express. Hence, they conclude that the chief function remaining for the visual arts is to create forms which a camera could not record and to express feelings for which no other adequate language can be found. Certainly it is correct to believe that art is, among other things, a language of emotion. And usually, when we speak of art and emotion in this context, we mean strong, intensely felt emotion.

In the visual arts, certain traits commonly recur in work which stresses the expression of feeling, and that is why we refer to a "style of emotion." Very often, the personality of an artist is such that he cannot "speak" in any language other than the language of feeling. Vincent van Gogh and Chaim Soutine were such men, and their paintings of people, flowers, trees, or even chairs seem to be bursting with intensity. For artists of this type, what matters most is not objective accuracy, or the measured and balanced expression of order; rather, the expression of excitement, anxiety, pity, or rage—any emotion—takes precedence over all other considerations.

THE STYLE

OF EMOTION

If we say that emotion is important to a certain kind of artist, however, do we refer to the emotion which the artist feels or to his arousal of emotion in others? Under certain circumstances, the reference might be to both. Usually, however, we have only a secondary interest in the artist's feelings; when studying art, we are mainly concerned with the way in which art *objects* are responsible for a viewer's responses. Sometimes the language used by writers to describe the emotional impact of a work may give the impression that the artist experienced the same feelings in advance of creating it. But, in fact, he may or may not have had such feelings. And it is not really our purpose to find out. Psychologists, of course, are interested in the connection between an individual's emotional life and his creative expression. Sigmund Freud's study of Leonardo da Vinci was, in part, an effort to explain the artist's work on the basis of psychoanalytic inferences about Leonardo's personality. In addition, certain theories of art criticism are based on the assumption that there is a close connection between artistic excellence and *genuineness* of emotional expression; that is, on whether the viewer is convinced that the artist truly experienced the emotions dealt with in his work. The study of style, however, focuses more sharply on the art object than on the artist's behavior. When examining a work of art, the viewer ought to be somewhat selfish: He should be more interested in his *own* biography and his *own* emotions than in those of the artist. He should ask, "Does the work convince me of the reality of the world it attempts to create?" rather than "Did the artist really undergo the emotions portrayed here?"

This latter observation raises an important question dealt with by aesthetics: Are emotions actually *portrayed* in a work of art, or do we merely project our personal feelings upon the art object? (The problem is dealt with in some detail in Chapter Ten, *Perceiving the Elements: Aesthetics.* However, a provisional answer is needed now if the discussion of an emotional style is to be understood.) There are, of course, differences of opinion about what constitutes the "expression of emotion" in art. The view taken here follows, in general, the position of the Gestalt psychologists, namely, that there are structural similarities between the neuromuscular behavior of a viewer and the physical features of the art object he is examining. Certain configurations of line, shape, and color induce corresponding kinaesthetic reactions in perceiving organisms. Emotions are the names the viewer gives to his neuromuscular reactions—his feelings—which have been "triggered" by the organization of elements in the art object. The *energy* for such feelings or emotions comes chiefly from the viewer, but the feelings are given form, they are *organized*, by the work of art. Consequently, the answer to the question raised above is, "Yes and no." In the sense that emotions are *caused* and *shaped* by the art object, they are *portrayed* in it. But, of course, only a living organism, specifically a person or a higher animal, can *experience* emotion.

Perhaps this theory of emotional perception in art accounts for the communication of feelings between an art object and a viewer. Yet what we are trying to discover is whether there is a *style* of emotion. Is there any difference, so far as emotional perception is concerned, between works belonging to this style and those in a style discussed earlier—the style of intellectual order, for example? The mechanisms of perception are the same, but there is a difference in the viewer's *disposition to behave* on the basis of his neuromuscular reactions. That is, a painting by Mondrian disposes him to stand still or sit, or to measure spatial intervals; a painting by van Gogh disposes him to discharge energy through his limbs, to move toward the work, or perhaps to clutch at the air around him. Why does van Gogh have this more massive, overt, and physical effect on the viewer? It is because van Gogh's painting has structural similarities to the neuromuscular behavior which the human organism, going back to its primitive origins, has always regarded as a signal to move—to run, to leap, to dance, to bob and weave, and so on. The Mondrian stimulates behavior which is more recent in the development of the human organism—perhaps as recent as man's discovery of agriculture: the measurement of property, the laying out of fields for cultivation, the calculation of dates for planting, the estimation of weight and bulk with the eye. When the eye is used to measure, it performs a more intellectual task than when it signals the organism to run or fight. Consequently, the difference between an emotional and an intellectual style can be understood as: (1) a difference in the "signals" which the work of art transmits to the viewer; (2) a difference in the viewer's disposition or readiness to act on the basis of the "signals"; and (3) a difference in the type and magnitude of neuromuscular behavior induced in the viewer, behavior based on involuntary habits or reactions inherited from the development of the human species.

There are also differences *within* the style of emotion. That is, works of art have the capacity to arouse a *range* of feelings and dispositions in viewers— all of which are emotional, but differing individually in their content. It is obvious that we can be elated by one work and depressed by another. Each particular emotional response may be caused by the subject matter or theme of the work; or it may be due to the type of aesthetic "signal" which the work transmits. For example, abstract art often has no apparent subject matter, yet it can cause complex emotional responses. Something in the visual organization of abstract works must be responsible for the emotional reactions of viewers. Consequently, we shall be dealing, in the following sections, with *two* sources of emotion in works of art: thematic or subject matter sources, and organizational or design sources.

The style of emotion properly designates works which rely on *any* means of arousing feelings in a viewer. Usually, its most stirring exemplars reveal the mutual influence of theme *and* design, resulting in a heightening or intensification of emotion. Examples might be observed in the *Side of Beef* by Chaim Soutine and *The Bat* by Germaine Richier (1904–59). Both subjects are distasteful, and the organization of forms in each case reinforces our normal feelings of revulsion. On the other hand, Henry Moore's *Falling Warrior* deals with

CHAIM SOUTINE, *Side of Beef* (c.1925), left. Courtesy Albright-Knox Art Gallery, Buffalo, New York.

GERMAINE RICHIER, *The Bat* (1952), right. Photo courtesy Peter Heman.

HENRY MOORE, *Falling Warrior* (1955–56). Courtesy The Joseph H. Hirshhorn Collection; photo, The Solomon R. Guggenheim Museum.

death also, but his simplification of forms and his freezing of movement divests the sculpture of any gory or horrific qualities the theme might ordinarily have. In other words, the drama of Moore's theme does not interfere with the formal order of his sculpture. The warrior's limbs are caught in a type of classic ritual—a ritual which confers nobility upon a valorous death on the battlefield. But the carcass by Soutine dramatizes the dumb, mutilated character of the eviscerated form which once housed organic life. The carcass records the slaughter of a beast, not the slaying of a hero. Richier's bat, with its webbed

limbs radiating from a mammalian trunk, strikes a note of primeval terror because of some instinctive fear it arouses in humans. At the same time, its resemblance to the human is openly stressed by the artist to arouse mixed emotions in the viewer—emotions of dread and of recognition. In this case, design is assisted by the *manipulation of symbolic meanings* to account for the effectiveness of the work.

Themes of violence and an interest in mutilated forms are not uncommon features of the art of this century. However, we are not concerned merely with discovering whether we like or dislike such style features in contemporary art. Rather, we want to examine them in order to gain some insight into the kind of world we live in. If art reflects the times as well as the personalities of artists, it is worth serious attention whether we enjoy it or not. Certainly, our study of the style of emotion should help us to see what it is about life in the twentieth century which leads to the expression of anguish and despair . . . or possibly even the expression of hope and joy.

Romanticism and Emotion

Although almost all works of art generate feelings in the viewer, whether intentionally or not, some appear to have been created largely *in response* to an artist's strong emotion, an emotion he was anxious to express. His attitude is unlike that of the artist working in an objectively accurate style: As a rule, the latter sort of person suppresses any revelation of personal feeling in his work and is indifferent to any

emotion an audience may experience in its presence. A prominent feature of the style of emotion, however, is the evident desire of the artist to *disclose*, even to *parade*, his feelings as frankly and as forcefully as possible.

The attitude of emotional candor, of giving primacy to the requirements of personal reactions, is also part of what is called Romanticism. The Romantic tends to believe that the important fea-

186

ture of any event, person, or place is *his* feeling about it. The claims of truth or of fact seem less urgent since his feelings are themselves facts: Truths are emotions which are intensely felt or expressed. Many of us sometimes speak of individuals as "losing themselves" in some project or idea, and this ability to "lose" oneself is characteristic of the Romantic also. We may on occasion speak of such a person as losing his "sense of proportion." Looking at Romantic art, it is not difficult for the viewer to feel *lost* in the work, to lose his "sense of proportion," that is, the common-sense idea of the correctness or rightness of things. The paintings of Henry Mattson (1887–   ), as in *Wings of the Morning,* encourage the viewer to feel drawn into the sea. He exhibits the typical Romantic reluctance to distinguish between subject and object, between the observer and observed. The ocean is shown not merely as a body of water, but as a mysterious world in which we could somehow live. By contrast, Winslow Homer (1836–1910), who also painted the ocean with great power, did not convey any sense of the sea as a complete cosmos, a place in which the soul could wander endlessly.

Another feature of Romanticism is interest in the exotic, the strange, and the dangerous. Romantic artists have often been attracted to far-off lands, as Paul Gauguin (1848–1903) was to Tahiti. Unfamiliar places and customs create the opportunity for the artist, and for us as viewers, to forget our present lives and environment: We can *lose* ourselves in a distant place, at least imaginatively. The emotion of wonder or of amazement is deliberately encouraged. Gauguin's *The Spirit of the Dead Watching* (1892)

DARREL AUSTIN, *The Black Beast*
(1941). Courtesy Smith College
Museum of Art; photo, Perls
Galleries.

RUFINO TAMAYO, *Animals* (1941).
Collection The Museum of Modern
Art, New York, Inter-American
Fund.

perfectly fits the requirements of Romantic art: Tahiti is an exotic place; the people are simple and unsophisticated—especially to a European, a Parisian; fantastic flowers and a mysterious inscription, "Manao Tupapau," occur in the background;° and most important, an atmosphere of supernaturalism is an integral part of the picture.

In contrast to the exoticism of Gauguin, there is the dreamlike and somewhat threatening world of the American painter, Darrel Austin (1907–   ). His work illustrates the fascination which the idea of violence has for the Romantic imagination. *The Black Beast* shows a fierce jungle cat at rest with a dead bird under its paws, both set in an eerie, marshy landscape. The animal seems to glow because the painter has illuminated her from below, creating a luminous, incandescent effect. Also, his paint is applied with a palette knife in thick ribbons of relatively unmixed color, so that the surface is exceedingly active and exciting, in contrast to the serenity of the animal in the night landscape. The source of Romantic emotion in this picture lies in the juxtaposition of the beautiful but fearsome jungle cat with the mangled bird. Thus the artist suggests the duality of natural beauty: Killing and suffering exist side-by-side with satiation and repose.

Another treatment of the Romantic theme of animal savagery lies in *Animals* by Rufino Tamayo (1899–   ). Here there is no contrast between repose and killing: The animals are not

°It is the title, or "The spirit of the dead remembers her." The dark figure in the background resembles, as does the entire composition, the very un-Romantic work by Manet, *Olympia* (1863), illustrated on page 246.

satiated; a few bones of their victims are shown and they howl for new prey. The artist's manner is more primitive and at once more abstract than Austin's; indeed, the animal heads owe something to the images of destruction in Picasso's *Guernica*. Tamayo's color is more tropical than Austin's; he achieves his effect through large areas of flat, warm color set among menacing, black shapes. We might contrast the essential attitudes of the two artists by saying that Tamayo is chiefly impressed with the pure, unalloyed savagery of his animals while Austin views the beast sentimentally although he knows she preys and kills.

In sculpture, a complex Romantic work exhibiting mixed emotions is *Spectre of Kitty Hawk*, by Theodore Roszak (1907–   ). The artist has created a frightening bird which we might regard as pure invention had he not told us it is a pterodactyl, an extinct predatory bird. Using steel, bronze, and brass, Roszak has built a flying monster which he intends to suggest the mixed consequences of the invention of flight at Kitty Hawk. Without the title and our knowledge of what the Wright Brothers accomplished at Kitty Hawk, would this work hold its significance? Probably we should still experience a similar set of emotions since the idea of a predatory bird communicates itself well through the head and claws; also the wings, body, tail, and remaining anatomical features hint at the airplane—perhaps a crashed plane. Finally, the hard, refractory material, which is hammered and brazed, suggests the metallic glint of a flying bird-machine.

The use of a literary or historical title is also characteristic of Romantic art, since the intent of the artist is to heighten and intensify our emotional reactions to the forms with any assistance from symbols, history, or literature, which he can legitimately include. Some artists of less creative power, craftsmanship, or formal invention may rely too heavily on titles, symbols, and literary association to communicate with an audience. In Roszak, however, we have a superb craftsman who can handle metal directly, achieving organic effects as easily as if he were modeling in clay. His forms—seen as a whole and apart

THEODORE J. ROSZAK, *Spectre of Kitty Hawk* (1946–47). Collection The Museum of Modern Art, New York, purchase.

THÉODORE GÉRICAULT, *The Raft of the Medusa* (1818–19). Courtesy Musée du Louvre, Cliché des Musées Nationaux.

EUGÈNE DELACROIX, *Entrance of the Crusaders into Constantinople* (1841). Courtesy Musée du Louvre, Cliché des Musées Nationaux.

from what they mean—have considerable abstract power. The jagged shapes, radiating out from the fuselage or body, imply danger and flight at the same time. This unity of form and meaning is what characterizes a successful work of art. It should also be added that because the Romantic artist deals with pure forms as well as with associations and symbols, he undertakes large risks because he attempts to control a complex vehicle of communication in the creative enterprise. The dangers of a trite or easily dated sentimentality are very great. For example, some of the works of the great Romantic masters, such as Delacroix and Géricault, may seem to us excessively melodramatic. However, *The Raft of the Medusa* by Géricault and the *Entrance of the Crusaders into Constantinople* by Delacroix survive as important paintings because of their magnificent formal organization, craftsmanship, color, and powerful execution.

Although Romantic art satisfies certain psychological needs of the artist and endeavors by any means to generate emotional reactions in the viewer, its genuinely great and enduring works survive only when they are well wrought. That is why an emotional temperament or strongly held convictions on the part of an artist will not by themselves guarantee artistic merit. The general public can be fascinated, excited, or shocked into admiration of works which are merely sensational. That is, their symbolic or literary meanings may be so strong as to obscure weakness of organization, craftsmanship, and invention. With the passage of time, though, sensational effects diminish in power. Then a more just assessment of the artist's real achievement is possible.

The Role of Distortion

The style of emotion relies heavily on distortion because a viewer's feelings are very readily aroused by any departure from what is considered "normal" or visually "correct." Particularly with respect to distortion of the human body, we find our attention arrested and our emotions almost immediately involved. But even distortion of other themes—objects in the natural or man-made world—also arouses the viewer, since there is an inevitable tension between what we "know" to be accurate and what we see represented as presumably faithful to reality. By "distortion" we usually mean stretching, twisting, enlarging, or otherwise deforming the customary shape and size of things. But distortion may also refer to exaggerating color and illumination, increasing the contrast between light and dark, or overstating textural and surface qualities. Generally, the artistic choice of one or several of these types of distortion is not so much a calculation as a spontaneous and largely unconscious result of an artist's emotional attitude toward his subject.

Because of his personality or because of his training, an artist may characteristically enlarge or suppress certain anatomical features; or he may prefer to view his subject when it *seems* agitated and deformed. Even a photograph can exhibit distortion if the subject is viewed at an atypical moment or from an unusual angle of vision. Michelangelo most notably portrayed the figure in writhing attitudes, employing particularly his famous *contraposto*

—an extreme twisting action through the trunk, shoulders, and pelvis. Some of the apocalyptic feeling of his *Last Judgment* fresco in the Sistine Chapel is due to the representation of muscles in tension. The viewer "feels" such tensions physically and emotionally. Michelangelo also tended to reduce the size of the head, except in his figure of *David*, where the slightly oversized head and hands help describe the subject as an adolescent. Gauguin, enlarged feet and drew their contours somewhat awkwardly so as to suggest the primitive quality in his people as a whole. Toulouse-Lautrec, one of the great draftsmen of modern times, distorted his cabaret people with extraordinary wit and *accuracy*—accuracy, because he approaches but does not fall into caricature: His delineations are truthful,

MICHELANGELO, *David* (1501–4). Courtesy Alinari–Art Reference Bureau.

Distorted imagery may grow out of the characteristic blurring of objects when seen by a moving rather than a fixed viewer.

MAURICE VLAMINCK, *La Nationale*.

the exaggerations are based on observation rather than fantasy, and they have a sure grasp of the characteristic forms that reveal character.

Distortion has many objectives: It may be comic observation and pity in Lautrec; anxiety in Munch (p. 195) and Soutine (p. 20); and a kind of isolation and despair in Giacometti (p. 7). Van Gogh, as mentioned earlier, seems to have distorted unconsciously as a result of his intense preoccupation with color and pigment and because of an almost mystical identification with the places and people he painted. The distortion of Francis Bacon (p. 196), the English painter, achieves a macabre effect and seems to suggest that beneath man's civilized surface, the mentality of the savage is in command. Some distortion is quite pleasant: The attenuated fig-

HENRI DE TOULOUSE-LAUTREC, *À la Mie* (1891). Courtesy Museum of Fine Arts, Boston, S.A. Denio Fund.

ures of the German sculptor Lehmbruck (p. 152) endow the adolescent form with harmony and grace. Modigliani's stretching of the figure and simplification of contours (p. 12) results in a heightening of sensuous and pleasurable qualities. But it is interesting that both these artists would be described as Classicists. Distortion in their hands is mainly attenuation for the sake of refining form, the elimination of incidental detail which would oppose the sense of eternal stability and poise. Even Modigliani's erotic nudes are endowed with a certain dignity, a kind of aloofness, because of the purity of line and simplicity of the large forms he uses to describe them.

Caricature employs distortion, but it has a different purpose from that of other art genres. Caricature is mainly intent upon ridicule of its object and consequently will subordinate artistic and factual considerations to the prime objective of making its target appear ugly, preposterous, hateful, or absurd. (Indeed, the German word for ugly, *hässlich,* also means hateful.) In *The Senate* by William Gropper (1897–   ), caricature is approached in the figure of the politician as exemplar of rant and bombast. We see gross exaggeration of gesture; an active, noisy figure juxtaposed with one asleep; a speaker with an overlarge mouth, large stomach, and bald head, full of seriousness yet having no effect on his potential audience. The senator is a stereotype of the garrulous politician who persuades no one with his oratory—and yet his perception of the office and of his role seems to require the empty performance. The painting is a caricature since the situation is greatly oversimplified; it is an exaggeration of the truth because it is meant to arouse feelings of derision and of indignation. In Jack Levine's *Welcome Home* (1946) we see distortion employed in a more artistically complex and thematically developed work. Here, too, the physical traits of the persons in the painting are held up to ridicule and contempt: We are encouraged to see their bodies as the physical containers of moral vices: pride and gluttony. At the same time the artist makes certain that moral deformity is joined with social eminence. He lavishes attention on the details of the sumptuous meal; the obsequiousness of the waiter; the formal dress of the diners; the female diner, upper left, who combines a certain emaciation with a ludicrous effort at glamor. Noteworthy also is Levine's use of foreshortening and a distorting perspective to enlarge the heads; the view from above lets us "look down" on the "celebrities" and hence feel superior to them as they gorge themselves—middle-aged heroes celebrating a victory won with the lives of boys who lived on "K" rations. The kind of satire which Levine practices calls for a tremendous capacity for indignation and a willingness to deform his targets remorselessly. Oddly enough, corruption and hypocrisy must have a certain fascination for the satirical artist. And Levine brings consummate draftsmanship and a Rembrandtian fascination with light and flesh to the task.

Distortion, then, is among the most necessary artistic devices, playing an especially large role in satiric art as well as in the comic and grotesque. Among classical artists it is used for the refinement and purification of forms, as in Botticelli or Modigliani; among those inclined to Romanticism, it is a means of intensifying the emotional reactions of

WILLIAM GROPPER, *The Senate* (1935). Collection The Museum of Modern Art, New York, gift of A. Conger Goodyear.

an audience. Many artists distort unconsciously because of a deeply personal manner of seeing and executing, or because their feelings toward the subject matter are exceedingly strong. Strong emotions—love or indignation—reduce anyone's capacity to speak clearly and accurately. But objective accuracy

JACK LEVINE, *Welcome Home* (1946). Courtesy The Brooklyn Museum.

is not a goal of Romantic art; passionate expression is. Consequently, if there is any single characteristic which most commonly occurs in association with the style of emotion, it is the liberal employment of distortion. Through distortion, the artist shocks the viewer into a mode of perception different from his habitual manner of seeing. For distortion ensures that emotion rather than the "clear light of reason" will govern the transaction between the art object and the persons who examine it.

Anxiety and Despair

Because men in the twentieth century have known two great wars and live with the knowledge of their possible extermination in a third, it is not surprising that art has expressed their symptoms of fear and occasional feelings of hopelessness. The style of emotion is used to describe man's periodic lapses into depression, his feelings of doubt that the world can ever right itself. Artists, like philosophers, social scientists, and theologians, have sought through their work to explain what is happening to the human species. Some condemn the social or economic conditions which make war possible; others look to the cause within man himself. Some artists do not attempt to explain the sources of their anxiety: Instead they express its consequences. For example, they may create images of struggle and slaughter; they may stress the ugly features of human nature; they may dwell on the persistent failures of civilization: poverty, injustice, and disease. They may fashion works which express the difficulty of practicing love of mankind in our depersonalized society. For such artists, pictorial organization, design, and formal order seem less urgent than the expression of their inner crises.

There is an eloquent artistic tradition of protest against the inhumanity of war itself, from Goya's *Disasters of War* etchings to Picasso's *Guernica*. But beyond that, what might be called the "side effects" of war, or preparation for it, are felt in many unhappy ways and these reveal themselves in visual art. In addition, there is a despairing art which is related only to personal grief or suffering without any apparent social or institutional connection. An example of this type of individual malaise or despair is *The Scream* (1895) by the Norwegian artist Edvard Munch. This painting shows a person on a bridge, hands held to the ears, with the mouth open in what seems to be a drawn out scream or howl. We are uncertain of the age or sex of the person, and we do not know the reason for the grief. There *is* something deathly about the face, as is true of most of the people in pictures by Munch. The silhouettes of two anonymous figures on the bridge suggests the indifference of the world to the private tragedy of the subject. The drawing is very generalized; the lines of sky and harbor seem to be echoes of the cry. Munch used the most economical means to describe what seemed to him the essential suffering and pain of life. He was an inventor of visual symbols for expressing the *inner* anguish of existence.

In sculpture, the figure *Cain* by

Lu Duble (1896–   ) constitutes an *external* image of torment in its extremely agonized portrayal of the biblical personality who murdered his brother. The artist uses a powerful diagonal line to express the agitation of Cain, and distorts the upturned head and out-thrust jaw to keep the diagonal. The work is a good example of the way a dancer would use his body to express the emotions of guilt and remorse. The body becomes the vehicle for externalizing the spiritual condition of its owner. There is very little subtlety in biblical narrative, and consequently this tense and dramatic portrayal seems appropriate to the moral scale of the crime and the character of the biblical account.

The English painter Francis Bacon (1910–   ) presents a frightening image in *Screaming Man*. Whereas the cry in the work by Munch suggests loneliness, suffering, and death, this scream is related to the savagery and pain of civilized life. The figure is in the portrait format, a reasonably well-dressed man sitting in a chair. Our expectations of a

picture in this kind of setting call for a study of character or the revelation of personality in repose. Instead, the connection between man and beast is emphasized. Of course, such a version of man is exceedingly disturbing; it certainly does not seem to tell the *whole* truth about the human condition. And yet Bacon has influenced many artists, even in the United States, where bitterness has not been a notable theme of artistic expression. In the so-called San Francisco school of painting, Richard Diebenkorn and Elmer Bischoff seem to have been particularly influenced by Bacon; outside the West Coast group, Hiram Williams (1917–   ) appears also to be attracted by the Baconian image of man. The blurring of the features and the apparently arrested movement—as in a photograph taken when the subject turns erratically—are characteristic of Bacon's work and to some extent of the work of artists he has influenced. Bacon is not a particularly facile artist; he concentrates instead on the ungraceful creation of images which disturb any

EDVARD MUNCH, *The Scream* (1893), left. Courtesy Nasjonalgalleriet, Oslo.

LU DUBLE, *Cain* (1953), center. Collection of the Whitney Museum of American Art, New York.

Edward Villella, right, in the title role of *The Prodigal Son* (Balanchine-Prokofieff); photo by Martha Swope, courtesy of the New York City Ballet.

FRANCIS BACON, *Screaming Man* (1952), left. Collection Mr. and Mrs. Edwin E. Hokin.

HIRAM WILLIAMS, *Guilty Men* (1958), right. Collection of Mr. and Mrs. Dalton Trumbo, courtesy of Nordness Gallery.

comfortable notions we may have about human dignity.

Rico Lebrun (1900–64) in *Migration to Nowhere* deals with the effects of war by making a macabre dance out of the flight of its crippled victims. The artist's superb draftsmanship and dramatic imagination create a strangely ambiguous reaction in the viewer when we consider the grimness of his subject matter. Through distorted perspective he has emphasized the feet and the idea of flight. The distant and vacant horizon symbolizes the hopelessness of escape or security for these maimed figures, which lose their corporeality as they recede into the picture space. Yet there is a curious grace in their movement, in their billowing garments, in their use of crutches with the apparent skill of

players in a horrible game. Compare them with the figure in a totally different context: *See Hockey at the Garden,* a poster by Martin Glanzman for Madison Square Garden. The similarity of the figures in both works shows how danger, exertion, and grace are fused in the Romantic imagination, no matter what theme is being treated. Lebrun reveals himself as an artist who uses his skill to make a desperate situation bearable by invoking the agility of the maimed, but Bacon finds nothing redeeming in the contemporary image of man; he endeavors to terrify us to the very marrow of our bones.

A subject similar to Lebrun's is treated by Ben Shahn in *Liberation.* But here, as in so much of Shahn's work, the figures are awkward; they seem maimed

RICO LEBRUN, *Migration to Nowhere* (1941). Courtesy Mrs. Rico Lebrun.

MARTIN GLANZMAN, *See Hockey at the Garden* (1951). Courtesy New York Rangers Hockey Club, Madison Square Garden.

BEN SHAHN, *Liberation* (1945). Collection James Thrall Soby; photo, The Museum of Modern Art, New York.

although they are not. Lebrun's figures, on the other hand, are graceful although they are crippled. Irony is a major quality in Shahn's work: The children play in a bombed-out setting; they pursue the normal pleasures of childhood under the most desperate circumstances conceivable. Just as Lebrun "needed" to discover a type of grace in deformity, Shahn gratified his aesthetic interest in texture and design through his slanting treatment of the sky, the leaning building and the painstakingly rendered rubble. But in his drawing of the children—especially of the one full face we see—he has dwelt on hunger and pathos. By examining the children as silhouettes, noticing especially the foreshortening of the legs, we can grasp the full horror of the scene with its suggestions of broken cities and human dismemberment.

The recurrent upheavals in Europe during this century, especially in Germany, have contributed to a characteristic Central European type of artistic anxiety, so well expressed in Expressionism, particularly by Oskar Kokoschka

OSKAR KOKOSCHKA, *Self Portrait* (1913). Collection The Museum of Modern Art, New York, purchase.

(born 1886). His *Self Portrait, 1913* reveals the typical distortions of Expressionist art: the large eyes and hand; gaunt, bony head; agitated paint application; flickering light; and a facial expression hovering between profound sadness and guilt. The hand seems to accuse the artist while his mouth endeavors to say what it is that assails and condemns him. The attenuation of the head and the restless contours of the face heighten the central idea of this work— that a man feels himself to be under a terrible judgment. Some of the same style features which El Greco employed to exalt the spirituality of the Counter-Reformation in the sixteenth century become the means of expressing Kokoschka's anguish and self-doubt in the twentieth.

Perhaps Kokoschka in his self-portrait best expresses the theme of anxiety in modern man without venturing as far as Bacon. His subject remains capable of feeling responsible for, and hence guilty about, the world he lives in. One would find it difficult to attribute such feelings to Bacon's *Screaming Man*. However, the Bacon painting was created in the 1950's and Kokoschka's portrait was executed one year before World War I. Hence, on the evidence of these two works, there has been a considerable moral deterioration in our civilization; but, of course, such evidence is exceedingly incomplete and may reflect only the highly subjective opinions of two atypical observers of human nature in our time. It remains to be seen whether the expression of joy strikes as responsive a chord.

Joy and Celebration

It should not be surprising that the style characteristics which serve to express sadness and anxiety can also be employed to celebrate and to enjoy human experience. In the theater we find comic performers who also have ability as tragedians. Indeed, students of acting believe that great comedians such as Chaplin are masters of their art because they closely approach tragedy and then swerve slightly to avoid it in an obvious way, meanwhile fully expressing the tragic dimensions of life. However, celebration in art is not *directly* related to the comic spirit; it deals rather with life's festive and exultant moments: the overcoming of fear, the consummations of love or ambition; the affirmation of the goodness of being alive.

The indirect connection between celebration and the comic is visible in *Hassidic Dance*, by Max Weber (1881–1961) where we see the members of a mystical Jewish sect who dance and sing to express their religious feelings of joy in the created universe. The dance is meant to be ecstatic, joyous, and genuinely reverent at the same time. And because the men wear high hats and long, somber garments while dancing in a spirit of complete abandon, they create a slightly comic effect. Weber has used twisted forms and a rather loose, sketchy, drawing line to suggest the hectic movement, the shouting, and the not very graceful figures of these enthusiastic men. Much of the appeal of this work derives from the contrast between the plainness of the men, the extreme formality and somberness of their dress, and the excitement and passion with which they throw themselves into the dance.

Using a totally different technique and subject matter, the painter, John Marin (1870–1953) displays a vigorous, uncomplicated approach to the American scene. Marin worked mainly in watercolor, painting landscapes alive with action and even the suggestion of noise. *Sun, Isles and Sea* is characteristic of Marin's use of a few slashing, wet watercolor strokes to suggest panoramic nature: air, sky, sun, water, vegetation, and mountains. Although highly individualistic, Marin was principally influenced by Cubism. He used an abbreviated, notational, straight-line style which may derive ultimately from the carefully hatched planes of Cézanne. His works were carefully composed, although executed vigorously so that they create a "slap-dash" impression. The generous use of the white paper and a rapid, wet brush gives his work considerable sparkle and freshness. Marin's picture is a happy one: He

painted a few sun rays almost as children do. His world is untroubled, full of radiant energy; the movement and noise implied by his bright colors and active brushwork are friendly to man.

Marc Chagall is the chief modern exponent of romantic love. His paintings seem naive because they exhibit an almost childlike belief in the power of love to remove anyone beyond the "here and the now," the world of problems, obligations, and conflict. In *Flying over the Town* a couple floats above a village as if in a fairy tale or a dream. He has been identified with Surrealism because of the fantastic and dreamlike elements in his work, but this label does not seem entirely accurate: He is not interested in shocking the viewer; his work grows out of the folk culture and the Hassidic legends absorbed during his youth in Eastern Europe rather than the theoretical views developed by André Breton and his circle in Paris. He literally illustrates the beliefs of his childhood and his people: that love overcomes physical facts and mystically transports individuals despite the laws

MARC CHAGALL, *Flying over the Town* (1914). Courtesy Mrs. Mark C. Steinberg.

of gravity and aerodynamics. Chagall's work as a designer for the ballet also contributes to his interest in a world of fantasy and romance since the ballet is an art that is much devoted to the rituals of courtship and love. He is a joyous artist because of his unique attitude toward romance: Its erotic aspects are very minor in his paintings although the color is rich, even sensuous. Even his portrayal of the female nude is devoid of suggestions of physical love. Rather, his models appear to be women as conceived by the minds of children. Chagall's distinctive view of love is that it is a joy which people take in each other. It is so intense they are liberated from terrestrial bounds: The world does not exist for them. This is an idea which anyone who has been in love can share, hence the popularity of this artist whose artistic forms are rather eclectic, deriving from Cubism, Orphism, Russian folk art, and, perhaps, individual painters like Redon and Ensor.

Eclecticism, the tendency to employ forms and stylistic devices from a variety of sources in the work of a single artist, is not necessarily a term of disapproval in connection with a personality like Chagall. His originality is essentially poetic and literary, and consists of his very individualistic vision of the world. All artists, of course, borrow in the process of arriving at their distinctive modes of expression. But it is important to recognize that originality of style or execution may seem less urgent to an artist than communicating effectively a certain kind of feeling or idea. The form-language of Chagall is adequate for his theme since his dreamers and lovers are acceptable and credible to the viewer. Very rich color and a type of primitive drawing combined with associations of theatrical sets and lighting are probably the principal devices which encourage us to abandon our logical, "everyday-life" mode of seeing in the presence of his work.

How does architecture deal with the themes of joy and celebration? It is difficult for a building to illustrate dancing or flight since it must, before anything else, solve the problems of stability and safety. Yet the Pavilion for the United States at the World's Fair in Brussels (now destroyed) was a structure with a festive air about it. The architect, Edward Stone (1902–   ), began with a round plan and with general proportions similar to that of a carousel, so that the association with an amusement park was quickly established. Using a large, circular reflecting pool before the building, he strove toward a sense of lightness. A perforated screen as opposed to a solid wall around the core of the building also contributed to the feeling of buoyancy. The columns which supported the shallow roof were as slim as possible. Modern

200

materials and engineering reduce the size of the safety factors architects must use in designing their structures, so their forms need not be as massive as in the past. Generous use of flags around the building, and fountains in the reflecting pool completed the holiday mood of the Pavilion. From the standpoint of the interests of the American government, this was a most effective building, since a World's Fair constitutes an occasion for projecting a favorable image as well as gaining customers for American manufactured goods. Clearly, a "happy" as opposed to a solemn or overdignified building can help overcome the impression of the United States as a colossus interested chiefly in money and power but indifferent to "little" countries and simple pleasures.

Another joyous building using different forms is Ordoñez and Candela's Los Manantiales Restaurant in Xochimilco, Mexico (p. 202). Here the principal engineering device, thin-shelled concrete shaped in the form of dramatic hyperbolic curves on a circular plan, solves the problem of structure and expression brilliantly. The thin-shell structure serves as roof, side wall, and window opening at the same time. While the shell is very strong, its visual effect suggests the delicacy and grace of artful paper folds. In contrast to the mathematical beauty of these curving shapes, the designers use a rugged, rubble masonry foundation and wide, gentle steps to create a powerful horizontal base for the soaring forms above. The large openings are inviting to the persons who approach the building while, for those inside, they create a maximum opportunity for unobstructed vision so that nature and passing events can be enjoyed while eating.

In buildings such as those of Edward Stone and Felix Candela we discover what the art of architecture can mean when it is applied to the solution

EDWARD DURELL STONE, U.S. Pavilion at the Brussels World's Fair (1958). Courtesy Edward Durell Stone.

of unusual problems. For them, it was not a matter of finding a standard, stereotyped or traditional building type and imposing it upon the unique requirements of a specific situation. They did not, to use an often-cited example, use a Greek temple for a twentieth-century bank. Rather, they used modern technology and an understanding of the distinctive problems raised by their respective commissions to create architecture which is technically successful and visually appealing. Without the use of the human figure or other obvious symbols, the inert materials of building, when skillfully organized, can become expressive of the whole range of human emotion. Here we see how architecture can meet the challenge of designing structures to express enjoyment, elegant leisure, lightness, and gaiety without becoming merely frivolous or sensational.

It appears that the choice of joyous or despairing themes in art is not entirely determined by the materials, media, technology, or type of artistic expression. Rather, the attitude of the artist or the influence upon him of some aspect of his culture also governs the ultimate meaning, the emotional content, of his work. We might imagine that architecture, because of its large scale and great cost, would be limited in its range of meaning. And often these factors *do* inhibit the architect. But the vast array of technology also serves to extend his expressive scope. Reinforced concrete, wide expanses of glass, and thin-shelled structures can be employed equally well in the design of sacred buildings, domestic dwellings, or restaurants, and the style of the structure, in each case, will depend on the way these elements are related to each other. However, architecture has mainly tended during the first half of the twentieth century toward classicism and austerity (notwithstanding exceptions like Gaudí, Wright, Stone, and Yamasaki), because powerful factors like mass production of building materials, increasing costs of labor, and the interest of financial groups in safe and predictable results influence designers in the direction of highly rational, stereometric design. The style of emotion, therefore, is most prominent in those art forms (painting, sculpture, and printmaking) which use modern materials and techniques but are not controlled by the huge costs of modern technology.

More recently however, there has been an upsurge of experimentalism in the cinema and in architecture, both of which can be described as art *industries*. The opportunity to carry out daring and costly projects in these art forms suggests that our civilization is entering

JOAQUIN ALVARES ORDONĚZ, architect, and FELIX CANDELA, structural designer, Los Manantiales Restaurant, Xochimilco (1958). Courtesy Felix Candela.

an era when *imagination rather than cost* will be the principal limitation felt by creative artists. And paucity of ideas, poverty of imagination, is an inner rather than an external restraint. But will a wealthier society in which there is a relaxation of economic inhibitions among artists result in significant changes in the themes and styles of art? Will celebration now displace despair? The answer depends on how the creative imagination is influenced by our culture as a whole . . . and art is one of the constituents of the culture.

CHAPTER   SEVEN

As artists become skilled in the manipulation of their materials, they often discover that they can invent forms which were never seen or imagined before. While one artist will not permit his work to stray from what is logical or probable—what is within the realm of common-sense reality— another may enjoy creating entirely new worlds. And most artists possess the skill to make such worlds seem real, however briefly. Ultimately, the creation of fantasies reflects the artist's perception of his role as one who obeys the rules implicit in reality or as one whose mission is to *change* the rules. Either he deliberately creates strange new forms which are logical and credible or he *lets fantastic forms happen,* regarding himself as an instrument that cooperates with the processes of creation in the universe.

From a social standpoint, fantasy is, of course, the prerogative of children since adults are not considered responsible or even entirely sane if they habitually disclose their dreams, much less take them seriously. Artists (and perhaps mathematicians) are among the few adults who seem to have the privilege of openly exhibiting their fantasies without incurring disapproval. Perhaps society indulges artists and mathematicians because it regards them

THE STYLE

OF FANTASY

as fools or madmen, or as children whose active imaginations may be safely encouraged since they have no significant connection with reality. In that case society is mistaken, because every familiar reality in the man-made world almost surely had its origin in someone's fantastic imagination.

It is very likely that architects imagine spaces and shapes which would make wonderful buildings before they think of any practical purpose such buildings might serve. This would be especially true of those architects who have sculptural inclinations (see pp. 434–440, "Constructors and Sculptors"). But even engineers, as Arthur Drexler says, "have subjective, if not actually arbitrary, preferences for certain kinds of shapes."° Painters and sculptors, being even more liberated from practical necessity, can pursue their inner vision wherever it leads without any obligation to "make sense." The important point is that fantasy—the imagination of unreal forms, places, and events—is a universal human trait, and art is the principal means of giving it public expression.

Although children do not have a well-developed ability to distinguish between fantasy and reality, adults do, and therein lies an important feature of the interest which a fantastic style arouses: Our knowledge that a work has little or no basis in objective reality yet can convince us of its authenticity. Art exploits the will-to-fantasy in all men by "improving" on dreams, since

°*Twentieth Century Engineering,* The Museum of Modern Art, 1964.

the artist, by his craft, makes dreams tangible, substantial, and alive.

All man-made realities were once fantasies, but all fantasies do not necessarily become realities. Nor are they intended to. Chagall's people flying through the air are fantastic, but they do not anticipate general diffusion of the gift of levitation. In his case, fantastic imagery represents an emotional state rather than a technical advance in courtship. But some artistic fantasies have utopian implications. The architect who conjures up an ideal but fantastic city may be instrumental in converting dreams into reality, modified from his original conception perhaps, but real and socially useful. In fact, most of the major architects of this century have proposed utopian communities or single structures which in themselves constitute utopian solutions to human problems. City planning, which is largely practiced by architects, might be regarded as the professionalization of the tendency to propose utopias. But the capacity of modern technology combined with human intelligence is so considerable that it is difficult to draw a sharp line between organized, rational planning and utopian fantasy. Certainly, many of the architectural fantasies of the 1920's and '30's are accomplished facts today. Private dreams *can* become public realities.

Some utopian fantasies deal with unreal spaces and flights of structural imagination; others deal with unprecedented personal and social relationships. The *Peaceable Kingdom* by Edward Hicks (1790–1849) is a fantasy based on the biblical description of a world in which natural enemies have learned to live together without conflict and men (exemplified by William Penn

EDWARD HICKS, *Peaceable Kingdom* (c.1848). Collection of the Philadelphia Museum of Art.

and the Indians in the background) negotiate all their affairs harmoniously. The work fits into the category of fantastic art because the world it *realistically* portrays is not the one we live in, yet the meticulous technique of this primitive artist convinces us at least of the intensity with which he holds the ideal of peace. Such works may not succeed in overcoming some of our doubts, but they persuade us that the ideal they embody is real.

Because fantastic art originates in both logical and irrational mental processes, it presents no common set of visual qualities. Fantastic works may be objectively accurate or subjectively distorted, orderly or chaotic, rectilinear or curvilinear. We are justified in speaking of a fantastic *style*, then, only because certain works exhibit a logic based on hallucination, dreams, utopian hopes, and speculative vision. That is why, in the following sections, we will discuss fantastic art in relation to science as well as mythology. So far as art is concerned, science and superstition are equally useful as sources of imagery. The cognitive claims of science afford material for the creation of art in the same manner as the magical practices of shamanism, the prophetic utterances of wise men, the redemptive hopes of religion, or the impersonal logic of geometry. Fantastic art demonstrates that it is very difficult for artists to know where reality ends and imagination begins.

JEAN COCTEAU (director), *Beauty and the Beast.* Stills from The Museum of Modern Art Film Library.

JEAN COCTEAU (director), *Blood of a Poet.* Stills from The Museum of Modern Art Film Library.

Myth

As children we read or listened to mythological narratives and usually accepted them without question: They were entertaining stories and seemed to explain the world in a manner which satisfied our curiosity and was adequate for the state of our knowledge. Subsequently, with increasing sophistication, myths or fairy tales were revealed to us as neither scientifically nor historically true. They remained entertaining as fiction but not as reliable accounts of real events or as accurate explanations of the way phenomena really "work." But some mythic material was not entirely abandoned: It was converted into folk wisdom to be ultimately enshrined in our mental lives in the form of unexamined beliefs and convictions. Officially, we think of myths, fairy tales, and nursery rhymes as the fantastic entertainments of a stage we have left behind; we try to forget that once we regarded them as truthful accounts of nature, man, and the world.

When an artist like Jean Cocteau (1891–1964) presents myth vividly and believably in a film—for example, *Beauty and the Beast* or *Blood of a Poet*—the shock to adult sophistication combined with what remains of our childlike will-to-believe creates an aesthetic experience of enormous impact. For we never completely lose our faith in the power and validity of myth. Folk tales possess the capacity to stir our deepest selves long after we imagine that we are immune to superstition. The great Swedish film director Ingmar Bergman (1918–   ) is fond of creating conflicts between characters representing the scientific, rational mind and the

INGMAR BERGMAN (director), *The Magician*. Stills from Janus Films, Inc.

mythic, poetic, or religious mind. Often, he shows how the opposed tendencies are present in the same person, as in his film *The Magician*, in which a physician ultimately succumbs to fantastic fears—fears to which he felt immune because of his training as a scientist.

Why does myth have the capacity to move us, frighten us, or compel our belief? It is not that myths are true as science defines truth. Rather, myths establish connections with the way our minds grasp reality. Men are not completely civilized, completely rational, or completely evolved from their earlier physical and psychological selves. Myths are truthful accounts of the way men have seen themselves and the world for most of their life on earth, and in that sense of truth, they accurately explain a great deal about the way we think, feel, and behave. Hence, the serious study of myth is an important means of uncovering valuable material about man as he was in former epochs and as he is now.

In visual art, as in life, myth-making goes on continually. Whereas narrative or poetic types of myth-making are employed in literature, the visual arts use plastic fantasy—the invention of strange forms or strange associations of known forms. These fantastic forms may be initially suggested by accidental technical effects, as in the "planned accidents" of Max Ernst (see p. 325), but the fact that they are permitted to stand, or are further enhanced, suggests that the artist is willing to rely on hidden, mysterious sources for the origin and partial determination of his work. Some artists, in other words, believe that the relatively uncontrolled creation of forms will connect their work with the mythic com-

ponents of personality. For them, surrendering to fantasy is not abandoning truth; it is a way of gaining access to *a type of truth*—a type which our civilization does not value very highly but which nevertheless explains a great deal about our inner lives.

One of the best-known fantastic paintings showing the mythic imagination at work is *Hide and Seek* by Pavel Tchelitchew (1898–1957). On first examination the picture is of a tree, then of a hand, a foot, a system of nerves and blood vessels, then of children, babies, and embryos. Everywhere we look in the painting, passages of wet flowing color appear to merge with forms of biological life. The artist's technique is at once loose yet fantastically meticulous and accurate. The blood vessels appear to be illustrations for a medical anatomy, and tiny lights occur throughout to illuminate beautifully the exquisite rendering of an ear, or the place where the veins of a leaf merge with fine capillaries feeding a human embryo.

Of course, children do not grow on trees, and the similarity between a hand and a tree is only superficial. But for the mythic imagination, things that look alike or can be made to look alike, are aspects of the same reality: Men once worshipped trees. Children are the "fruit" of our bodies as is the fruit on a tree. To see the way blood is circulated to feed our bodies both frightens and fascinates us. Our arteries and nervous systems branch out like the limbs of a tree, the fingers of the hand, or the tendons of the foot. But the painting by Tchelitchew is not a treatise on biology or physiology; it *is*, however, a treatise about how the primitive portion of our personality confronts such themes as the life of the unborn, the drama of

PAVEL TCHELITCHEW, *Hide and Seek* (1940–42) [whole and detail]. Collection The Museum of Modern Art, New York, Mrs. Simon Guggenheim Fund.

nourishment, the connection between plants and human beings, the tension between consciousness and unconsciousness, the teeming activity beneath the shell of a living thing.

In this same work, then, different types of imagery and different levels of observation tumble over one another. At once we have *both* the implied comparison between a hand and a tree—a plastic metaphor—and a directly observed and accurate rendition of a human embryo. *Hide and Seek* is thus a prime example of fantastic art which yet retains connections with empirically observed reality. It shows how the mythic imagination uses science and fantasy to deal with themes that are of monumental and absorbing human interest.

Dreams and Hallucinations

Our dreams are further examples of the connection between fantasy and the real world. They appear, however, to lack logical organization after we reflect upon them in the waking state. But while we sleep, they seem very real, sometimes frighteningly so. An artist employing vivid dream material can exploit irrational, disturbing qualities for the purpose of jarring peo-

A Surrealist strategy of surrender to unconscious impulses and hostilities during the act of execution may account for the exaggeration and distortion of figurative forms in this example from the artist's Woman *series.*

WILLEM DE KOONING, *Woman, II* (1952). Collection The Museum of Modern Art, New York, gift of Mrs. John D. Rockefeller, 3rd.; photo, Geoffrey Clements.

If you think a fur-covered cup and saucer is funny, it is probably because the whole idea is so fantastic or revolting that only a humorous response permits it to be tolerated at all.

MERET OPPENHEIM, *Object* (fur-covered cup, saucer, and spoon) (1936). Collection the Museum of Modern Art, New York.

ple out of their habitual modes of perception. Such an art, using a realistic mode of representation, can employ images as they appear to us in dreams or in hallucinations, images similar to those caused, for example, by a high fever. Such an art was Surrealism, which was, and to some extent, persists, as an artistic movement, seeking to shock viewers by the employment of just such a strategy as is outlined above. As a formally organized artistic movement embracing the visual arts and literature, Surrealism is largely spent; but its influence is a permanent part of the creative approach of all artists who wish to make use of it. That is, an artist can deliberately create images which look as if they might have been dreamed; or he may endeavor to recollect his dreams and then represent them accurately; or he may employ the kind of creative strategy which eliminates preparatory plans and anticipation of the final product in favor of seeking to exploit spontaneous impulses during the process of execution. Abstract Expressionism constitutes an entire school of painting which stresses the impulsive and spontaneous character of execution. This school also tends to use the agitated paint quality developed by Central European Expressionism, especially after World War I. Although it does not deal with dreams or with images, Abstract Expressionism does owe to Surrealism the idea of reliance on unplanned or irrational impulses as an organizing principle for the creation of art.

It is easy to see that an artistic strategy which relies on dreams and the irrational and which encourages accidental technical effects would encounter considerable resistance from those who think of art as a planned and reasoned approach to creation. However, it can be argued that even the most rational of artistic approaches employs some kind of intuition, some reliance on sources of imagery hidden mysteriously in the self; otherwise, if artistic planning and execution were entirely a matter of the application of known principles to known objectives, artists could easily be replaced by computers programed by technicians.

In their interest in dreams, the Surrealists were, of course, influenced by Freud. From Freud they learned that dreams are only *seemingly* illogical, that they have important meanings if certain principles of interpretation are known. Not that Surrealist paintings necessarily constitute a puzzle, a collection of symbols requiring of the viewer a key for interpretation. Rather, Surrealism employs fantastic imagery in order to shock the viewer. Shock is believed to have an educational effect in that it obliges the viewer to reorganize his customary habits of perception in the act of experiencing the work. Behind this interest in shock is the conviction that man and society are hopelessly enmeshed in traditional and false modes of thinking and acting. Presumably, fantastic art helps the individual to break away from inherited forms of thought and perception and opens him to the possibility of new kinds of behavior. Oddly enough, Surrealist and fantastic art can be regarded as having an educational purpose: It quite literally seeks to change behavior, a goal which is one of the fundamental objectives of any system of education.

Salvador Dali (1904–) executed *Soft Construction with Boiled Beans: Premonition of Civil War* in 1936 before he abandoned his serious artistic efforts in the interest of using his talent to illustrate the flamboyant aspects of his public personality. In it we see a highly naturalistic technique combined with truncation and distortion of the figure—devices which are characteristic of this painter. He also employs a Caravaggesque system of illumination: strong contrasts of light and shadow plus careful modeling to add to the illusionism of his fantastic forms. The sky and landscape are very conventional and are presented in hues which might be seen in a Technicolor travelogue. This almost banal naturalism increases the shock value of the figurative elements. A small figure in the lower left portion of the picture establishes the monstrous scale of the central subject. We recognize portions of female anatomy, stretched, skeletal forms, and a horrible grimacing head. A supporting element seems to be a tree trunk which merges into a foot. The melting of objects—the manmade into the natural, or the organic into the inorganic—is characteristic of Surrealist art in particular and of fantastic art in general. It is also a feature of dreams where persons and objects turn into something else. It is noteworthy also that in mythology, metamorphosis is a common occurrence—persons and objects change their identity readily. Dali relies a great deal on the portrayal of plump, fleshy forms which he then merges into dessicated forms or into stones, trees, and manufactured objects. He has a characteristic Spanish obsession with death and with love of the land, and to the extent that these concerns are universal, his art possesses the power to hold our interest, notwithstanding our knowledge that these fantasies are highly theatrical, often seeming to be staged more to amaze us

than to express feelings sincerely held by the artist. Dali's literary title, combining an absurd or flippant idea with a serious reference to an historical event, is very much a part of the total work. Thus, the attempt to shock is carried out in the imagery of the work, in the title, and, as the artist's biography reveals, in his behavior as well.

A sculptural fantasy is seen in *Secretary* by Richard Stankiewicz (1922–   ), a work which also contains an element of humor. The torso consists mainly of a cylinder with a typewriter embedded in the abdomen.

SALVADOR DALI, *Soft Construction with Boiled Beans: Premonition of Civil War* (1936). Courtesy Philadelphia Museum of Art; The Louise and Walter Arensberg Collection.

RICHARD STANKIEWICZ, *Secretary* (1953). Collection of Mrs. Martin Cannon, Jr., Charlotte, N.C.; photography by Sandak, Inc.

Advertisement, "A Christmas gift with keys so lively, they can go 115 words a minute." Courtesy Royal Typewriter Company.

Pipe-stem arms seem to operate the typewriter, which is also part of the secretary's body, thus we have absurdity in the incongruous association of the mechanical and the human. A large part of contemporary art deals with the theme of the assimilation of people by machines: Here we see an only slightly human figure as it absorbs a machine into itself and then operates upon its own mechanical innards. Although welded sculpture is now a well-accepted contemporary medium, Stankiewicz was one of the first sculptors to use machine parts which have not completely lost their original identity. Thus, he can manipulate meanings and associations at the same time that he manipulates the physical materials themselves.

This sculptor, like many others engaged in a similar effort, runs the risk that his constructions will rely too heavily on the original meanings of the parts and that the contribution of the artist will not consist of much more than having brought the parts together. The art of *assemblage,* as it has been called, raises interesting problems in aesthetics and criticism revolving around the role of the artist as discoverer of form or as creator of form. Contemporary critical opinion has frequently tended to de-emphasize the necessity of *creating* form and meaning out of anonymous materials, and has been willing to attribute artistic value to works in which the artist's effort has been more nearly akin to that of impressario than craftsman.

A variation of the Stankiewicz fantasy placed at the service of advertising art appears in an illustration for the Royal typewriter. The idea of the typewriter emerging organically from a French horn is at once whimsical and shocking,

so that the viewer's attention is arrested and the chances that he will read the message below are increased. Since the written copy makes no explanation of the incongruous combination of objects above, we assume at first that the purpose of the illustration was mainly to startle and demand attention. In addition, the French horn is a beautiful instrument, the product of elaborate hand craftsmanship. Hence, when we see it presenting the typewriter as if on a pedestal or, if you will, giving birth to the typewriter (which is carefully related to the horn in color and in some of its curvilinear features), we are encouraged to associate the grace and craftsmanship of the horn with the industrially produced commercial machine. Furthermore, the copy assumes that its idea of a beautiful machine has been communicated, hence stresses the speed, ease of operation, and *ruggedness* of the product.

Although the photographic illustration here is sensitive and the typewriter itself has the clean sculptural lines of a work by, say, Arp, the *art* of the advertisement consists of ingeniously assembling images and copy to produce a persuasive total idea: It is effective from a marketing standpoint without introducing qualities which might conflict with those of the product. In the Stankiewicz sculpture, the assembly of incongruous elements serves to heighten the characterization of the secretary, the person who assimilates and is assimilated by, a machine. In the advertisement, on the contrary, the incongruous juxtaposition of elements serves to enrich and intensify our perception of the machine.

One of the great monuments of modern fantastic art is Picasso's etching *Minotauromachy* (1935). The work embodies almost all the elements of fantastic art: myth, dream, history, sex, incongruous juxtaposition, the literal vs. the absurd, shock, and distortion. The artist deals with the Cretan myth of the Minotaur as well as with bullfighting today, and he refers obliquely to the ancient Greek legend in which Jupiter carried off Europa in the guise of a bull. The horse, which carries a sleeping or unconscious female matador, is badly wounded, losing its entrails through its torn belly. But the violence of this scene is viewed calmly by faces of almost classical beauty. A flower girl holds a light against which the minotaur, a symbol of erotic violence and civil chaos, shields himself. Like a dream, the work does not readily lend itself to a simple narrative explanation; yet it makes us symbolically aware of most of the elements of modern European history, and of the recurrence of the same themes in the art of Western Civilization. For a Spaniard like Picasso, the tauromachy, the killing of a bull, is a dramatic reenactment, not only of a pre-Christian sacrifice—possibly a fertility rite—but also of the structure of personal and collective life in the West. In other words, both the myth and the modern spectacle are short, concentrated versions of what our history has been. Picasso employs his Spanish heritage, his fascination with the ritual murder of the bull, his sexual fantasies, and his ideas about the events and outcomes of history to create a work which, as much as any, embodies the meaning of Western Civilization from its Mediterranean origins through Greece to Europe and the modern crises of man. Two years later, the artist created his famous *Guernica* to commemorate one of the most violent events of the Spanish

PABLO PICASSO, *Minotauromachy* (1935). Collection The Museum of Modern Art, New York.

Civil War. He appears to have anticipated this work in 1935, with his *Minotauromachy.*

In *The Dream* by Henri Rousseau (1844–1910), we encounter a particular type of fantastic art, that based on the imagination of an unsophisticated, untrained artist—a so-called primitive

HENRI ROUSSEAU, *The Dream* (1910). Collection The Museum of Modern Art, New York, gift of Nelson A. Rockefeller.

artist—who takes up painting without any formal instruction and, in faithfully reproducing his inner vision, arrives at a curious blend of heightened realism and pure dream. In this gentle work, Rousseau, a retired customs inspector, lovingly portrayed a dream about a nude woman on a couch, mysteriously located in the jungle with its wild animals and birds, exotic natives, and lavish natural growth. Not only is this the dream of the woman in the picture, but also it must be the dream of the artist—naive and mildly erotic at once—in which the wealth of nature is arranged as a benevolent environment in which man can find food on the trees, visual fascination in the natural forms, friend-ship from the animals and natives, and love from the naked woman. The artist achieves a magnificent decorative effect with his painting of foliage and flowers, and although his drawing of the nude is somewhat stiff, he has been able to dramatize her figure and make her credible through his careful modeling and intense illumination. In painting this dream, Rousseau probably painted the universal dream of male adolescence, an achievement made possible by his naivete: He lacked the technique or the desire to conceal the literal presentation of his imaginative vision, and as an adult seriously involved in the art of painting, he labored to give each detail an overwhelming veracity.

Scientific Fantasy

Because the character of our time is so much determined by science and its technological applications, it is not surprising that art uses the common symbols and effects of science and technology. Science raises questions about the nature of outer space and of submicrocosmic matter—questions which fascinate the popular imagination and lead to speculation. Speculation and fantasizing about such questions by nonscientists is part of a natural process of *humanizing* the new concepts which modify our conventional notions of space, time, matter and energy. The characteristically human manner of dealing with events and information which promise to alter our lives and our world radically is to talk about the events, create fantasies and jokes about them, anticipate the changes they may bring, and attempt to adjust our own typical ways of feeling and thinking to the new realities they imply.

Art does not merely illustrate—that is, make visual—the consequences of science and technology. Artists play with, or speculate about, the new principles. They endeavor to discover whether new materials can be harmoniously or expressively employed. They wonder whether physical discoveries about the motion and energy of subatomic particles can or should change the way they think about pictorial composition, the methods and themes of sculpture, artistic conceptions of order, the forms expressive of motion and repose, the relations between container and contained. And although artistic speculation and fantasy does not add to the common fund of knowledge regarded as scientific truth, it *does* add to our fund of humanistic knowledge, that is, about the effects of science on man's personal and social existence.

The Conquest of the Air by Roger de la Fresnaye, which was executed in 1913, seems a relatively tame work of scientific fantasy when compared with the actualities of space exploration today. This painting uses cubistic forms with their geometric-mechanical associations to cope with the intellectual aspects of extraterrestrial travel. A balloon is shown in the distance, the French flag is prominent in the sky, and a sailboat floats at the right. Presumably, the artist wishes to symbolize the connections between sailing and flight and at the same time relate the scientific achievements in space travel to French nationalism. Any association between science and nationalism may seem naive to a world which has seen the international character of science and technology amply demonstrated in two world wars. However, we can regard this work, painted before the first of those wars, as reflecting an optimistic, essentially nineteenth-century attitude toward science, notwithstanding its use of a form language which belongs to the present century.

In the work of Matta (Echaurren), we have a very frank effort to come to terms visually with the world which modern physics has revealed. The foundation provided by Surrealism, particularly its invitation to the artist to surrender to his unconscious and automatic plastic impulses, enables this painter to create a universe of visionary forms. These forms seem to grow out of an interest in the problems of physics —problems such as heat, energy orbits, the motion of subatomic particles, their velocities, collisions, radiation, and brief life spans. However, the

Romantic heritage of Surrealism is present in Matta's rich color as in *Here Sir Fire, Eat,* in which a luminosity similar to Tanguy's moonscapes is visible in the general background (see *Infinite Divisibility* by Yves Tanguy, p. 217), although Tanguy's silvery luminescence gives way here to a more tropical palette, possibly because Matta (1912–   ) is of Chilean origin. As the orbits of the particles become more complex and begin to overlap and combine with one another freely, they seem to describe forms of almost architectural meaning. Some of Matta's paintings are more austerely geometric, but he never totally suppresses the organic in his physical fantasies, so that a biological note, a humanistic idea, is always present. That is, we can sense ocean, air, sunlight, breeze, moonlight, stars, and all their romantic meanings behind the movements of the particles which are so strange and yet so obviously guided by the laws which physics attempts to describe.

ROGER DE LA FRESNAYE, *The Conquest of the Air* (1913). Collection The Museum of Modern Art, New York, Mrs. Simon Guggenheim Fund.

MATTA (Sebastian Antonio Matta Echaurren), *Here Sir Fire, Eat!* (1942), left. Collection James Thrall Soby, photo, The Museum of Modern Art, New York.

HIERONYMUS BOSCH, *Hell* [detail of *The Garden of Delights*] (c.1500), right. El Prado, Madrid.

It should be stressed that Matta does not create models describing the physical properties of the universe. He *does* establish a setting that suggests a model of what might be seen by some superior eye which can translate the mathematical-symbolic formulations of science into visual images. However, such a setting is intended more to encourage the credence of the viewer than to manage physical phenomena with the kind of precision which could claim scientific validity. In short, we are dealing with art, that is, imagination, rather than talented technical illustration. Perhaps the best analogy to Matta's effort can be seen in Hieronymus Bosch's paintings of the fantastic creatures supposed to inhabit Hell. Bosch represented in detailed, credible terms what no one had seen but what everyone speculated about—the tortures of the damned according to then current notions of punishment within the framework of medieval cosmology and theology. Just as medieval and sixteenth-century science and theology found their visual expression (devils, demons, tortures) in the art of Bosch, modern science and speculation about its characters and events (ions, mesons, antimatter, particle collisions) are given visual expression in the fantastic world of Matta.

Fantasy and Illusionism

In connection with the style of objective accuracy, we considered some of the devices used by artists to heighten the realistic or naturalistic impact of their works. Now we shall examine some works which employ traditional and new devices to create fantastic illusions, occasionally substituting the real object for the illusionistic treatment of it.

Infinite Divisibility by the American Surrealist Yves Tanguy (1900–55) employs the naturalistic illumination and modeling we would expect in a conventional painting of still life. Light comes from a single source and causes the strange objects to cast sharp, distinct shadows which obey the laws of perspective as they move toward an infinitely receding horizon. In the distance are glowing light centers as if from strange suns, but their light comes to us through the atmosphere much as sunlight sometimes reaches us on earth—through a cloud haze. The forms of the objects themselves are arresting, appearing to derive from a skeletal system—but whose? They suggest organic origins along with mechanical origins. They also are painted to resemble stones and other geological forms. Yet a machine is distinctly suggested by the geometric arrangement of shapes at the left.

The infinite horizon so much employed by Surrealists helps create the mood of a dream and the sense of silence. The deep space also supports these feelings. And the perspective effects are mainly those of converging lines, diminishing size of objects and shadows, increasing loss of focus in the distance, and sharp, almost photographic focus in the foreground. In Tanguy's work, everything tends to dissolve into a luminous haze in the distance after we have had the opportunity to examine highly detailed and carefully rendered fantastic shapes in the foreground. Since Tanguy's color is usually a silvery gray we can easily associate his imagery with photographic realism.

The effect of this work is not to shock, but rather to induce a calm and serene acceptance of an environment which might be plausible to an astronomer. We can accept this environment, which is so bare of the essentials needed to sustain human existence as we know it, because of its all-pervading atmosphere of emptiness and silence. There is no violence in Tanguy's "lunar" landscape; it seems to exist at a time *after* violence and passion have been spent. There is a sense of stillness, peace, and abstraction from human reality that we might associate with the fate of forms which are no longer alive. We may have here, in other words, a calm, contemporary portrayal of the world as it would appear after we, and everything alive, are dead.

A different kind of illusionism is seen in *The Bride* by Marcel Duchamp (1887–1963). Here we have the convincing representation of geometric solids connected by a kind of mechanical-biological plumbing system. The title assists the effect of Surrealistic irony as it contrasts the romantic-erotic meanings of the bride with a mechanical, quasi-cubist representation of her person. We are shown what might be the interior of a complex mechanical system and are given visual hints of human internal organs, arteries, glands, and so on. The manner of representation is the same as would be employed in illustrating a catalogue for a manufacturer of equipment serving, let us say, a biological or medical laboratory. This theme, executed as a painting in

YVES TANGUY, *Infinite Divisibility* (1942), left. Courtesy Albright-Knox Art Gallery, Buffalo, New York; The Room of Contemporary Art Fund.

MARCEL DUCHAMP, *The Bride* (1912), right. Courtesy Philadelphia Museum of Art; The Louise and Walter Arensberg Collection.

1912, would probably be carried out in three dimensions today.

The illusionistic devices of early Surrealist art relied on discoveries made as early as the Renaissance. However, many contemporary artists, eschewing illusionism, nevertheless pursue a kind of realism by employing the objects themselves which formerly would have been represented through a traditional artistic technique. That is, instead of representing the human figure by forms painted or modeled to appear as if they were hammered, cast, sawed, turned, or stamped, artists now assemble such objects *themselves* to create the figure. An example is seen (p. 218) in *Masculine Presence* (1961) by Jason Seley (1919–   ). The figure here consists of welded automobile bumpers and a grille. The result suggests the muscular and skeletal system of a man, the chromium finish and convex forms of mechanical parts being skilfully employed to achieve an organic effect. A relationship between industrial design and sculpture is implied by this work: The purpose of automobile bumpers, as we know, is to provide a sturdy

JASON SELEY, *Masculine Presence* (1961). Collection The Museum of Modern Art, New York, gift of Dr. and Mrs. Leonard Kornblee; photo, Charles Uht.

MARISOL (Escobar), *The Generals* (1961–62). Courtesy Albright-Knox Art Gallery, Buffalo, New York, gift of Seymour H. Knox.

defense for the easily damaged metal skin of the car. However, over the years, designers have given a variety of curvilinear shapes to the sturdy and serviceable bumper. That is, they have tended to treat it like sculpture, endowing it with the *qualities* of the human figure but avoiding "museum art" representational effects. In reassembling these automobile parts, the artist has located their organic qualities in the setting from which they were originally derived, and where, as sculpture, they appear perhaps more appropriate and authentic.

Marisol (Escobar) (1930–   ) creates a whimsical fantasy, *The Generals,* out of painted wood, plaster, and other common materials. We recognize what appear to be a barrel in the body of the horse and an ordinary table or bench in the legs. This construction moves among several modes of representation and meaning at once: There is a hobbyhorse quality to the whole, particularly in the neck and head; the two Generals seated on the "barrel," in their stiffness and box-like construction, suggest children's soldiers. But their painted faces have the traits of a Byzantine icon. Their boots—symbols of military command—are painted on the side of the barrel just as a uniform might be painted on a child's wooden soldier. Hence it is difficult to take their generalship seriously, notwithstanding the somber mein of their painted portraits. And for an heroic equestrian statue, the horse will not do.

The illusionism of these latter two works lies in the employment of "real" materials or of materials we normally associate with other real con-texts. The artist is the beneficiary of all the conventional associations we make with the objects he uses. His illusions are not of the "fool-the-eye" variety; no particular craftsmanship is required to mount boxes on a barrel, and with some visual hints, it is easy to imagine them as soldiers on horseback. The art here consists in using the viewer's *knowledge* that boxes are being represented as generals or that an automobile grille is a man's abdomen. Our *knowledge* that a horse's legs represented by table legs will not, therefore, carry the generals into any battle, constitutes the distinctive aesthetic material of this kind of artistic effort. In conventional illusionistic sculpture, the artist labored to convince viewers that bronze or stone was in fact muscle and sinew, and hence we could briefly disbelieve in the inertia of these materials. By his craftsmanship, the traditional artist "persuaded" paint, clay, or stone to look like flesh or cloth, for example. But the contemporary artist is more inclined to employ real objects or materials along with illusionistic fragments (as in the painted portraits of the Generals) to create several levels of reality in a single work. Thus, an artist "plays with" the viewer's frame of reference, offering cues to reality at first, second, and third hand. The result can be a disorientation in our perception, leading to the possibility of discovering new meanings in the reality of commonplace things. Fantastic art, then, through the manipulation of illusion and reality, moves beyond shock and disorientation of the senses to the creation of opportunities for new perceptions of the real world.

PART THREE

THE STRUCTURE

OF ART

When as children we learned to talk, we tried almost from the beginning to express ideas, desires, and feelings. Adults may have helped us to pronounce words. But they did not provide us with definitions of nouns, verbs, adjectives, and adverbs and then ask us to put them together to make language. We learned somehow to talk and to understand at the same time, and through trial and error, through successful or meaningful reactions to our speech, we learned to understand and use the language. It was not until some time later that teachers dissected the language for us, broke it down into its parts of speech and rules of usage. Before that, without knowing the rules, we had managed to convey and to understand meaning. Only when we grew older did we discover, like Molière's *Bourgeois Gentilhomme*, that we had been speaking prose all our lives.

So far in this book we have examined works of art comprehensively and have tried to understand them in terms of their functions and their styles. Such meaning as we have discovered has resulted first from seeing the art object *as a whole*. Later we may have looked within the object, into its parts, to find clues to its operation and purpose. But the meaning of the parts of a work of art is always governed by its meaning as a totality: In art, *the whole is greater than the sum of its parts*.

Now we are about to embark upon a study of the *structure* of art. Sometimes, art is compared to a language, a visual language, which one learns to understand by studying how it is put together. But, as has been observed above, we first learned our spoken language as a whole *and then* were taught parts of speech, rules of usage, and the rest. Without knowing the definition of some noun or verb, we derived its meaning in particular contexts from the way people used it and reacted to our own speech. Consequently, it would appear that studying the *construction* of language or of art is not absolutely necessary for the apprehension of meaning. There must be some other good reason for studying the parts and structure of linguistic or artistic forms, or the effort might well be abandoned.

The point of view taken here is that the parts and organizational devices of a language have meanings of their own and are worth studying for their own sake. Words and techniques for putting them together poetically have inherent interest and beauty quite apart from the comprehensive meaning of the poem. The values generated by word combinations in a poem or the organization of visual elements in a work of art are called formal or syntactical values, and they constitute an additional source of satisfaction and pleasure. Hence, my discussion of the elements and organization of art is an effort to draw your attention as a viewer to additional sources of aesthetic pleasure and meaning.

There is another reason for approaching the study of art by examining its fundamental units first and then proceeding to the way they are organized and perceived: Works of art are created step-by-step and part-by-part. They do not spring into existence as finished wholes; it is doubtful that artists initially conceive of the finished work and then go on to execute its parts methodically. An artist may have a vague idea of what he is seeking at the outset, but he improvises, modifies, or even totally changes his original objective before he is done. He is guided by goals, but the goals change as he works. We might say that the changing goals of the artist during the process of execution give *aesthetic form* to his use of materials. Otherwise the creative act would be mere manipulation, mere play. By studying the structure of art, we may not learn to be artists ourselves, but we can learn something about *the decisions* the artist makes in the light of his formal objectives.

The experience of art is not based entirely on what is objectively, physically present in an art object. Even if viewers could agree on the objective existence of a red circle in a particular painting, its meaning would vary to some degree according to the personality of each observer and to a large degree in relation to his habits of seeing, his perception. Some works of art are deliberately created with the expectation that the viewer's perception, his act of seeing, will play a role in the meaning of the whole work. Such works are incomplete without the perceptual contribution of the viewer. Accordingly, we shall look into aesthetic perception as a constituent of the structure of art. We are primarily interested in perception not as physiologists and psychologists study it (although their researches are helpful) but as artists manipulate it. Painters, for example, may not understand color as physicists do, but they use it to affect the way people see their pictures. And we, in turn, try to discover what the painter seems to have done with our perception of color to complete his picture.

If our study of structure is carried out properly we should learn three things: (1) the nature of the constituents, or the elements of visual art, (2) the way these elements are organized, the so-called principles of design; and (3) the way people see and respond to what has been organized, that is, the viewer's contribution.

CHAPTER   EIGHT

People see images not things. The sensations of light falling on the retina are transmitted as energy impulses to the brain where they are almost simultaneously translated into a meaningful entity called an image. Not that there is a picture, an optical projection, in the brain itself. The optical processes are in the eye, of course. But perception is a function of the mind. We cannot experience sensation without characterizing it in some way, giving it a label, loading it with meaning. An image, therefore, can be defined for our purposes as *the result of endowing optical sensations with meaning.*

For practical purposes, the common images in our lives have labels like house, tree, boy, and sky. But we can train our perception to identify the constituents, the elements, of ordinary images. That is, we can learn to focus our attention on the shape, color, texture, light-and-dark which are parts of images. In fact, when we focus our attention on *part* of an image—its shape, for example—that part, that element, *becomes* the image because it becomes the meaningful locus of our interest.

Artists working in all media and styles have trained their perception so that they not only see the images common to us all, but also can readily shift gears to see in terms of contrast, brightness, line, and space. Their practice of

THE VISUAL ELEMENTS:

GRAMMAR

fashioning images for others to see has accustomed them to think in terms of image constituents, the visual elements.

We are concerned, of course, with the visual elements of works of art: lines, shapes, and textures as they are employed by artists. After we have learned to see them in art, we may discover these same constituents in nature, although, obviously, no artist is responsible for the texture of trees or the linear properties of the veins in a leaf. To see the visual elements of art in the natural world is to project upon nature certain acquired habits of perception which we find pleasurable or useful. Consequently, one of the indirect dividends of studying art in general and the structure of art in particular is the added satisfaction we can get in ordinary perception of the world outside art.

When art was largely naturalistic, before the abstract and nonobjective became the central tendencies of painting and sculpture, the visual elements received little attention. Traditional painting and sculpture were studied mainly in terms of their literary meanings, their narrative values, and the sentiments and emotions they aroused in viewers. Architecture and applied art were subjected at times to formal and structural analysis because of their nonrepresentational character. But even so, proportions, shapes, spatial properties, and dominant forms received less attention than the allegorical figures and naturalistic ornaments applied to the basic structures. However, with the advent and increase of abstraction, it became necessary to find a language which is common to all modes of visual expression.

The labels used to designate the visual elements tend to vary according to the user, but what the labels denote in the art object is uniform. It does not matter greatly if one authority uses "form," another "contour," and a third "shape." These terms are common and clear; and in any case they are defined by the context in which they occur. Such synonyms are used fairly interchangeably, but precisely, in this book. What is important, however, is that you, the viewer, *understand* the real properties of the structure of art which these several words designate.

The discussion of the visual elements which follows does not constitute a grammar or set of rules which artists follow or disobey at their peril. Rather, I have tried to present a visual grammar based on artistic *usage*—a *functional* explanation of the visual elements.

Line

There is a difference between *a* line and line-in-general. A line, of course, is the path made by a pointed instrument: a pen, a pencil, a crayon, a stick. In geometry, a line is "an infinite series of points." This definition calls attention to a line as a dynamic entity; a line implies action because action was necessary to create it. Line-in-general can also mean direction, orientation, motion, and energy. The effect of movement may be achieved by a series of shapes, none of which is thin, sharp, or linear, but all of which collectively imply a direction. In other words, *a* line is an actual mark made by a sharp, moving instrument, whereas line-in-general is the result of a conclusion by the viewer that forms have an orientation, a direction. For the most part, we shall be talking here about *a* line, the sharp, definite series of points.

Because we all have used lines to write, to make marks in the sand, in dirt, or on sidewalks, we know that muscular exertion is required and that choice has to be exercised about where the line will go. In learning to write we discovered that making "wrong" lines resulted in letters or words which could not be understood. Since line forces an individual to commit himself, there are, from a certain standpoint, right and wrong lines. A "wrong" line is one we cannot control sufficiently to achieve our intent or it is the result of incorrect knowledge. In writing, a convention about what letter forms should look like, together with the muscular coordination of the writer, produces linear structures that others can read. Thus, among our earliest personal experiences with line was the effort to use it "correctly" so that others could understand what we had written. In attempting to draw, we wanted to exercise a similar control over line so that others would see the resemblance between our lines and visual reality. Therefore, the idea that there is a linear convention, an agreement about how lines communicate information, was established early in our lives.

We did not know the *basis* for the agreement about combinations of line standing for certain sounds and images, but we used the conventions and they worked. Line combinations acquired magical properties: A circle could be a letter, a ball, the sun, a face, the world.

PABLO PICASSO, *Guernica* (1937) [details]. On extended loan to The Museum of Modern Art, New York, from the artist, M. Picasso.

Line was thus alive with possibility, potent with meaning. In art, however, the agreements about the meaning of line operate differently from those in writing. The artist *goes behind* the conventions of writing to the magical-symbolic origins of linear properties. Indeed, the artistic employment of line, when it is very expressive and widely approved, can become the basis of new linear conventions which people recognize and understand almost immediately. This would seem to be the case with Picasso's linear formulations of the crying woman and the horse's head in *Guernica*.

THE MEANINGS OF LINE

We know that our present phonetic letters grew out of a pictographic language, letter forms being derived from pictures of oxen, ram's horns, the sun, people, agricultural tools, and so on. Over the centuries, pictographic symbols became increasingly abstract, and in alphabets have come to stand almost solely for sounds, although in China and Japan they continue to designate words and ideas nonphonetically. Although our Western letter forms may have lost their descriptive-pictorial function, we still recognize the relation of certain line combinations to fundamental material conditions. Vertical lines look like trees in a windless landscape. They also look like erect men as opposed to running men, falling men, sleeping men, or dead men. Obviously, verticality stands for lack of movement, and for life as opposed to death. The meaning of verticals can be extended, depending on context, to include dignity, resistance to change, timelessness, and so on. All the meanings are based ultimately on the fact that man is an erect, two-legged creature, who through the millenia of his evolution has developed reactions to verticality which are now part of his so-called human nature. It is doubtful that insects or fish or other creatures older than man, would have similar reactions to verticality. If man's age-long associate, the dog, speculates about these matters, he must interpret verticality in some unique dog-like way, since he is himself a horizontal creature.

The associations with horizontal lines are betrayed, of course, in the word itself. The mountain rising abruptly from a plain may be a dramatic focal point in the uninterrupted horizon: It is also an obstruction to unimpeded movement as represented by the horizon. Turbulent wave forms break up the horizontality, the *calm*, of the sea. They are also the probable origin in nature for many of the artistic forms employed in Romantic art to symbolize tempestuousness, *sturm und drang*. At six or seven years of age, children begin to employ a "base line" in their drawings— a horizontal line at the bottom of the sheet which stands for the ground plane we walk upon, and, in a cosmological sense, for the *foundation* of the world or the basis of civilization.

The combination of vertical and horizontal lines provides us with the right angle, which is the whole basis of the art of some men—Mondrian, Burgoyne Diller, Mies, and many others. The absolute, precise, right angle introduces the man-made element into the natural world of irregular and approximate forms. Two verticals connected by a horizontal at the top stand for two posts and a lintel, or beam, hence, a doorway, a house, a building, and so a solid, safe place. To the simple balance of the verticals is added the constructive horizontal member; thus, man builds, putting things together so they will stand. A single vertical might be blown or pushed down; connected horizontally to other verticals, it has a better chance to remain upright. Note the stability of the letter H.

When applied to the human figure, the horizontal calm of the ocean, land, or sky means sleep or death, but death understood as the absence of strife, as man at one with mother earth. Danger is associated with diagonal lines—suggestive of man or the structures he has built *falling* to earth. Just as the right angle suggests stability, the diagonal suggests instability, loss of balance, uncontrolled motion. The two-legged creature fears a physical fall and in his religions translates that movement into a symbol for a moral fall. Only when the diagonal forms a triangle resting on its base (△) or when it connects the corners of a rectangle (▱) can it be regarded as safe. In the latter it forms a truss, strengthening the rectangle against any force that would make it an unstable parallelogram (▱). To these engineering associations of man the builder, we can add the catastrophic meanings seen in lightning, a jagged, diagonal line (⚡). Splits and cracks in stone or wood also often take a jagged, diagonal path. Hence, in man's tools and in nature, these lines symbolize breakdown and destruction.

Circular, ovoid, and curved lines are exceedingly complex in their meaning because they are less definite, predictable, or measurable than straight lines. These qualities alone are enough to connect them with femininity. Since so many of the meanings of lines derive from the human figure, it is obvious that curves describe the fleshier portions

Helical Chambered Nautilus shell.
Photo, H. Rinehart.

of the anatomy. Circular lines, then, are inevitably associated by men with the female bodily attributes which arouse their erotic interest and which are related to procreation and nurture. Because of what feminists regard as tyranny, these essentially masculine interpretations of curvilinear forms are shared in the main by both sexes. That is why rounded hills in nature or in art are rarely compared to a man's shoulders. On the other hand, active and inactive volcanos—Vesuvius, for instance—bear male appelations and male roles in folklore.

Curved lines also suggest the motion of certain natural phenomena. Light rays, of course, travel only in straight lines, but water flows *around* objects. Thus, we speak of curved lines as *fluid* lines. Bodies of water contain eddies and whirlpools, or spirals and concentric circles. The human ear, too, is shaped like a helix, or spiral. So also is the ram's horn, the volutes of Ionic column capitals, and snail shells. When children are born they still maintain a spiral position; in some primitive cultures, therefore, spiral designs on amulets are considered effective in promoting female fertility. Women living in modern, mechanized cultures also wear spiral-formed jewelry, but doubtless they are unaware of the fertility implications. For our society, such forms probably resemble coil springs which are useful in watches, instruments our sophisticates have been taught to associate with Salvador Dali's painting *The Persistence of Memory*.

This discussion of line had led inevitably to a discussion of linear symbolic forms. We have mentioned only a few of the many meanings associated with these basic linear forms. The meaning and function of the visual elements vary greatly according to the context provided by an artist in specific works. The combination of angles and curves with shape, texture, and color complicates the situation immensely. Now I shall examine a few works, paying principal attention to the operation of their linear elements. But it should be plain from the discussion above that no matter how finely we dissect a work of art, we can never arrive at a line which is meaningless, purely itself, and nothing more. The problem is rather one of selecting the best meaning among the many meanings which are possible.

USES OF LINE IN WORKS OF ART

For a demonstration of line employed simply, powerfully, and accurately, let us turn to Picasso's drawing of the ballet impressarios *Diaghilev and Selisburg*. The artist who has given the world so many truncated and distorted images of the figure here shows his mastery of drawing as it was understood by the academic art tradition. But he goes beyond a simple display of representational skill, and, dispensing with light-and-dark modeling, uses line darkened or accented by varying pencil pressure to describe the volume and movement of the forms within. The lack of shading imparts a classical elegance to these already elegant, fashionable, and well-fed gentlemen. The hands of M. Selisburg constitute a set of complex, foreshortened, intermeshed forms and together with his fleshy face are executed with a line of dazzling precision and simplicity. Even in a naturalistic vein, Picasso knows how to use the power of abstract forms—underlying ovals, cones and cylinders—to strengthen the work. In this

PABLO PICASSO, *Diaghilev and Selisburg* (1919). Collection of the artist; photo, The Museum of Modern Art, New York.

JOSEF ALBERS, *Aquarium* (1934). Courtesy Philadelphia Museum of Art, Print Club Permanent Collection.

PAUL KLEE, *Family Walk* (1930), left. © Cosmopress and SPADEM 1966 by French Reproduction Rights, Inc.; photo, Kunstmuseum Bern.

PAUL KLEE, *Flight from Oneself* (1931), right. © Cosmopress and SPADEM 1966 by French Reproduction Rights, Inc.; photo, Kunstmuseum Bern.

case, the tilted bowler hat on Selisburg enhances the characterization of the face, just as the angular lines of Diaghilev's top hat help cancel the bulbous effect of a second chin.

Josef Albers (1888–   ), known for his many variations of "homage" to the square, has created an ovoid composition within a rectangle in his woodcut *Aquarium* (1934). This work shows line produced indirectly—at the edges where flat, contrasting areas meet. The artist uses line and shape here to play with the viewer's perception: One sees alternately the *lines* created by the juxtaposed forms and the *shapes* contained by the ovoid lines. He opposes vertical ovals, at the left, to large horizontal ovals center and right. Negative shapes —that is, shapes of non-solids—and positive shapes exchange places. We can even "see" a fairly naturalistic fish if we try. The thickened black bar along the top defines the water surface, thus locating the figure as a floating form in the white rectangular space below, which then becomes water. The artist has even managed to balance out two white triangles by having them point in opposite directions. Finally, the refusal of the figure-and-ground relationships to resolve themselves may be regarded by the viewer as a brilliant visual device for making the fish "swim."

The idea of a line going on a journey is best expressed in the work of Paul Klee (1879–1940). He continuously reminds us that line can be used not only to describe the shapes of things, as in conventional drawing, but also to call attention to the act of making the line itself. He indulges in a type of metaphysical wit, creating illusions of reality with his drawn lines and then employing some device to let the viewer know he has been briefly deceived about the existence of an image. Actually, Klee lets the viewer in on a private joke: The artist is not too sure whether the image he draws is "out there," somewhere inside him, or created by unseen hands. Thus, the play between the objectivity and the subjectivity of Klee's images becomes the real image the viewer sees. *Family Walk* is a typical example of Klee's wit which illustrates our discussion of line perfectly. In this abstract performance, a few geometric figures and lines are sufficient to describe the characters, suggest their procession, evoke the family associations, and carry off the artistic point that reality can be described eloquently with line combinations which embody the structure and movement but not the *appearance* of people. In *Flight from Oneself,* Klee attempts a more serious and penetrating study: a visualization of alienation, or split personality. At first the repeated gestures appear to be decorative in purpose until we realize they represent the dual aspects of a single soul. The meandering line, apparently a disciplined scribble, turns out to be sufficiently controlled to repeat itself exactly in different scale. The figures are separate but joined, made of something like string and attached to each other by the same "string" which accounts for their being. Klee, with great economy, can portray the reality of the psyche and the illusory character of the body at the same time. His magical way with lines, his play with levels of reality, has been imitated for comic effect by Saul Steinberg (1914–   ), although in the cartoon, entertainment is the primary objective. No one has approached Klee in the originality of his linear invention. And as a metaphysician who "happens to be" an artist, he ought to be ranked, perhaps, with professional philosophers who specialize in that branch of their discipline.

Line employed as in a map is shown in a *Drawing in Color* by the Belgian artist Corneille (Cornelis van Beverloo). The work can also be regarded as an aerial view of the varying densities of a populated area seen from a plane as it travels from the countryside to the

CORNEILLE (Cornelis van Beverloo), *Drawing in Color* (1955). Courtesy the artist.

tangled core of the city. It is not a real map; rather it exploits and imitates the linear *qualities* of real maps. There are some black blots which, in a genuine map, might stand for bodies of water but which here function as do the knots in Jackson Pollock's paintings, as places where things get "tied up." Notice that the freer lines are ungraceful, their movement hesitant and awkward; in places they are childlike. The open blocks do not have the rhythmic, undulating qualities of nature; they look like lots which formerly had buildings which have been torn down, while the neighboring areas await further "clearance." The awkward, scratchy line accompanied by blots here and there is an expressive comparison between bad pen-writing and the urban experience. To make the metaphor more specific, the artist is probably referring to one of the old steel pens, rather than one of the modern, smoothly gliding ballpoints which write so efficiently under water.

The drawing line occurs in sculpture, too, except that it moves in three rather than two dimensions. A good illustration is a humorous little work, *The Hostess,* by Alexander Calder. The penetration of formerly solid sculptural forms has encouraged linear tendencies, especially in welded sculpture, since iron and steel obviously can be employed in

JACKSON POLLOCK, *Number 1* (1948) [detail]. Collection The Museum of Modern Art, New York.

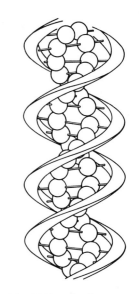

Model of the DNA molecule.

ways foreign to clay and stone. One of the first modern sculptors to exploit the linear properties of iron was Julio Gonzalez (1872–1942) who, logically enough, grew out of the rich Spanish tradition of decorative ironwork. His association with Picasso and Brancusi contributed to his adoption and personal assimilation of the form-language of modernism. In *Maternity* (1933), he used iron rods and a late-Cubist approach to the figure to create an aloof, stately, monumentally dignified version of a woman. The converging lines, which meet at the waist and at the head, represent the gathered folds of the skirt and her hair yet create just enough density to suggest the corporeality of the body. This sculpture eliminates a great deal, arriving at form by implication rather than addition of appendages. Squint your eyes in looking at the sculpture to gain some idea of the masses which are so sparingly suggested by the sweeping lines of the rods and the cage-like structure of the skirt.

A recent, more attenuated sculpture which builds on the pioneer work of Gonzalez is *Organic Form* (1951) by Joseph Goto (1916–). Its symmetrical and delicate treatment of figurative forms carries the work to the edge of architecture, suggesting the linear tracery of a Gothic church spire. The fact that line is versatile aids the sculptor: He can use it as a drawing line, describing the contours of objective forms; or he can use it as the skeletal framework upon which a skin may or may not later be placed. Because line is precise and unambiguous in character, it well expresses "systems"—the nervous system, the skeletal system, wiring diagrams, maps and charts, even the structure of life itself, as in a two-dimensional model of the DNA molecule which carries genetic information in the cell. Line gives us a map of life's secret.

The linear character of early American cooking accessories made of wrought iron derives from utilitarian considerations and the nature of the material itself. Some of the forms are not unlike those of Gonzalez and are strongly suggestive of the anthropomorphic candlesticks also made in colonial America. The late David Smith (1906–65) plays a geometric game with eating utensils and tableware in *The Banquet*, using line to stand for the objects and also to locate them in relation to each other on the table. A biomorphic work by Smith employing a dominant horizontal line is his *Royal Bird*, made of steel, bronze, and stainless steel. Here as in Theodore Roszak's *Spectre of Kitty Hawk* (p. 189), visual metaphors of the bird's skeleton are used as the primary sculptural forms. The calm associated with horizontals, however, is counteracted by the fierce beak-and-jaw construction, the spikes darting out from the head, and what we know to be the aggressive stance of a fighting bird. The linear pattern of the rib-cage, when translated into metal, suggests the intricate armor of medieval knights more than Thanksgiving leftovers. But if we can suppress our associations with the bird and see the horizontal pattern primarily as a cursive script with fascinating contrapuntal angles and curves, we can almost read the construction as a kind of metal calligraphy. There is no question that David Smith has been strongly influenced by the written line in his sculpture. In one sculptural landscape, he drew within space—blending descriptions of hills, rocks, and clouds with a mysterious, metallic penmanship.

Contrasting attitudes of the artist toward line can be seen in the *Nude* (*face partly showing*) (1914) by Matisse

Ironwork cooking accessories. Courtesy Henry Francis du Pont Winterthur Museum.

Eighteenth-century iron candlestand and rushlight holders, above top. Courtesy The Art Institute of Chicago.

DAVID SMITH, *The Banquet* (1951), above bottom. Collection Governor Nelson A. Rockefeller.

DAVID SMITH, *Royal Bird* (1948), below. Collection Walker Art Center, Minneapolis.

HENRI MATISSE, *Nude (face partly showing)* (1914), above left. Collection The Museum of Modern Art, New York, Frank Crowninshield Fund.

FERNAND LÉGER, *Big Julie (La Grande Julie)* (1945), above right. Collection The Museum of Modern Art, New York, acquired through the Lillie P. Bliss bequest.

PAUL KLEE, *And I Shall Say* (1934), below left. © Cosmopress and SPADEM 1966 by French Reproduction Rights, Inc.; photo, Kunstmuseum Bern.

WILLIAM STEIG, *No One Is Exactly Like Anyone Else* (1944), below right. Courtesy the artist.

and *La Grande Julie* (1945) by Fernand Léger (1881–1955). The line which Matisse uses is firm, knowledgeable, and confident: While using it to represent the swelling curves of the figure, he does not lose sight of its independently abstract quality. It is both a drawing line and an ornamental arabesque. In the hand, he abandons a strict naturalism in favor of a semiabstract shape; he was apparently tempted by the sculptural possibilities of the hand and forearm thrust toward the viewer. Happily, the

empty space in the left half of the print adequately balances the weight and thrust of the forms in the right half. Léger, in his painting of 1945, employs a heavy, mechanical line of unvarying weight and antinaturalistic intent throughout. Julie is perhaps a symbol of mechanized young womanhood, a bicyclist who has created a new Christ out of sprockets, wheels, gears, and handlebars. In place of the sensuous and sophisticated linearity of Matisse we are given blatant color, stark contrasts of light and dark, and a rigid line which could be made of cable. It is difficult to say whether Léger means simply to indict mechanization or whether, in his flight from sensitivity and sentiment, he is trying to prepare the way for a new world with a tough-minded, uncompromising presentation of the impending female type as she really is. The painting is concerned more with the description of an idea than of an image; it has only an apparent relation to visual reality. Even its superficial rigidity is deceptive. It is not Julie who is rigid, mechanical and depersonalized but the *idea* she symbolizes.

A use of line by Klee which is difficult to place in any neat category appears in his drawing *And I Shall Say* (1934). The torso seems to have been executed with a slightly directed scribble. The hands and feet are good imitations of drawing by children. But the head could only have been done by a skillful draftsman. He has united all three modes of drawing in a single, psychologically convincing characterization. Once again we see the prototype of an approach to the visualization of personality employed by contemporary "cartoonists" like William Steig and Abner Dean. But they are more literal than Klee in the portrayal of the "psycho-pathology of everyday life." Beyond the cryptic title, which laconically describes a practice we are all familiar with, Klee relies on linear invention to do the job for him. The figure's position, the device for showing the eyes directed inward, the immaturity of the hands, the uncertainty of the body—all combine to describe a person confidently but pathetically wrapped in her fantasy. Her mouth is closed, her mind is speaking. She listens to herself making reply in an imaginary dialogue. The work is truly modern in that it is totally original, has a twentieth-century type of psychological understanding, and, like most masterpieces, it is remarkably economical.

Line is perhaps the most crucial of the visual elements. The reasons for this decisiveness might be summarized as follows: (1) Line is familiar to everyone because of our almost universal experience with writing and drawing. (2) Line in itself is not indefinite (although its windings and patterning may be infinitely complex); it is precise and unambiguous. It commits the artist to a specific statement. (3) Line conveys meaning through its identification with fundamental natural phenomena. (4) Line leads the viewer's eye and involves him in its "destiny." (5) Line permits us to do with our eyes what we did as children in getting to "know" objects: We handled them and felt their contours. By handling an object we trace its out*lines*, in effect, with our fingers. In our growth toward maturity, the outlines of objects became more important for identification than their color, size, or texture.

Shape, which is an extension of line, seems to take priority over color and texture in our perception of visual phenomena. Hence, we shall devote the next section to an examination of shape as one of the visual elements.

STUART DAVIS, *Composition No. 5* (1934). Collection The Museum of Modern Art, New York, gift of Abby Aldrich Rockefeller.

Shape

According to the purist philosopher in Molière's play *The Forced Marriage*, form is "the outward physical manifestation of an animate object" whereas shape is "the outward physical manifestation of an *inanimate* object." One speaks of the *shape* of a hat, not its form. One speaks of the *form* of a lady, but reference to her shape is not quite proper. Clearly, the difference between form and shape hinges on whether the object is alive or not. For art, such distinctions are much too fine; in fact, they may constitute distinctions without a difference; the terms have been used here interchangeably. We are interested in shape *or* form as one of the visual elements and the manner of its operation in works of art.

Our discussion of line necessarily touched on shape since closed lines become the boundaries of shapes, such as triangles or circles. But shapes can be created without lines, as when a painter establishes an area of color or a sculptor creates a three-dimensional volume. Drawn lines need not be used in either case. The resultant shapes may have *linear* quality if our attention is drawn to their boundaries; but these contours usually have the effect of making us aware of the *shape*, that is, they present the silhouette of the area or space they enclose. We may, if we wish, think of *shape* merely as an extension of *line,* but that would be a quibble about categories. The important point is that shape is something we perceive, something which has meaning, something which operates structurally within art objects.

The shapes which artists create have a wide variety of sources: Some are directly drawn from nature or the man-made world; others reflect the characteristic mark of the tool used to create them; there are also shapes which do not apparently occur in nature or the manufactured environment but are "invented" by the artist. However, a viewer cannot help seeing these shapes— no matter how abstract—in terms of his experience with reality. That is, he cannot see a triangle without regarding its corners as "sharp" and hence related, however remotely, to something which has a point, which can puncture, which is potentially dangerous. This does not mean that triangles are necessarily dangerous. A triangle resting on its base also suggests stability, like a football lineman crouched in a three-point stance. The meaning and operation of a triangular shape ultimately depend on which of the potential properties of a triangle the artist chooses to emphasize. If an artist uses a triangular shape to describe or embody something which in life is ovoid or curved, his departure from the expected provides an important clue to the meaning of the work as a whole. Why does the horse's tongue in Picasso's *Guernica* come to a sharp, dagger-like point?

Let us examine some of the fundamental shapes which occur in art or in reality and summarize their most obvious and common properties. We shall find, in examining specific works, that the artist often endeavors to *redefine* the conventional properties of shape through his total organization of the visual elements. His efforts always take place, however, within the context of broad, common experience with the properties of shapes as we encounter them in life.

Leonardo was supposed to have been able to draw a perfect circle freehand—that is, without any aid or tool. But whenever we encounter any perfect geometric shape, we are inclined to believe it was not made by hand. Perfect straightness or absolutely regular curvature in visual phenomena imply a mechanical origin. Recall that the characteristic beauty of machine-made objects, as opposed to handcraft, lies in their geometric precision and regularity of form. Irregularity and variation of shape characterize hand-made forms. Hence, when we perceive works of art which contain shapes that appear to have been produced with a straight-edge and compass curves, even though the artist has used his hands and hand tools to create such forms, we "read" them as mechanical forms. Machine forms, we realize, do not grow as natural objects do, but are the result of human planning and design, activities which are essentially intellectual. Consequently, geometric shapes possess cerebral qualities, since, like mathematics, they appear to be pure products of the intellect. Geometry can be found in nature, of course, especially in the microscopic examination of crystals and snow flakes, and even in certain geological formations, but nature confronts the unaided eye overwhelmingly in the form of irregular, assymmetrical, uneven shapes.

PABLO PICASSO, *Guernica* (1937) [detail]. On extended loan to The Museum of Modern Art, New York, from the artist, M. Picasso.

Our own bodies and the bodies of animals are a source of the irregular ovoid and curvilinear shapes which seem to have organic or biomorphic qualities. They are modeled ultimately on the pattern of organic growth through the division and integration of cells. What designers of coffee tables used to call "free-form," and builders of outdoor swimming pools called "kidney-shaped," constitutes a correct although banal application of biomorphic form. Of course, crustaceans defy this principle since they are organic, yet possess jagged, sharp, almost geometrically shaped outer armor. But their armor, which has been so suggestive to sculptors working with welded metal is like our fingernails—lacking the nerves, muscles, blood vessels and capacity for sensation of flesh and hence not "organic."

The Star by Jean Arp (1887–1966) is a good example of organic

Snowflake, left. Courtesy The American Museum of Natural History.

Giant's Causeway, Northern Ireland, center. Courtesy Sheldon Judson, Princeton University; photo, David Owen.

The crystalline world exhibits a regular geometry which is normally associated with man-made creations; perhaps human egotism explains the tendency to attribute order to man and irregularity to nature.

Electron micrograph of the southern bean mosaic virus protein, above. Courtesy Ralph W. G. Wyckoff, The University of Arizona.

The weapons, sense apparatus, and armor of crustaceans offer a form language which has a curious fascination for contemporary painters and sculptors, Graham Sutherland and Theodore Roszak, for example.

Spiny lobsters. New York Zoological Society photo.

THEODORE ROSZAK, *Sea Sentinel* (1956), far right. Collection of the Whitney Museum of American Art, New York.

JEAN ARP, *Star* (1939–60). Courtesy Etienne Bertrand Weill, Collection Eduard Loeb.

CONSTANTIN BRANCUSI, *Fish* (1930), at right. Collection The Museum of Modern Art, New York, acquired through the Lillie P. Bliss bequest.

LE CORBUSIER, Chapel at Ronchamps (1950–55). Photo, Lucien Hervé.

shape given to a phenomenon traditionally conceived in geometric terms. A star is, after all, light from a distant body. We do not really see the body, just the light-wave emanations. But Arp has chosen to construct a biological model of the conventionally pointed diagram we use to symbolize a scientific concept. The star has lost its geometry, its absolute regularity, and its radiating points. It has gained skin and flesh, with bones implied underneath, and an opening in the center which might be any bodily aperture. The contradiction between the standard idea of the star and its beautifully organic embodiment is no obstacle to enjoyment of the sculpture. In fact, the very freedom from the constraints of common sense and tradition is an asset.

Architecture seems to be an unlikely source of organic shapes since its fundamental structural devices are geometric in form. However, the modern development of reinforced concrete has vastly enlarged the vocabulary of forms available to the architect. Indeed, one of the criticisms of some contemporary buildings is that the architects are too flamboyantly sculptural, seeking to create exciting shapes at the expense of functional efficiency. Le Corbusier's chapel at Ronchamps, however, satisfies structural and functional requirements while using shape to enhance the symbolic expressiveness of the chapel. The roof, particularly, resembles in profile a sculpture by Brancusi, the *Fish*. Although it might be forcing the comparison to suggest that Le Corbusier designed the roof as a literal image of the fish, which is a central symbol in Christian iconology, the biomorphic shapes in the building do increase its capacity to express the idea of the Church as the body of Christ.

Another instance of the architectural use of organic shapes is seen in the Casa Milá apartment house in Barcelona. Antonio Gaudí (1852–1926), the architect, avoided geometric shapes wherever possible, and in the stone columns, particularly at the ground level, created the impression of dozens of elephants' legs. We would have to go back to Hindu-temple construction of the eighth century to find a comparable approach to architectural form. The entrance to the Shrine at Elephanta, which was carved and excavated from solid rock, bears an interesting resemblance to the Gaudí apartment house. In Gaudí's work and the Art Nouveau movement in general, organic shapes were employed quite uniformly without

ANTONIO GAUDÍ, Casa Milá (1905–10), near right. Courtesy Amigos de Gaudí, Barcelona.

General view of entrance to the shrine, Cave No. 1, at Elephanta, India, far right. Photo, copyright Archaeological Survey of India.

regard to the purpose of a work of art, the character of its materials, or the processes employed in forming the material. Hence, although the style often appears to be a triumph of the imagination over the obduracy of materials, it sometimes approaches the ludicrous because of its curvilinear obsession.

Arp's *Madame Torso with Wavy Hat* is clearly frivolous in shape and comic in purpose. We can readily identify the basic hourglass figure, while the head, hat, and hair develop into shapes like an Ionic capital, ocean waves, or an inverted handle-bar mustache. The several convex, rounded forms are balanced by the negative, *concave* shapes located where the thighs would fit into the torso. And the raised relief of the figure casts shadows which strongly define the negative shapes and accent the formal organization. But why are these forms frivolous? We might hazard a guess that organic shapes without a suggestion of firmness seem to wriggle, to describe a biological entity without bones (as in Miró's *Harlequinade*), im-

Through the scale and location of his positive, convex shapes, Ellsworth Kelly manages to generate sensations of expansion and squeezing in the visual field of the observer.

ELLSWORTH KELLY, *Aubade* (1957), below. Photo, Carnegie Institute.

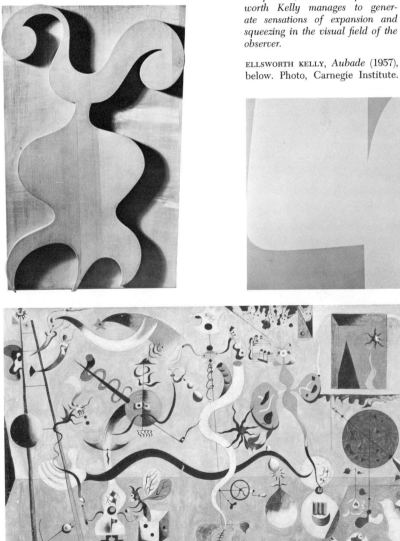

JEAN ARP, *Madame Torso with Wavy Hat* (1916), above at left. Photo, Hermann and Margrit Rupf Foundation, Museum of Fine Arts, Berne.

JOAN MIRÓ, *Carnival of Harlequin (Harlequinade)* (1924–25), at right. Courtesy Albright-Knox Art Gallery, Buffalo, New York, The Room of Contemporary Art Fund.

plying the movement of a gelatin dessert. Excess human flesh develops a power of motion independent of the body of its owner. The result, depending on the viewer's outlook, is ungraceful or lyrically pleasing, superabundant or delightfully comic. The *Wavy Hat* is reminiscent of the curly, feathery shapes Miró is fond of using, as in his *Harlequinade*, a party of a picture, replete with squirmy, biomorphic shapes. Some of its fantastic insects would arouse the envy of that redoubtable illustrator of children's books, Dr. Seuss.

Adolph Gottlieb (1903–) in *Blast II* gives a splendid laboratory demonstration of the properties of shape. The canvas is occupied by two forms of approximately the same area and mass, but the upper one is smoothly rounded whereas the lower one is ragged and chaotic, smeared at the edges, seething with conflict. The title and the visual aspect suggest that the work is an abstract version of a nuclear explosion. The circular form above represents the familiar mushroom cloud while the agitated shape below stands for the destructive process. There is a serene quality to the cloud which heightens the contrast with the "noisy" chaos below. An interesting feature of the lower shape is the random, smeary quality of the brush strokes at the periphery. They tell us that the artist does not emphasize the destructive force of a nuclear blast so much as its "dirty" character. And, since scientists and military men speak of "clean" bombs, the idea is appropriate. An *un*clean bomb is, of course, one which yields a large amount of radioactive fallout. Obviously, the artist has attempted to express this concept by the use of dark, smudged, disorderly shapes against an immaculate back-

ground above which floats a clean, bright, carefully brushed-out cloud form.

From the fertile imagination of Paul Klee comes a striking illustration of the two major types of shape—the biomorphic and the geometric. *The Great Dome* is a triumph of philosophic statement employing a modest, unassuming line and symbolic shapes in the guise of architectural description. The structure on the left represents the culmination of the age-long effort to bear the weight of a dome continuously around its edge. At the same time, the dome is the architectural expression of the female breast, the symbol of maternal nurture. In the right half of the picture, Klee portrays a tower, symbol of the male principle, which is essentially geometric, a system of triangles. The two basic shapes are quite starkly presented, each occupying one half of the picture space. They are connected somewhat (not really joined)

ADOLPH GOTTLIEB, *Blast II* (1957). Courtesy Joseph E. Seagram and Sons, Inc.

PAUL KLEE, *The Great Dome* (1927). © Cosmopress and SPADEM 1966 by French Reproduction Rights, Inc.; photo, Kunstmuseum Bern.

at the base of both buildings, but it is worth noting that Klee employs no compositional device to harmonize the two shapes, to connect them visually, to mitigate their essential opposition. Furthermore, he ignores the tower in his title. If we may permit ourselves some amateur psychologizing, Klee here is expressing (1) the eternal war between the sexes and (2) his admiration, as a man, for woman. As in his *Flight from Oneself*, the artist shows his interest in the duality of all unities. Just as human personality struggles with itself and sometimes succeeds in becoming alienated, the sexes, which must unite to be creative, are nevertheless in open opposition by the very nature of their appearances—and this dichotomy is expressed in the contrasting monuments that are built as reminders of these differences.

Perhaps an extreme version of the employment of geometric shapes to represent human beings is seen in *Composition: The Cardplayers* (1916) by Theo van Doesburg (1883–1931). Did the *Cardplayers* by Cézanne of 1885–90 anticipate, with its hint of Cubism, the complete dematerialization of the innocuous gamesters in van Doesburg's work? We are aware of progressively smaller forms, more densely packed at the center of the picture, where hands and cards and a drink, perhaps, may come together. A few large, right-angle shapes suggest the location of shoulders, knees, seat, chairs maybe. The surface organization takes precedence over representation and much of its interest stems from our knowledge that this organization is based upon, is abstracted from, something real. The movement, the recession in space, and the complexity of visual reality are presented. Only the imitation of appearances is absent. The organic shapes of reality have been converted into the geometric shapes of a mechanized, completely rationalized art. Consequently, it is not surprising that a modern device now exists which can create patterns representing the electronic circuitry of computers, patterns which bear a remarkable resemblance to van Doesburg's painting. The electronic patterns are made by a technician using an instrument called a "coordinatograph." Did van Doesburg unwittingly anticipate printed electronic circuits? Will more sophisticated coordinatographs supplant painters? Do electronic engineers wish to create art?

Technician using coordinatograph to prepare pattern for microelectronic circuit, left. Courtesy General Instrument Corporation Microelectronic Division.

Printed circuit (used in television sets) (1958), center. Collection The Museum of Modern Art, New York, gift of Warwick Manufacturing Company, U.S.A.

H. DOUGLAS PICKERING, *Pomegranate* (1955), right. Courtesy the artist.

One of our operating assumptions about shape has been that geometric forms suggest machine technology whereas irregular, curvilinear, and ovoid forms have biological origins. Now this assumption is refuted by a printed circuit for a television set which is not only devoid of geometry but which could have been drawn by Arp, Dubuffet or Henry Moore. Some of the forms

have figurative connotations, although they are only the result of translating the functions of resistors, condensers, and electronic tubes into two-dimensional patterns. If such quasi-artistic phenomena are created by engineers unintentionally in the course of designing a television set, we might, out of innocent curiosity, insert Douglas Pickering's drawing *Pomegranate* into a television circuit and watch the screen for the results.

We have seen some curiously amusing shapes in the work of Arp and Miró. Now we look forward to new frontiers of shape organization as electronic engineers reveal their latent artistry in the design of circuits for television.

Light and Dark

PAUL KLEE, *Self Portrait* (1939), left. © Cosmopress and SPADEM 1966 by French Reproduction Rights, Inc.; photo, Kunstmuseum Bern.

KASIMIR MALEVICH, *Suprematist Composition: White on White* (1918), right. Collection The Museum of Modern Art, New York.

Goethe on his deathbed is reported to have uttered the phrase, "More light." Rationalist philosophers of the En*light*enment spoke of "the light of reason." In this context, light means that which clarifies, that which dispels darkness. Darkness, by contrast, stands

for ignorance and obscurity. In the humanist tradition, light is a symbol of the activity of mind operating to clear away and illuminate what is dark, hidden, and mysterious, to reveal the shining face of truth. It is also a masculine symbol; all the ancient sun gods were male: Apollo, Mithra, Mazda and Horus. Such light symbolism, of course, bears a close relation to reality because, without light, we could not see. Our eyes are light-sensitive organs, equipped to receive stimuli caused by light energy falling upon objects—energy which is then absorbed, or reflected back to our eyes to form the sensory data of images. Darkness is not a positive phenomenon, it is the absence of light.

The world of art, however, is created by man, not by nature. Artists use darkness as a positive tool: They work with shadows to imply light. The light in Klee's *Self-Portrait* is the absence of shadow; the exposed paper is seen as light because of its *contrast* with the black areas painted in by the artist. Without *some* contrast, we would have the sensation of light but would be unable to perceive line and shape. The famous *White on White* painted by Kasimir Malevich (1878–1935) shows how the virtual elimination of light-dark contrast almost results in the inability to discriminate any form. Actually, Malevitch used two kinds of white—warm and cool—so that perception is possible on the basis of a subtle color or "thermal" difference rather than light-dark contrast. But for the most part, artists employ distinct contrasts of light and dark or of hue to delineate form.

A drawn line is visible because of contrast, whether a dark line on a light ground or a white line on a dark ground. Since colors, even when pure, differ in degree of lightness or darkness, they can be used to establish light-dark differences and thus visible form. As pure pigment, yellow is lighter than red, blue is darker than green. Sometimes, however, colors are mixed to the same degree of lightness or darkness and then the eye is obliged to discriminate between them on the basis of their chromatic quality alone—a matter we shall discuss later. I should point out that, although the works created by sculptors, architects, and craftsmen are seen in terms of light and dark, it is chiefly the two-dimensional media of painting and drawing which employ the device of light-dark contrast for the creation of form. Sculptors build their forms directly: Painters create the *illusion* of forms in space, and light-dark contrast is one of their principal tools.

The simplest type of light-dark contrast is seen in the silhouette. Usually a solid black against a white ground, the silhouette provides a maximum of contrast and visibility. But it directs the viewer's eye to its shape as a source of information or identification. Its interior is uniform and flat, it has interest only by virtue of what can be implied through its contour. Silhouettes occur in nature, as when we see an object against the light. But usually, objects are illuminated by one or several light sources. The play of light over their forms, when imitated by an artist, results in a naturalistic appearance. Artistic manipulation of light and dark to reveal form or to create the illusion of volume on a two-dimensional surface is called modeling—a term borrowed from sculpture. An object can be "modeled" with only the stark contrast provided by two "values"—black and white. But a more convincing and subtle representation of natural appearance can be created by imitating a wider range of light intensities. This type of modeling, which was perfected during the Renaissance, notably by Leonardo da Vinci, is called *chiaroscuro*.

By taking great pains and introducing a wide range of gradation of shadow, an artist can almost simulate photographic naturalism. However, the eye can discriminate more degrees of light intensity than the skill or materials of the artist will permit. Consequently, artists do not usually attempt to compete with the camera, even when they are trying for objective accuracy. Instead, they look for *patterns* of light and dark which can reveal form effectively: They simplify and generalize shadows in some places and represent them with great accuracy in others. Thus, we can

Silhouette used to create pictorial space and to direct the spectator's vision.

HENRI DE TOULOUSE-LAUTREC, *Maxime Dethomas* (1896). Courtesy National Gallery of Art, Washington, D.C., Chester Dale Collection.

AUGUSTE RODIN, *The Kiss* (1886), left. Courtesy Musée Rodin, © SPADEM 1966 by French Reproduction Rights, Inc.

DAVID SMITH, *Drawing 1959 — 8* (1959), center. Courtesy Marlborough-Gerson Gallery, Inc.

In this lithograph, the artist employs light and dark patterning not only to describe an event but also to endow a Mexican religious ritual with a spirit at once solemn and macabre.

LEWIS RUBENSTEIN, *Good Friday* (1951), right. Courtesy the artist.

look at equally convincing representations of the form of the same object and find that they affect us differently, because of the varying emphasis placed on the patterning of light and dark. Chiaroscuro as a tool is subject to an almost infinite variety of uses: Light-dark contrast can be exaggerated or underplayed; the artist may simplify shadow and accumulate detail in the light areas or vice versa; he may superimpose linear conventions upon forms modeled by chiaroscuro. And color and texture are inevitably involved in the representation of form. It is almost impossible for an artist to create forms by an absolutely mechanical imitation of the varying intensities of light and dark visible in the model he may be attempting to represent. Some process of selection, some evidence of emphasis, some sign of exaggeration by inclusion or suppression of visual facts will be apparent in the drawn or painted work. However, the evidence that an artist has *attempted* naturalistic imitation will have some bearing on our critical judgment of his work.

Much of the symbolism of light and dark is literary and philosophic in character. Yet in the visual arts, the transitions from light to dark have meanings of their own, that is, distinctively aesthetic meanings, as do the shapes of shadows also. The gentleness or abruptness of half-tones, or transitional areas, participates in the creation of emotional reactions for the viewer. The type of illumination—from above or below, from one source or from many sources—affects our perception. The distinctness or indistinctness of shapes is controlled by line and also by the manipulation of light and dark. Some shadows appear to be empty or opaque; others are luminous and mysterious. They invite closer inspection for themselves or they may direct our attention back to the light areas they define. We have already noted that some architects design interiors which are bathed in strong light while others create spaces and volumes which will cast shadows or break up the intensity of direct light. The sculptor Rodin was especially sensitive to the effect of light in the perception of his work. He would move a lighted candle along the contours of his figures to help him see and control the animation of his sculptural surfaces. The welded sculptures we have seen by David Smith are highly effective in silhouette, and, indeed, some of his preparatory drawings show that he conceived his works largely in terms of their silhouettes.

As with the other visual elements, our perception of light and dark is guided by our experience of it in life. And in life we avoid too much of either: We can be as "blinded" by the absence of light as by light itself. Strong light-dark contrasts are equated with sharpness of focus, and since only near objects come into sharp focus, the degree of contrast in artistic forms provides information about their location in space. Once again, it was Leonardo who knew this first and advised painters to make distant objects less distinct than near ones—that is, less bright in color and less marked in contrast. The degree to which forms melt into one another or retain their separate identity is often a function of light-dark manipulation. The resulting distinctness or indistinctness of form is one of the important indices of style according to Heinrich Wölfflin°; we shall return to this subject in our discussion of perception. At present, we may note one of the practical advantages of the eye's preference for avoiding the extremes of light or of darkness: So far as natural light is concerned, the late afternoon seems to afford, not the best visibility, but the most interesting shadows and half-tones compatible with the pleasing delineation of form. Consequently, it is a good time for the conduct of social life. Ladies beyond the

bloom of youth seem always to have known this important fact. Only American teenagers have the temerity to brave a coke date at noon in the fluorescent glare of a modern soda-drug-and-pill emporium.

One of the consequences of the unrestrained use of color in modern painting has been the tendency to think of light and dark in terms of color. Even black-and-white prints have color and tonality. The paper has a certain color, so light areas may be slightly yellow or blue; and all black inks are not the same: Students of painting are taught to describe forms, not by tonal painting (that is, by variations of one hue), but by playing on the different colors which reside in the light, dark, and half-tone areas. Nevertheless, our perception of objects seems to be affected primarily by the distribution of light and dark on their surfaces. Only *after* we have identified objects in this manner do we go on to perceive their color qualities. And, as we know, some persons are color-blind in various degrees; this deprivation may handicap them in certain respects, but most of them function quite adequately. The primacy of form as determined by shape and by light and dark, therefore, accounts for the heavy reliance on these visual elements throughout the history of art. We shall discuss in the following pages some examples of the dramatic use of light and dark in traditional and modern art.

BAROQUE EXPERIMENTS
WITH ILLUMINATION

After the masters of the Renaissance perfected chiaroscuro, the later Mannerist and Baroque painters went on to employ unusual illumination to drama-

°Heinrich Wölfflin, *Principles of Art History*.

CARAVAGGIO, *The Calling of St. Matthew* (c.1597–98), left. Courtesy Art Reference Bureau.

GEORGES DE LA TOUR, *La Madeleine* (1625–33), right. Courtesy Musée du Louvre, Cliché des Musées Nationaux.

EL GRECO, *Agony in the Garden* (c.1598). Courtesy The National Gallery, London.

tize their subjects. In Caravaggio's *The Calling of St. Matthew* (1597), for example, the source of light from the right, so clearly indicated by the modeling of the figures, the cast shadow on the wall, and the direction of the angel's hand provide a means of endowing the event with a highly theatrical quality. About eighty per cent of each figure is in shadow; bright light creeps around the

edges of the forms to perform its descriptive function and also to seize the eye of the viewer. Study of the abstract patterning of the sharply defined light areas will reveal that they carry the real burden of the work. Georges de La Tour (1593–1652) went a step further, using *artificial* light to construct dramatic forms of classic simplicity. His *La Madeleine à la Veilleuse* (1625–33) shows the remarkable lengths to which this Baroque artist would go to create quiet pictorial drama through light-and-dark patterning while remaining within the confines of realism. The painting is very "modern" in its simplification of form, its anticipation of Cubism, and its manipulation of light to arrive at essentially abstract patterns. Distracting detail and a descriptive inventory are suppressed; the dark areas are handled so as to maximize their mystery. Although about three-quarters of the picture surface is in darkness, it is a very comfortable darkness, made so by the calm and reasoned shaping of the lights.

El Greco is known to us as a superb colorist, having carried the tradition of Titian and Tintoretto to Spain, yet he was also the master of a so-called flickering light—a light more animated than that of La Tour. Although both are Baroque painters, La Tour exhibits a formal order which relates him to modern classicists like Seurat and even Mondrian, while El Greco has an emotional, agitated style which may be felt in modern Expressionists like Munch, Kokoschka, and Soutine. His *Agony in the Garden* (1580) appears to be artificially illuminated, especially in the Christ figure, in which the light-dark contrast is powerfully distinct. Of course, El Greco's technique of monochromatic underpainting followed by transparent overglazing (pp. 317–319), permits separation in the execution of two crucial phases of pictorial composition: light-dark modeling and color application. Modern painters attempt to deal with color and light and shape all at once: What is gained in spontaneity, though, is lost in the opportunity to calculate in advance the shape, color, and dramatic impact of the total composition. El Greco, too, seems very "modern" in that he did not feel constrained to be consistent or uniform in his light sources or in the naturalistic rendering of visual forms. The angel receives a different illumination from that of the Christ; the difference is partly explained by a shaft of light, but to our modern eyes the lighting simply seems appropriate for the mystical-religious theme.

In Rembrandt we encounter perhaps the most moving synthesis of Baroque experiments with dramatic light-and-dark illumination. The simplification of forms in the light, the cultivation of mystery in the darks, the use of spot-lighted effects as in El Greco, and many other technical and structural devices are readily at his disposal and are used with maximum eloquence and discrimination. Rembrandt underpaints and overglazes, but he is not averse to painting in spontaneous passages opaquely on top of transparent areas. His transitional tones bear the closest study because it is there that he departs from the abstract patterning of light and dark and reveals the distinctive insight into the human condition which raises his art above merely skillful pictorial organization. In *Man with a Magnifying Glass,* the loss of light in the half-tones and shadows serves not only to model the forms but also to symbolize all that is human—that is,

REMBRANDT VAN RIJN, *Man with a Magnifying Glass* (1665–1669) [whole and detail]. Courtesy The Metropolitan Museum of Art, bequest of Benjamin Altman, 1913. Photos, John Pitkin.

vulnerable—in his subject. The light areas consist of a vigorous, masculine impasto swimming among liquid, colored glazes which begin the transition to the luminous shadows. The light might be regarded as the virile, affirmative element—meeting our eyes first, establishing the shapes of the principal forms, struggling to expand and assert its dominance. The half-tones represent the modifications of light, the feminine element which seeks to find an accommodation to the incursion of light, through resistance, compromise, and yielding. Half-tones operate in those areas which light cannot entirely occupy. In the shadows we see death and defeat, their luminosity being the visible record of invasions by light which failed. However, while the darks in Rembrandt allude to death, they do not symbolize the final frustration of life, but merely a stage in an on-going process. That is, the light is dynamic; it has been where the shadow is now, and one feels that it will return.

LIGHT AND DARK IN MODERN ART

The modern use of light and dark was most spectacularly inaugurated by Édouard Manet, especially in his "scandalous" painting, *Le Déjeuner sur l' Herbe.* But his *Olympia* (1863) may be an even more dramatic example of the use of flat lighting in figures set against a sharply contrasted dark background. It was this merciless flat light as much as his subject matter which aroused the indignation of the French public. That is, they may have believed they were objecting to his theme, but most likely they were aesthetically repelled by his realistic and unsentimental application of paint and glaring treatment of light. Manet tended to eliminate half-tones and subtle modeling effects. He painted directly, without glazes, but with a

preference for bluish-black in the shadows and transitions. The *Olympia* lighting has some of the quality of a candid camera photograph in which the flash bulb has flattened out the forms. This flattening was to influence the progress of subsequent painting in bringing all forms up to the picture plane. By 1892, Paul Gauguin, in *The Spirit of the Dead Watching,* could benefit from the innovations initiated by Manet in the flattening of forms and stark light and dark contrasts. Gauguin was able to concentrate on symbolism and psychological expression while exploiting the compositional devices pioneered in Manet's *Olympia.*

The woodcut, *Prophet* (1912), by Emil Nolde (1867–1956) shows how powerfully expressive the simple contrast of black and white can be when all middle tones are eliminated. Of course, the woodcut medium is highly suited to this treatment of light. But we would not accept it as readily as we do if it were not for the process of simplification of light and dark set in motion by Manet.

ÉDOUARD MANET, *Olympia* (1863), left. Courtesy Musée du Louvre, Cliché des Musées Nationaux.

PAUL GAUGUIN, *The Spirit of the Dead Watching* (1892), right. Courtesy Albright-Knox Art Gallery, Buffalo, New York, A. Conger Goodyear Collection.

EMIL NOLDE, *The Prophet* (1912). Courtesy National Gallery of Art, Washington, D.C., Rosenwald Collection.

GEORGES ROUAULT, *Dura Lex Sed Lex* (1926). Collection of the Philadelphia Museum of Art.

The bridge of the nose and the nostrils in Nolde's *Prophet* are entirely dark, though the logic of illumination would dictate otherwise. But by 1912, an artist could mix abstract and descriptive elements freely, in this case producing a harrowing impact through the continuous pattern of darks connecting the brows, nose, and mustache. The light areas are not only patterns of light falling on the bony structure of the face and skull; they also become abstract symbols which we can read. The tool used in cutting the wood block imparts a characteristic shape to the forms; it does not change direction easily or gracefully because it must contend with the resistance of the wood grain. Consequently, the harshness of the shapes becomes an attribute of the subject: The prophet is ignored or despised because he announces truths which the multitude does not wish to hear.

Rouault's *Dura Lex Sed Lex* (Harsh Law, but Law) (1926) is a print very much in the spirit of Nolde's earlier woodcut. Here, too, the pictorial structure is basically an extreme light-and-dark contrast, with the inclusion of a few half-tones which modulate the light intensity somewhat. The texture Rouault is able to achieve with the printing plate creates a painterly richness of surface, so that this work seems less obedient to the character of printmaking than the Nolde. But it is clearly the emotional expression of an idea which is paramount in Rouault, and he accomplishes his purpose mainly through an uncompromising use of the extremes of black and white combined with shapes which are painfully astringent.

As we mentioned earlier, the modern movement has increasingly stressed the function of color as a determinant of form. Even architects have bravely incorporated bright primary colors into exterior wall panels. Painters, in their training and in their mature work, now spend less time on the consideration of problems of modeling by chiaroscuro, contrast by light and dark, and emotional affect through unusual illumination. Technology has produced a very large array of safe, durable, and brilliant colors which may be used without mastering the complex techniques of older eras. Consequently, the limits to the aesthetic potential of color will probably be determined, not by the tools and techniques which technology can devise, but by the perceptual capacity of the human organism. However, it would appear that, although there is much that we know about color, we presently know a great deal more about how to employ the expressive potential of light, and its opposite, dark. Now it would be appropriate to discuss color, which may be the visual element that holds the most *future* promise for enlarging the realm of aesthetic effect.

Color

I shall discuss color *theory* in summary fashion because it is treated exhaustively and expertly in a number of specialized works on the subject. Besides, color theory provides speculative answers to questions which are not often asked in the course of examining works of art. Some color systems seem related to the physiology of perception more than to the aesthetics or psychology of perception. Others may have evolved from industrial needs for the classification and description of dyes, pigments, and colored objects. At any rate, artists work with color—pigment, to be exact —more on an intuitive than a scientific basis. The so-called Op artists may have a more sophisticated understanding of color and of perceptual theory than is usual among painters. But ultimately, even so knowledgeable a colorist as Josef Albers must paint his pictures by making intuitive adjustments to the organismic requirements of vision rather than by applying the data of color physics to the problems of pictorial organization. Even the Impressionists, who were supposed to have been influenced by the color theory of Helmholtz, cannot be accused of knowing as much about color theory as today's high school student of physics. Their opportunity to see, in 1870, the work of Turner and Constable in England may have been a more potent influence on their subsequent painterly development. One might say the aesthetic value of their painting transcends the discovery that objects *en plein air* have purple shadows. And teachers who have inflicted color wheels, color triads, and intermediates on generations of students appear divided about the ultimate effectiveness of this material for influencing the use or understanding of color by the public at large.

COLOR TERMINOLOGY

Nevertheless, there is a terminology of color based on scientific study and theoretical classification which facilitates discourse about it and permits orderly reference to the properties of color which we believe generate aesthetic emotion. Following are brief definitions of the terms most commonly used in connection with color, chiefly the color attainable through the use of artists' pigments.

Hue is the quality we commonly label by the names of the so-called primary colors: red, yellow, and blue. Note that these are different from the colors of the light spectrum as taught in physics: red, orange, yellow, green, blue, indigo, violet. The primary hues are theoretically the basis for mixtures resulting in orange, green, and violet; and presumably, the primaries are *not* the result of a mixture. But in practice with artists' pigments, the most intense hues are achieved by mixture. The names given by manufacturers to colors are usually a form of proprietary advertising, designed to identify a product with a color such as "Lucky Strike Green."

Value refers to the lightness or darkness of a color. As white is added, the color becomes "higher" in value until pure white is reached. Conversely, as black is added, or some other color which has a darkening effect, the value becomes "lower" until pure black is reached. As you approach pure white or pure black, you become less aware of the chromatic, or color quality, and more aware of the lightness or darkness, which is to say, the *value* of the color. Yellow is already high in value. It can be used to raise the value of colors darker than itself. Blue is already low in value. It can lower the value of lighter colors.

Intensity refers to the purity of a color, the absence of any visible admixture. As mentioned above, pigments are not often absolutely pure, thus they seldom present a hue at its fullest intensity.

For example, the pigment called alizarin crimson can be made into a very intense red by the addition of a small amount of yellow or cadmium orange. Ultramarine blue is very dark as a pigment and becomes an intense blue hue only with the addition of white. Of course, too much white will "kill" its intensity and give it a faded appearance.

Local Color is the color we know an object to be as opposed to the colors of the object we actually see. We know a fire engine is red, but depending on the light conditions when we see it, its distance, its reflective quality, and so on, it will appear red, violet, yellow, orange, and even green in some places. Its sparkling highlights might be almost white. At least, a painter would use these colors in representing the "redness" of the fire engine. Similarly, distant mountains appear to be blue or violet although we "know" that the local color of their foliage is green. The blue or violet which the green becomes when it reaches an observer's eye is called *optical color.*

Complementary colors are opposites. They are opposite each other on a color wheel; more fundamentally, they are opposite in that the presence of one denotes the complete absence of the other. In this sense, no other color is as different from red as green. To the human eye, the after-image of red is green; the after-image of green is red. If red and green are placed side by side, the red looks redder and the green looks greener because the after-image of each enhances the actual image of the other. If, instead of being juxtaposed, complementaries are mixed, they cancel each other out—that is, they produce a gray, or, more likely, what painters call mud. Thus, they neutralize each other. A

small amount of red added to a large amount of green will gray the green; white added to the mixture will raise the value, and thus a variety of interesting grays can be mixed without the use of black.

Analogous colors are relatives, kinsmen, as opposed to strangers like complementaries. They are related because they share the same "blood lines" —red and orange, orange and yellow, blue and green, violet and blue, red and violet. Analogous colors are contiguous on the color wheel so that families of color do not end distinctly at any point, but seem to "intermarry" with their neighbors. Being relatives, they "get along," if that is true of relatives. They are harmonious next to each other; they mix with each other without becoming gray.

Warm and cool colors are so called perhaps because of our psychological associations with blood, fire, sky, and ice. Reds, yellows, and oranges are warm; blues, greens, and some violets are cool. But these "thermal" properties are relative. Yellow-green would be cool next to orange but warm next to

Derain tried to exploit the emotional qualities of color, unlike the Impressionists who used it to describe atmospheric conditions (see p. 251).

ANDRÉ DERAIN, *London Bridge* (1906). Collection The Museum of Modern Art, New York, gift of Mr. and Mrs. Charles Zadok.

Color here is not only being liberated from the description of objects, but also begins to generate its own spatial properties (see p. 251).

ALEXEI VON JAWLENSKY, *Still Life with Blue Can* (c.1906-7). Courtesy Andreas Jawlensky; photo, Frankfurter Kunstkabinett.

blue. Gainsborough introduced some purple into the shadows of his *Blue Boy* to warm up what would have been a chilly blue figure otherwise. Picasso has done the same thing in his "blue period" paintings. Painters often create forms by contrasts of warm and cool rather than of light and dark. The warm colors seem to advance, the cool colors tend to recede. This illusion results not only because of association, but also because the wave lengths at the warm end of the light spectrum are "stronger"—that is, more visible, than those at the blue-violet end. *Ultra*-violet, of course, cannot be seen at all.

Tonality refers to the generalized, over-all color effect of a work of art, when one color and variations of it, produced by admixtures of light or dark pigment, seem to predominate in our vision of the whole. Rousseau's *The Dream* (p. 213) has an essentially green tonality, for instance. At times we speak of warm or cool tones, which is a way of referring to variations of color built around a dominant warm or cool hue. A painting with a blue tonality may contain reds and yellows, but, because of the *quantity* and *distribution* of blue and its *tonal* variations, the single comprehensive effect is of the prevailing blue. Tonality imposes at least a color unity upon a work, reducing and simplifying the problems of composition by reducing the number of color variables the artist must endeavor to harmonize. If he is particularly concerned with problems of shape, volume, or illumination, the artist may deliberately limit his range of colors, employing variations of one or two pigments plus black and white. Such a practice is called working with a *limited palette*. Yet great subtlety and expressiveness is possible

while working within a single tonal range. The major works of Analytic Cubism were executed by Braque and Picasso with a limited palette, largely an umber, blue, and burnt sienna tonality. (Notice that it is easier to designate their prevailing color, or tonality, in terms of the painter's pigments than by the hues drawn from the light spectrum or the color wheel.)

COLOR AS LANGUAGE

It should be plain that very little can be asserted with certainty about colors in isolation. They always occur in a context or relationship—in art and in life. The *quantity* of a color in a particular context may overturn some of our assertions about advancing/receding, expanding/contracting, warm/cool relationships. And, of course, the *shape* of a color area affects its impact, as does the visible manner of its *application*. In addition to the optical properties of color, there are its symbolic properties to consider. Needless to say, there is an enormous accumulation of folklore about color as well as a theoretical and practical discipline called the psychology of color which endeavors to deal systematically with this material. Professionals called color consultants apply the body of knowledge about color to a variety of practical problems in manufacture, communication, safety, decoration, illumination, and so on.

One of the prominent goals of the modern movement in art has been the use of color as a direct and independent language of meaning and emotion. Abstract and nonobjective art liberated painters to the extent that they could abandon or minimize the use of the other visual elements and endeavor to communicate by color exclusively. The intention of some painters was to imitate music, which communicates feelings through "nonobjective" sound. There have even been attempts to combine painting and music through the invention of "color organs" which would project colored light on a screen as one "played" on a keyboard. The artist Wassily Kandinsky, who seemed to think of color in terms analogous to musical notes and of painting in terms of musical composition, is credited with the creation of the first nonobjective paintings, works which were not abstracted from anything, which set out to use color—not descriptively or symbolically —but arbitrarily, as a visual language of the emotions.

The Fauves ("Wild Beasts")— chief among them Matisse, Derain, Friesz, and Vlaminck—were responsible for carrying the coloristic advances of Impressionist painting into the realm of arbitrary color, making possible the conception of painting as an art of color solely, using line, shape, and symbol, if at all, in supportive roles. Several artistic movements during the first part of the century were concerned with carrying the color innovations of post-Impressionism, especially of Cézanne, into new realms of expression. Among them were Synchromism (founded by two Americans, Stanton MacDonald-Wright and Morgan Russell), Orphism, Die Brücke (The Bridge), Der Blaue Reiter (The Blue Rider), and Expressionism as a whole. Although it would be difficult to think of any modern painter or painterly movement that did not carry on serious experimentation with color, those mentioned gave strong emphasis to color as a nonverbal language. In the following pages we shall discuss the coloristic

advances made by a few of the leading personalities of contemporary art.

London Bridge (p. 249) by André Derain (1880–1954) might be taken as a typical transitional work from Impressionism to Fauvism. Dated 1906, it has the crisp, bright touch characteristic of Impressionist paint application and the use of blue and blue-violet in the shadow areas. But the blurring of edges and the pursuit of atmospheric effects by the admixture of white is absent. Black masses and outlines are used for emotional and visual shock, something the Impressionists would not have done because it would not have been optically "right." Intense yellow marks on the bridge do not locate themselves properly in space, but jump out of their places and begin to function independently as color. Color is exaggerated everywhere. The sky is vividly orange without any optical "explanation" of how that color was arrived at. Yellow and pink reflections in the water are theoretically possible, but not probable in the manner we see them here presented. The drawing is adequate for identifying the site, but it is clearly subordinate to the activity of the brushwork and the dynamism of the pigment. At a time when the coloristic innovations of Impressionism were still controversial, it is understandable that the exaggerated color and departure from natural drawing by the Fauves would arouse violent reactions from conventional critics and the public in general.

Still Life with Blue Can (p. 249) by Alexei von Jawlensky (1864–1941) dates from the same time as Derain's; it has moved still further in the direction of independent color while retaining only a nominal connection with its point of departure in visual reality.

WASSILY KANDINSKY, *Landscape with Houses* (1909). Courtesy Kunstmuseum der Stadt Dusseldorf; photo, Walter Klein.

WASSILY KANDINSKY, *Composition No. 2* (1910), left. The Solomon R. Guggenheim Museum Collection.

WASSILY KANDINSKY, *All Saint's Day* (1910–11), right. Courtesy Stadtische Galerie Im Lenbachhaus; photo, Joachim Blauel.

straction in which pictorial structure is based on color intensities; the drawing, illumination, subject matter, and spatial representation are fairly impersonal. It should be remembered that, at this time, French developments in abstraction were often monochromatic, since Cubism was chiefly concerned with the analysis of shape and space. Synthetic Cubism permitted itself the indulgence of arbitrary color and texture, but always within the framework of its own logic of shape and space. It is as if Gallic logic would not permit, for long, any thoroughly irrational development in pictorial composition. Yet Matisse, the informal leader of the Fauves, was thoroughly French. The apparent "wildness" of his color was inspired not by a desire to escape rationality but rather by an urge to discover color which could directly express emotions. He was fairly well convinced that color imitation or exactitude not only failed to convey the emotions felt by the artist, but constituted instead an impediment to successful expression.

Although the structural organization of the painting is strong, it offers no particular eloquence in shape or line. The design is simply a scaffold upon which to hang the intense, vigorously applied color. Jawlensky's subsequent Expressionist development is foreshadowed here in his rather coarse and unrefined design and execution. But he is well on the way in this work to a type of ab-

The *Landscape with Houses* of 1909, by Wassily Kandinsky (1866–1944), although later than the Derain, is closer to Impressionism in its gradations of color and traces of color-vibration technique. His edges are not as harsh as Derain's and the drawing is not as assertively rebellious in the Fauvist manner. But the spots of pure color in the roof tops begin to "jump out" of their spatial locations. The pictorial space is pressed forward, although Kandinsky has not reached the control of the picture plane which Cézanne had achieved in the 1890's. He never became as interested in pictorial architectonics as Cézanne and the French Cubists in general. For Kandinsky, the emotional and metaphysical possibilities of color were central. By 1910, Kandinsky had almost departed from subject matter in the traditional sense, as in his *Composition No. 2*. Landscape and figurative elements are present as well as conventional scale relationships, if we assume a traditional composition. But independent color has now asserted itself in a cheerful, bright picture which *does* seem to exhibit the visual equivalents of a musical composition—possibly the qualities of Slavonic dance music. We should not overlook the influence of Russian folk art in Kandinsky's color choice, even in his completely nonobjective works, Indeed, the heritage he shares with another Russian, Marc Chagall, is very evident in *All Saints' Day* (1910–11), a fantasy employing the same flying figures and folkloric elements we have come to associate exclusively with Chagall. Later in his career, Kandinsky was to develop a geometric style of painting in which mechanical shapes and lines share with color the burden of expression. His Fauvist phase (until

about 1914) appears to have been the period of his most vigorous and painterly experiments with color. At this time he produced the paintings which have been so influential in the evolution of contemporary Abstract Expressionism. His subsequent geometric style has also affected abstraction through its "hard-edge" line of descent. Compared to Matisse, there is a certain naïveté in Kandinsky, particularly with reference to the drawn line, but he was strikingly original and single-minded in his pursuit of one goal, a goal which has been of immense historical value for the subsequent development of painting:

MARK ROTHKO, *Earth and Green* (1954–55). Collection Mr. and Mrs. Ben Heller; photo, courtesy Dell Publishing Co.

He separated color and paint from subject matter, thus giving abstract color an impetus which would be fabulously exploited by subsequent generations of painters.

In Mark Rothko (1903–   ) we have a contemporary painter who endeavors to employ color as if it were a mystical light which can surround the viewer and engulf his vision. *Earth and Green* (p. 253) consists of two unequal rectangles superimposed on a blue field. The pigment is applied to the canvas by staining it, hence we have no awareness of it as a brushed-on substance. It seems to be an integral part of the canvas which radiates or emanates a colored light. Within the rectangles there are subtle changes of tonality of the sort we have seen in the painting of Baziotes. The simplicity of Rothko's means recalls a similar quality in the *Blast* paintings by Gottlieb, but the expressive effects are quite different. Rothko appears to be seeking a way of changing the viewer's mode of consciousness through color, an objective unlike that of Kandinsky who sought to communicate emotions, while Gottlieb seeks to communicate an *idea* through form and color. It appears that Rothko wants painting to seize the consciousness, to get behind man's thought and feeling. This achievement would be comparable to affecting human experience through color in a manner which now is possible only through drugs or some mystical discipline. Since color is one of the most powerful instruments available to painting so far as its capac-

ity to affect the nervous system is concerned, it is quite possible that Rothko has introduced a revolutionary new phase into the history of painting. It is interesting that this ambitious goal for painting is expressed through works which are quiet, serene, deceptively simple, and very pleasing to the eye. Unlike Op art, which also endeavors to change or "shake up" consciousness through the eye, the art of Rothko involves no pain, shock, dizziness, or other threat to the viewer's poise and equanimity.

The last previous artistic movement which sought the alteration of consciousness was Surrealism. Its principal instrument was shock arising from the hallucinatory juxtaposition of incongruous material. But its capacity to shock, particularly to change seriously the viewer's frame of reference, diminished as the public grew familiar with the strategy and the devices which were meant to surprise. However, contemporary painters like Rothko seem to have found a way to create pictures which temporarily change one's color and shape environment, thus inducing a very pleasant, contemplative state of being. Matisse was also interested in an art which would afford, through visual means, an opportunity for contemplation. We are perhaps about to enter an era when paintings, largely through color and shape, will offer occasions for relaxation and meditation—occasions from which the individual can emerge calm and serene, his being having been quietly renewed.

The Op(tical) pathway to the nervous system.

BRIDGET RILEY, *Current* (1964). Collection The Museum of Modern Art, New York, Philip C. Johnson Fund.

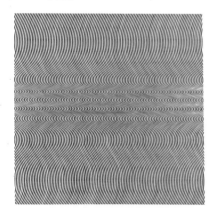

Conclusion

This chapter is entitled "The Visual Elements: Grammar" because it is devoted to explaining the "parts of speech" in visual art. Selected works, in which the performance of a certain visual element was crucial for the total meaning, were also examined. In attempting to concentrate on the role of line, light, shape, or color, we found the function of an element to be invariably affected by the nature of its association with the other elements. In verbal language, the way parts of speech "associate" with each other is called syntax, hence the chapter touched briefly on what might analogously be called visual syntax.

But rules of syntax or usage do not operate in art (if they exist at all) as strictly as rules of usage in language. Nevertheless, there are principles of organization in art which seem to be employed consistently and which serve to maximize the effectiveness of a work of art, no matter what its function or purpose. We turn in the next chapter to these principles, which are sometimes called principles of design.

In the chapters on the functions of art we discussed the variety of purposes for which works of art are created. But no matter what the purpose or function of a work of art, its parts or elements are organized to be seen. That is, the purpose of a chair is to support someone and *to be seen*. The purpose of a poster is to persuade someone and *to be seen;* indeed, to state it more accurately, a poster *must be seen first,* before it can be persuasive. Consequently, organization of the elements of art has one common goal along with the variety of personal, social, and physical goals that are normally pursued. The common goal might be called *organization for visual effectiveness.*

A painting that has no relation to physical utility, that functions by providing an opportunity for significant *seeing,* requires purposive design of its elements if it is to be effective. Here, the term *design* has been substituted for *organization. Design* is a process which is common to the creation of all works of art. No essential distinction is made in this book between the design of paintings and the design of objects of daily use, such as chairs. According to another point of view, though, the word *design* is confined to the organization of the visual elements for creating utilitarian objects, while the organization of visual elements for creating "nonuseful" objects like paintings and sculpture is

ORGANIZATION

OF THE ELEMENTS:

DESIGN

called *art.* However, that distinction is not used in this book for the following reasons:

1. The useful objects of the past frequently become the "use*less*" objects, the *fine art,* of the present.

2. So-called nonutilitarian objects *do* have a purpose, but not a physical one. They function by being seen, by arousing feelings, by "explaining" the world in visual terms.

3. The different functions of works of art affect the way their visual elements are designed, but the need for design —that is, for organizing the elements so as to be visually effective—remains constant.

By insisting that design is common to the creation of all works of art, and by refusing to set up a hierarchy among art objects—designating some *art* and others *designed objects, applied art,* or *artifacts*—we gain certain theoretical advantages. We avoid being embarrassed by history, as when the magical—that is, useful—African fertility sculpture becomes a fine art object in a culture which does not believe in certain kinds of magical rite. We are not caught in classification dilemmas by having to make arbitrary distinctions, for example, about the physical utility or aesthetic value or psychological expressiveness of stained glass in Gothic cathedrals, of medieval tapestries, and of Romanesque sculpture. Is the Brooklyn Bridge symbolically less potent because it was *designed* to carry people across a river, as well as to perform its function with a maximum of visual and structural effectiveness? As we know from the example of stained glass, it is possible for a work of art to perform several functions at once, to be *designed* to operate at several levels, and to be apprehended by viewers at one or more levels according to their needs and interests.

As soon as materials are formed or assembled, they constitute a visual organization, an organization which operates with greater or lesser effectiveness depending on how well its visual elements work together. Works of art of all kinds exhibit certain common patterns of "working together" that are called *principles of design*. These principles are ultimately based on the way people see most effectively and pleasurably and on the way materials can be formed most satisfactorily from the standpoint of effective and pleasurable vision. In a sense, the so-called principles of design are the result of long-term experimentation both empirical and intuitive. The history of art can be regarded, in part, as a revelation of the types of design or formal organization which have been effective in different times and places.

It cannot be claimed that any single design precept—for instance, unity in variety—constitutes a "rule" for artistic and aesthetic effectiveness. Distinguished works can be found that defy the principles of design cited here or in other places. Furthermore, the capacity to experience unity in variety differs among cultures: The unity of a Hindu temple may be less apparent to Western than to Indian eyes; the unity of Gothic architecture was doubtless absent for persons habituated to classical Mediterranean forms of artistic order—in fact, the term "Gothic" as applied to art originally meant something like "barbarian" to those who first employed the label. Nevertheless, these variations aside, the principles of design are based on habits of visual perception which, in turn, are greatly influenced by the common physiological equipment of the human race.

The habit of reading from left to right, or top to bottom, or right to left, affects perception variably. But everyone has to measure size relationships, the rate of speed of moving objects, the distance of objects from the viewer. Binocular vision and perceptions of size, brightness, color, shape, texture, speed, and depth probably confer more uniformity than diversity on mankind's vision. And it is on the basis of similarities in vision and perception that we dare to speak of design elements and principles as if they applied to everyone. In fact, as languages go, the language of vision may, like the languages of science and mathematics, tend more often than not to communicate the unity than the disunity of man.

The visual language is capable of disseminating knowledge more effectively than almost any other vehicle of communication. With it man can express and relay his experiences in object form. Visual communication is universal and international: It knows no limits of tongue, vocabulary, or grammar and it can be perceived by the illiterate as well as the literate. Visual language can convey facts and ideas in a wider and deeper range than almost any other means of communication.[*]

Unity

Perhaps unity is the only principle of visual organization, and the other principles merely constitute different ways of achieving it. For unity may ultimately represent the desire of the individual viewer to relate the multitude of visual facts and events he sees to one person—himself. Therefore, no matter how well or badly an artist organizes the visual elements, they *will be seen as a whole*. The viewer must be able to conclude, or close, his visual experience so that he can move on to perceive other things which require his attention. In addition, closure is required to make sense of, to understand, what has been seen. If an individual must leave the theater before a motion picture is completed, his mind usually requires him to complete the film himself. He will recall what he saw and impose a meaning on the fragment of the picture by adding something of his own to the material presented by the film-maker.

But if the viewer requires unity in his visual experience and is capable of supplying it when it is absent, what is the purpose of deliberately trying to achieve unity in the art object? Our answer must be that the artist or designer is theoretically engaged in an effort to communicate *his* unity, that is, *his* vision of form, to the viewer. Ineffectiveness of design will result in an abrupt termination of the viewer's experience. In simple language, the viewer will stop looking. The act of "not looking" is a type of completion; it is a critical judgment, made but not spoken.

We have seen works of art that consist of only one of the visual elements—shape, for example, or color—and thus the problem of unity is substantially simplified, although the problem of sustaining interest becomes more difficult to solve. But usually, all the visual elements occur in a single work and in several manifestations: that is, there are many shapes, colors, lines, and patterns of light and dark. Thus, a variety of visual events occurs within the type of organization we call a work of art. One of the objectives of design, then, is to create some kind of order, or unity, among those events *before* they are seen by a viewer. (Of course, the artist himself acts as a sort of surrogate viewer for the public.) What are the principal devices of design for creating unity within the variety of

[*] Gyorgy Kepes, *Language of Vision*, Theobald, 1944, p. 13.

visual events taking place in a work of art?

Dominance and *subordination* are the devices through which the artist attempts to control the *sequence* in which visual events are observed or the *amount of attention* which is paid to them. The dominant element of a work is the one on which all other elements depend for their meaning, or perceptual value. Dominance is achieved most easily by *size,* the largest form being seen first. Secondly it is achieved by *color intensity.* Other things being equal, an intense area of a warm color will dominate an intense cool area of the same size. A third way of achieving dominance is through *location:* The viewer's eye is usually drawn toward the center of any visual field; objects located there are more likely to receive earliest attention. That is why the head

in most portraits is centered between left and right and above the mid-point of the canvas; it corresponds to the viewer's idea of the location of his own head when he looks at the picture. The *convergence* of lines and principal directions on a point in the visual field can impart dominance to that point without the aid of size and color. The eye finds it difficult to resist the point from which lines or strong light radiate. For instance, we are tempted to look at the bright sun although we know it will hurt our eyes. Hence, a very light area will dominate its darker surroundings by analogy to the sun in the sky. Finally, dominance can be achieved by *difference* or *exception.* We know that nonconformity stands out. If an ovoid shape appears among a number of squares, it will be seen as the exception; it will stick out like the proverbial "sore thumb" and thus seem to dominate the others. Similarly, in a field of similar shapes, the shape bearing a different color or texture will be able to assert its individuality. Subordination, as would be expected, results from the employment of devices opposite to those which create dominance: small size, peripheral location, dull or grayed color, remoteness from converging lines, and similarity to other forms in shape, color, and texture.

Coherence refers to the sense of *belonging together* that characterizes the components of a successful work of art, one whose various parts have an independent existence but appear to have become what they are through harmonious adjustment to the requirements of each. When Paul Cézanne (1839–1906) painted a picture, changing any single area, he felt, would oblige him to reorganize the entire

Coherence or the sense of organic relatedness is achieved in Cézanne's work by adjusting each color area to the spatial requirements of the areas around it.

PAUL CÉZANNE, *Mont Sainte Victoire Seen from Bibemus Quarry (near Aix)* (c.1898–1900). Courtesy The Baltimore Museum of Art, The Cone Collection.

composition. All the parts were so adjusted to one another in color, shape, and size that they functioned organically: The parts were objectively independent but they were completely *interdependent* so far as aesthetic effect was concerned. If an organization is so carefully adjusted that change in one of its parts ruins its effectiveness, we are justified in regarding it as a *unique, coherent,* man-made organism. Its unity is based on the viewer's feeling that the organization as it stands is inevitable: It could not be otherwise and exist properly. The apples, lemons, trees, or rocks of Cézanne must be precisely where and as they are.

Coherence or organic unity can be achieved, as mentioned earlier, through analogous color and color tonality—the prevalence of a single color or admixtures of it throughout a work. *Similarity* of any kind—of shape, color, size, illumination, character of line and edge, and texture—will promote the impression of coherence and hence of unity. The use of this device has its perils, however, since sameness also leads to monotony. Any device for achieving unity runs the risk, if employed too mechanically, of losing the viewer's interest. Our tolerance for sameness is limited; we require variety to satisfy our visual appetites and yet not so much variety that the sense of unity is sacrificed.

Forms which are *dis*similar can be unified by the device of clustering. If they are unlike in shape or color, their *closeness* suggests coherence. In a sense, the eye is deceived by propinquity into accepting a relationship among incongruous forms. If they are surrounded by open space, dissimilar forms located near each other tend to be perceived as

a unit. This principle of unity is frequently illustrated in the paintings of Braque following his Cubist period. *The Round Table* contains a variety of objects and shapes, no two of which are alike. But they are held together by the dark, encircling form of the table top which imposes the unity of a container upon the things contained.

Unity based on converging or radiating lines is very common and easily employed. The design problem in such cases is to avoid the obvious. We have seen this type of unity in a very pure manifestation in the wire constructions of Richard Lippold. But Lippold creates subsidiary centers of interest at the periphery of the space he controls, and the color and shimmer of his fine metal lines appeal to the eye directly, thus mitigating what might be a too-insistent stress on the radiant center. In *"and the bush was not consumed,"* Herbert Ferber (1906–) presents a radiating

GEORGES BRAQUE, *The Round Table* (1929). Courtesy The Phillips Collection, Washington, D.C.

RICHARD LIPPOLD, *Variation Number 7: Full Moon* (1949–50), left. Collection The Museum of Modern Art, New York, Mrs. Simon Guggenheim Fund.

HERBERT FERBER, *"and the bush was not consumed"* (1951–52), right. Courtesy the artist.

composition based on the V form; but although the directions converge at the point of the V, a number of minor variations in shape and direction serve to avoid a too obvious, hence monotonous, reliance on the basic organization.

A classic instance of unity by central location occurs in *Nachi Waterfall,* a silk scroll painting of the Kamakura Period of Japanese art (1185–1333). Although paintings of this type had a religious function in medieval Japan, they can be perceived by modern eyes largely in terms of their mastery of pictorial structure. In this case, the subordination of rich and complex landscape forms to the waterfall is superbly accomplished. The dead-center location of the

water could easily lead to monotony if it were not for the sensitive adjustment of dark weights, left and right, top and bottom. A rugged, rocky profile is dramatized at the point where the eye is led by the falling water, enabling the artist to introduce several diagonals to modify the dominant verticals. He also reserves his strongest light-and-dark contrasts for the spot where the water crashes against the rocks, after which it trickles away to a different tune. As the eye penetrates the darks, it grows aware of rhythmic vertical repetitions in the rock forms of the cliff as they support the dominant central waterfall, while balancing horizontal shapes are found in the tree foliage and the mysterious mountain forms across the top. The great virtue of this work is that, although an obvious, almost mechanical device for the achievment of unity has been chosen, the artist has managed to sustain the viewer's interest by ingenious use of subordinate measures for creating variety without in any way detracting from the principal dramatic event.

The problem of artistic unity might be compared to the dilemma of Scheherazade, the Persian princess who had to entertain the Sultan with a different story each night for "a thousand-and-one nights." If the Sultan were not amused, the princess would lose her head. The common element in the situation, the unity of the thousand-and-one nights, was that the same narrator was engaged in the effort to divert the same listener. Scheherazade managed to keep her head by introducing sufficient variety into her stories to obscure the fact that the same situation experienced a thousand times can become exceedingly dull—especially for a sultan.

Nachi Waterfall (c.1300), left. Nezu Museum, Tokyo.

MARSDEN HARTLEY, *Smelt Brook Falls* (1937), right. Courtesy City Art Museum of Saint Louis.

Balance

Aside from the legend that Galileo dropped unequal weights from it, the reason why the Leaning Tower of Pisa is popularly renowned is that it is out of balance yet manages to stand. The building is a world-wide curiosity. Our normal expectation is that the forces at work in the structure will be resolved —one way or the other. The building will either "balance itself" or fall. That it does neither is visually disturbing. Balance is the resolution of all forces in a structure leading to equilibrium or equipoise. It is evident in nature, in man, and in the man-made world.

Balance in the structural world is largely a matter of the reconciliation of weights and stresses leading to stability. It may be a chemical process in the biological world without which life itself could not be supported. In art, balance is, of course, an optical condition, and terms like weight, stress, tension, and stability, which are borrowed from physics and engineering, take on perceptual meanings. It would not be surprising if the parallelogram-of-forces problems that students of mathematics and physics solve, are intuitively solved by artists and viewers as they calculate whether certain visual forms are pleasing. One thing is certain: Having gone through a period of instability during infancy, we are very sensitive to signs of imbalance in all phenomena.

Architectural and sculptural structures must be in balance or they will not stand. The first cantilevered structures created some unease among persons accustomed to buildings whose support was visible, for the cantilever is a form of *hidden* balance. If we cannot intellectually imagine the balance of forces that provides its strength, we are likely to feel endangered when walking under a canopy which is unsupported by posts. The imbalance of graphic or painted forms does not endanger us physically, but is nevertheless disturbing. Hence, several design devices are employed to create for viewers the experience of optical balance which they seem to require.

The simplest and least interesting type of balance is *symmetrical balance,* usually understood as bilateral symmetry. The left and right halves of the visual field are identical—mirror images of each other. This form of balance has a spontaneous appeal which may relate to the bilateral symmetry of the human body. Also, it requires a minimum of perceptual effort to understand. The elements in each half may be very complex and in themselves difficult to comprehend, but as soon as they are recognized as echoes of each other, they acquire an interest which is curiously satisfying. Perhaps the pleasure which even children take in bilateral symmetry is related to the manner in which electrical charges are distributed over the hemispheres of the brain during perception. The other main type of balance, *asymmetrical balance,* is more complex and interesting, although it may, by a more devious route, provide the viewer with the same pleasurable reaction he experiences in symmetrical balance.

The cantilever—a form of hidden balance.

AMMANN & WHITNEY, hangar at Miami Airport (1958). Courtesy National Airlines.

Symmetrical balance.

ANTOINE PEVSNER, *Construction in the Egg* (1948). Collection Albright-Knox Art Gallery, Buffalo, New York.

Asymmetrical balance.

JEAN GORIN, *Composition No. 9* (1934), left. Courtesy Jean Gorin, Paris.

Horizontal balance by weight.

JEAN ARP, *Olympia* (1954), right. Courtesy Mrs. Jean Arp.

Balance by weight (usually asymmetrical) suggests analogy to a lever and fulcrum, or a see-saw. It is assumed that the center of a picture, or of the visual field in the case of sculpture and architecture, corresponds to the fulcrum on which a lever or see-saw is poised. A heavy weight can be counterbalanced by a lighter weight which is located at a further distance from the center. But we are dealing with visual weight rather than physical weight. (Although gravity does not *actually* operate on the objects in paintings, we *perceive them as if it does.*) What are the properties of the visual elements with respect to weight? Clearly, size is the first consideration. Other things being equal, the larger, more massive shape is heavier. Color, too, is important, in that it always occurs in *relationships.* In general, warm colors are heavier than cool colors; those of strong intensity heavier than those of weak or faded intensity. As between warm colors—for example, yellow and orange—an area of yellow would appear

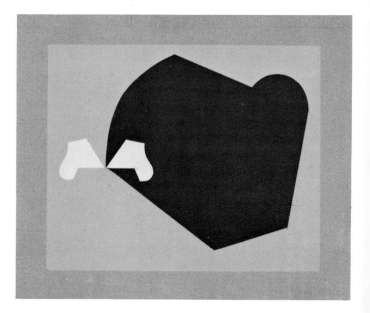

larger than an equal area of orange, because yellow is higher in value; but orange has a stronger wave length than yellow and so would advance before it; their apparent weights, therefore, might be equal. Coarsely textured surfaces appear to be heavier than smooth surfaces, perhaps because the tactile feeling excited by coarseness alerts the organism to the possibility of cutting or abrasion if the surface were handled. In this case, weight is associated with concern about danger. The *location* of forms also affects visual weight. Above the mid-point they appear lighter than they do below. We can only speculate that this is due to the viewer's assumption of a horizon at the mid-point, forms above it being seen as if in the air, in defiance of gravity. In most pictorial traditions, "up" is interpreted as "in"; the top of the picture recedes while the bottom advances. Gravitational "thinking" affects perception; the bottom is where heavy objects appear to have landed. Also, the unusual excites interest and interest confers weight. Peripheral position was noted in connection with unity as a type of subordinate location. For purposes of balance, however, a small object at the left or right edge of a field can cancel the weight of a larger object closer to the center—a case of lever action in the pictorial field.

The "action" in most contemporary painting takes place on the picture plane itself. Even when some of the conventions of depth representation have been employed, as in Picasso and Braque, we have been conditioned to "read" the forms as if the existence of deep space were not implied. This results in a certain amount of ambiguity regarding the visual weight of objects that have been reduced in size because

of their location *back* in the implied picture space. The viewer can only look for other structural cues to guide him to the correct reading of the visual weights and the pictorial location of the forms he is examining. Cézanne is perhaps the most skillful painter in eliminating confusion about the spatial location and weight of forms, although he takes many liberties with the conventions of linear perspective. From the standpoint of critical judgment (see p. 486), the failure to resolve the spatial location of forms or to balance visual weights may lead to an unfavorable estimate of the work as a whole, assuming that visual balance and spatial consistency are implied objectives.

Balance by interest is another asymmetrical device. It is based on the excitation of the viewer's *curiosity*, perhaps to counteract the impression of weight caused by size, color, or location. The idea that psychological interest adds visual weight may be open to question. But we can say, with some confidence,

Vertical balance by weight.

ADOLPH GOTTLIEB, *Blast II* (1957). Courtesy Joseph E. Seagram and Sons, Inc.

Balance by interest.

Lacquer table with gold design (Japan, Muromachi period, fifteenth century). Courtesy The Cleveland Museum of Art, Edward L. Whittemore Fund.

that artists have long employed interest to balance shapes of obviously greater mass. Hence, interest operates *as if* it possesses weight. Visual interest, in turn, is generated by formal complexity. Therefore, a simple, large, brightly colored form can be balanced by a small, neutrally colored form if the latter's shape is complex. Interest is related to the whole realm of psychological affect and therefore it can upset the logical operation of structural forces in visual art. That is, once symbols and explicit signs are employed in a work of art, they arouse complex emotions and associations; they can influence perception in ways which are irrelevant to formal structure. For example, it is difficult to perceive Surrealist works apart from their symbolic meanings. Most viewers say they enjoy the color of Chagall's paintings, but it is very likely they are chiefly attracted by his romantic and poetic imagery. Perhaps they really enjoy their *feelings* about his images and *believe* the color causes their feelings. At any rate, the pictorial structures of Chagall owe any order or balance they possess to the *interest* he can create by his symbolic and narrative episodes. They are not balanced by weight, which is to say, they do not possess *formal* balance.

Balance by contrast might also be called balance by difference or opposition. It is the type of asymmetrical, dynamic balance which is most difficult for the artist because it involves calculating the visual demands of varying quantities of different elements. It includes not only oppositions between colors (as in warm vs. cool) or between shapes (as in geometric vs. organic) or between light intensities (as in light vs. dark) but also oppositions between color

and shape, between weight and interest, and between shape and illumination. Although the balancing of weights is difficult, it is not overwhelmingly complex. Indeed, it is implied in the elementary design problems given art students, who are asked to find the "best" arrangement of black or of black and gray rectangles on a white field. It turns out that there are several good solutions, and also some that do not work. However, balance of interest by shape and color begins to approximate the complexity of art beyond that in a student exercise. The selection of one solution among others (none of which can be known in advance) transcends more-or-less skillful manipulation of the visual elements and approaches the difficulty of mature artistic expression.

It is possible that balance by contrast is the closest visual analogue to musical harmony. That is, in both musical and visual structures there is a unified effect which is pursued through the combination of dissimilar elements. In each case, the work increases in interest when the dissimilar elements combine to create something new, for example, a third voice. Most of us recognize that the consonance created by playing or singing the same melody at the same time in a different octave is rather insipid. Dissonance is favored by some modern composers to avoid the monotony resulting from the reiteration of consonant harmonies. In visual art, the unities based on similarity and likeness are most common and most predictable. Perhaps the reason we admire the skylines of New York or Chicago (although we *know* that those cities are chaotic when seen up close) lies in the vigor of their unity wrested from so many dissimilar elements.

Balance of weight by interest.

JOAN MIRÓ, *Maternity* (1924). Courtesy Penrose Collection, London.

Balance of weight by interest is very conveniently illustrated in Joan Miró's *Maternity* in which the artist virtually sets up a laboratory experiment for us. Two straight lines cross in the center of the picture, forming an X. The point where they cross acts as a fulcrum. A large form at one end shaped like a wedge of pie is balanced by a small, insect-like form at the other end. A worm shape also joins the insect although it does not seem attached to the lever arm. The heavy shape is closer to the center, so that the moment of its forces (distance times weight) is about equal to the moment of forces created by the insect which is further from the center of the fulcrum. This element in its entirety stands for the male, the hole in the wedge serving to characterize it as the eye of a cockscomb, while the wormlike shape symbolizes the spermatazoa aimed at an ovum. The other arm of the X is, of course, the female, divided by the fulcrum point into two equal segments, one presumably internal, where the ovum is located, and the other external, where we see a hemispherical shape suggesting a breast. The feathered little creatures at both ends, which look like the female biological symbol, ♀, seem to be engaged in a see-saw game wherein the ovum may swing closer or further away from the sperm. The position in the picture and the title suggest that they will meet. In addition to the principles of balance, this work illustrates the highly individual and whimsical type of Surrealism developed by Miró. He has created a playful enactment of the biological drama of human conception and divested the process of much of its dark, clinical mystery, presenting it as a slightly comic natural event in which delicate timing and physical forces play a crucial role.

Rhythm

The term rhythm applies basically to poetry and music, and relates to measures of time. But seeing also takes time, and from the standpoint of the viewer, it is most efficiently and pleasurably done in a rhythmic way. Therefore, events or works of art that aid and abet the rhythmic tendencies of seeing are likely to promote a pleasurable reaction when the total organism concentrates on vision. Some examples from sports may make this clear. Tennis is a pleasurable game to watch, in part because of the rhythmic alternation of long volleys. A service ace is dramatic, but less satisfying to the rhythmic sense. American football seems rhythmically more satisfying than its English ancestors, Rugby and soccer, because football has distinct, alternating rhythms of attack and defense, like fencing, whereas the rhythms of soccer or Rugby are more difficult to perceive.[*] The action in the British games is more continuous, and, to American eyes at least, less distinct in structure.

In the visual arts, rhythm is the *ordered or regular recurrence of an element or elements.* The main types of

[*] See the essay, "Football in America: A Study in Culture Diffusion," by David Riesman and Ruel Denney, in David Riesman, *Individualism Reconsidered*, The Free Press of Glencoe, 1964.

rhythm are labeled *repetitive, alternative, progressive,* and *flowing.* The repetition of the same or almost the same shape, color, line, or direction would constitute rhythm. The recurrence of similarly shaped spaces between lines, the recurrence of colors and of positive shapes are also rhythmic. In architecture, the rhythmic development of interior space is vital, possibly more important than the appearance of the external forms that enclose the interior. Ideally, rhythm should characterize the enclosing forms and those which are enclosed through correspondence between inside and outside. But medieval building technology, for example, did not permit such a relationship; hence the cathedral,

with its complex skeleton on the outside, afforded little insight into the open character of the space within. Nevertheless, the exterior membranes and buttressing exhibit a rhythm of their own which is fascinating as sculpture, apart from the interest derived from its structural performance.

We know that men march, lift, or pull together with more effectiveness if their effort is regulated by a recurrent, rhythmic stress or beat. They tire less easily, too. In performing repetitive tasks, people try to find a comfortable rhythm. Up to a certain point, *repetitive* rhythm helps to sustain attention, to reduce weariness, to maximize efficiency. But early experimenters in

Rhythm accomplished through the repetition of shape, while variations in tonal value and spacing are subtly introduced.

MU CH'I, *Six Persimmons* (c.1269), left. Daitoku-ji, Kyoto.

JOERN UTZON, model of Sydney Opera House (in construction), right top. Photo, Australian News and Information Bureau.

WAYNE THIEBAUD, *Seven Jellied Apples* (1963), right bottom. Courtesy Allan Stone Gallery.

industrial psychology discovered that operators performing repetitive tasks on dangerous machinery—such as punch presses, stamping machines, and sawing machinery—tended eventually to suffer injuries. Injuries could be reduced (aside from the use of safety equipment) by rotating operators after a certain length of time. Apparently, the human organism finds repetitive motion boring if experienced for too long, and resists by breaking the rhythm.

Visual repetition such as we encounter in fabric patterns can be very monotonous. Of course, all-over, repeat designs in fabrics are rarely perceived in a simple, flat plane: We see them broken up, draped, and in association with the movement of the shapes or volumes they cover. Some Op art is more tolerable in the form of fabrics draped over attractive models than it is when seen as a flat plane. Op is an art style which uses repetitive rhythm effectively so far as its physiological impact is concerned. Its practitioners introduce subtle variations after setting up a strong pattern of visual expectation. These variations have a rhythm of their own while participating in the rhythm of the primary pattern. But the viewer is disoriented by the deliberate ambiguities of the rhythmic optical patterns: His eye finds it impossible to integrate the stimuli it receives into any single, consistent image, or *gestalt*. This lack of integration has been variously described as exhilarating, confusing, exhausting, or pleasurably exciting.

The usual objective of artists and designers is to exploit the comfortable qualities of repetitive rhythm without incurring monotony. Hence, they employ repetition with variation, com-parable to theme and variation in music. Simple *alternations* between black and white, warm and cool, for instance, can be varied by the introduction of an unexpected element, a slight change in emphasis that does not destroy the rhythmic pattern of the whole. Rhythm, therefore, exploits the viewer's expectation. It can achieve variety within unity by frustrating expectation temporarily—in other words, by an occasional surprise.

The establishment of a rhythmic sequence in art does not occur as the result of accident: It has to be planned and calculated. Such calculations can easily become mechanical patterns requiring not artistry but the capacity to follow directions. But when the viewer senses the noncreative character of rhythms so achieved his experience of the work tends to be wearisome. Some Pop art works by Andy Warhol seem to fit this category. We can think of many examples from painting, sculpture, architecture, and industrial design which exhibit a deadly, unrelieved sameness. Art seems to consist of the saving variation which enlivens the rhythmic whole.

Progressive rhythm involves the repetition of an element with a consistently repeated change leading from one color, shape, or type of illumination to another. The expectation of the viewer is aroused in terms of a goal, a culmination. It is exploited in architecture very often by the sequence of the steps or set-backs of tall buildings. As one moves through a building's interior, one may experience a sequence of progressively enlarged or diminished volumes, thereby arousing the expectation of a certain kind of volume, shape, or type of illumination at the conclusion. The architect may

Model in paper dress of Op design. Dress, courtesy Scott Paper Company; photo, H. Rinehart.

Repetitive rhythm.

ANDY WARHOL, *Brillo Boxes* (1964). Courtesy Leon Kraushar Collection.

Progressive rhythm.

KASIMIR MALEVITCH, *Eight Red Rectangles* (1916). Courtesy Stedelijk Museum, Amsterdam.

Flowing rhythm in modern structural materials.

EERO SAARINEN, TWA Terminal, Kennedy International Airport (1962), left. Courtesy TWA by Ezra Stoller Associates.

ALVAR AALTO, experiment with bentwood (1929), center. Courtesy Artek.

FRANK LLOYD WRIGHT, The Solomon R. Guggenheim Museum (1959), right. Courtesy The Solomon R. Guggenheim Museum.

choose to satisfy this expectation or he may work for a dramatic effect through surprise. But an architectural surprise that is totally unrelated to what precedes it would sacrifice the unity of the whole. Some qualities of the introductory sequence must be present in the dramatic climax. In other words, there are good surprises and bad surprises.

Rhythm as continuous flow is suggested by the movement of waves: regular recurrence of shapes; emphasis or stress at the crests and pause in the troughs; measured, periodic intervals; and smooth transitions from one wave form to the next. The crucial feature of this type of rhythm is the connection between forms. The eye is arrested at various points of interest in the visual field: How is the movement of the eye from one nodal point to the next accomplished? We feel that when the eye is encouraged to move along a curvilinear path, which is punctuated by undulating swells (waves again) with no breaks or sudden changes of direction, it describes rhythmic or continuous flow. There are, of course, staccato rhythms described

by the movement of the eye. We see them in the paintings of Stuart Davis, Bradley Walker Tomlin, and John Marin. Flowing rhythm, on the contrary, is associated with sculptors like Jean Arp, Aristide Maillol, and Henry Moore; painters such as Georgia O'Keefe, David Siquieros, and Amadeo Modigliani. In architecture, fluid rhythms are more difficult to achieve, although, as we know, the Art Nouveau designers carried curvilinear forms to an extreme. The late Eero Saarinen (1910–61) employed fluid rhythmic lines in his TWA terminal building at Kennedy Airport as he did also in the Administration Building Lobby for the General Motors Technical Center. And the principal structural element of Wright's Guggenheim Museum interior is the continuous spiral flow of the ramp following the curved inside walls of the building, which is like the shell of a huge crustacean. Aalto's bentwood experiment seeks a practical application in chair design, but also is a good abstract illustration of flowing rhythm based on human contours. Plowed fields photo-

THOMAS EAKINS, *Man Pole Vaulting* (1884–85), above. Courtesy The Metropolitan Museum of Art.

MARCEL DUCHAMP, *Nude Descending a Staircase, No. 2* (1912), at left. Courtesy Philadelphia Museum of Art, The Louise and Walter Arensberg Collection.

GINO SEVERINI, *Dynamic Hieroglyphic of the Bal Tabarin* (1912), below. Collection The Museum of Modern Art, New York, acquired through the Lillie P. Bliss bequest.

graphed from the air illustrate flowing rhythm and also exhibit the moiré effect now employed by Op artists. (Moiré fabrics, usually silk, have been watered to create a pattern of wavy lines which shift and shimmer as the light changes or the fabric moves.)

A photograph of a pole vaulter, by the painter Thomas Eakins, illustrates repetitive rhythm. Eakins, a serious student of anatomy, shared with the photographer Eadweard Muybridge a scientific interest in motion, and the results of his investigations happily exemplify the design principle of rhythm. In painting, the well-known *Nude Descending a Staircase* by Marcel Duchamp makes the same point, as do all Futurist works which give to motion the central place in art. A variety of rhythmic qualities is evident in Boccioni's *Unique Continuity* sculpture (p. 29), while the *Dynamic Hieroglyphic of the Bal Tabarin* of Gino Severini (1883–1966)

ALAIN RESNAIS (director), *Last Year at Marienbad*. Stills from The Museum of Modern Art Film Library.

is possibly the best single example in modern painting of rhythm in its repetitive, alternating, progressive, and flowing varieties. It contains color, line, and shape repetitions and progressions which can occupy the eye for hours. The painting also has the quality of a sedate explosion; it is similar to, but less raucous than, Joseph Stella's *Battle of Light, Coney Island* (p. 54). The Futurists, fascinated by mechanization

and motion, clearly made rhythmic capital out of the austere Cubist analysis of form.

Notwithstanding the many outstanding examples of rhythm in painting, sculpture, and architecture, the most spectacular manifestations today are very likely visible in motion picture imagery and the animated film. Certainly, continuous-flow rhythm is one of the main objectives of film cutting. As the time needed to see a work of art increases (in the film, in murals, in vast architectural projects) the principle of rhythm requires more attention. Rhythm is essentially a temporal concept which becomes increasingly prominent in the visual arts as duration becomes a ponderable factor in their perception.

Proportion

LE CORBUSIER, Modulor.

Proportion refers to the *size* relationships of parts to a whole and to one another. The visual context determines whether size is read as area, width, height, or depth. The size of a shape in itself has no proportional meaning: It must enter into a relationship with other shapes before we can be aware of proportion. It should be understood at the beginning of any discussion of the subject that there are no permanently valid *rules* fixing "correct" or harmonious proportions. True, in criticism of representational art, the phrase "out of proportion" may be used, but it means that the proportions of the representational image do not correspond to the proportions of the actual model being drawn, painted, or modeled.

There have been attempts to set

up a rule or canon of perfect proportion, one that would automatically confer pleasing intervals on all artistic structures.° (The Vitruvian man, discussed earlier, p. 164, attempted to derive architectural proportions from the human figure.) The most enduring has been the so-called Golden Section. It divides a line into two segments so that the smaller has the same ratio to the larger as the larger has to the whole.† Another attempt, the Module or Modulor devised by Le Corbusier, was mentioned on page 95. The Golden Section has been used in many works

° See Erwin Panofsky, "The History of the Theory of Human Proportions as a Reflection of the History of Styles," Chapter II in *Meaning in the Visual Arts*, Doubleday, 1955.

† The algebraic formula for the Golden Section is: $(a + b)/a = a/b$.

of art and in many periods, but there seems to be nothing remarkable about it as a formula beyond its indirect recognition that a line divided in half makes a dull pair of intervals. Nor are segments of thirds much better than halves. Efforts to discover a magical geometric ratio that underlies all pleasing or beautiful proportion will no doubt continue. But the history of art will in all likelihood continue to afford examples of great works that do not conform to the canon. Of course, the validity of a rule of proportion can be "proved" consistently if one takes measurements at points convenient for the purpose of demonstrating the rule. But modern aesthetics has been greatly influenced by the *perceptual field theory* of Gestalt psychology, and the perceptual field of an art object is not easily reduced to a set of dimensions (although it is not independent of the dimensions of forms, either).

The lack of eternally valid rules for perfect proportion does not, however, mean that we recoil from making judgments about proportion. In any given era, people seem to have fairly common conceptions about what constitutes good proportion in buildings, pictures, sculpture, useful objects, and even in people. We are taller and larger today than the men who wore medieval armor, so it is likely that our conceptions of pleasing height, if not width, in men and women, have changed. Hence, if there has been a change in proportional preference, it has been caused, not by a rule of geometrical ratio but by better nutrition.

The figures in contemporary fashion illustrations are some ten or twelve heads high, although this ratio changes from time to time. Art students used to be taught that seven-and-a-half heads

was the correct measure for men, and six-and-a-half for women. If a model did not conform, the head was drawn larger or smaller according to need. Aside from the ratio of head to height, it is probable that the average, or presumed average, size of the human figure, and the relationships among its parts, constitute the model for *thinking about proportion* for most visual phenomena. *We tend to perceive sizes, dimensions, and proportional ratios in terms of multiples of the human figure as a whole* and in terms of proportional ratios *within the human figure.* In other words, we see a doorway or ceiling height as providing so much open space above the *height of a man.* Drivers may perceive in terms of car lengths and widths. But when we see only for the sake of seeing—when vision is self-conscious, so to speak—the referent is the dimensional self-image, the figure.

According to this view, people are continuously if unconsciously engaged in making visual calculations and comparisons. They may use a scale of feet and inches, as when they say, "That man is six foot two." They may also say, "She is about my height, but a little stouter." In the latter statement, there is a hint of proportional judgment. We may visit friends in a new apartment and feel uncomfortable during the visit without knowing why. Did the builder skimp on the ceiling height, so that we felt squeezed? A proportional feeling was experienced here although unexpressed. We walk along the downtown canyons of a large city and feel depressed for no apparent reason. Are the buildings so high that we cannot perceive them as multiples of the human figure? There is nothing wrong with height in itself. If we approach a tall building

M. S. BIGELOW, Fashion drawing (1966).

Female figure. Photo of Debbie Drake from jacket of Debbie Drake's *Easy Way to a Perfect Figure and Glowing Health*, Prentice-Hall, Inc., 1961.

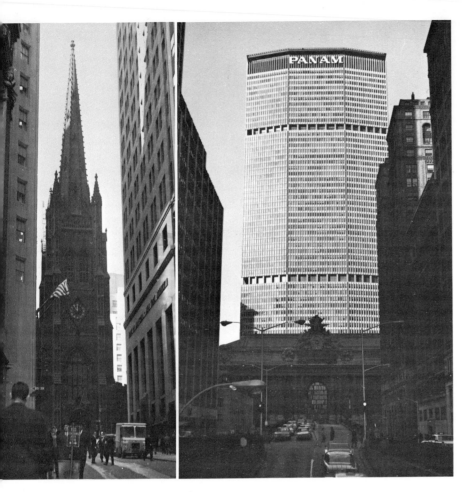

The Trinity Church permits pleasing perception in relation to the
surrounding structures. But the
design qualities of many buildings
are lost to the viewer if he cannot
see their parts in relation to their
architectural environment.

RICHARD UPJOHN, Trinity Church
(1846) between skyscrapers, left.
Photo, H. Rinehart.

WALTER GROPIUS and others, Pan
Am Building (1963), right. Photo,
H. Rinehart.

from sufficient distance, it begins by
occupying a small area of the retina; we
see it *in relation* to other visual phenomena with which we have already established a *proportional understanding*. We
can gradually advance toward the building, accumulating and enriching our perceptions of its size relationships through
other cues in the visual field. The space
around the building, which corresponds
to the area of the retina the building
does not occupy, is necessary for the
establishment of a proportional understanding. But few skyscrapers are situated
so that we can see them at a distance,
especially on foot. Rarely can we see a
tall building continuously as we advance
toward it. In summary, it is very difficult
for contemporary tall buildings to have

what is called "human scale." The fault
does not necessarily lie in their design,
or their proportions, but in the insuffi-
ciency of optical space around them.

The function of design, however,
is to manage proportion so that the
disadvantages of the *spatial envelope*
and inherent problems of shape can be
minimized or overcome. Manipulation
of the visual elements can create "adjustments" in the ratio of width to height,
for example. Isolating a large shape
makes it appear smaller. Horizontal
patterning and segmentation of a tall
shape reduces its apparent height. The
size of repeat designs in a fabric effects
its advancing/receding qualities: A large
motif brings the pattern closer. Coarseness and fineness of texture too can be
regarded as a dimension of proportion,
coarseness tending to approximate the
large motif, which advances relative to
the small figure or the fine texture.

Any large, immeasurable form,
when represented graphically, needs
some familiar object or shape to give it
"scale." We have a very vague understanding of the proportions of a landscape painting unless we are granted a
human or architectural cue. Knowing
the size of a man or a barn, we can
calculate ratios visually and then understand how high, distant, or menacing
the mountain is. In abstract works, the
viewer's knowledge of the size of real
objects is not exploited, although his experience with size relationships in life *is*
used. For example, in Matta's painting,
The Disasters of Mysticism we cannot "know" whether the work is structured according to the scale of a conventional landscape, a situation in outer
space, or an event seen under the microscope. But we are inclined to perceive
motion, direction, light, shape, and size

relationships in terms of our ordinary terrestrial experience. The same observation can be made in connection with nonobjective works by Kandinsky, Bauer, and Malevitch.

A final point needs to be made about the exploitation of conventional norms in proportion: Since we tend to perceive variations from these norms as distortion, proportion can be used for expressive effect. We are familiar with the effects of attenuation in the sculpture of Lehmbruck and Giacometti; and Modigliani and Picasso in their painting have placed small heads on large bodies to convey the quality of massive stability. Viewers see not only the head size but also, more importantly, the proportional *relationship* between the size of the head and the bulk of the body: It is the *proportion* which carries the expressive burden. Monumentality is a matter of proportion and of generous spacing rather than mere height and magnitude.

In architecture, viewers have been habituated for centuries to the intervals found in classical Greek and Roman buildings. As we know, modern buildings, even tall office buildings, have been adorned with miniature Greek temples at the ground level and also on their roofs. Aside from offering on obeisance to tradition, this practice represented a recognition of the fact that the classical civilizations solved the problem of proportion while we were not able to do so. The severe flat roof of International Style architecture in the 1930's seemed dreadfully stark, naked, and arbitrarily cut off. Viewers required psychological interest at the top of a building as well as at the entrance— whether overhanging eaves, entablatures, and triangular pediments were functional or not. Apparently, the earliest skyscrapers were perceived by de-

MATTA (Sebastian Antonio Matta Echaurren), *The Disasters of Mysticism* (1942), left. Courtesy The Museum of Modern Art, New York, James Thrall Soby Collection.

PABLO PICASSO, *Seated Bather* (early 1930), right. Collection The Museum of Modern Art, New York, Mrs. Simon Guggenheim Fund.

Buttress of the state capitol, Lincoln, Nebraska (1922). Courtesy Edholm & Blomgren Photographers, Lincoln, Nebraska.

signers as structures requiring a capital, a "head." It was felt that a building had to be "topped off" by something that would endow its entirety with *proportion*. The designer's "block" in this case was his inability to free himself from the idea of the building as a symbol of the human figure. This idea is expressed quite literally in the buttresses of the State Capitol, Lincoln, Nebraska. The Nebraska State Capitol is dated 1922. Only nine years later, however, the Radio City complex was begun by Harrison and others (see pp. 105–106). The proportions of its individual buildings expressed the technology of construction and the solution of functional problems. The vocabulary of form and proportion was now based on the abstract creations of the machine rather than figurative symbols and analogies imported from the past. Figurative relief sculptures over the entrances to several of the buildings now seem to be quaint survivals. This does not mean that architecture and sculpture are permanently divorced: But the means of reconciling them is still in process of being discovered. Humanistic interest has shifted to the space between the buildings and the people moving through that space, *their* movement and visual opportunities reflecting the designer's approach to the enclosure of outdoor areas. Thus, we gain some hint of a new, *kinaesthetic* approach to form and proportion: the shaping of space to be seen and felt by people in motion.

Conclusion

Although unity, balance, rhythm, and proportion have been treated mainly as objectives of the designer, we found it necessary to discuss the contribution of the viewer to the achievement of these goals. That is, in addition to knowing some of the devices artists use to reach their design objectives, we needed to know why viewers are interested in them. To some extent, an artist's effectiveness depends on his understanding of the way people respond to his organization of the visual elements. But as we know, he is mainly guided by his own personal responses to his work in estimating its visual effectiveness for others. The principles or goals of design we have discussed are rarely the *conscious* aims of artistic creations: From the artist's standpoint they are labels that viewers give to his often intuitive efforts to discover form, express meaning, organize materials, and solve problems.

These "labels" should help us as viewers to understand the underlying principles of visual organization which seem to make works of art effective. There may be a temptation to set up the principles of design as standards of excellence against which specific works can be measured. But that would be a mistaken employment of them. Their use should be limited to *explaining* the organization of visual events in works of art. The problems of judgment and art criticism, discussed in Chapters Fourteen and Fifteen, are more complex because they involve philosophic as well as structural considerations. Notice that in the chapters on *Structure* we have talked chiefly about the effectiveness of visual organization; and in the earlier chapters on *Function* we discussed the *uses* of art. But we said less about the *value* of the uses or purposes which art serves. That is a question for the philosophy of art; determination of excellence is a problem of art criticism. However, we have been acquiring the tools which should help in the performance of critical tasks. As for a philosophy of art, *informed* persons can build their own, and, hopefully, you have been encouraged in that undertaking by the material presented thus far.

CHAPTER TEN

We have examined the visual elements and the principles of their organization, design. Now we are about to examine the principles which account for our perception of what has been organized. Before doing so, we must make an important distinction between *visual form* and *aesthetic structure* if later confusion is to be avoided. Visual form refers to the features of a work of art which are responsible for its organization, its existence as a coherent, intelligible whole. In other words, form designates whatever it is in the object that holds the work together.° Aesthetic structure refers to those features of the act of perception which give wholeness and coherence to our experience of a work of art. From this definition you can see that I intend to treat aesthetic structure as a psychological problem. It might be said that aesthetic structure exists *inside* the viewer, but only because the potential for visual form exists *outside* him in the art object. Both form and structure are primarily caused by the art object but, to oversimplify, visual form is used as an objective term and

°I like the statement about form which Vivas and Krieger use to describe the views of Isenberg and Bradley: ". . . they see form as the manner in which everything that is to be found in the object is put together, as the total interrelation of whatever is discriminable (the expressive as well as the formal elements) in the object." Eliseo Vivas and Murray Krieger, *The Problems of Aesthetics,* Holt, 1960, p. 181.

PERCEIVING

THE ELEMENTS:

AESTHETICS

aesthetic structure is used as a subjective term.

What is the purpose of making this distinction? It allows us to recognize the contributions of the viewer to the "creation" of a work of art without ignoring the responsibility of the artist for determining the crucial events that underlie the structure of the aesthetic experience. It helps to account for the fact that different viewers perceive the same work differently, and that even a single viewer perceives a work differently at different times. It maintains the integrity of the objective existence of the work of art, a point which has some philosophic value. If we did not define visual form in terms of an objectively existing organization, we might find ourselves in the embarrassing position of ascribing the aesthetic experience almost wholly to the effort of the viewer. The artist would be credited only with some minor physical activity in providing the raw sensory materials for the experience. He would not be regarded as responsible for the organizational effort which results ultimately in visual form.

At the other extreme, if viewers saw *only* what is physically present in the work of art—the colored patches of pigment on the canvas, for example— all experiences of art would be identical, assuming all viewers had normal vision. It would be unnecessary to instruct them in what to look for. There would be no variation in perception based on the maturity, culture, or interests of different viewers. But clearly, viewers *do* vary in background, they *do* see differently, they *do* have varying capacities for understanding or enjoying what they see. We know that perception is not merely a passive activity, that it requires work—the *active* organization of psychological energies. In other words, perception is a *creative* process. The perception of works of art involves the *creative integration of the sensory excitations and psychological expectations aroused in the viewer by the organization of elements embodied in visual form.*

It might be helpful at this point to summarize the steps in our discussion which have led to the present position about the structure of art as a whole:

1. *The visual elements* are constituents of perception which have been fashioned by an artist. They are not materials, like paint, concrete, and clay: The elements represent intelligible qualities and relationships—line, shape, and so on—*resulting from* the handling of materials like paint, concrete, and clay.

2. *Design* is the organization of the visual elements for the sake of objectives such as unity, balance, or rhythm. *Designing* is not painting or drawing: It is an intellectual and controlling activity; it is *thinking about* how to paint or draw or model to achieve certain ends.

3. The *art object* is the physical result of artistic execution with materials such as paint, concrete, or clay. It has a similar meaning to "artifact," the kind of man-made physical object which an archaeologist might dig up. An art object *possesses the potential* for visual form; it is the repository where form lies waiting to be discovered.

4. *Visual form* is the *perceived* result of artistic execution which has been undertaken in the light of design objectives. When someone looks at an art object, its *potential* for visual form becomes *actual.* The *viewer* brings its dormant potential to life.

5. *Perception* is the viewer's act of seeing and attempting to understand visual form. It is more than an optical process since it also involves what the viewer's brain and nervous system do with the sensory data they receive.

6. *Aesthetic experience* is the vividly apprehended sum of a viewer's perceptions of visual form on any given occasion. Individual perceptions are very brief because of limitations in our nervous and physiological equipment. *Funded perception* is the accumulation and integration of perceptions which are separate in time. Funded perception becomes *aesthetic experience* when it occurs in connection with the unifying quality of visual form.

7. *Aesthetic structure* designates the forces at work in the aesthetic experience which bind our separate perceptions together. Aesthetic structure does not designate the *content* of aesthetic experience. It designates the psychological operations in a viewer which account for his *awareness* of the content or substance of a work of art.

The term "aesthetics," as used in the title of this chapter, is not intended to be confused with the philosophy of art, which deals with the questions surrounding the meaning, creation, and purposes of art, its relation to society and history, its role in the lives of individuals and communities, its character as knowledge, pleasure, expression, and so forth. Aesthetics here is confined to questions about the way perception occurs and is organized in the experience of art.

Empathy

Empathy is the English translation of the German word, *einfühlung*, which means "feeling into." The term is used in attempting (a) to describe what happens to a viewer as he perceives a work of art and (b) to explain the origin of the viewer's feelings about visual form.

We can gain a general idea of what empathy is by recalling our reactions during a play or film. As the narrative unfolds, we become not only acquainted with the characters but also *concerned* about them. We may dislike some of the characters (not the actors, but the characters they impersonate) and admire others. The play seems to encourage us to become personally *involved* in what happens to the people in it. We worry and rejoice *with* them. Then we even forget that they are performers and we are in the audience: We *identify with* the characters and actually feel the emotions they express on the stage. No doubt measurements of our blood pressure, pulse, and breathing rate would indicate changes associated with our experience of emotions in "real life."

At the beginning of the play we had a very clear idea of the separate identities of the performers and ourselves. Yet at several points during the play that clear idea was lost. Why? Further, what is the connection between witnessing a dramatic performance and looking at a painting or a building? We identified with the characters in the play because, according to theories of empathy, watching and listening are themselves forms of mimicry, forms of imitation. The only way we can "see" the emotion of fear expressed by an actor is by summoning up that same emotion in ourselves. Fundamentally, we cannot understand or perceive an emotion felt by another person unless we feel it ourselves. The more skillful the actor, the more intense will be our effort to imitate the feelings he is pretending to have. All the circumstances surrounding the performance are designed to encourage our effort to "suspend disbelief," to identify, to become a participant in the events we are witnessing.

Empathy is, in part, a motor response. That is, one way we endeavor to imitate what we identify with is by setting our muscular equipment into motion. We clench our fists, draw our lips back and bare our teeth. (Is this the part where John Wayne confronts his antagonist or grimly rides into the face of a howling gale?) We tap our feet or rock our bodies in time to music because it is the only way we can imitate regular intervals of sound with our muscular-skeletal systems. These motor activities are not the *result* of felt emotion, they *cause* emotion to be felt. Actors realize that an audience is watching them closely for motor cues; hence actors learn how to use their bodies, voices, and facial muscles to signal the audience about which motor activity to imitate in order to experience the appropriate feelings. In the theater, actors must "telegraph" their cues quite broadly. On the huge cinema screen, with its enormous close-ups, the merest twitch on an actor's face or glottal stop in his voice can send oceans of feeling through the sensorimotor apparatus of the audience.

However, if it is possible to imitate a performer with our bodies and thus feel the same emotions he is "acting out," how is it possible to imitate a bowl of apples painted by Cézanne, a building by Le Corbusier, or an abstract work by Mondrian? It is understandable that human beings imitate other humans in order to share feelings, but how do we imitate, empathize, "feel into" objects, some of which are inanimate? The answer lies in the fact that perception is accompanied by physiological movements and kinaesthetic feelings of which we may or may not be aware. We know that looking at a church steeple involves an up-and-down movement of the head.

The feeling of being "squeezed" in a low-ceilinged apartment, as mentioned earlier, is based on the restricted physiological movements which accompany perception in that apartment. Conversely, we are familiar with the open, expansive feelings we have when walking into a great hall. In addition to these rather obvious, largescale movements, of which we are often quite aware, there are also minute movements of the eye and associated activities of the nervous system, breathing apparatus, indeed of the whole organism, which we do not consciously feel or know about. Nevertheless, such activity causes an individual to experience feelings and sensations which he attributes to the visual forms he is examining. The retinal image is not the only factor affecting perception. We are aware, of course, that the muscles which move the eyeballs as well as the muscles which regulate the opening and contraction of the pupils are continuously active in vision and that the design of the forms we see affects their activity.

In addition, the viewer is unconsciously engaged in summoning up the feelings and ideas which have been previously experienced in association with neuromuscular sensations similar to those taking place as he perceives a work of art— whether naturalistic or abstract. The organism does this work, without the viewer's conscious awareness, because of what the psychologist Karl Groos called "inner mimicry." We see and think with our physiological equipment, particularly with our muscular, skeletal, neural, circulatory, glandular, and cutaneous systems. Consequently, seeing abstract colors, shapes, lines, and patterns of light and dark opens up or closes neural pathways which were *previously* affected in a similar way by similar patterns of motor activity. For example, circular shapes may have been experienced in a thousand different contexts in life. When experienced abstractly in art, the organism tends to *relate* and to *fuse* those earlier meanings of circularity with the present experience of it. The context and the cues provided by the work of art helps the organism select from many previous encounters with circularity those feelings, meanings, or "traces" which are most appropriate—that is, most related to the character of the present stimulus. Because the viewer is not consciously aware of these processes taking place within him as he looks at a work of art, he attributes the feelings and sensations he is experiencing to the objective forms he sees. And the viewer is right to do this, since his "inner mimicry" is indeed a response, a creative response, to the visual material before him.

You will recognize that many of the observations made earlier about the visual elements, their organization and meaning, were based essentially on an empathic understanding of perception. There is a considerable amount of experimental evidence to support theories of perception as empathy. However, the version of empathy advanced by one of its earliest advocates, Theodor Lipps (1851–1941), includes elaborations which cannot be experimentally verified. Lipps believed that in the process of "feeling into" the work of art, an individual *identifies* with the work and its constituents by projecting his ego

into it. Through this "projection," the viewer takes hold of the feelings and ideas embodied in the forms. Lipps recognized that motor sensations, which he called "sense feelings," are often aroused by the contemplation of works of art. But, he felt, to the extent one is aware of these bodily feelings one cannot regard them as properties of the art object. He argued that enjoyment of one's bodily feelings is not enjoyment of art. Unfortunately, Lipps' idea, the "projection of the ego," is not very satisfactory as an explanation of aesthetic perception. The phrase adequately describes the *results* of perception, our sense of identification and empathy, but it does not explain the process, the inner mimicry, the subliminal awareness of feelings which are experienced as qualities, not of one's own constitution, but of the work of art itself.

What emerges from the discussion is a convincing argument that empathy exists, that it is empirically observable in others and in ourselves, and that it originates in a motor response to perceived phenomena. There is no debate about that. The questions of whether ego projection is a sound concept, whether bodily awareness interferes with aesthetic experience, and whether perception involves organismic imitation—these remain open. It is interesting to note that the concept of empathy applies not only to the visual arts, but that it also applies to music, drama, and literature. We can accordingly feel confident that the idea constitutes a useful instrument for understanding and probing further into the nature of our reactions to art.

Psychic Distance

As was just mentioned, Theodor Lipps, the early advocate of empathy as projection of the self into the object, found serious difficulties in a viewer's awareness of bodily sensations during aesthetic perception. Such awareness, according to Lipps, prevented the viewer from perceiving the qualities of the art object: He would be too involved with his own kinaesthetic reactions. Lipps' objection to this type of self-involvement is an approach, of a sort, to the concept of "psychical distance" as developed by the British psychologist Edward Bullough (1880–1934).

According to Bullough, psychic distance (I prefer "psychic" to "psychical") does not refer to physical space; it is not a spatial or temporal concept, although, obviously, there is a physical separation between the viewer and a work of art, and time is required to see or listen to a work of art. By psychic distance, however, he means the *degree of personal involvement* of a viewer in a work of art. In other words, psychic distance begins with the assumption of empathy: There *is* identification or projection or "feeling into" the work. The important question for Bullough is: How much personal identification in the work of art is desirable?

Before proceding to Bullough's answer, we should look further into what he means by "distance." Distance is a matter of attitude or outlook. We do not approach art in practical terms, as we approach ordinary experience. We seek no personal advantage or useful knowledge. Bullough shares with the philosopher Kant the view that aesthetic pleasure is "disinterested" or detached. The attitude of the viewer is contemplative, reflective, not oriented toward action. Any motive beyond disinterested satisfaction would be regarded as placing the ordinary goals of the viewer ahead of the proper perception of the work for its own sake. It is easy to see the influence of Kant upon Lipps, who also was concerned with "disinterested" perception. According to him, the viewer would not be capable of truly seeing the work if his perceptions were focused on his bodily sensations.

In order to escape practical involvement in a work of art, then, the viewer must suppress his customary habits of seeing. An effort is required to "hold in abeyance" those normal attitudes and interests which characterize our daily perception. When viewing films or plays for example, we sometimes have to remind ourselves that what we are seeing is unreal. Consider children. They identify so readily, and have so indistinct an idea of the separation of the identities of others from themselves, that we must deliberately develop in them the concept of psychic distance. Otherwise, they may have nightmares and unexplained depressions. Although Bullough does not mention it, the concept of "aesthetic frame" helps to establish distance, or the attitude of disinterest. The frame around a picture, or, for that matter, the proscenium arch around the stage, serves to separate the events taking place within the frame from those in the ordinary world around it. Of course, when distance is lost, when complete identification occurs, we lose "sight" of the frame. (In this connection, it is worth noting that older works of art usually had massive frames around them, whereas modern paintings increasingly employ thin wooden or metal strips, or no frame at all. Can we conclude that contemporary artists want to eliminate the separation of art and life?) In addition to isolating the work of art from the rest of the world, the frame serves to remind us that the work contains material intentionally organized for aesthetic as opposed to practical perception.

At this point we can define psychic distance as *any awareness* by a viewer that there is a separation between the reality of his own life and the reality of the feelings he experiences in connection with a work of art. The viewer is *desirous* of having feelings through art; he *does* "cooperate" with the work of art by trying to believe in its reality. But he recognizes that these feelings do not belong to his day-to-day "practical" existence. He understands that there is or must be a separation between art and life. Like a scientist, he realizes that he must be objective about gathering data and making measurements at the same time that he has a strong *personal* interest in the fruitfulness of his experiments or investigations.

Loss of distance can be defined as complete involvement or identification with the realities present in the work of art. It occurs, according to Bullough, when perception becomes *practical* as opposed to *aesthetic*. At the other extreme, there is *excessive distance*, not caused primarily by the attitude of the viewer, but by the work of art. Its lack of concreteness, credibility, or relevance

to the life of the viewer does not permit *any empathy*, as we might say, to take place. This overdistancing is not only a feature of perception, but also is traceable to qualities in the design and execution of the art object. Excessive distance, the inability of a viewer to develop any interest in the work, thus becomes one of the factors in critical judgment. That is, while one "sees" the work, one cannot become sufficiently involved to experience its formal, expressive, and other relationships. The situation is comparable to attending a social event where one is not an invited guest. In the same vein, it is difficult to enjoy certain sporting events unless you know the players or root for one of the teams. Some identification is necessary.

In discussing psychic distance, Bullough speaks of it as being operative in artistic production as well as aesthetic perception. He recognizes that the artist must detach himself to some extent, even from an experience which has affected him deeply, if he is to express himself effectively. The Romantic view of the artist as achieving excellence entirely because of the depth and intensity of his inspiration is rejected. Loss of distance would interfere with his intelligent and skillful employment of the techniques he possesses. This point is illustrated in life by the fact that when we are deeply moved by an emotion, it is difficult to speak about it coherently. Do good actors learn how to *simulate* emotions or do they find it necessary to *experience* the emotions they are called upon to portray? This seems to be the question which divides proponents of "classical" acting and advocates of so-called "method" acting, followers of Konstantin Stanislavsky and Lee Strasberg. Our discussion of empathy suggests that good actors express or project emotion by knowing how to create motor signals which the audience can simulate. Perhaps they undergo genuine and exhausting emotions during training and rehearsals, acquiring the technique they can exhibit in a detached manner during actual performances.

Bullough's understanding of the distance factor in the creation of visual form as well as in aesthetic perception leads him to propound what we might call the *law of psychic distance:* The most desirable degree of empathy or identification with the work of art "is the utmost decrease of Distance without its disappearance." At one extreme lies apathy, at the other lies the confusion of art and life. A moderate degree of disinterestedness results in a moderate degree of pleasure. But vividness and intensity of perception require as much involvement as possible without actual loss of personal identity.

Having established what he considers the ideal psychic distance for aesthetic perception, Bullough goes on to classify the arts according to their tendencies toward overdistancing or underdistancing. The dramatic arts, as we know, run the risk of underdistancing. Bullough suggests that the problems of censorship arise, particularly in connection with theater, because people lose their distance too readily. It is difficult also to maintain any distance toward the dance because, as with theater, the human figure is so prominent in the medium. And sculpture, insofar as it uses the figure, is close to the dance. Although the figure is not actually alive in sculpture, our attitudes toward its corporeality and its state of dress cause distance to be kept with effort. (The mythical sculptor, Pygmalion, fell in

love with his statue, Galatea.) Painting as an art most nearly approaches ideal specifications for distance: Its reduction of life-size scale and its stylization of presentation render it the least subject to confusion with reality; hence the proper degree of distance is more easily attained. Music, especially "serious" music, tends to be overdistanced, and architecture is most distant of all.

These observations by Bullough, which were made in 1912, may seem somewhat quaint today. For example, he could not have anticipated the nonfigurative character of much contemporary sculpture. Both classic ballet and, to a lesser extent, modern dance employ the figure in a formal and stylized manner. Still, it is not difficult to maintain psychic distance from these art forms. Architecture is far from inducing apathy, even without the aid of such distance-decreasing factors as figurative ornamentation and the appeal of utilitarian use. Painting in its abstract examples has similar distance-potential to that of architecture. Despite these particulars, though, the principle which Bullough employed in making his distance classification seems to have continued validity: Naturalism in art, whatever the particular medium, tends to encourage loss of distance and identification; stylization and abstraction promote overdistancing and apathy.

It does seem necessary, however, to take exception to Bullough's radical separation of *practical* and *aesthetic* concerns. Although he is in honorable company when he stresses the *disinterestedness* of aesthetic perception, the *definition* of disinterestedness he used—nonpractical, nonutilitarian concern—is too negative. He and philosophers who share his view tell us what aesthetic perception is not, but they do not tell us what it is. Their difficulty may be due to an effort to establish the existence of emotions and ideas which are "purely" aesthetic, unmixed with crass, work-a-day motives. Such thinking may betray the sociological frame of reference in which it was conceived: Aristocrats can perceive pure beauty, merchants can only perceive money, and workmen only see things. Or, it may represent an idealistic or religious world-view which assumes hierarchic levels of experience within men similar to differences of rank and purpose which exist in the world men have created. Nevertheless, a psychologist operating on scientific foundations would be hard put to demonstrate experimentally the existence of interests, values, or concerns which are detached from biological survival, social utility, or practical function. Bullough tried to deal with these problems by asserting that men seek satisfaction in art by suspending any interest in practical advantage from it. However, he does not make his case. One's motive *in advance* of perception may be as detached and nonpractical as one would wish. (Even then, self-deception is possible.) But the meanings one attributes to perceptions are based on the practical experience, the concrete interactions, of the organism with life. In seeing, there is no escape from the memory of our visual progress through the world.

Fusion and Funding

The concept of funding in the perception of art was originally employed by John Dewey and was further developed and refined by the aesthetician Stephen Pepper.° Although the terms "funding" and "fusion" are used almost interchangeably, we can think of funding as including remembered perceptions and the accumulation of separate perceptions of the same work, and of fusion as the process of integrating those perceptions into a whole so that it is characterized by a single dominant quality.

°In acknowledging Dewey's interest in fusion and in bringing the concept more emphatically to our attention, Pepper has occasion to say: "He [Dewey] has much, of course, to say about quality, but never, so far as I have found, does he stop to write on the topic of fusion or funding. He used the concepts all the time but never held them up for long and careful scrutiny." Stephen C. Pepper, *The Work of Art*, Indiana University Press, 1955, p. 153.

I have already asserted that people tend to perceive the whole of a work of art before they become aware of its parts. That seems to be a paradox, since we know that the whole work, at least the *physical* whole, is the sum of its parts. In any given perception or series of perceptions, however, we do not see *all* of the work which is there to see. Almost any art object is capable of yielding far more sensory data than we are capable of perceiving on a given occasion. In the world outside of art, we do not wait to see the color of the license plates when an automobile is coming our direction. We are satisfied to identify the existence of a car moving at a certain speed along a certain path . . . and we get out of the way. The perception of events, in other words, is perception *infused* with a primary quality which makes meaningful action of some kind possible—a process of a few seconds, at most. In the case of a moving object, action is embodied in a "decision" by the whole organism to change its distribution of energy: to relocate itself. In the case of fine art, action consists of an immediate and vivid intuition of the quality which pervades the object, a quality which is simultaneously felt as pleasing or displeasing. Although a situation may not be urgent, perception is hastily integrated; it does not last long enough to exhaust all the sensory possibilities within it. We cannot claim that the habits of perception drawn from daily life do not also carry over into the experience of art. Hence, a person tends to perceive the whole work quite rapidly and, if more time is available, forms several qualitative perceptions of the work.

This tendency of the perceiver to "jump to conclusions" is apparent if we think of our behavior when reading a mystery novel. At any number of points before the end, we assemble the evidence for the detective and decide who

the culprit is and how he committed the foul deed. If the mystery is well written, we turn out to be wrong, intentionally led astray by the author. The skillful writer of mysteries exploits the tendency of readers *to form a comprehensive perception of the quality of the whole before all the potential meanings of the material have been experienced.*

Theoretically, a work of art that is complex beyond the most rudimentary level can never be perceived completely, totally, finally, once-and-for-all. We know that the plays of Shakespeare, for example, seem inexhaustible to the people who know the most about them. At least one reason why an excellent work continues to be rewarding after we have experienced it several times lies in the fact that we, the perceivers, have changed and hence view the same organization of forms differently. But on a single aesthetic occasion, our perceptions of the whole change because the later perceptions or "evidence" change the meaning or import of the earlier "evidence." And the changed earlier evidence affects the meaning of the later evidence, so that collectively they change the significance of the whole work which we are engaged in examining. Because perception of visual form takes time, just as does the perception of musical form, there is a rich and complex interaction among our separate successive perceptions of that form.°

When we examine *Sunday Afternoon on the Island of La Grande Jatte* by Georges Seurat (1859–91), a number of expectations are aroused by our initial

GEORGES SEURAT, *Sunday Afternoon on the Island of La Grande Jatte* (1884–86). Courtesy The Art Institute of Chicago, Helen Birch Bartlett Memorial Collection.

°One of the functions of art criticism is to form an interpretation, that is, a description of the single quality or idea which best accounts for our several successive perceptions—the aesthetic evidence—of the work.

perceptions of the work. As the examination proceeds, these expectations are confirmed, disappointed, or supplemented. We may have expected social description and encountered instead a treatise on sunlight and cast shadows. Our perception of sunlight and shadow was transmuted into a perception of the pointillist treatment of surfaces under varying conditions of illumination and distance from the viewer: The perception of light and distance gives way to a perception of colored pigment resting on the flat picture plane. The perception of the picture plane yields to an apparently opposed perception of the figures as sculptural solids floating in pictorial space. Furthermore, perceptions of form mingle with perceptions of the thematic material. Our personal experience with similar events may affect the way we see the somewhat stately and dignified visual organization. Previous experience with art—say, *Le Moulin de la Galette* (1876) by Auguste Renoir (1841–1919) —may introduce a contrasting view of the material which Seurat presents. In recollection, other works of art which seem to deal with related forms introduce new perceptions at the same time that they color those we have already made. For example, *A Vision of Antiquity—Symbol of Form* by P. C. Puvis de Chavannes (1824–98) exhibits the same devotion to Classicism but with far less control of pictorial space relationships.

Clearly, a multitude of qualitative perceptions—consistent with each other, building upon each other, or opposed to each other—can be formed by a single viewer in the presence of a work which possesses the formal organization to sustain his interest. Now arises the problem of how they are funded or fused into a unified experience.

Perhaps the discussion of the different ways in which the same work can be understood has obscured the fact of the technical unity and the design unity in the art object itself. First, it is we, the viewers, who have the capacity for "reading" the same work variably. Second, we are all the while aware that our several perceptions of the work are caused by the same organization of visual forms. Third, and most important, fusion designates a *qualitative* unity in aesthetic perception rather than a log-

AUGUSTE RENOIR, *Le Moulin de la Galette* (1876), left. Courtesy Musée du Louvre, Cliché des Musées Nationaux.

PIERRE PUVIS DE CHAVANNES, *A Vision of Antiquity—Symbol of Form* (c.1885), right. Collection Museum of Art, Carnegie Institute, Pittsburgh.

CLAUDE MONET, *Old St. Lazare Station, Paris* (1877). Courtesy The Art Institute of Chicago, Mr. and Mrs. Martin A. Ryerson Collection.

ical or thematic unity. In other words, at any given moment during our examination of a work of art, we have a dominant, controlling impression of all the elements of visual form which we have seen in the work. That controlling impression, or fused perception, is of the pervasive quality which seems to characterize the various parts of the work, no matter what its official title or theme. With respect to the Seurat, at a given moment all the parts seem to be permeated by a single feeling, which might be poorly verbalized as a *sense of controlled relaxation*. This fusion or qualitative perception having been made, our more analytic reading of the work becomes *qualitatively* consistent. The motion of the sailboat and of the bandleader seems to be arrested. The cast shadows do not shift or flicker: They are fixed. Even our recollections of related themes are governed by the quality of *this controlling perception*. The informality of

Renoir's dancers and diners appears extraordinarily intimate and flirtatious by comparison with Seurat's sedate parade; we are made aware of an almost Surrealist quality in the airless landscape of Puvis de Chavannes because of the masterful control of atmosphere and edges in Seurat's painting. For the time being, at least, everything we perceive in the work, or relate to it from the outside, is understood in the light of a *controlling quality* which is seen as the unifying element of the work under scrutiny. Renoir's painting may not be noisy when seen for itself on another occasion, but it seems so *now* in the light of our perception of the Seurat.

Incidentally, this capacity of aesthetic perception to color the experience of other places and events which are not currently the focus of our attention, can lead ultimately to a romanticism of the Oscar Wilde type: *All* experience is then regarded in terms of its effect on one's aesthetic perception. Thus, taking a train trip might be felt in terms of its influence on one's perception of Monet's *Old St. Lazare Station, Paris*. Then, as such an attitude grows, life can be experienced *only* in terms of its influence on the perception of works of art: Human relationships cannot be felt directly, but only as they are or might be felt in novels or plays. However, extreme forms of this sort of Romantic attitude are rare. If anything, the qualitative perceptions we experience in art are too uncommon in perceptions of our daily life, our work, and our personal and social relationships.

Even if the concept of fusion is fairly well accepted as the binding factor in the qualitative perception of form, the descriptions by Dewey and Pepper do not explain, from an experimental standpoint, the operation or the causes

290

of fusion, although their discussion is very suggestive. Consequently, we shall turn to the Gestalt psychologists and their concept of closure and "good *Ge-* *stalt*" (which is not unlike the concept of fusion), for what might prove to be an explanation of aesthetic fusion from another angle of attack.

Closure and "Good Gestalt"

Closure is the term used by Gestalt psychologists to explain the tendency in all human perception to seek completeness of structure and meaning. So long as the perception of wholeness is denied to a viewer, he experiences tension, discomfort, suspense. Forms which are in some way incomplete are therefore regarded as unstable by Gestalt psychologists. The perceptual energies of a viewer are always organized to endow unstable forms with stability—that is, to complete them, to bring about *closure*—because only then can his discomfort and tension be dissipated. Gestaltists hold, therefore, that perception is always of wholes, of total *gestalten*, or configurations. They deny that the perception of a whole configuration is the sum of sense impressions of component parts. In this contention, they are supported by Dewey and Pepper in their concept of fusion. Dewey maintained, as we know, that the fused quality of the whole work of art is immediately grasped—"seized," he said—by the viewer. Only *after* perceiving the quality of the whole does the viewer become aware of separate sensations and perceptions. These separate perceptions are bound or fused together by the original perception of over-all quality, but neither Dewey nor Pepper explains how this comes about.

In Gestalt psychology, closure is a single instance of the operation of the *Law of Prägnanz*, other instances being unity, uniformity, good continuation, and simple shape. According to this law, the viewer's organization of the perceptual field will always be complete and as "good" as possible, "good" in this case meaning as good a *gestalt* as possible given the objective character of the stimulus. The viewer, furthermore, will always seek the route of maximum simplicity to arrive at closure of his perception. However, closure does not result from the recollection of similar unities previously encountered by the viewer. Neither does Gestalt theory accept the empathic theory of perception in which the viewer is motivated to imitate what he perceives and thus arouse in himself emotions corresponding to those expressed in the work of art. Gestaltists maintain that there are independent laws which govern the organization of psychological energies during perception, and that the organization of energies in perception does not imitate the organization of energies in the stimulus object.

Gestaltists make a distinction about sensory stimulation which is important for psychology *and* aesthetics. They speak of the *distant*, or geographical, stimulus as the object which receives energy from the sun or elsewhere, absorbing some of it and reflecting some of it back to a perceiving organism. The energy from the *distant stimulus* excites our sense organs and sets up a new pattern of local, or *proximal, stimuli* which become the objects of perception. We do not, according to Gestalt psychology, perceive the *distant stimulus* although we do receive its reflected light energy. What we perceive are proximal stimuli. While the distant stimuli—a tree, a face, a picture—remain relatively unchanging, the proximal stimuli vary a great deal. Now we can understand Claude Monet's numerous paintings of haystacks as his effort to give objective form to the many proximal stimuli which could be based on the same distant stimulus. This distinction is not particularly difficult when we consider that something like it is incorporated into every school child's study of the stars. In the fifth or sixth grade, children learn that in "looking at the stars," they do not in fact see the stars but see light which left the stars perhaps millions of years ago. Gestaltists maintain that they do not even see the light, but rather their own local sensory excitations which have been stimulated by light (now much diminished) from the distant bodies.

Consequently, we have a fundamental split affecting aesthetic theory: Some aestheticians believe that perception replicates, or re-enacts, the processes of organization which were involved in the creation of the work of art. Others believe that aesthetic perception proceeds according to independently operating processes of the organism. Lipps and Dewey would be in the first category and Gestalt psychologists in the second. According to the Gestalt view, the energy or fuel for the conduct of perception comes mainly from within the perceiving organism. The art object *ignites* the fuel and sets the energies into motion. In that sense, the art object is the *cause*, the event prior to perception as well as the focus of visual interest. But our *experience* of the art object does not correspond to the structure of the distant stimuli. The perception of a shape or color in no way resembles the objective shape or color itself. In other words, there is no blue color or triangular shape to be found in the brain of a perceiving organism.

If perception does not involve imitation, or re-enactment by the sensorimotor system of events perceived in the object, how do we learn anything *about* the object? Also, how does the organism bring about closure or "good *gestalt*" when confronted by unstable or ambiguous forms? In partial answer to the first question, Gestalt psychology advances the concept of *isomorphism*, which maintains that there is a correspondence between physiological proc-

CLAUDE MONET, *Two Haystacks* (1891), left. Mr. and Mrs. L. L. Coburn Memorial Collection. *Haystacks in Setting Sun* (1891), center. Potter Palmer Collection. Both photos, courtesy The Art Institute of Chicago. *Haystacks in Snow* (1891), right. Courtesy the Metropolitan Museum of Art, bequest of Mrs. H. O. Havemeyer, 1929. The H. O. Havemeyer Collection.

esses and consciousness in the organism. That is, thoughts and feelings are the same as the activity of atoms and molecules in the brain. But how is such activity in the brain initiated? It is "ignited," as mentioned above, by the "distant" stimulus of the art object. As Kurt Koffka says, "We see, not stimuli—a phrase often used—but on account of, because of, stimuli."° The proximal stimuli (the sense excitations in the organism caused by the "distant" stimulus, the art object) take the form of combinations of the conventional visual elements we have discussed earlier: line, shape, color, and so on. Then the specific character of the visual elements in combination causes the viewer to integrate them in a *gestalt*, or configuration, according to one or more illustrations of the Law of Prägnanz: regularity, simplicity, and so forth. We have discussed some of these laws indirectly in Chapters Eight and Nine when speaking of the properties of the visual elements in isolation and the properties of the elements when designed to achieve, say, rhythm or balance. Our discussion, however, included recollected and symbolic qualities of the elements in addition to those properties which, according to Gestalt psychology, are independently determined by the organization of energies in the visual field. For example, Gestaltists maintain, on the basis of scientific experiment, that the space *inside* a closed shape is perceived as a different, denser substance than the space *around* the shape, although we "know" the space to be the same substance—for instance, ordinary paper. The Gestalt psychologists have developed a considerable body of such mate-

rial, so that they feel confident in propounding "laws" about the perception of the main types of visual forms. They would claim that their laws describe physiological processes in the viewer which cause corresponding mental states or "experiences," as we might say.

You may recall that in Chapter Eight, in describing the visual elements, we spoke of them as "image constituents." Images, we said, were "the result of endowing optical sensations with meaning." In the light of the Gestalt distinction between distant and proximal stimuli, we can identify the visual elements with proximal stimuli. That is, they are *local* organizations of sense data which might be called *percepts of the visual elements*. The problem raised by our earlier question (If perception does not involve imitation or re-enactment, how do we learn, that is, know, anything about the object?) becomes for Gestaltists a question of how the many percepts based on local stimuli relate or correspond to the "real," or *distant*, stimulus. Their answer is equivocal. They introduce problems of constancy in *size, shape, color*, and *brightness*, and carry out observations and experiments showing differences between the *retinal image* and the perceived image one would expect to be produced by experimental changes in the distant stimulus. Clearly, psychological factors are at work which govern the *constancy* of the percept despite the fact that the retinal image has been distorted by the experimenter's manipulation of the distant stimulus. Certain forces tend to prevent distortion of the percept despite objective changes in the stimulus. But Gestalt psychologists are unwilling to explain the stability or constancy of percepts in terms of previous experience with the stimulus

°Kurt Koffka, *Principles of Gestalt Psychology*, Routledge and Kegan Paul, 1962, p. 98.

object. They state one hypothesis to the effect that "the percept depending upon the *proximal* stimulus approaches the properties of the distant one."° In addition, "central factors" cause proximal stimuli to remain similar to distant stimuli. But this is what we would suspect from common sense and from the traditional psychologies which Gestalt rejects. Elsewhere, Koffka suggests that strong stimulus forces tend to produce a retinal shape which resists distortion, resulting, in turn, in a percept which corresponds closely to the retinal shape. The "stimulus forces" he refers to are within the organism—that is, proximal as well as external. Those who have no doctrinaire commitment to Gestalt psychology might aver that the local stimulus forces, which resist distortion, which cause the viewer's percept to approach the distant stimulus, are affected by something called *previous experience*. In other words, granting that perception is the organization of energies under conditions set by the organism and the field with which it interacts, our seeing is strongly influenced by experiential cues (*umstandsdaten*). Gestalt psychology rejects the concept of fusion but reintroduces it in terms of forces tending to maintain the constancies, or as "phenomenal regression to the real object."†

Let us return to the second question propounded above: How does the organism bring about closure? The best answer we can get from Gestalt relies again on the Law of Prägnanz, which appears to be a psychological version of principles derived from physics, notably Kirchkoff's Law. Applied to per-

ceptual organization, Kirchkoff's Law would assert that the current intensities in a system of circuits (the perceptual forces within the organism) will be distributed in a pattern which produces or uses a minimum of energy while functioning as a system. This amounts to asserting, as we have above, that the organism tends to seek the route of maximum simplicity (the least expenditure of energy) to achieve closure. A common illustration of this physical law is the shape of a soap bubble or a rain drop. The spherical shape of the soap bubble represents the best and smallest surface area for containing its volume. The rain drop arrives at a shape which is most efficient for carrying out its function: maintaining its volume against the resistance of its environment while falling as quickly as possible. The shape of the bubble or of the rain drop performs a function; it does a job; it is not the result of irrational forces. Likewise, closure in human experience performs a function: It permits perception to take place according to the most economical expenditure of energies.

The Law of Prägnanz, which we can understand as a requirement that perceptual energies be organized in "good" *gestalten*—that is, in patterns of maximum efficiency—further implies that such patterns must contain three properties: regularity, symmetry, and simplicity. You will readily note that these properties have been discussed in Chapter Nine as *principles of organization* under the headings, respectively, of *rhythm, balance*, and *unity*. According to the Gestalt principle of isomorphism (see above), rhythm, balance, and unity are actually physiological processes which give rise to corresponding conscious processes during perception. Thus,

°Koffka, *op. cit.*, p. 225.

†Koffka, *op. cit.*, p. 225; quotation from Thouless.

Gestalt completes the circle in its presentation of solutions to the problem of how perception takes place, how characteristics of the art object are communicated to the perceiver, and how the organism is enabled to experience feelings and thoughts.

Since the Gestalt theory of perception is very important for aesthetics, but also quite difficult, I shall summarize its main contentions below without, it is hoped, doing them violence through oversimplification.

1. Perception is of whole *gestalten,* or configurations, which are the fundamental units of experience.

2. The organism imposes wholeness upon the objects of its perception because of the way it organizes psychological energies during the perceptual process.

3. If visual forms are unstable or incomplete (and they always are, in some sense), the human organism completes them according to psychophysical laws governing its perceptual behavior. Such completion is called *closure.*

4. Closure is needed to form a *gestalt* because the organism will not tolerate instability in its perception.

5. The completion of the *gestalt* takes place according to the Law of Prägnanz, which maintains that the resulting configuration will be as "good" —as unified, balanced, and constant— as objective conditions (visual forms and constitutional factors) permit.

6. The Law of Prägnanz is a psychological application of the physical principle that forces distribute themselves in a system according to a pattern of minimal energy production to maintain a maximum of stable, systemic function.

7. Regularity, symmetry, simplicity, and closure are characteristics of energy distributions during perception. These psychophysical terms correspond to these aesthetic terms: *rhythm, balance, unity,* and *coherence.*

8. *Isomorphism* is the principle which asserts that consciousness corresponds (has structural affinities with) physiological processes.

9. Perception results from physiological processes in two ways: (a) through sensory activity caused by energy received from the *distant* stimulus (the art object); (b) through neural and other somatic activity caused by the organization of energies *within* the viewer following "ignition" by the *proximal* stimulus.

10. The organism perceives, *is conscious of,* qualities and properties of a work of art because the physiological processes of perception induce states of consciousness in the brain that correspond to functional activites of the body. These physiological processes are organized during perception along patterns of symmetry, simplicity, and so on. They do the work of forming a "good *gestalt,*" using the material provided by the distant and proximal stimuli.

It appears, then, that the principle of isomorphism, propounded by Köhler, is not very different from the empathy theories of Lipps, Groos, and Vernon Lee. The *correspondence* between physiological and mental or psychological states is not substantially at odds with "inner mimicry"—the induction of thoughts and feelings through motor imitation, that is, physiological processes. There is, however, a difference in the Gestaltists unwillingness to employ voluntary imitation, association, and recollection as an explanatory factor for the perception of quality. Since Gestalt theory will not rely on previous experience as a source of meaning and emotion during present perception, it must derive meanings and feelings from the patterns of energy distribution in the organism triggered by the proximal stimuli. The result is an ahistorical explanation of perception, a description of vision without memory which seems to fly in the face of common sense. (Of course, science often conflicts with common sense.) In reacting against the excesses of associationism, stimulus-response bonds, nerve-synapse theory, and atomistic sense perception, Gestalt psychologists may ultimately arrive at another extreme, namely, a rather impoverished description of aesthetic perception in terms of the distribution of electrical energy in the brain and neural network. Such an analysis may be truthful from a scientific standpoint, but it leaves out much that seems to present itself to consciousness in aesthetic experience.

Nevertheless, we are indebted to Gestalt psychology for its key concept of the total configuration as the fundamental unit of perception, its important distinction between distant and proximal stimuli, the concept of isomorphism, and especially its rigorous experiments in perception. The latter have been particularly welcome to artists, since they tend to confirm scientifically the validity of artistic knowledge and practice which has been intuitively or empirically gained.

Artistic Perception: Wölfflin's Categories

The discussion of perception has been conducted thus far mainly from the standpoint of the person who views works which others—artists—have created. It may be useful to change our perspective and examine perception from another vantage point—that of the artist. I do not wish to assert that artists perceive differently from others. Indeed, it is possible that they best illustrate how *everyone* perceives at a given time. It is instructive, however, to draw inferences about perception in general from the evidence of visual art. Fortunately, a systematic approach to the study of such evidence is available in the influential book *Principles of Art History* by the art historian Heinrich Wölfflin. His categories of visual analysis, which will be discussed in this section, deal with characteristic "forms of beholding," as manifested in drawing, painting, sculpture, and architecture.

Wölfflin attempted to show that variations in the media and subject matter of art conceal underlying commonalities in style and that style results from a way of perceiving, an outlook or mode of imagination, which characterizes individuals, nations, and races at certain stages of their development. We have also studied style in Part Two, but the discussion there was conducted largely along the lines of *style as expression*. Wölfflin's approach to visual style is psychological or perceptual. The perceptual approach has the advantage of avoiding the excesses of literary, moral, and social association to which expressivistic theories of art are vulnerable. It is also obviously well suited to the visual arts. Wölfflin said he believed that the discussion of style as the *expression* of a school, a country, or a region could not deal with the unique qualities of works of art. Hence, he saw his task as an art historian to be the exposition and analysis of the history of vision and the description of necessary stages in the visual development of mankind.

It is likely that Wölfflin thought of himself as a psychologist of style as well as an historian of style. Although he recognized that there is more to art than the artist's eye, he relied heavily on a *psychology* of vision. Despite his distaste for the analysis of art as expression, he was perhaps too prone to draw racial and nationalistic inferences from the modes of perception he found embodied in art. But we can ignore this material which seems, in any event, to be superimposed upon essentially sound observation of artistic modes of beholding. We can make use of his visual categories while passing over his "blood and soil" psychologizing. ("It has long been realized that every painter paints 'with his blood.' " "Different times give birth to different art. Epoch and race interact." "The linearity of the Latin race was apt to look cold to Germanic feeling . . ." and so on.) It might be said that Wölfflin diluted the value of his excellent eye by rather second-rate ethnic and racial explanations of the visual differences he perceived and taught others to see.

He understood the history of art as the history of modes of representation which, in turn, are based on a characteristic or typical mode of perception at a certain time and place. These modes of perception are broken down into five categories, or pairs of concepts. There are two poles in each category, and development is from the first pole to the second. For example, the first category deals with the development from a linear style of art to a painterly style. This means that when we encounter a painterly style of art, it is the creation of an artist who has already passed through the linear stage: He has made the transition as an individual, or it has been made for him by the group or tradition to which he belongs. Nations and schools of art pass through the developments at different historical times. Thus, one country may be arrested at the linear stage while another has arrived at the painterly. Wölfflin occasionally suggests that ethnic and other factors may predispose artists, because of their heritage, to prefer the earlier phase of a stylistic category to the more highly evolved phase of development, but he stresses that neither pole is inherently—that is, aesthetically—superior to the other.

The five categories of stylistic development are as follows:

1. From a linear mode to a painterly mode.
2. From plane to recession.
3. From closed form to open form.
4. From multiplicity to unity.
5. From absolute clarity to relative clarity.

As the first concept of representation in a category yields to the second, new possibilities of visual satisfaction become available. Although these concepts serve as ways of representing or imitating visual reality, they also perform a "decorative" function: They have the capacity to afford pleasure as well as to describe the objects of percep-

In painterly works by Albright and Paolozzi, unlike the Marini, the viewer's eye is obliged to examine areas rather than contours to gather information about the meaning of the whole.

IVAN ALBRIGHT, *That which I should have done I did not do* (1931–41), left. Courtesy The Art Institute of Chicago.

EDUARDO PAOLOZZI, *Japanese War God* (1958), center. Courtesy Albright-Knox Art Gallery, Buffalo, New York, gift of Seymour H. Knox.

MARINO MARINI, *Horse and Rider* (1947–48), right. Collection The Museum of Modern Art, New York, acquired through the Lillie P. Bliss bequest.

tion. In other words, any artistic style, based on any concept of perception, is quite capable of carrying out the usual artistic functions of representation or imitation, decoration or aesthetic enhancement, personal and social expression, and so on. However, stylistic change offers new ways to perform these functions and makes it impossible, according to Wölfflin, to turn back, to regress to a previous stage. This is so because *psychological law* governs the changes in perception which ultimately manifest themselves in art forms. We are therefore interested in Wölfflin's psychological explanation of the changes in perception from the first to the second concept in each of the five categories.

FROM THE LINEAR
TO THE PAINTERLY MODE

First, what is a *linear* mode of perception? It is a style of seeing which, as the term would imply, stresses the contours or outlines of things. In addition, it is

concerned with the tangible (that is, the grasp-able), or material, qualities of things. This is not to be confused with an exclusive interest in texture. Rather it is the opposite of any non-material, spiritual, or idealistic view of the physical world. Emphasis is on boundaries, on definite separations between things. The drawings of children sometimes reveal this kind of linearity: They are afraid to permit objects to touch because that would interfere with or confuse the boundaries of objects. Although color and chiaroscuro are employed in linear works, the eye of the viewer finds the edges to be the principle source of information about form.

On the other hand, a *painterly* mode (*malerisch* in German) stresses the masses and volumes of things in the perception and representation of their forms. Because boundaries and limits are of secondary importance, objects can and do merge. Perception is of the continuities among objects rather than of their differences. Instead of perceiving things in isolation, one sees them in relationship. With the linear mode one is impressed with the stability and fixity of objects while with the painterly mode one is aware of their shifting quality, their refusal to remain stationary.

Now, these modes of perception apply to architecture and sculpture as well as drawing and painting. For example, a sculpture by Eduardo Paolozzi (1924–), *Japanese War God*, is clearly a painterly work. Its contour is not particularly interesting: The eye is drawn to the interior of the shape. Emphasis is on light and dark as the delineator of form. By contrast, *Horse and Rider* by Marino Marini (1901–) is a distinctly linear work. The eye of the viewer is drawn to its contours first, and then it moves inward. Even when perceiving the interior of the forms, one is aware of the clarity and distinctness with which they present themselves: Their flow into each other is precisely and logically articulated.

It is apparent that the concepts of linear and painterly style correspond to what we have earlier described as the style of formal order and of emotion respectively. Now, however, we are concerned with linearity as an attitude toward perception. It represents a total *weltanschauûng* (world-view). Wölfflin's categories have the value of demonstrating that what is seen and artistically portrayed is not what is objectively available to perception (in this respect he anticipates Gestalt psychology) but is rather the result of a choice by the artist from available modes of perceiving what is objectively present. Wölfflin adds that at certain times and places the perceptual alternatives are very limited. That is why art history classifies art according to geographic and chronological categories. The student should know what perceptual modes were available at a particular time and place. Wölfflin wrote primarily of the transition of Renaissance to Baroque art in the countries of northern and southern Europe. For contemporary art, however, nationality and geography tend to mean less, although psychological differences in perception remain useful tools for the analysis of artistic style.

FROM PLANE TO RECESSION

The second pair of concepts deals with the development from *plane* to *recession*. The artist employing a planar style sees action occurring not only on the picture plane but also on a succession of planes *parallel to* the picture plane. In other words, the movement implied among his forms is from side-to-side and up-and-down. But it is not *recessional* movement, which is to say, in-and-out. As far as painting is concerned, the illusion of depth can be managed through both modes. However, only the recessional mode conceives of balance through angular movement *forward and backward* in the visual field. In painting, a classic instance of the planar would be, once again, the *Grande Jatte* by Seurat (p. 288). Although many levels of pictorial depth are represented, each level occurs on a plane which is parallel to the picture plane itself. A good case of recessional movement is seen in *Blue Horses* by Franz Marc (1880–1916). The manes of the horses, particularly, describe curvilinear movements back into the picture and forward to the frontal plane. Foreshortening of the forms is obviously an important recessional device in painting. Sculpture, on the other hand, which need not employ illusionistic devices, nevertheless shows recessional move-

FRANZ MARC, *Blue Horses* (c.1911). Collection Walker Art Center, Minneapolis.

HERBERT FERBER, *Homage to Piranesi* (1962–63). Collection of the artist; photo, The Museum of Modern Art, New York.

JOSÉ DE RIVERA, *Construction "Blue and Black"* (1951), above top. Collection of the Whitney Museum of American Art, New York.

IBRAM LASSAW, *Sirius* (1951), above. Courtesy Samuel M. Kootz Gallery, Inc.

PHILIP JOHNSON, glass house in New Canaan, Connecticut, the living area (1949). Courtesy Philip Johnson.

PAUL RUDOLPH, Art and Architecture Building, Yale University (1963). Courtesy Yale University News Bureau.

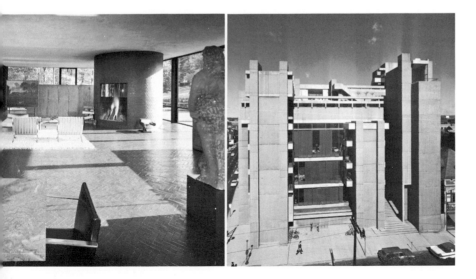

ment as in the constructions of José de Rivera and the work by Herbert Ferber, *Homage to Piranesi*. Ibram Lassaw (1913–), by contrast, is a planar sculptor. All the movements of line are rectilinear and parallel to the frontal plane from which the work is clearly intended to be seen. The sculptures of Lassaw also have a similar planarity to the early analytic cubist paintings of Braque.

FROM CLOSED TO OPEN FORM

Wölfflin calls closed form "tectonic" and open form "a-tectonic." It is a subtle pair of concepts, dealing with the sense of enclosure in *closed form,* and of freedom to move infinitely in any direction in *open form.* Once again, the notion of boundaries and delimitation occurs, this time in connection with the space in which the artistic forms are located and in which they have the opportunity to move. In general, Renaissance art was tectonic; it did not permit the eye to wander freely, but confined it within carefully designed enclosures—either real space as in architecture or virtual space as in painting. Baroque art tended to be a-tectonic, its space representations were infinite; it valued movement above stability. Obviously, the space in Philip Johnson's living-room is a a-tectonic since it tends to merge with the space around it. But Paul Rudolph's Yale Art School is distinctly tectonic or closed: It has a powerful, fortress-like quality which leaves no uncertainty about the distinction between indoors and outdoors. The pair of concepts is clearly architectural; how does it apply to painting? Certainly, Cézanne's pictorial space is closed and tectonic. Impressionism in general is open. Kandinsky is open. But Expressionists vary: Soutine and van Gogh present open space; Rouault is planar and tectonic, while in Max Beckmann there is a struggle between tectonic and a-tectonic forces. Abstract expressionist painting of the present period can be regarded as the modern continuation of Baroque recessional, a-tectonic movement. It represents a breaking away from the tectonic restraints of the School of Paris when it was dominated by such masters as Matisse, Picasso, and Braque.

FROM MULTIPLICITY TO UNITY

The fourth category deals with multiplicity and unity. Although some type of unity is the aim of all artistic effort, it is achieved in one case by the balancing of individual co-equal parts, that is, by unity through *multiplicity*. In the second case, it is achieved through dominance and subordination, through a principle of hierarchic order among parts. A style of multiplicity approaches unity as a problem in the addition and subtraction of known and distinct parts or quantities. It is opposed by a style of unity based on accent, emphasis, domination, subordination, and building to a climax. Naturally, the mode of perception which stresses the separate identity of things will pursue unity in the form of "checks and balances." It does, indeed, resemble one philosophy behind our system of government: Unity as the symbiosis, the "living together," of *independent,* sovereign states, a confederacy; the emphasis is on mutiplicity. The opposed philosophy, that of the government as a federal union, stresses the sovereignty of the whole in which subordinate centers of interest play various minor roles producing a single harmony. (According to Wölfflin, the sovereignty

of independent parts evolves into a federal type of unity.)

Miró certainly represents the point of view of multiplicity. Mondrian, however, is an interesting case: His is an art of carefully calculated balance among independently existing elements. Yet his verticals and horizontals quickly enter into relationship so that the viewer becomes aware that the objects of his perception are the areas and visual weights established by the related lines. But, on balance, he is a classical artist, hence a "confederate" rather than a "federalist."

Among contemporary artists, the style of unity in multiplicity is evident in Jackson Pollock, Mark Tobey, and Louise Nevelson, while the style of unity through subordination is visible in Richard Diebenkorn, de Kooning, and Giacometti. Ben Nicholson (1894–   ) in *Still Life* (1929–35) presents an inter-

BEN NICHOLSON, *Still Life* (1929–35). Courtesy C. S. Reddihaugh; photo, O. H. Wood (Bradford) Ltd.

esting case of unity through repetition of shape and dominant color. Since he employs sharp edges to describe his shapes, one would expect him to be a linear painter who is intent on establishing the separate identity of the parts in his pictures. But his use of line is misleading. The forms, in fact, merge and overlap. They fuse. The objects are united, as in Braque, by the container which encloses them and by the white color tonality. The fine line Nicholson employs is a decorative or sensuous element rather than a device for establishing limits. Indeed, the only firmly delimited form, which is of the table top, employs no outline, but achieves its edge by contrast in color and value. Hence, applying Wölfflin's categories to this work, we would find some intriguing departures from any consistent pattern: It is painterly, not linear; planar not recessional; closed in form rather than open; in the style of unity rather than multiplicity; and relatively clear rather than absolutely clear or distinct.

FROM ABSOLUTE TO RELATIVE CLARITY

Wölfflin's final category, from absolute to relative clarity, constitutes a summary, perhaps, of his entire argument concerning the development of artistic perception. By *absolute clarity,* he means "the exhaustive revelation of form." Everything which is known about a form must be told. The view of it which best explains its character should be chosen. Coloristic considerations and dramatic treatment of illumination must not be permitted to obscure the clear, objective, and complete account of what is there to be seen. Thus, linearity is regarded as an instrument of greater precision than painterliness. Planarity shows what is "going on" while recessional movement is devious. From the standpoint of absolute clarity, the unity achieved through dominance and subordination involves the suppression of visual truths. Relative clarity, then, represents a somewhat sophisticated artistic attitude.

As Wölfflin observes, Impressionism is the natural and logical outcome of this point of view. It employs suggestion instead of exposition, mystery instead of revelation. Forms which had been exposed in an even, clear light are half-covered in shadow or lost in a haze. The viewer must participate more actively in the "creation" of the work of relative clarity, whereas formerly,

HOWELLS & HOOD, Chicago Tribune Building (1924), left. Courtesy Chicago Tribune.

HOWELLS & HOOD, Daily News Building (1930), right. New York Daily News photo.

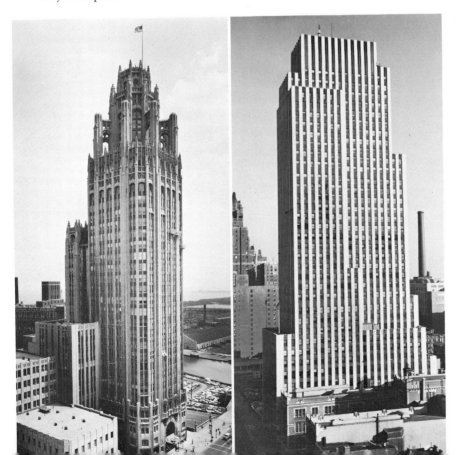

he could view absolutely distinct forms with a detached, relaxed eye. Instead of *taking in* the visual experience, he must actively *inquire after* it with his eye.

In architecture, two buildings by the same firm illustrate the styles of absolute and relative clarity. However, the direction of development is the reverse of that described by Wölfflin. Howells and Hood designed the Chicago Tribune Building in 1924 and they designed the Daily News Building in New York in 1930. The Tribune tower is, of course, Gothic in inspiration, hence it is a "painterly" structure, its parts tending to fuse and merge into the impression of the whole. The Daily News tower, on the contrary, is made up of clear, distinct, cubical volumes. The reverse development by Howells and Hood does not necessarily invalidate Wölfflin's scheme of visual evolution; it merely illustrates the emergence in modern times of "synthetic" developments in

style. That is, stylistic development does not grow "naturally" out of changes in the outlook of artist and designers. Instead, it is "other-directed," to use the terminology of David Riesman. Style is responsive to shifts in technology, client preference, and, of course, the prevailing taste. Thus, we find modern revivals of planarity, multiplicity, or closed form, although these are, according to Wölfflin, the earlier stages of development to which it is impossible to return once they have been thoroughly explored and understood.

Given these exceptions to Wölfflin's theories of perceptual development, what is the value of his system? First, we must think of his categories in psychological rather than historical terms. Second, we should consider that one or the other of his pairs of concepts is remarkably suitable for the explanation and description of art he could not have seen or known about. For example, Willem de Kooning's *Woman* series is

WILLEM DE KOONING, *Woman, I* (1950–52), left. Collection The Museum of Modern Art, New York, purchase. *Woman, IV* (1952–53), center. Courtesy Nelson Gallery-Atkins Museum, gift of Mr. William Inge, Kansas City, Missouri. *Woman, VI* (1953), right. Courtesy Museum of Art, Carnegie Institute, Pittsburgh.

very adequately described in terms of relative clarity. Third, we are assisted by Wölfflin in seeing the connection between an artist's perception of the world and his presentation of form. Wölfflin helps explain why details are suppressed or obsessively recounted, why the viewer's eye is drawn to the contour or the interior of a shape. Such explanations are made without the benefit of scientific experimentation and yet are not inconsistent with Gestaltist studies of the outline as being (a) *part of* the figure or (b) the separating boundary between the figure and its ground.

In his *History of Art Criticism*,° Lionello Venturi takes Wölfflin to task, as I have, for insisting on the necessary succession from closed form to open

° Venturi, *History of Art Criticism*, p. 294.

form. But he grants the usefulness of Wölfflin's "schemes of visibility" for interpreting works of art. (Remember that Wölfflin does not favor the analysis of the *expression* of art.) Innovations in expressive meaning such as might be seen in the work of Picasso or Klee are not easily explained with Wölfflin's categories. Perhaps this is due to a defect of the purely perceptual approach to art, or perhaps it means that we should refine our approach to the perceptual study of artistic form. At the present time, therefore, it seems likely that experimentation and empirical research into visual perception can be carried out with the expectation of useful discoveries. However, such findings will probably supplement rather than entirely displace our present humanistic models for the analysis of the structure of art.

PART FOUR

THE INTERACTION

OF MEDIUM

AND MEANING

W hat are the differences among these three terms: material, medium, and technique? We should have a clear idea about them before investigating the interactions between the various media and artistic expression. *Material* causes no difficulty: It designates the *physical elements* of art, such as paint, stone, glass, clay, and metal. They are available to the artist or designer in a variety of manufactured or natural forms, and he either works with them directly or directs workmen in shaping and assembling them according to his intent.

Medium is a more difficult term. In the dictionary definition it is the "substance through which a force acts or an effect is transmitted." In other words, it is the vehicle by which materials are converted into artistic form. In painting there is also a narrower, technical meaning of medium: It is the liquid in which pigment is suspended—linseed oil, casein glue, egg yolk, varnish, synthetic resin, and so on. But that definition does not apply to architecture, sculpture, and film. A definition of *medium* that can apply to all the arts is as follows: A medium is a characteristic use of particular materials for an artistic purpose. Architecture is not a medium, it is an art. Cast concrete, however, is a medium employed in architecture. Sculpture is an art, not a medium. But metal which is welded, hammered, or cast constitutes a sculptural medium.

Technique and medium tend to overlap in ordinary usage, but we can define *technique* with more precision here: *Technique is an individual or personal way of using a medium.* For example, many artists employ the medium of oil paint in their work. But Jackson Pollock developed a very *personal technique* in his employment of the medium. Ibram Lassaw has a different technique from that of Richard Stankiewicz, although both employ the medium of welded metal. Le Corbusier, Nervi, and Candela employ personal techniques in the cast-concrete medium. Incidentally, their use of building *technology* may be similar, but personal technique is evident in their highly individual results.

Our problem in the following chapters is to show how the nature of a medium influences what is done *with* it and what is expressed *through* it. Each medium has inherent possibilities and limitations. Some artists submit to the limitations and achieve

306

excellence through their sensitive awareness of what can or cannot be accomplished within them. Other artists choose to ignore the known limitations and either fail or succeed in extending the range of the medium. *Craftsmanship* can be understood as the knowledge of what can be done in a medium and the ability to do it. But we can never be certain that all the possibilities are known. Hence, any artistic medium, whether of ancient vintage or recent development, holds out a challenge to the skill and judgment of the person who uses it.

Art, however, is not identical with technology, which continually develops new ways to perform existing tasks, because in art, skills and technical mastery are not pursued as ends in themselves. Although artistic skill is necessary and admirable, it is a *means* to an end. In judging art works, we are always concerned about the suitability of the ends and means, that is, of the *quality of interaction between medium and meaning.* We try to discover, in our examination of a work, how the medium has influenced what appears to be expressed. At the same time we are interested in how the expressive content has affected the employment of the medium. It goes without saying that viewers must have experience with the observation of many works in the various media; otherwise, they will not be able to tell in what ways the medium and its meaning have interacted. Some authorities even believe that personal experience with artistic creation is necessary if these relationships are to be fully understood. (This question is discussed in Chapter Fourteen, under "The Tools of Art Criticism.") The purpose of the following chapters, therefore, is to provide information about medium-meaning interactions in the principal art forms. This is a difficult objective because we are attempting to communicate in verbal form the sort of knowledge which is normally gained by direct observation or practical experience. Furthermore, technology or artistic ingenuity can render obsolete any pat generalizations about media. However, if we make observations about medium and content on the basis of specific works of art, they, at least, will stay put. You may extend these observations, or *extrapolate,* as the scientists say, to other artistic phenomena at your own risk.

CHAPTER ELEVEN

Of all the visual arts, painting is the most widely practiced. Children and grandparents, life-long professionals and the rankest of amateurs, physicians and prize-fighters, sick people and well —all paint, apparently with considerable satisfaction to themselves if not always to others. Is there any reason why this art form should have attracted so many more devotees than sculpture, for example? There are, of course, several reasons, but one of them concerns us especially: the flexibility and versatility of painting, particularly in oil.

The discovery of oil painting, allegedly by the Flemish painter Jan van Eyck in the fifteenth century, opened up a pictorial realm which could not have been realized or even anticipated before then. The suspension of pigment in linseed oil was the type of technological innovation which exemplifies our theme: the interaction of medium and meaning. Oil paint has blending and modeling qualities unobtainable with the earlier tempera paint. Its drying time is much longer, hence "wet-in-wet" effects are possible, effects which the quick-drying tempera would not permit. The slow-drying oil vehicle permits the artist to modify a still-wet paint film by adding paint, wiping it out, introducing darker or lighter tones, adding lines, scraping out lines, and even manipulating the paint with his fingers. Yet the paint film will dry as a single "skin"

PAINTING

in which all of these applications and afterthoughts are physically united. Since oil paint dries to a fairly elastic film (years ago our kitchen floor covering, linoleum, was made of a coarse fabric impregnated with the same tough, durable linseed oil which is the base of oil paint), it can be applied to canvas without great danger of cracking when the canvas buckles a bit. Large areas of canvas can be painted as opposed to the small wooden panels required for tempera, although prepared wooden panels continued to be preferred for oil painting until the end of the Renaissance. Before the perfection of painting in oil, mural-size works had to be executed in fresco—which is to say, fresh plaster

MICHELANGELO, *Isaiah* (from the Sistine Chapel ceiling) (1508–1512). Courtesy Anderson-Art Reference Bureau.

—and on the site of the wall itself. It was much later that artists took advantage of the possibility of executing mural-size canvases in their studios, transferring the canvas afterward to the building for which it was intended. Michelangelo still painted the Sistine ceiling on his back, supported by scaffolding under the ceiling.° Even so, fresco did not afford the sharpness of delineation he wanted, so he used *fresco secco* (which is really a type of egg tempera), applying it over the fresco to bring out the forms. But oil paint permits huge canvases—canvases which can include dozens of life-size figures and animals; landscapes; atmospheric effects; bright, fresh color; liquid, bravura passages; ample detail where desired; and all resting on a paint surface which may look today as if it were executed "in one skin" a few weeks ago.

Painting is about as old as sculpture, but it is difficult to think of any sculptural medium with the flexibility and easy working qualities of oil paint (or its modern synthetic variants, which preserve the advantages of oil and extend the permanence, stability, and strength of the medium still further). Consequently, we can understand why painting is attractive to persons varying greatly in skill and sophistication, while sculpture appears to be an art for the hardy few. But more important than ease is the limitation of subject matter and treatment in sculpture as compared to painting. To be sure, Bernini could

°Michelangelo gained no particular advantage by painting on the site. The individual panels are composed as wall paintings rather than ceiling decorations, the ceiling is poorly lit, and if the viewer wishes to see the entire sequence he must lie on his back as Michelangelo did. We see the Sistine ceiling frescos more steadily in reproductions than on the site.

execute lace in stone and create sculptural shafts of light behind his St. Theresa, but such effects seem inappropriate according to contemporary taste. Indeed, they appear to be painterly effects, an observation which brings us to another of the distinctive qualities of painting—its capacity to create *veritable illusions.* Sculptors who sought naturalism had to build replicas of actuality, going so far in the ancient and medieval worlds as to *paint* their figures in order to close the gap between reality and its representation. But key inventions in painting—linear perspective, chiaroscuro, oil painting, foreshortening, aerial perspective, glazing, color complementarity, and color vibration—opened up immense potentials for naturalistic representation, fool-the-eye illusionism, the portrayal of depth, the capture of fleeting impressions, and the creation of elaborate but credible fantasies. Finally, in comparing painting to sculpture or architecture, we should observe that poorly executed sculpture cannot easily conceal its lack of craftsmanship, and poorly designed buildings are at least inconvenient and at most dangerous. Bad paintings, however, survive physically in spite of their craftsmanship. Painting possesses no "built-in" characteristics which might discourage ineptness in technique or lack of invention. Everything survives. As a result, there is a wide range of expression in painting; and individuals who, as playwrights or architects, might never have seen their plays performed or their buildings erected, manage to persist in this art until they eventually make some contribution of value.

Because the media of painting are versatile, flexible, durable, and also inexpensive; because human temperaments

in wide variety are attracted to painting; because almost any theme can be
treated in the art; and because works of
modest imagination and indifferent
technique survive physically as well
as masterpieces do—painting is one of
the most popular, perplexing, and exciting of the visual arts. Exhibitions of
painting are held in museums, universities, and shopping centers, where they
constitute cultural and social events
comparable, let us say, to attendance
at a Puccini performance in a middle-
sized Italian city. The point to be stressed
is that the popularity and accessibility
of painting is a result, in part, of the
distinctive qualities of the painting
media. Oil paint is mainly responsible
for the size and character of the public

which sees paintings, and of the public
(there is no better word) which creates
paintings.

Having made this observation
about the social climate in which painting exists today—a climate resulting
substantially from the character of the
painting medium—I shall move on to a
discussion of the technical and expressive
qualities of painting itself. With regard
to art, it would be wrong, however, to
succumb to a type of technological de-
terminism. No matter how revolutionary the invention of oil painting or fixed-
point perspective appears to be, remember that these developments grew out
of a search for color luminosity and control of space because cultural factors
rendered such objectives important.

The Fugitive and the Permanent

It is readily apparent that
architectural form grows out of structural requirements. In a well-designed
building we quickly see that a truss, an
arch, a dome, a post-and-beam, or a
cantilever is *doing the work* of supporting weight and enclosing space. Although
the forms can be appreciated for their
decorative or expressive role, they are
also felt as a physical system which is
or is not likely to hold together as we
live in and use it. No such consideration, however, enters into the perception
of painting. Nevertheless, the art of
painting has a physical basis which,
like architecture, is concerned with
durability.

The stone vaults of Gothic churches
were developed, as we know, because
fires were so common in the medieval
world that wooden-roofed churches

burned down repeatedly. We can be
sure, therefore, that the durability of
man-made structures was one of the
most important practical goals of medieval communities. This interest in durability also reflected a concern with the
timeless and eternal in social, philosophical, and theological systems. For the
art of painting, physically considered,
durability meant permanence—resistance to fading, chipping, cracking,
warping, and splitting. Consequently,
since painting was regarded not only as
a means of communication, but also as
a valuable material commodity, questions of permanence led to the study of
"correct"—that is, permanent—technique. So-called fugitive colors could
fade, especially the blues and violets.
Others might turn black or "bleed
through" (**that is, show through** super-

imposed layers of paint). Colors applied to a ground which was too absorbent would "sink in," especially if the color were too lean (that is, mixed with insufficient binder or excessively diluted with a thinner, for when dry it might present a dead, grayed appearance). A thousand perils hovered over every painter's brush.

Artists were members of the goldsmiths' guild during the Renaissance, and although masters like Leonardo, Titian, and Michelangelo had risen socially above the artisan class, they were nevertheless deeply immersed in problems of technique. Their training and professional roots were in craftsmanship and in the guild system. (Unfortunately, a number of works by Leonardo, who was an inveterate experimenter, have not survived because he often did not follow the standard technical recipes of his day.) Leonardo and Cennino Cennini wrote treatises on the art of painting which contain lengthy discussions of technical methods. Cennino's however is more like a cookbook, while Leonardo's penetrates beyond cookery into psychology, composition, and philosophy.

But whereas permanent painting technique began as an interest in physical durability, it ends as an aesthetic requirement. What began as a concern about *means*, concludes as a concern about *ends*. In artists' contracts with their medieval patrons, specifications were stipulated for the amount and quality of lapis lazuli (the semiprecious source of blue pigment), gold leaf, and other costly materials, much as architectural specifications today require a particular brand of a product or materials with certain performance ratings. Later contracts were more likely to

specify the size of the canvas, the number of figures (whether full-length or three-quarter-length), the visibility of hands, type of costume, and so on. But with the social and professional status of the painter more firmly established, the intangible qualities of his art were primarily sought, and although sound technique was assumed, it was realized that genius consisted of more than the use of costly materials. Nevertheless, the grace, subtlety, and inventiveness of painterly forms were almost surely perceived as triumphs of technique as well as imagination. The modeling of Leonardo and Raphael were based not only on a good understanding of illumination and anatomy, but also on the artist's capacity to force paint to resemble light and shadow, skin and bone.

For the contemporary student of art, it is important to know that technical methods inherited from the medieval past, with its pronounced interest in permanence, survive as aesthetic goals in the present. For example, blues were used sparingly, because good blue was expensive, and others faded or turned green. Hence, a predominantly brown tonality survived in painting well into the nineteenth century. Paint was applied thinly in the shadows, more heavily in the lights, for several reasons: Tempera underpainting was often preceeded by a thinned-out drawing of ink washes which took care of the shadows; dark pigments tended to peel if applied heavily; and illusionistic effects were defeated by raised ridges of paint in the shadow areas. But modern colors resist fading and peeling, illusionism is not often pursued, and glazing over a tempera underpainting is uncommon. Nevertheless, one can find many contemporary paintings which observe the ancient painterly traditions because they seem to afford aesthetic gratification even though they have no foundation in the current requirements of permanence.

The resemblance of Jack Levine's technique to Rembrandt's has been mentioned. The same can be said of Soutine. *The Madwoman* by Soutine, however, exhibits more direct brushwork in the darks than Rembrandt would have used. The brilliant cadmium reds, alizarins, and madders used by Soutine were not available to Rembrandt and El Greco, for example. Or perhaps, it would be better to say they were not available in such stable, light-proof colors as are now readily and cheaply at hand. Hence, the masters used a reddish glaze over a greenish tempera underpainting which itself rested on a luminous white ground. Soutine used opaque reds and alizarins mixed with umber applied directly to the primed canvas. The colors retain their brilliance because they are chemically almost inert compared to the colors available to Rembrandt. Consequently, Soutine could apply the paint for his twisting shadows with loaded brush quite spontaneously and the agitation

of the result owes a great deal to this direct execution. El Greco's turbulent and flickering effects had to be planned in advance and can be partly attributed to direct painting into his wet glazes. But laying opaque paint crisply into a wet, transparent glaze, which itself rests on a modeled monochrome underpainting, calls for sureness of hand and a fairly clear idea of the effect desired in the outcome. Today, Willem de Kooning, who seems to be influenced more by Rubens than El Greco, is prominent among contemporary painters who practice loaded-brush, wet-in-wet painting technique.

There has been an important change in the contemporary attitude toward permanence, one which inevitably influences any examination of painting done now. Just as scarcity characterized the economies of all nations in the past, affluence characterizes the economies of the industrially advanced nations today, particularly that of the United States. And, as the economist J. K. Galbraith has noted in his book, *The Affluent Society*, a disproportionate effort of the economy is devoted to its private sector, that is, to the production and distribution of goods and services for individual

CHAIM SOUTINE, *The Madwoman* (1920), left. Courtesy The National Museum of Western Art, Tokyo, presented by Mr. Tai Hayashi, 1960; photo, Thames and Hudson, Ltd.

REMBRANDT VAN RIJN, *Old Woman Cutting Her Nails* (1648), center. Courtesy The Metropolitan Museum of Art, bequest of Benjamin Altman, 1913; photo, John Pitkin.

EL GRECO, *Agony in the Garden* (c. 1598), above right. Courtesy The National Gallery, London.

PETER PAUL RUBENS, *Judgment of Paris* [detail] (1638–39), below left. Courtesy The National Gallery, London.

WILLEM DE KOONING, *Woman, VI* [detail] (1953), below right. Courtesy Museum of Art, Carnegie Institute, Pittsburgh.

consumption. He argues that insufficient economic effort is devoted to the maintenance and expansion of publicly owned instrumentalities like schools, transport systems, hospitals, recreation facilities, riverbank development, and so on. As a result of greater personal prosperity and of our freedom to make ever-increasing expenditures in the private sector of the economy, individuals find that they can buy more consumer goods, replace possessions more frequently, and discard their possessions before they are "worn out." The process of quick obsolescence has already been discussed (p. 124) in connection with industrial design. It would be strange, indeed, if the idea of quick obsolesence in manufactured goods did not also affect our notions of permanence in works of art.

The medieval idea of craftsmanship and durability was ultimately based on economic scarcity: There was not enough of the necessities of life, not to mention the luxuries, to go around. The lives of kings and nobles in the Middle Ages were unspeakably crude and primitive when compared with the standard of living of our own citizens of even modest means. Human labor was abundant and the political-economic organization existed to extract the maximum of effort from it. By contrast, the modern idea of craftsmanship has to be related to economic abundance and an increasing *scarcity* of labor. Today, the prosperous nations of western Europe have labor shortages and must import workers to supply the needs of their expanding economies, just as the United States did during the first quarter of the twentieth century. Furthermore, the actual manufacture of goods is done by machines, with human labor employed to direct and operate them. Hence we have an abundance of goods, an increasing value set upon human labor in nations with advanced economies, and a reduction of human participation in the direct forming and fabrication of goods.

Inevitably, the durability and permanence of goods has a different meaning in an economy such as ours compared to its meaning in the scarcity economies of the past. Although many of us have had experience with scarcity, an enormous number of citizens, perhaps the majority, is unaware of any obligation to make things last or to acquire only those goods which appear to be durable. Instead of fixing a broken part, we replace it. And this practice makes economic sense, since the labor cost of repairs is often greater than the purchase cost of a replacement. In such a context, an artistic concern with permanent technique can seem to be an anachronism. Furthermore, as was observed, technology has created new painting media which are durable no matter how they are used. Consequently, the *fact of permanence*, the physical durability of the art object, ceases to be an important problem. The *idea of permanence* remains important, however.

Since we are reasonably assured of the physical permanence of a painting, our concern shifts to its durability as a significant statement in the medium. We want to know whether it will continue to survive as a vehicle of sustained aesthetic interest. Our concern about this kind of survival is not rooted in an artist's technique so much as in his capacity to make a statement *through* his medium and *through* personal technique which can survive changing standards of taste and competing art forms. The traditional artistic effort to master technical methods which would insure physical survival often led to the creation of such values indirectly—ideas about man and the universe which were manifested by the artist's own search for enduring technique, sound principles of composition, and exalted subject matter.

The *time* required to execute a work by traditional methods militated against a casual approach toward technique and theme. As the oil-painting medium was perfected, however, as painters used it with increasing ease and facility, accomplished technical skills were applied to rather insignificant themes. For example, the subject matter of Fragonard (1732–1806)—courts of love, and the general foppishness of French aristocratic life before the Revolution—seems trivial in the extreme, especially for modern, democratic taste. However, the execution of his painting *The Meeting* is exceedingly able. Beyond the situation that Fragonard has illustrated, the drawing, color, and composition are managed with a high degree of competence. Some contemporary painters, on the other hand, undertake themes of portentous import or utmost solemnity while employing a technical approach which seems rather casual and off-hand. *La Mort d'Atilla* by Georges Mathieu (1921–   ) is such a work. *Number 21* by Hans Hofmann (1880–1966), executed in oil on paper, is another. Hofmann's work appears to have been created by a combination of liquid paint spatters and blobs. (Oil on paper is not, of course, a permanent technique. If the paper is unsized, the acids in the linseed-oil medium may cause it to rot eventually. But physical permanence is not at all a consideration in the execution of this work.) The value of painting for many contemporary artists has been relocated: *It now lies in the act of execution.* For the viewer or the collector, value lies in his immediate experience. Modern man does not look at a painting as medieval man did, making visual inquiry into its craftsmanship and durability, its likelihood of surviving through eternity. The contemporary collector is aware of the work as a possession which he may eventually sell if it ceases to interest him or if its market value increases. But more importantly, modern men have a *different sense of time*. Under the impact of science, and particularly of relativity physics, the belief in eternal values and in fixed systems of thought has broken down. The idea that man-made structures can or should survive forever now seems slightly absurd, just as it would have seemed absurd to medieval men that anything be made *not* to last.

We know that the physical permanence of painting is a relative matter.

JEAN HONORÉ FRAGONARD, *The Meeting* (1773), left. Copyright The Frick Collection, New York.

GEORGES MATHIEU, *La Mort d'Attila* (1961), right top. Courtesy Galerie Jean Larcade, and the artist.

HANS HOFMANN, *Number 21* (1962), right bottom. Courtesy David K. Anderson.

Although scientific methods of conservation are now highly advanced, we are acutely aware of the transience of taste: Works of art may cease to be interesting long before they have decayed, their decay being a matter of certitude. Considerations of this sort account for the general indifference to craftsmanship and permanent technique in painting as they were traditionally understood. Consequently, contemporary painting rarely exhibits a painstaking technique, conscientious attention to detail, and a quality of "finish." That is why a painter like Andrew Wyeth is so unusual: His distinction is not that he employs the traditional egg-tempera medium, but that the medium is evidence of an *attitude* in a contemporary artist which most of us thought had disappeared.

If the virtual disappearance of older ideas of permanence has cost us the loss of certain artistic values, there have also been gains. Experimentation with design, with materials, and with the subject matter of painting has re-sulted in considerable visual variety. Painting is perhaps more entertaining than it was formerly. At the same time, it has not ceased to be concerned with serious matters. Although the invention and perfection of still photography and of motion pictures during this century poses a serious threat to the survival of painting as an art form, painting appears to be responding to the challenge with vitality. Indeed, painting is more widely practiced and exhibited than ever before; it has extended the range of social and personal functions it performs; and, as will be seen in the following discussions, painting has acquired many of the characteristics of sculpture, architecture, and even of drama. If it were not for the museums and libraries which serve to remind us of what painting has been, we might not be so acutely aware of the revolutionary changes now taking place in the arts, especially in painting. If one's vision is too retrospective, the experience is very unsettling; otherwise, it can be exhilarating and uniquely satisfying.

MICHELANGELO, studies for the *Libyan Sibyl.* Courtesy The Metropolitan Museum of Art, Purchase, 1924, Joseph Pulitzer bequest.

Direct and Indirect Techniques

Simply stated, direct painting involves the pursuit of the final effect immediately, or *alla prima.* Indirect painting calls for a stage-by-stage approach to the final effect. These two approaches represent fundamental contrasts in technique, in artist psychology, and in style. In general, traditional methods are indirect and rationally planned in advance. Modern approaches tend to be direct and spontaneous

So long as painting is regarded as an elaboration of drawing, the indirect method prevails. That is, if painting is seen as the application of color to a scheme which has already been worked out, it clearly makes sense to employ the indirect method. The choice amounts to a problem in the logical division of labor. First comes the conception of the general idea of the work, its theme, its specific content, its over-all setting, and so on. Next, drawings can be undertaken to explore the spatial representation, landscape, and architectural features, and the figures. For the Renaissance painter, drawing was not only a way of making visual notations, as it is for the contemporary architect or designer, it was also a means of *studying* the things he would later paint. Indeed, we refer to such drawings as "studies." As mentioned in our discussion of line (p. 233), drawing obliges the artist to *commit* himself, and commitment of this sort cannot be undertaken without knowledge. The Renaissance artist regarded drawing *primarily* as a mode of investigation and only secondarily as a display of his facility. It is the modern era which has made drawing an end rather than a means.

Studies of drapery, of hands, of facial expressions, of the anatomy of a figure (which may not be seen finally because it is covered by clothing)—these were undertaken by the artist so that he could be assured of his intellectual and visual grasp of the subject matter. Then he felt ready to transfer his drawings to a prepared surface. Following transfer to the scale of the final work, the artist could begin painterly execution according to his inherited technique or his personal variation of

it. If the work were to be completed in oil or varnish glazes, the preliminary painting in tempera would be monochromatic or limited in color. Division of labor extended to separation of drawing from painting; and within painting, coloring was separated from modeling. The monochromatic underpainting served as a guide for translating the drawing into paint, establishing the compositional scheme, placing lights and

LEONARDO DA VINCI, study for *Adoration of the Magi*. Courtesy Uffizi Gallery.

GENTILE DA FABRIANO, *The Adoration of the Magi* (1423), below left. Photo, Scala, Florence.

Van Eyck's use of oil paint permits a much wider range of color and tonal values than the egg tempera medium employed by Gentile da Fabriano only ten years earlier.

JAN VAN EYCK, *A Man in a Red Turban* (1433), right. Courtesy The National Gallery, London.

darks, modeling large forms, and solving any unanticipated problems which might arise. Because tempera paint dries quickly, and because it is quite opaque, corrections which cover mistakes can be easily made. Oil paint dries more slowly, and becomes more transparent as it grows older; hence passages which have been painted out or blended over tend to show through eventually. However, tempera does not blend easily; consequently it is difficult to conceal any uncertainty on the artist's part by a wide, blended passage. Egg tempera, especially, is difficult to spread on in large areas. Large forms have to be built up by "hatching" (creating a small *area* of color or tone by a series of lines painted close together) and with small washes: It is a linear technique.

When the indirect method is employed, underpainted shadows can be executed in cool tones if warm-tone glazes will be applied over them at the end. Then, by glaze manipulation, the painter will be able to achieve a warm-cool balance as well as a rather Impressionist color vibration as he models and "drowns" some of the light with his glazes. The light areas are usually painted "higher" or "chalkier" than they will finally appear because overpainting and glazing will lower their value. In traditional painting techniques, it was assumed that white pigment (usually white lead), together with final varnishing, would tend to yellow the painting. That tendency constituted another reason for favoring a cool tonality in the underpainting. Some painters added a little blue to their white pigment in anticipation of subsequent yellowing.

At this point, mention should be made of the mischief done to painting and aesthetics by final varnishes. Varnishes served primarily to protect the paint surface from impurities in the air —smoke, sulphur, carbon, and so on— which menaced painting before the development of modern heating systems. These impurities became embedded in the cracks and crevices of older works, especially those with an irregular surface, or those having impasto passages (thick, rough-textured paint surfaces). In the nineteenth century especially, dealers would revarnish paintings to endow them with a fresh, glossy appearance. Rarely did they give the painting a thorough cleaning or remove the old varnish before applying a new coat. As a consequence, old paintings acquired a soupy brown patina which could not be attributed entirely to the darkening of their colors. They were, in a sense, too old for their years. Rembrandts suffered in this manner, notably the famous *Night Watch*, which upon being cleaned was revealed to be not a nocturnal work at all. With regard to the formation of taste among art students and collectors, a "museum brown" convention came to be operative, so that the appearance of numerous coats of varnish over a dirt-embedded paint surface was sought from the outset.

Since glazes are mixtures of varnish or thickened oil with pigment, it is possible to confuse a glazed surface with one which merely has a final varnish applied over a direct painting. Perhaps that is why frequent coats of varnish were applied by dealers. Titian claimed to use as many as eighty glazes in a single painting: Such pains and craftsmanship might be simulated for the unwary by several varnishings. But a conscientious examination of Rubens, Rembrandt, and El Greco should enable the viewer to recognize the difference between underpainted monochromatic passages which have colored glazes resting over them and canvases whose colored pigment has been laid on directly, followed by clear varnish on top. It should be added that very glossy color reproductions in art books sometimes create a spurious impression of glazing where it does not exist. You can be reasonably certain, for instance, that a glossy reproduction of a van Gogh or a Cézanne is misleading.

Before the discovery and wide use of oil painting—either in the form of glazes over tempera or in direct application of oil paint to the primed canvas—most paintings were completely executed in tempera (the other principal forms were encaustic, which is a wax-based medium, and fresco, which employs water, lime, and plaster as its medium). Tempera is usually understood as any painting medium based on a glue. Older glues came from cooked animal skins—rabbit skin, for instance. As you may know from scraping breakfast frying pans, eggs act as a powerful adhesive. Casein, a milk derivative, is a modern glue, one that makes an excellent tempera. Polymer tempera comes close to being an ideal medium since it possesses all the assets and none of the liabilities of the traditional tempera and oil media. However, tempera paintings until the 1940's were mostly executed with the traditional egg-yolk medium which was often diluted with water. Today, for example, Andrew Wyeth employs the classic egg-tempera medium, whereas Ben Shahn uses egg tempera, casein tempera, and gouache (a type of opaque water-color medium).

Many painters presently active were taught Cennino's recipes for preparing a gesso ground (a thin, white plaster-of-Paris layer usually applied over a coating of size) on a wood panel (today Masonite hardboard is usually

employed), and learned how to puncture the egg yolk sac, "cook up" an egg-and-water or egg-and-oil emulsion, and then mix the emulsion with powdered dry pigment. The pure egg-tempera medium is permanent, does not darken with age, and provides clean, bright color. But it usually calls for a rigid support, and, as mentioned above, is not well suited for covering large areas. Furthermore, it virtually dictates a slowly-built-up, step-by-step mode of execution. It tends to force a linear conception upon the artist; the style Wölfflin calls "painterly" is possible but difficult for the artist working in egg tempera. It is interesting to note that Shahn and Wyeth both tend toward the linear and distinct as opposed to the painterly and undistinct poles of the stylistic categories.

Direct painting begins when the artist starts to load his glazes with more "body" pigment. The Venetians are credited with introducing a loaded-brush technique (instead of being used to spread a thin, liquid paint film, the brush is loaded with paint of a pasty, viscous consistency which is then applied in short "touches" rather than evenly brushed out). The technique is accompanied by free departures from the controlling tempera underpainting. There is a line of development in the use of the oil medium from Titian to Rubens to Delacroix to Monet. Delacroix, perhaps, represents the critical departure from reliance on the underpainting; with him, spontaneous execution begins to assert itself forcefully. His contemporary, the classicizing Jean August Dominique Ingres, practiced an impeccable indirect method of painting with nowhere a brushstroke evident. But Eugène Delacroix quite consciously and effectively exploited the emotional possibilities of brushwork. His oil **sketch** for *The Lion*

Encaustic on wood.

Panel from a mummy—portrait of a man, Egyptian (second century). Courtesy The Metropolitan Museum of Art, Rogers Fund, 1909.

EUGÈNE DELACROIX, sketch for *The Lion Hunt* (1861), above left. Private collection.

EUGÈNE DELACROIX, *The Lion Hunt* (1861), above right. Courtesy of The Art Institute of Chicago, Potter Palmer Collection.

RICHARD LYTLE, *The Possessed* (1959), below left. Courtesy the artist.

JON CORBINO, *Stampeding Bulls* (1937), below right. Courtesy The Toledo Museum of Art, Toledo, Ohio.

Hunt, executed in about 1860–61, shows how the artist created forms directly with the brush. Drawing is felt or understood, but it is distinctly subordinate to the painterly establishment of form. Brushwork as the artist's handwriting now begins to be a prominent feature of painting. The dynamism of this composition derives basically from its underlying pattern of whirling forms which appear to have radiated from the center and then begun to rotate in a clockwise direction. But Delacroix is not content to rely on the dynamics of the compositional arrangement: He supports its movement with writhing brushstrokes which have a life of their own. It is interesting to compare this oil sketch with the final work, which is much modified in composition and, of course, more "finished" in execution. From the standpoint of contemporary taste, the sketch is more abstract, less finicky, and fresher in its use of paint. The contemporary quality of the Delacroix oil sketch is vividly brought home when we examine a painting by a young American artist, Richard Lytle, (1935–), *The Possessed*. The contemporary painter is clearly the beneficiary of Delacroix's form language, as was Jon Corbino (1905–64), before him in his painting, *Stampeding Bulls*. The antecedent of these works, both in subject matter and in painterly execution was created almost two-hundred-and-fifty years earlier —Peter Paul Rubens's *Lion Hunt* (1616–21). Although Rubens employed a preliminary underpainting, he clearly relied on a direct type of overpainting executed in what appears to be a very spontaneous fashion. Hence, notwithstanding the many innovations introduced into painting through the ages, there is considerable continuity of outlook and of method, from Rubens in 1616 to Delacroix in 1861 to Richard Lytle in 1959.

The connection between brushwork and emotional expression has already been mentioned several times. Now the question arises about *how* brushwork performs an emotional function. Furthermore, how is this function related to direct oil-painting technique? Perhaps the earlier discussion of empathy (p. 281) may help to explain the role of brushwork. Fundamentally, a viewer's perception of the artist's brushwork involves an internal "acting out" of the process of wielding the brush and applying the paint. It is for this reason that the term "action painting," coined by the critic, Harold Rosenberg, is so appropriate as a designation for the work of the so-called New York School of painters—the Abstract Ex-

PETER PAUL RUBENS, *Lion Hunt* (1616–21). Courtesy Pinakothek, Munich.

pressionists. Most viewers have had experience with the use of brushes, either in art instruction or in some other, more prosaic connection. Hence, it is relatively easy for them to identify with and to simulate inwardly the motions implied by the brushwork they see. This does not mean, of course, that viewers perform a series of gymnastic maneuvers before a painting which has a rather active surface. But it does mean that a variety of physiological reactions are set in motion within the viewer by such a work and that these reactions produce feelings in the manner described by the Gestalt principle of isomorphism (p. 292). Such feelings are similar to kinaesthetic emotion; that is, emotion felt in association with bodily movement.

Indirect technique, for the most part, does not rely on brushwork to express emotion. Because indirect paintings are executed in separate layers, or "skins," distinct marks of the brush tend to be lost. If pronounced ridges of paint are employed in the underpainting, they will, of course, show through as textures; hence they must be anticipated, or the final effect may be spoiled or at

J. A. D. INGRES, *Madame Moitessier Seated* (1851). Courtesy The National Gallery, London.

least confused. The element of planning tends to reduce the appearance of spontaneous execution, which is one important means of arousing empathy in the viewer. Masters of indirect painting technique such as Ingres and David brushed out their paint, leaving no surface sign of the process of execution; any empathic response of the viewer to their works had to be based on subject matter and on the design of the forms rather than their technical execution. For artists who favored historical themes and allegorical compositions, however, such a response was intended. Clearly, then, indirect technique draws attention to the subject matter of the picture whereas direct technique emphasizes the way it was painted.

Although indirect painting involves a division of labor in the process of execution, direct painting combines al-

most all the crucial decisions in the single act of applying paint. The artist may make preliminary sketches and he may transfer his general idea of the drawing and composition to the canvas before beginning to paint. But the final effect is not built up: Color, drawing, value, shape, weight of pigment, and paint quality are decided at once as the paint is laid on. A spontaneous appearance is usually sought even if the painter works slowly and deliberately, calculating his brushwork in advance. If he does not achieve the desired effect at once, he is likely to scrape the paint off until he succeeds. Oil paint, of course, is ideal for this sort of trial-and-error execution. When an artist does not succeed in his first attempt but continues to paint over his earlier efforts rather than scrape them off, a labored, rather tortured paint surface often re-

The impression of swiftness and spontaneity in direct painting technique calls for considerable assurance on the part of the artist—assurance based on solid knowledge, power of observation, and shrewd grasp of character.

FRANS HALS, *Governors of the Old Men's Almshouse, Haarlem* (1664) [whole and detail]. Courtesy Frans Halsmuseum, Haarlem.

A painterly approach to drawing. The artist does not use line to establish contours so much as to anticipate paint application, the direction of brush strokes, and the dominant rhythms of his composition.

EUGÈNE DELACROIX, *A Mounted Arab Attacking a Panther* (c.1840), at right. Courtesy Fogg Art Museum, Harvard University, bequest of Meta and Paul J. Sachs.

VINCENT VAN GOGH, *The Ravine*
(1889), left. Courtesy Museum of
Fine Arts, Boston, bequest of Keith
McLeod.

PAUL CÉZANNE, *Self Portrait* (c.1879),
right. Courtesy Tate Gallery, London.

sults. Direct technique is not well suited to frequent "overpaints." The color, being largely opaque, tends to become muddy; it begins to look tormented, as if it had been "pushed around" too much; clarity of color and crispness of brushwork are lost.

Since direct technique usually emphasizes the performing aspect of painting, the attention of the viewer is drawn to the visual evidence of paint mixing and application, because they constitute an integral part of the artist's performance. Cézanne and van Gogh are both instructive performers to watch. There is more building up of planes in Cézanne, but his "touch," while careful, is rarely hesitant. He does not push the paint around indecisively but seems to know the color and value of each stroke or series of strokes before he commits himself. Frequently, Cézanne's canvas shows through as the white paper does in some water-color paintings. Consequently, his paint surfaces have a freshness and sparkle which a more labored technique would not yield. Certainly glazing would sacrifice the vividness of directly applied opaque color. The luminosity of glazed painting depends on light striking through to the whitish underpainting (which acts like a mirror) and then bouncing back in modified form through the translucent colored glaze to the viewer's eye. Thus, the light by which the viewer sees becomes an ally of the indirect painter. But the artist who employs direct technique cannot rely on such refractive effects: He must usually mix and apply any color effect he expects the viewer to see. However, with Impressionist painting (which is executed in direct technique), the artist relies on the viewer's eye to "mix" new colors optically, using the pigments the painter has *actually* applied to the canvas. The color vibrations of van Gogh's *The Ravine* might be regarded as a demonstration of Gestalt principles of perception: The blues and yellows are juxtaposed, for example, so that they "complete" each other by forming greens. But they are also what they are —blue and yellow. Hence, the viewer's energies are organized to perceive the colors alternately as blue and yellow, or as green. It is the *alternation* of perceptual organizations, or *gestalten*, which causes the experience of color vibration. In addition, van Gogh's short, distinct brush strokes set up staccato rhythms which reinforce the impact of the vibrating color. Thus, the colors of the paint, as well as its application, contribute to the tormented motion one "feels" in the water. A brushed-out technique or a luminous glaze in the traditional manner would surely ruin this effect. The flickering light of El Greco's *Agony in the Garden* (p. 313) is a different phenomenon entirely; it was achieved by the *shape* of the light and dark patterns. El Greco came as close as one could to conveying an agitated movement of light and form while using indirect painting technique.

If we trace direct painting technique from its beginnings among the

Employing direct technique, modern painters use pigment as a vehicle of candid self-revelation (de Kooning), or as an anonymous element subordinated to the requirements of the total design (Glarner).

WILLEM DE KOONING, *Woman, II* (1952), left. Collection The Museum of Modern Art, New York, gift of Mrs. John D. Rockefeller, 3rd; photo, Geoffrey Clements.

FRITZ GLARNER, *Tondo No. 54* (1960), right. Courtesy Richard Zeisler; photo, Rudolph Burckhardt.

Venetians during the fifteenth century to its full development in our own time, it seems that this method of painting has paralleled the growth of individualism among men in general and of autonomy among artists in particular. Since direct technique emphasizes the uniqueness of the painter's execution, it is best suited to individuals who set a premium on the expression of their personalities no matter who their patron may be or what the theme of their work is. Indirect technique has served painters with lofty and ambitious aims, but it has best suited artists who did not wish to display their "handwriting," their technical idiosyncrasies. In recent work, these two contrasting attitudes toward

the disclosure of technique remain visible although almost all artists paint directly. The so-called "hard-edge" and geometric painters employ an anonymous technique, relying on design qualities and optical effect of color quantity and shape to carry the burden of their work. For the "action" painters, the execution of the painting, the path of the painter as he travels across the canvas with loaded brush, is the subject of the work of art. Such works of art constitute evidence of the extraordinary development of personal freedom in the present era. Indeed, this emphasis upon individual personality to the exclusion of virtually any other value has aroused the hostility of some observers. Perhaps they are offended by such forceful assertions of freedom; or perhaps they cherish classical ideals of moderation and balance—of a mean between the extremes of "inner-directedness" and "other-directedness." But such Aristotelian counsels are rarely heeded in contemporary art: Media and techniques serve to celebrate the individual—his freedom, his anxiety, his indifference to the form and content of yesterday's masters, and his search for new meaning.

Frottage, Grattage, and Decalcomania

The spontaneous application of paint with a loaded brush was one type of liberation from the methodical approach to painting as it was traditionally practiced. In this technique the artist recognizes and exploits the fact that the *marks of the tool*—the brush marks—are expressive of meaning in themselves, apart from the import of representational forms and the stated

subject matter of a work of art. Once this form of expressiveness was discovered, it was a simple step to the realization that changing the tools of painting results in new possibilities of meaning. Although painting remained an art of fashioning images, some artists devised new techniques for manipulating the paint, which *itself* became the source of their imagery. Among the most inventive of these innovators has been Max Ernst (born 1891), an artist who has also been a prolific creator of nonpainterly pictorial devices. In this section, however, we are concerned only with the application of his techniques to painting because they have been so influential in the work of other artists.

Ernst has for most of his career been associated with the Dadaist and Surrealist movements. Hence, irrational impulse has played a major role in his art. *Chance arrangement* is a principle of Dadaist composition while the juxtaposition of unrelated images is a principle of Surrealism: Clearly, the movements are closely connected in their creative approach. Ernst's technical discoveries can be seen as the result of a search for sources of imagery which are not known in advance, which cannot be calculated consciously, but which must be developed in response to "accidents" caused by interactions between paint and process. Still, although the resulting images appear to be irrational and unplanned, the artist works hard at a conscious level to create the accidental situations which, in turn, establish the basis for his adventitious forms.

Frottage is the best-known of Ernst's techniques. You may be familiar with it as the popular art of making rubbings: Pencil or crayon rubbed over paper placed on a textured or relief surface transfers to the paper a negative image of the texture underneath. Archaeologists use rubbings to make transportable copies of stone or metal reliefs. Children use the technique on coins or whatever else comes to hand. Purely abstract patterns such as wood grains can be transferred, and then, because of their suggestiveness, worked up into specific, recognizable images. *Frottage* then, is a technique which has a practical, record-keeping value, and which also can be used to stimulate the creation of fantastic forms. For Ernst, it was a means of exploiting unplanned images of natural or accidental origin such as those one sees in clouds, wall stains, rock fissures, and so on. He found a way to use *frottage* in oil painting by placing a freshly painted canvas over a relief texture and then scraping away the paint. The unscraped paint remaining in the valleys and crevices of the canvas creates a pattern corresponding to the texture below. The process really does not involve rubbing, but it results nevertheless in a transfer of the pattern underneath by a technique similar to *frottage*. As with *decalcomania* (see below), the key concept is *transfer,* or, in other words, *informal printing.* Another informal printing process involves the dip-

MAX ERNST, *The Eye of Silence* (1944). Courtesy Washington University, St. Louis.

ping of leaves, kitchen utensils, fabrics, or toy parts—virtually anything which can be held in the hand—into wet paint; then the object is used like a hand stamp to transfer the pattern to canvas. However, we must distinguish between printmaking, as the intentional contrivance of images on a stone or metal plate for the purpose of making many reproductions, and *frottage*, as the transfer of "found" textures and patterns for the purpose of enhancing them in the context of a single painting.

Grattage, another Ernst technique, is the grating or scratching of wet paint with any of a number of tools: a comb, a fork, a pen, a razor, an irregular-shaped piece of glass, a needle, and so on. *Grattage* takes advantage of the plastic character of wet oil paint just as the paint brush does. But the brush is designed primarily to *apply* paint and to blend it—only secondarily to leave its mark. These other tools manipulate paint which is already applied. *Grattage* involves an almost sculptural or architectural working of paint, the pigment being regarded as a type of building material like concrete. (In this connection, it should be mentioned that Le

Corbusier liked to "scratch" images into his poured-concrete wall surfaces. As would be expected in an architect who was a serious painter, several of his buildings contain incised relief figures created by pouring concrete around a shallow mold incorporated into the wooden formwork for the wall.) The conception of paint as a material which can be scratched, modeled, abraded, or otherwise tortured, represents a significant departure from the idea of paint as a descriptive substance. In traditional painting, the pigment was not really "there." It always designated a different substance from itself, usually one occupying a spatial location different from the pictorial surface. In the terminology of aesthetics, it was *transparent* rather than opaque; it pointed to something beyond itself. Today, pigment with its various admixtures can function "transparently" *and* "opaquely": It can describe something else or it can be the focus of interest because of the operations which have been performed—not *with* it, but *in* it. Clearly, this new role of pigment carries painting closer to sculpture.

Decalcomania is used by Ernst in a special way: Wet blobs of paint are squeezed between two canvas surfaces which are then separated. Variations in motion and pressure force the paint into random patterns forming crevices and rivulets which, when dry, can be worked on directly and exploited for their formal and thematic suggestions: fantastic geological structures; volcanoes, caves, and valleys; landscapes of unknown planets, of prenatal memories; and projections of the fevered imagination. It is, of course, the artist's imagination which acts as creative instrument while decalcomania, frottage, and the rest

The painter builds a surface which he then carves, scratches and abrades; his picture is something "real" rather than a system of illusions.

ANTONIO TAPIES, *Painting* (1962), left. Courtesy Martha Jackson Gallery.

MAX ERNST, *Swamp Angel* (1940), right. Collection Kenneth MacPherson, Rome.

serve as strategies of imaginative stimulation. Another Ernstian technique, *éclaboussage,* has been widely practiced by painters. It involves the dropping of paint or turpentine from a height to a prepared canvas. Ernst dropped the paint from a perforated tin can which swung from a string suspended above the canvas. The paint splashes are used in the same manner as the squeezed pigment in decalcomania. Turpentine dropped on a freshly painted canvas is also used to create splash patterns which expose the bare canvas or dilute the wet paint partially, depending on the force of the drop and whether the turpentine is blotted up or permitted to stand, puddle, or run in random paths. There is only a short step from dropping paint to throwing paint from a brush or dripping it from a stick in the manner of Jackson Pollock.

It is interesting that, when these techniques are employed, the connection between the artist and the canvas becomes mechanically more indirect and physically more distant. For centuries, the brush was an extension of the painter's hand, but when used to spatter paint it is a different tool. Among the more bizarre methods of distributing paint on a surface is the technique of a young woman, Niki de Saint Phalle (1930–), who used to fire a rifle at bags of paint suspended before a wall covered with random relief sculptures. The explosion of the gun and of the bag of paint created two dramatic events— the performance itself and the record of its violence on the paint-bespattered wall. As compared with the Ernst technique of stimulating the imagination, this latter method shifts attention from the *result* of the creative process to the act of execution, which becomes the

Niki de Saint Phalle about to paint with a rifle. Courtesy Alexander Iolas Gallery.

primary focus of interest. Another bizarre technique consists of driving an automobile back and forth over a prepared canvas laid on the road. This performance represents the interposition of a very complex machine between the artist and his working surface. Aside from its theatricality, however, it is no more absurd than composing music with a computer (which is a very complex machine) or employing the coordinatograph (see p. 240) to create abstract pictures.

Once the brush lost its central position in painting and pigment could be combined with new admixtures held together with new glues and binders— once, indeed, that pigment was abandoned altogether—then the tools and materials of painting became capable of almost infinite extension. If an automobile could be substituted for a paintbrush, then a bulldozer might logically be employed as a sculptor's carving tool. César (Baldaccini) (1921–) has in fact created objects in collaboration with the powerful hydraulic press used to squeeze junked automobiles into compact cubes of anonymous metal. He calls the method "governed compression." His relief is a good example of the combination of painting and sculpture in a crushed automobile. One cannot escape the impression, once again, that so theatrical an artistic gesture rep-

CÉSAR (Baldaccini), *Portrait of Patrick Waldberg* (1961). Courtesy the artist; photo, Luc Joubert.

resents a shift of focus from the object to the symbolic meaning of the act of creating it. In such "sculpture" and in the "paintings" of Miss de St. Phalle, we see the crossing of the line from plastic art to dramatic art: The object is of relatively minor importance; it serves to remind the viewer of a previous *dramatic enactment.*

The tendency of painting to seek assimilation by the dramatic arts will be discussed in further detail in a following section. But with reference to the technical and imaginative innovations of painters like Klee, Ernst, Duchamp, and Dubuffet, I want to stress that these men have been essentially engaged in

devising strategies for the artistic imagination. These strategies remain tools whose major goal is the creation of art objects. It would appear, however, that another generation of artists has been impressed by the dramatic qualities of such painterly strategies. The *process* of throwing, dripping, or exploding paint has opened up possibilities which are felt to have aesthetic value independent of the outcome as it is embodied in the conventional art object. In a subsequent section of this chapter, "Beyond Collage: Assemblage, Environments, Happenings," we shall analyze these more recent developments in painting and/or drama.

The Picture and the Wall

Abstract Expressionist painting, which dominated the international art scene from 1946 until approximately 1960, reintroduced the huge canvas, an innovation which has been retained by succeeding styles such as Pop art and Op art. Canvases containing dimensions of up to twelve feet are not unusual today. However, they represent a departure from the preceding easel-painting styles in more than dimension; the

new scale of painting signifies a fundamental change in the way painting is intended to operate in its setting and for its public.

Critics at first questioned the huge scale of the post-World War II works which seemed to contain visual ideas that could be comfortably accommodated within much smaller dimensions. Habituation to small-scale painting had been abetted by an increase in the

CLAUDE MONET, *Water Lilies,* triptych (c.1920) [detail at far right]. Collection The Museum of Modern Art, New York, Mrs. Simon Guggenheim Fund.

publication of art volumes of good quality after the War, resulting in the wide dissemination of reproductions of contemporary painting. But reproductions create a homogenized scale, and, for persons who have not seen the originals, they convey a misleading impression of the authentic experience of the work. "Action painting" was dependent for its effectiveness upon the communication of the artist's brushing gestures—gestures accomplished mainly through the movements of the large muscle groups of the body. This point is obvious in a work such as de Kooning's *Merritt Parkway*. The viewer's reaction must be substantially kinaesthetic as well as optical if he is to appreciate the painting. Hence, the same composition executed on a small scale, or the reproduction of the work in a book, will not succeed in stimulating the appropriate kinaesthetic responses.

Large pictures have been created, of course, during almost all periods of art history. However, their large size was based on the need to accommodate many figures, buildings, landscape details, and so on. The figures rarely exceeded life size: The fundamental scale and format were keyed to the imitation of visual reality. Hence, the perception of them was easily related to a close or distant view of the same material seen in reality. Only with Impressionist painting did the distance of the viewer from the picture—the *size* of the area occupied by the image on his retina—become crucial for the understanding of the work. At one distance, the perception would be mainly of fragments of the work, of color patches and color vibrations. At a greater distance, the color areas and fragments would come into *focus*, yielding a relatively stable image of the whole comparable to conventional representations of similar subject matter.

Paintings executed with direct technique had always exhibited indistinctness when seen from a close distance. But the vital discovery brought about by the color divisionism of Impressionist painting was that unfocused color areas had interest and emotional possibilities by themselves. As mentioned earlier (p. 250) the potential of color for independent emotional expression could be exploited in painting only after it was substantially detached from a descriptive function. The combination of almost free color and active brushwork with large-scale abstract design was beautifully managed in a huge canvas mural, *Water Lilies*, painted by Monet in 1925.

WILLEM DE KOONING, *Merritt Parkway* (1959). Courtesy Sidney Janis Gallery.

The work is over eighteen feet wide and is executed with very loose and free brushwork. Although its over-all design is somewhat governed by the requirements of the natural setting portrayed, it is difficult to see the whole canvas at once because of its size. Hence, one views only a succession of its parts, and these are quite abstract, the color and pigment taking precedence over description. As with the art of Delacroix, the drama of the painting performance is heightened in Monet. But in the *Water Lilies* canvas, the *scale* of the work becomes more prominent than the dexterity of the brushwork. Therefore, aside from its inherent visual appeal and its demonstration of mastery of color and paint application, this work constitutes an important monument of large-scale abstract painting.

The large scale of modern works has several important implications for contemporary painting. The first is that passages of color and texture are frequently larger than the viewer, making it difficult to maintain an attitude of detachment and objectivity during perception. (Traditional aesthetics is based on detached perception, disinterestedness. Contemporary art, in general, militates against the maintenance of distance or detachment.) Areas and shapes in a painting become not so much the objects of perception as *part of the environment* in which perception takes place. A color area, in other words, surrounds the viewer. Mark Rothko is one painter who makes especially effective use of this factor. There is an analogy between the relation of the new scale of painting to the old scale and the relation of the wide-screen motion picture image to the television image. Empathy is easier to achieve with the motion picture image than with the home screen; psychic distance is lost more readily. The motion picture image in the main communicates meaning visually, while the television image seems to be more of an extension of radio, of sound, of the spoken word. The small-scale image in television or painting, in other words, bears a closer relation to literature than the more visual, large image.

A second implication of large-scale painting lies in the tendency of the picture to merge with the wall and so to become an architectural element rather than a separate work of art *attached to* a wall. In this development, painting is, of course, returning to a condition enjoyed by its mosaic and stained-glass antecedents. The modern development began with the flattening of space by Cézanne and the Cubists. Illusionistic effects—the creation of pictorial space through perspective and chiaroscuro devices—were regarded as violations of the integrity of the wall and the reality of architectural space. Now the imagery of painting, in the work of artists as different as Antonio Tapies, Jean Dubuffet, and Robert Rauschenberg, rests on the surface; it makes no claim to occupy space other than what it needs for two-dimensional support. If texture or depth is desired, it is built in sculpturally rather than created illusionistically as in traditional painting. Because it does not conflict with the spatial identity of the wall and may have almost the same dimensions as the wall, the large painting—in visual terms, at least—*is* the wall.

The return of painting to architecture is part of a general development, already noted, to create environments. In this tendency, painters have been encouraged by modern architectural practice. Some architects, of course, see their role as extending beyond the creation of space: They endeavor to control not only the location of the elements which articulate space, but also the character of surface on interior and exterior wall structures. To the extent that they design wall *surfaces*, architects perform a painterly function. Certainly Wright and Le Corbusier designed surfaces as well as volumes. As we know, Le Corbusier was a painter, and it would not be wrong to say that Wright composed like a painter. Consequently, buildings by Wright and Le Corbusier seem quite satisfactory without painting and sculpture (although painting and sculpture can be and have been added). Some painters feel that Wright's Guggenheim Museum dominates the pictures displayed in it: Wright's interior design satisfies the visual and plastic requirements of viewers in the museum; hence the paintings may be superfluous. Buildings by Mies, on the contrary, seem to welcome painting and sculpture. Perhaps that is why his former colleague, Philip Johnson, has become the leading designer of new museums in the United States.

Since Miesian architecture is by far the most common influence on the construction of new buildings in this country, there is an abundance of anonymous space and plain wall surfaces in American building. Perhaps the lack of decoration and the absence of drama in much of our public architecture helps to create a vacuum which painters instinctively endeavor to fill. Furthermore, the large scale of modern painting has fairly effectively removed it from the domestic dwelling so that public buildings are becoming its natural habitat. Increasingly, the new painting is intended for the spacious walls of galleries and museums (designed by Philip Johnson) or for the corridors and executive suites of banks and public buildings (designed by Skidmore, Owings and Merrill or by Philip Johnson).

Small works are still created for homes and apartments, but usually they are minor efforts by major artists, preliminary studies, drawings, or works by amateurs. Very few major works by "important" modern painters can fit into the homes of even the affluent middle class. Collectors of means are obliged to design special facilities to exhibit their collections. Clearly, painting has departed from the category of Victorian knick-knacks. It is too insistent, too large, too bright, too disturbing, to rest quietly against the wallpaper, surrounded by an ornate frame, sharing soft light from a table lamp with a collection of china, family photographs, and travel souvenirs. Painting has become an art of public statement and public performance. Increasingly, public and quasi-public institutions support artists and pay for paintings. The economics of art is such that even private collecting requires the existence of public museums and government tax policies which are politically determined.

Although a novel represents a private statement by a writer, it would be absurd to think of publishing it for

FRANK LLOYD WRIGHT, The Solomon R. Guggenheim Museum, interior ramps (1959), left. Courtesy The Solomon R. Guggenheim Museum.

The office of David Rockefeller, interior (1961), right. Courtesy The Chase Manhattan Bank, N.A.; photo, Alexandre Georges.

DAVID TENIERS, *The Picture Gallery of Archduke Leopold Wilhelm* (c. 1650), left. Courtesy Museo del Prado.

HONORÉ DAUMIER, *Connoisseurs* (c.1862–64), right. Courtesy The Cleveland Museum of Art, Dudley P. Allen Fund.

one person, no matter what his means. Perhaps the major works which painters create are approaching the condition of the novel. At any rate, it is difficult to believe that large-scale paintings are created without any awareness that they

are destined ultimately for public ownership and display. The small picture, the easel painting, is diminishing in importance. "Happenings" and environments have become possible as the dimensions of the canvas approximate the dimensions of the wall in a room. And the flattening of space and the elimination of figurative subject matter have conspired to identify the painted canvas with the wall. Hence, pictures as wall ornaments, traded like furniture or related household items, may continue to be created; but they are not likely to occupy a position that is very close to the heart of painting as an art form.

Beyond Collage: Assemblage, Environments, Happenings

In every generation, painters feel that their elders have carried the medium as far as it can go in its prevailing direction and that they must strike out in radically new directions —in theme, in technique, in materials, and in creative approach. The feeling that inherited methods and media are at the stage of exhaustion has been especially intense among painters of the twentieth century. One reason, conceivably, for their sense of dissatisfaction with conventional materials has been the powerful attraction of the film—an attraction which is quite understandable, since motion pictures are a modern technological extension of the art of creating images which has been practiced by artists since paleolithic times. Many painters today are strongly drawn to cinema, either as spectators or as

film-makers themselves. Others have felt, perhaps unconsciously, the need to change the fundamental painting situation. Spurred by the need they feel to compete effectively with the new media of communication, painters have crossed the line separating their art from sculpture. They have abandoned the representation of objects and have created works of art which are made of "real" objects. They have created works which disintegrate or destroy themselves as one views them. They have created works which spectators do not merely observe, but which they enter into, which they participate in physically, as actors in a drama. The innovations may be regarded as acts of desperation intended to retain the interest of a public which was beginning to seek visual satisfactions elsewhere. On the other hand, they may be understood as the logical and inevitable adjustment of the art of image-making to available new materials and the unique visual challenges and opportunities of the contemporary world.

Assemblage, as the word implies, is the creation of art objects by putting things together—usually by taking them from their accustomed environments and combining them in a new context to form a pictorial composition. There is also a type of three-dimensional assemblage—in other words, sculpture. But, as was mentioned above, painting has "crossed the line," and it is very difficult to say when a work ceases to be pictorial and becomes either relief sculpture or sculpture in the round. Such classifications, at any rate, do not seem to be important. Outstanding painters, from Picasso and Braque forward, have employed assemblage of one sort or another. What is important is that a pictorial manner of seeing and organizing is evident in works of assemblage. Painters seem to think of the debris and the found objects they incorporate into their works in terms of the customary visual elements: line, shape, texture, color, light, and so on. Instead of simulating these qualities of objects with brush and pigment, the artist employs the object itself. It might be argued that this procedure relieves the painter of the obligation to employ skill and imagination in the *re*-presentation of reality, that he may be concealing his ineptitude in the handling of paint. There are several answers to this charge. First, representational skills, even if not of so low an order as is frequently maintained, have grown progressively less vital to painting as photography and the film have advanced. Secondly, the display of skill in imitation of appearances seems to be

one of those achievements of the past which contemporary artists feel cannot be surpassed. Finally, we cannot claim to judge a work of art properly in terms of the skills its maker does *not* seem to have: We must examine it on its own terms, seeing the materials the artist *has* used and the techniques he *has* employed in an effort to endow the materials with significant meaning.

In addition to the psychological and cultural conditions which led to the emergence of assemblage, the technical ground for assemblage was prepared by *collage.* The media are similar except that collage, as the name implies, (the French verb *coller* means "to paste, to glue"), calls for the glueing of materials to a surface. Assemblage employs *any* method of joining or fastening: nailing, glueing, stapling, riveting, screwing, welding, soldering, and so on. The latter methods carry it into sculpture, whereas collage has been traditionally conceived as a two-dimensional medium. For a long time, entry into the third dimension was a formidable barrier for painters. Although many practiced sculpture, they restricted their three-dimensional explorations, as painters, to textural elaboration and the creation of *illusions* of depth. But such fastidiousness about categories began to break down under the assaults of Dada artists such as Kurt Schwitters, Jean Arp, Max Ernst, and Marcel Duchamp. Today, artists do not seem to be particularly inhibited about working in any dimension they can penetrate. The old distinctions still survive somewhat in the education of artists. That is, separate courses in two-dimensional design, three-dimensional design, painting, and sculpture are still taught. But painting studios in college and university art departments display almost as much three-dimensional work as do sculpture studios. The principal difference seems to be the relative absence of paint among the sculptors. Unlike their painterly brothers, they are less inclined to "cross the line."

Among practitioners of collage and assemblage today, the French artist Jean Dubuffet (1904–) can be compared to Ernst in imaginative and technical fertility. Although he too has abandoned the paintbrush in his later work, Dubuffet has a more authoritative command of pigment and color than Ernst. No matter how much he experiments with discarded materials as sources for his imagery, his work grows out of an authentic "feeling for paint," something

JEAN DUBUFFET, *The Maestro* (1954). Private Collection.

JEAN DUBUFFET, *Corps de Dame— paysage, sanguine et grenat* (1950). Courtesy Alfonso Ossorio.

The coarse, heavily textured surface of Rouault's painting is an additional weapon in his arsenal of savage characterization; furthermore, he anticipates the incised, scratched, and tormented surfaces of later artists such as Dubuffet and Tapies.

GEORGES ROUAULT, *La Loge* (1929, 1941). Courtesy Jacques Gelman.

one misses in the elaborate technical fancies of Max Ernst. Indeed, Dubuffet's preparations of pigment, asphalt, tar, cement, varnish, glue, sand, and so on seem to be efforts to convert the artist's canvas into a *wall* which can be scratched, modeled, and then painted. He appears to be creating a contemporary kind of fresco or wall painting, inspired by *graffiti*, the wall and sidewalk markings which are a type of popular art found in all human communities. Perhaps writing or drawing on walls is a primitive expression of primitive personalities; or it may be the universal manifestation of that fear of empty spaces which has been the origin of so much decorative and magical art in the past. In our own time, graffiti may symbolize the remoteness of the dominant "museum" art from the lives and interests of the people as well as an expression of displeasure with the austerities of metal-skinned architecture. At any rate, Dubuffet has been powerfully attracted to graffiti as a source of imagery and to debris as a source of materials. He has created works out of butterfly wings, tobacco leaves, papier-mâché, metal foil, driftwood, banana peels, fruit rinds, coal clinkers, and dirt. In his art we see a special case of the general interest among artists in discarded and worthless materials.

The refuse of an industrial civilization strongly oriented to the production of consumer goods is, of course, enormous in amount and variety. Moreover, it possesses a built-in visual history: We can see what it set out to be, how it was used, and how it came to be discarded. For an artist like Dubuffet, there seems to be an obsessive delight in employing garbage of one sort or another *in place of* conventional oil paint or in conjunction with it. Like so many contemporary artists, he seems to be anxious to demonstrate that the excellence of a civilization is not measured by its rate of consumption; that values can be created out of apparently insignificant materials; that the human contribution is the most important ingredient of all.

Industrial debris, garbage, botanical fragments, and the earth itself—stones, minerals, dirt—provide the materials of "painting" now that the brush and pigment are being either displaced or combined with varieties of refuse and other common substances. In many respects, they are more difficult to work with than paint. Inventing problems with materials—problems which must be overcome so as to reach some significant level of artistic statement—may be an unconscious expression of the burdens and frustrations of painterly freedom. The constraints of indirect technique are gone. There is no hierarchy of subject matter. Any theme is as good as any other. The hostility of the art-interested public toward experimental art has all but evaporated. Moving from a social position of alienation, painters are often celebrated personages—culture heroes who are supported by foundations, employed by universities, and encouraged to exhibit their work in the new museums and cultural centers springing up each month. This combination of social acceptance and absence of technical restraint seems unnatural, not only to the older artists who remember the years in the wilderness, but also the younger performers who have not known any other creative environment. Their uneasiness stems from the nature of artistic effort, which seems to require some kind of resistance: The recalcitrance of materials; the lim-

JEAN DUBUFFET, *My Cart, My Garden* (1955). Collection James Thrall Soby; photo, The Museum of Modern Art, New York.

itations and requirements of sound technique; the philistinism of the public; poverty; outrage; indifference. When these elements are absent, the artist contrives somehow to re-introduce them into his technical procedures, or his subject matter, or both. Such an explanation would help to account for the extraordinary variety of materials in assemblage and the pronounced interest in themes which might shock the apparently unshockable middle classes of the mid-twentieth century.

POP ART AND COMBINE PAINTINGS

We know that everything in the manmade environment has been designed, given an appearance to help it perform some function. In much of the environment, design is commonly used to communicate, to persuade, to entertain, to sell, or to decorate. An enormous amount of visual material is produced and reproduced in the carrying out of these functions. Not only are signs, labels, pos-

TOM WESSELMANN, *Still Life No. 15* (1962). Collection of the University of Nebraska Art Galleries, Lincoln.

ANDY WARHOL, *Marilyn Monroe* (1962), left. Courtesy Dwan Gallery, Los Angeles, California.

WAYNE THIEBAUD, *Pies and Cakes* (1963), right. Collection of the Whitney Museum of American Art, New York; photo, Allan Stone Galleries, Inc.

ters, and packages designed, but the products they advertise are also designed. Hamburgers and hot dogs, soft drinks and bathing suits, automobiles and rocking chairs—all have shape and color more or less arbitrarily given them by designers; and their images saturate our surroundings, greeting us on television, jumping out from road signs, enveloping the reading matter in newspapers and periodicals, mounted on groceries in supermarkets, and carried aloft by airplanes and dirigibles in the sky. When we do not see this imagery, we hear it described for us through other media. To carry on our normal lives, we have become *adjusted* to the world of public images; that is to say, we do not really see them, or we learn to see them selectively. Pop (for popular) artists have chosen this world as the source of their *own imagery,* and appear determined to make us see what our nervous systems have mercifully managed to suppress.

Large scale is an important part of the strategy of Pop. An enormous slice of pie by Claes Oldenburg; a magnified comic strip by Roy Lichtenstein (1923–   ); a bread-and-catsup

ad by Tom Wesselmann—these drive home with all the subtlety of a hard-sell radio commercial the blatancy of our visual environment. A second feature of Pop is repetition, mechanical repetition, as in *Marilyn Monroe* by Andy Warhol (1931–   ). One persuasion technique of radio and television spot commercials is constant repetition—a device which eventually overcomes indifference or resistance. Warhol uses visual repetition without variation in his painting and in his three-dimensional "sculptures"—reproductions of containers for soap, soup, breakfast foods, and so on. Obviously, he is not selling the product, he is pointing out the fact of visual repetition.

Anonymity is another feature of Pop. Robert Indiana's paintings of stenciled signs betray nothing of the personality of the artist except his lettering skills and determination to paint the sign. Warhol's Campbell Soup labels—hundreds of them—might have been painted by some other, equally meticulous, painter, Lichtenstein's choice of a comic strip image may be his, but we cannot see anything in its execution which refers to the artist except that he created the work. Some skill and much effort are visible but they do not seem to belong to any particular artist. In this respect Pop echoes the homogenized character of the designed environment as contrasted with the highly individualized, egoistic creations of contemporary fine art. Some of the Pop artists seem to be saying that the way to be truly original is to suppress all visual evidence of originality.

Other Pop artists, such as Robert Rauschenberg, Jasper Johns, and James Rosenquist, betray a more personal approach to painting while still drawing on popular imagery with varying degrees of literalness. Rauschenberg (1925–   ) appears to control his material more as a conventional painter of "pictures" does, using devices of visual dominance and subordination, as opposed to the "straight," unadorned presentations of Warhol and Lichtenstein. His work grows more organically out of Abstract Expressionism than that of his fellows. However, as compared with action painting in general, he is more inclined to paste up or silk-screen an image than to paint one. He applies paint and attaches objects to images already manufactured by the world of commerce, his vision being that of the collagist, essentially. Perhaps the work of Rauschenberg and the other, less painterly Pop artists signifies that the "hand-painted" image is dead. Henceforth, imagery will be *confected* of interchangeable parts manufactured in many distant places and for purposes unrelated to art.

Rauschenberg's "combine" paintings exhibit the free association of many of the stylistic and technical developments of twentieth-century painting. In such a work as *Canyon* (1959), the principal ingredient is collage together with attached three-dimensional objects—a stuffed eagle and a suspended pillow—plus painted areas, paint drippings, and a stick nailed to the wooden picture support. The work does not easily lend itself to interpretation in terms of any meaning or idea which the materials and their organization seem designed to embody. Like other examples of Pop art and of Dada art before it, the prevailing theme is nonmeaning, the absurd, or anti-art. But the choice of poster fragments, of banal or sentimental photographs, and of material from the world of display provides some indication of

the ideological realm in which the painting dwells: It is a work of simultaneous fascination and disgust with the visual environment, particularly as it is manifested in hard-sell advertising, packaging, labels, trade-marks—in the printed forms of popular culture. The early use of printed matter by collagists like Picasso, Braque, and Gris was based on the color, texture, and "reality level" of these materials. Pop artists, however, are interested in the *content* of the material they paste up and assemble: They seem determined to present its original

KURT SCHWITTERS, *For Kate* (1947), left. Courtesy Kate T. Steinitz.

Does this enlargement of the comic strip version of romance constitute a critique of our mores? Or does it search for significance in the meticulous rendering of the banal?

ROY LICHTENSTEIN, *The Kiss* (1962), right. Private Collection.

ROBERT RAUSCHENBERG, *Canyon* (1959), below left. Collection Leo Castelli Gallery.

ROBERT RAUSCHENBERG, *Odalisque* (1955–58), below right. Collection Ileana Sonnabend, Paris.

ROBERT INDIANA, *The Beware-Danger American Dream #4* (1963). Collection Joseph H. Hirshhorn; photo, John Schiff.

purpose and meaning in the ugliest or silliest context. Rauschenberg has gone so far as to use paint smears and drippings which simulate mud or other substances thrown at a wall. The "splatter" idea is pervasive in modern painting— from Ernst, to Hofmann, to Pollock, to action painters, to Miss de Saint Phalle. It may be the most graphic symbol of defiance and contempt which can be applied to a flat surface. In the work of Rauschenberg, however, the splattered paint is more nearly a gesture of annoyance . . . with the subject? with the viewer who persists in trying to read meaning? with himself for approaching a pretty surface too closely? We are not likely to find out.

A principal problem of some Pop artists lies in their inability to decide what stance to take toward the visual phenomena included in their work. It is difficult, when viewing works of Andy Warhol, Robert Indiana, or Roy Lichtenstein, to discover whether they are repelled by the "ordinariness" and commercialism of the environment or whether they are endeavoring to *embrace* the environment, accepting it uncritically, and seeking to merge with it. One looks for signs of a point of view, an artistic statement of approval or aversion. But we seem to receive only an exclamation point! It is fairly clear that Pop offers no new "internal" developments for painting; its formal and technical language is not original. It is a thematic art; hence it raises question of attitude and value orientation. Perhaps the movement will produce significant statements of an aesthetic, social, or formal character as its members have the opportunity to develop, to gain insight as artists and as human beings. But since styles of painting suc-

ceed each other rapidly in the present artistic climate, a new style is given wide exposure and acceptance somewhat prematurely; then it is displaced quickly by another vogue before, it would seem, there has been enough time to exploit its distinctive vision of the world.

HAPPENINGS

Architecture has traditionally been the art of creating a physical environment in which people can live or work. Painting and sculpture were originally *part* of architecture: They were features, focal points, of the architectural environment. Now some painters are involved in an endeavor to go beyond architecture, to create a living environment which changes while it exists in space and time. Instead of being a statement *about* life, painting becomes an activity which is co-extensive *with* life, *which is lived as it is created.* Unlike ordinary pictures, the new "paintings" are not perceived from the outside, but are created from within by the spectators who move through them (in collaboration with the artist who prepares the setting). Such works have been designated "Happenings" or "Environments."

The Happening grows out of collage and the type of Environment created by the Dadaist, Kurt Schwitters (1887–1948), in his famous Merzbau constructions of the 1920's. Built in his home in Hanover, the earliest Merzbau might be described as an architectural collage, a division and modulation of interior space using refuse and found objects as structural and decorative elements. Schwitters worked on it for several years, bringing it to completion around 1924 and giving it the title *Ca-*

thedral of Erotic Misery. A subsequent Merzbau (*Merz* may be an abbreviation of *Kommerz,* commerce, or of *Schmerz,* pain; *bau* means construction or building), dated about 1933, is more architectonic, less reminiscent of collage techniques. It appears to bear the influence of the design experiments conducted by the de Stijl group, especially by van Doesburg. Schwitters built little grottoes into his constructions, dedicated them to friends and incorporated in them discarded clothing and similar "nonart" items, much as Robert Rauschenberg (1925–) includes old socks in his paintings, or as James Dine (1939–) makes bronze casts of light bulbs. Schwitters is quoted as having said, "Anything the artist spits is art." The aesthetic outcome of such a viewpoint is the glorification of scabrous materials and unimportant objects which have nonart or antiart connotations.

Schwitters had conventional academic training and painted conventional portraits to earn his living. His collages and Merzbau constructions stemmed partly from his rejection of traditional painting as a serious form of expression and the generally nihilistic climate of Europe in the 1920's—a climate which accounts for the strange humor of Dadaism, its inversion of all established values, its peculiarly negative wit. On the positive side, however, Schwitters was attempting through collage and his constructions to arrive at a synthesis of the arts of poetry, architecture, painting, and drama. He was apparently a versatile and spectacular personality. But his creativity flourished in the Central European environment of general disillusionment following defeat in World War I, disastrous postwar inflation, deterioration of the European economy,

and the rise of Fascism. These conditions combined to create a watershed in history for many artists and intellectuals. The end of the war initiated a new mode of feeling which was taken up by many Europeans who felt trapped by the war and betrayed by their civilization. For them, the forms, values, and institutions that had existed up to and through World War I were associated with systems of thought and behavior which had miserably failed. It is against this background that Dadaism and its products must be seen.

The Happenings and Environments of the contemporary painting scene may be regarded in part as more formalized and ritualized versions of the Dadaist events and antiart of the 1920's. In one reported incident, Schwitters took the discarded socks of a friend, cast them in plaster, and incorporated the casting into one of his Merzbau grottoes. Such gestures, which are repeated in contemporary art with or without knowledge of their earlier occurrence, exhibit features common to other expressions of revolt in the visual art of the twentieth century: (1) As already mentioned, discarded materials and debris are used. (2) There is a positive avoidance of "beauty" or conventional notions of artistic form.

Perhaps the most cynical and contemptuous version of postwar German life was found in the painfully satirical drawings of George Grosz.

This "environment" is the more-or-less exact replica of a time and place, an "event" whose cosy squalor has aroused the artists's obsessive affection as demonstrated by his extraordinary effort to replicate its myriad detail. Amid such realism the clock-faces cannot function as symbols; they do not succeed in redeeming the essential grubbiness of the work.

EDWARD KIENHOLZ, *The Beanery* (1965). Courtesy Dwan Gallery, Los Angeles, California.

Clarence Schmidt in residence (1964). Photo, *The New York Times*.

(3) The gesture of creation is as important as its outcome. (4) Humor is sought in the defiance of authority, of established norms, or of the values authorities presumably admire. (5) Nonmeaning or absurdity is intentionally pursued. (6) The gap between art and life is narrowed as much as possible. (7) Caves and grottoes appear—for example, both Happenings and Merzbau constructions are explorations and decorations of interior, womb-like spaces.

A relatively little-known American primitive artist, Clarence Schmidt, has created a series of grottoes within his winding, cave-like house on a hill in Woodstock, New York. Schmidt, who has general carpentry and building skills, has had no formal artistic training, and is almost certainly unaware of the Dada art of the 1920's, much less of Schwitters. Yet his truly fantastic house can be compared in all important respects with the Merzbau constructions. Like Schwitters, he also recites poems of his own composition, but probably thinks of them and of himself as following in the tradition of Walt Whitman. The Happenings of Allan Kaprow and his group (the principal Happening impresarios are Claes Oldenburg, Jim Dine, Red Grooms, and Robert Whitman) are also a syn-

thesis of poetry and space organization. Apparently the primitive artist and the sophisticated artist are equally stirred to recite, perform, gesture, and *live* in their elaborate constructions. Schwitters' Merzbau was located in the basement of his house and grew by accretion until an attic tenant had to be evicted. Schmidt lives in his "house" and adds to it continuously, so that, on the inside, it resembles a "many-chambered nautilus," with new rooms and grottoes emerging almost organically as the construction winds down the hill or burrows into the earth.

The Happenings of Allan Kaprow are more formally staged. They call for a script or scenario which serves to articulate the time element, while people, as spectators or actors, move through the garage or gallery where the event takes place. Kaprow says that these events grew out of his work in collage and assemblage, and he lists the typical collage materials used: "painted paper, cloth and photos, as well as mirrors, electric lights, plastic film, aluminum foil, ropes, straw; objects that could be attached to, or hung in front of, the canvas along with various sounds and odors. These materials mutiplied in number and density, extending away from the flat canvas surface, until that pictorial point of departure was eliminated entirely and the whole gallery was filled. I termed this an environment." As the two-dimensional confines of the canvas were left behind, real environments were simulated: "a subway station, penny-arcade, forest, kitchen, etc." The gallery gave way as a place for staging Happenings to "a craggy canyon, an old abandoned factory, a railroad yard, or the ocean side."*

Unlike conventional theatrical performances, Happenings do not have a developed dramatic structure—that is, a beginning, a middle, and an end; plot and character development; climax and dénouement. They retain their connections with assemblage as orchestrations of the visual elements with new elements introduced from other art forms —physical movement, sound, speech, and odors. They are, in short, paintings or assemblages moving in space, with the addition of nonpainterly elements which function as extensions of shape, color, texture, and light. Kaprow defines his Environments as "slowed-down,

*Allan Kaprow, "A Service for the Dead" *Art International,* Jan. 25, 1963.

quieter, happening[s]"—in other words, as large-scale dioramas which can last for several weeks, while the Happenings compress time and endure for only a few hours. Of course, motion pictures have not only better technical devices for the compression or expansion of time but also the further advantage of being reproducible many times; in contrast, the Happening contains so many spontaneous elements that it is confined to a single viewing and enactment. However, the impermanent character of Happenings is intentional. Happenings deliberately stress the transient nature of what man creates and anticipate the ultimate obsolescence of any work of art by causing themselves to disintegrate almost immediately as objects and events.

What is the future of the Happening and what is its meaning for painting? The Happening bears a superficial resemblance to theatre, but is dramaturgically clumsy because complex spatial-temporal events cannot be structured with sufficient precision to maintain control of its form. Only in the film, with its cutting, montage, and flashback techniques, can one manipulate the time dimension without losing pictorial con-

ALLAN KAPROW, *A Service for the Dead* (1962). Photo, Robert R. McElroy.

JIM DINE, "Santa Claus in Cellophane" from *The Shining Bed* (1960), below left. Photo, Robert R. McElroy.

ROBERT WHITMAN, *The American Moon* (1960). Photo, Robert R. McElroy.

trol. As sculpture or as painting, the Happening surrenders the monumental and durable character of these art forms, their capacity to linger before our vision, for a while at least, and thus to permit the kind of visual exploration which the human organism seems to require and to enjoy. Yet the collage and assemblage antecedents of Happenings and Environments suggest different objectives. Happenings by Kaprow and Environments-plus-Sculpture, like those George Segal creates, appear to be efforts to discover the hidden ritual—that is, the sacred ceremonial element—which lies just beneath the surface of ordinary events in everyday life. Like Schwitters and Dubuffet, these younger men are trying to find the meaningful in what is apparently worthless and meaningless. In this respect they are following the honorable tradition of Chardin, who painted common kitchen utensils, and of Courbet who painted ordinary men doing menial tasks. Art has always tried to redeem the world by finding significance in rejected elements of experience.

The Happening, however, is not in my opinion of major importance as a vehicle of aesthetic value. It serves better as a type of creative discipline for the artist, as a means of stimulating and focusing his perceptual energies on realms of experience which must eventually find their way into painting and sculpture. Some art forms and some artistic operations perform an instrumental function for the creation of other works of art.° Painters, for example, are often stimulated by literature, music, the dance, and the film. Drawing and collage serve to collect a variety of sensations and experience on a two-dimensional surface where they may be conveniently exploited by the painter or sculptor. But the kinds of experience which drawing and collage can compress into manageable and useful form appear to be too limited for many contemporary painters and sculptors. They require an instrument which does more than reflect what is seen in concise form. Like scientists, artists need a device which *interferes with* observed reality, which can take events apart and reveal their new or unsuspected meanings. It would appear that Happenings and other similarly bizarre manifestations of creativity constitute new artistic strategies—strategies which were foreshadowed in techniques like frottage, Merzbau constructions, Surrealist automatic writing, and in the nihilistic stunts and gestures of that troubled generation which lived between the two Wars.

GERALD OSTER, *Conic Sections II* (1964). Courtesy Howard Wise Gallery.

° Jim Dine, who no longer creates Happenings says of his work in that mode: "I do not feel that there was enough of a perspective between art and life in them. . . . . And I also felt that it was taking too much from my painting, which I really wanted to do." Quoted in Michael Kirby, *Happenings,* Dutton, 1965.

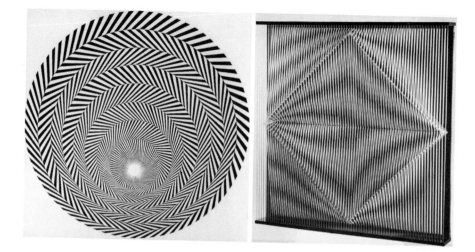

In Op, or optical, art, which followed the premature decline of Pop art in 1964, painters attempted to construct works that would rely for their effectiveness solely on the viewer's act of vision. In a sense, the color divisionism of Seurat (with its dependence on afterimages to create colors that were not present as pigment), and Joseph Albers' chromatic venerations of the square were precursors of Op art. Its practitioners employ mechanical motion, artificial light filtered through prisms, images which shift depending on the viewer's angle of vision, and a variety of other technical devices to produce optical sensations which conventionally painted canvases could never arouse. The sophisticated optical knowledge of modern physics has been brought into the realm of aesthetics by Op; the sociological contents by Pop gave way to an art which by-passed the mind and imagination of the viewer, appealing to him as a physiological entity. And the effectiveness of Op on its own terms is undeniable; it produces feelings of disorientation or exhilaration purely by visual means, without recourse to alcohol or drugs.

The desire to transform the physical basis of consciousness has always been latent in painting, and in Mark Rothko's work, as was mentioned earlier, it has become an explicit objective. Op art appears to be a systematic attempt to take hold of the human organism through its visual sense and to change first its somatic, and then its psychic, state.

The similarity of Op's objectives to those of modern biochemistry may be only coincidental. (Control of attitudes and emotions now seems within the grasp of biochemistry; hence the information-and-education approach to attitude-formation may, in the future, be less efficient than biochemical or medical methods.) Nevertheless, Op has brought about the discovery of new powers in painting; and painting, as a result, has found a new *raison d'être*, a new claim on human attention. Now art can compete with tranquilizers and "pep" pills as a depressant or a stimulant. Even Matisse said he dreamed of an art "which might be for every mental worker ... like an appeasing influence,

BRIDGET RILEY, *Blaze I* (1962), left. Collection Mrs. Louise Riley, London; courtesy Richard Feigen Gallery; photo, Eric Pollitzer.

YVARAL, *Acceleration Number 19, Series B* (1962), right. Collection The Museum of Modern Art, New York, gift of Philip C. Johnson.

AGAM (Yaacov Gipstein), *Double Metamorphosis II* (1964), left. Collection The Museum of Modern Art, New York, gift of Mr. and Mrs. George M. Jaffin.

VICTOR DE VASARELY, *Kalota* (1963), right. Courtesy City Art Museum of Saint Louis, gift of Mr. Henry B. Pflager and Members of the Shoenberg Family through the Shoenberg Foundation, Inc.

like a mental soother, something like a good armchair in which to rest from physical fatigue." For the present, Op seems more effective as a stimulant than as a pacifier. A psychoanalyst, Anton Ehrenzweig, has compared it to a plunge into a cold shower. But surely an art capable of producing such physical effects will also be able to induce the soothing feelings Matisse longed for.

As objects of aesthetic value, Op works are not easy to judge. They cause precisely the difficulties which Professor Lipps (p. 283) regarded as obstacles to an aesthetic response—awareness of one's bodily feelings. Also, the single-minded pursuit of purely optical responses results in an experience of impoverishment for those who expect more explicit emotional, intellectual, or formal nourishment from art. Compared to the Neo-Plastic art of Mondrian and the de Stijl group, Op art arouses reactions which are quicker, easier, more physical, and less intellectual. It is doubtful that Op can have the influence on design which Mondrian's Neo-Plasticism has had (with the exception of the ladies' stockings designed by Richard Anuszkiewicz). Moreover, the movement has not as yet articulated a philosophic rationale, which would be needed to guide its further evolution. Therefore, it remains to be seen whether Op—at present more related to physics than aesthetics—can carry its discoveries and effects back into the humanistic mainstream of art.

Conclusion

The employment of trashcan contents in collage by Schwitters; the use of botanical materials, fruit rinds, and butterfly wings by Dubuffet; the incorporation of "real" objects in paintings by the Pop artists; and the Happenings which create a fugitive art of short duration—these developments suggest new connections between painting and the culinary arts, gastronomy, spectator sports, psychodrama, and the theater. There is an analogy between the machines fashioned for self-destruction by the Swiss artist Jean Tinguely and the elaborate dishes created by a chef to be eaten and thus visually destroyed in the act of consumption. The aesthetic element in food preparation as well as dining has often been the subject of speculation by philosophers, and now the connection between a collage and a salad does not seem remote or absurd. There are works of art which seem to echo the processes of food preparation, eating, collecting the leftovers, discarding the refuse, and assembling it again. The ritual of dining is not very different from the ritualistic self-destruction of a machine or of a "happening" which creates itself and is destroyed at the same time.

For many years, a popular act of the comedian Jimmy Durante was the tearing apart of a piano before a nightclub audience. The process of decomposition possesses its own aesthetic fascination as might be confirmed by anyone who has watched the wrecking of a building, a staged auto crash, or even a child knocking down a house of blocks he has laboriously built up. The "controlled compression" sculpture of César (p. 325) represents an effort to convert the ultimate destruction and transformation of an automobile into a constructive act. Thus, it constitutes a model for other artistic and quasi-artistic activities which have crushing, breaking, and dismemberment as their theme: They are efforts to discover an affirmative meaning in all the acts of needless destruction, senseless consumption, and nihilism which mark our contemporary civilization.

Obviously, tearing down good buildings, ripping trees out of the landscape with bulldozers, scarring the earth with open-pit mining, disfiguring men's faces in prize fights, producing goods which break easily, testing thermonuclear bombs and missiles, and other normal activities which involve destruction or preparation for it are strangely attractive to many of us; otherwise they would not be so widespread. Some artists, then, are engaged in seeking a constructive version of the all-too-human impulse to dismember things. Artists may not always know the import of their work: But civilization operates through them nevertheless, exploiting their fascination with materials and processes for what are, hopefully, humanizing ends.

CHAPTER TWELVE

Like painting, sculpture had its origin in the forming of figures for primitive magic and, later, for religious ritual. In viewing all subsequent sculptural developments, we should keep in mind as an ever-present influence this early association of sculpture with magic. The ancient Greek myth of Pygmalion and Galatea symbolically expresses a number of fundamental insights into what sculpture is about. Pygmalion fell in love with Aphrodite and, because she would not have him, made an ivory figure of the goddess and prayed to her. Eventually she took pity on the sculptor and entered into the figure, giving it life as Galatea. Pygmalion then married Galatea who bore him two sons.

All the essential ingredients of sculptural creation are present in the myth: The artist's motive for creating the work arises from an emotional crisis —a combination of personal yearning and cosmic anguish. The sculptor tries to control reality by fashioning an object that portrays the ideal outcome he desires. It is the pity of the goddess (a symbol of the magical power animating sculpture) which gives life to the artist's effort. He falls in love with the image he has created; hence art can acquire an autonomous life of its own. Out of the union of creator and creature comes the continuation of his family line. That is, the somewhat morbid longing of the sculptor for the goddess is con-

SCULPTURE

verted into a healthy and living reality
by his compelling skill with palpable
materials. As always in magical art, there
is an underlying assumption that materials cunningly wrought will oblige the
gods to do what man wants.

Painting, too, has magical associations, but it requires the capacity to
create and believe in airy illusions,
whereas sculpture can give corporeal
reality to man's hopes, memories,
and fantasies. Consequently, sculptural
works have served more prominently
than painted images as vessels for the
souls of departed kings and Pharaohs,
and as totems and cult objects among
primitive men. The painted image seems
to call for more capacity for symboliza-

tion than the sculptural image: The viewer must be able to conceive of the representation of space, volume, and texture in painting, whereas, for the primitive mind, sculpture does not represent or symbolize—it actually *is* what its maker says it is. Indeed, ancient sculpture was painted in order to fortify its claims *to be*, rather than represent, human personality.

The capacity of sculpture, no matter what its materials, to occupy real space and to compel belief in its claims to be alive, distinguishes it from painting and graphic art in general. Consequently, sculpture has remained, throughout its history of changing form, material, and social function, the same art which Pygmalion practiced—the art of making three-dimensional materials come alive in order to objectify human fantasies, record human personality and achievement, and satisfy human longings for perfection.

Modeling, Carving, and Casting

The sculptural processes are simply the most suitable ways of working available materials and, where there is a choice of materials, the process chosen most likely reflects compatibility with the sculptor's personality. Obviously, stone can only be carved, drilled, abraded, and polished. It appeals to artists who are comfortable with highly resistant, obdurate materials. Wood lends itself to the same processes more easily; but in thin sheets it can be stamped, while modern technology permits it to be permanently bent and molded, as in Thonet and Eames chairs. Results come more easily here than with stone, but at the sacrifice of durability. Metals can be cast, cut, drilled, filed, extruded, polished, bent, forged, stamped, and assembled. More recently, metals have been combined with plastic binders so that they can be modeled, almost like clay. They can be assembled durably by welding, soldering, and riveting, and by applying adhesives also. Plastics were brought prominently into sculpture by the Constructivists, although tasteless employment of plastics in imitation of other materials has created unfortunate associations which are only now being overcome. But there seems to be ready acceptance of metal sculpture no matter how it is fashioned. Metal is, after all, a plastic material which has had thousands of years of artistic use and visual familiarity.

HENRY MOORE, sculpture for UNESCO building (1958). Courtesy UNESCO Information Office.

It might be said that for traditional sculptors, mastery of the basic processes —modeling, carving, and casting—constituted the principal artistic challenges. Such mastery remains important, but it is not indispensable in today's sculptural expression because, as in painting, technology permits the forming and assembling of materials by other means. However, the modern sculptor confronts new problems of aesthetic choice due to greater variety and flexibility in the processes and materials available to him. When there are many alternatives, selection of material and process becomes a vital element in the meaning of the work. If the sculptor carves or casts, it is because these methods have a particular aesthetic significance, not because alternative processes are unavailable.

Monumental statuary has in the past been cast in bronze or carved in marble. Occasionally, concrete casting has been employed, but the material is suitable only for work which does not require subtle detail, which is to be incorporated into walls, or which is meant to be seen at a distance. Today, welded metal is growing more common in public sculpture, especially as the human figure recedes in importance and as abstract works gain acceptance. Naturalistic statuary, of course, must be modeled, then cast in bronze; or it must be carved in stone. Public buildings and parks still abound with statuary of this kind, and it continues to be commissioned by conservative patriotic groups and municipal bodies. But sculptors who can or will create such works are a diminishing minority. Contemporary buildings seem to be more friendly to sculpture which is, in general, more open, less monolithic in form than older works. Sculpture carved

AUGUSTE RODIN, *Burghers of Calais* (1889). Photo, H. Rinehart.

in marble, moreover, does not lend itself easily to the perforations, extensions, and surface qualities possible with forged, cast, or welded metal.

It is difficult, however, to conceive of a sculptural group like Rodin's *Burghers of Calais* being created through any process other than bronze casting. The psychological characterization of several figures; the naturalistic treatment of flesh, bone, and sinew; the range of surface subtlety in Rodin's group— these would be hard to achieve with modern welding or assemblage proc-

WESSEL COUZIJN, sculpture for Unilever building (1963). Courtesy Unilever N.V., Rotterdam.

esses. Still, monumental work has been attempted by contemporary sculptors, and they seem to have found an idiom which, while fulfilling the requirements of a monument, avoids the limitations of classic pediment sculpture and its rather stuffy imitations. If the detail and nuance of modeling possible with clay or marble are sacrificed, still, a marvelous freedom of extension into space together with generous scale is now possible. Also, many of the techniques of industrial production and building have been assimilated by sculptors today. The mallet and chisel have been joined by the acetylene torch.

The Greeks knew the art of bronze casting and they also had an abundance of good white marble. Nevertheless, they must have prized marble largely for its durability since their statuary was painted. It was not the whiteness or texture of marble they admired so much as its capacity to reveal their love of clear and stable forms, their understanding of the body and its anatomy in action or repose, and their conception of the ideal as embodied in the form of a surpassingly real and beautiful human figure. The Greek mode of thought and art was an effort to locate perfection in the here and now of men's vision and behavior. The Greeks chose marble to fix the "now" forever and they used a refined naturalism because they did not believe meanings or values should exist apart from men's bodies and behavior. Sculpture for them was a means of demonstrating that perfection and reality could meet in forms which have human appearance and which can endure eternally.

The greatest sculptor to follow the Greeks was Michelangelo, who believed his art was mainly one of releasing the forms and meanings hidden (perhaps imprisoned) within marble. Such an idea is not surprising in an artist influenced by neo-Platonic thought; it also typifies the sculptor who is a carver, one who begins with the stone block or the wood log and cuts away until the form in his mind's eye is revealed. Carving, a subtractive process, has always been considered the most difficult of sculptural processes because it calls for a well-defined conception of the result before the work of execution is begun. The carver subtracts the nonessential material in or-

POLYCLITUS, *Spear Bearer* (c.450–440 B.C.), above. Courtesy Museo Nazionale, Naples.

MICHELANGELO, unfinished slave, from tomb of Pope Julius II (1513–16), at right. Courtesy Alinari-Art Reference Bureau.

der to liberate *the idea* which already exists. And yet—the grain of wood, ivory, or stone; its texture and density; its high compressive and low tensile strength—these significantly determine what forms will emerge and how they must be created. For example, diorite and basalt, used by the sculptors of ancient Egypt, are extremely hard granitic stones which resist detailed carving; consequently, Egyptian sculpture is characterized by large, simplified forms which adhere closely to the shape of the stone block as it was quarried. The well-defined prior conception of the work is therefore substantially at the mercy of the material when the actual carving takes place.

Michelangelo quarried his own marble and carved it himself directly. Subsequent carving practice permits the sculptor to make a small plaster model to serve as a guide for a pointing machine which enlarges and roughs out the major forms and dimensions accurately in marble or stone. The final detailed carving and polishing can then be executed by the sculptor. This *indirect* method of execution guarantees a faithful and less laborious translation of the earlier sculptural conception to large scale. But it also creates aesthetic problems: The small plaster model is usually based on a clay original, that is, on forms which where built up by addition, not subtraction. And, of course, the working properties of clay are different from those of stone or marble. Of course, the sculptor can anticipate the structural problems of enlargement and change of material. However, his original conception must necessarily be influenced by clay built around an armature (the wood or metal "skeleton" which supports the wet clay). As in translation from one language to another, some loss of meaning inevitably occurs. Hence, the indirect method, which is also involved in any casting process, stands between the sculptor and his intimate contact with materials.

Casting, which we have noted as a very ancient process, accurately reproduces the forms and tool marks of an original clay or wax model. Its advantage lies in the translation of clay or wax into a material which is more durable than the original, which can be transported without danger of breakage, and which, of course, can also be duplicated. But durability and surface quality rather than duplication are the chief motives for the use of casting techniques in modern sculpture. Bronze, which is the most common casting material, also has surface and color characteristics that can be controlled for heightened sensuous satisfaction. The surface of a bronze casting develops a rich patina with age; it can also be burnished or

Bronze casting.

REUBEN NAKIAN, *Voyage to Crete* (1964), located in New York State Theater, Lincoln Center for the Performing Arts. © 1964, Lincoln Center for the Performing Arts.

Polychromed terra cotta.

LUCA DELLA ROBBIA, *Madonna and Angels* (c.1460). National Museum, Florence.

Painted stone.

The Lady Nofret (c. 2650 B.C.). Egyptian Museum, Cairo.

treated with chemicals to produce a wide range of color from gold to deep brown or greenish black. Its surface can be made dull or glossy, depending on the sculptor's intent. Similar surface possibilities are available with other metals, such as copper, brass, gold, lead, steel, and the new alloys. Clearly what is involved is direct work on the metal surface in a manner which is almost painterly. But it should be remembered that the earliest sculpture—whether of wood, stone, metal, or clay—was painted, glazed, or inlaid with gems and other materials, in an effort to create convincing and vivid effigies. Terra cotta sculpture was frequently polychromed—that is, it was glazed in the manner of modern colored ceramics—and achieved thereby a considerable degree of naturalism. (Polychromed terra cotta was carried to a high art by the della Robbia family of Florence during the fifteenth and sixteenth centuries.) Today, a similar degree of naturalism might be achieved, if desired, with the use of plastics. For example, Frank Gallo's *Swimmer*, executed in polyester (a plastic also employed in painting), reinforced with fiber glass and wood, offers conventional form in an unconventional material. The work is painted and is deliberately "pretty" in the Pop style. Often this sculptor seats his figures in real chairs, thus creating a juxtaposition of art objects with "real" environments made anonymously

Sculpture combining subtlety of surface with monumental scale can be created through the use of modern industrial metals, plastics, and forming processes. (Cast aluminum and fiberglass).

WILLIAM THOMPSON, *Archangel* (1965). Courtesy the artist.

in the culture. Gallo (1933–) is similar in this to George Segal, although his figures are more sculpturally described, modeled, and "prettified" than Segal's. Perhaps the closest modern counterpart to ancient painted sculpture is found in the store-window manikin, which is made of painted papier-mâché or plastic; synthetic hair and eye lashes are attached, and the whole is then decorated by an assemblage technique known to window dressers. The manikin's parts appear to be interchangeable. But, like their ancient predecessors, they have a certain cultic significance.

Unlike Michelangelo, Rodin defined sculpture as "the art of the hole and the lump." Although he produced many carved marble works, Rodin's statement is characteristic of the sculptor who models to achieve form, who builds a surface additively. Clay is more responsive than wood or stone and it requires few tools. The sculptor's hand creates the forms and leaves the marks

of thumb and figures in the soft, pliable material. Nothing is so personal and direct as clay; painters need a brush, and even those who abandon the brush must substitute some other tool or process. Yet even if clay offers little resistance to the sculptor and permits him to give form to the most transient impulse, it has distinct limitations when compared to wood or stone. It possesses little strength in tension or compression and hence requires an armature for support, as mentioned above. The building of an armature already commits the sculptor to a certain type of result. Clay is not itself a permanent material. If it is to be fired as a ceramic sculpture, it is subject to size limitations of the kiln and a variety of engineering considerations: It must be constructed to withstand high heat, complex internal stresses based on the weight of its projections, wall thicknesses, shifts in dimension during firing, and so on. Hence, clay is usually used to make preparatory "sketches" for sculp-

FRANK GALLO, *Swimmer* (1964). Collection of the Whitney Museum of American Art, New York, gift of the Friends of the Whitney Museum of American Art, and the artist.

PAUL VAN HOEYDONCK, *The Couple* (1963). Courtesy Iris Clert.

PAUL VAN HOEYDONCK, *Space-Boys* (1963). Courtesy Iris Clert.

NICCOLO DELL'ARCA, *The Lamentation* (c.1485–90), left. Courtesy A. Villani Studio.

JACOB EPSTEIN, *Madonna and Child* (1927), right. Courtesy The Riverside Church, gift of Miss Sally Ryan.

ture to be executed in other materials, or for casting in metal. As ceramic sculpture, however, it is cheap, durable and reproducible. It can be given a wide range of glossy or matte color, has many textural possibilities, and very honestly reflects the marks of the tool used to give it shape.

One of the unique satisfactions of bronze sculptures by Epstein or Giacometti, for example, arises from our knowledge that we are perceiving a very soft, plastic material which has been "frozen" into a hard, very resistant material. Bronze castings are, of course, hollow, with rather thin walls. But they *look* solid and massive; they often manage to retain the earthy quality of clay or rock. Cast iron is too coarse and granular to reflect the nuances of clay: It has its own character and does not simulate other surfaces and materials as well as bronze, copper, and brass do. Hence, clay seems to call for bronze casting if it is to be per-

manent. For a master like Rodin, the capacity of clay to yield a surface of great variety—one which modulated light at the same time that it described shape—was perhaps its principal attraction. That bronze casting of clay models is a difficult and expensive process has not diminished the virtue of clay as a cheap and versatile material for sculptors; it remains one of the quickest, easiest, most direct, and most endearing ways of thinking in three dimensions.

Wood appeals for its grain, its color, and its origin in a living tree. It has greater tensile strength than stone, hence can be given long projecting forms without fear of breaking. As might be surmised from its wide use in handles and in furniture, wood is warm and pleasant, even sensuous to the touch. It is not cold like metal or abrasive like stone. It acquires a patina with time as does bronze. The disadvantages of wood lie in its dimensional instability—its tendency to warp or crack. Wood can be carved, filed, drilled, and polished more easily than stone, yet it offers enough resistance to cutting and carving to require similar carving tools which leave similar marks. A great advantage of the material, much exploited in contemporary work, is its versatility in techniques of constructed or assembled sculpture. There is a particular expressiveness in wooden joints, whether those of the skilled cabinet maker or of the sculptor employing improvised methods of attachment. In the present climate of unconcern for permanence, the fact that wood may warp or crack counts little as a liability. Also, the new adhesives, some of which bind on contact, form joints which are stronger than the materials they join. Finally, there is a long tradition of painting wood, covering it with fabrics, and embedding foreign materials in it. Hence, it fits well into the creative strategies of sculptors influenced by collage and assemblage. One has only to think of the many materials with which wood is combined in practical objects, from plows and guns to furniture and home appliances, to realize how useful it is to the contemporary sculptor.

The contemporary use of wood is shown in *Wall Piece* by John Anderson (1929–   ). It is a combination of carving and construction techniques in a work that pretends to have some mechanical

action. Forms projecting from a slot appear to be levers, gear shifts, door knobs, or faucet handles, suggesting to the viewer that he should pull, twist, or thrust them, depending on their shapes and his mechanical experience. That these operations cannot in fact be performed does not prevent the sculpture from arousing our expectations of performance anyway. *It looks as if it could work.* Here we find a remarkable similarity between the visual operation of myth for modern man and for ancient man. Their magical sculptures *looked as if* they could be repositories of the souls of departed personalities; our magic

GABRIEL KOHN, *Nantucket* (1960). Courtesy The Joseph H. Hirshhorn Collection; photo, Rudolph Burckhardt.

JOHN ANDERSON, *Wall Piece* (1963), left. Courtesy Allan Stone Galleries, Inc.

ROBERT CREMEAN, *Swinging Woman* (1960), right. University of Nebraska Collection, gift of Mrs. A. B. Sheldon.

H. C. WESTERMANN, *The Big Change* (1963). Courtesy Allan Frumkin Gallery, New York; photo, Nathan Rabin.

sculpture *looks as if* it could throw a switch, turn on an electric motor, or put an engine into neutral. The viewer projects prevailing associations and expectations upon objective reality. Anderson's sculpture at the same time retains anthropomorphic features from the past—suggestions of bones and limbs among the several handles. The association is logical enough, since levers and knobs are meant to be grasped and wood is inviting to the touch. Consequently this work can function at several imaginative levels simultaneously: It suggests a curious mechanical device and it makes connections with primitive animistic sculpture through its carved figurative forms and limb fragments.

The sensuous potential of plywood, a construction material which is usually covered or hidden, is beautifully revealed

MEDARDO ROSSO, *The Bookmaker* (1894). Collection The Museum of Modern Art, New York, acquired through the Lillie P. Bliss bequest.

EDGAR DEGAS, *Statuette: Developpé en avant* (modeled in wax 1880, executed in 1920). Courtesy The Metropolitan Museum of Art, bequest of Mrs. H. O. Havemeyer, 1929. H. O. Havemeyer Collection.

in a laminated plywood sculpture by H. C. Westermann (born 1922), *The Big Change.* A huge, sculptured knot made of wood, it constitutes the sort of contradiction in form and material, the play with levels of reality, which appeal to the Surrealist interests of this sculptor. Aside from its meticulous rendering of the absurd and its use of a material without ancient credentials, the work possesses the unity of form, consummate craftsmanship, and monolithic stability of classic sculpture.

Few final sculptures are done in wax, although this material combines the responsiveness of clay with a special, translucent quality of its own. But it is not a very permanent material for sculpture; it can be too easily changed or damaged in handling. Wax, however, was a congenial material for the nineteenth-century sculptor Medardo Rosso (1858–1928). In *The Bookmaker,* which was done in wax over plaster, we see a painterly interest in light similar to that of Rodin and Degas, both of whom also executed sculptures in wax. The figure by Rosso, dated 1894, is extraordinary for its delicate treatment of a heavy body reminiscent of Rodin's monumental *Balzac* figure, and for its subtle, melting forms which do not, however, weaken or oversentimentalize the total work. The transitions from form to form are so gently accomplished that they appear to be painted or blended with a soft brush. As a result, the sculptor can direct the viewer's eye to the more defined forms with great precision. Although the sculpture is small, it suggests a large scale because wax has no grain, no texture visible to the eye. Hence, it is capable of almost infinitely detailed modeling. It is easy to see that the capacity of wax to confer its own liquid, melting quality upon form has great appeal for Rosso. The medium seems well suited to his Romantic, evocative art. But its small scale and sympathetic application to the figure are precisely the virtues which become liabilities for contemporary sculptors who are interested in materials suitable for *art brut*—harsh effects on a huge scale.

A tremendous change in sculptural attitude has taken place since Rosso modelled his delicate wax figures in the 1890's. An excellent summary of the new view is given in the following quotation by the American critic Clement Greenberg:

Space is there to be shaped, divided, enclosed, but not to be filled. The new sculpture tends to abandon stone, bronze, and clay for industrial materials like iron, steel, alloys, glass, plastics, celluloid, etc., etc., which are worked with the blacksmith's, the welder's and even the carpenter's tools. Unity of material and color is no longer required, and applied color is irrelevant: a work or its parts can be cast, wrought, cut or simply put together; it is not so much sculptured as constructed, built, assembled, arranged.°

Clearly, we are in the midst of a revolution in sculptural materials and technique, a revolution which responds to the unprecedented themes and emotions of modern life. But changes in tools and materials themselves dictate new artistic ideas and aesthetic effects. The following sections will examine some of the more prominent technical and aesthetic developments in contemporary sculpture.

°Clement Greenberg, "The New Sculpture," *Art and Culture*, Beacon Press, 1961.

LEONARD BASKIN, *St. Thomas Aquinas* (1962), left. Courtesy St. John's Abbey, Collegeville, Minnesota.

AUGUSTE RODIN, *Balzac* (1892–97), right. © SPADEM 1966 by French Reproduction Rights, Inc.

Working directly with bronze over monel metal, Lipton has elaborated the forms of cymbals to create a sculpture which seems to declare a resounding optimism and faith.

SEYMOUR LIPTON, *Archangel* (1964). Collection Philharmonic Hall, Lincoln Center, New York City.

Easter Island stone images (seventeenth century or earlier). Courtesy The American Museum of Natural History.

From Monolith to Open Form

The sculpture of the old agrarian civilizations reflects the stone block, the marble slab, or the tree log from which it was carved. Even where the raw material permitted major extensions and protuberant shapes, the stresses involved in wielding hammer and chisel might break off or split parts of the work. That is why totemic sculpture, for example, so closely resembles the tree trunk and Egyptian statuary closely follows the granite block. Only the casting process, perfected mainly by nomadic peoples, was capable of reproducing very complex open shapes. But metal casting was used largely to fashion weapons, amulets, harness decorations, and the like, rather than the monumental figures we associate with the settled peoples of the old Mediterranean world. Sculpture in general, and carved sculpture in particular, was monolithic (similar in form to a single stone). That is, whether it was hewn out of a single stone or not, it tended to adhere to the shape of the stone unit. An exception, a Hellenistic sculpture, the *Laocoon*, was carved from several blocks of marble, and although it represents a remarkable technical achievement, it is not generally considered aesthetically successful because its parts are disunited and the feeling of a single, embracing shape, the *monolithic feeling*, has been lost.

In addition to considerations of material and process, monolithic form prevailed in sculpture for religious and psychological reasons. Stability, per-

Calf-Bearer (c.570 B.C.), near right. Acropolis Museum.

Laocoon (late second century B.C.), far right. Courtesy The Vatican Museum.

manence, and resistance to change are qualities associated with uncomplicated shapes. Openings, extensions, and protuberances have dynamic implications, and motion is the enemy of the timeless and eternal. As we know, Rodin's *St. John the Baptist* was criticized because the figure appears to be walking off its pedestal. The pyramids of Egypt and the temples of Greece rely heavily on the triangle resting on its base, or the triangle supported by repeated massive verticals. Since one of the religious functions of sculpture is to *arrest* change, to create monuments which can resist the ravages of time, the sacred sculpture of the ancient Mediterranean world (excepting the later Greek, or Hellenistic, development) was largely solid, frontal, and monolithic. Sculptural movement, open form, and extension in space occur when the archaic styles are left behind, when the worship of effigies of the old tribal gods gives way to philosophic speculation about divinity, and when travel and navigation begin to displace agrarian space conceptions and Euclidean geometry.

Another source of open form in sculpture comes from the art of the barbarian peoples whose incursions through Europe from the steppes of Asia eventually succeeded in destroying Graeco-Roman civilization. Their nomadic lives and their skill in metal-working, especially as goldsmiths, predisposed them to an art of linear dynamism. Heated metal lends itself to curved, serpentine, and spiral shapes. And since the total nomadic economy was adjusted to continuous movement, early Celtic, Scandinavian, and Germanic art, created by the European descendants of the Asian nomads, reflected a fascination with, and mastery of, complex abstract movement.

Their sculpture in wood or metal was not primarily naturalistic because the faithful imitation of appearances requires, first of all, the concept of a model fixed and motionless in time and space. But the barbarian consciousness was nourished on incessant travel, hunting, and battle. Furthermore, from the standpoint of people accustomed to the freedom to move indefinitely in any direction along the seemingly endless Asian plains, the concepts of balance, stability, and enclosed space are not easily discovered. Consequently, the art of the wanderers who eventually settled Europe from Russia to Ireland was predominantly one of endless convolution on a flat plane. Their three-dimensional or sculptural expression consisted mainly of the visual *assembly* of two-dimensional, abstract linear structures.

The development of Western art, particularly of Christian religious sculpture, represents the alternating struggle and synthesis of Mediterranean closed-form or monolithic conceptions and nomadic open-form ideas. On the one hand, sculptors from Michelangelo to Maillol have endeavored to preserve classical sculptural order; on the other hand, Romanesque and Gothic sculpture reveal the barbarian obsession with infinite movement, convulsive forms, and abstract ornament as opposed to naturalistic rendering of the human figure. If the Gothic cathedral is regarded as the culmination of Christian glyptic (carved, sculptural) art, then the nomadic conceptions of form and space can be said to have prevailed. Indeed, the revival of classical order during the Renaissance never succeeded in displacing entirely the taste for complex motion which had been whetted by barbarian art. In the styles of Mannerism and the

AUGUSTE RODIN, *St. John the Baptist Preaching* (1878). Collection The Museum of Modern Art, New York, Mrs. Simon Guggenheim Fund.

Animal head from the Oseberg find (c.825). Courtesy Universitetets Oldsaksamling.

In Moore's penetrated forms we see the culmination of a long process of accommodation between the nomadic obsession with open serpentine shapes and the classical Mediterranean concern for balance and stability.

HENRY MOORE, *Reclining Nude* (1937). Courtesy The Baltimore Museum of Art, gift of Mr. and Mrs. Albert Lion.

GIANLORENZO BERNINI, *Ecstasy of St. Theresa* (1645–52), left. Courtesy Alinari-Art Reference Bureau.

ADRIEN DE VRIES, *Mercury and Psyche* (1593), right. Courtesy Musée du Louvre, Cliché des Musées Nationaux.

Baroque, restless movement, representations of indefinite space, and linear complexity were again reasserted. To be sure, some classical restraint characterized the now civilized and Christianized sculptors of Western Europe during the sixteenth and seventeenth centuries, but they had surely left the monolith far behind. Although Bernini's sculpture is situated in the very house of Latin Christianity, its animation and its tendency to expand into every space around it reflect the artistic inclinations of those barbarian hordes that swept down into Italy and captured Rome in the fourth century.

Modern critical opinion generally maintains that very few major sculptors intervened between Bernini and Rodin. Although many sculptures were created, the art form was increasingly dominated by academicism, which is to say, by ideas and institutions devoted to the support of an art which is reasoned, calculated, and created according to rules. If this definition of academicism is sound, then it is similar in spirit to Classicism. And, indeed, the history of art bears out such a similarity. Hence, today's low critical estimate of academic sculpture may reflect the view (a) that it is unoriginal, anachronistic, and not truly classical; or (b) that the classical bias in favor of monolithic form and stable composition is no longer meaningful. Probably both views are partly true. Consequently, contemporary sculpture would be expected to reveal anticlassic tendencies, that is, resistance to distinct, naturalistic form and balanced relationships among parts. Furthermore, it should display shapes created by puncture; twisting, rope-like knots and coils; and an almost infinite degree of linear detail—as in the paintings of Jackson Pollock.

Such expectations are, in fact, borne out in the most recent sculpture. As in painting, antiacademic tendencies predominate, although a minority continues to create balanced works of classical order. But even with them, the feeling of the monolith, which derives so much from the carving tradition, has been abandoned. It survives conspicuously in the work of a master like Henry Moore, although his penetrations of solid forms betray a distinctly modern consciousness.

A rare monolithic work is seen in Leonard Baskin's *Seated Man with Owl.* Baskin's sculpture is a version of a theme which appears frequently in Egyptian art, as in the *Pharaoh Khafre,* behind whose head is the hawk god, Horus. But in the modern work, the bird—now an owl—is much inflated, and stands forward on the man's arm, almost obscuring him from view. Baskin's sculpture shares the frontality and immobile expression of the Pharaoh but is otherwise a modern personality. Where *Khafre* is slim, athletic, and youthful, the modern man is overweight, stolid, and middle-aged. The Egyptian sculpture conveys a powerful sense of enduring mass, in part because it is carved from diorite, but also because it is absolutely without a trace of motion. Baskin's figure, carved in wood, has the ponderous bulk of a flabby person whose sitting down is an act of collapse. The Pharaoh looks confidently toward a future which he expects to dominate eternally, while Baskin's image of man is somewhat bored; he is resigned to the future since he knows too much to be hopeful about it. Thus the monolithic quality of Egyptian sculpture, when present in a modern work, is used for a different purpose and embodies different qualities. Instead

LEONARD BASKIN, *Seated Man with Owl* (1959), left. Courtesy Smith College Museum of Art.

Pharaoh Khafre (c.2600 B.C.), right. Courtesy Hirmer Verlag, Munich.

EDWARD RENOUF, *Chow* (1960). Courtesy the artist and Mr. and Mrs. George Zabriskie.

of playing a role in the funerary culture of an ancient despotism, it becomes a tool of psychological analysis. The king's strategy for guaranteeing his victory over death is exploited by a contemporary artist to portray man's resignation in the face of life's everlasting sameness.

Additional illustrations—from the work of Maillol, Brancusi, and Arp—could, no doubt, be brought forward to show that monolithic form survives in the present era. However, these sculptors are among the "old masters" of modernism. As we approach the present day, even artists who seem to possess some classical feeling nevertheless choose media and techniques which yield dynamic, perforated, predominantly abstract form. The nonfigurative bias of modern sculpture is also an indication of the collapse of the classical, Mediterranean, monolithic tradition. One of the most persuasive signs of this collapse is evident in contemporary ceramic sculpture (to be discussed below). The clear, stable, and functional forms which have characterized pottery since the Neolithic era are now giving way to busy, indistinct, and frequently nonfunctional shapes in earthenware and ceramic sculpture. Since clay thrown on a potter's wheel inevitably assumes distinct, regular form, wheel-thrown shapes and hand-built shapes, too, are truncated or smashed together to create the cracks and fissures, lumps and perforations which are congenial to the contemporary artist's *formgefühl* (preference for form) (see Voulkos sculpture, p. 393).

It is conceivable, however, that the taste for dynamic, broken forms will eventually be oversatisfied and that a desire for its opposite will arise. In that case, the stylistic pendulum may swing back to monolithic form. But then it will not be granite blocks or wooden logs which determine the forms; rather it will be our visual appetites which require that reason and geometry once again govern the organization of shapes.

Constructivism

Constructivism was the twentieth-century movement which formally abandoned the monolith as the basic sculptural form and the central axis as the core around which sculptural volumes must be organized. It introduced new materials into serious sculptural practice—materials like plastics, plexiglass, and metal wire—on the ground that several kinds of material could be combined in one work. Finally, it made a complete break with the figurative tradition, placing geometrical shapes and volumes at the foundation of sculpture. Its leading personalities were Vladmir Tatlin (born 1885), and two Russian brothers with dissimilar names, Naum Gabo (1890–1965) and Antoine Pevsner (1886–1962). They advocated an approach to sculpture which would bring it into harmony with new concepts in physics and mathematics, and hence, via engineering, with production and industrial design. But although the communist government of Russia supported the movement following the Revolution of 1917, it became unsympathetic to abstract and experimental art by 1921, even though Constructivists hoped, ultimately, to revolutionize architecture and industrial design as well as painting and sculpture.

Leaving Russia in 1922, the Constructivists disseminated their ideas through associates at the Bauhaus in Dessau, from Berlin, and from Paris, where Pevsner settled (and where, incidentally, the art world received its principal leadership until the end of World War II). Naum Gabo settled in the United States in 1946 and died here in 1965. But the influence of Constructivist conceptions of form and space had taken firm hold in America and throughout the world many years earlier.

Cubism had begun the development toward geometric abstraction well before World War I, although its primary impact was on painting. Futurism, a descendant of Cubism, had carried the geometric analysis of movement into sculpture, notably in the work of Boccioni and Balla. The Dutch de Stijl group and the German Bauhaus group however, were more concerned than the French Cubists or the Italian Futurists with the problems of practical design. Thus, while manifestoes issued by Futurists, Constructivists, and even Surrealists had as stated aims the reconstruction of society, or, at least, the transformation of the visual environment, it was ultimately the Bauhaus which had the most practical effect. And, through exhibitions in Germany in the 1920's, and through an exchange of ideas with members of the Bauhaus faculty, Constructivism affected Bauhaus thinking and teaching.

What bearing does Constructivism have on the techniques and meaning of sculpture today? Its principal traits, as expressed in the sculptures of Gabo and Pevsner, are abstraction, transparency, openness and penetration of sculptural form, overlapping of planes, and the employment of lines in tension to describe direction and movement in depth. Gabo's *Linear Construction #1* (1942) exhibits many of the qualities of a mechanical drawing executed in three dimensions. Its curves do not betray any irregularity because they are divorced from the effort to record organic shapes. The construction endeavors to provide the viewer with the kind of satisfaction he normally experiences in a suspension bridge or in a microphotograph of a crystalline structure. The key word and idea is *structure*—the visual rendition of lines of force which are transferred from point to point within a sculpture whose only work is holding itself together. The useful function of engineering structures is set aside in Constructivist work so that, presumably, the pure, mathematical beauty of energy transmission may be demonstrated.

Torso, executed by Gabo's brother, Pevsner, in 1924–26, is, by contrast, a fig-

urative abstraction very close to Cubist painting. Like the sculpture of another Russian, Archipenko, it stresses negative —that is, concave—volumes, in the presentation of forms which in life are convex. The materials used are translucent, brownish plastic sheets, and copper. In this work, the doctrinaire Constructivist determination to avoid volume or solid forms in the representation of space is especially evident. The translucency of plastic enables Pevsner to stress lightness, that is, the negation of mass or weight. Hence, two basic characteristics of the monolith are undermined in Constructivist sculpture: (1) solidity or volume: the occupation of space by opaque three-dimensional forms; (2) mass or weight: the determination of forms by gravity requirements and the need for immobility. As with Cubism, the influence of concepts in physics is present.

NAUM GABO, *Linear Construction #1* (1942–43). Courtesy Joseph H. Hirshhorn Collection.

ANTOINE PEVSNER, *Torso* (1924–26). Collection The Museum of Modern Art, New York, Katherine S. Dreier bequest.

The idea that negative forms can express matter occupying space seems to violate common sense. Yet modern physics has discovered antimatter, and we realize that apparently solid materials are really collections of energy paths. Gabo's *Monument for a Physics Observatory* (1922), very appropriately expresses his interest in physics and his elimination of any distinction between sculpture and architecture. Although the model is made of plastic, metal, and wood, and follows strictly geometric curves, as sculptural form it bears an interesting resemblance to a later (1931) wrought-iron sculpture, *Woman Combing Her Hair*, by Julio Gonzalez (1908-   ). Since Gonzalez followed Picasso's precedents primarily, there is no question of direct influence from Gabo. The work of both artists, however, demonstrates

JULIO GONZALES, *Woman Combing Her Hair* (1936). Collection the Museum of Modern Art, New York, Mrs. Simon Guggenheim Fund.

NAUM GABO, *Monument for a Physics Observatory* (1922), above right.

ANTOINE PEVSNER, *Developable Column* (1942). Collection The Museum of Modern Art, New York, purchase.

ANTOINE PEVSNER, *Construction in the Egg* (1948). Courtesy Albright-Knox Art Gallery, Buffalo, New York, gift of The Seymour H. Knox Foundation, Inc.

the new openness of sculptural space. From its age-long condition of rooted-ness in the earth, from its resemblance to masonry-wall construction, sculpture had moved confidently, during the period between the two world wars, into a kind of interstellar space.

Although modern physics has permanently altered our ideas about the concreteness of matter and the nature of space, sculptors could not entirely abandon the use of massive, opaque, volumetric materials in favor of plastics, wire, and glass. Pevsner, who was trained as a painter, inclined to use solid met-als, particularly bronze rods bonded in-to curved planes, in his later work, like *Developable Column.* Apparently, the sensuous appeal of metals counteracts tendencies toward dematerialization with transparent substances. In any event, sculpture cannot be created without some substance which has mass and volume. Heavy, opaque materials continue to be used along with light, transparent substances, but open space is now treated with immense sophistication, as if it were one point on the continuum of matter rather than as an element totally foreign to matter.

Sculptural Assemblage

The efforts of painters to "annex" sculpture have already been noted. Largely as a result of collage experiments, painters found themselves assembling three-dimensional objects, and so, in a certain sense, they invaded sculpture's domain. Is there any significant difference in result when artists who call themselves sculptors employ assemblage processes? It would appear there is none. There are more differences *among* artists employing assemblage than there are between painters and sculptors. For example, there are obvious differences between the work of Louise Nevelson (p. 381) and Jason Seley (p. 218), both of whom are sculptors using assemblage techniques. However, Nevelson is closer to a painter like Kurt Schwitters (p. 339) than to many of her sculptural colleagues. Therefore, one cannot assert, for example, that painterly assemblage retains the sense of the wall and that sculptural assemblage occurs in the round.

Sculptural assemblage is significant with respect to the *history* of sculpture in that it represents the abandonment of carving, modeling, and casting. It begins with materials and objects which already have a rich accretion of meaning. It parallels the flight of painting from the creation of illusions. The sculptor apparently does not wish to participate in a process which pretends that stone is flesh or that metal is hair. Seley's automobile bumpers are very sculptural in the spatial sense, but they do not cease to be bumpers. In other words, assemblage does not involve any *transmutation of materials.* Rather it involves composition with the reality of existing materials.

The reluctance of sculptors to engage in transmutation of materials represents a profound change in art and in sculpture. As we know, medieval alchemists, the precursors of modern chemists, labored to transmute ordinary materials into gold. There was, for them, a hierarchy of substances. Modern men are less willing to accept such a hierarchy. Certainly, science and technology have encouraged this attitude, since so many things we value are derived from relatively abundant and cheap substances like coal, petroleum, nitrogen, soy beans, and so on. Secondly, the entire process of creating illusions has acquired some of the associations of deceit. "Honesty of materials" was one of the goals of the pioneers of modern industrial design, but that goal or principle was a reaction against practices like marbleizing wood or painting wood grains on metal. Nevertheless, the honesty-of-materials idea has helped to create an aesthetic climate in which any transformation of the inherent properties of a material seems faintly unethical.

The influence of democratic ideas should not be minimized. Particularly in the United States, democratic beliefs militate against the existence of social classes in ascending or descending order: Speech, manners, and dress are not as

reliable indicators of status or income as they are in Europe. There is an inclination to evaluate persons in terms of their performance rather than their origins or presumed status. Although this attitude may not be strong in all sectors of American life, it is certainly powerful among artists. It is logical and, I believe, empirically justified to expect that the social ideas of artists will find their way, perhaps unconsciously, into matters of technique, into the "proper" handling and purpose of materials.

Another reason for the rise of sculptural assemblage lies in the sense of inadequacy a sculptor may feel when confronting the forming and fabrication achievements of industrial production. When Cellini made his famous salt cellar, he could rightly feel that it represented the highest degree of technical mastery which his age was able to produce. But the modern artist is daily exposed to miracles of miniaturization in electronic components, for example, which make hand carving and casting

BENVENUTO CELLINI, Salt Cellar of Francis I (1539–43), left. Courtesy Kunsthistorisches Museum.

Ultra-small electronic circuit, a high-speed binary electronic counter for use in a spacecraft, right. Courtesy National Aeronautics and Space Administration.

seem to be puny achievements. Space flight represents a social organization of technology so remarkable that meticulously carved stone and marble appear, from a technical standpoint, to be medieval survivals. Aside from their often tasteless shapes, mass-produced auto bodies or bathroom fixtures represent forming and shaping achievements which would tend to frustrate any sculptor inclined to attempt the same thing.

From the standpoint of creating form, the resources, versatility, flexibility, and control available in the tool-and-die shop of a modern machine-building concern are enormously greater than anything available through the older techniques and processes of sculpture. Consequently, there is a certain practical wisdom on the part of the sculptor who takes possession of these resources by incorporating the products (usually worn-out) of industry into his work. His creative strategy shifts from an emphasis on forming skills to an emphasis on ideas and composition, which is to say, on *design.*

There is always a danger, however, that the sculptor as welder or riveter will lose the "feeling" for materials which carvers and modelers had. Tactile contact with the work, particularly in modeling clay, was one of the main sources of humanistic value in sculpture. The clay sketch functioned for the traditional sculptor very much as the drawing did for the painter (although sculptors also draw). However, drawing and clay modeling become increasingly less relevant to the assemblage of found objects. Drawing and modeling constitute a means of thinking in advance of final artistic execution. But they do not adequately convey in advance the textural and volumetric qualities of rusted metal parts, for example. The sculptor must compose with the materials themselves. Such an approach to design with materials has been advocated from the days of the Bauhaus. One of the most trenchant criticisms of the older practice of industrial design was its excessive reliance on design conceived on the drawing board. It was held that design should grow out of direct work with three-dimensional materials. Today, almost all industrial-design firms employ model-makers who build prototypes of new products in plaster, clay, wood, or plastic. They are, in a sense, the industrial sculptors behind manufactured reality. The assemblage sculptor, however, is one step closer to reality since he makes no model but builds the final object directly.

Some of the richness and variety of sculptural effect possible through assemblage is suggested in the works which follow. They seem virtually a new art form. Even so, the viewer with a good visual memory will not find it difficult to discover echoes of historical form and idea among contemporary themes and materials.

AN ASSEMBLAGE ANTHOLOGY

Lee Bontecou (1931–   ) employs a personal and craftsmanlike assemblage technique in her untitled relief (p. 368) made of canvas stretched over bent steel wire mounted on a metal frame. But the forms of this construction appear to have a strong resemblance to primitive masks and to the totem pole sculptures of the Northwest American Indians. The technique is similar to one employed in early aircraft manufacture—stretching and glueing fabric over a wire-frame skeleton; and its alternating light and

LEE BONTECOU, untitled relief (1962). Collection Mr. and Mrs. Seymour Schweber; photo, Leo Castelli Gallery.

Front view of man's shirt, woven by the Tlingit Indians of Alaska. Courtesy Museum of the American Indian.

gant demonstration of the interactions among material, construction technique, and meaning in sculpture.

Europa on a Cycle by Richard Stankiewicz (1922–) is one of this artist's most fully realized works in the assemblage idiom of welded junk metal. The artist's debt to Gonzalez and to David Smith is clear, and there is also a hint in this work of the kinetic sculpture of Tinguely. In committing himself to rusted metal as his basic material, Stankiewicz arrives at the same unity of material, color, and texture traditionally achieved with a classic metal like bronze. He draws and constructs with old chains and rods, builds with parts as they are found, or cuts metal shapes with his torch. The several forms of metal—wire, pipe, sheet, rod, spring, tube, bar, and plate—all are united by a single process of attachment—welding, and a single color and surface texture—rust. The sculptor is thus free to deal with problems of volume and contour, movement and balance, illusion and reality. The silhouette of the *Europa* has some of the graphic interest of a print by Gabor Peterdi (1908–). That is, it sustains interest as a two-dimensional, linear work. Its idea might be derived from Picasso's *Minotauromachy*, but Stankiewicz has replaced the bull of Cretan and Picassoid memory with a unicycle dating from the era of the auto graveyard. The notion of a beautiful woman carried off by a rusty wheel would surely amuse Picasso, who made good use of bicycle handle bars in his *Goat Skull and Bottle.* As for the maiden, she seems to descend, via Gonzalez, from one of Picasso's bathing beauties, *Seated Bather* (1930), who has left her abode by the sea to join the motorcycle set.

dark canvas areas suggest the painted wood effects in masks carved by Nigerian sculptors in the nineteenth century. But the most prepossessing element in her sculpture lies in the ovoid apertures which can be experienced as eyes, as openings in a curiously abstract mask, or as the entrances to mysterious caves.

The fundamental sculptural metaphors here are the mask and the membrane. The light, sturdy construction of the mask permits a massive yet buoyant organization of positive and negative spaces. It suggests the Indian practice of building a canoe by stretching hides over a frame rather than hollowing out a log. The membrane, which we know would vibrate if it were snapped, is the source of a primitive, animistic feeling; air trapped inside the sculpture seems to be exerting a force outward, a living, invisible force which holds the forms away from the wall surface, just as an invisible, "magical" force holds up the airplane wings in flight. The ability of the sculptor to sustain and encourage the viewer's illusion that expansive forces are at work inside the mask, creates surface tensions which are further supported by the visible stretching of canvas over the wire frame. The work is an ele-

The use of a form language developed by his predecessors is not a negative reflection on the artist's creative capacities or artistic integrity. Surely Picasso has borrowed heavily from the whole of Mediterranean civilization, extracting meaning from the play of old forms against their new contexts. If anything, the Stankiewicz sculpture illustrates the recurrence of perennial themes in the most modern media, and the artist's wit—his ability to make a kind of sculptural "crack" about the human and the mechanical. The lady and the bicycle theme has attracted several contemporary artists—Léger, Lucchesi, and de Kooning, for example. It would be interesting to compare the Stankiewicz approach to that of Léger in *La Grande Julie*. Without doubt, the lady and the wheel constitute a theme which attracts a variety of artistic temperaments.

RICHARD STANKIEWICZ, *Europa on a Cycle* (1953).

GABOR PETERDI, *The Black Horne* (1952). Courtesy the artist; photo, Grace Borgenicht Gallery.

PABLO PICASSO, *Goat Skull and Bottle* (1951–52). Collection The Museum of Modern Art, New York, Mrs. Simon Guggenheim Fund.

PABLO PICASSO, *Seated Bather* (early 1930). Collection The Museum of Modern Art, New York, Mrs. Simon Guggenheim Fund.

BRUNO LUCCHESI, *Woman on Bicycle* (1962). Courtesy Forum Gallery, Private Collection.

ROBERT MALLARY, *The Juggler* (1962), left. Courtesy Allan Stone Galleries.

CLAES OLDENBURG, *The Stove* (1962), right. Collection Mr. and Mrs. Robert C. Scull.

The Juggler by Robert Mallary (1917–) is executed in particularly exotic materials for sculpture—plastic-impregnated fabric and wood. Using a man's shirt and trousers, which are soaked in plastic and attached to a burnt-wood support, Mallary can arrive at the figure through the suggestions of the clothes meant to cover it. The hollow arms and legs, now given a certain structural rigidity, exist as real limbs and as heavy rags at the same time. The plastic manages to "freeze the action" of the fabric stretched apparently by its own weight and suspended from a wooden frame in the manner of a crucifixion. Burnt wood is, of course, one of the primal materials of religious sacrifice, and so Mallary has brought together in new form some of the basic symbols of suffering, destruction, and transfiguration. As he "puts on his act," the juggler falls into the position of the Christ on the Cross, thus expressing the dying-in-living and the failure-in-success which are implicit in all of man's enterprises.

Mallary's form and vision are traditional in many respects; he seems to resemble Rouault in point of view. Assemblage, in his case, means giving a type of stiffness, hence quasi-permanence, to a material—fabric—which wears out quickly and is normally associated with softness and formlessness. But swatches of fabric have long been used in collage and assemblage. It is the distinctive manipulation of *clothing* which awakens a host of existential ideas about the human predicament. The empty tuxedo often included in Mallary's constructions, becomes, not a fabric shell or covering for a man, but the man himself. Literary metaphors expressed by phrases like "hollow men" or "stuffed shirt" are thus transmuted into sculptural reality by a plastic-impregnated empty sleeve.

The Stove by Claes Oldenburg, an example of Pop art *and* assemblage sculpture, consists of painted plaster "food" displayed on a real, slightly antiquated cooking range. The range is similar to the "ready-mades" of Marcel Duchamp. But the luridly colored provisions are the contribution of Oldenburg alone. Further, the authentic kitchen environment helps explain why Pop art has been called "the new realism."

Sculpture as the pleasing organization of forms and volumes is completely irrelevant here. The design principles of unity, rhythm, balance, and so on are not considered either. Instead the viewer is encouraged to perceive food and food preparation as a supremely vulgar, if not disgusting phenomenon. The artist seems to be directing a program of sabotage against what the housekeeping magazines, with all their delicious color plates, attempt to accomplish. The absence of any attempt to create logical or ingratiating sculptural form and space contribute to the shock value of the work as a whole. We seem to be seeing the nakedness of groceries and cooking. A familiar event thus divested of the glamor, zest, and comfortable associations in which we normally attempt to clothe it, becomes hideously ugly. Such an anti-art objective is not only legitimate, however; it is also aesthetically valuable if it can stimulate new perceptions and sustain new meanings beyond its initial shock.

John Chamberlain's assemblage of crumpled automobile parts seems to constitute an earlier stage in the process of machine destruction than is seen in the final "compression" sculptures of César Baldaccini. Although these parts are "found" in junkyards, Chamberlain (1927–) bends, paints, and welds them himself, constructing works which tend not to rely heavily on their automotive origins. In other words, the dead automobile serves this sculptor as a source of

cheap raw material. His *Essex* acknowledges that venerable vehicle as ancestor but is more closely influenced by action painting than by philosophic speculation on the destiny of machines in Western civilization. The scale of the work (nine feet high by seven-and-a-half feet), and its aggressively jutting forms create some difficulty for the viewer if he attempts to see it as a very large, colored metal painting. But that is clearly one of its objectives. The work adheres to the rectangle; its holes, valleys, and crevices occur in the consistently shallow space one encounters in Abstract Expressionist painting. However, the achievement of unity of form and expression seems to elude the sculptor. Why is this so?

Crumpled auto metal inevitably records a history of violence. When assembled in the context of a work of art, this history of violence is present as a palpable idea just as much as the shape and gauge of the metal. Consequently,

JOHN CHAMBERLAIN, *Essex* (1960), left. Collection The Museum of Modern Art, New York, gift of Mr. and Mrs. Robert C. Scull and Purchase.

CÉSAR (César Baldaccini), *Sculpture Picture* (1956), right. Collection The Museum of Modern Art, New York, gift of G. David Thompson.

the application of bright enamel paint creates a contradiction between form and appearance which upsets the viewer's effort to achieve unified perception, closure. Clearly, the artist is aiming at an original transformation of a common material, but his color interferes with the attempt; we remain unconvinced. The effort to carry sculpture into painting runs these perils: Crumpled metal occupies "real" space, applied color creates "optical" space, and the two kinds of space are inclined to fight with each other. Signs of age in the metal conflict with the new and shiny paint film given to the old surfaces. A "logic of materials" is not permitted to assert itself. César's *Sculpture Picture* would appear to be a more successful attempt to integrate sculpture in a painterly format.

The painted plaster food of Claes Oldenburg also contradicts its form, and does so intentionally. But the total work succeeds because the sculptural forms, which are large and simple, establish their identity quickly and unambiguously. They are, without doubt, oversized hamburgers. The contradiction works because we clearly see that the forms exist only to be decorated, embellished, or ridiculed. The *Essex* does not succeed in establishing an initial sculptural concept—simple or complex—hence there is no "leverage" for the subsequent painting to exert force, that is, convey meaning. But the effort is very ambitious: It is an endeavor to transform materials and meaning three or four times in the context of a single work of assemblage. Perhaps such failures are more commendable than easier successes.

A ceramic relief panel by John Mason, designed to be seen against the marble wall of a building lobby, illustrates the assemblage attitude applied to ceramic sculpture. Slabs and strips of clay are joined and pressed together in a manner similar to John Chamberlain's assembly of auto parts. An impression of ruggedness which the sculpture conveys is due, in part, to its resemblance to natural rock formations. But its loops and perforations and the shapes which run *across* each other suggest the arbitrary constructions of man rather than the geologic formations of nature. As in the "action" sculpture of Peter Voulkos (see *Gallas Rock*, p. 393), the unadorned clay slabs of the ceramist, together with his characteristic way of compressing or throwing them together to form a bond, constitute the "subject matter" of the work. Although such sculpture is abstract, it performs a humanistic function when located against the austere walls of modern buildings: It sounds a note of earthiness and hand fabrication within our soaring machine-made structures of glass and steel.

Edward Kienholz works in the Pop-art vein but is more bitter and explicit in his social criticism than other members of this group. His *John Doe* is an assemblage consisting of a manikin, a perambulator, paint, wood, metal, and plaster. A lettered placard at the bottom reads:

Riddle:
    Why is John Doe like a piano?
Answer:
    Because he is square, upright and grand . . .
                    —Old Soothe Saying

The "square-ness" of some Americans is not a new idea; it has been well developed in literature by H. L. Mencken and Sinclair Lewis. Finding plastic expression for the idea, however, is another

JOHN MASON, relief panel in Wilshire-Flower Tishman Building (1961).

matter. There may be something "square" about Grant Wood's *American Gothic*, although "plain" would be a more appropriate term. Kienholz approaches the square American in the characteristic manner of satirists—viciously and with loathing. The regular features of the manikin's head (which includes, perhaps unintentionally, an archaic Greek smile) have been "abused" with painted stripes and spills; the eyes have been crudely outlined in paint, in an effort to endow the usually inoffensive store-window dummy with a gruesome countenance. John Doe wears an out-sized, gleaming badge over his heart—an unsubtle reference to the square passion for insignia which declare lodge membership, loyalty, patriotism, and good fellowship. The paint runs and spatters are similar in function to those employed by de Kooning in *Woman, II* (p. 324) to express contempt for the creature the artist has created and now holds up for scrutiny. And, of course, placing an adult in a child's perambulator, without *saying* he is a clown, is a brutally direct statement about his level of maturity. The statement is bitter, not compassionate. It reveals little inclination to indulge the square. He is offered as a monument fit for oblivion.

In other works, such as *The Widow*, Kienholz exhibits the same corrosive wit but relies somewhat more on his construction to tell the story. The use of aged, discarded objects seems to combine well with the artist's deliberately crude paint application (Kienholz was trained as a cabinetmaker) and inelegant assembly of parts. The disdain for "finish" and for any display of sculptural virtuosity characterizes the art of many (although not all) workers in as-

semblage. The artist's ability to create form by fastidious carving or modeling is now beside the point. Such skills are embodied in already created manikin heads which he exploits for their thematic values. The artist "changes" them (assuming that *changing* a material is a prerequisite for art) by smearing the busts with paint, or battering them a bit to create among all the objects a harmony of age, wear, and disintegration.

The Widow, now a faded relic among relics, rides a see-saw which elevates her periodically in front of a

EDWARD KIENHOLZ, *The Widow* (1961), at right above. Courtesy Dwan Gallery, Los Angeles, California.

Head of the Rampin Horseman (c.560 B.C.), below. Courtesy Musée du Louvre, Cliché des Musées Nationaux.

EDWARD KIENHOLZ, *John Doe* (1959), at right below. Courtesy Sterling Holloway.

MICHELANGELO, *The Rebellious Slave* (1513–16). Courtesy Musée du Louvre, Cliché des Musées Nationaux.

wrinkled mirror. Kienholz has chosen the kind of manikin which used to grace the windows of beauty shops, the type of head which is more finely modeled than figures for displaying apparel. Consequently, the widow's falling away from the look and fashion of young womanhood is heightened. He deals with the same theme which occupied Ivan Albright (*Into the World There Came a Soul Called Ida*, p. 150). Albright, however, offers the portrait of a particular individual, whereas Kienholz is more of a sociologist: He is concerned with human types as they occur in a certain cultural milieu.

The employment of *wrappings* in assemblage has enlarged the now-popular artistic vocabulary of terror. Using ideas and methods we associate with prisons, mortuaries, or shipping rooms, two sculptors, Bruce Conner (1933–) and Christo (1935–), have independently developed a gruesome and enigmatic sculptural rhetoric. Both create an imagery in which enshrouded figures or objects seem struggling to escape their wrappings. The situation has clinical as

well as sculptural overtones, relying as it does on the viewer's fear of close confinement. That is its funereal side. But the chained or bound figure has a history as old as the legend of Prometheus. Michelangelo's *Rebellious Slave* describes a drama of imprisoned form which, under various disguises, appears in all his portrayals of the figure. And the nineteenth-century American sculptor William Rush in 1828 carved a life-size wooden sculpture, *The Schuylkill Chained*, which today rests in Fairmount Park, Philadelphia, serving as an allegorical reminder to Philadelphians of the Prometheus myth and the fate of a river condemned to flow through the industrial confines of a modern city.

Conner's *Child* shows a wax figure on a highchair enmeshed in a transparent, gauze-like material made of torn nylon stockings. Bank robbers have used nylons to conceal their identities; here the device suggests the flimsy but entangling concealment of cobwebs. The nylon also functions like Francis Bacon's blurred form to create the illusion of movement and to project the quality of

WILLIAM RUSH, *The Schuylkill Chained* (c.1828). Courtesy Commissioners of Fairmount Park; photo, Philadelphia Museum of Art.

an anguished, silent, and agonized scream.

The Wheelbarrow by Christo describes the quiet, somewhat ghoulish struggle of an unknown thing against a random but effective system of knots and bindings. Its wrapping, a sheet, maintains the anonymity of the imprisoned figure, and the wheelbarrow keeps the secret, adding only the possibility that the writhing form (why else is it tied?) will be carried away. As a result, the viewer's fear and curiosity enable him to experience the nameless tensions which are usually sustained by "abstract" sculptural form. But, of course, a lively imagination nourished on horror films may discover a taste for the macabre rather than abstract art at the root of its perceptions.

Little Hands by Arman (1929–) continues the macabre note struck by Conner and Christo (p. 376). Consisting of dolls' hands (some of them broken) glued in a wooden drawer, it readily initiates a series of grotesque perceptions, beginning with a collection of mutilated toys and ending with the uncovered mass

BRUCE CONNER, *Child* (1959), left. Collection Philip Johnson; photo, Geoffrey Clements.

FRANCIS BACON, *Screaming Man* (1952), right. Collection Mr. and Mrs. Edwin E. Hokin.

CHRISTO (Javacheff), *The Wheelbarrow* (1963), left. Courtesy Leo Castelli Gallery.

FRANCISCO GOYA, *Disasters of War: It Will Be the Same* (c.1810), right. Courtesy The Metropolitan Museum of Art, Dick Fund, 1932.

ARMAN (Fernandez), *Little Hands* (1960), left. Collection Robert C. Scull.

ARMAN (Fernandez), *Chopin's Waterloo* (1962), right.

JEAN TINGUELY, piano before its incorporation into *Homage to New York:* a self-animating and self-destroying work of art (1960). Photo, Alicia B. Legg.

graves discovered after the last war. The drawer functions at first as a frame, then as a container, and finally as a tomb (see section below, "Niches, Boxes and Grottoes"). To equal its content of horror one would have to go back to Hieronymus Bosch. Even then, the images wrought by hand lack the clinical detachment possible for the artist who assembles hands or limbs originally meant to function in a normal context.

In a humorous vein, Arman created *Chopin's Waterloo* (1962). Many citizens, it seems, harbor a secret desire to tear a piano apart. Arman has done it for them (as Jimmy Durante or Harpo Marx used to do), and has given the dismemberment permanent form in a type of piano collage. The idea of this work may be trivial, but the visual effect is one of beautiful destruction—the splinters, ivories, and piano wire in gorgeous disarray. It seems that a music-making device sustains more visual interest in its disintegrated state than it does when healthy and whole, awaiting the pianistic attack of a tail-coated virtuoso. By tearing a piano open, the sculptor reveals it as a type of machine and then employs assemblage techniques to gratify the per-

verse human desire to see machines break down, fall apart, or ball things up. For these or similar reasons, Jean Tinguely (1925–), a Swiss sculptor celebrated for machines which destroy themselves, included a flayed piano in his kinetic sculpture performance at the Museum of Modern Art, *Homage to New York*. Arman's piano collage might represent the aesthetic vindication of small boys who take clocks apart and fail to put them together again.

The interest in violent, macabre, and gruesome phenomena is today visible in all forms of art and popular culture. There has been, for example, a vigorous and sustained market for the horror films of Vincent Price; and revivals of the early (1933) film *King Kong*, have been enthusiastically received. Sculptural assemblage has been technically congenial to the expression of extreme emotions, or, more accurately stated, it seems capable of dealing with ordinary themes which are very acutely felt. The advantage of the medium lies in the extraordinary range of objects and qualities which are accessible to the sculptor when he does not have to fashion forms *ex nihilo*—out of nothing, so to speak. In assemblage, the sculptor *begins* at a fairly well-developed level of meaning and is able to devote much of his effort to exploring the outermost reaches of the ideas and emotions suggested by his materials.

It would be a mistake to attribute the prolific assemblage activity of today's younger sculptors to reluctance or inability to master the traditional sculptural materials and processes. Rather, the classic techniques must seem sterile to many of them, or, at best, inadequate for the expression of the ideas which they feel are significant. When the pres-ent artistic interest in agitated movement, symbolic destruction, and the exploration of urgent emotions has abated; when a preference for stable forms, controlled movement, and moderate feeling reasserts itself; then the vocabulary developed by assemblage sculptors may turn out to be adaptable to the new aesthetic demands placed upon it. In other words, while it is not possible (or desirable) to offer a final requiem for carved and modeled sculpture, it can be asserted with reasonable confidence that assemblage will occupy sculpture's mainstream for a long time to come.

Niches, Boxes, and Grottoes

The niche is a recessed place in a wall where a sculptured figure or bust can be located. It was used in Roman architecture but is known to us primarily through its evolution from Romanesque relief carvings: As low relief was succeeded by high relief, as more stone was cut away behind the relief forms, the sculpture emerged fully in the round. In the fourteenth century, high relief reached its three-dimensional fulfillment in Gothic sculpture. Then the niche became part of a wall *built around* a sculpture rather than an *excavation in* the wall. However, the sense of the sculpture as originating *in* the wall, and belonging to it, remained, even if it were executed elsewhere and set into the niche already erected.

It is important to think of niche sculptures as *born from* walls, conceived out of the necessity to endow the plane at a particular point with dramatic meaning. The niche encloses the forms physically and psychologically. It governs the angle of vision from which the sculpture can be seen, and it strongly influences the incidence of light and the amount of light admitted to reveal the forms. Psychologically, the sculpture is *protected* by its enclosure; it is removed from full exposure to the elements and thus can be perceived as something precious—something which requires shelter, possibly because it contains a highly valued secret.

These psychological meanings of niche sculpture also adhere to the box sculptures and constructions which figure prominently in twentieth century art. The box sculpture can be regarded as a detached niche, a contemporary secular shrine which has been lifted from an architectural setting that never existed. When we look at box sculptures (which are involved in the abstract and symbolic form language of modern industrial civilization), it is difficult to avoid projecting on them all our associations of the cathedral niche, of a mys-

BENEDETTO ANTELLAMI, *King David* from the façade of the San Donnino Cathedral (c. 1180–90). Courtesy Alinari-Art Reference Bureau.

Detail of the *Last Judgment* from the Orvieto Cathedral façade (c. 1320). Photo, Raffaelli-Armoni & Moretti.

FREDERICK KIESLER, Endless House (1949–60), left. Courtesy Mrs. Kiesler; photo, The Museum of Modern Art, New York.

ANTONIO GAUDÍ, Casa Milá, original attic (garret), (1905–10), right. Courtesy Ampliaciones y Reproducciónes MAS.

Mammoth Cave, Kentucky, left. Courtesy National Park Concessions; photo, W. Ray Scott.

AARON BOHROD, *Grotto* (1964), right. Courtesy Mrs. David Martin.

terious and sequestered hiding place which is seen and addressed in the intimacy of private worship.

The grotto, like the niche, is a man-made recess or excavation. But it is not associated with the wall. It relates instead to the vault or the convoluted inner spaces of natural caverns. The sculpture of interior space is, of course, a type of architecture, and the work of the architect Frederick Kiesler (1896–1965) does indeed resemble such a hybrid art form. But the grotto as a modern sculptural type has no concern with shelter: It is better understood as the opposite of modeling surfaces; it is interior sculpture. Certainly Schwitters' Hanover Merzbau (p. 339) was a quasi-Cubist grotto, employing geometric solids instead of the organic forms Kiesler used to shape interior environments. And in the grotesque—that is, grotto-like—passageways and roof structures of Antonio Gaudí, we see not so much the expression of architectural ideas, as the creation of purely sculptural concavities. The interior sculpture of architects like Gaudí and Kiesler reflects the modern survival of man's eternal attraction to the cave. As Siegfried Giedion observes, prehistoric men lived beneath overhanging rocks or near cave openings, but never in the depths of a cave. They ventured into the interior recesses only to carry out sacred rituals. Hence, caves are not architecture.[*] But the cavernous spaces created by natural action and barely visible in the feeble light available to early men must have been tremendously impressive. Such spaces may constitute unconscious models for those contemporary architects and sculptors who seem so powerfully drawn to the grotto form.

[*]Siegfried Giedion, *The Eternal Present: The Beginnings of Art*, Pantheon Books, 1962, pp. 525–526.

The *Room* by Lucas Samaras (1936–) is a twentieth-century grotto, a three-dimensional interior assemblage. It consists simply of the aggregate of possessions collected and attached to the walls of a teen-age cave. Its claim to style lies in a total lack of style, and its vividness is reinforced by the viewer's knowledge that the room is utterly real and quite typical. If the clutter and visual disorganization of the grotto seem to constitute a scandal, a poor reflection on adolescents growing up in America, then we should remember that it accurately mirrors the space organization of the large-scale environment created by generations of adults in our society. There is also the possibility that modern conceptions of order—influenced by the austerities of Mondrian and Mies—fail to perceive a logic hidden in the apparent illogic of the Samaras room. But as art, the room comes too close to life to fall within a frame of aesthetic relevance. It is really a manifestation of a new, quasi-art fashion called "camp"—a set of attitudes about film-viewing, interior decorating, curio collecting, personal dress, and word choice.

Camp seems to be deliberately perverse, as with the Samaras assemblage. It chooses to celebrate films, novels, decorative objects, book illustrations, fabrics, paintings, sculptures, and so on, which have either been universally condemned by prevailing critical opinion, treasured in primitive regions and cultural backwaters, prized by children before they become aware of aesthetic alternatives, or cast aside by households, museums, and even rummage shops. Much of Pop art is influenced by campy attitudes, and therein lie some of its assets as well as its liabilities. Pop has been imperiled by its addiction to the garish and banal; its practitioners may lose the capacity to take pleasure in anything which is not superficial or tawdry. And we who enjoy Pop run a similar risk. The willingness to admire and prize what has been passed over and discarded is the way we contribute to the just evaluation of art by history. Moreover, the relics of fashion are always instructive and frequently valuable. But uncritical admiration of yesterday's trivia, which may have been sensibly discarded, is no better than the unthinking accept-

LUCAS SAMARAS, *Room* (1964) [detail]. Courtesy The Pace Gallery of New York.

A sculpture in which one could live, or a dwelling which invites the plastic responses appropriate to sculpture.

ANDRÉ BLOC, *Sculpture Habitacle No. 2* (1965). Courtesy André Bloc.

GEORGE SEGAL, *Girl in Doorway* (1965). Collection of the Whitney Museum of American Art, New York.

ance of all novelty in the arts. When this happens, the enjoyment and understanding of art becomes ritualistic and cultic. We lose contact with our intelligence and capacity for feeling, substituting mechanical reactions, "inside" jargon, and the doubtful security of repeating the right words and liking the right things without knowing why.

Boxes differ from grottoes and niches in that they close and become a package. The niche is part of a stationary wall; the box is a portable container for something worth keeping. It has many of the ancient associations of a reliquary—a container for the bones of a saint, the remnant of a precious scroll or garment. The Ark of the Covenant in Jewish houses of worship, for example, is a chest in which are kept the Scrolls of the Law. Originally the ark was portable; now it is usually built into the wall behind the altar and is opened only on special occasions. These religious uses of box-like containers suggest the ancestry of boxes in modern sculpture. And boxes in ordinary usage provide additional connections between everyday behavior and sculpture; we have tool boxes and lunch boxes, silver chests and hope chests, strong boxes and wall safes. The kitchen shelf-units of modern homes are collections of wall boxes and base cabinets; every drawer or closet can be perceived as a type of reliquary. How often housewives perform the modern ritual of opening the door to a kitchen cabinet, casually reaching for a package which has been extolled, reproduced, and *glorified* by the best resources our civilization has for conferring the magical power to banish care! But the most remarkable box we have—transcending even the radio and the refrigerator—is the television set. It is more magically potent

than the motion picture screen because its sounds and images are not projected upon it but come from within, and, in addition, it possesses sculptural interest when viewed from behind. Indeed, the television box may be the twentieth-century shrine which reveals to contemporary man the hypnotic potential of all niche sculptures.

The authority of the niche is revealed in the sculpture of Louise Nevelson (1904–) which usually consists of a collection of boxes or cells—little rooms. Painted in monochrome—black, white, or gold—her constructions convey first of all the impression of compulsive neatness and order, of well-arranged, frequently cleaned drawers. Without knowing what the contents are, one senses they have been carefully classified, reviewed from time to time, and periodically dusted. They consist, in fact, of pieces of wood molding, bowling pins, newel posts, chair legs, plain wooden boards, and lumber yard odds and ends. What distinguishes *Royal Tide I*, for example, is not so much the origin of each fragment as the precision and control one senses in its location. Since no significant meaning can be attributed to the wooden shapes themselves, how can one explain their oddly gratifying power?

Just as the monolith is a basic sculptural type for the expression of order, so also is the box a type which automatically commands belief; it is convincing on sight. The box-form in general, and Mrs. Nevelson's work in particular, constitute a latter-day magical art. The artist employing this form becomes a shaman or sorcerer, and the box sculpture becomes a potential container for fetish objects. It is not necessary to know what the wooden shapes mean inherently so long as we believe they will ward off

LOUISE NEVELSON, *Royal Tide I* (1960), left. Photo, Rudolph Burckhardt.

LOUISE NEVELSON, *Dawn's Wedding Feast* (1959), right. Photo, Rudolph Burckhardt.

LOUISE NEVELSON, *Totality Dark* (1962). Courtesy The Pace Gallery of New York; photo, Eric Pollitzer.

An application of box sculpture to the needs of advertising; but emphasis is on the security of many closed containers rather than the compelling magic of their contents.

Air freight advertisement, from *New York Times* (1964). Courtesy American Airlines Freight System.

evil spirits, that is, the tensions and anxieties we normally treat with aspirin and tranquilizers. Indeed the anonymity of the boxes sustains faith in their magical influence. It is a case of the *form of presentation* taking possession of and governing the material which is presented. The monochrome paint changes each wooden object into a talisman, a kind of charm. Since five sides of the box are enclosed, the sixth side surely has been opened to us as a special privilege, just as the doors of an altarpiece are opened or the curtain on a stage is parted. The mystery of the work is supported by its asymetrical arrangement and the absence of any clearly discernible pattern. Individual boxes could be relocated without weakening the magic of the whole because sorcery compels belief in each cell;

such art is not governed by the principles of design taught in art schools.

Marcel Duchamp's *Boîte-en-valise* is a craftily compartmented little museum contained within a box which resembles an attaché case. Its carefully dimensioned spaces make room for small reproductions of each of the sixty-eight principal works Duchamp created before abandoning art for chess. In all, three hundred editions of the "museum" and its contents were built. But the box is more than a handy container for the artistic output of the pioneer Surrealist. Its identity as a work of art lies in the relationship between the contents and the container. It is not merely a portable educational device designed to introduce students to miniaturized but "real" versions of genuine art objects, though the serio-comic possibility of such a device is raised by Duchamp in order to dwell on the distinctive ironies which appeal to him as a man and as an artist: (1) There is irony when the enthusiasm, productivity, and intellectual ferment of an important artist's ca-

reer can be neatly contained in a small valise. (2) There is irony in Duchamp's resolution of the conflict between Dadaism and Design; all the antiart, antimeaning, and glorification-of-chance tendencies in Dada must submit to the precise, orderly, engineering requirements of the box form. (3) There is irony in the domestication of Dada; in a box it becomes tame. By miniaturizing works of art which were originally considered scandalous and giving them neutral locations in a container according to the impartial logic of space requirement, their disturbing possibilities are minimized; the barbarian ideas are civilized; the objects and reproductions become a type of inventory—merchandise which can be displayed as in a salesman's sample-case.

The comprehensive irony of Duchamp's traveling case lies in its existence as a metaphor for liberal education as a whole. The box can be understood as a symbol of educational institutions— libraries, museums, colleges, and universities: The compartments are subjects,

MARCEL DUCHAMP, *Boîte-en-valise* (1938–42), left. Courtesy Dwan Gallery, Los Angeles, California.

Crafts for Tour advertisement (1963), right. Courtesy The 7 Santini Brothers Fine Arts Division, New York City.

courses, disciplines, and curricula; the objects are equipment, books, slides, and catalogs; their arbitrary arrangement corresponds to the elective system. Finally, their miniaturized resemblance to reality suggests some of the artificiality of the art world as well as the remoteness from life of educational institutions.

The boxes of Joseph Cornell (1903–) are also surreal containers—collections of objects which seem related until the viewer suddenly realizes that the logic of common sense leads to a series of uncommon questions he cannot answer. For example, *Soap Bubble Set* (*Nostalgia Group*) (1950) has all the serenity and simplicity of a Chardin still life. The objects are not anonymous as are Louise Nevelson's wood fragments, and they assume no magical or fetishistic role. But they have the capacity to induce dreams of old possessions and places, recollections of childhood, and images which seem to belong to the future. Many observers have reacted in this nostalgic manner to Cornell's work. Apparently, he manages to scramble one's time sense, which is fitting and proper for Surrealist art. And the experience is entirely pleasant and nonviolent; it leaves no scars. The collections have no erotic suggestion; if they awaken a desire it is not to possess, but to be in another place or time briefly and then to return to the present.

Cornell has been creating his enigmatic and delightful constructions since the 1930's, apparently uninfluenced by contemporaneous developments in art. In his work the connection with sculpture is very tenuous; he is really an Imagist poet who uses objects in space to create opportunities

for reverie, or an occasional ironic comment. *Habitat for a Shooting Gallery,* for example, communicates more explicitly than is the artist's custom. Still, its cutouts and dated printing matter introduce some Victorian evocations at the same time that the shattered glass cracks the silence of the collection. *Blériot* (1956), on the other hand, has the

JOSEPH CORNELL, *Soap Bubble Set* (1950). Collection Dr. and Mrs. Nathan Alpers; photo, Dwan Gallery, Los Angeles, California.

JOSEPH CORNELL, *Habitat for a Shooting Gallery* (1943), left. Courtesy Ferus Gallery, Los Angeles.

JOSEPH CORNELL, *Blériot* (1956), right. Collection Mrs. Eleanor Ward.

H. C. WESTERMANN, *Memorial to the Idea of Man, If He Was an Idea* (1958). Collection Mr. and Mrs. Lewis Manilow, Chicago; courtesy Allan Frumklin Gallery; photo, Nathan Rabin.

spare open structure of Constructivist sculpture. It is also a prime illustration of quietly stated visual wit. The rusted spring mounted on a kind of trapeze or parrot's perch is intended as a symbol of the first Frenchman to fly across the English Channel. Ever economical with his means while seeking to encompass the widest span of time and space, Cornell extends the metaphor to bird and machine flight, to planetary orbits in space, and back to the bird in its cage.

H. C. Westermann's boxes are distinguished by their careful craftsmanship and their grotesque connection with the human figure. *Memorial to the Idea of Man, If He Was an Idea* is a large (fifty-five inches high), well-made cabinet-and-Cyclops who has for a crown crenellations just like the battlements on a castle tower. The door of his torso, when opened, reveals an interior that is lined with bottle caps and includes the figures of a headless baseball player and an armless acrobat, and a black ship sinking in a sea of bottle caps.

It is not unusual for primitive sculpture to include magical substances in the abdominal cavity,° and Westermann, responding to a similar impulse, lavishes considerable effort on the interior finish of his boxes and contained forms. Since the inside of the construction will not be seen in a casual inspection, his approach to box sculpture embodies a totally different concept

°"A figure is a fetish and can be used as one only when it is charged with some magic content . . . Every conceivable thing is used as a magic content: bits of bone, teeth, animal claws . . . They are often placed in a cavity hollowed out in the head or belly, or, too, in a little horn on top of the head." Werner Schmalenbach, *African Art*, Macmillan, 1954, p. 132.

from previous examples. The artist does not rely entirely on the outward visual aspect to make his statement; he feels obliged to fabricate the visceral contents too, although they will not necessarily be seen. Together with the evidence of superior joinery and the obvious durability of the box, this completeness of construction suggests that Westermann is not merely concerned with the creation of artistic illusions. He appears to be fashioning real beings who exist by virtue of their own built-in-equipment and according to their own laws. The fact that their insides are lined with the debris of an afternoon at a baseball stadium is no more remarkable than the fact that the insides of other creatures contain partly digested hamburger and coke.

The arms akimbo are a reference to the famous Leo Durocher stance before angry baseball umpires. Indeed, the whole work is a scathing "memorial" to man as sports fan. But these symbols function within a new conception of the sculptor's role: The sculptor is an architect. His constructions, like architecture, exist to be used and seen, but they also possess operative parts which are not seen. These unseen operations are essential to the validity of the work as a whole. So, just as the architect builds heating, cooling, plumbing, and electrical systems into a building, the sculptor builds a consciousness into his creations: memories, visceral emotions, ideals of heroism, fears of defeat, undigested experiences, and the assorted rubbish of the creature's personal history. *Memorial* is a monster, of course, but only in those respects wherein it resembles a human being. Otherwise, it is a fine job of cabinetry—inoffensive and soundly put together.

Kinetic Sculpture

Sculpture in motion has a history as old as the Trojan horse and as recent as the figures which strike the hour in the Piazza San Marco in Venice or in New York's Herald Square, in front of Macy's Department Store. It is demonstrated in the widely owned but aesthetically unmentionable Swiss clock, as well as the millions of spring-driven, motor-driven, and rocket-actuated Christmas toys which children manage to break before Easter. The combination of sculpture with mechanical motion occupied some of the great minds of the Renaissance, including that of Leonardo da Vinci who, among his multifarious activities, designed sculptural-mechanical devices for princely entertainments and city festivals.

As we know, Leonardo also designed an early flying machine, repeating the exploit of the Greek sculptor, Daedalus, who, according to the myth, achieved successful flight but with disastrous results for his son, Icarus. Flying too close to the sun, which melted his wax wings, the boy fell into the sea and was drowned. Thus did the ancients describe the fate of men who attempt to share the prerogatives of the gods. But the myth may have other meanings. According to Robert Graves,° the idea of melted wax wings is connected with the *cire-perdue,* or lost-wax, method of bronze casting, which was brought from Crete to Greece by Daedalus. Daedalus may also have been the mythical progenitor of all kinetic sculptors, since he is

° *The Greek Myths,* Braziller, 1959.

supposed to have devised dolls with movable limbs for the daughters of the king of Sicily. At any rate, the ability to make objects which can move by themselves—whether machines or sculpture, whether on land or in the air— has always seemed to be one of the great mysteries. Men who possess this capacity must be more than ordinary mortals: They must somehow have gained access to secrets about the movement of the universe itself.

It is the mystery surrounding motion as an idea and as a phenomenon which fascinates artists. We realize that science possesses a vast body of knowledge about motion and we are familiar with the useful applications of that knowledge in technology and especially in mechanization. With respect to motion, science is like a runner who drives his body as fast as he can to win a race; the goal is realized at the end of the race through increased knowledge of energy and matter. But art is like a dancer who moves her body as gracefully as she can because it feels better to move that way; the goal is realized *during* the dance by her feelings of pleasure in bodily movement for its own sake.

Static sculpture, like painting, is obliged to use optical devices to convey an illusory impression of movement. In figurative art, the position of the body, the twisting of the trunk, the contraction of certain muscles, or the portrayal of postures associated with exertion, can be read directly as frozen action or, by arousing kinaesthetic responses in the viewer, can communicate some of the

RICHARD HUNT, *Icarus* (1956). Courtesy Albright-Knox Art Gallery, Buffalo, New York, gift of Seymour H. Knox.

Movement and precarious balance conveyed by static sculpture.

BRUNO LUCCHESI, *Seated Woman #2* (1963), left. Courtesy Forum Gallery.

LUCIANO MINGUZZI, *Woman Jumping Rope* (1954), right. Collection Alfons Bach.

NAUM GABO, *Blue Construction in Space* (1920). Courtesy Wadsworth Atheneum, Hartford.

bodily feelings described in the work of art. In kinetic sculpture however, motion becomes one of the visual elements, like shape or color.

Futurist art was, as we know, officially dedicated to the expression of movement, especially of mechanical movement, which was considered "more beautiful than the *Victory of Samothrace.*" But for the most part, the Futurists stayed within the static conventions of painting and sculpture; their work portrayed motion and mechanization, but did not *absorb* them into the art form itself. Similarly, the Impressionists were interested in light, but they continued to paint pictures with pigment rather than create works of art with light itself as Laszlo Moholy-Nagy° was to do later.

In 1920, Naum Gabo created the first modern work to be designated "kinetic" sculpture and exhibited it in Berlin in 1922. The statement which he and his brother made in their *Realist Manifesto* (1920) serves as a foundation

°See his experiments with photograms and light modulators in *Vision in Motion*, Theobald, 1947.

principle for kinetic sculpture as well as Constructivist aesthetics:

We free ourselves from the thousand-year-old error of art, originating in Egypt, that only static rhythms can be its elements. We proclaim that for present-day perceptions the most important elements of art are the kinetic rhythms.

But Gabo concentrated on constructions which penetrate volume and minimize mass. He executed few works which actually employ movement as an element. It remained for the American sculptor Alexander Calder to create in the 1930's an art form—mobiles—which successfully integrates motion into art without abandoning any of the essential traits of sculpture.

Calder's mobiles do not sacrifice the material, spatial, or design properties of static sculpture, and, although he has occasionally used motors to impart movement, his best-known works move seemingly by themselves. They are sensitively balanced systems which are set into motion by the gentlest of air currents. But while they receive their motive force from the invisible environment, the parts and subsystems of mobiles move in orbits designed by the sculptor. Hence, the energy which actuates the mobile is random, whereas the character of its movement is largely anticipated, which is to say, formed.

It is possible to discuss the meaning of the shapes in Calder's sculpture as if they were parts of static sculpture. The original contribution of mobiles, however, is to raise the possibility of responding to qualities of movement as attributes of an organized art form. Calder's shapes appear to be biomorphic forms similar to those used by Arp and Miró. For the most part, they are play-

386

ALEXANDER CALDER, *Spring Blossoms* (1965). Collection The Pennsylvania State University.

ful, reminiscent either of child and primitive art or of natural forms—fish, animals, leaves, flowers, planets, and stars. But his sculptural movement interests us here, and it is expressive both of nature and the man-made world. Some works suggest the stately motion of great tree branches in a deep forest; others are as comic as Charlie Chaplin strolling, hopping, and dancing his way down a street after stubbing his toe. The fact that mobiles are widely imitated (they have become virtually an American folk art) suggests that it is their organized motion which has caught the popular imagination, since abstract forms do not usually evoke such broad acceptance, and especially the kind of approval which is implied by imitation.

While Calder is the best known of kinetic sculptors, there are other men who employ motion—either in elaborations of Calder's works or in new kinetic forms of their own. Furthermore, the artistic "breakthrough" which kinetic sculpture represents has introduced new problems related to the study of kinetic art. Just as *motion* pictures require a conceptual framework and terms of reference which differ from those used to study *still* pictures, so also does motion sculpture require its own categories and special terms.

Kinetic sculpture might be classified according to its *source of energy*, in which case the following two categories can be set up: natural kinetics and artificial kinetics.

NATURAL KINETICS

This category describes the operation of invisible, nonmechanical forces which drive Calder mobiles, for example—wind currents, gravity, temperature and humidity changes in the environment of the work. The weathervane and the windmill exploit such energy sources, although for different purposes, in the out-of-doors. Inside a room, as we know, warm air rises naturally and its upward movement can be used to impel sculpture. If it is directed against forms shaped to act like fins or sails, they can be set in motion; they might also be used in conjunction with controlled light to cast moving shadows. A chemical or mechanical heating device to accomplish such a purpose would seem to violate the "rules," although the movement of air by convection is invisible. Another type of motion derives from sculptural forms which have an insecure, rocker-like base; its energy comes from the force of gravity working on the sculptor's shapes and assisted by his location of the masses. We are, of course, mainly familar with the operation of gravity to promote stability and the absence of motion in sculpture. But the swing, the seesaw, and the pendulum are instances of stability *and* motion which pleasurably or usefully employ the force of gravity and they constitute models for kinetic sculpture. Water falling against

JOSÉ DE RIVERA, *Homage to the World of Minkowski* (1955). Collection The Metropolitan Museum of Art, Fletcher Fund, 1955.

Whistle: Swinging Girl; Veracruz, Mexico: Remojadas. Courtesy of The Museum of Primitive Art, New York.

387

The action of a rugged natural waterfall is simulated by the organization of hovering metal planes in an abstract fountain sculpture.

JAMES FITZGERALD, *Fountain Sculpture* (Plaza Level, IBM Building, Seattle) (1961). Courtesy University Properties, Inc.

LEN LYE, *Fountain* (1963), still and in motion. Courtesy Howard Wise Gallery; photos, Geoffrey Clements.

man-made forms, pouring into container systems, or spilling out of them in a calculated sequence also constitutes a source of naturally available energy. But its use, as in the water wheel, involves a more-or-less sophisticated machine. In fact, all of the above-mentioned arrangements for using natural energy in sculpture involve relatively primitive ways of harnessing air, heat, gravity, or moisture to create motion, to do work. However, they do not obviously—that is, visually—introduce mechanical force, fuel combustion, or electricity.

Thin metal or plastic rods fixed at one end can exhibit vibratory motion based on their resonance and elasticity; such energy is a property of the material and its shape, as in the case of a watch spring. But a spring must be wound, and a metal rod requires outside energies to make it flex and vibrate—a controlled electrical force, say, if the resultant motion is to achieve the aesthetic objectives of the artist, as in the *Fountain* by Len Lye (1901–). Kinetic sculptors are understandably tempted to use gadgetry of one sort or another to manipulate the energy available in natural forces and materials. But there appears to be a group among kinetic sculptors who would rather avoid the introduction of "outside"

energy sources. Perhaps they feel that motion should *seem* to be independent of any mechanical assistance or obvious manipulation of nature.

ARTIFICIAL KINETICS

This category designates man-made motive force used to drive sculptures which would not achieve motion either spontaneously or by the introduction of a small initial "push" from the outside. All energy sources arise ultimately in nature, but some kinetic sculptors are willing to interpose artificial devices between nature and art in order to operate their creations and to regulate the energy flow and movement which nature might provide. Since small electric motors are now very efficient, they are often used to drive kinetic sculptures. Their power comes from batteries or house current. But electrical energy, like wind energy, is invisible, and must be translated into mechanical action to create the visual movement which is the actual content of kinetic sculpture. Similarly, energy from other sources, such as watch springs or electromagnets, must find mechanical expression to achieve visible results. Eventually, perhaps, photochemical effects will become part of the visual repertory of kinetic art, and then mechanical movement may not be necessary. But at present, kinetic sculpture is largely dominated by what can be done through mechanical and electronic devices.

TYPES OF MOTION

Clearly, the *source of energy* has a bearing on the *type of motion* which a kinetic sculpture will exhibit. That is why natural and artificial sources of energy have been distinguished here. We are ultimately interested, however, in types of motion because they constitute (along with the visual forms) the embodiment of aesthetic quality in kinetic sculpture. Wind, the flow of water in a stream, air convection in a room, or the casual gesture of a hand against an object—all are intermittent forces. If they are employed as energy sources, they will not influence sculptural movement in the same fashion as the regular output of energy from an electric motor or a gasoline engine. An electrically driven Calder mobile does not move as his wind-driven works do, although there are some similarities. In general, artificial energy causes regular rhythms, recurrent events, intentional motion whereas the unpredictable and irregular character of natural energy imparts some of its own random quality to the sculpture it animates.

There are several types of motion which could potentially be imitated and abstracted in kinetic sculpture. As with the other visual arts, sources arise in nature, in man himself, in the man-made world, and in the interactions among all these. Kinetic sculpture permits treatment not only of the color of clouds or the shapes of fruit but also of atmospheric movement, of leaves blown from trees, of hail striking cobblestones, of airplane shadows moving across cattle grazing in a field. That is, kinetic sculpture can deal with qualities of motion in these events apart from the appearance of the participants in them. It can be highly abstract, similar to the musical organization of sound. The movement of the human figure, varied according to age, sex, or occupation, now becomes available to plastic art—not ephemerally as in the dance or the film—but in a

form which is relatively permanent, concrete, and durable.

Mechanical motion is understandably attractive to kinetic sculptors because they must use it themselves to combine sculptural form with movement. In addition, the machine as an idea and as a feature of the visual environment is inevitably part of the artistic expression of our time. The problem of the kinetic sculptor lies in going beyond the mere incorporation of machines and machine forms in his work. Since mechanical action is often fascinating in itself, some kinetic sculptures consist of machines designed for no purpose other than to exhibit their own operation. They are distinguished from "real" machines in that their "working" parts are exposed although they perform no practical work. In his fantastic designs for machines, the cartoonist Rube Goldberg based his humor on one idea—the absurdity of an enormously complex apparatus for the performance of a simple, really unnecessary job. Our fascination with the precision, reliability, and mathematical order of machines is mixed with various kinds of resentment and hostility toward them: They seem perfect and absurd at the same time.

Music Machine by Arthur Secunda appears to exhibit Goldbergian absurdity in a craftsmanlike, operational form. It consists of a gilded construction of wood, metal, and machine parts which has a music box concealed within. Its associations with the mechanics of sound are abetted by radio antennae, a built-in xylophone, a guitar handle, and other noise-making and electronic odds and ends. Here the externalization of gears, sprockets, springs, and so on is part of a total effort to derive visual poetry from mechanized innards. Furthermore, it is

TAKIS (Takis Vassilakis), *Signal Rocket* (1955), left. Collection The Museum of Modern Art, New York, Mrs. Charles V. Hickox Fund.

ARTHUR SECUNDA, *Music Machine* (1964–65), right. Courtesy the artist and *Craft Horizons* magazine.

KONSTANTIN MILONADIS, *Flower Garden* (1961). Courtesy Dr. Malcolm A. McCannels; photo, George Rickey.

7000 locomotive. Union Pacific Railroad Photo.

JULIUS SCHMIDT, untitled iron sculpture (1962). Courtesy Marlborough-Gerson Gallery, New York.

LIN EMERY, *Homage to Amercreo* (1964), still and in motion. Courtesy Lin Emery.

consistent with the general tendency in contemporary art to avoid concealment of working parts.

The steam locomotive, for example, was a more dramatic and visually interesting combination of forms before it was streamlined, endowed with a skin, and made to resemble a fountain pen. But although we still cover machines with metal or plastic skins—cosmetic operations for the purposes of "styling" —we have overcome the Victorian distaste for mechanical forms. Victorians were enamored of mechanically duplicated imitations of handcraft. Consequently, artists like Secunda, Edward Paolozzi, or Julius Schmidt (1923–) see meaningful ornament, power, and

grace in the parts and operation of complex machines, much as in a bygone era small boys, who wanted to be locomotive engineers, saw magnificence in those steam engines and in the men who commanded them.

EXAMPLES OF KINETIC SCULPTURE

A practical application of kinetic sculpture is seen in Lin Emery's *Homage to Amercreo*, a mobile fountain whose forms fill with water until they tilt over, empty themselves, and then return to position to be filled again. Although the work functions as a machine, its mechanical operation is clearly subordinate to its visual performance. Perhaps this idea could be applied to other machines in our civilization with immense visual and psychological benefits. Of course, the purpose of a fountain is to create visual entertainment by the display of water in motion. In the past, sculptured figures were usually employed to hold a spout in position, but, from a certain standpoint, the frozen figure of a human being forever holding a water spray is faintly ridiculous. Emery's abstract forms, on the contrary, appear entirely suitable to their visual and mechanical function. The viewer may be grateful that they are not nymphs and sea creatures acting out an allegorical charade.

Study Falling Man by Ernst Trova presents an aluminum figure strapped to an apparatus with clinical-experimental overtones. The work is terrifying because the apparatus is so obviously clean, efficient, and well calculated to carry out its job of scientific dehumanization. The figure is a model of urban, middle-aged man—slightly paunchy, sway-backed, faceless, and curiously without arms. In some respects he resembles the manikins used in place of drivers in auto-crash experiments. Trova has created an image of man as ideal subject for clinical experiment, the "patient etherized upon a table" of T. S. Eliot's poem "The Love Song of J. Alfred Prufrock." He seems to be a willing victim of technology. But we do not know the purpose of the experiment. The figure is about to be rocked, whirled, and rotated as if he were an astronaut undergoing a simulated experience in weightlessness. Another of Trova's works, which is entitled *Landscape #1,* constitutes a deadly portrayal of a frail human organism beset with mechanical equipment to regulate its movement. The nakedness of the man, the Buck Rogers accessories strapped to his body, and the shiny aluminum surface he has for skin, convey eerie evocations of that depersonalized humanity described by George Orwell in his not-very-fantastic novel, *1984.* A rather harmless creature is about to go through several very sophisticated gyrations. Precautions have been taken so that he will emerge whole, but will his manhood survive?

Jean Tinguely's kinetic sculptures are essentially mechanical poems about the absurdity of machines and, by implication, of a civilization which permits itself to be governed by them. His

Homage to New York was a type of mechanized Happening. In addition to the battered piano mentioned earlier, drums, bicycle wheels, coke bottles, a typewriter, a drawing-machine, and a weather balloon figured as performers. Fifteen rickety motors powered the rather shabbily constructed affair. The entire assembly was designed to make music, create drawings, issue reports, give birth to machine offspring, set itself on fire, and finally to destroy itself. The noise, the drawings, the typed reports, and the bursting activity in general were aimless in true Dada fashion. At the same time, the suicidal machine constituted a junkyard parody of contemporary civilization.

Man-size manikin, from advertisement (1966), above left. Courtesy Ford Motor Company.

ERNEST TROVA, *Landscape #1* (1964), above right. Courtesy the Pace Gallery of New York; Collection P. Johnson.

ERNEST TROVA, *Study Falling Man* (1964), at left. Courtesy The Pace Gallery of New York.

JEAN TINGUELY, *Homage to New York* (1960). Copyright David Gahr 1961.

The short career of *Homage* was witnessed by a distinguished audience, on March 17, 1960, in the garden of the Museum of Modern Art. But the machine did not destroy itself entirely as expected and M. Tinguely's intervention was required to set its course finally on the path to self-immolation. Following the ministrations of its maker, the entire whirring, flapping spectacle began to smoke, and finally, it exploded into flame, its "useful" life ended with the assistance of a fire extinguisher.

Homage to New York, like the Happenings of Kaprow and associates, falls more conveniently into the category of dramatic performance than of sculpture because its existence is so brief. However, Tinguely has created other works which resemble *Homage* but do not attempt to explode. *Méta-Mécanique* exhibits the sculptor's fascination with mechanical movement and his addiction to bicycle wheels, discarded metal, and belt-driven systems for transmitting motion. Tingue-

ly's kinetic sculptures move and sound something like a one-man band, with motors substituting for the embattled musician. They thump and pound, vibrate and oscillate, producing repetitious movement, sometimes to-and-fro alternations, sometimes simple ongoing cycles, as in *Homage*, where the machine endlessly dispatches soft-drink bottles down an inclined plane to a crashing finale.

Ever since Henry Ford perfected the assembly line and made ownership of a complex machine feasible for average citizens, Europeans have tended to identify America with both the triumphs and excesses of mechanization. Consequently, it is not surprising that the Swiss Tinguely should create in *Homage* a device which symbolizes a somewhat stereotyped understanding of America —Coca-Cola, rhythm and blues, automation, big business (typed reports), and explosive potential—perhaps to express his resentment of the American eco-

JEAN TINGUELY, *Méta-Mécanique* (1954), left. Courtesy Alexander Iolas Gallery.

Jean Tinguely at work, right. Courtesy Dwan Gallery, Los Angeles, California.

nomic and cultural colonization of Europe. By employing the quasi-ritualistic action of kinetic sculpture to smash Coke bottles, the artist presumably gave form to his aggressive feelings about the North American colossus of mechanization.

From the water clocks of Greece to Leonardo's mechanized entertainments for the Duke of Milan, to the Swiss cuckoo clock, to Calder's mobiles, to the parodies of Rube Goldberg, to the automated protest sculpture of Jean Tinguely is a long kinetic voyage. But it is altogether likely that Tinguely's work is a belated reaction to what Lewis Mumford° has called the "paleotechnic" phase of civilization. Tinguely's machines have not come abreast of modern, electronically guided tools; they more nearly resemble the equipment which must have adorned the bicycle shop of Orville and Wilbur Wright during the first decade of the twentieth century. That comfortable old noise and clangor has today been supplanted by new, quiet, and more subtly insidious processes of mechanization and automation. Perhaps that is why *Méta-Mécanique* is not at all frightening, but quaint, in the manner of antique coffee mills and sculpture which stands still.

BRUCE W. KOKKO, *Paint Can with Brush* (1965). Courtesy the artist.

PETER VOULKOS, *Gallas Rock* (1959–60). Courtesy Dr. and Mrs. Digby Gallas, Los Angeles, California.

The Crafts and Sculpture

The crafts have been involved in a maneuver of disengagement from useful manufacture, steadily fortifying their claims to fine-art status, that is, to being sculpture. Even though they are defended vigorously as useful art forms, the crafts are increasingly prized for their sculptural values rather than their practical function. Hand-made ceramic pots, for example, serve as containers, but cannot compete economically with mass-produced containers made of metal, plastics, or clay. Nevertheless, they continue to be made by potters, exhibited by museums, and purchased by collectors. Clearly, they satisfy aesthetic as well as utilitarian needs. This argument is strengthened by the fact that pottery forms—that is, shapes created from clay thrown on a wheel—are often assembled with no claim to function as containers. The potter's wheel is a tool of sculpture; clay formed in the characteristic man-

ner of potters is a sculptural material, as it always was.

Peter Voulkos (1924–) is perhaps the best-known of American potters who have extended their efforts to sculpture. He has been in the vanguard of artists who saw and explored the expressive possibilities of forms developed over the centuries by ceramic craftsmen. There are overtones of assemblage in his *Gallas Rock*, which was created by combining hand-built pottery forms. The act of putting them together, of crushing the former containers against each other, endows the result with some of the violence and kinaesthetic excitement one associates with action painting. Voulkos might be regarded as an "action potter," one who has taken the crucial step away from the pot as container and into the realm of sculpture as assembled, nonfunctional container.

°Lewis Mumford, *Technics and Civilization*, Harcourt, Brace, 1934.

The aspirations of the crafts to sculptural scale and expressiveness can result in grotesquely spectacular effects as in these jewels, or in the rings, pins, bracelets, and lavalieres worn by the late Edith Sitwell.

Jewels from Helena Rubinstein's collection. Courtesy Parke-Bernet Galleries.

DORIAN ZACHAI, *Complacent Man,* tapestry (1962).

Similarly, jewelry and metalwork, silversmithing, and enameling may be regarded as small-scale sculpture practiced with special materials. Woodworking in combination with metal, clay, fabric, or leather, or as employed in furniture, falls into the same sculptural category. Blown glass corresponds to clay shaped by the potter's wheel: It is a sculptural material which employs a specialized forming process. In addition, of course, glass can be cast like metal or cut like jade. The important point is that the crafts seem to be emerging from their "previous condition of servitude." Although they may continue to serve practical ends, they also perform the expressive functions of sculpture, and hence they should be seen in the same light.

Conclusion

Of sculpture it can truly be said that in the midst of change there is also abiding sameness. Magic and sorcery persist in the art while its materials and techniques undergo radical transformations. Through all the innovations of form and concept, sculpture has retained its identity as an art of physical material occupying real space, compelling men to believe that the resultant forms are somehow alive. Consequently, the history of sculpture is a history of innovation in material and technique, changes in form concept, and shifts in the interrelations of the various media. But the pursuit of vitality remains constant.

Ancient conceptions of volume and mass have been revised under the impact of modern science and technology. Classical notions of order and stability have given way to new emphases on dynamism. That is, the moderns are looking for ways to express vitality through agitated movement just as the Hellenistic Greeks did. Kinetic sculpture appears to be a departure from static sculpture, a "spin-off" which is similar in some respects to the departure of motion pictures from painting. In assemblage, sculpture and painting have come together and both are periodically returned to architecture, to become a wall, vault, niche, or grotto.

Perhaps assemblage has been responsible for calling attention to the sculptural character of the crafts. The use of exotic materials and found objects in "fine art" has had the effect of breaking down the old hierarchies among sculptural materials: marble, stone, bronze, and wood, with ivory, jade, and precious metals at the periphery. It is, of course, obvious that the material is important in any art object. But the importance of a material lies in the way it influences form and meaning, not in any arbitrary rank it possesses by virtue of its rarity, cost, or resistance to the artist's effort. The transformation of metal in sculpture is a case in point. Because metal is ductile, it can be drawn into long, thin strands called wire, a material used mainly for industrial purposes during the past two centuries (although the barbarian metalsmiths of northern Europe and Asia excelled in the use of serpentine metal forms at least one thousand years ago). Now wire has become an important sculptural material—and not only for armatures.

Threads, strands, and filaments are themselves expressive elements. Wrought iron, too, has changed in status from a decorative and structural material to one of the major media of sculpture. As was seen in the work of Gonzalez, wrought iron approximates wire in that both can describe form and enclose volume with a minimum of solid material and a maximum of open space.

Wire constitutes, of course, a metal line in space. Hence, it would seem to be an extension of drawing rather than an authentic sculptural material. But in addition, as was noted in connection with Constructivism, the line can be regarded as a more legitimate way of expressing volume than the solid. At least, the line in space conforms with contemporary ideas about the energy trails of particles of matter as they move through their orbits. In the wrought-iron sculpture of Gonzalez (*Maternity*, p. 230), we saw how converging lines could be employed to describe volumes. And in the sculptures of David Smith (p. 231), metallic line was used as a type of calligraphy. Do handwriting and particle physics constitute the only sculptural metaphors for which drawn wire or wrought iron are the media?

There are many others. Richard Lippold (see p. 178) has used filaments of gold-and silver-colored wire to suggest light emanations, mostly from celestial bodies. Of course, light rays are an obvious instance of the role energy particles play in daily life, but sun rays have been so conventionalized in art, even in the earliest efforts of children, that we do not find the sculptural representation of light energy especially strange. And, as mentioned earlier, Bernini used metallic lines to represent light behind his *St. Theresa* (p. 360). In the seventeenth century, the light represented by metal had a mystical connotation; but in the twentieth century the mysteries of science are intended.

Painting and sculpture have long dealt with light, but indirectly—in terms of its effect upon the grosser forms in the world which we can grasp or see with the unaided eye. Since the materials of sculpture have always been palpable, however, it is difficult to deny their physical existence. Consequently, the effort to use polished and anodyzed wire or fine metallic filaments to symbolize the very light which permits us to see, represents an ambitious but ultimately frustrating artistic undertaking. As an alternative, artists have endeavored to trap light itself, to bend it and bounce it between mirrors and prisms or to fire it like a gun against photographic film, in order to create new optical effects. But such adventures risk becoming unsophisticated versions of experiments in physics. They cease to be sculpture. The motion picture represents, for the time being, our best model of the artistic application of light physics; and its aesthetic possibilities have just begun to be exploited.

Sculpture's loss of volume and mass —from the monolith to the metal filament—and its gain in motion—from the static statuary of Old Kingdom Egypt to the kinetic sculpture of the twentieth century—find art knocking at the door of physics. But it is interesting to observe that artists like Gabo, Pevsner, and Moholy-Nagy—men with strong scientific interests—become increasingly attracted to the sensuous qualities of matter as their artistic careers unfold. To the extent that they are sculptors, the medium continues to make tactile claims which cannot be denied.

CHAPTER THIRTEEN

A building results from the interaction of many factors: function, style, site, climate, materials, structural design, financing, client requirements, building codes, workmanship. For any given building, one or more of these factors may assume crucial importance. But *all* of them must inevitably be considered at some time in the solution of an architectural problem. That is, from the standpoint of the architect, factors such as cost, site, and client must be dealt with realistically in working toward a design solution. We who are not architects see the result, but rarely do we know the priorities among the factors which affected the architectural solution. Consequently, it is al-most impossible to know every relevant fact about a building's design and construction. It *is* possible, however, to know in general terms what materials and devices are available to architects and to know how they work—visually and symbolically.

In the introduction to this Part, media were defined as materials used in a characteristic way. The fundamental media of architecture are structural devices like arches, domes, trusses, and cantilevers. They can be made of materials like wood, stone, or steel. The structural devices are fundamental because they determine the kind and amount of space which can be enclosed in a building. Materials are important

ARCHITECTURE

because they determine the effectiveness and mode of operation of structural devices. A truss can be made of wood or metal, a post can be made of stone or steel. But different materials require different dimensions to do the same job; hence, the visual result depends on the architect's choice and design of particular structural devices and materials.

Now, in these choices the art in architecture begins to appear. There are usually several ways to enclose space, to support weight, to manage circulation, to admit light, to shape an exterior, to finish a surface. The architect makes his choices and solves his problems in the light of *an idea*—usually an idea about the impact of space on people. If he had no choice among materials, structure and plan—if he did not know how to *design* solids and voids—his services could be provided by a computer, and architecture would not be an art. Some buildings indeed appear to have been designed by computers, which means, in practical terms, that the same architectural solution has been used over and over again. Similarity of needs—in office buildings and hotels, for example—plus the standardization of building components have led to a certain amount of computer-like efficiency and monotony in modern architectural design. Despite the existence of insensitive design, however, the distinguished buildings which *are* constructed demonstrate that all architectural problems are *not* alike, that design alternatives *do* exist, that architecture *is* an art.

Meaning in architecture results partly from the viewer's capacity to understand how materials and structural devices affect his perception. Conse-

quently, the following pages will be devoted to discussion of the principal ways men have built with the materials available to them. When materials were few and architectural devices limited, labor and patience were apparently abundant. Consequently, the architecture of the past offers monuments of extraordinary richness and beauty notwithstanding the fact that its creators possessed less knowledge and fewer resources than we do. Today, engineering knowledge is immense and the variety of materials is almost bewildering. But labor is costly and not always very skilled; also, we are impatient to complete our building projects—and impatient to tear them down after a few years. Consequently, when we see a magnificent modern space, it represents not only an architectural achievement but also a triumph over an array of social and economic obstacles which were probably never imagined by Egyptian pharaohs, Athenian aristocrats, Roman emperors, medieval bishops, Florentine bankers, or absolute kings.

The Classic Materials

The earliest builders used construction materials which were close at hand and in good supply. Then as now, building devices and techniques resulted from a combination of human ingenuity and the inherent possibilities of available material. The African villager today builds his hut with sticks and grass because vegetable fibers are the most profuse material in his environment. For the same reason, the Eskimo builds an igloo of ice when he settles down for the winter. When on

the move, he makes shelter from reindeer skins and bone much as the American Indian used to fashion his teepee of wooden poles and animal hides. The humble igloo is a domical structure resting over an excavation in the ice, solving in its modest way the same problem Michelangelo's dome of St. Peter's does; and the Indian's conical teepee may be preferable as portable housing and as architectural form to the modern auto trailer. The African hut of grass and twigs often consists of a cone-shaped roof resting on cylindrical walls. Its materials may be primitive, but their geometric form is, from a modern standpoint, quite sophisticated.

During the great periods of Egyptian and Greek architecture, stone grew to be the favored material as the tools for quarrying, transporting, and erecting it were developed. But the Mesopotamians, having little stone, used brick and glazed tile for building. In most places, however, wood probably preceded stone and mud as a structural material, or at least it was used as the supporting framework for "curtain-wall" surfaces of vegetable fiber and mud. Early men used stone for religious and commemorative purposes as in their mighty *menhir* statues (upright stones serving as homes for departed souls) and *dolmens* ("table" slabs set on upright supporting stones and serving either as altars or as open tombs). Such stone arrangements, which must have involved enormous energy expenditures and engineering difficulties for prehistoric men, found more complex expression in the *cromlechs* at Carnac and Stonehenge. Cromlechs were circular arrangements of menhirs around a dolmen, which could have served as a primitive type of altar. The total plan of this organization of stone, with its axis, regular spacings, and orientation toward the sun, prefigured later architectural developments such as the temple, the amphitheater, and the cathedral.

It is important to recognize ecological influences on the beginnings of architecture. Egypt had not only an abundance of stone but also a great river, the Nile, along which heavy stone could be carried to construction sites. The wood of native palm trees was not very strong and the importation of bet-

ter woods was too expensive. Hence, the Egyptians used stone roof lintels rather than timbered ceilings. As a result, their interior spaces look like forests of massive columns, since stone cannot span a very wide space. Understandably, Egyptian architecture favors tall, narrow spaces. Of course, the passageways inside the pyramids had to be narrow because of the enormous weight overhead. In effect, their vaunted pyramids were virtually solid volumes surrounding a relatively small space for the king's burial chamber. The Egyptians built with monoliths that for size, hardness, and weight would be rejected by contemporary builders, despite the mechanical aids at our disposal. But the Egyptian builder, who worked with little more than the lever, the pulley, and the inclined plane, had, in his slaves,

Stonehenge. (c. 1800–1400 B.C.), left. Photo British Travel Association.

Aerial view of Stonehenge, right. Photo, British Information Services.

Model of Hypostyle Hall, Temple of Karnak, Egypt (1350–1205 B.C.). Courtesy The Metropolitan Museum of Art, purchase, 1890, Levi Hale Willard bequest.

SMITH & WILLIAMS, church in California City, California (1964) [whole and detail of plywood supports]. Courtesy Smith & Williams, Architects and Engineers.

thousands of efficient human engines. For the Pharaohs, it was economical to raise grain in the fertile Nile valley, feed it to human beings, and exploit their labor for a lifetime greater than that of a modern machine. *Our* civilization would rather convert the grain to alcohol and use it as fuel to operate machines devised by the creativity of people released from animal toil.

Following is a brief survey of the classic materials—wood, stone, and brick—with observations on their working properties, principal advantages, and liabilities.

WOOD

Wood appears in nature as a working, structural material rather than as an inert, mass material like stone. Its wide distribution in all but the most arid regions, and its strength, ease of handling, and adaptability to a variety of tooling enable it to compete successfully with many specialized materials. Wood can serve as a covering surface as well as a structural member. The variety of its grain, the principal source of the beauty of wood, also accounts for its structural unreliability. In its natural state, wood varies in strength; consequently, wood construction requires inefficient safety factors: larger dimensions than would seem needed, and frequent reinforcement to defend against failure due to hidden defects. Recently, lumber manufacturers have developed scientific methods of grading lumber reliably, eliminating much of the uncertainty about the inner structure of each board. Their efforts should result in substantial modification in the design of American houses, which are usually built by the balloon-frame method,

using far more lumber than is really necessary. The typical wall made of two-by-four studs spaced at sixteen-inch intervals is not only wasteful of lumber, but it also inhibits open and flexible design.

American building has always been lavish in its use of wood, but design considerations, the disappearance of the frontier, prudent conservation practices, and the development of competing materials will probably reduce at least the excessive and ill-considered uses of wood. Furthermore, wood has distinct disadvantages. It is combustible. What must have been magnificent Japanese temples and Scandinavian churches are lost to us because of fire. Besides, wood is highly responsive to temperature and moisture changes: It warps. Therefore, its dimensions are not stable; Nails shift and slip as the wood in which they are embedded dries out and shrinks; wooden joints loosen; furthermore, as an organic material, wood is subject to attack by rot, fungus, and insects.

Some of these liabilities have been overcome by technology. Plywood, for example, is a remarkable building material. It is made of sheets, or veneers, of wood glued together at right angles, thus virtually cancelling out the tendency to warp. The veneers, made by a rotary shaving of the log, constitute a very economical use of the raw material. Plywood is more consistently uniform in strength than natural wood and, as we know, can be molded and stamped into complex shapes. It can be used in skeletal structures or in stressed skin and shell structures. Wood in general is remarkably light for its strength; for plywood, the ratio between strength and weight is even better than that of steel. Consequently, in the construction of small and medium buildings, boats, and aircraft, where strength and lightness are desired as well as resistance to chemical and insect attack, plywood is very useful to designers. Laminated wooden beams (to be discussed below) create a vast new array of architectural possibilities. Indeed, plywood, molded wood, and pressed wood, or fiber-board, constitute wholly new materials which use trees as a raw material much as perfumes or synthetic rubber employ coal or petroleum.

STONE

Men originally found shelter under stone ledges and in the mouths of caves. Later they dwelt in circular holes in the ground, protected by a low wall made of piled stones which was surmounted by a roof of sticks and pine branches. They used stone for their earliest tools and weapons and kindled their first fires within stone enclosures. The stone fireplace is still a symbol of warmth and safety in dwellings otherwise bearing no resemblance to a cave. Heavy, resistant, but virtually indestructible, stone was probably the first material erected by early man to commemorate the dead, to express his belief that powerful personalities live on. But erecting monoliths or piling up stones was not building. Construction with stone began with the building of the so-called Cyclopean walls—made by placing rough stones on top of each other (as in dry-wall masonry today), a type of masonry in which sheer weight and bulk produce a crude form of stability. When satisfactory cutting tools were developed, it became possible to shape stones, to fit them accurately together,

to create true masonry. It was then feasible to build stone shelters not only for the dead, but for the living as well.

The earliest construction employed no mortar. In most of the ancient civilizations, instead, stone and marble blocks were fitted together with great skill and accuracy. A knife could not be inserted into the joints of the masonry used to face the Pyramids. The same can be said of stone walls built by the Incas of Peru. Since the Greeks did not develop mortar until the Hellenistic period, in the classic monuments of the Acropolis they used metal dowels and clamps to prevent any shifting of the marble. But their engineering and craftsmanship, based on fundamentally simple structural devices, produced virtually immovable structures. Stone masonry employing mortar has additional assets: It does not require the extraordinary precision of dry masonry, and it offers greater resistance to shifting. The weight and bulk of stones joined together by mortar create a structural fabric of tremendous durability. While stone and mortar may chip or erode somewhat over the

Ruins of the seventeenth-century Spanish mission at Abo, New Mexico, exhibit thick-walled rubble masonry construction similiar to that of the Romanesque churches of medieval Europe.

Abo ruin. Photo, John V. Young, Los Alamos, New Mexico.

years, the walls they create are likely to survive indefinitely if placed on a sound foundation and protected from human depradation.

But stone is heavy, costly to quarry and transport, and expensive to erect. Like brick, it is rarely used in modern building as a structural material: Stone and marble veneers are laid over structures of steel, concrete, or cinder block. As such, stone masonry becomes a cosmetic operation—a far cry from the pure stone engineering of the Parthenon, the great pyramids, or the Gothic cathedral. The Romans may have been the first large-scale builders to face brick or rubble masonry with stone or marble slabs. Babylonians used what little stone they could secure for statuary, but followed a practice similar in principle to veneering by facing brick walls at key locations with glazed tiles assembled in the form of large, colored reliefs.

The prestige of stone today is such that great cities and important buildings must exhibit a large expanse of it, even if some commoner material lies beneath. The Sam Rayburn House Office Building for the House of Representatives in Washington, D.C. cost some 80 or 100 millions of dollars; much of that expense was due to the mountains of marble and limestone required to clothe its steel and concrete fundament. Almost universally regarded as an architectural disaster,° the building is, hopefully, the last governmental structure which endeavors to overcome the defects of unimaginative design with simulated classical masonry. The United Nations Building, on the other hand, employs marble veneers on its end walls more honestly. Authentic stone masonry could never reach that high in a single plane: The marble quite frankly declares that it is a thin, crystalline covering that accents the severe planarity of the tall, slab-like building.

The outstanding characteristic of stone is its great strength in compression and its relative weakness in tension. Classical building took advantage of this compressive strength by creating structural systems which consisted essentially of one stone resting on top of another. The load was almost always transferred directly downward. But stone walls must be very thick to support their own weight and yet remain stable. Any substantial height calls for the kind of reinforcement and buttressing so marvelously developed in Gothic architecture. Indeed, the great achievement of Gothic engineering was to transfer heavy roof loads to the ground by multiplying the paths they could take downward. Small stones and mortar used in the arch and flying buttress enabled stresses to

The Sam Rayburn House Office Building, Washington, D.C. (1965), left. Photo, United Press International.

WALLACE K. HARRISON and others, permanent headquarters of the United Nations in New York (1949), right. Photo, United Nations.

° ". . . not only the most expensive building of its kind in the world but probably also its ugliest." Wolf von Eckardt, *Saturday Review,* May 23, 1964, p. 23.

be carried away horizontally to piers located some distance from the wall. Later, a massive, load-bearing wall became unnecessary: Weight could be concentrated in the piers and pilasters alone. But achieving the greater height of modern buildings with stone walls, columns, piers, and pilasters would call for impossible thicknesses regardless of transverse buttressing. Notwithstanding the engineering superiority of the stone arch to the stone post and lintel, pure masonry construction is limited by the very quality which accounts for its stability—weight. The loads on bearing walls and columns of stone build up too quickly. Today, when "Gothic style" churches are built, their characteristic forms cover "working" structures of steel and reinforced concrete. "Collegiate" Gothic libraries and towers are usually air-conditioned shams from the standpoint of architectural structure. And yet, this reluctance to abandon the appearance of masonry, even when structural deceit is called for, reveals the extraordinary sense of satisfaction men derive from a building system of stone piled on stone. Let the stone be expensive and damp; let it cover electrical conduits and steel reinforcing rods unimagined by the medieval Abbot Suger; let elevator shafts be hidden behind compound piers while the clatter of IBM machines is heard in the side aisles; memory and imagination will nevertheless feel life in the stone ribs, warmth in the slanting light, and protection under the vaulted ceilings.

BRICK

Lacking fuel to fire brick, and living in an arid land where wood was scarce, the Sumerians made sun-dried bricks much like the adobe bricks of the Southwestern American Indians. Even in a relatively dry climate, however, the so-called "mud-brick" wall is subject to erosion and needs to be repaired or replaced regularly. Fired brick, however, constitutes one of the earliest of manufactured materials. (Prefabrication in building began when bricks made in a distant brickyard were transported to the construction site.) It is really a type of artificial stone—not "reconstituted stone" as Le Corbusier designated concrete—but a truly artificial, man-made type of stone which has several advantages over natural stone: standardized dimensions, uniform quality, variation in shape and size within the limits of hand use, strength and lightness, wide range of color and texture, and adaptability to mass-production manufacture from inexpensive raw materials—clay or clay-and-concrete mixtures.

Since brick is usually made of clay fired in a kiln, it is a ceramic material and tends to resemble a ceramic mosaic when laid up in a wall. But a mosaic is a type of wall "painting" whereas brick is a structural material capable of constituting the wall itself. Today it is most commonly used as a brick veneer—that is, it is really employed as a mosaic applied to a wall built of some

PIETER BRUEGEL (the Elder), *Tower of Babel* (1563). Courtesy Kunsthistorisches Museum, Vienna.

Spiral minaret of Samarra (ninth century). Courtesy Ministry of Culture and Guidance, Baghdad.

other structural material. For modern usage, then, brickwork is valued for its textural and coloristic properties—its painterly qualities—as well as for its remembered association with the hand-fabricated wall. Because it is such an ancient material, brick confers familiarity and acceptability on architectural forms which would otherwise seem unconventional. Its warm colors and its weather- and fire-resistant qualities inspire confidence. The viewer also knows that a brick wall has been laboriously built, so that costliness as well as durability seem to characterize brick masonry even though clay is a cheap and common substance.

The mortar joints of brick masonry constitute one growing disadvantage of the material: Brick masonry is expensive, especially where skilled labor is costly. A large proportion of the area of a brick wall consists of mortar joints which require careful hand labor, and mortar joints are also subject to far more shrinkage than the brick itself, which is fairly stable. Finally, a brick wall is fabricated slowly; for tall build-

ings, an elaborate scaffolding is required by the workmen. That is why metal panels are being used increasingly for the exterior walls of large structures. Bricks offers good sound insulation but tends to transmit dampness, as does stone, unless combined with additional insulating material.

Using mud bricks which had little strength in compression or tension, the Babylonians built their ziggurats (huge, stepped, pyramidal structures with a shrine at the top) with heavy walls as much as twenty-eight feet thick. The massiveness of the biblical Tower of Babel was really necessary to compensate for the structural weakness of sun-dried bricks as well as to create a mountain top where, it was believed, the gods dwelt.

Such man-made mountains on the plains of Sumer, like the pyramids in the valley of the Nile, were also expressions of the monstrous egotism of ancient despots. Even then, the attempt to reach the sky by piling up mountains of masonry symbolized "towering" pride, not to mention limited architectural imagination. The ziggurats of today—our own setback skyscrapers—have different origins: high land values, steel-frame construction, high-speed elevators, and, in the case of Manhattan, a bed of solid rock which makes an excellent foundation for high-rise structures.*

In the stone and brick architecture of Egypt and Babylonia, the amount of interior space compared to the

*The "setback" restrictions on American skyscrapers were presumably intended to let light into the street, although they also reflected economic and aesthetic considerations. For a full discussion, see John Burchard and Albert Bush-Brown, *The Architecture of America*, Little, Brown, 1961, pp. 348–351.

amount of exterior volume was exceedingly low. Such construction seems to us not only inefficient from the standpoint of labor and material, but also appalling in its social and political implications. Perhaps the ratio of interior space to exterior volume in the architecture of any civilization is an index of the freedom of its people. Slave labor inhibits architectural imagination whereas today's light and thin-walled buildings create interior space almost equal to the volume of the whole—a remarkable triumph of engineering. Aside from aesthetics, such structures may reveal the sort of valuation our civilization places on human labor, since they reflect, in part, a response to the high wages paid in the construction industry. But does our architecture indicate a major concern for human skill and personality, or does it merely seek to avoid the costs of handcraft for economic reasons, finding answers in prefabrication and mechanization to the problems of constructing buildings quickly and creating inexpensive space?

To say that wood, stone, and brick are classic materials does not imply that they have been totally displaced in contemporary architecture. They continue to be used, but less frequently for structural reasons. Their contribution is now aesthetic and symbolic, since they have been divested, in most cases, of their weight-bearing and space-enclosing function. The classic materials may linger a while in the intimacy of the domestic dwelling. But even there, glass, steel, aluminum, and plastics yet unheard of will probably supplant them in their structural role. When a material begins to be simulated, when it becomes part of the vocabulary of "interior decoration," its structural career can be considered waning if not finished. Now that marble, stone, brick masonry, and wood graining can be convincingly imitated, we shall not long see the classic materials performing their authentic roles except in museum restorations and in monuments which society has the good sense to preserve.

Modern Materials

Steel, concrete, and glass are, of course, old materials, but their structural use in architecture is comparatively new. The Romans mixed stone rubble with mortar in the construction of walls, a practice which was really an extension of masonry. But the use of *poured* or *cast* concrete, reinforced with steel rods, is entirely different from stone masonry. Similarly, the tempered-steel weaponry of medieval warriors has little in common with the rolled-steel I-beams which make modern steel-frame construction possible. And the lovely opalescent glass bottles of ancient Egypt are only distantly related to the large sheets of plate glass which fill rectangular openings in cage structures today.

Architecture has been radically transformed by these "new" materials because, in the case of glass and steel, the specialized techniques of mass manufacture produce a superior product, on a large scale, and at reasonable cost. Factory manufacture and prefabrication

The prefabrication of complex architectural forms now replaces many laborious and time-consuming operations formerly performed on the site.

Tecfab Industries Plant, concrete section (1965), left. Courtesy Tecfab Industries, North Arlington, New Jersey.

The versatility of concrete is demonstrated in this church whose seemingly precarious support is a strong and graceful hyperbolic paraboloid form springing from a single ferroconcrete post.

KIRK, WALLACE, McKINLEY, Church of the Good Shepherd (1964), center. Courtesy Church of the Good Shepherd, Swedenborgian, Bellevue, Wash.

Reinforced concrete rooms, cast on this site, are lifted into place at a housing project in Israel.

Prefabricated stack houses in Israel housing project (1965), right. Photo, Michael Maor, Jerusalem.

Laminated wood beams.

The shrine chapel of Our Lady of Orchard Lake (1963). Courtesy National Gypsum Company.

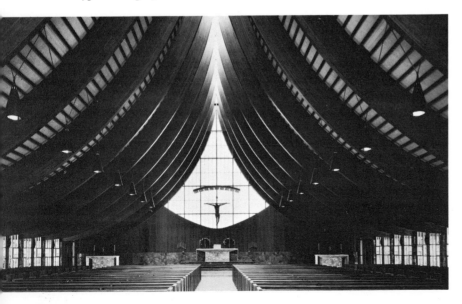

reduce costs and improve quality, while the handcraft operations which still survive in building are often associated with waste of materials, uneven quality, and frequent delays and confusion. Reinforced concrete structures are usually fashioned at the building site although some prestressed concrete beams and slabs are factory-produced like steel beams to standard size and strength specifications. But ferroconcrete fabrication at the site is not a handcraft process in the classical sense; it is better described as a collective manufacturing operation, the plywood forms and steel rods being set locally while concrete mixed in transit to precise engineering specifications is brought in from a plant which may be several miles distant.

Laminated wooden beams have to be manufactured in a factory and carried to the site. Here again, the techniques of bending and glueing wood were known to tradition. But the older, animal-skin glues cannot compare with today's powerful adhesives. As a result we possess the technology to exploit the lightness, strength, and resilience of wood in continuously curved, load-bearing members of considerable beauty and grace. They permit the spanning of good-sized spaces without interior supports, creating some of the dramatic structural excitement of Gothic stone arches. Laminated beams and arches are monolithic members, hence can be erected by cranes, thus avoiding the complex scaffolding of stone masonry. And they can be chemically treated to make them fire-resistant although not fire-proof. The warmth of wood, the pattern of its grain, and the rhythmic effect created by the repeated laminations, make such beams attractive and practical devices for homes, churches, auditoriums, shops, and so on. They show that prefabricated materials are compatible with architectural excellence; mass-produced structural devices can be visually exposed without the application of handmade cosmetics if the designer is sensitive to their distinctive qualities.

Prefabrication of building materials and industrial production of whole buildings or of large, interchangeable building units has steadily advanced—both in quality and amount—during recent decades. Many of the new products used for wall partitions, roofing, insulation, and utilities have been developed in the course of mechanizing and industrializing architecture. Plastic tubing replaces copper and cast-iron piping; various new exterior wall- and partition-"sandwiches" replace the old masonry, lath, and plaster walls. These "substitutes" may or may not be qualitatively superior to the materials they supplant. It is certain, however, that their development is substantially due to the inertia and resistance to innovation of the building industry. Here, architecture is inevitably influenced by social and economic factors. Trade unions, lending institutions, municipalities, federal government agencies, manufacturers associations, and a host of others are interested in building materials and construction methods. Frequently they exercise restraints through building codes which necessarily affect design and the total character of architecture. The costs of land, the availability of credit, the rate of amortization, subsidies for housing, the selection of builders, the award of construction contracts—all of these nonarchitectural factors have an ultimate bearing on materials, design, and the quality of construction that goes into a building. Therefore, the materials of modern architecture not only constitute the bricks and mortar of structures, but they also provide a reflection of the society which develops and uses them.

CAST IRON

Cast iron, the first metal substitute for wooden posts and stone columns, has some characteristics similar to stone: great compressive strength, brittleness, heavy weight, and hidden internal flaws or strains which develop as the molten iron cools in its mold. Nevertheless, the second half of the nineteenth century saw the construction of magnificent and often exceedingly delicate structures built with prefabricated cast-iron columns and beams. They were often manufactured by a resourceful American promoter of prefabricated construction, James Bogardus, or sometimes by his competitors. They tended to imitate the stone masonry of Italian Renaissance buildings, hence the palatial magnificence of the facades for factories, shops, and warehouses built in

J. P. GAYNOR, The Haughwout Building (1857), left. Photo, H. Rinehart.

GEORGE HERBERT WYMAN, Bradbury Building (1893) [interior], right.

lower Manhattan in the 1850's and now, alas, threatened with extinction. The Haughwout Store, designed by J. P. Gaynor and erected in 1857, was a cast-iron version of a Venetian palazzo, but today it faces demolition to make way for a major expressway. The Bradbury Building in Los Angeles, designed by G. H. Wyman in 1893, is chronically in danger of destruction and yet it ought to be preserved, not only for historical reasons, but to show the delicacy of wrought iron in the hands of a gifted designer and the splendid lightness and openness of interior space which Wyman could achieve at a time when the rusticated Romanesque masonry of H. H. Richardson was very popular.

Cast iron set the stage for steel-skeleton construction in a number of nineteenth-century railroad sheds, exhibition halls, libraries, market halls, and so on. Bridge engineers appreciated iron and steel better than architects, who used iron structurally (as in the dome of the Capitol in Washington) but made sure to conceal it. Even today, few designers are willing to expose steel structural members if it can be avoided. When cast iron was brought out of hiding by nineteenth-century designers, it was

often given some sculptural form based on work in stone or wood which branded it forever as a utilitarian but aesthetically inferior material. Unlike steel, which usually is employed by engineers and architects in a straightforward manner (that is, in the form of the process of rolling or extruding which shapes it), cast iron lends itself to a variety of derivative and uncongenial shapes. Since it is a plastic material like concrete, though capable of being modeled in greater detail, it has been fair game for some questionable sculptural impulses. The Paris Métro Stations by Hector Guimard (see pp. 78–79) and the ornamental cast-iron columns, bannisters, and canopies by the other Art Nouveau designers show how the material can imitate terra-cotta panels or high-Gothic stone filigree. On the other hand, engineers like Joseph Paxton, John Roebling, and Gustave Eiffel were among the most clear-sighted designers with metal in the nineteenth century. Henri Labrouste (1801–75), designer of the Library of Sainte-Geneviève (1843–50) and the Bibliothèque Nationale (1858–68), both in Paris, was unusual in that his career combined conventional Beaux Arts training in architecture with an advanced and original mastery of cast-iron engineering.

John Roebling's Brooklyn Bridge (1867–83) made use of the compressive strength of stone masonry for its massive piers, while demonstrating a dramatic new combination of delicacy and strength in its steel suspension cables. Roebling (1806–1869) pioneered in the development of data for suspension bridges, but his contribution to architecture lay in his design of a metal structure whose elegance stirred men's imaginations and emotions while it also performed its practical function superbly.

The soaring and graceful qualities of the bridge grow out of the magnificent curves of the supporting cables and the vertical web of spun steel strands which carry the deck. Perhaps admiration for the venerable shape of the arch explains the extraordinary affection in which suspension bridges are still held. The great Spanish structural engineer Eduardo Torroja° compares the suspension bridge to a reversed arch, the piers serving as posts, while the deck, suspended from the crown of the arch formed by the cables, corresponds visually to the tie rod sometimes used

° Eduardo Torroja, *Philosophy of Structures*, University of California Press, 1958, pp. 207–8.

to counteract lateral thrusts in a conventional arch.

Although suspension bridges made of wood and rope may have been used in Asia thousands of years ago, the nineteenth-century development of suspension engineering, so dramatically advanced by Roebling, revealed the distinctive structural and aesthetic possibilities latent in metal under tension. In the twentieth century, designers like Pier Luigi Nervi (1891–   ) and Eero Saarinen would employ suspension engineering daringly to create architectural space.

The Crystal Palace (1851) owed its originality in material and construc-

HENRI LABROUSTE, reading room of Bibliothèque Sainte Geneviève (1843–50), left. Courtesy Caisse Nationale des Monuments Historiques.

JOHN ROEBLING and A. WASHINGTON, Brooklyn Bridge (1867–83), right. From the collection of the Library of Congress.

EERO SAARINEN AND ASSOCIATES, Dulles Airport, Washington (1962), left. [interior]. Photo, © Ezra Stoller Associates.

PIER LUIGI NERVI, Burgo Paper Mill (1964), center and right [detail]. Courtesy Studio Nervi.

JOSEPH PAXTON, Crystal Palace, Hyde Park, London (1851). Courtesy British Information Services.

DUTERT & CONTAMIN, Halle des Machines (1889), left. From Nikolaus Pevsner, *Pioneers of Modern Design;* courtesy the publishers, Penguin Books, Ltd.

GUSTAVE EIFFEL, Eiffel Tower (1889), right. Courtesy French Embassy Press and Information Division.

tion to the fact that its designer was not formally trained as an architect, hence did not have to overcome the Beaux Arts addiction to classical construction methods and canons of style. Joseph Paxton (1801–1865) had design experience in building large greenhouses. His structure for the London Exposition in 1851 consisted almost exclusively of prefabricated wrought- and cast-iron units and glass panes, manufactured throughout England, and bolted together on the site, one story at a time. The Crys-

tal Palace was the largest building in the world, enclosing seventeen acres under one roof. Yet it was constructed in six months, easily dismantled when the Exposition was over, and erected again at another site, where it stood until 1935. The construction method and the use of an iron skeleton anticipated the present-day bolting, riveting, and welding of prefabricated steel girders into a cage-like structure. Manufacture of standardized parts for on-site assembly was shown to be practical and economical. Masonry vaults and domes whose strength depended on mass and, as in St. Peter's, on ten iron chains embedded in their mortar, could be supplanted eventually by thin membranes of concrete or glass. Strength could be achieved by substituting lightness and precision for heaviness and bulk. Although nineteenth-century critics like Ruskin did not realize it, the architecture of large spaces would never be the same.

The Eiffel Tower in Paris, built like Paxton's Crystal Palace for a large industrial exposition (1889), was made of wrought iron. Even though steel produced by the Bessemer process was available, Gustave Eiffel (1832–1923) built with iron since he lacked enough data about steel performance for highrise structures. (Nevertheless, his fellow designers at the exposition, Dutert and Contamin, constructed the immense Halle des Machines using steel in arched trusses.) For the same reason, Eiffel used masonry rather than reinforced concrete for the foundations. In his specifications, however, he anticipated steel-girder and ferroconcrete construction. His boldness lay in erecting an open structure without the expected masonry facade— a boldness for which he was severely criticized. Nevertheless, the thousand-foot tower went up, despite objections from leading architects and artists, and became one of the most popular symbols of Paris. The entire structure was prefabricated and was assembled by only one-hundred-fifty men using scaffolds, winches, and rigging designed by Eiffel. The project was completed without accident in seventeen months and established a crucial precedent for skyscraper architecture.

STRUCTURAL STEEL

Much of the distinguished work of the "Chicago School" of architecture, leading to the development of the skyscraper, was carried out with wrought-iron or rolled-iron framework. Rolled-iron "I" beams were a vast improvement over the cast-iron columns so extensively used in American commercial architecture earlier in the century. The principles of skeleton construction, known in the 1890's as "Chicago construction," were developed with iron. But iron is not as strong as steel (particularly under tension), hence its members cannot be as slender as steel girders. High-rise structures (above twelve or fifteen storeys) could be built with iron, but not as economically as with steel. Consequently, steel has almost completely replaced iron in modern construction.

The cost of steel per pound, however, is higher than that of any other structural material. And, since steel has high tensile strength, rolled steelplate beams are designed in shapes which exploit that strength while keeping weight and cost to a minimum. The I-shaped beam is most common because the vertical section can be quite thin while resisting any force which seeks to bend it, and the horizontal flanges defend the beam against lateral bending. But large structural members, such as trusses and built-up girders, cannot be manufactured in the form of a single rolled steel beam. They must be assembled, usually in the form of lattice work, to keep the weight of the member down and to take advantage of the tensile properties of the material. The visual result, as seen in bridges, factories, elevated railroads and highways, airplane hangers, and the like, is of complex geometric openings and web-like patterns of metal. Viewed from a distance, the poetry of steel construction is often very striking, as in the Golden Gate Bridge, for example. When seen up close, however, steel construction often appears crude and brutally harsh, because designers must work with standardized rolled-steel shapes. In addition, the common methods of fastening steel—riveting and bolting—further limit the designer in that he must organize connections and joints so that construction men will have adequate space to work on

JOSEPH B. STRAUSS (chief engineer), Golden Gate Bridge, San Francisco (1933-37). Courtesy American Airlines.

them. Open steel work must be painted periodically to prevent rusting, consequently, finished structures expose their bolts, rivets, and methods of assembly with more frankness than is evident in other construction methods. Notwithstanding the value placed on structural honesty and the general antagonism to concealment or embellishment, steel construction often exhibits an almost deliberate indifference to aesthetic effect. Indeed, when we think of engineering as inhospitable to art, we probably have reference to the insistently technical, defiantly ugly character of some highly visible steel structures.

But the technology of steel manufacture and fabrication advances in response both to the competition of other structural metals—notably aluminum—and the requirements of designers.

A joint of the Eiffel Tower, above top.

EDUARDO TORROJA, a joint of the Tordera Bridge, above bottom. From Eduardo Torroja, *Philosophy of Structures;* courtesy the publishers, University of California Press.

LUDWIG MIES VAN DER ROHE, Crown Hall (1952), at right. Courtesy Illinois Institute of Technology.

PAUL SCHWEIKHER, Fine Arts Center, Maryville College (1950), below. Courtesy Maryville College, Maryville, Tennessee.

Welded connections may eventually yield cleaner joints and greater continuity within a structural system. Tubular, extruded, and corrugated steel products may open up new formal possibilities. Nevertheless, covering steel with a skin of another material will probably continue to be practiced because it is so difficult to achieve appealing surfaces with the material although it remains indispensable for many structures.

A few architects have successfully exposed steel members, thus converting a practical necessity into an aesthetic asset. In Maryville College, Maryville, Tennessee, the designer, Paul Schweikher (1903–   ), has shown how exposed steel I-beams can be exploited to give linear emphasis to large planes of brick masonry. And Crown Hall at the Illinois Institute of Technology, by Mies van der Rohe, is a brilliant demonstration not only of exposed steel but also of structural function in the suspended roof. The rolled-steel I-beam, of course, offers a precise edge and a clean surface—qualities difficult to obtain in the lacy webs of built-up girders and latticework trusses. That open steelwork looks better at a distance suggests that the color, texture, and joinery are mainly responsible for its poor aesthetic performance. Perhaps metallic sculpture can serve as a type of experimentation with the aesthetics of form and fabrication in steel. Admittedly, such sculpture does not confront the problems of scale and engineering encountered in architecture. But experiments and pilot projects are usually conducted on a small scale and with variable factors limited. At present, the example set by metal sculpture (often inspired by architectural forms) may be partly responsible for our feelings of dissatisfaction with open steel construction which is not carefully handled.

Furthermore, the essentially technical and aesthetically indifferent character of steel is responsible for the anonymous quality of so many modern buildings, the Seagram building and Lever House being conspicuous exceptions. In general, the very versatility of the steel frame has placed designers in a quandary. So far as the skyscraper is concerned, they do not know whether to emphasize its verticality or horizontality. Should it resemble a slab, a honeycomb, or a crystal? Is it an obelisk or a layer cake? As a young man, Mies proposed a circular steel-and-glass skyscraper. More recently, Gropius collaborated in the design of the Pan Am building, a huge slab with tapered ends. But the building is not considered a brilliant success. The glass skyscraper proposal of Mies was not accepted, although other circular towers have since been built, and they have not been highly admired either. Perhaps we have been overconditioned to the rectilinearity imposed by rolled steel girders to accept rounded towers gladly. At any rate, major construction in steel proceeds furiously in a variety of directions, with the Miesian rectilinear idiom dominating high-rise architecture. But when horizontal space is available, when the problem is an arena, a library, a chapel, or an airport, the most exciting buildings seem to be made of reinforced concrete.

REINFORCED CONCRETE

Although the Romans developed a mortar based on volcanic ash, it was not until 1824 that the first Portland cement was produced by Joseph Aspdin in

LUDWIG MIES VAN DER ROHE, circular glass skyscraper (1920–21 project), left. Photo, Hedrich-Blessing.

DEETER-RICHEY-SIPPEL (architects), circular dormitories, University of Pittsburgh (1963), right. Courtesy University of Pittsburgh.

Leeds, England. In 1868, a French gardener, Jacques Monier, hit on the idea of reinforcing concrete flower pots with a web of wire, thus creating a small-scale reinforced structure. However, reinforced concrete, or ferroconcrete, was not widely employed as a building material until the 1890's. As mentioned earlier, Eiffel was reluctant to use it for the foundations of his tower, although he contrived a similar result through wrought-iron bars embedded in masonry piers, thus joining the superstructure to its foundations. The development of reliable performance criteria for ferroconcrete is generally credited to two French engineers, Hennebique and Coignet; and two other Frenchmen, Perret and Garnier, pioneered the use of ferroconcrete in the skeletons of buildings as well as in their membranes. But once again, an engineer—a Swiss, Robert Maillart (1872–1940)—best exploited the plastic quality of the material for bridges, reducing the thickness of concrete beams so that they became slabs, and then bending or warping the plane

ROBERT MAILLART, Schwandbach Bridge (1933). Reprinted by permission of the publishers from Sigfried Giedion, *Space, Time and Architecture,* Harvard University Press, Cambridge, Massachusetts, Copyright 1941, 1949, 1954, 1962, by the President and Fellows of Harvard College.

ANDRÉ MORISSEAU, marketplace in Royan, France (1958). Courtesy the architect.

of the slab to produce structural forms of great sculptural beauty and precision.

The continuously curved and warped ferroconcrete slab results in a structural member which does not imitate masonry, wood, or metal. Since complex stress patterns are distributed throughout the slab, there is *no distinct break between the functions of supporting and being supported.* Thus, the curved ferroconcrete slab is the logical and organic fulfillment of older types of supporting structure. It also is vastly more efficient than stone-masonry piers and arches, while serving as an exceedingly versatile structural device.

Although curved slabs and shells enclose space in a manner which is efficient and pleasing, their curves must be correct from an engineering standpoint. The distribution of reinforcing rods as well as their thickness and shape must be confirmed by testing and by mathematical calculation. But it is worth noting that as engineering criteria are refined and perfected, their visual results tend to approximate natural forms. The egg shell, for example, is one of the strongest and most beautiful of natural containers because its curvature constitutes the simplest, most efficient, and accurate relationship between its

contents, the shell material, and the environment. Consequently, it is interesting that some of the most dramatic ferroconcrete structures exhibit curves which resemble organic forms such as one sees in sea shells, honeycombs, mushrooms, tree limbs, soap bubbles, coral, and so on.

It is generally conceded that the joints are the weakest points in classical structures: They are the places where loads frequently change direction and where a multitude of complex stresses are situated. One of the assets of the curved ferroconcrete member consists in its virtual elimination of such joints. As with the egg shell, loads are distributed over the entire fabric rather than concentrated at particular points. This feat is accomplished by locating the steel rods at the points of greatest tensile stress, that is, the points where the concrete particles would tend to tear or pull apart. The concrete is thickest at points of greatest compression, that is, places where the particles would tend to be crushed, causing the member to fracture. The steel rods are covered with sufficient concrete to prevent rusting, and they are given slight irregularities of surface to prevent slippage after the concrete is hardened and subjected to a live load. As a result, ferroconcrete possesses the virtues of steel *and* of stone without their disadvantages. Stresses are transferred back and forth between the two materials. A slab of ferroconcrete can span a much greater space than a stone slab which is subject, over any large span, to breakage from its own weight. The slab can also support more weight at less cost than rolled steel, which is subject to deformation and failure under high compressive loads. Steel surpasses ferroconcrete when light weight is essential, as in a suspension bridge. Concrete, however, is fire-resistant whereas steel is not. Steel does not, of course, feed flame itself, but exposed steel will twist, deform, and fail when exposed to intense heat. Consequently, most building codes require that steel skeletons be covered with insulation such as firebrick or poured concrete.

Aside from its practical advantages, ferroconcrete appeals to the designer because it is not usually manufactured in standardized shapes and sizes. It must be designed for a specific structure and usually manufactured at the site. The designer can choose among several structural solutions and he can also give expression to his forming and shaping impulses. Of course, his sculptural aspirations are limited by the wooden forms which can be built, the setting of the steel rods, and the process of placing the concrete. As the technology of ferroconcrete is advanced, more and more is known about the interactions between the steel and concrete; the size of the stone aggregates and the amounts of mortar needed to bind them together; and the usefulness of additives which lower weight, speed drying, add color, or transmit light. Such knowledge not only permits the designer to work with greater precision and certainty, but also enlarges the range of potential aesthetic effect.

One of the supposed disadvantages of concrete, reinforced or not, is its alleged unsuitability as a surface material. Many architects use concrete for structural purposes only, covering it with veneers of brick, stone, marble, opaque glass, metal, plastic, wood, and so on. Others try to cover it with stucco and various more-or-less ineffective concrete paints. One of the unsatisfac-

tory qualities of Wright's Guggenheim Museum (completed after his death) lies in the thin stucco covering applied to its bold, poured concrete forms. Any applied surface treatment of a Wright building is ironic since he denounced even painted wood. Could he condone painted concrete? He had shown himself an original master of surfaces in concrete-block masonry, for example— the blocks cast to his own design. But although he used ferroconcrete in the Kaufmann House and in the Guggenheim Museum, he may have felt the surfaces of brick and stone masonry more congenial. Small fissures and minor variations in the stucco do not follow the underlying concrete forms and hence the heroic effect of the structure is somewhat spoiled by what is apparently an unsatisfactory cosmetic operation. Quite possibly, the cosmetics were unneccessary. Le Corbusier, followed by many others, has shown what vitality and textural interest can be obtained by exposing the concrete aggregate and the marks of the formwork. Furthermore, rough concrete surfaces function very effectively as a foil for smooth, machine-made materials, like glass and metal, whose precise, gleaming, and reflective skins shine more brilliantly in contrast to the coarse, granular, stone-sand-and-cement mixture which constitutes concrete. Pigments added to the cement do not seem to help much. Apparently gilding and cosmetics are not the answer either.

Along with the steel-frame skeleton, ferroconcrete has revolutionized architecture by eliminating the weight-bearing masonry wall. Windows used to be small openings in a wall, openings whose width was governed by the strength of a stone or wood lintel, a metal plate, or a masonry arch. Skeleton construction combined with recessed columns permits a skin almost totally composed of glass, if the designer wishes. Such buildings as Lever House and its numerous imitators show how appealing the tinted-glass curtain wall has become. The structural revolution brought about by ferroconcrete and steel has changed many of our deep-rooted attitudes about inside and outside, privacy and exposure, skeleton and membrane. Great spaces are spanned without visible support; prodigious strength is developed without convincing bulk. But we are so accustomed to handling wood and stone that there is some tendency to feel insecure under a concrete dome whose weight is not carried down by a system of trusses and posts we can see. Perhaps these fears will be overcome in a generation of children who have seen for themselves how strong constructions can be made with folded paper, drinking straws, toothpicks, raffia, and wire.

PRESTRESSED CONCRETE

Prestressed concrete is a refinement of reinforced concrete which further strengthens the material and improves its structural performance. It involves the stretching of high-tensile steel strands within concrete forms before the concrete sets. After the concrete has bonded to the tensioned or stretched steel, the tension is released and the strands, now encased in concrete, attempt to return to their former length. As a result, the steel "squeezes" the concrete particles together. Concrete, as we know, is weak under tension, that is, it tends to crack or break when subjected to forces which seek to pull it apart. Since the bottom of any beam is under tension while the top is under compression, the bottom of concrete beams will develop cracks due to their own weight as well as the weight of a live load. (Steel beams resist forces which would pull them apart, but may deform under compressive or crushing forces which concrete would resist. In other words, a steel beam is vulnerable along its upper portion, where concrete is strong.) But prestressing gives the concrete a slight upward arch, neutralizing the beam's own weight and developing a continuous resistance to tensile forces along its bottom portion.

In practice, beams are prestressed in two ways—by *pretensioning* and *post-tensioning*. As the terms imply, the steel strands are stretched either before the concrete is poured or after it has

J. C. WOMACK (state engineer, designer), Elysian Viaduct over Arroyo Seco flood-control channel near Los Angeles (1964), left. Courtesy California Division of Highways.

S. MAYNARD LOVELL, CBE, ERD, TD (Chartered Civil Engineer), Wentbridge Viaduct (1961), center. Courtesy Ministry of Transport, Agent Authority, County Council of the West Riding of Yorkshire.

Elevated highway, Berlin (*Bundesautobahn*) (1963), right. Courtesy Der Senator für Bau- und Wohnungswesen, Berlin.

been poured and has set at a certain strength. Both methods yield the same results, but pretensioning is usually done at a plant, thus lending itself to standardization and prefabrication. Post-tensioning is usually done on the site, the steel strands being first encased in tubes or channels, especially for large and specialized beams. Sometimes the tensioning of the steel wires in post-tensioned beams is increased long after the concrete has set. This is possible if the channel around the tension wires has not been filled, or grouted, and if the anchorage at the beam ends is accessible.

Prestressing means ultimately that stresses—that is, forces within the material tending to move in certain directions—are built into concrete during the process of manufacture. They are calculated to counteract the loads and stresses which the structural member will undergo when in use. Since concrete is the heaviest of modern materials, concrete beams must support their own "dead" weight before they can begin to carry "live" loads. It is easy to see that in bridges with long spans, the dead-weight load of concrete beams would be immense. But through prestressing, the dead weight is counteracted and the strength of the beam and its built-in upward thrust can be used entirely for the support of live loads. The dead weight can then be transferred to the bridge towers or foundations.

The plastic quality of concrete, combined with the great strength of steel wire, makes prestressed concrete a superb architectural material, as is beautifully demonstrated in the work of Maillart and Freyssinet. One disadvantage of the material lies in the difficulty of tensioning wires in a member which has more than a slight curve. Conventional reinforcing rods must be used in complex or sculptural concrete forms and thus the advantages of prestressing are lost. But it is very likely that technology will find ways to prestress complex forms. In that case steel-truss construction will face a worthy aesthetic and economic competitor.

The Structural Devices

One of the aims of architecture is to enclose space. To carry out this aim, materials must be organized so that they define the space around them as inside and outside, protected and exposed.

But materials will not perform space-enclosing tasks of their own accord; and nature, in the form of gravity, tends to oppose human efforts to organize materials so that they will stand —safe, stable, and secure. Architectural structure, therefore, is the science and art of shaping, arranging, and fastening materials to resist successfully the continuous opposition of gravity, the intermittent attacks of the weather, the wear caused by human use, and the processes of fatigue and decomposition within the materials themselves.

The problem of structure is to find the best ways to pit the resistant qualities of materials against the steady, predictable force of gravity in order to produce equilibrium and stability. To show how structural devices function in this task, I devoted the previous sections to a discussion of the inherent strengths and limitations of ancient and modern materials used in building and their effects upon construction. The following section carries the discussion further into the interaction of materials and specific structural devices.

The emphasis on structure and building in this chapter should not be equated with indifference to the role of architecture as a vehicle of ideas and emotions. On the contrary, an understanding of how structures are designed and put together should enhance your capacity to experience architectural forms intelligently and with an intuitive grasp of their structural role. The meanings we discover in architecture are partly derived from our perception of buildings as symbolic configurations of form. Such perception is not highly dependent on a knowledge of structure. On the other hand, the ability to make a sound critical judgment about a building depends on a knowledge of the manner in which its materials and structure operate objectively. Since architecture is a social art, and frequently is publicly supported, such "technical" knowledge may be more vital in a civic sense than it is in painting or sculpture. Perhaps the best argument for an understanding of structure as necessary for the designer *and* the layman is that of Eduardo Torroja as follows:

This matter of the unseen thickness of dimensions is fundamental in construc-

tion. It might be said that it constitutes a fourth dimension in the interplay of volumes enclosed by the apparent enveloping surfaces. "It is this quality of depth that alone can give life to architecture," says Frank Lloyd Wright; the designer must be continually reminded of the necessity to make it easy for the viewer to sense and feel these thicknesses. The work cannot be appreciated without that "fourth dimension" essential to the nature and beauty of the whole. [*]

In another place, Torroja gives to designers advice which, with less urgency, might be useful for anyone seeking a genuine understanding of architecture:

One should become so familiar with the structure as to have the feeling of being, in full vitality and sentiment, part of it and of all its elements.

The discussion which follows constitutes only a beginning of that endeavor to "feel" structure. But you will surely improve your powers of judgment and your capacity for enjoying architecture if you carry your study of structure beyond the foundation presented here.

THE POST-AND-LINTEL

The post-and-lintel is the most ancient of construction devices and it continues to enjoy wide use today. In it, two vertical supports are bridged over by a horizontal beam. The dolmen of prehistoric man was an approximation of the post-and-lintel—the upright stones serving as posts and the horizontal table rock acting as a lintel. In this system there is a sharp and visually distinct demarcation between the supporting and the supported members. Certainly

[*] Eduardo Torroja, *Philosophy of Structures,* University of California Press, 1958, p. 273.

its clarity of function appealed to the Greeks, who were admirers of reason and clarity in all things. It was also used exclusively by the Egyptians, since the post-and-lintel is very secure and capable of withstanding great weights.

Stone, as we know, was the principal material employed in ancient post-and-lintel construction; in modern times wood-frame construction involves post-and-lintel as well as truss features. But ferroconcrete and steel are mainly used in modern post-and-lintel construction, especially in large buildings. Perhaps the contemporary architect has different motives for using this system than did ancient designers: The resolution of the principal resistant forces into vertical and horizontal components permits a high degree of rationality in the planning of space and considerable efficiency and precision in the use of materials. Further, since the structural members are very specialized, performing the function for which they are best suited, standardization makes possible prefabrication, mass production, and lowered material costs.

The post-and-lintel system is also responsible for the strong emphasis on window walls in modern building: Large openings are available for wide windows, wide vision, excellent ventilation for interiors, and generous display possibilities for outside viewers. As a result, the design of fenestration for steel-cage construction was a major architectural problem before the wide use of central air conditioning. The most common solution involved a large, fixed pane of glass in the center of each horizontal rectangle, with vertical bands of louvered windows at the sides. When supporting posts are set back from the curtain wall, no structural interruption of

Temple of Hera, Paestum (c. 460 B.C.). Photo, R. Nelson.

POST-AND-LINTEL

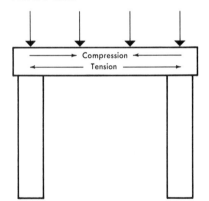

the fenestration is necessary; window design is restricted only by the optimum size of glass panes and the framework needed to hold the glass in place. The Bauhaus designed by Walter Gropius (1883–   ) in Dessau was an early instance of the use of continuous horizontal bands of glass uninterrupted by exterior posts (p. 420). This type of design became common in all kinds of buildings—but especially those containing activity which requires a great deal of light. In the 1930's, factories were the main beneficiaries of the recessed posts and continuous window walls made possible by steel-cage construction. Today, designers rely far more on artificial illumination for industrial plants, office buildings, department stores and so on, but the glass wall is retained because, viewed from the outside, reflections in the glass enable the frequently austere forms of contemporary architecture to harmonize with the environment.

In addition to its role in glass-wall design, the post-and-lintel system as used in steel- or ferroconcrete-cage construction, affords regular spacing of

WALTER GROPIUS, Bauhaus workshop wing, Dessau (1925–26), left. Photo, courtesy The Museum of Modern Art, New York.

SKIDMORE, OWINGS & MERRILL, B.M.A. Tower, Kansas City (1964), right. Photo, © Ezra Stoller Associates.

posts and thus of partitions, creating interchangeable cubical spaces. Like the grid plan of land subdivision, such spaces lend themselves to the rational—that is, measurable and calculable—methods required by modern commercial and industrial enterprise: the efficient sale and rental of space; the standardized design of fixtures and furnishings; the rapid and orderly transportation and circulation of people; and the maximum utilization of the space which has been created. It is easy to see how space created by arches, vaults, and domes is "wasteful" from a commercial standpoint. What is lofty and inspiring in a church or the reading room of a library represents an uneconomic expenditure of funds in a commercial office building.

Cage construction based on the post-and-lintel also permits the raising of a building on stilts, or pilotis, as Le Corbusier called them. In effect, the first floor is eliminated and the entire weight of the structure is supported by a series of strong, built-up girders along the bottom of the building. The load is carried from these members to the ground through the stilts very much as it is in a chest of drawers or a dresser on legs. Only a steel or ferroconcrete beam, of course, would have the necessary

strength to do the job without creating intolerable bulk or multiplying the stilts, which would nullify the advantages of ground level circulation beneath the building.

The steel posts of skyscrapers are so slender that when visible they are commonly encased with bulkier materials, not only for fireproofing and concealment of plumbing, wiring, and so forth, but also to provide psychological assurance that the building is being supported. Although the post-and-lintel is an old device, we are conditioned to its use in the dimensions appropriate to wood or stone. Only during the construction process do we see the lightness and openness of the steel cage. Its strength is a product of the material and the structural system. Stone lintels *rested* on their supports, but steel posts and lintels are *fastened* together: Their joints resist lateral and rotary movement so that the inherent strength of the material is enhanced by the strength of the joint system. Consequently, it is a mistake to think of modern cage construction as merely a translation of the ancient post-and-lintel into new materials. Similar cubical spaces are created, but the modern system does not rely on gravity for its strength.

Our cubical spaces, unlike those in classical buildings, require fewer interior supports. Design emphasis is not on columns and capitals, or lintels and architraves. Instead, the principal design problem lies in the treatment of the curtain wall and the total space envelope. That is why it is not unusual for an architect commissioned to design a large office building to employ a firm specializing in the organization of interior space and utilities to handle those details while the designer applies himself to refinement of the skin, and planning of the elements visible at the ground level. Thus, the post-and-lintel system combined with modern materials has created a number of constructional advantages as well as architectural dilemmas.

THE CANTILEVER

A cantilever is basically the horizontal extension of a beam or slab into space beyond its supporting post. Its free, or external, end is unsupported and the point where it rests on its post acts like the fulcrum of a lever. If the internal end of the beam were not bolted down or counterweighted in some fashion, the cantilever would rotate around its fulcrum. But since the inside end is fixed, the free end is rigid. The overhanging front and rear ends of an automobile function as cantilevers. The thumb extended on the hand acts like a cantilever. But a bracket is not truly a cantilever as some suppose, because, although its upper surface resembles an extended beam, it is really supported by a diagonal brace in compression. The cantilever, like a beam supported at both ends, relies simply on the resistance to breaking of its material and the secure fastening of its internal end.

The cantilever principle has been known at least from the time of the first overhanging stone lintel. A tree branch resembles the cantilever, and the strength-to-weight ratio of lumber makes the material suitable for light cantilever construction. But steel and ferroconcrete are the ideal cantilever materials. Some steel bridges that resemble arch construction are in fact the product of a pair of beams projected out from their supports and meeting in the center of the span. Bracket-type bracing in the shape of a half arch creates the impression that the whole span is supported by an arch.

As an architectural device in major construction, the cantilever has become increasingly feasible and popular with the availability of strong materials at reasonable cost. For domestic dwellings in the moderate price range, the steel needed for cantilevers of any substantial projection may be somewhat expensive. Although wooden cantilever beams are used, they cannot be extended as dramatically as steel. As noted earlier, multiple dwellings employ narrow cantilever balconies as design clichés or as sun-breaks. But the dramatic impact of

FRANK LLOYD WRIGHT, The Kalita Humphreys Theater, Dallas (1959), left. Photo, Messina-Dallas.

MARCEL BREUER, Begrisch Hall, New York University (1961), right. Courtesy New York University Photographic Bureau.

TREE

THUMB

CANTILEVER

WELTON BECKETT AND ASSOCIATES (architects and engineers), First State Bank of Clear Lake City, Texas (1965). Courtesy the bank and the architects.

cantilever construction is not felt unless an extension approaching the limits of the material is created. As with the suspension bridge and the light-weight truss, the defiance of gravity by strength of material and ingenuity of design accounts for the distinctive beauty and excitement that are characteristic of the cantilever.

The continuous band of windows discussed in connection with post-and-lintel construction is based on columns recessed back from the outside wall. The portion of the floor projecting beyond the columns in such buildings, is, of course, cantilevered. The supporting columns may be concealed within wall partitions, so that no interior posts are seen. Instead of being extended freely in space, the edge of the cantilevered floor becomes an attachment for a curtain wall of glass, or metal panels, or the support for bands of brick veneer. Hence the cantilever is not visible, al-though its operation is essential for this type of curtain-wall treatment.

Among the most exciting uses of the cantilever are ferroconcrete canopies, roofs, pavilions, grandstands, air-craft hangars, and theater balconies. Here the imagination of the architect and the ingenuity of the structural designer combine to create some of the most striking and uniquely modern structures of the age.

THE TRUSS

The truss is an application of the geometric fact that no angle of a triangle can be changed without altering the dimensions of the sides. It is a system of triangles (with the exception of the rectangular Vierendeel truss) arranged to work like a beam or lintel. Such systems of triangles can be made very rigid, and thus capable of bridging exceedingly wide spans. Truss construction is used

WOODEN ROOF TRUSS

Reconstruction of the façade of the Treasury of the Siphnians in the sanctuary of Apollo at Delphi (c. 530 B.C.), near right. Photo, copyright by Dr. Franz Stoedtner.

Roof truss, Fairbanks House, Dedham, Massachusetts (c. 1636), far right. Photo, Sandak, Inc.

where great spaces must be spanned with few or no interior supports. Wood and metal are the principal materials used to build trusses because these materials possess high tensile strength for their weight, and most of the members of a truss are in tension. In bridges, theaters, convention halls, gymnasiums, assembly plants, and most dwellings featuring gable roofs, the truss is almost indispensable.

The pediment of the Greek temple constitutes the most beautiful application of the truss in the shape of a triangle itself. This triangle has so firmly established itself in the consciousness of men of almost all cultures that it is difficult to conceive of a house or barn or church which does not have a triangular gable. Even though the comparatively short distances between the walls of domestic dwellings can be spanned by other means, the triangular-gable roof "feels" safe and stable because of our long conditioning to its use. A flat roof is accepted very reluctantly, if at all, in low structures. Of course, for many centuries the space *within* the gable roof has been useful in the form of a sleeping loft, grain storeroom, attic (an appropriately Greek word), or merely as an insulating space. In the sturdy Cape Cod cottage, Yankee ingenuity found space for extra bedrooms, which accounts for the wide popularity of the New England saltbox dwelling even today. In contemporary homes, less economical of space, the flat ceiling is raised or eliminated, converting the gable space into the prestigious "cathedral ceiling." Furthermore, the gable roof not only encloses the space between the walls of a dwelling, it also sheds snow and rain conveniently and offers a profile of low resistance to wind.

Although trusses are usually systems of triangles, their over-all shape is not necessarily triangular: Most trusses are long rectangles in the shape of a beam. As mentioned above, they are indeed a type of beam which substitutes stiffening struts, braces, or bars in place of the solid wood, metal, or stone of a beam. Other trusses may be straight along the lower edge and arched or paraboloid along the top—the so-called bowstring truss. Usually the upper chord of a truss and its vertical members are in compression while the lower chord and the diagonals are in tension. The stresses on these members correspond to the stresses which would operate within the solid material of a beam. In effect, the truss designer locates bars of appropriate length, direction, and cross section in places of greatest stress, eliminating the intervening solid material which does no work. Some trusses—the lattice type—superficially resemble the so-called open-web or trellis-work girders. But such girders are essentially built-up beams whose weight has been reduced by substituting steel web bracing for solid metal. They do not possess the lightness and strength of genuine trusses whose triangulations are designed specifically for the requirements of a particular type of load. A truss can span a much greater distance than a built-up girder because a girder is a standardized building part while the calculated design of a truss is responsible for its great strength in relation to its weight.

Surely anyone who has traveled over a bridge supported by a truss or stood in a great hall whose roof is supported by trusses has wondered how such vast spaces can be spanned by what are apparently fragile and slender members. Any insecurity we may feel

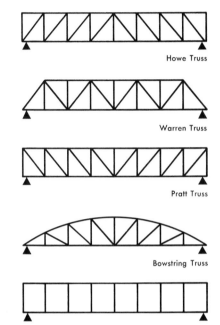

TYPES OF TRUSSES

Howe Truss

Warren Truss

Pratt Truss

Bowstring Truss

Vierendeel Truss

is usually based on our proneness to believe in the strength of materials under compression and to underestimate the strength of materials—especially of steel—in tension. Most of the members in an overhead truss have been designed so that the weight of the roof works to *pull apart* rather than *bend* the steel braces. But the crystalline structure of steel is such that it is almost impossible to pull it apart, and the designer has usually given each brace a length and cross section which will powerfully resist bending. So, those fears based on stone-age memories can be put aside. Few of us can estimate the enormous tensile strength of steel visually, just as we cannot form any kind of percept for a billion dollars. This observation may point to fundamental distinctions between art and engineering: Art deals with visually ponderable effects; engi-

neering employs mathematics to manipulate data with which our senses cannot deal adequately. But the results of engineering are visible to the senses and ought to be pleasing, since mathematical calculation is a tool of design just as imagination and sensibility are tools of art. If steel and wood are remarkable materials because they tenaciously resist being pulled apart, isn't human ingenuity even more remarkable in being able to design structures—with or without mathematical calculation—which magnificently exploit the properties of materials?

THE ARCH

The post-and-lintel represents the simplest and most direct means of using gravity to enclose space; the arch is considerably more sophisticated. In both cases, vertical supports or columns are used. But the means of bridging over space, which has always been the central problem of architecture, is vastly different. The arch originally relied on the compressive strength of bricks or cut stone: The separate units of an arch, called *voussoirs*, are in effect "welded" into a single curved member as they are squeezed together by the weight above and around them. The arch does not begin to function until the voussoir in its center, called the *keystone*, is set into place. As the keystone is the last stone to be placed, the arch has to be supported by a structure of wooden forms, called *centering*, while the arch is being constructed. The curve of the arch carries weight to its columns along a path which is not only graceful but which also corresponds to the pressure line of forces over the opening which the arch protects. In other words, if a door-

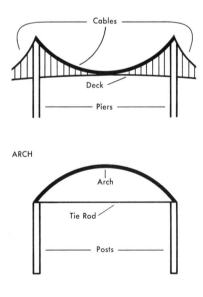

SUSPENSION BRIDGE

— Cables —

Deck

— Piers —

ARCH

Arch

Tie Rod

— Posts —

Claudian Aqueduct near Rome (c. 39 A.D.), at right. Courtesy TWA.

shaped opening were cut in a solid wall, and if we could see the distribution of the stresses in the wall over the opening, they would meet over the door to form a curve similar in shape to an arch.

The arch was probably developed by the Mesopotamians some four thousand years ago. They found that wedge-shaped bricks could be fitted into a semicircle to hold each other in place and to support weight above them. However, the load which the arch carries to its supporting posts develops almost horizontal reactions, called thrusts, which tend to force the posts outward, bringing about collapse. That is why arches appear in series or in walls but rarely alone. The outward thrust of the arch must be resisted by some type of buttressing or by a heavy masonry wall. The area of masonry which surrounds an arch is called a *spandrel*. It prevents bulging or deformation of the arch under pressure, no matter what its shape. It was the principal type used by ancient builders. A *free* arch, on the other hand, requires some buttressing, but it relies mainly on the correctness of its design and the strength of its own materials for security. It is the principal type used in modern construction. The systems of abutments and buttresses employed in place of solid masonry to counteract the outward thrusts of the free arch grew out of engineering necessity, yet they are responsible for much of the aesthetic effect of late medieval and Gothic architecture.

The arch was heavily employed in Renaissance construction, in combination with the post-and-lintel, but usually as part of a wall and without external buttresses. The triangular pediment shape, which is based on the roof truss, was commonly alternated with the arch over windows and portals, frequently *as a decorative rather than a structural element.* Although builders of this period possessed the engineering knowledge and capacity of their Gothic predecessors, their architectural tastes differed: Structural functions were frequently concealed, while pilasters, blind arcades, arches, pediments, columns, architraves—the entire panoply of the classical building orders—were employed for visual purposes. The Greeks and Romans, from whom the Renaissance architects derived their inspiration, also employed decorative and constructional details for visual effect, but their buildings rarely included nonfunctional structural members. And even Gothic building, which is more closely identified with pure engineering than any of the other great architectural traditions, possesses features which perform visual and symbolic rather than structural functions. Still, the arch tempts builders to become great engineers. Only in Italy was the arch a compositional device among others: It was a shape employed to decorate a wall.

The arch permits high and large openings and the successive positions of its frames help to establish a rhythmic pattern of forward or upward visual movement. It also is an extremely versatile device, lending itself to the rugged honesty of early Christian architecture, in which coarse masonry walls and piers were used for abutment, or to the delicate, soaring effects of Gothic architecture, in which weight-bearing walls were virtually eliminated. In both cases, tall, vertically shaped space was the objective. The early Romanesque basilica, however, emphasized a darkly mysterious interior, lit mainly from

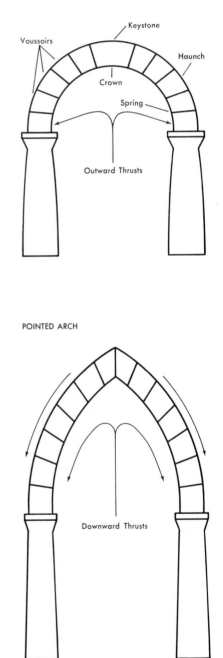

ROUND ARCH

Voussoirs

Keystone

Haunch

Crown

Spring

Outward Thrusts

POINTED ARCH

Downward Thrusts

Crypt of Speyer Cathedral, Germany (1040). Courtesy Marburg—Art Reference Bureau.

EERO SAARINEN, The David S. Ingalls Hockey Rink, Yale University (1958). Courtesy Yale University News Bureau.

within; those chapels, like early Christians themselves, were indifferent to their outer garments. In contrast, Gothic interiors were illuminated from without by light passing through colored glass. Their exteriors revealed not only the bones of their construction but also a host of sculptured images formerly visible in the flickering light of nave and apse mosaics. Romanesque builders could not go very high because their method of vaulting and abutment—the masonry wall and the buttress hidden under the roof of the side aisles—contained limitations inherent in the amount of stone which could be safely piled on stone. The Gothic method of abutment—the pier and flying buttress (which is really a half-arch)—permitted as much height (up to one hundred fifty-seven feet at Beauvais) as could be managed without setting up bending and twisting stresses in the fabric of the stone arches and ribs. The stability of the masonry arch, it must be remembered, depends on the compressive strength of relatively small stones or bricks bonded together with mortar. These materials fail when subjected to tension or torsion. Apparently the vaults of Beauvais fell, in 1284, because the builders made their arches too light and too high, leaving the structure vulnerable to bending or twisting stresses from live loads caused by wind and weather.

The capacity of an arch to withstand uneven and moving loads is increased if heavy stones are used to build it. Heavy stones, in turn, require strong and well-engineered *centering* (the hemispherical wooden framework used to support the arch under construction before it is subjected to load), sophisticated machinery to raise them into place, massive piers to sustain their dead weight, and, of course, a sacrifice of the slenderness to which Gothic vaulting aspires.

The pointed Gothic arch had the effect of directing its thrusts more nearly downward than in the almost horizontal direction of the round arch. As a result, the flying buttresses could be quite slender and the stained glass windows could be relatively unobstructed by thick masonry abutments and cast shadows. In addition, the pointed arch raised the height of interior space. Gothic ribbed vaults based on the pointed arch became, in effect, segmented domes, the area between the cross ribs being filled with a masonry fabric which functioned much as the membrane materials in contemporary geodesic domes designed by Buckminster Fuller.

In modern architecture, the free arch is used mainly to support bridges and viaducts and in association with large domical and vaulted structures. Made of reinforced concrete, steel, and also of laminated wood, the modern arch is a monolithic member which is much stronger than its brick or stone ancestors. In wide-spanning concrete arches, such as the Ingalls Hockey Rink at Yale by Eero Saarinen, the supporting posts are omitted; the arch virtually springs (begins its curve) from the ground. Consequently, the action of the

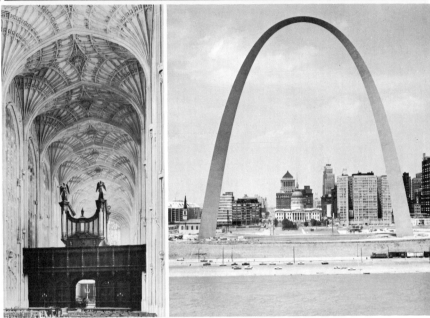

arch resembles the action of a huge bowstring truss, or a beam employing a single, curved brace. Nevertheless, true arch action is involved, since the entire member is in compression while the ground level serves as a tie rod or as the lower chord of a truss.

The modern free arch, because of the strength of its materials and the precision with which engineers can calculate lines of pressure, is capable of spanning great distances and it also is capable of considerable variation in shape. Frequently its shape results from its function as the opening for a curved shell structure as in Saarinen's Kresge Auditorium at M.I.T. or in Freyssinet's Airport Hangar at Orly. But the assimilation of the arch into stressed skin shells and vaults recapitulates the development of the classical arch and the Romanesque cross vault into late Gothic vaulting, as in the Cathedral at Exeter and the Chapel of King's College, Cambridge. The mastery of structural devices and building materials reaches the point where an almost organic unity is achieved; there is hardly any separation between skin and bone, between support*ing* and support*ed* members; the designer tends to use his mastery and freedom to disperse the structural function through the entire building fabric. The dissolution of the weight-bearing arch into fan vaulting, as at Cambridge, may represent a decline in straightforward structural performance. Perhaps the modern imagination pines for the drama of a single arch springing unassisted over open space. If so, it can find contemporary designers using the arch for its emotional properties and as a structural device of enhanced strength and reliability.

THE VAULT

The classical vault was a succession of identical arches in file order—one behind the other. The wall was a masonry plane punctuated by arches. Bridges and aqueducts were arcades, successions of arches in rank order—side by side:

EUGÈNE FREYSSINET, airport hangar, Orly, France (1921), top left. Photo, copyright by Dr. Franz Stoedtner.

EERO SAARINEN, Kresge Auditorium, Massachusetts Institute of Technology (1954), top right. Photo, Sandak, Inc.

The Chapel, King's College, Cambridge, England (1446), bottom left. Photo, British Information Services.

EERO SAARINEN, Gateway Arch, St. Louis (1965), bottom right. Arteaga Photos, St. Louis.

Barrel vault.

Nave, St.-Savin-sur-Gartempe, France (c. 1095–1115), left. Photo, Jean Roubier.

Groined vault.

Nave, St.-Étienne, Caen, France (vaulting, c. 1115–20), right. Photo, Jean Roubier.

Ribbed vault.

Vaulting of the choir of the abbey church of Asnières, France (early thirteenth century).

Interior space of any size was spanned by arches in the form of a semicylinder—the so-called barrel vault. (Even the dome, which was also employed to enclose large spaces, can be thought of as a shape which results from the rotation of an arch around a vertical axis formed by a line drawn through its keystone, or mid-point.) The groined vault of Romanesque and Gothic building resulted originally from the intersection at right angles of two barrel vaults.

Since the intersecting barrel vaults were of the same size in early construction, the *bay*, or space below the cross-vault they formed, was square. As a result, the groined vault over a square bay, usually found in Romanesque construction, produced a shape which was like a segmented dome. Italian builders employed this type of vaulting even after the introduction of ribbed vaults permitted long, narrow bays. Symmetry is a pervasive quality in Italian culture and in classical culture in general. In Gothic building, rectangular bays and vaults were preferred, hence the transverse, longitudinal, and diagonal arches had to be carefully adjusted in their rise and curvature so they would meet in the same place at the top of the vault. The vaults of classical construction, then, were created from a solid succes-

sion of arches, followed afterward by groined cross-vaults. Subsequently, with greater sophistication, the groins were succeeded by a network of arch-like members called ribs, between which a fill-in fabric of stone masonry was set to complete the enclosure. The important point is that the choice of the rectangular bay created problems in the design of the ribs whose solution demanded considerable ingenuity and led to a steady reduction in the weight of the vault, increased height, and further penetration of the walls.

The disadvantage of the barrel vault, going as far back as the Romans and Chaldeans, was that it could not be pierced by windows without being substantially weakened. That is one of the reasons why early Romanesque naves were so dark. The replacement of barrel vaults by a succession of groined vaults enabled the nave to go higher because the vaulting had become lighter, hence did not require such heavy walls and abutments for support. By the twelfth century, however, pointed arches and rib vaulting began to replace the round arches, heavy groins, and square bays of Romanesque construction. The ribs were lighter than the groins they replaced, and could be built wherever they were needed—not just at the points where the old barrels would have intersected. By multiplying ribs, the stone panels between them could be narrowed, and lighter weight stone could be used, greatly reducing the total weight of the vault. As the ribs multiplied, both for decorative and structural reasons, the panels between them grew lighter, and the weight-bearing function was distributed throughout the surface of the vault. The result, as mentioned earlier, was a dynamic pattern of stresses which resembles modern stressed skin or shell construction. The ribs tended to prevent lateral slipping, a danger of groined vaults which discouraged their use over very wide spaces. The rib vault, the pointed arch, and the flying buttress—all variations of the same device—made possible the triumph of Gothic construction.

THE DOME

The vault evolved as a solution to the perennial problem of bridging great spaces without interior supports while avoiding wooden trusses—which might burn—or stone lintels—which would break of their own weight. The solution was based on arch combinations. The dome represents another solution. A dome is a hemisphere essentially, although it can bulge to approximate the bulbous shape of an onion, as in the famed multiple domes of the Cathedral of St. Basil the Beatified, Moscow (1555–60), or seem to be somewhat flattened at the equator, as in St. Peter's. Like the vault, the dome must be made of stone, brick, or concrete to resist fire. Usually a circular opening or skylight

is left at the top, called an *oculus*, or a *lantern* if the opening is surmounted by a tower. The weight of a tower, of course, increases the tendency of the dome to bulge. That is why chains or metal rings were embedded in the masonry of classic domes. The Pantheon in Rome, built in 120 A.D., although hemispherical when seen from inside, has on the outside a very high, thick mass of masonry surrounding it up to the haunch (the area on the curve of an arch or dome which is about halfway up to the top, or crown), so that the dramatic exterior form of the dome is almost lost. It appears to be a shallow mound resting on a high drum (the cylindrical ring of masonry upon which the dome rests).

The placement of a dome on a cylindrical drum over a circular foundation is logical from the standpoint of geometry and construction. But most domed structures rest on rectangular foundations, because a rectangular ground plan lends itself to a more logical (to Western eyes) subdivision of space. (Domes totally unrelated to their supporting structure appear in the Corn Palace in Mitchell, South Dakota.) The

Cathedral of St. Basil, Moscow (1555–60). Photo, Air France.

The Pantheon, Rome (120–124), left. Courtesy, Foto ENIT, Roma.

Domes, turrets, and annually rotated mosaic panels made of corn illustrate the uninhibited expression of folk architecture.

Corn Palace, Mitchell, South Dakota (1921), right, Courtesy Mitchell Chamber of Commerce; Photo, Dorothy Prather.

dome emphasizes a vertical orientation of vision, while the rectangle, preferred in Western churches, stresses a forward-looking orientation. The dome appears to be a very extravagant device for focusing dramatic attention on a point directly beneath its center. In the Middle East, where the dome probably originated, its ceiling was regarded as an image of the cosmos and was frequently covered with stars. (Even the modern planetarium is dome-shaped.) It had religious and cosmological meaning, then, and was not devised merely to create a difficult and spectacular construction problem. The cosmological function survives in Western churches in the semidomes of apses with their mosaic representations of Christ as Pantocrator (ruler of the cosmos). For the same cosmological reason, perhaps, the Pantheon, the Roman temple of all the gods, is not especially impressive from the outside. From within, however, it conveys the sense of a world apart, self-contained and secure. Doubtless these qualities of the dome appealed to the emperor Hadrian, its builder, and

later motivated Pope Julius II in 1505 to rebuild the wooden basilican church of St. Peter as a great stone structure under a central dome.

A number of devices were used to manage the transfer of load from the circular edge of the dome to the rectangular foundation on which it ultimately rested. The most commonly used were called *pendentives* and *squinches*. The pendentive system, in effect, rests the drum of the dome on four arches springing from four powerful piers located at each corner of the square plan. The arches meet the rim of the drum at only four points, however. Between these points are four triangular sections of a sphere—the actual pendentives—which serve to connect the entire rim of the drum to the curves of the arch and carry its weight down to the piers. A bold modern use of the dome on pendentives—this time made of reinforced concrete ribs and arches—is seen in Max Berg's Centennial Hall, Breslau, built in 1913. Hagia Sophia in Constantinople, built by Justinian in 532 A.D., as well as being an unsurpassed building

MICHELANGELO, St. Peter's, Rome (1546–64; dome completed by GIACOMO DELLA PORTA, 1590; colonnade by GIANLORENZO BERNINI, 1657), left. Courtesy, Foto ENIT, Roma.

MAX BERG, Centennial Hall, Breslau (1913), right. From *The Language of Art* by Philip C. Beam. Copyright © 1958, The Ronald Press Company, New York.

achievement, is the supreme example of a dome on pendentives. The great outward thrusts developed in the arches and pendentives are carried down by a system of half domes and powerful exterior abutments. The dome itself has no oculus but is pierced instead by windows running continuously around its lower edge, a device which creates the impression that the dome is floating. The narrow spaces between the windows seem to define vertical ribs which transfer the dome's weight to the drum. In the interior of the Pantheon, a system of hollow rectangular shapes called *coffers* defines vertical and horizontal ribs, although the dome was in fact built of horizontal courses of brick laid to form two shells between which concrete was poured. The coffers therefore emphasized the thickness and stability of the dome for Hadrian while the shaft of light from the oculus may have strengthened his consciousness of divine descent. Similarly, the windows piercing the thick base of St. Sophia's dome must have reassured Justinian by their depth and dazzled him by the ring of light

they shed on his imperial person and court.

The system of squinches, used by Mohammedan and some Byzantine builders, is not as rationally articulated as the pendentive solution. It too rests the dome on four arches sprung from four corner piers, creating a square support for a circular edge. But in place of pendentives in the corners, smaller arches called squinches are substituted, forming an octagonal support at eight points. The octagon approximates a circle better than a square, and so, with some adjustments in the masonry, the dome can rest on what is, in effect, a polygonal drum. Squinches have the visual advantage of creating niches in the corners between the main supporting arches, forming semidome shapes which rhymically repeat the shape of the major dome they support, as is seen in the detail from the dome interior of the Mosque at Isfahan (p. 432). But otherwise they represent an approximate solution as opposed to the pendentives, which are found in some of the world's great domed buildings: St. Sophia and the Mosque of

Interior of Hagia Sophia, Istanbul (532–537), left. Courtesy Turkish Tourist and Information Office.

Sultan Ahmet Mosque (The Blue Mosque), Istanbul (1609–16), right. Courtesy Turkish Tourist and Information Office.

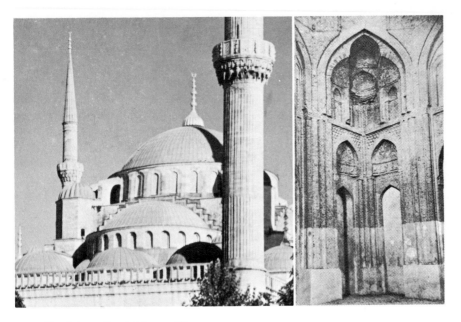

The Sultan Ahmet Mosque (Blue Mosque), Istanbul (1609–16) [detail], left. Photo, Pan American World Airways.

Congregational Mosque, Isfahan, Iran, interior of the north dome (1088), right.

R. BUCKMINSTER FULLER, Monohex Dome, for Cinerama Theater, Los Angeles (1965). Photo, copyright by R. Buckminster Fuller.

Ahmet I in Istanbul, St. Peter's in Rome, and St. Paul's in London.

SHELL STRUCTURES

Modern shell structures are the beneficiaries of reinforced concrete and superior mathematical tools for the calculation of stresses and the resistant strength of materials. As a result, the classical masonry dome as a distinct structural type has been virtually supplanted by shell structures which are usually much flatter and wider than their predecessors. Concrete shells are so thin that their dead weight is negligible, and the engineering problem becomes the maintenance of stability and resistance to buckling because of stresses caused by rain, snow, wind, or uneven heating by the sun. Since shells enclose a great deal of space with a minimum of material, they are very economical. Also, the plasticity of ferroconcrete permits the shell to be thickened where its curvature and the concentration of stresses require. Of course, if necessary, the thin-shell dome can be stiffened by visible internal or external ribs as classic domes were.

Shells can also be made of metals, such as aluminum, steel, or copper. Geodesic domes designed by R. Buckminster Fuller (1895–   ) have been made of aluminum, steel, wood, concrete, plastics, and even of paper. Plastic and fiberglass sheets stretched over cable systems or metal-mesh supports may eventually compete with concrete for the construction of shells. These materials would create forms similar to those seen in tents, kites, and umbrellas. Shell structures have already been constructed by spraying cement over an inflated rubber balloon, then deflating the balloon after reinforcing members have been embedded and the concrete has set. Sprayed plastics and impermeable fabrics also have design potentials which are now being seriously investigated.

Since fair and exposition architecture is temporary, it is frequently the source of new material applications and structural devices. The Berlin Pavilion at the New York World's Fair of 1964-65 was a type of shell or tent structure made of vinyl-coated canvas stretched into a stressed skin and supported by tension cables and steel masts. The "drum" of the structure consisted of a steel ring resting on steel columns. Buildings of this type are not only very pleasing visually, they are also quite inexpensive. If problems of long-term durability and weather resistance can be overcome, their use will unquestionably spread to permanent buildings. Like the tents of nomads, or the geodesic domes of Buckminster Fuller, these structures may cause a general revision of our attitudes toward temporary and permanent architecture. By radically lowering the costs of construction, the new space-enclosing methods may alter philosophies of design. That is, designers have conceived of roof structures, building shapes, and interior spaces which have never been built because of the economics of traditional construction. In the future, such structural ideas may be found thoroughly practical.

The ability to enclose enormous spaces, combined with the steadily increasing wealth and productive efficiency of modern societies, can lead to the design of total communities in single structures. Our technical ability to carry out such enterprises has been apparent for some time—perhaps since Le Corbusier planned his *Unités d'Habitation* as comprehensive structures for the vital activities of society. Similar ideas are implied by huge hotels, ocean-going superliners, great shopping and entertainment centers, industrial parks, and resort centers. By locating all of their building units on a single raised platform, designers of academic centers and office building complexes suggest the direction of future plans: comprehensive design of communities through integration of their

major solids, voids, and utilities in a single structure. This idea does not represent a sharp break with the past, nor does it constitute a threat to individualism. Rather it confirms in architectural terms what is already a fact—namely, that communities are multicelled organisms increasingly interrelated by common systems of power, transport, communication, government, recreation, and so on. The structures in communities of the past were always huddled together; their separateness was only nominal, imposed by the inability of materials and design to unite structurally a multitude of building units. Today's communities, particularly cities undergoing urban renewal, are not only single organisms in the social sense, they are also effectively single structures in the architectural sense. That is why one speaks of the New York or Chicago or Dallas skyline as a single entity. The unity that was formerly imposed by imagination and perception is now becoming a structural fact.

Umbrellas over Trade Section, Swiss National Exposition (1964), left.

Berlin Pavilion, New York World's Fair (1964), right. Courtesy Roy Bernard Associates.

Dallas skyline. Photo, American Airlines.

Constructors and Sculptors

Is any pattern discernible in contemporary architecture as a whole? Is there any common idea about building shapes, structural systems, or interior and exterior space which seems to pervade architectural practice now? The answer has to be that no single idea of structure or of space dominates architecture either in the United States or in other major countries. In almost any given place, buildings are being erected which express divergent philosophies of architecture while using similar materials and structural devices. Yet to the extent that the variety of contemporary architectural expression can be generalized and placed in categories, two camps—with individual members varying in their distance from each other—can be described: constructors and sculptors. These labels may be unfair to any given architect. Certainly the work by designers within each category is not visually similar. What is common to each camp is an attitude toward form, engineering, architectural emotion, and the purposes of design.

From the preceding discussions, we can see how the structural and technological developments of the past seventy-five years have liberated architecture from decorative, ornamental, and constructional systems which had existed for centuries. A revolution against applied ornament, the classical orders, facades false to their interiors, eclectic mixing of styles, and imitation of materials, has been won. The turning point may have come with the great nineteenth-century engineers,—Paxton,

Roebling, Labrouste, and Eiffel; or it may have been the writing and examples of the Americans—Sullivan and Wright; or the central Europeans—Gropius, Mies van der Rohe, and the Bauhaus designers; or the genius of Le Corbusier alone; or the great modern engineers—Perret, Maillart, Nervi, Morandi, Freyssinet, Candela, and Torroja. At any rate, all living designers possess tools and enjoy freedoms inherited from these figures of recent or current activity. A heritage of design freedom has come down to everyone, and it has been used to generate architectural quality through an emphasis on (1) the revelation of structure, or (2) the subordination of structure to sculptural form.

The label "constructor" can be applied to designers who favor the dramatization of engineering devices to create architecture which is exciting, stirring to the imagination. The word "constructor" is also used, mainly in Europe, to designate the person who practices what Americans call structural engineering. In both Europe and America, architecture and structural engineering are independent although cooperating professions. But their separation is fairly recent. Although designing major structures has almost always been regarded as an art, the responsibility was not divided between two professions —one aesthetic and the other structural —until after the Industrial Revolution. Today, though the professions are formally distinct, each shares many of the competencies of the other. That is why

WIMBERLY, WHISENAND, ALLISON & TONG, Waikiki branch, Bank of Hawaii (model, 1965). Courtesy Bank of Hawaii, Honolulu, Hawaii.

it is accurate to think of some architects as constructors—designers who try to exploit the emotional qualities of engineering. For them, the engineering solution is fundamental; architecture is, as Nervi called it, "structural truth."

The label "sculptor" characterizes designers who are interested in pictorial and symbolic form as a source of architectural emotion. They must, of course, use engineering devices to build, but these devices are regarded as a means rather than as ends. The sculptural architect is also interested in the play of light and texture among his forms for the sake of visual excitement. He endeavors to create space-enclosing shapes which symbolize the purpose of a building or some attribute of its users. Such designers believe that, in addition to being utilitarian, architecture should be expressive of ideas and feelings.

Today, many buildings exhibit an elaboration of form which goes beyond the strict requirements of structure and utility. Giovanni Michelucci's Church of the Autostrada is a good example; it also reveals the influence of Le Corbusier's Chapel at Ronchamps carried to a sculptural extreme. This tendency is very apparent in the work of Edward Stone, Paul Rudolph, and Minoru Yamasaki, architects who have received a growing number of important commissions in recent years. Philip Johnson (1906-), notwithstanding his former association with the austere constructor, Mies van der Rohe, can also be grouped with the sculptors. He belongs with them because his "sculpture," while restrained, betrays a devotion to surfaces and a primary emphasis on composition with the sensous qualities of materials which is often at the expense of the revelation of structure.

The arbitrary cross-section of the columns and the rather ornate chandeliers in his New York State Theater at Lincoln Center reflect this designer's growing concern with the pictorial effect of architecture, the achievement of elegance through sensitive adjustment of intervals and size relationships which are addressed to the viewer's eye, as was the Greek temple. The forms do not necessarily grow out of the building's structure or the plain requirements of physical function. Johnson's rich orchestration of domes for the museum at Dumbarton Oaks involves the decorative rather than structural employment of a building device. The numerous interior space divisions indicate that the engineering advantage of the dome—enclosure of large-scale interior space without internal supports—does not constitute the reason for its use. Instead, the symbolic function of the dome, its creation of a whole and separate world, its shaping of space around the individual at its

Domestic architecture or free-form sculpture?

JACQUES COUELLE, houses, Castellaras, France (1965). Photos, René Isnardon, Cannes.

GIOVANNI MICHELUCCI, Church of the Autostrada (1962).

PHILIP JOHNSON, wing for the Pre-Columbian collection, Dumbarton Oaks (1963). Courtesy Dumbarton Oaks; exterior photo by Ezra Stoller.

Steel arches at ground level covered with marble.

NARAMORE, BAIN, BRADY, & JOHANSON and MINORU YAMASAKI & ASSOCIATES, IBM Building, Seattle (1961). Courtesy University Properties, Inc.

EDWARD DURELL STONE, Beckman Auditorium (1960), left. Courtesy California Institute of Technology.

Court of the Myrtles, The Alhambra, Granada, Spain (1368), right. Courtesy Ministerio de Información y Turismo, Madrid.

center—these properties have been exploited to create a contemplative and mystical atmosphere for the viewer's examination of small, exquisitely presented art objects.

It is easy to see that from the standpoint of the constructors—designers like Gropius, Mies, Neutra, I. M. Pei, Marcel Breuer, and Gordon Bunshaft—the work of the sculptor might represent a turning away from the tenets of modernism. It may appear to be a revival of the old architectural traditions, with the exception that modern materials and structural devices have been substituted for classical orders and systems of embellishment. In Yamasaki's work, for example, Gothic arches of metal or pagoda-like roof canopies in ferroconcrete are employed, not only in modern adaptations of still viable ancient devices, but also in the spirit of architectural revival. His buildings appear to be engaged in "borrowing" some of the symbolic meaning of older systems of construction without indulging in the obvious eclecticism of the nineteenth century. Edward Stone, too, uses modern materials and devices to create architectural reminiscences—particularly of the lacey arabesques of Persian and Moorish structures of the

late Middle Ages. But while his arcades, forests of columns, and perforated metal or concrete walls may exhibit some of the qualities of the great periods of Islamic building, they also represent a search for living symbols in architecture by a designer who is not too proud to base his style on the past. It might be more accurate to say that Stone endeavors to satisfy with modern devices the same human appetites for richly patterned surfaces and stately abstract shapes which were so successfully appeased in the medieval architecture of India and Iran. Compare his Beckman Auditorium at the California Institute of Technology with the colonnade in the Court of the Myrtles of the fourteenth-century Moorish-Spanish palace, the Alhambra. Although the forms are not identical, the designer of the modern building has clearly drawn on the qualities of the colonnade in the older building, employing ferroconcrete to achieve continuous curves and regularity of shape which only a machine technology could fashion.

It is ironic that a Moslem mosque recently built in Malaysia breaks with the medieval tradition of Asian and African mosques. The new National Mosque in Kuala Lumpur, designed by Baharuddin bin Abu Kassim, features a huge prayer hall whose pleated roof of reinforced concrete constitutes acceptance of the most modern structural idiom for large interior spans. Rather than revive memories of the Alhambra, a potent influence on Stone and Yamasaki, Abu Kassim has built more in the spirit of the Harrison & Abramovitz Assembly Hall for the University of Illinois or the market at Royan, France (p. 414). The single minaret may harken back to traditional Islamic architecture, but it also bears a remarkable resemblance to modern airport control towers and particularly to the television tower at Stuttgart, Germany, designed by Fritz Leonhardt.

In contrast to the sculptural architects, the constructors take pride in an unsentimental approach to design. Indeed, the term "new brutalism" was used to describe the work of a British group of structural architects in the 1950's. An example, by no means harsh, of this philosophy of design is seen in a Canadian art school, the Central Technical School, Toronto, designed by Fairfield

and Du Bois. The building is framed in ferroconcrete, employs generous glass areas to light its studios, quarry tile floors which are easy to maintain and almost indestructible, concrete block walls, and movable plaster partitions. The rugged strength of the structure is not merely the result of a rough, poured concrete, exterior surface; it grows also out of a highly rational solution to the specific light and space requirements of an art school and the typical operations which must be performed in its studios.

The drama of a pure engineering solution is seen in Eduardo Torroja's

GUILHERMO ROSELL & MANUEL LA ROSA (architects) and FELIX CANDELA (structural design and construction), entrance to a housing development, Tequexquitergo, Mexico (1957), top. Courtesy Felix Candela.

MANO PANI (architect) and FELIX CANDELA (structural design and construction), band shell, Santa Fé, Mexico, D.F. (1956), center. Courtesy Felix Candela.

EDUARDO TORROJA, Grandstand of La Zarzuela Racecourse, Madrid, Spain (1935), bottom. Courtesy Instituto Eduardo Torroja.

Grandstand for the Madrid Hippodrome, in which the great cantilevered roof over the grandstand is anchored in, and tied to, the roof of a betting hall under the stands. The stands themselves act as a half arch or flying buttress, serving to resist any lateral movement of the single post from which the huge shell is cantilevered. Another exciting cantilevered form is seen in Felix Candela's band shell for a housing development in Mexico. It, too, lets the engineering speak for itself.

Although Pier Luigi Nervi (1891–   ) is one of the great constructors, he has probably used more columns than are structurally necessary in his Palazzo del Lavoro Exhibition Hall in Turin, Italy. The same is true of Wright's Administration Building for the Johnson Company in Racine, Wisconsin (p. 82). Nervi has designed a modern equivalent of Gothic fan vaulting, and Wright's mushroom columns, like all man-made "trees," serve to establish a sense of scale, a structural reference to which man can relate himself and thus "feel" the dimensions of a great interior space. Anthropomorphic suggestions are not necessarily absent from the work of constructors: Morandi's Parco del Valentino Exhibition Hall in Turin and Freyssinet's Pius X Basilica in Lourdes, convey a sense of powerful supporting legs, arms, and ribs. It is interesting that both structures are earth-covered and employ prestressed concrete arches and braces. From within, one gains the impression of an enormous cavern or grotto. The inclined pillars, the absence of rectangles or of cubical spaces, encourage an underground feeling. In the Basilica at Lourdes, of course, such associations serve to enhance the mystical atmosphere of this famous pilgrimage shrine.

Architectural emotion, therefore, arises from several sources: It can result from the careful adjustment of purely visual spaces and intervals, from the magic of geometry; it may rely on immemorial recollections of masonry, and conceivably, from memories of life under ledges, in front of caves, in the tops of trees, underneath woven boughs and bundles of straw, or in small earthen craters—memories carried in the old brain stem and never brought

PIER LUIGI NERVI, Turin Exhibition Hall (1959). Photo, courtesy Jan C. Rowan, *Progressive Architecture*.

to conscious awareness; it may depend on the model of a tent in which a thin membrane just barely separates a private world from the vastness of infinite space, a tent whose capacity to control openings, promote circulation, admit light, and move air remains a goal of architecture even yet; it may recall huge stones modeled to resemble human bodily parts, the imagined dwelling places of procreative power and fertility. At different stages of his development man has sought to live in the bowels of the earth or on the summits of mountains. Depending on his luck and his mood, he reverts back to one or another of these widely divergent, dimly remembered locations for shelter. That is why architecture is so various, so perplexing, so personal, so inconsistent. If we interpret the art as the evolution of spatial envelopes from closed to open forms, we are certain to be disappointed by modern caves and grottoes. If we believe engineering defines architecture, visual contradictions

RICCARDO MORANDI, Turin Exhibition Hall (1959), left.

EUGÈNE FREYSSINET, Pius X Basilica, Lourdes, France (1958), right. Courtesy H. Baranger & Cie.

PIER LUIGI NERVI, Little Sports Palace, Rome (1957). Courtesy Studio Nervi.

abound in painted, colored, and ornamented structures which obviously satisfy a still persisting need for symbols, for glitter, for exhibition of status or technique. The moral and aesthetic superiority which constructors feel toward their sculptural brethren who are less inhibited in the pursuit of "exciting" space, may turn out to be, on close inspection, the perennial conflict between abstraction and empathy, between the geometric and the pictorial. For one camp, architecture is structure, and structure is measure, and measure is geometry, and geometry is reality. For the other, architecture is sculpture, and sculpture is magic, and magic is illusion. And so the architectural conflict is in the end a conflict between views of the world as real or illusory. Although the conflict cannot be settled to everyone's satisfaction, it reveals, at least, that architecture and art deal with matters of ultimate importance. Architecture is both the end product of a philosophy of design and also the concrete source of a philosophy of community—of men sharing common structures and facilities as they pursue their individual destinies.

PART FIVE

THE PROBLEMS

OF ART CRITICISM

A lmost everyone fancies himself an art critic. At least, most people are willing to deliver critical opinions, no matter how unfamiliar they may be with art or with the theory of art criticism. This may be so because a democratic society encourages its citizens to feel that their views on any subject have importance and equal weight just as their votes count equally in our political life. As a result, a great deal of heat is generated in critical discussions of contemporary art, and this heat is one of the factors which brings contemporary art so forcibly to the attention of us all. It is interesting to observe, however, that formal education at all levels fails to devote much time to the establishment of a systematic foundation for critical judgment. Hence, even well-educated persons find themselves delivering the authoritative opinions of others, or offering their

442

own views about art without really knowing how they arrived at them. In an effort to overcome this deficiency, I devote this section of the book to critical theory and critical method as applied to contemporary art. No attempt will be made to deal comprehensively with the body of material known as aesthetics or philosophy of art. Rather, my goal is to assist in the development of an intelligent *approach* to the business of making critical judgments about art. Although I do not believe there are eternally valid, permanently correct evaluations of particular works of art, I *do* think there are systematic procedures for making evaluations which are fairly durable and defensible. Hence this discussion of art criticism as a practical activity in which one can gain proficiency as one's critical grounds and procedures are subjected to logical scrutiny.

CHAPTER FOURTEEN

The Purposes of Criticism

The chief goal of art criticism is understanding. We wish to find a way of looking at objects of art and thinking about them which will yield the maximum of knowledge about their real or alleged merits. Works of art yield information to the trained viewer, and this information is useful in the forming of critical judgments. But we are not interested in the information for its own sake; for the purposes of criticism, we want to know how that information is related to the excellence of the work. It is for this reason that archaeological, historical, or social information derived from works of art may be fascinating but not necessarily useful in art criticism. In short, we seek to understand the causes *in* the work of the effect the work has upon us.

Another goal of art criticism, perhaps as important as the first, is quite frankly delight or pleasure. To be sure, we derive some pleasure from understanding, from knowing what it is in art that gives rise to our feelings

444

THE THEORY

OF CRITICISM

and our total sense of approval. But the critical process enables us to carry on the search for meaning or pleasure systematically, that is, more carefully and for a more sustained period than would be the case if we had no logically organized approach to art. The trained viewer should be able to extract most of the satisfactions which a work is capable of yielding. Hence, the practice of art criticism yields a certain *quantitative* benefit—the increase of satisfaction derivable from any particular work.

Some persons, artists among them, believe that careful and systematic scrutiny of art kills the satisfaction, dessicates the values, particularly the emotional values, which art can yield. They assume, however, that careful study is aimed only at finding information. And such may be the case with the archaeologist or anthropologist who sees the art object as evidence for the reconstruction of a buried culture. But the information sought by the art critic is mainly about the sources of his satisfaction or about the reasons for his admiration or disapproval. As we look, we discover that we are pleased or displeased. Then, because we are human, hence curious, we want to know what combinations of color and shape or subject matter and execution cause our feelings of pleasure.

The purposes of art criticism are not entirely hedonistic, however, nor centered exclusively on introspection. There is a very real interest in sharing what we have discovered in art. It is very difficult, perhaps impossible, to experience any satisfaction absolutely as an individual without so much as a thought for the reactions of someone else. That is why we talk about art, about music, about literature. We wish to find out if others share our feelings when they have been exposed to the same work. Or, if they have not, we want to tell them about its worth to us. Negatively, we may want to persuade others that a work is inferior, an artistic failure. There is, then, a social motive in art criticism—assuming that, whatever else it may be, *art criticism is talk about art.*

Why do all of us, experienced critics or not, enjoy talking about art? Is it not sufficient to see a work, to enjoy it or dislike it, and to set the experience aside privately and move on to the other business of life? Talk about

art, or art criticism, is probably one of the ways we share the contents of our inner lives without embarrassment. Consequently, very few of us can resist the impulse to deliver at least our concluding opinions about a work of art, whether or not we can go into the details of the experience itself. Great art critics have an unusually rich and varied capacity for aesthetic pleasure, so that when they disclose discoveries they have made about art, they are also assisting us to enlarge our own capacities for understanding and delight. In this sense, art criticism is very much like teaching; it is the sharing of discoveries about art, or, in some cases, about life, where art has its ultimate source.

One of the most commonly accepted purposes of art criticism is to make some objective statement of the worth or rank of an art object. Indeed, the purposes mentioned above are often held to be preliminary to the ultimate judgment of "how good" a work is. Here again, we are confronted with a persistent human tendency—the need to say that something is "better than" or "poorer than" or "worth more than" something else. Obviously, part of this need derives from our wish to possess what is valuable, both materialistically and spiritually. This particular motive for making critical judgments is not especially elevated although it is plainly very human. But its pervasiveness may account for the development of art criticism as a serious discipline. Clearly, many persons want to have a sound foundation for their judgments about what is good, better, or best. And, in the case of many works of art, large sums of money are connected to those judgments. To some extent, even a scholarly, academic discipline like art history is based on the need to establish firmly that an art object is what someone claims it to be: that its authorship, place of origin, or date of execution are what a seller asserts before a potential buyer. In the course of answering questions of authorship, provenience, and so on, the historian discovers information which is humanistically valuable, quite apart from the data required to secure a transaction. In connection with modern works of art, there is usually little question (except for forgeries) about the authenticity of a work. Hence, critical evaluations become more crucial in the establishment of monetary values for contemporary works. Even when no financial transaction is involved, critical evaluations are important in the determination of prestige among artists and current styles in the art world. And, of course, prestige is sought for its own sake as well as for its connection to fame or wealth.

It is apparent, therefore, that the purpose of art criticism which we might consider least important—ranking and valuation—absorbs most of the energy of the contemporary art world and has most influence on the destinies of artists, the aspirations of art students, perhaps the teaching of art, and the complex business of exhibiting and selling art.

Collecting art is related to art criticism since the collector, by his purchase, confirms his own or someone's critical judgment about a work. In our society, many people have the opportunity to collect art since the range of prices is so great, works are so widely available, artists are so productive, and we are, in general, so affluent. And,

since money is a very potent symbol in our culture, all the activities leading to or following the purchase of works of art have enormous cultural significance. Clearly, art criticism as carried on in newspapers, magazines, and universities, and by implication in galleries and museums, has the function of influencing what artists create. Thus we encounter a cultural anomaly: Criticism of art—that is, informed talk about art—tends to affect the production of what it talks about. This anomaly should not really surprise us, though, since talk about automobiles or television shows tends to influence what car manufacturers design and sell as well as the programs networks produce and sponsors support. Therefore, our conception of the relation of artist or producer to the public is changed. We realize that, among the materials an artist works with, there is the *critical material* coming to him from a great variety of sources. He does not confront his muse privately nor create in a vacuum. Consequently, one of the indirect functions or purposes of art criticism is to create a body of critical material which constitutes *a set of standards* against which artists measure their work. Of course, some artists may deny that critical opinions influence them, much less that critical opinions constitute standards for their work. Nevertheless, many other artists, in their desperate pursuit of recognition, endeavor as well as they can to discern the critical standards which seem to be most prominent in the places where they wish most to be admired.

If the purposes of criticism begin with the need to understand art and to seek out its satisfactions, they conclude with the formulation of a body of opinions and reactions which serve as *standards* for the creation of art. As individuals, we may not have set out upon the critical enterprise with the goal of influencing what artists create. But in the course of discovering what art means, searching for what we like, and talking about it, we may have indirectly brought critical standards into being. Such standards shift, of course, and are difficult to formulate with precision at any particular time or place. Nevertheless, a social process of communication and interaction seems to be constantly at work, involving popular discussion of the meanings and values of art, together with artistic efforts to discern the direction of this discussion and its implications for the further creation of art.

The Tools of Art Criticism

What kind of equipment must an art critic possess in order to function adequately? What kinds of knowledge must he have, or what skills need he have mastered, to be qualified beyond the layman who so freely offers unsupported critical judgments?

Obviously, wide acquaintance with art and especially with the kind of art he proposes to deal with, is a fundamental requirement. Usually, this acquaintance is acquired through formal study, especially of art history. It is most important that knowledge of art be gained by direct experience of original works as well as through reproductions. Many artists who are also sound critics have gained their knowledge from intensive examination of works in museums as well as from studio experience. But it is very difficult, if not impossible, to gain an authentic understanding of art from lantern slides or reproductions alone. These devices should serve mainly to *remind* us of qualities we have found in original works.

Wide acquaintance with art implies more than visual recognition of the principal monuments of art history. It also calls for understanding of the styles and functions of art, the social and cultural contexts in which artists have worked, the opinions of critics and scholars during the principal periods, and the technical factors governing artistic execution in various media. However, the chief benefit conferred upon a critic by a wide acquaintance with art is breadth, or catholicity, of taste. He should know and appreciate an extended range of artistic creativity as it has been manifested in many places and times. This knowledge would be at least one defense against critical narrowness, the tendency to invoke standards which are derived from scant knowledge of styles or limited experience with technical methods. Art historians, for example, do not usually gain through their training as much technical knowledge as do artists. However, this lack can be in some measure compensated for by extensive examination of works in many styles and by study of works in various stages of execution. Such experience enables the prospective critic to gain some understanding of the gap between artistic intent and artistic achievement.

Many critics of contemporary art also have a wide acquaintanceship among artists. This situation is almost inevitable since artists and critics are thrown together by work and common interests. But acquaintance with artists may act as a critical handicap if it leads to bias in favor of or against works of art because of the personalities of the artists who have created the work. It almost seems preferable for the critic, particularly the journalistic critic, to be acquainted with artistic personalities through biographies and other documents. Thus, he may be assisted in achieving some measure of critical distance or objectivity. However, the interest we all have in persons who are successful creators, or who are prominent in artistic circles, militates against social distance between artists and critics. Consequently, it is most important that the critic have some means of defending against undue bias or sympathy for the work of artists he knows personally. Certainly it would assist critics if they were more familiar with the education of artists—that is, if they spent some time in art schools— for it is useful to see the struggles of the novice if one is to understand the achievements of the professional.

Many artists would hold the judgment of critics in greater esteem if they knew their judgments to be based upon some experience with artistic execution and technique. Of course, a number of practicing critics have had artistic experience, and some are artists themselves. But usually, the criticism we read emanates from persons with only avocational artistic experience or with purely literary and theoretical preparation for the task. It would be safe to say that most artists have very little

respect for the criticism of persons having only theoretical training, although artists are concerned about the influence of criticism, no matter who writes it. On the other hand, critics and scholars readily recognize emotional distortion and partisanship in the critical opinions of artists. Indeed, some feel that artists are almost constitutionally incapable of making critical judgments objectively and dispassionately. The question will doubtless continue to be argued as long as there are artists and critics. For a long time, universities employed only theoreticians to give art instruction. Now there is a growing tendency for educational institutions to employ theoreticians *and* practitioners, or individual instructors who have both kinds of training.

In summary, it would appear that a critic with mainly theoretical and verbal preparation may be ill-equipped to assess properly the elements of skill and technique in works of art. Indeed, there is a tendency among critics so trained to denigrate technical ability, to regard it as a fault, as evidence of superficiality. In addition, such critics do not recognize poor craftsmanship when they see it, or they may construct theoretical grounds for consigning craftsmanship and the well-wrought object to the junk-heap of history. As a consequence, the art world is annually embarrassed when the work of amateurs, neophytes, practical jokers, or animals is given serious attention, and occasionally prizes, in art exhibitions. These stunts, which are probably intended to indict the entire modern art movement, do not have anything to do with the genuine achievements of serious artists. Nevertheless, they *do* constitute a kind of scandal in the practice of art

The artist's mischievous image of the critic—a ridiculous, top-hatted figure who rides around the galleries on roller skates wielding a vacuum cleaner.

ARTHUR G. DOVE, *The Critic* (1925). Courtesy The Downtown Gallery; photo, Geoffrey Clements.

criticism and cannot be casually ignored when regarded as a comment on the quality of criticism so frequently encountered in newspapers and art journals. Conscientious critics are eager to be fair, to be open to the legitimacy of artistic expression no matter how unusual, shocking, or experimental. Hence, it is possible for them to be occasionally deceived by a fraudulent or insincere work, unless they have sufficient technical experience and connoisseurship to *recapitulate imaginatively the technical execution of the work.* In short, the critic, if he is to be more than an essayist on the themes of the works he evaluates, must know in general terms how the work was made. This knowledge is the *sine qua non* for critical expertise; without it critical judgments may be useful or interesting but only valid by grace of good fortune.

Another term, "critical sensibility," designates mainly the ability to react to the variety of meanings in a work of art. It could also be defined as the capacity for discriminating among one's feelings in the presence of a work of art. People vary in capacity for feeling, in the range of emotions they can experience in connection with events in life. Likewise, individuals vary in their capacity for feeling or understanding in connection with art. A critic, however, must have access to a wide range of aesthetic emotions, else his usefulness is severely limited. Many of the heated controversies about contemporary art may, indeed, be based on a restricted range of aesthetic perception on the part of critics. An oversimplified example might be the following: a person who regards straight lines, rectilinear composition, simplified planes, and crystalline structures as harsh, cold,

impersonal, mechanical, repellent, and so on, but who has strong preferences for curvilinear compositions, for the S-curve which some theorists considered the "curve of beauty." The reasons for his set of preferences and antipathies might be traced by a psychologist and quite possibly the set could be changed. However, the sensibility of the individual would prevent his dealing in an adequate critical manner with the work of Feininger, Mondrian, Mies van der Rohe, Albers, Gabo, and many others. Before a negative judgment could be made about the work of any of these men, it would first be necessary to experience the meanings in their work. And a critic who dislikes planimetric art would be emotionally prevented from experiencing fully the architecture of Mies or the paintings of the Analytic Cubists.

It is important that a critic be able to experience a work in its fullness. Some of us may be debarred from the fullness of experience by strongly held preferences, as cited above. Or we may be limited in our emotional range and reluctant to extend that range further. Much of education, particularly education in the fine arts, should be directed toward enlarging the range of aesthetic reactions we are capable of having in the presence of art. Needless to say, the extension of our aesthetic range is also a humanly enriching enterprise, a chief goal of liberal education. That is why emphasis upon critical capacity is as important as the accumulation of information in the study of the fine arts.

Not that a critic has no preferences, or that he sees himself as a *tabula rasa* in carrying out his critical responsibilities. He carries with him, as everyone does, a host of experiences, predilections, biases, and constitutional affinities, together with gaps in his knowledge and experience. However, the seasoned critic possesses devices, critical techniques, which permit him to act judiciously in the presence of the work of art. Hence, another item of critical equipment might be called judicious temperament. By this, I mean essentially the ability to withhold judgment until all the evidence is in. Persons untrained in art criticism make judgments too quickly; they state conclusions first and then set about finding reasons why their conclusions are valid. Naturally, the experience of a work of art takes place in an interval of time, and *during* that interval a number of impressions present themselves to the critic, impressions which in themselves seem to lead toward a particular interpretation or judgment. But the virtue of a judicious temperament is to grant time for the multitude of impressions, associations, sensations, and half-formed judgments to interact, to permit intelligence to operate in the task of sifting and sorting and organizing. In short, we need time to exercise logic and rationality when our feelings are being skillfully assaulted, and the judicious temperament supplies that time. (In Chapter Fifteen, *The Critical Performance*, the specific operations of the critical intelligence will be described in some detail.)

It follows from the remarks above about a judicious temperament that art criticism is mainly an empirical enterprise, as opposed to a deductive process. As in a legal trial before a jury, the process of arriving at a verdict involves the orderly gathering of facts and presentation of evidence and the suspension of judgment until the end. We begin without knowing what the critical judgment will be, and we gradually adduce facts and feelings until a valid conclusion seems warranted. This is the best way to avoid the pitfalls of excessive subjectivity, of partisanship, of emotional intoxication. In general, forming conclusions on the basis of "first principles" or axioms about art—in other words, proceding *deductively* from premises which may or may not be applicable to the work in question—results in bad art criticism. It is difficult to avoid deductive critical procedures entirely, and sometimes they are useful, but in general it is best when confronting a difficult contemporary work to gather the data systematically, relying on the soundness of one's critical technique to lead logically to a valid conclusion.

Types of Art Criticism

Although I have referred to a type of person called an art critic, there are in fact several levels and types of art critic, differing according to the social or professional role each performs. We are most familiar with the journalistic critic, the person who writes reviews of exhibitions, plays, books, and concerts. There are several varieties within this category, since a newspaper may employ one reporter to "do" art, music, and drama criticism, while an art journal may employ several critics with considerable specialized training. Another kind of criticism occurs in schools, art schools, colleges, universities—wherever art is taught. Such criticism, conducted by teachers of art, might be called pedagogical criticism. In addition, scholars, usually associated with universities but also with museums, write criticism which is distinctly different from the journalistic or pedagogical varieties. Finally, there is popular criticism conducted by nonprofessionals; they are clearly the majority of critics and they vary greatly in the degree of their expertise.

JOURNALISTIC CRITICISM

The chief characteristic of journalistic criticism is that it is a category of news. It is written for the readers of a newspaper or magazine to inform them of transient events in the art world and also to retain their interest as readers of a particular newspaper or journal. Hence, we speak of the "review," which is only a brief summary of an exhibition and rarely is long enough to constitute a systematic analysis of the works of art in a show. Indeed, a style of review writing has emerged which endeavors to create verbal equivalents of the works which a reader might see if he were able to attend the exhibition. Obviously, a form of criticism which endeavors to be news and at the same time to substitute words for visual experience, while also passing critical judgment, labors under an almost impossible burden. The brevity of journalistic criticism obliges the writer virtually to eliminate analysis and to rely instead on critical conclusions and heavily weighted descriptions to create exciting and vivid copy. Unfortunately, this style of critical writing also appears in some longer

magazine articles on art, where there is less excuse for offering page after page of opinion and assertion as if these constituted reasoned and responsible analysis.

Notwithstanding the obligation of a journalistic critic to satisfy the curiosity of a wide variety of readers, to entertain perhaps, to avoid writing "over their heads," and despite necessary limitations of space, some excellent critical writing is found in outstanding newspapers and in some of the weekly news magazines. The specialized monthly art journals differ considerably among themselves as they sometimes become engaged in promulgating a "party line" or in castigating the museums and foundations for failing to support their favorite artists. In general, the magazines serve to stoke the fires of critical controversy and, by expressing their biases very forcefully, they are largely responsible for the atmosphere of vitality and internecine rivalry which surrounds the contemporary artistic scene. Critics like Hilton Kramer and Frank Getlein, by questioning some of the established and well-fortified views of advocates of action painting such as Harold Rosenberg and Thomas Hess, helped to create a freer market of ideas in the late 1950's at a time when significant critical dissent was virtually nil.

Because journalistic critics write so frequently and under the pressure of deadlines, their output suffers from the perils of much newswriting: inaccuracy, hasty conclusions, the substitution of opinion for analysis, and a tendency to exercise wit at the expense of the unseen artist. But the discriminating reader of such writing learns to discount the biases of a critic in advance, to compensate by reading several critics, and to check for accuracy by viewing the work himself. Without such safeguards, the individual who relies excessively on journalistic criticism finds, after some time, that his knowledge and critical understanding of contemporary art consist chiefly of a body of received opinions about the principal current reputations. Coteries and intrigues abound in the art world, and one's critical judgment can easily become a by-product of the incessant jockeying for position and prestige which necessarily characterizes a realm where talented persons struggle for recognition.

PEDAGOGICAL CRITICISM

Pedagogical criticism is intended to advance the artistic and aesthetic maturity of students. It does not so much seek to render authoritative judgments upon work by students as to enable students eventually to make such judgments themselves. The teacher of art ought to be aware of critical opinion in the professional art world, and should be capable of functioning as a critic of mature work; but he is not mainly engaged in holding student work up to contemporary professional standards. For the pedagogical critic, contemporary opinions and standards may represent possibilities for stimulation and discussion, but they should not represent absolute goals for achievement.

A difficult task for the teacher of art, one which involves his critical capacities in the process of instruction, is the sensitive analysis and interpretation of a student's work *to the student*. From this criticism, the student learns how to conduct analysis and interpretation himself, and also gains some insight into the direction and character of his achievement. In their early artistic efforts, small children require serious responses to their work as much as more skilled adolescents and adults. Since the creation of art has social implications (art is made for someone else to own, use, or admire as well as to satisfy one's self), art instructors must respond critically during the process of execution and at its conclusion. Indeed, the decision about when a work is "finished" has immense critical meaning and is often the result of collaboration by an instructor with a student.

Art instruction until the period of the 1930's usually involved the invocation by a teacher of his personal critical standards in the evaluation of student work. Students sought out teachers whose work they admired and may have wished to imitate. It rarely occurred to teachers or students that criticism might be based on standards or achievement other than those embodied in the teacher's own work. The instruction and criticism which resulted from this assumption were effective and educationally valuable insofar as the teacher was himself an artist whose stature and maturity did not require that he reproduce his style and artistic personality endlessly among his students. Certainly Robert Henri (1865–1929) was an inspiring teacher whose instruction grew out of his personal discoveries and convictions about painting, and yet these did not constitute a constricting influence upon his students. Thomas Hart Benton (1889–   ), on the other hand, from the force of his personality or the narrowness of his standards, succeeded in producing a host of "little Bentons." One such little

THOMAS HART BENTON, *Arts of the West* (1932), top. Courtesy New Britain Museum of American Art, New Britain, Connecticut.

JACKSON POLLOCK, *Deposition* (c.1936), center. Collection Lee Krasner Pollock; courtesy Marlborough-Gerson Gallery Inc., New York.

ARSHILE GORKY, *Waterfall* (c.1943), right. Courtesy Sidney Janis Gallery, New York; photo, Geoffrey Clements.

Benton was Jackson Pollock, whose early work was touchingly Benton-esque. He moved on to stylistic affinities with Picasso, Arshile Gorky (1904–48), and others, before arriving at the style of dripped and thrown paint for which he became famous.

The prevailing philosophy of pedagogical art criticism would seem to call for a certain self-abnegation on the part of the artist-teacher. His function is to assist in the gestation of critical standards within the student—standards which are congenial to the *student's* artistic personality as it appears to be emerging. Needless to say, some students, as they go through adolescence, have exceedingly well-developed conceptions of the direction and value of their work; others are painfully lacking in confidence. For the art instructor, both types constitute genuine challenges for his critical and teaching skills.

SCHOLARLY CRITICISM

Academic art criticism is the fully developed product of scholarship, critical sensibility, and judicial temperament. Its function is to provide the thorough analysis, interpretation, and evaluation of recent or traditional art and artistic reputations which ample time, space, and the best available evidence can make possible. Generally, such efforts can only be accomplished with the sponsorship of universities. Scholarly criticism represents the closest approximation to "the judgment of history" about an artist who is still alive, and it constitutes part of the changing judgment of history for an artist who is dead. Presumably, the academic critic, settled in the safety and security of tenure and undergirded by university traditions of scrupulous research and disinterested truth-seeking, is least vulnerable to special interest. Like a Justice of the Supreme Court who holds a life appointment, he can function as well as his critical equipment will permit, without regard for fear or favor.

Unfortunately, as academic criticism directs its attention toward contemporary art, it becomes vulnerable to some of the disabilities which afflict journalism. That is, notwithstanding the advantages and the protected place of the university professor, his sensibility is involved in the current way of seeing and feeling, and he is thus subject to the same enthusiasms and aversions as journeyman critics who have less time for reflection. In addition, the academy now contains living, practicing artists as teachers, and they have an influence on professorial critics who in the past were wont to turn their gaze away from the modern "chaos." As the university confronts contemporary life, it begins to lose its precious detachment and objectivity.

A very useful function of academic critics is their re-examination of artistic reputations which most of us have already categorized and set aside. Each new era has its characteristic way of seeing, and thus an artist who may have been regarded as banal in his time is discovered to have fresh meaning for the present era. Museums frequently function in this manner when they resurrect the reputations of a school or style of art which has fallen into disesteem. Such an operation was carried out by the Museum of Modern Art and its then curator of painting and sculpture, Peter Selz, in an exhibition and scholarly catalog on Art Nouveau. Hitherto regarded as a *fin-de-siècle* art movement of only minor decorative value, Art Nouveau was shown by the exhibition and its catalog to have had a most significant influence on many of the leading painters, sculptors, architects, designers, and craftsmen whose work we regard as modern classics today. However, the exposition of historical influence was not the only benefit conferred by the exhibition. A skillful installation, combined with a thorough and keenly analytic publication, enabled the public to discover in Art Nouveau a comprehensive artistic approach which conceivably meets certain contemporary aesthetic needs. That is, the linear approach to imagery in Art Nouveau may have served as a refreshing "new opening" for contemporary painters, wedded so closely to massive, loaded-brush attacks upon the canvas, with little attention paid to line, design, or drawing as it was conceived in 1900. In addition, we saw how a total aesthetic approach permeated all of the visual arts, from magazine illustration, to jewelry and industrial design, to architecture and sculpture.

POPULAR CRITICISM

Throughout this discussion, I have referred by implication to popular art criticism, to the judgments made forthrightly or indirectly by the great majority who have no claim to critical expertness. Quite clearly, this majority of our citizens will continue to make critical judgments whether or not they are regarded as exercising their judgment properly. Therefore, the existence of a vast body of popular critical opinion, more or less informed and experienced, has to be considered in its effect on the total contemporary art situation. As mentioned earlier, critical opinion constitutes an important influence on what artists create. And this would be true of popular criticism as well as expert criticism. The concept of an avant-garde, of a body of artists working in advance of existing popular taste, assumes, of course, the existence of popular taste as a sort of huge, laggard collection of conventional preferences. But if it were not for this popular majority, there would be no body of conventional preference for the avant-garde to rebel against! The idea of progress in art, of advanced and retarded preferences, is very misleading, and a misapplication of the idea of progress in history.

There will always be large numbers of people who judge art intuitively, who regard their possession of normal vision as satisfactory equipment for the conduct of art criticism. The number of such persons is so large, and their critical consensus so consistent through history, that their opinions and intuitive standards have to be regarded as constituting a foundation for at least some of the creativity in the visual arts. Their desire for an art which is faithful to the visual facts, an art of verisimilitude, has been discussed in connection with the style of objective accuracy. Of course, the popular success of cinematic and television imagery has served to satisfy the desire of the popular majority for realism and has also created the opportunity for the older visual arts to depart from realism or naturalism. Nevertheless, we can expect that the contemporary artist of each new era will work in a context which is mainly determined by the obvious and candid preference of the majority for an art which imitates appearances. We can hope, however, that the improvement and extension of aesthetic education will enable most people to discriminate among the types of realism, so that a vulgar or "tricky" realism will be disdained. It should not be impossible for most people to learn to see the difference between a mechanical sort of realism in art and a mimetic style which reveals the *character* of things through imitation of their appearances or typical modes of being. Popular criticism, in other words, can become discriminating within its own standards of fidelity to the visual facts.

Kinds of Critical Judgment

What are the ultimate grounds on which a critic justifies his evaluations? Assuming that a critic is knowledgeable and disciplined, and that he has the appropriate temperament and sensibility, are there any final standards to which he can repair?

It would be enough in most cases if the art critic possessed the right credentials and practiced a method which was open to reason and discussion. Such equipment would satisfactorily enable him to carry on the work of description, analysis, and interpretation. But evaluation must take place in the light of some idea of what artistic excellence is. Hence, I shall discuss here a few of the principal ideas of artistic excellence which seem to underlie what critics and others say is good.

NICOLAS POUSSIN, *Landscape with the Burial of Phocion* (1648). Courtesy Musée du Louvre, Cliché des Musées Nationaux.

FORMALISM

Once we have abandoned the notion that artistic excellence consists of the accuracy with which art imitates reality, or of the amount and kind of information a work yields, we can turn to what is called formalist criticism. Such criticism locates excellence in the integrative quality of the formal organization of a work of art. By formal organization we mean the relationships among the primary visual elements of the work, independent of any labels or associations or conventional meanings which these elements may have by themselves. For example, any visual beauty or excellence in a building by Mies depends on the formal relationships established by the building as a whole, since the individual parts are neutral: They do not look like anything other than themselves, and we have difficulty forming associations with the glass and the steel members. On the other hand, it is easy to form associations with shapes and textures in a house designed by Frank Lloyd Wright; he was a Romantic architect whose houses deliberately carry the viewer beyond their structural elements to a host of meanings and associations connected to the land, rocks, the sky, and other natural forms.

For a formalist, successful relationships are designed; they must be the result of calculation and planning by the artist rather than personal variation in the viewer's perception. Obviously Mondrian appeals to the for-

malist since he minimizes accidental effects. There is no uncertainty on our part about the artist's formal means or method: It is to put together the parts in as simple, interesting, and unified a manner as he can without permitting "extraneous" considerations to enter.

Formalist excellence, however, does not require a geometric style or a totally abstract style. In the paintings of Poussin we have naturalism and a multitude of complex shapes, but the entire composition is organized so that the various masses, contours, directions, and representations of mass and space are related to each other with precision; they balance, or cancel out, almost like the books which have been audited by an accountant.

In viewing a work of art, the formalist critic may encounter value in the meaning of the subject matter or the sensuous appeal of the materials used. However, he is willing to confer the judgment of excellence upon the work only insofar as its *form*, its organization, is responsible for his *perception* of the meaning or the sensuous qualities of the materials. For example, he would admire the bronze metal skin of Mies van der

Rohe's Seagram Building not because bronze is an inherently beautiful material, but only because Mies has given the bronze members precisely the right dimensions and located them at the best intervals in relation to the quantity of tinted glass, the height of the building, and the total spatial envelope which affects our perception of the whole.

Formalist criticism takes some interest in craftsmanship since putting things together soundly and properly working them to the "right" degree of finish necessarily invoke formal criteria of pleasing relationships. However, craftsmanship is ultimately based on durability and the logical use of tools and materials, utilitarian concerns which are not of primary interest to formalist criticism. If we try to penetrate to the heart of the formalist critique, we should probably encounter a wish that works of art depend for their effectiveness *solely* on the principle of *unity in variety,* with that unity achieved through the non-symbolic properties of the materials employed in the work.

Formalism has had a healthy influence on art when it has been negative in its strictures, that is, when it has insisted on the elimination of literary and associative elements as the principal vehicles of meaning. In its positive implications, however, formalism experiences some difficulty in establishing just what its canon of excellence is. That is, how do we know that the formal relationships in a work are pleasing or significant? The great formalist critics Roger Fry and Clive Bell never succeeded in defining the criteria of formal excellence; they merely associated it with the capacity to generate disinterested, aesthetic emotion.

If the formalist were pressed further, he might say that a formal organization is best or most significant when it *embodies the ideal structural possibilities of the particular visual elements present in the work.* But how do we know whether the organization we are viewing represents the *ideal* possibilities of its particular components? Here, the formalist must fall back upon the quality of perception of the viewer—that is, he must rely upon the viewer's conviction that his perceptions in the presence of the work are intrinsically satisfying. The late connoisseur and critic Bernard Berenson was relying on formalist ideas of aesthetic value when he employed the term "life-enhancing" to describe the characteristics of great works of art. The term "life-enhancing" represents a judgment by a viewer that his perception of formal quality is solely responsible for a feeling of exaltation.

This criterion of aesthetic value may not be as subjective as it appears. The qualities in the organization of the art object which elicit from the formalist critic the designations "excellent" or "beautiful" or "life-enhancing" are the qualities which a reasonably intelligent, reasonably perceptive person discovers to be pleasing. That is, they approximate an *ideal standard,* or *norm,* which establishes connections with whatever is within men that seeks or requires the *perception of an ideal standard, or norm.*

Now we have come, in effect, to a theory of communication which underlies the formalist idea of aesthetic excellence: The formalist shares with the Platonist the view that there is an ideal or perfect embodiment of all things, and that art, when it is successful, reveals, represents, or *communicates* that ideal embodiment. The formalist and the Platonist might quarrel about whether the ideal embodiment exists *before* or *after* the work of art is created. But they agree that art approximates to a greater or lesser degree some idea or form of perfection; and the normal man, *l'homme moyen sensuel* (the man of moderate feeling), as the French put it, has, because of his biological and psychological make-up, the ability to perceive, to recognize ideality of form. Thus, excellent form communicates itself to individuals, not only because of learning or personal culture but also because they as normal persons cannot help responding to it.

These views about the foundations of aesthetic excellence are held by artists as well as laymen. Mondrian and Kandinsky, notably, were interested in discovering the combinations of forms which would embody to perfection certain feelings or ideas. It is interesting that Mondrian used mainly a measured, geometric path to formal perfection and that Kandinsky, although he used geometry, is best known for irregular, "expressionistic" colors and shapes. Formalist criteria are intuitively employed by artists as they create, particularly when they are faced with the problem of deciding when a work is finished. There is a strong artistic tendency to "perfect" the forms in a work, long after the theme or subject matter has become plainly visible. The artist continues to adjust and modify the formal relationships until *he feels* they can be carried no further. In measuring the finish or perfection of the work against his ideal requirements, he is proposing his own ideas of what is normative for the ap-

proval of a reasonably sensitive and intelligent viewer, thus demonstrating the formalist theory, that universal norms or ideal possibilities communicate themselves among men who are attuned to apprehend them. Such men are those regarded by their group or society as having all the normal appetites and capacities in proper measure.

Part of the task of art criticism, if one is a formalist, is deciding whether the artist has carried the adjustment of his forms precisely to the point where they should be carried or whether he has "spoiled" them in some way. Clearly, the exercise of such judgment calls for knowledge of the formal possibilities open to the artist as well as appreciation of the technical possibilities employed or left unexploited by the artist. Consequently, the formalist critic must be a widely experienced

PIET MONDRIAN, *Painting I* (1926). Courtesy The Museum of Modern Art, New York, Katherine S. Dreier bequest.

WASSILY KANDINSKY, *Study for Composition 7* (1913). Courtesy Mrs. Nina Kandinsky; collection Felix Klee.

person, yet he must avoid the temptation of all critics to condemn the artist for failing to create the work which he, the critic, would have created. Obviously, the critic cannot evaluate a work of art which does not exist, one which someone *might have* executed; he must hold the work up to the standard of formal perfection *toward which it appears to be striving.* He tries to learn through *internal evidence,* that is, through visual hints and signs *in* the art object, what goal the work is striving to reach.

Many artists and critics are probably formalists without knowing they are. Their criteria of excellence, however, consist ultimately of feelings of sympathy with the organization of the art object, feelings derived from design qualities, and communicated perhaps by pleasing or affirmative signals received from their glandular, nervous, muscular, and skeletal systems.

One can only suspect that these sources participate in the formalist awareness of aesthetic value. Formalism as a theory provides us only with a guide to the values it rejects as aesthetically irrelevant: social, historical, and psychological description; literary and emotional association; and imitation or representation of real objects. Beyond the *form preferences of the normal person,* confirmed by his experience of a distinctively aesthetic emotion, it offers no certain guide to artistic excellence.

EXPRESSIVISM

Expressivist criticism, as might be surmised from the term, conceives of excellence in terms of the ability of art to communicate ideas and feelings effectively, intensely, and vividly. It is at the opposite pole from formalism in its lack of interest in the niceties of formal organization for its own sake. A good

Child's chalk drawing, left. From George Conrad, *The Process of Art Education in the Elementary School* (Prentice-Hall, 1964). Courtesy the author.

JEAN DUBUFFET, *Person in Red Costume* (1961), right. Collection The Museum of Modern Art, New York, gift of Mr. and Mrs. Ralph F. Colin.

OTTO DIX, *Lens Bombed* (1924), left. Collection of The Philadelphia Museum of Art.

Air attack on tank, World War I, right. Photo, United Press International.

example of art admired by expressivist criticism is seen in the work of children. Children rarely possess the skill or the desire to arrive at perfect organizations of form. For them, the impulse to communicate, to objectify some inner need, is much stronger than the desire to embellish, modify, or adjust the results so that they are "beautiful" as adults understand beauty. The art of children may often be enjoyed for the delight afforded by its uninhibited color, design, and imagery. Yet the principal reason for its appeal lies in the naîveté of the child's *view* of the world. Some expressivist critics believe that children (and primitives) portray a world of ideal possibilities since they can see through to the "heart" of things without the associations and distortions which plague adult vision. This suggests that we are interested in the ideas and emotions expressed by child art more than we are attracted by the technical and organizational qualities of their work. The expressivist critic, in short, sees the formal elements and their combinations as vehicles for the communication of ideas or the sharing of specific feelings.

Now, all art, regardless of style, and no matter whether it is successful or not, to some extent communicates ideas or feelings. Consequently, expressivism as a criterion of aesthetic value must provide some way of deciding whether we are in the presence of something *beyond* the mere sharing of feelings and ideas. To meet this problem, expressivist criticism offers us the idea of *intensity of experience* in the presence of art. That work is best which stirs us most deeply, which arouses feelings in connection with the material communicated, feelings which

are stronger than we would experience if the same material were encountered in everyday life. Furthermore, the intensity of our experience is based in part upon our knowledge that the artist's skill is responsible for the way we feel. For example, if a photographer presents us with straightforward, purely descriptive views of a terrible catastrophe, such as an earthquake, a sea disaster, or an airplane attack, we may respond with strong feelings of shock and sympathy, but we do not especially regard the photographer as being responsible for our feelings. However, when an artist (who might be a photographer) deals with the same material, we are aware that he is in some manner governing our imagination and our responses. The expressivist critic, therefore, is interested in art which (1) carries him beyond his customary range of intensity in the apprehension of ideas and the awareness of feelings, and (2) achieves this result because it communicates an idea of importance through technique or through the sheer force of feeling and depth of emotion experienced by the artist.

It thus appears that the expressivist critic believes that art should "have something to say," which implies that the artist should have something to say. This school of criticism, therefore, shares with large numbers of laymen the preference for art as a source of insight about life. It sees the artist as in some sense wise in a way that the officially designated wise men in our society are not. That is, the artist has taken hold of some truths about life, possibly through intuition, and because of his skill, talent, and imagination, found the means of embodying those truths. Consequently, the *originality, contemporary relevance,* and *cognitive validity* of the ideas communicated by art become important criteria for judgment. Although the expressivist critic recognizes the desirability of excellence in technique and formal organization, he regrets that these qualities are often associated with the communication of trivial ideas or that they have themselves become the subject matter of art.

It is not uncommon for expressivist critics to apply the criterion of truthfulness to life in judging art. Certainly critics of the drama or of novels talk about the credibility of characters and situations. This criterion does not necessarily require that art be an imitation, a tape-recorded account, of life. It *does* require that the viewer or audience be sufficiently convinced of the possibility of what is presented to be willing to suspend disbelief and enter imaginatively into the aesthetic experience. However, although the theory of imitation, or mimesis, has influence on the criticism of drama and the novel through the criterion of credibility, it obviously has less applicability to the visual arts and music, especially in modern times. The idea of art as credible imitation of life survives in the expressivist demand that art be *relevant* to life; works of art need not look like recognizable objects, places, persons and events, but they must support ideas and emotions which have immediate meaning for the reasonably perceptive person. We have come again to the normal individual, *l'homme moyen sensuel,* who serves to establish a standard of emotional and intellectual relevance for the expressivist critic as he established a standard of satisfying structural relationships for the formalist critic.

In relying on that mythical person, the normal individual, for standards of emotional relevance or formal coherence in art, we are, in effect, approaching a criterion of universality for the judgment of excellence. Not that everyone must admire a work for it to be deemed excellent, but great works of art must have the capacity to elicit admiration from the *majority of persons* who are reasonably well informed, sensitive, and open-minded. A survey among such persons could never actually be taken, particularly since they have lived in all historical eras; hence, it is one of the tasks of art criticism to establish procedures, standards, and criteria in order to function *as if* such a body of persons existed and could be consulted, *as if* one could appeal to their preferences and capacities for feeling. Because of the indeterminate character of the group of persons to whom art criticism appeals to support ultimate judgments of excellence, art criticism is not, of course, a science. It is rather one of the humanities, one of those continuous inquiries about questions men are interested in, and only tentative conclusions are offered as the evidence of present taste and historical judgment about art accumulates.

INSTRUMENTALISM

Instrumentalist theories conceive of art as a tool which helps to advance some moral, religious, political, or psychological purpose. Artistic excellence, according to such theories, is not based on the ability of artists to solve problems inherent in the use of their materials or the solution of problems *internal* to the artistic enterprise. Neither is artistic excellence based on the expressivist criteria of vividness, credibility, and intensity in the communication of ideas or the sharing of feelings. The instrumentalist is concerned with the *consequences* of the ideas and feelings expressed by art. He wishes art to serve an end more important than itself, or, stated in another way, art is excellent when we are not aware of it but rather find our thoughts and emotions involved with the purpose art is supposed to subserve.

An ordinary illustration of the instrumentalist idea of art is found in the background music which accompanies a film. Ideally, the music should not be obtrusive, the audience should be unaware of it. The music should support the dramatic action we see, heightening its meaning or possibly anticipating climactic moments, but never calling attention to itself. The relation of art to social, political, or moral ends thus should be the same as the relation of background music to the dramatic action on the cinema screen.

The history of art is rich in illustration of the instrumentalist theory of art. In a sense, the history of art is the history of its service to the principal institutions and dominant classes of civilized society: priesthood, church,

nobility, mercantile aristocracy, princely court, imperial monarch, democratic public, totalitarian despot, and corporate elite. It has only been in the modern era that art has functioned to a considerable extent as a free-floating activity, unattached and unpatronized by a single, dominant social class or institution. More recently, modern museums, universities, and foundations have emerged as sponsors of art or of artists; but they have for the most part taken great care not to change the free-floating, unattached character of contemporary artistic creativity. They have tried not to have their support seem to be contingent upon any loyalty of the artist to the institution which aids him. Certainly they have not consciously endeavored to influence the *content* of art. Hence, the instrumentalist theory of art finds support in the institutional practices of the past. In the present, instrumentalists must accept the freedom of the *artist*, his detachment from institutions, but they can argue for the subservience of *art*, the necessity that art shall advance some purpose, usually a purpose embodied in an institution.

One difficulty with the instrumentalist interpretation of historic art —art, for example, in the service of the Christian Church—is that today we admire ancient art for different reasons from the ones it was created to serve. Romanesque sculpture, for example, was created to teach religion, to communicate the doctrines of the Church to people who could not read. We, on the contrary, can read about and receive religious teachings through books and other sources. Nevertheless, we admire Romanesque sculpture for the vigor of its forms, its relatedness to the

King David from the Cathedral of Santiago de Compostela, Spain (c.1077–1124). Photo, Boudot-Lamotte.

South portal, Abbey of St. Pierre, Moissac, France (early 12th century).

architectural structures of which it was a part, and for its symbolic and expressive power. For us, such sculpture is art *about* religion, while for its contemporaries, Romanesque sculpture was inevitably *part of* the religious life.

A strong argument in favor of the instrumentalist theory lies in its implied analysis of artistic creativity. The instrumentalist recognizes that art which formerly served some purpose outside itself is now prized for its formal or expressive qualities. These qualities are present, he believes, because they had to be "built into" the art object so that it would function adequately in the service of church, or state, or aristocracy. In other words, the creation of excellent works of art calls for proper motivation, the motivation of a cause, or institution, or profound psychological need. The desire to place skill, energy, and imagination at the service of an idea or institution in which one strongly and sincerely believes, results in the creation of forms whose aesthetic potential is very great. Another type of motivation which the instrumentalist must accept, and which history illustrates, is the incentive of continuous support from a patron, or generous payment for individually commissioned works. There is no evidence that such support or payment had more disastrous artistic consequences than present arrangements or nonarrangements for the patronage of art and artists.

However, is the instrumentalist critic really a formalist or expressivist critic, differing only in his requirement that art have extra-artistic motivation in order to be excellent? This view would be incorrect since it converts instrumentalist theories of art into theories of artistic motivation or of pedagogy, when in fact, instrumentalism *derives* artistic motivation from the transcendent value of the institution art serves. Instrumentalists are unwilling to accept the view that aesthetic values exist independently, that satisfactions or meanings in artistic forms can be experienced apart from their employment toward some external purpose. The reason, they would argue, that Michelangelo's *Pietà* is a great work is not only that it illustrates a central event in Christianity, but also that its formal organization supports ideas of death, grief, and maternal love.

MICHELANGELO, *Pietà* (1498 or 1499).

These ideas are the *purposes* for whose expression the forms were created. We have a psychological need to understand maternal love, and the extremity of the situation represented in the *Pietà* challenges the artist to organize a work whose forms express love, grief, and resignation. These ideas, to be sure, support moral and religious teachings at the same time that they satisfy the universal human concern about the sustenance of life through motherhood and the denial of life through social practices like execution or war. The meaning of the forms and our judgment of their excellence, however, depends on our perception of the purposes or ends which the forms are clearly intended to support. There is a clarity in the relationship between the formal organization and the purpose of the work, which provides the instrumentalist standard of judgment. Unlike the formalist critic who must speculate about whether the organization he perceives has realized its ideal possibilities, the instrumentalist critic can more readily discern the purpose of the work. Hence, he can direct his critical energies to the estimation of the artist's success in fulfilling his purpose.

There is a vulgar kind of instrumentalist criticism which requires of art that it illustrate ideas or endeavor to stimulate emotions which have been shown in prior argument to have political or social value. Thus, certain Marxist critics require that art illustrate the class struggle, the impoverishment of the masses under capitalism, the heroism of workers, and so on. At more sophisticated levels, Marxist critics tend to evaluate artistic excellence in terms of its ability to present or re-present "correct" versions of the operation of dialectical materialism in history. At its best, Marxist thought is mainly convincing in its explanation of the social relations having to do with the creation and use of art, but it tends to be unsatisfactory in the formulation of criteria of artistic excellence. Diego Rivera was an artist, himself a Communist, whose work met with ap-

DIEGO RIVERA, *Two Women* (1914). Courtesy The Arkansas Art Center, gift of Mrs. Jean Mauzé, New York, 1955.

EDWARD LANING, *The Role of the Immigrant in the Industrial Development of America*, mural at Ellis Island [details] (1930's). New York Public Library.

proval by Marxist canons of taste but who is also widely admired by non-Marxist critics. His murals and paintings dealing with the exploitation of the Mexican Indian masses were intended to present both a dramatized version of history and the motivation for revolutionary change. It is likely, however, that the foundation of Rivera's enduring reputation as an artist is established more securely on formalist than instrumentalist grounds. He was a superb designer and draftsman, with great skill in organizing large, complex surfaces whose cumulative effect is exciting, dramatic, and well related to their architectural settings.

The more recent efforts of the Soviet government, and of authoritarian governments in general, to stimulate the creation of art which supports and illustrates the official views of the regime have been almost uniformly productive of mediocrity. We should not hastily conclude that such failures are due to the employment of instrumentalist theories of art by government officials. It is more likely due to the promulgation by the government of an "official style"—socialist realism—and to excessive bureaucratic caution and rigidity, not to say, ignorance. Citizens and politicians in all societies however, can adhere to critical theories of vulgar instrumentalism: Art is excellent when it illustrates the achievement of our officially proclaimed goals; it must never reveal our personal or collective inadequacies; it must conform with official characterizations of hostile or competitive social systems. To this it must be added, however, that notwithstanding occasional uninformed criticism of art from prominent persons, artists in America, and in Western societies in general, enjoy substantial creative freedom, and some are prosperous also.

Notwithstanding the vulgar application of instrumentalist theories—especially in censorship—they often provide useful grounds for the criticism of art. They encourage the critic to seek out the social, moral, or psychological purposes which art has historically served and to assess the degree to which these purposes are satisfied in contemporary creativity. They also serve to emphasize the legitimacy of art which is related to the dominant concerns of life and thus act as a corrective to the artistic tendency to become excessively involved with narrow, purely technical problems.

CONCLUSION

Philosophers and aestheticians have described a number of other theoretical grounds for critical judgment in addition to, and in distinction from, those mentioned here. I have tried to indicate in this section some of the main kinds of argument used to justify critical assertions of aesthetic value. For the beginning student, it is perhaps useful to know that such theoretical and logical justifications exist and must ultimately be relied on to support judgments of value in the realm of art. Individuals may wish to develop critical theories which stress the hedonic or pleasurable element in art, or they may prefer to view aesthetic value chiefly as communication of personality, the character of the age, or man's aspirations for a better world. In connection with the criticism of architecture, handcraft, and industrially produced objects, it may be advisable to rely on theories which analyze social utility, workmanship, formal coherence, and the expressiveness of processes of forming and fabrication. The forms and purposes of art are so varied that no single critical theory is likely to be adequate for the evaluation of all works. Indeed, the adequacy of some theories of art criticism results from ruling certain classes of objects as aesthetically irrelevant, thus confining consideration to the kinds of art where a particular set of critical principles can be applied. The layman who says, "Such and such a work is not art," avoids the task of criticizing work he does not like or understand simply by refusing to examine it. He probably does so because he knows of no critical theory which will allow him to examine the object in question intelligently. But obviously, if we want to understand art and assess its value, formal or informal theories of art criticism which exclude works or art from consideration are not very useful. We would be wise to employ a definition of art which is as comprehensive as possible, which includes potentially everything that man makes. Then, reasonably equipped with the apparatus of art criticism, we can proceed to examine the merits of any work which presents itself for judgment.

CHAPTER FIFTEEN

Having discussed the theory of art criticism—the qualifications of a critic, the purposes of his activity, and the kinds of argument he can use to support his judgments—let us turn now to a consideration of the actual critical performance. Throughout the text, in the course of discussing works of art, I have functioned informally as a critic. Indeed, any statement about art is likely to contain examples of critical performance, since it is difficult to talk about specific art objects without carrying out some of the functions of art criticism. In this chapter I shall describe in some detail the principal features of the critical performance.

My guiding assumption is that there is a form, a systematic way of behaving like a critic, just as there is a systematic way of behaving like a lawyer. In presenting an argument for his client, a lawyer presumably has some method of offering evidence, of refuting his adversary, of citing appropriate precedents, of appealing to his hearers, and so on. Art criticism does not have the form of legal debate, but it *does* have a form. And if we wish to be effective as critics, we must become conscious, *critically* conscious, of the form or process or system (if any) we use in arriving at our critical conclusions.

THE CRITICAL

PERFORMANCE

I have divided the *performance* of art criticism into four stages: Description, Formal Analysis, Interpretation, and Evaluation or Judgment. It would be possible to break down these categories further, and it is also likely that they overlap. Nevertheless, they consist of fundamentally *different* operations which a critic must perform, and their *sequence* follows the order of the easiest operation to the most difficult operation. And since art criticism is more empirical than deductive, the stages proceed from the specific to the general. That is, we focus on particular visual facts before drawing conclusions about their collective value.

Description

Description is a process of taking inventory, of noting what is immediately presented to the viewer. We are interested at this stage in avoiding as far as possible the drawing of inferences. We wish to arrive at a simple account of "what is there," the kind of account about which any reasonably observant person would agree. A legal analogy is pertinent: A witness in a courtroom is usually cautioned by the judge not to draw conclusions, *no matter how he feels* about the case. He must reply as factually as possible to the questions put to him, but it is for others to interpret what he has said and to deliver a verdict. Likewise in critical description, interpretation must be deferred. The language of the critic should be as "unloaded" as possible. That is, it must not contain hints about the value of what is described.

The reason for deferring inferences and value judgments about what is described is to make certain that the description, or inventory, is complete. "Inventory" is an appropriate term here: It comes from the Latin *invenire*, meaning "to find," "to come upon," and it is the critic's function *to find* what is objectively present in the work. If the critic became involved in assertions of value at this stage, he might also, quite possibly, proceed to justify his evaluations. Such activity would tend to prevent the critic from completing his description, that is, from finding everything which is "there" to be discovered. We can assume that an art object, which may have engaged the skill, imagination, and craftsmanship of an artist over a long period of time, contains a number of things which are not superficially visible. Indeed, it is common for people to remark that they have made new discoveries in works they have owned for a long time. Another reason for deferred judgments is that we do not wish the final critical statement to be based on a nonreflective perception of the work.

You might say that there is no such thing as observation without value judgment, that we see everything in terms of its value or meaning to ourselves. However, I am trying to describe a *system* of criticism, which implies a *discipline* of seeing, interpreting, and judging. The natural mode of perception, which inevitably involves valuing, has to be resisted in an enterprise which claims to be disciplined and systematic. Consequently, although our perceptions appear to lead toward certain interpretations and evaluations, we defer or postpone them —they will not be forgotten—while we complete out inventory. Furthermore, a good critic does not wish to be embarassed subsequently by the necessity of changing a premature interpretation, one that was made before all the evidence was collected.

What are the kinds of things in a work of art which we are interested in describing? First of all, we should mention what is most obvious. If we are dealing with a naturalistic work, we note the *names* of the things we see.

In description we use words at a level of generalization which will minimize disagreement. For example, we might say of Picasso's *Les Demoiselles d'Avignon* that it contains the figures of five young women. But, notwithstanding the title, it may not be immediately apparent that one of the figures is a woman. We should say, then, that the painting contains five *figures*, four of whom appear to be women. It would be better for the critic *to prove* that the fifth figure is a woman. Quite possibly, the uncertainty about the nature of the figures may in itself be useful in forming an interpretation subsequently. In noting the things which cannot be a source of disagreement, we should mention the title. (It constitutes a gratuitous clue, assuming that art criticism can be compared to detective work.) We know that the title may be misleading or irrelevant, but there are safeguards against being misled by titles.

As works increase in degree of abstraction from nature, it becomes difficult to name objects, trees, persons, and so on. In other words, the subject matter we are accustomed to recognize easily in traditional works disappears or shifts to something else. We are obliged now to describe the principal conformations, colors, and directions which meet our inspection. In noting such matters, we should try to give information without offering any hints to their meaning. A shape is ovoid or rectangular; the edge of a contour is sharp or indistinct. But we should not say a shape is gentle or grotesque, a color harmonious or harsh. The trained critic can, moreover, perceive compositional features in a work, and he can describe them without making value judgments. That is, he can readily recognize repetitions of shapes and colors; he can identify the axes or directions which forms take. He can direct the attention of viewers to visual characteristics which the viewer would not have found for himself.

One of the more difficult, but necessary, tasks in description of modern works is to call attention to characteristics of execution, since these affect the ultimate interpretation. In examining sculpture we should not only mention the obvious fact that a bronze has been cast from a clay model, but also observe how the clay has been built up—compare it, for instance, with the surface of a bronze casting by Rodin, Epstein, or Maillol. The application of paint, too, is significant and should be noted. The critic with technical knowledge can discern whether the paint has been thinned or not, how it has been brushed out, how it has been mixed, whether it contains additives, and whether the surface is built up of transparent layers or applied in one coat, *alla prima*. In architecture, obvious technical features, such as the use of cast-concrete or steel-frame construction, should be considered. In craft objects as well as manufactured objects, final critical judgments must be informed by a description of the process of fabricating: Is a container turned, built up by hammering, stamped out, cast? Are the distinctive marks of the tools or forming process visible or concealed? The answers to these questions must affect our perception of the object, our understanding of it, and our critical judgment.

It would appear, therefore, that critical description involves (1) making an inventory of the names of the things we see in the art object and (2) per-

PABLO PICASSO, *Les Demoiselles d'Avignon* (1907). Collection The Museum of Modern Art, New York, acquired through the Lillie P. Bliss bequest.

forming a technical analysis or description of the way the work seems to have been made. It is an operation intended to permit the viewer to "take in" the whole work and to defer the task of interpretation and appraisal. In this respect, critical description has some of the character of a "delaying action," a postponement, in the interest of greater critical acuity later on, of our immediate impulse to draw conclusions. We realize that asserting a patch of color is sky or land or clothing or skin is itself a process of drawing inferences from sensory data. Therefore, we invoke our rule that in critical description a level of generalization must be used which is sufficiently broad to minimize disagreement among reasonable observers. With abstract or non-

SKIDMORE, OWINGS AND MERRILL, Beinecke Rare Book and Manuscript Library, Yale University (1963). Courtesy Yale University News Bureau.

objective works, our descriptions become highly generalized and we also tend to make greater use of technical analysis. For such analysis, the viewer must depend on the authority of the critic. In architectural criticism, for example, we may have to rely on a critic who knows building techniques to the extent that he can distinguish between a curtain wall and a load-bearing wall. But this distinction is not, of course, a matter of personal taste or subjective judgment. The question whether a wall is load-bearing or not can be empirically verified. An *aesthetic* question may subsequently arise about whether a curtain wall appears or "feels like" a load-bearing wall. Here, too, objective visual evidence can be discovered to take into account our feelings about the wall.

A good example of such criticism at work is the following comment by Professor Vincent Scully:*

Moreover, the Beineke Library wall is actually a Vierendeel truss; it thus need be supported only at the four corners of the building. But the truss does not look structural to the eye, which therefore sees the building as small, since the span looks to be a little one. Yet the building is huge and therefore disorienting to the viewer."

Note in this comment that Mr. Scully implies a criterion of architectural excellence in his distinction between the way in which the building *is* constructed and the way in which it *appears* to be constructed. There should be a *correspondence*, he implies, and since there is none, the building "is disorienting to the viewer." Thus, we see, in a brief

*Vincent Scully, "Architecture and Man at Yale," *Saturday Review*, May 23, 1964.

excerpt, how technical analysis leads to an aesthetic percept, "disorientation," which this critic holds up to a standard concerning visual and structural correspondence, and which then culminates in his critical judgment, as follows:

It all ends, I think, by creating an atmosphere of no place, nowhere, nobody, matched only by some of de Chirico's images of human estrangement and by a few similarly motivated Italian buildings of the Thirties and early Forties.

Although it is not pertinent to our discussion of critical description, it is interesting to observe the form in which Professor Scully offers his critical estimate. We know his judgment is negative, that he regards the building as unsuccessful, and that he has given what are for him adequate technical reasons for his view. However, he also endeavors to *persuade* us of the correctness of this position by sharing his subjective impressions of the building with

us, by citing an analogy to the forlorn imagery of Giorgio de Chirico (born 1888), and by a comparison with the generally condemned architecture of the Fascist era in Italy. The judgment, in short, begins as a conclusion and concludes as an attack.

In ordinary journalistic criticism, subjective impressions and unflattering comparisons frequently constitute the whole of the critique. Hence, while such criticism may be exciting or entertaining to read, we are never very certain whether it is responsible—that is, based on objective description and analysis and on assumptions about aesthetic value which can be examined. In Professor Scully's short critique, however, his aesthetic assumption is apparent and he possesses the knowledge to give us a technical description of what is, for him, the crucial failure of the building. Whether we agree with his conclusions, this critic has *earned* the right to make them.

Formal Analysis

In formal analysis, we endeavor to go "behind" the descriptive inventory to discover how the things we have named are constituted. We may have found five female figures in *Les Demoiselles*, but now we want to know how they have been organized as shapes, as areas of color, as forms with particular contours, textures, and locations in space. Formal analysis is also a type of description, but with it we are no longer engaged in naming things or describing the technical features of the work. We describe the qualities of line, shape, color, and illu-

mination which are responsible for the existence of the things, the subject matter, included in our descriptive inventory. (For color, see p. 484.)

In *Les Demoiselles*, we note that some of the figures appear to be made of sharp, flat planes of color, whereas the two central figures are more curvilinear, have gentler transitions of flesh-toned color, and seem less distorted from a naturalistic standpoint. One of the central figures also uses white lines for the delineation of shapes. The outer figures have heads which are in marked contrast to their bodies. The central

PABLO PICASSO, *Les Demoiselles d'Avignon* (1907) [whole above and details below and on pages 475, 476, 477, and 485]. Collection The Museum of Modern Art, New York, acquired through the Lillie P. Bliss bequest.

tant perception of this work which will affect my interpretation of it.

Although the color in *Les Demoiselles* varies in value and seems to be deployed as if it were modeling forms, we have in general very little impression of depth, of hollowed-out space in which the figures are contained. There is only a quite shallow space, implied by the overlapping of the forms, that is, by the location of figures in front of or behind each other. But there are no perspective devices used, no changes in size relationships, no changes in focus, color intensity, or sharpness of edge to suggest a representation of space deeper than the picture plane.

Notice that the drawing of the hand in the central figure involves some skill in foreshortening; it is more or less believable, but the other two hands in the painting are crudely drawn, one a child-like representation, while the other is schematic and stiff—part of an arm which resembles carved material more than flesh. But that arm, at the left of the canvas, is painted in the typical rose tones of conventional European art. Thus, there is a conflict between the drawing in this single arm and its color and paint quality. Is this the kind of conflict which Scully noted in his architectural critique, or is it an intended conflict which has relevance to our interpretation of the work?

We should also notice that in the three outer figures, there are three kinds of distortion in the heads. In the head at the left, color shifts from pink to brown, the eye is enlarged and the planes of the nose are simplified in a way characteristic of African carving and also perhaps of Egyptian or Peruvian renderings of heads. The *shape* of the head remains naturalistic, however.

figures, while more naturalistic, show the nose in profile, and one seems precariously based, like a statue which may fall from its pedestal. Her torso is erect but the position of her feet could not possibly permit her weight to be supported.

My notion that the figure seems to be falling illustrates one of the sources of our inferences about form: the erectness of man's posture and the influence of gravity. No matter what style of art we examine, certain assumptions about man are shared by artist *and* viewer. We cannot view a tilted representation of the human figure without concluding that it is falling. The idea of falling, the expectation of collapse, therefore, can be an impor-

This head also has conventional illumination with a logically implied light source which accounts for its convincing sculptural quality. Moving to the upper right head, we depart from logical representation; indeed, there is hardly any bow in the direction of naturalism; very pronounced, really harsh, green lines are employed to indicate part of the nose plane in shadow; inconsistent treatment of the eyes, and a rough, unfinished kind of execution characterize the head in general. The breast is also reduced to a diamond shape with no subtlety in the transition from light to shadow. (Obviously, with this head the artist has abandoned the effort to convince us that we are looking at a representation of something which exists in reality somewhere else. In other words, the painting at this point begins to depart from the simple imitation of appearances as the goal of art.)

Nevertheless, the upper right head has a normal attachment to the body. The head on the seated figure, lower right, however, is uncertain in its relation to the body. The nose with its shadow plane has been flattened out, and the convention of a shadow plane has been employed as a decorative element, or an element of pure form in a total composition based on the head. The alignment of the eyes is now completely illogical. A collection of forms based on different views of the head *and* different modes of representing the head have been reassembled and located in the approximate place where the head would be. But only the left shoulder carries out this treatment, as the rest of the figure is consistent with the two central figures. From the head alone, we cannot deduce the sex, race, age, or any other features of the figure. Only the

hips and thighs, plus the title, confirm that the figure is a woman.

At the extreme left position of the canvas is a brown area which seems to be a close-up, a large-scale detail of a female figure, employing the typical forms of African sculpture. It is clearly not one of the *demoiselles*, but seems to be an echo of some of their forms, this time carried out in the brown color of carved wood sculpture. Perhaps it is an announcement of the *leitmotif* of the painting as a whole. In purely formal terms, however, we might guess that the area shows an enlarged version of the forms which might be seen in a rear view of the figure at the left.

The material discussed above constitutes an example, albeit incomplete, of formal analysis. In describing the forms, I touched on their possible meaning, thus anticipating the work of interpretation. I attempted to take notice of formal treatment varying from what might be normally expected: straight lines where we expect curves, flat forms where we expect modeling, distortion where we expect naturalistic representation, harsh changes of surface or shape or direction where we expect gentle transition.

The idea of the viewer's expectation is very important in formal analysis. As mentioned earlier, there are certain

Guardian figure from the Bakota area, Gabon (19th–20th century), above. Collection of the University, Zurich.

Shirt, or poncho, tapestry, Peru, (1300–1532), below. Courtesy Dumbarton Oaks.

universal expectations based on our erect posture and our experience with gravity; our associations with the horizon affect our visual expectations when we perceive horizontal lines; likewise our expectations are conditioned by natural phenomena which have jagged, zig-zag, spiral, circular, ovoid, crystalline, triangular, and rectangular directions or shapes. In art schools, students learn, usually in classes in design, to organize forms employing combinations of these directions and shapes. In this way they gain skill in controlling the viewer's perceptions and purely formal reactions, without the employment of illusionistic devices. However, in addition to our reactions based on experience with nature, we respond to forms on the basis of our experience with other works of art as well as our cultural conditioning to what artistic forms should look like. The artist is usually well aware of the viewer's cultural conditioning and uses it in planning the total impact of his work. Picasso knows how to use linear perspective, and knows very well that viewers in the Western world are accustomed to a logic of picture-making which calls for perspectivist illusions to create the space occupied by the *demoiselles*. Nevertheless, he deliberately breaks up any opportunity for the perception of illusionistic space. The still life in the bottom center of the picture provides the merest hint of a flat plane leading *into* the picture space. But the artist does not follow through on that kind of spatial representation. Indeed, he locates the foot of the figure on the left in the same plane and at the same height as the still life. The foot must be standing on the floor! Yet the floor cannot be at the same level as the table top on which

the still life rests! Obviously, the logic of spatial representation we have been conditioned to expect is destroyed in this painting.

It is plain that in making a formal analysis, we have been accumulating the evidence which will help us to attempt interpretations of the work and also to make judgments of its excellence. Under certain circumstances, the breakdown of spatial logic would justify a conclusion that the work we are examining is unsuccessful. However, we must first ascertain whether a different kind of logic has been created to supplant the one we expected. Or, perhaps a logic of spatial representation is irrelevant for the purpose of evaluating this particular work. In the case of *Les Demoiselles*, it is sufficient for the purposes of formal analysis to say that the activity of most of the forms we see takes place mainly in a shallow space parallel to the plane of the picture. We arrive at this conclusion by elimination, since no consistently employed pictorial device carries the eye *into* a convincingly real representation of space. Rather, the linear and coloristic clues keep us fairly close to the surface. In a sense, as soon as our eyes begin to penetrate inward, they are turned to one side. This is the effect of the two central heads which begin conventionally enough in front view, and then turn our vision to one side by presenting the nose in profile. The tradition of looking at pictures, from the Renaissance forward, was based on the assumption that the viewer did not move. (Children, of course, have never shared this tradition; they *learn* it at sometime approaching puberty.) Picasso's picture makes the viewer feel he must move in order to make sense of the profile view of the nose. A fixed position for the viewer will not enable him to deal adequately with a front view of the face and a profile of the nose in the same head. In fact, *we are obliged to move imaginatively from left to right as we view the two central figures.* And this imaginative movement of ours is in the same direction the "falling" central figure seems to be taking; furthermore, we in the West read from left to right, and tend to examine pictures and other visual phenomena from left to right. Thus, we encounter a pictorial reinforcement of our cultural tendency to "read" everything in a clockwise direction, together with numerous violations of our other expectations. By the time we reach the seated figure at the right, we are almost willing to accept the joining of the shoulder, arm, forearm, and hip in a single continuous form, with the emphasis shifted from the anatomy of the limbs to the *shape of the opening* which they form.

Our formal analysis has begun to move now from an objective description of the forms to statements about the way we perceive the forms. We appear to be groping for a principle of organization, an idea or set of ideas which accounts for the way the work of art is structured. As our observations of the work increase, as the information begins to accumulate, it becomes increasingly difficult to defer the work of interpretation. However, we can undertake the task of interpretation with certain modest feelings of security: We have *tried* to be objective in our descriptive account of the work; we have tried *not* to overlook evidence which might affect our conclusions; and we have endeavored to make assertions about the work which would not in themselves be the subject of disagreement.

Interpretation

By interpretation in art criticism, I mean a process through which the critic expresses the meanings of the work under scrutiny. I do not mean that the critic is engaged in finding verbal equivalents for the experiences which the art object yields. Neither do I mean that interpretation is a process of evaluating the work. Evaluation, or judgment, is an independent operation which necessarily follows interpretation. Obviously, we are not in a position to evaluate a work until we have decided what it means, what its themes are, what problems—artistic and intellectual—it has succeeded in solving.

All works of art require interpretation if we propose to deal with them critically. Even the object which on first and superficial examination appears to be weak can sustain meanings—meanings which can be expressed and which enter into our consideration of the value of the art object as a whole. If our method of art criticism is sound, it should be capable of dealing with the work of serious artists, with work by children and by untrained or primitive artists, and to some extent, with the work of emotionally disturbed persons (although special clinical training is also needed in the latter case).

The work of interpretation is tremendously challenging and is certainly the most important part of the critical enterprise. Indeed, the business of evaluation or appraisal can often be postponed or dispensed with, if we have thoroughly interpreted a work. Generally, academic instruction about art is heavily centered on analysis and interpretation, with only passing attention paid to appraising a work in terms of its excellence. One of the faults occasionally found with art instruction is that value judgments are too rarely expressed, that the exclusive emphasis in teaching is on interpretation and explication. But such a bias or emphasis is understandable, since the task of arriving at an explanation of a work of art is exceedingly stimulating to teacher and student alike.

Explaining a work of art, which may be understood as interpreting the work, involves discovering its meanings *and also* stating the relevance of these meanings to our lives and to the human situation in general. Now we come to another educational implication of art criticism: As mentioned earlier, art criticism is a humanistic enterprise because, through it, men not only acquire information but also relate that information to the vital questions they are interested in. We study art not only to learn the facts about *its* existence but also to learn the bearing which art has upon *our* existence.

Certain assumptions underlie our work in the critical interpretation of art. We assume that art always has, clearly or by implication, some ideological (in the nonpolitical sense) content. We assume that an art object, being a human product, cannot escape some aspect of the value system of its maker. Just as a human being cannot go through life without consciously or unconsciously forming a set of values, so also an art object, which is the very intimate result of an individual's encounter with ideas, materials, and experiences, cannot avoid being the vehicle of ideas. As critics, we are not particularly interested in whether the ideas expressed by art are faithful to the artist's deliberately or publicly expressed views. That is, we are not primarily interested in using art to find out what an artist thinks; we do not wish to invade his privacy. It is necessary, however, to observe that an art object somehow becomes charged with ideas—ideas which are frequently very significant. They may, indeed, be present in the work without the conscious knowledge of the artist. But it is our function as critics to discover what these ideas or meanings are.

From the discussion above, an important conclusion for criticism is that *the artist is not necessarily the best authority on the meaning of his work.* Some artists readily agree to this proposition; others vehemently disagree. Whatever they believe, however, the conduct of serious art criticism is fraught with difficulties if we accept the artist as the most authoritative interpreter of his own work. As critics we are, of course, interested in what the artist thinks about his work; we are interested in anything he can tell us about it. We should examine his views as we would those of anyone else who cared to offer them; but we must regard such views as material which requires confirmation by our own methods of analysis and critical interpretation.

It is not uncommon for books and catalogs about art to quote statements by artists alongside reproductions of their work. Such statements are at times enlightening or entertaining or both. They are also at times misleading. Artists, like other people, vary in their ability to write or speak clearly; also, like others, they vary in their willingness to be candid about their motives; finally, like others, they vary in the degree of their self-knowledge, their understanding of what factors are involved in their behavior, especially with regard to something as complex as their artistic behavior.

For persons accustomed to viewing naturalistic works of art with obvious thematic meanings, the interpretation of abstract and nonobjective art is quite difficult. This difficulty may account for the recourse to the artist's statements, his diaries, and the views of his close associates to throw light on the mystery of his work. Then, too, certain theories of artistic creativity assume that the artist "knows" what he is trying to express or what problem he was trying to solve, and often he does know. The critic, however, should not confuse artistic *intent* with artistic *achievement*. As critics, we should follow the rule of making statements of explanation about a work only when such statements can be confirmed by visible characteristics of the art object itself. In confronting contemporary art it is not difficult to be influenced unduly by the reputation of the artist or the quantity of written material devoted to his work. However, the literature of art and the reputability of artists, especially of contemporary artists, should be used as a *guide* to the meanings to be found in specific works; ultimately the critic must discover these meanings for himself.

In the discussion of critical theory I referred to the common opinion that analysis of art is a deadening or desiccating process. Likewise, it may be similarly felt that interpretation of art objects inevitably does scant justice to the qualities of art which are not readily verbalized. That is, how can one verbalize the sensuous appeal of the object? Since criticism is "talk about art," how can one talk about colors and textures and shapes except in very imprecise, possibly inaccurate terms? My reply is that art criticism is not intended to be a substitute for aesthetic experience. I realize that if the content of a work of art could be expressed verbally, it would not be necessary to paint, model, or construct the object in the first place. Discovering the meaning of art does not involve the discovery of verbal equivalents of the visual qualities of the art object. Unfortunately, some writing about art endeavors to do just this, with disastrous results for art criticism. In critical interpretation, however, we deal with sensuous and formal qualities of the art object by examining the *impact* these qualities have upon our vision. As we perceive the work, the formal and other qualities become organized into a kind of unity, and it is this unity which becomes the meaning of the work, the meaning we wish, however badly, to verbalize.

During the process of description and analysis we talked about colors and shapes in order to *direct the attention* of viewers to *actual* colors and shapes in the art object, not our language about them. One of the central problems of aesthetics and of art criticism is that there is no way to avoid the perception of art by organisms called human beings. When we are involved with human perception we are inevitably involved with the distortions and biases of human learning and culture. Unlike scientists, we cannot use instruments to gather sense data and then convert the data into mathematical symbols. Indeed, if there were such instruments we would not wish to use them, since the variations in human perception of the same work (often by the same person) create a substantial part of our interest in art and in aesthetics. Variation in perception is itself a source of delight and part of the joy of being alive, but it is troublesome when we are faced with the problems of art criticism, of making statements about art which others can accept without surrendering their uniqueness as individuals. In the following discussion about forming an hypothesis, I shall attempt to offer a solution to the problem of the subjectivity of our perception as it affects critical interpretation.

FORMING AN HYPOTHESIS

How can we begin the task of interpretation? Fortunately, the tasks of description and analysis have preceded interpretation and several possible explanations of the work may already have presented themselves spontaneously. Now we must consciously and deliberately attempt to formulate a specific explanation which will fit the evidence we have been assembling. The explanations which seemed to suggest themselves as we analyzed the art object may have been based on an incomplete examination of the work as a whole. Yet we can try one or more of them as hypotheses to see if they are satisfactory. Of course, explanation or interpretation in art criticism is somewhat different from the same process in science, which also employs hypothesis. In science, we seek a cause or set of causes which can account for an observed phenomenon. Scientists are willing to *interfere* with the phenomenon, that is,

experiment with it to find what causes it to occur. In art criticism we are not so much interested in what caused the creation of an art object; we are interested in the *idea or principle of organization which accounts for the effect which the work has upon us.* That effect, unlike the phenomena which science studies, is not observable. Indeed, there is a strong suspicion that the same art objects affect individuals differently. Science, on the other hand, is partly based on the assumption that different individuals will make the same observations of a given phenomenon if they follow the same experimental discipline. Because the *effect* of art, the aesthetic experience, takes place "inside the skin" of an observer, so to speak, I have tried to develop a method which would minimize the subjectivity inherent in the nature of our problem. I have attempted to find a way to be reasonably certain that art criticism, "talk about art," can be talk about something we have perceived in common. Hence, I have insisted on description and analysis, and on the principle of making only those assertions (or observations) about which reasonable persons could agree. In other words, since we cannot very successfully study the effect which art has *inside* us, it has seemed best to study the statements, assertions, observations, and perceptions which have been made *about* particular art objects and which are *outside* our persons; although they arise within us, they are capable of being scrutinized by everyone.

For the purposes of interpretation in art criticism, *an hypothesis is an idea or principle of organization which seems to relate the material of description and formal analysis meaningfully.* And, just as in science, where more than one hypothesis can account for a given phenomenon, more than one hypothesis can adequately explain a work of art. The reason more than one hypothesis or "theory" may be entertained by scientists to explain a phenomenon (for instance, the wave theory and the particle theory about the emission of light and other radiant energy) is that *the current state of knowledge* in science seems to support both theories equally well. Presumably, new knowledge will cause the preponderance of evidence to favor one of the theories or to favor their being supplanted by a new theory entirely. Science always regards its current knowledge as tentative and subject to revision. In art, explanations of works and estimations of their value change also, but not chiefly because new knowledge has made the old estimations obsolete. I do not subscribe to the idea of improvement or progress in art. However, changing social and cultural conditions change our individual perceptions. The things we see and hence value or *disvalue* are literally changed by historical and environmental circumstances so that we are quite justified in finding more than one satisfactory hypothesis to serve in the interpretation of a work.

If more than one hypothesis can adequately explain a given work, should the critic abandon his efforts to furnish a single explanation? The answer to this question depends partly on the public or publics the critic believes he is serving. If he is functioning mainly to increase his own understanding and enjoyment, he may be satisfied with a single explanation at a given time, or he may revise his interpretation of the same work from time to time because his own experience and insight have

been enlarged. The critic who serves others, as does a teacher or scholar, may determine to advance a single interpretation which can most adequately satisfy the interest of his particular audience or public at its stage of development and capacity for understanding.

For example, the teacher of children may explain Seurat's *Sunday Afternoon on the Island of La Grande Jatte* as a picture of ladies and gentlemen enjoying a day off by strolling along the river bank, by resting in the shade, by watching fishermen and sailboats, and by playing games. In other words, an adequate interpretation for small children might consist of little more than an account of the kinds of subject matter visible. For other children the tapestry-like quality of the picture's surface might be explained in terms of the pointillist technique of Impressionism employed by the artist and the relation of this technique to the representation of light, the flattening and simplification of forms, and the control of contours. One could speak further of the dignity, silence, and order of the painting as opposed to the noise and

481

random movement which must have characterized an *actual* Sunday afternoon. Finally, we might offer the hypothesis that the picture is "really" an abstract work of pictorial architecture which only uses familiar objects, people, and subject matter to arouse the interest of viewers, to sustain their attention until they become aware of the complex relationships of pattern, light and shadow areas, silhouettes, flat and deep space representation, atmospheric effects, and imitations of sunlight and shadow effects with pigment. Another hypothesis, not incompatible with the others, is that the picture constitutes a *game* played by the artist with his viewers, in which he uses pictorial conventions of drawing, cast shadows, light and dark, perspective, and a new way of applying pigment, to induce their recognition of familiar things in forms which are almost exclusively painterly inventions. What the viewer believes is quite familiar is in fact a set of quite unfamiliar constructions in pigment. The viewer has been "taken in" by a few contours and perspective devices; he has been "fooled"—to his own advantage and delight, it must be said.

This latter interpretation of the *Grande Jatte* introduces an idea about the artist's designs upon his viewers as expressed in this and possibly other of his works. That may be a superfluous idea for some persons so far as their appreciation of the picture is concerned. And it may not be possible to support the idea with material from the artist's biography. However, it may legitimately be used in the interpretation of the picture if it seems to give *a plausible explanation of our perceptions* in the presence of the work. Our interpretation or hypothesis, at least,

is useful as a tool in explaining the simplification and flattening of the forms combined with the diminishing size of the figures as our eye moves from the bottom to the top of the canvas. It also explains the uniform pointillist treatment of water, foliage, grass, and fabric. We might have tried the hypothesis that the work is an investigation of the leisure-time activities of the French middle classes, or an admiring portrait of the decorum with which certain people use their leisure time. Some objective evidence would support these explanations (and we came close to such an interpretation in presenting the picture to small children). However, such interpretations are essentially frivolous and would not do justice to the material developed in a description and formal analysis of the work.

THE MIMETIC THEORY

We have offered examples of hypotheses for the interpretation of a single work, a painting executed in the 1880's, one which is not very difficult to fathom, at least superficially. But how is the hypothesis formed? A hint about the process can be gained, curiously enough, from the remarks people make about very "experimental" works of art, works which seem "wild" or "crazy." In museums and galleries we are accustomed to the things people say when they are frustrated in their efforts to understand difficult works of art. Sometimes they express their frustration by attempting to be funny. "That looks like a picture of a cow eating grass, but the grass is gone and the cow went back to the barn." A freeform sculpture reminds someone of a "dog taking a bite out of a mailman's

SEYMOUR LIPTON, *Cerberus* (1947). Courtesy the artist.

pants leg." The humor is dubious and yet amazingly recurrent. It probably indicates embarrassment as much as anything else. But it also reveals the normal impulse to use what might be called the "looks-like-feels-like-and-reminds-me-of" reaction. The mind confronted with visual material it cannot meaningfully organize struggles to find some correspondence between present, confusing perceptions and past experience which has already been organized and understood.

The mimetic theory of art is immediately employed by persons who never heard of mimesis: The art object must look like or resemble in some way, something they have seen, experienced, heard of, or read about. They search their experience for configurations which might resemble what is presently under scrutiny. The unprepared viewer is at a disadvantage, compared to the person who has formally studied criticism, since the former usually attempts to interpret the work before analyzing it very thoroughly. His "looks-like" and "reminds-me-of" reactions are correct in their form, but tend to be superficial and not very enlightening, because the viewer has not searched his experience systematically, has not really "looked" at the work, as art teachers are wont to say.

At a certain level of analysis, the sculpture *does* look like a dog biting a mailman, if you wish. But if we are satisfied with that hypothesis, we are denying ourselves a number of potential meanings which are more valuable than the saga of dog and mailman celebrated so frequently in the adventures of Dagwood Bumstead. Consequently, we must employ the " looks-like" reaction, which is an easy and spontaneous response, at a more sophisticated level. That is, what is there about an episode in which a dog bites a man corresponding in some manner with the art object which suggested the episode in the first place? Are we dealing with a lofty, philosophic idea such as the inability of a noble creature like man to avoid becoming entangled in the ordinary, low concerns of creatures far below him in moral and intellectual stature? That would be a potential line of exploration for an artist like Charlie Chaplin. Is the episode an "excuse" for an artist to create some forms which play among the categories of structure, organism, and animality? That idea is explored by Seymour Lipton (1903–   ) in *Cerberus*. The ideas which are suggested by a simple "looks-like" or "reminds-me-of" reaction are plentiful. Fortunately, our previous analysis of the art object enables us to select among them and to modify our statement of them so that we begin to approach an adequate explanation of the work itself.

INTERPRETING "LES DEMOISELLES"

Let us return to Picasso's *Demoiselles*, which was used to illustrate formal analysis in the preceding section. Perhaps the same work can be employed to illustrate interpretation. We can discard some hypotheses first. The work is not on the surface a celebration of female beauty. (But it does evoke references to works of that type, such as Rubens *Judgment of Paris* or the same theme executed by Raphael, *The Three Graces*.) The work does not involve any display of artistic virtuosity—that is, skillful drawing and brushwork, painterly modeling of forms and representa-

PABLO PICASSO, *Les Demoiselles d'Avignon* (1907). Collection The Museum of Modern Art, New York, acquired through the Lillie P. Bliss bequest.

PETER PAUL RUBENS, *The Judgment of Paris* (1638), left. Courtesy The National Gallery, London.

RAPHAEL, *The Three Graces* (1500), right. Courtesy Musée de Chantilly; Ektachrome, Giraudon, Paris.

tions of light. Color and shape are not employed as if they were intended to be a source of sensuous delight in themselves. In other words, this is not a *decorative* work whose values and meanings lie in the optical enjoyment of its surface. Rather, the forms we have analyzed previously exist in order to symbolize ideas. And, if this work is a truly significant one, the ideas it symbolizes could not be as well expressed in any other medium of artistic creativity. Indeed, it is quite possible for this work to express ideas uniquely *and also* to express ideas which are original from a cognitive standpoint, that is, in terms of the history of ideas. Let us form our hypothesis on the basis of the clue offered by the left-central figure which *looks like* a statue on an insecure base; the figure is falling, but, being a statue, maintains a serene expression; the statue does not *know* it is collapsing: *This work of art, it seems to me, deals with the idea of falling.*

We observed earlier that the artist used white lines instead of dark ones to delineate the forms of the torso in the central figure. One of the earliest historical uses of white line drawing in the figure occurs in Greek vase painting, especially in the so-called black-figured style of the sixth century B.C. The faces of the two central figures also have the expressionless, wide-eyed stare which is characteristic of early Greek portrayals of the female in vase painting and in sculpture. A more recent ancestor of the central figures might be found in a highly sentimental work, *Venus Anadyomene* by J. A. D. Ingres (1780–1867). Even without this information, however, we sense the classical origins of the two central figures. They stand for the ideas of feminine beauty which began in the ancient cultures of the Mediterranean world and which are part of the heritage of Western civilization—a heritage which Picasso has amply shown that he feels deeply. Another clue lies in the Greek hair style of the right-central figure. By contrast, the other two standing figures are derived from non-Western sources—African or Peruvian or pre-Columbian Mexican imagery. And, as observed earlier, they employ angular as opposed to curvilinear shapes. These figures deliberately disappoint the expectations of pulchritude aroused by the central figures. The upper-right figure is aggressively ugly. The leg of the left figure is unfeminine, it belongs to a human type which is not at home in the cities of the Western world. We have here a change of race along with a change of artistic treatment. Picasso has intentionally juxtaposed Western and non-Western racial and plastic representational types to express the *fall* of Western

J. A. D. INGRES, *Venus Anadyomene* (1848), at left. Courtesy Musée de Chantilly; Ektachrome Giraudon, Paris.

Female figure from a Greek amphora, below.

ethnocentrism. The classical beauty as symbolized by the central figures is at first contrasted with the form ideas of the other two standing figures and finally is synthesized in a new development which appears in the lower-right figure. Its head is based on non-Western plastic forms subjected to a Westernized, cerebral kind of play.

The relaxed calm of the classical figures is contrasted with the primitive intensity of the others. In the *fall* of the classical figures we can also see the fall of a culture in which beauty is the object of serene contemplation. This ideal is displaced by ideals of frenetic activity, beauty as procreative potency, and the victory of magical ritual over rational reflection.

Historians tell us that Picasso originally intended to paint a scene showing a sailor surrounded by nude women, fruit, flowers, and a symbolic intimation of death. The final version of the canvas does not, of course, carry out this plan. But it should be stressed that an interpretation of the work need not follow Picasso's original or modified intent; indeed an interpretation could easily be misled by the artist's plan or the history of changes in the plan, interesting though they may be. Our critical procedure should be designed to get at those meanings which can be visually confirmed in the present work—meanings of which Picasso may not have been consciously aware.

In 1907, well before World War I and the beginning of the dissolution of European colonialism in Africa and Asia, Picasso's painting represented, at the very least, a remarkable anticipation of the political and cultural developments which came into prominence some forty years later. If this analysis and interpretation are correct, then Picasso's painting has value for the history of ideas as well as for internal development of artistic styles. Not only does it anticipate social and political developments, but it also serves a didactic function in the history of art. By employing the artistic devices tradi-

tionally used to create the illusion of deep space and of verisimilitude, the artist creates expectations in the viewer of seeing a typical figure composition, a kind of *tableau vivant*. But he uses these pictorial conventions to frustrate the usual expectations, to teach us that a picture is made of painted forms resting on a flat surface. These forms are not veritable substitutes for reality; they are symbols of reality as seen and thought about. Painterly forms employed as symbols are capable of functioning at several levels of meaning. Consequently, the art of painting becomes, with this work, capable of dealing with a much wider range of experience and meaning than was thought possible hitherto.

My interpretation of *Les Demoiselles* has led, almost imperceptibly, into a discussion of evaluation, or judgment. It should be plain from what has been said about the work that it is regarded as having tremendous importance. In the following section on evaluation, I shall discuss some of the considerations which lead critics to make their rankings of artistic value.

Judgment

Evaluating a work of art by critical method means giving the work a rank in relation to other works in its class—deciding the degree of its artistic and aesthetic merit. As mentioned earlier, this aspect of art criticism is much abused and is for some purposes unnecessary if a thorough and satisfactory interpretation has been carried out. Nevertheless, for a variety of motives, human beings seem unable to dispense

with ranking art objects. Even artists, who do not have critical obligations, commonly indulge in the ranking of art and of other artists. And there are many practical situations where ranking and evaluation are unavoidable. For example, a museum usually has a limited amount of money for acquiring works of art. Obviously, the museum's trustees and staff are anxious to expend their limited funds on works which are judged superior and important. The same problem arises for individuals who wish to collect works of art. They are encouraged to buy what pleases them. But usually, and especially if a large outlay is involved, collectors wish to know that what pleases them also possesses substantial intrinsic value to justify the investment. That is, a work of art must be valuable for reasons other than the pleasure it gives us aesthetically. To put the problem in another way, we should like to be assured that works of art which afford us aesthetic pleasure afford comparable pleasures for others, thus rendering the works durably valuable.

If a preference survey could be taken in connection with a particular work or group or style, we should gain some information about their current acceptability and presumably we could draw limited inferences about the "value" of the works, even their money value. But such surveys are impractical, they are probably unreliable for any extended period of time, and we should like to think there are better methods for arriving at evaluations—evaluations which are also more lasting.

Certain kinds of art scholars are called connoisseurs, that is, persons who "know" a great many things that relate to judgment about artistic excellence. When dealing with older works, such as the art of the Renaissance, a considerable part of connoisseurship is the determination of the authenticity of a work. Since the importance of an artist like Botticelli, for example, has already been well established, problems of connoisseurship involve deciding whether he did, in fact, execute a certain work; when in his career the work was completed; whether other versions exist; whether the work is a good example of his style; what the judgment of collectors and connoisseurs has been about the work; and so on.

In the case of contemporary art, somewhat different problems of connoisseurship exist. Authenticity is usually not a problem. Most of the facts about the execution, display, sale, and ownership of a work are known. There is also likely to be a large body of critical opinion about the artist and about particular works he has created. However, the short time during which these opinions have been accumulated tends to limit the reliance we are willing to place upon them. Furthermore, collectors and some museum directors desire to acquire significant works of art *before* their artists have become well known. They wish to exercise critical judgment in the form of a risk, a wager, a "bet." Such persons would like to believe that they can identify artistic excellence before the multitude discovers it. Hence connoisseurship of modern art is more related to the prediction of durable aesthetic value rather than exhaustive knowledge about art which has already been judged valuable. This game is one of the excitements of connoisseurship and of art collecting, apart from the aesthetic excitement which specific works yield. Art is, after all, a commodity as well as a type of experience, and as a commodity which fluctuates in money values, it gives rise to methods of anticipating the fluctuations. It is also possible, alas, that methods for *controlling* as well as anticipating the fluctuations of art values may be devised. This is to say that, where there is a market for a commodity, persons will be found who endeavor to manage market conditions for the sake of financial gain. However, these are extra-aesthetic considerations, and we are here concerned only with the development of critical instruments which will enhance aesthetic satisfactions.

COMPARISONS WITH HISTORICAL MODELS

In making a critical evaluation, it is important that the work under scrutiny be related to the widest possible range of comparable works. One of the errors made by youthful artists and neophyte critics is to form estimations of value with reference to a very recent or narrow context of artistic creativity. Perhaps this is done because the critic may sincerely believe that a certain date, say 1875, constitutes a watershed in history and that artistic events preceding and following that date must be treated as if they belonged to separate, self-contained categories. It would appear that many persons who make judgments about art operate unconsciously on some such assumption. But if they do, their assertions about artistic value should be qualified in terms of the time span over which they are intended to be regarded as applicable. The important point is that if we are to take critical judgment seriously, statements of value ought to specify or imply the range of art objects in time and space which have been considered relevant in making the judgment. Since we know of examples of artistic creativity beginning approximately twenty thousand years ago and continuing through to the present day, the range of relevant objects is enormous. I do not cite the long history of art in order to multiply the difficulties in making

critical judgments. But I wish to stress that it is essential for the critic to be acquainted with as large a number of artistic styles and genres as possible, because modern artistic communication and exchange, the dissemination of reproductions, and the display of original works extend through the entire known history of art. This development is quite recent, but as André Malraux has eloquently demonstrated in his book *Museum without Walls*, artistic creativity today is inevitably conditioned by the fact that almost every artist is aware of, and has seen, South Pacific primitive stone carving, Cycladic figures, Roman fresco painting, Pop art, and Indian temple sculptures. The critic who judges according to standards derived only from familiarity with the works of artists in a certain "school" or geographic location or historical epoch is severely limited.

If we examine a portrait, a figure painting, or a landscape painting, it is natural that we relate it to works of similar purpose in the history of art. The same point applies to our examination of a house, a church, or a government building. We know that modern developments in technology and patterns of living change the way we think about domestic architecture, for example. But it is neccessary to know the forms and types from which modern innovations have departed in order to judge properly the full value of the modern achievement. Philip Johnson's glass house becomes more significant as a valid contemporary architectural solution if we understand the evolution of the domestic dwelling. His house must be judged not only in terms of the possibilities afforded by glass-and-steel-frame construction, but also in terms of social change from a closed to an open society.

We can decide about the adequacy of public buildings, particularly our state capitols and city halls, if we know that they are based on ancient models often erected for different purposes (temples, palaces, fortifications), at a time when modern notions about the operations of representative government were unknown. That is, judgment of architectural excellence must obviously be preceded by analysis of the function which the building is intended to perform. The formal excellence of the building has to be related to the activities which will take place within and around it. The reason our banks and libraries were often derived from Greek and Roman temples is that the symbolic effectiveness of those ancient structures was admired for its own sake and was thought to be applicable to any modern building type, no matter what its use. But we realize now that a building intended to house the statue of the female deity worshiped by the citizens of Athens is not ideally designed for carrying on banking transactions in a modern industrial community.

Thus, we approach a criterion of excellence which applies with special force to architecture: We expect buildings to express, as authentically as possible, the spirit of the time in which they are built. This does not mean that a building must reflect in some obvious way the popular opinion of the character of our age. After all, buildings are examples of technology as well as art, and hence they are a *cause* of the character of a period as much as its reflection. Perhaps our criterion can best be stated negatively: A building should

not express the character of an age other than its own. In other words, the Gothic style covering a working structure of steel girders or reinforced concrete makes little sense in contemporary architecture.

There may seem to be a paradox in our requirement that evaluating art calls for relating it to historical examples at the same time that we require it to express current needs and aspirations. But a comparison with the best work of the past does not imply *imitation* of the past. Historical examples are misused if they are reproduced, but they are intelligently employed if they serve as indexes, touchstones of excellence. When we are confronted with the problems of judging excellence, Shakespeare, Rembrandt, and Beethoven give us some idea of the capacity of genius to approach perfection in art. Architecture which successfully "expresses" its time does not deliberately and mechanically reflect the obvious or banal interpretations so glibly proffered by editorial writers and Fourth-of-July orators. Its expressive excellence is an indirect *consequence* of having applied the best analysis of function, the best employment of the available technology, and the most imaginative organization of forms to the problems presented by the commission from the client.

Our discussion can be summarized thus far by asserting that critical judgment or evaluation calls for: (1) relating the work under scrutiny to the widest possible range of similar works; (2) ascertaining the purpose or function of the present work; (3) determining in what ways the present work has departed from its historical antecedents; and (4) relating the work to the charac-

BRONZINO (Agnolo di Cosimo di Mariano), *Portrait of a Young Man* (c.1535–40). Courtesy The Metropolitan Museum of Art, bequest of Mrs. H. O. Havemeyer, 1929. The H. O. Havemeyer Collection.

MAX BECKMANN, *Self Portrait in a Tuxedo* (1927). Courtesy Busch-Reisinger Museum, Harvard University.

teristic needs and point-of-view of the time in which it is created.

If we examine a contemporary portrait, we know that its function as an historical record of appearance has been to some extent superseded by photography. We also know that modern investigations in psychology and personality theory can influence an artist's perception of his sitter. Such knowledge conditions our expectations and ultimately our estimate of a contemporary portrait. Knowledge of history frees us from the past rather than making us its slave. We can admire the *Portrait of a Young Man* by Agnolo Bronzino (c. 1502–72) at the same time that we understand *Self-Portrait in a Tuxedo* by Max Beckmann (1884–1950). Both portraits tell us something about their subject, of course. Bronzino, in addition to establishing the grace, poise, and self-confidence of the young man, takes pains to create a highly credible illusion of his skin, clothing, and architectural surroundings. The hand at the waist, for instance, is magnificently drawn and modeled. Beckmann, dealing with himself (which always involves special problems of objectivity and introspection) portrays an older person with a more experienced and cynical appearance. Although the pose has a certain grace, the portrait as a whole is hardly a celebration of manly beauty. Despite the evening clothes and the effort to exhibit nonchalance in the hands, and in the holding of the cigarette, we gain the impression of almost brutal power, held in check perhaps, but close to the surface and ready to erupt. In the Bronzino portrait, the element of psychological analysis is minimal. In the Beckmann portrait, psychological analysis is dominant, especially in the grim set of the mouth, the dramatic lighting of the face, and the exaggerated sharpness of the planes of the head. Bronzino's young man is a specific person, but we interpret him as a symbol of an age and of an attitude toward youthful masculine grace, rich but restrained dress, and elegant classical surroundings. He holds a book to symbolize the intellectual interests of the Renaissance, just as Beckmann's subject holds a cigarette to symbolize modern neurotic tendencies and the desire to achieve a measure of poise, social assurance, and pseudo-serenity through smoking.

The more we penetrate the Beckmann portrait, the more apparent it becomes that we are in the presence of a work of the highest order. Obviously its values are strongly at variance with those of the Bronzino. Both pictures are of the same type or genre. It is this typological similarity which enables us to compare them, to seek a range of meaning and a power of expression in the modern work which is comparable to the range we find in the classical work. We do not seek the *same values,* but we *do* seek the same *capacity to support values.* A formal analysis would reveal that the technique and organization of each work is directly responsible, for the meanings we are able to discover. The flawless surface of the Bronzino is a vehicle of aesthetic value just as is the harsh manipulation of planes in the Beckmann.

I advocate, consequently, that in making critical judgments, contemporary works be held up against their outstanding prototypes in the history of art. If a contemporary model is to be used, it should be employed carefully. That is, one should compare works that are typologically similar; one should not seek the same meanings but comparable power to support meanings; and one should be discriminating in the choice of models for comparison.

EVALUATING ORIGINALITY

Another instrument of critical judgment needs to be employed, especially in connection with those highly original modern works for which it is difficult to discover an historical prototype. Some contemporary paintings and sculptures seem to have almost nothing in common with older work in the same media. This "excess" of originality is what accounts for the activity of critics who appear to regard even the recent history of art as irrelevant. For them, the span of relevance (and hence of comparability) extends as far back as the most recently celebrated "breakthrough." A "breakthrough," as journalistic criticism seems to understand it, is similar to a scientific discovery like the equivalence of matter and energy. Previous conceptions become dated, obsolete, interesting but irrelevant. Just as Copernicus supplanted Ptolemy, and Newton supplanted Copernicus, de Kooning supplanted Rubens and was, in turn, supplanted by Robert Rauschenberg. However, I have maintained here that progress is a meaningful idea for technology but not for art. Thus, we can admire Rubens *and* de Kooning, without concern about their distance or proximity to the most "advanced" modes of artistic creativity during the time in which they worked.

If a modern work cannot be related to some comparable work, and if we do not wish to judge it in terms of how "advanced" it is—that is, with respect to the vanguard of stylistic change —how can we decide whether it is excellent or not? First, we must rely upon our techniques of description, formal analysis, and interpretation, since they can be employed almost independently of historical comparison. Second, we can shift our emphasis in the task of interpretation: Instead of attempting to discover the meaning of the work by advancing an hypothesis in the form of an *idea which explains the work,* we should try to *identify the artistic problem* which the art object endeavors to solve. Works of art are difficult to interpret and judge when they employ unusual, "excessively" original artistic devices. The functions of art, the purposes art serves in human affairs, tend to be the same, however, regardless of historical era, since human needs tend to be the same. Hence, it is innovation

GEORGES MATHIEU, *Painting* (1952), above left. Courtesy The Solomon R. Guggenheim Museum Collection.

JEAN ANTOINE WATTEAU, *Embarkation for Cythera* (1777), above right. Courtesy Musée du Louvre, Cliché des Musées Nationaux.

MARK TOBEY, *Written Over the Plains* (1950), below. Courtesy San Francisco Museum of Art, gift of Mr. and Mrs. Ferdinand Smith.

in the *means* of artistic expression which throws us into a quandary. Once we recognize that Georges Mathieu, for example, is coping with a new *artistic* problem, some of our confusion may be dispelled. Indeed, we may even be able to discover relevant antecedents with whom Mathieu can be compared.

Let us identify the artistic problem of Mathieu as finding a way to use linear movements so that they express the elegance, grace, and excitement of a dance, say a minuet, or the movement of the feet and action of the

sword of a skillful fencer—doing so, that is, by implication without in any way depicting a dancer or a fencer visually. If this statement of the problem is correct, the artist is trying to make paintings which are expressive in the same manner as music. We know that linear movement suggests motion, but the artist here tries to *characterize* motion, just as a composer organizes sounds so that they express feelings and ideas, attributes which sound, physically considered, does not have. Mathieu's historical antecedents would appear to be Watteau and Fragonard, both very French, very close to the revelry and *fêtes galantes* of courtly life before the Revolution. Watteau's *Embarkation for Cythera* is not a visual prototype of Mathieu's *Painting*, but it anticipates his work in spirit. Watteau also attempted to express a type of aristocratic, frolicsome commotion and gaiety. This he accomplished using the full range of pictorial imagery and compositional maneuver available to the eighteenth-century artist. Mathieu is the beneficiary of modern developments in abstraction, Surrealist experiments with automatic writing, the scientific study of scribbling, and the "white writing" of such contemporary American painters as Mark Tobey and Bradley Walker Tomlin. But to cite the relationship with certain contemporaries is not to detract from the originality of Mathieu. His work is quite personal and unquestionably elegant. Having said this much, we must also judge the work frivolous. Notwithstanding the elegance of the artistic solution, one searches in vain for the relevance of his theme to contemporary life. The artist entertains by the deftness and facility of his performance, but his work seems unable to support any other significant human interests. My judgment, therefore, is that the work by Mathieu is successful in solving an original artistic problem, that it possesses its own unique distinction, but that it is not memorable or important because it does not deal with ideas or emotions which make more than a temporary claim on the imagination of the viewer.

This evaluation of the Mathieu, if it is sound, illustrates the case of art which is technically adequate (even brilliant), original, and successful in its approach to the problems of artistry, but insufficiently *ambitious* to attain the highest rank. There is, of course, a legitimate need for art which does not strain mightily for significance; and all works are not required to be masterpieces. However, it may be useful for critics to observe that aesthetic worth is likely to result from the effort to solve formidable problems of both artistic meaning *and* contemporary human relevance.

The question of originality is inevitably brought into discussions of critical judgment. In spheres of activity outside of art, we often set a high value on originality. Certainly this is so in science, where originality is valued provided that it is also productive of reliable knowledge. One of the criteria of art criticism in the Renaissance was "invention," the capacity to create new forms and novel elaborations of traditional forms. Yet, at other times in the history of art, conformity to established models was valued, even demanded. Our own period seems to set a higher value on originality than any other historical era. In art instruction in the schools, a premium is often placed on originality, and the tendency of children to copy and imitate is discouraged, although not with conspicuous success. Emphasis on originality in art might also be understood as emphasis on rapidity of stylistic change. In this sense, artistic originality may be a reflection of tendencies in our commercial culture where style changes, model changes, and "revolutionary new principles" are employed to increase sales. Opposed to originality as an index of value is the view of a contemporary master architect, Mies van der Rohe, who is supposed to have said, "I would rather be good than original."

Obviously, originality is not an absolute good so far as art criticism is concerned. The enormous influence of the long and productive career of Pablo Picasso has probably had a strong influence on modern notions about the desirability of innovation in content, style, and technique within the career of a single artist. However, these innovations are characteristics of the production of a remarkable artist and are mainly relevant to him as a personality and prominent figure in the history of modern art. His individual works of art must be assessed on the basis of the aesthetic values they support. The reputation of an artist so remarkable as

Picasso tends to intrude on the critical evaluation of his individual works. It is quite possible that some of his production which is evidence of high originality and versatility will be less admired by future generations than it is today, although it has been, for a good part of the twentieth century, heretical to suggest such an idea. The impact of originality, especially on those in our civilization who have been conditioned to crave it, is such that, in the face of it, critical judgment is quite often suspended.

The art of ancient Egypt or of Byzantium exhibited uniformity for one-thousand to fifteen-hundred years. To moderns, it appears hopelessly monotonous and slavish, the expression of people who did not or could not "improve" themselves. We value change for its own sake. We are willing to give "points for excellence" to originality. We want to see and possess "the latest thing." It would be strange indeed if art did not respond to these strong and pervasive cultural influences. The critic, however, must be professionally cynical if he is to be socially useful. He must ask of originality that it not be novelty for its own sake, but that it provide truly new insights, that it illuminate rather than merely dazzle. Art can be ingeniously entertaining, as in the work of Mathieu discussed earlier, and when it is, our critical discrimination should enable us to recognize and admire it as such. But the normal human desire for entertainment, for relief from the monotony or sameness of experience, should not distract us from seeking values in art which possess some durable significance as well as immediate relevance and which are, at the same time, well expressed.

CRAFTSMANSHIP AND TECHNIQUE

Our final consideration in connection with critical judgment has to do with the last phrase above, "*well* expressed." What is the role of craftsmanship, mastery of technique, skill and facility in the use of materials, for the purposes of art criticism? To answer, let us begin with the proposition that *art is making*. It is what the Greeks called *techne;* they recognized no distinction between art and technical skill. Art is not thought which is subsequently embodied in materials through the employment of technique. This influential philosophic error has bedeviled education, aesthetics, and art criticism for hundreds of years. Art is in the first instance making or forming; we cannot afford in criticism to ignore the *character* of that making and forming. The *result* of making and forming is the embodiment of ideas through materials, and we legitimately study those ideas, but we must also study the manner in which they have been brought into being, given expression.

Earlier, technical analysis was mentioned as an important phase of art criticism. There we endeavored to gain information for the ultimate interpretation of a work from clues discovered in studying how the work was executed. Now we wish to study artistic execution with a view toward making judgments about artistic and technical excellence. Craftsmanship and technique are legitimate subjects for critical judgment because they are themselves supportive of aesthetic value. Technique is not merely a means toward an end; it is an end in itself. In other activities we readily admire technique for its own sake, especially in sport, where an athlete's performance is often praised for its form and execution even if he loses a contest. Conceivably, the roots of aesthetic pleasure in skilled technique arise from our tendency to identify closely with any exhibition of the effects of using our hands and hand tools, and by extension, machine tools. The logical and effective use of tools is one of the most fundamental demonstrations of man's mastery over his environment. Man is called, after all, "the tool-using animal." With his hands and their extensions, tools, he leaves his uniquely characteristic marks upon materials, and these materials in the form of art survive after the man who formed them is dead.

How do we judge whether a work is technically successful? Some critics evaluate technique by ignoring it in favor of judging expression. If a work is expressive as a whole, if it pleases us or yields meaning, then the technique is adjudged adequate for the expression of the meanings which have been apprehended. But this argument amounts to asserting that every effect has a sufficient cause. It does not treat adequately the aesthetic values which inhere in the *cause* of art, which is technique, workmanship, skill. It avoids the fact that works of expressive power may be technically deficient, just as works of technical excellence may be expressively inferior. The modern era has seen many departures from traditional craftsmanship, departures from the rules and formulas of artistic technique which used to be taught quite academically and which were thought by some to be guarantees of excellence. Also, modern media and materials have been developed by technology so rap-

idly that a logic or tradition of using them has not had time to grow. Consequently, contemporary art is frequently weak in craftsmanship; and modern critical theory tends to focus upon other matters.

In other eras, craftsmanship may have been chiefly a concern with the *durability* of whatever an artisan built, formed, or fabricated. It may also have been a visible sign of the labor expended in fashioning an art object and, hence, a symbol of its cost and so a further sign of its owner's power to command the labor of artisans. But in modern times, craftsmanship or technical excellence has come to mean *logic in the use of tools and materials* and *correspondence between the appearance of an art object and its function.* Durability remains one of the meanings of excellent craftsmanship, but it is less prominent today because modern materials permit even poorly executed works to survive. The evidence in an art object of much expenditure of human effort is less valuable as a sign of status since some of the most costly things we possess are made by machines. Thus, the older meanings of craftsmanship have given way to the idea of a logic of materials and of function.

Logic in the use of tools and materials can be illustrated simply, for our purposes, in the observation that one would not use a nail to join two pieces of paper. The idea is absurd because something within us rebels at the thought of the disproportion of the means to the end. We *know* there are other and better ways to join paper together. The physical properties of materials tend to govern what may or ought to be done with them. A sculptor should not attempt to execute forms in stone which are more appropriate to wood, metal, or fabric. Craftsmanship may consist of extracting the maximum of performance and meaning from materials without violating their essential nature. It is possible to train a dog to walk on his hind legs, but the sight of the performance is not especially inspiring. Plastics can be formed and treated to resemble a variety of materials from marble to wood but we invariably feel cheated when we discover the deception. Fortunately, contemporary product designers have learned to use plastics in ways appropriate to their versatile character. Our ideas about the "appropriate" use of tools and materials are derived from our own direct experience with the material and from conditioning by prevailing custom. Manufacturers, engineers, and designers are continually engaged in enlarging and extending our ideas of the appropriateness of new or conventional materials used in new ways. Moreover, the designer is also an artist, and one of the materials he works with is the expectations of an audience.

As an artist he may employ a perverse logic of materials so that a viewer's shock in connection with his *anticraftsmanship* becomes one of the intrinsic meanings of the work.

Certainly this is the case with "Pop" art. In *Dual Hamburgers* by Claes Oldenburg (1929–) we have a "sculpture" of an everyday object. The oversized hamburgers are constructed of plaster painted in vivid, garish colors to drive home to the viewer the banality of the commonplace features of our environment. Because of the crudely painted plaster, the distortion of scale, and the general lack of "finish" of the craftsmanship, the sense of vulgarity which the artist is trying to achieve is heightened. Technique in art of this sort is employed not only for identification of the object, but also it seeks a deliberate violation of our sense of the logic of materials so as to arouse a powerful feeling of disgust. There is enough naturalistic accuracy in the work to remind the viewer that he is looking at something intended to be eaten; then the viewer realizes that he might be sinking his teeth into painted plaster. Thus, the "aesthetic" reaction approaches physical revulsion. Anticraftsmanship becomes a positive instrument for the achievement of the artist's aesthetic intent.

By *correspondence between appearance and function*, we mean that craftsmanship should be employed to suggest the use, meaning, or operation of an art object. Oldenburg's anticraftsmanship becomes operative because we have expectations of *craftsmanship* which he can intentionally offend. Without our expectations, his hamburgers would merely be bad or unsuccessful art. Industrially produced art

CLAES OLDENBURG, *Dual Hamburgers* (1962). Collection The Museum of Modern Art, New York, Philip C. Johnson fund.

often illustrates the violation of our criterion that objects should *look like* what they do. Automobiles commonly reveal a separation, a disjunction, between their appearance and their operation and purpose. An automobile can be regarded as a type of moving sculpture which is often designed to conceal the way it works. But one of the modern maxims of art calls for "honesty of materials," that is, revelation of what an object is made of and how it functions; hence, as sculpture, the automobile is frequently dishonest. The desire to conceal the operational features of utilitarian art is a survival of the nineteenth-century aversion to machine imagery, to practical functions in general. Contemporary ideas of design encourage the creation of forms whose function need not be concealed and whose material need not be imitative. We insist that the inside and the outside of a machine or a house be equally considered, well designed, and excellently constructed. We are opposed to the creation of objects with shoddy workmanship or inferior materials on the inside which are then covered with a gleaming "skin," a package which is all pretense and deceit. These principles of handcraftsmanship, now extended to the design and production of industrial art, almost constitute an ethical position while they are employed as an aesthetic foundation for art criticism. By "inferior materials" we do not wish to imply that some materials are intrinsically superior to others. All materials are suitable for some purpose which the ingenuity of art and design can discover. Materials become "inferior" when they are employed improperly, from the standpoints of reasonable durability, honesty of appearance, and logic of forming or fabrication.

While craftsmanship can be seen as an important aspect of the criticism of handcraft, manufactured objects, and three-dimensional objects in general, it is a somewhat more elusive problem in the criticism of painting, drawing, prints, assemblage, and other "fine art" objects. This is because craftsmanship in painting and related arts has been closely associated with the technical capacity to create convincing illusions. Another consideration of tradition was permanence, or durability—resistance to peeling, cracking, crazing, and fading. But modern control of temperatures and humidity, plus superior media and supports, permit many works to survive whose craftsmanship is bad by traditional standards. Technique in modern painting therefore is almost independent of two of its principal reasons for being: illusion and permanence. Thus, when examining contemporary art, critically, we look for signs of *technical mastery* in the artistic *performance*. We study the application of paint, the development of shapes, the control of edges, the employment of drawing, the deployment of pigment for surface quality, the pursuit of coloristic effects, with the aim of learning whether these aspects of performance have been managed by the artist's understanding of his medium, or whether they represent failures of the artist to achieve what he apparently set out to do. The knowledgeable critic should recognize awkwardness and artistic or technical immaturity; he should not confuse technical inadequacies with aesthetic innovation; he must distinguish between *artistic intent* and *aesthetic effect*.

Artistic intent is not properly within the realm of investigation of the critic. We cannot always know the artist's intent; and, in any case, it may be aesthetically irrelevant. The artist may want to paint a picture which is more vivid in some way than that of a rival whose work is going to be exhibited along with his own. Artistic intent has to do with *the motivation of the artist which leads him to create*. We might speak of artistic intent as the biographical factors in the creation of a work of art which do not enter into our perception of the pervasive quality of the work as a whole. Aesthetic effect, on the other hand, refers to the qualitative goals of the artist which we discover from (1) our total perception of the work, and (2) our examination of the technical performance itself. When a music critic gives his judgment of an operatic singer, for example, he offers his judgment of the artist's interpretation of the role *and also* employs technical criticism: the singer's audibility, his range, his acting ability, his fluency, his diction, *the quality of sound he can create*. The critic of painting like the music critic must be able to evaluate the *performing* aspects of the art. To do so, he must be able to recognize or identify those qualitative effects the artist is endeavoring to reach, the so-called aesthetic effect. Here, critical judgment will, in many cases, rely on technical criticism, which in turn is based on (1) discernment of the artist's goals as craftsman and (2) estimation of his success in achieving those goals.

It would appear, then, that although permanence and illusion have receded in importance so far as craftsmanship is concerned, art criticism must nevertheless rely on analysis and evaluation of technical performance. When we study art, we are studying the results of technique, the consequences of a process of making. As critical experience increases one becomes more skilled in discerning aesthetic effect and thus more authoritative in judging the success of technical performance. Technical evaluation, then, is an instrument of aesthetic judgment which is indispensable for the completion of the critical act.

One of the most crucial decisions an artist needs to make about his work is the decision to stop working. The process of execution is strewn with difficulties but it also yields pleasures which are only reluctantly set aside. A time arrives, however, when the artist's critical faculties begin to overcome his desire to embellish and tinker with a substantially completed project. Since there is no rule which tells him when to quit, no buzzer signal announcing that the roast is done, no aesthetic policy of compulsory retirement from his labors, only prudence can stay the artist's hand. Prudence suggests that further elaboration *may* enhance an effect, but is more likely to imperil those effects already achieved. This is true of a book, especially one that undertakes to discuss the art of criticism: The author of such a book ought to cherish conciseness more than exhaustive explanation; he should exhibit critical discrimination if he has not always displayed scholarly depth; he should be prudent if he has not always been wise. And he can demonstrate these virtues, or such portions of them he may possess, by showing that he knows when it is time to conclude.

BIBLIOGRAPHY

Following is a selected list of books and articles related to the major themes discussed in this volume. It is by no means complete. Rather the list is intended to be suggestive of the range and type of published material which can be consulted in connection with questions raised in the text. Specialized monographs and publications about individual artists have been omitted as much as possible. The listing of periodicals, too, has been kept to a minimum. World histories of art such as H. W. Janson's *History of Art* (Prentice-Hall) are not included on the assumption that the reader is already familiar with them or has access to a bibliography of the outstanding works of comprehensive art history.

The Functions of Art

Dorner, Alexander, *The Way beyond "Art,"* New York: New York University Press, 1958.

Feldman, Edmund B., "Homes in America," in *Arts and Architecture,* October and November, 1957.

Gotshalk, D. W., *Art and the Social Order,* Chicago: University of Chicago Press, 1947.

Hauser, Arnold, *The Social History of Art,* 2 vols., New York: Knopf, 1951.

Hauser, Arnold, *The Philosophy of Art History,* New York: Knopf, 1959.

Hudnut, Joseph, *Architecture and the Spirit of Man,* Cambridge: Harvard University Press, 1939.

Huyghe, René, *Ideas and Images in World Art: Dialogue with the Visible,* New York: Abrams, 1959.

Huyghe, René, *Art and the Spirit of Man,* New York: Abrams, 1962.

Larkin, Oliver, *Art and Life in America,* New York: Rinehart, 1949.

Malraux, André, *The Voices of Silence,* New York: Doubleday, 1953.

Meier, Norman C., *Art in Human Affairs,* New York: McGraw-Hill, 1942.

Morris, William, *On Art and Socialism,* London: John Lehmann, 1947.

Pelles, Geraldine, *Art, Artists and Society: Origins of a Modern Dilemma,* Englewood Cliffs: Prentice-Hall, 1963.

Read, Herbert, *The Grass Roots of Art,* New York: Wittenborn, 1947.

Shahn, Ben, *The Shape of Content,* Cambridge: Harvard University Press, 1957.

The Styles of Art

Adam, Leonhard, *Primitive Art,* Baltimore: Penguin Books, 1949.

Barr, Alfred H., *Fantastic Art, Dada, Surrealism,* New York: The Museum of Modern Art, 1936.

Barr, Alfred H., Jr., *Masters of Modern Art,* New York: The Museum of Art, 1954.

Baur, John I. H., *Revolution and Tradition in Modern American Art,* Cambridge: Harvard University Press, 1951.

Boas, Franz, *Primitive Art,* New York: Dover Publications, 1955.

Clark, Sir Kenneth, *The Nude,* New York: Doubleday Anchor, 1959.

Hitchcock, Henry-Russell, and Philip Johnson, *The International Style: Architecture since 1922,* New York: Norton, 1932.

Hunter, Sam, *Modern American Painting and Sculpture,* New York: Dell, 1959.

Kroeber, A. L., *Style and Civilizations,* Ithaca: Cornell University Press, 1957.

Myers, Bernard, *Expressionism in German Painting: A Generation in Revolt,* New York: Praeger, 1947.

Ortega y Gasset, José, *The Dehumanization of the Arts,* New York: Doubleday Anchor, 1956.

Panofsky, Erwin, *Meaning in the Visual Arts,* New York: Doubleday Anchor, 1955.

Rewald, John, *Post-Impressionism from van Gogh to Gauguin,* New York: The Museum of Modern Art, 1956.

Ritchie, Andrew C., *Abstract Painting and Sculpture in America,* New York: The Museum of Modern Art, 1951.

Rosenberg, Harold, "The American Action Painters," in *Art News,* December, 1952.

Rowland, Benjamin, *Art in East and West: An Introduction through Comparisons,* Cambridge: Harvard University Press, 1954.

Seitz, William C., *The Art of Assemblage,* New York: The Museum of Modern Art, 1961.

Selz, Peter, editor, *Art Nouveau: Art and Design at the Turn of the Century,* New York: The Museum of Modern Art, 1959.

Seuphor, Michel, *Abstract Painting,* New York: Dell, 1964.

Shapiro, Meyer, "Style," in A. L. Kroeber, editor, *Anthropology Today,* Chicago: University of Chicago Press, 1953.

Soby, James Thrall, and Dorothy

C. Miller, *Romantic Painting in America,* New York: The Museum of Modern Art, 1943.

Taylor, Joshua C., *Futurism,* New York: The Museum of Modern Art, 1961.

Venturi, Lionello, *Impressionists and Symbolists,* New York: Scribner's, 1950.

Wölfflin, Heinrich, *Principles of Art History,* tr. by Mary D. Hottinger, New York: Dover, 1950.

Worringer, Wilhelm, *Form in Gothic,* tr. by Herbert Read, London: Putnam, 1927.

Zucker, Paul, *Styles in Painting,* New York: Viking, 1950.

The Structure of Art

Arnheim, Rudolph, *Art and Visual Perception,* Berkeley: University of California Press, 1954.

Arnheim, Rudolph, "A Review of Proportion," in *Journal of Aesthetics and Art Criticism,* Vol. XIV, No. 1, September, 1955.

Bernheimer, Richard, Chapter XIV, "Similarity and Recognition," *The Nature of Representation: A Phenomenological Inquiry,* edited by H. W. Janson, New York: New York University Press, 1961.

Dewey, John, *Art as Experience,* New York: Minton, Balch & Co., 1934.

Ehrenzweig, Anton, *The Psychoanalysis of Artistic Vision and Hearing: An Introduction to a Theory of Unconscious Perception,* New York: The Julian Press, 1953.

Gombrich, E. H., "How to Read a Painting," in *Saturday Evening Post,* July 29, 1961.

Henle, Mary, editor, *Documents of Gestalt Psychology,* Berkeley and Los Angeles: University of California Press, 1961.

Kepes, Gyorgy, *Language of Vision,* Chicago: Theobald, 1944.

Klee, Paul, *Pedagogical Sketchbook,* New York: Praeger, 1953.

Koffka, Kurt, *Principles of Gestalt Psychology,* London: Routledge and Kegan Paul, 1935.

Moholy-Nagy, Laszlo, *Vision in Motion,* Chicago: Theobald, 1947.

Moholy-Nagy, Laszlo, *The New Vision,* New York: Wittenborn, Schultz, 1949.

Pepper, Stephen C., "The Concept of Fusion in Dewey's Aesthetic Theory," in *Journal of Aesthetics and Art Criticism,* Vol. XII, No. 2, December, 1953.

Pepper, Stephen C., *The Work of Art,* Bloomington: Indiana University Press, 1955.

Weyl, Hermann, *Symmetry,* Princeton: Princeton University Press, 1952.

Wölfflin, Heinrich, *The Sense of Form in Art: A Comparative Psychological Study,* New York: Chelsea Publishing Company, 1958.

Painting

Doerner, Max, *The Materials of the Artist,* tr. by Eugen Neuhaus, New York: Harcourt, Brace, 1949.

Haftmann, Werner, *Painting in the Twentieth Century,* 2 vols., New York: Praeger, 1960.

Henri, Robert, *The Art Spirit,* Philadelphia: Lippincott, 1923.

Hitchcock, Henry-Russell, *Painting Toward Architecture,* New York: Duell, Sloan and Pearce, 1948.

Janis, Harriet, and Rudi Blesh, *Collage: Personalities, Concepts, Techniques,* Philadelphia: Chilton Company, 1962.

Jensen, Lawrence N., *Synthetic Painting Media,* Englewood Cliffs: Prentice-Hall, 1964.

Kandinsky, Wassily, *Concerning the Spiritual in Art* (and painting in particular) first published in 1912, New York: Wittenborn, Schultz, 1947.

Kirby, Michael, *Happenings,* New York: Dutton, 1965.

Leonardo da Vinci, *The Art of Painting,* New York: Philosophical Library, 1957.

Mayer, Ralph, *Artist's Handbook of Materials and Techniques,* New York: Viking, 1947.

Read, Herbert, *A Concise History of Modern Painting,* New York: Praeger, 1959.

Ritchie, Andrew C., *Abstract Painting and Sculpture in America,* New York: The Museum of Modern Art, 1951.

Seitz, William C., *The Art of Assemblage,* New York: The Museum of Modern Art, 1961.

Selz, Peter, *New Images of Man,* prefatory note by Paul Tillich, New York: The Museum of Modern Art, 1959.

Venturi, Lionello, *Modern Painters,* New York: Scribner's, 1947.

Williams, Hiram, *Notes for a Young Painter,* Englewood Cliffs: Prentice-Hall, 1963.

Sculpture

Arnheim, Rudolph, "The Holes of Henry Moore," in *Journal of Aesthetics and Art Criticism,* Vol. VII, September, 1948.

Geist, Sidney, "Miracle in the Scrapheap," *Art Digest,* Vol. 28, December, 1953.

Giedion-Welcker, Carola, *Contemporary Sculpture: an Evolution in Volume and Space,* New York: Wittenborn, 1955.

Goosen, E. C., R. Goldwater, and I. Sandler, *Ferber, Hare, Las-*
saw: Three American Sculptors, New York: Grove Press, 1959.

Kramer, Hilton, " 'Recent Sculpture U.S.A.' Exhibition at the Museum of Modern Art," in *Arts,* Vol. 33, June, 1959.

Modern Sculpture from the Joseph H. Hirshhorn Collection, New York: The Solomon R. Guggenheim Museum, 1962.

Read, Herbert, *A Concise History of Modern Sculpture,* New York: Praeger, 1964.

Rickey, George W., "The Morphology of Movement," in *The Art Journal,* Vol. XXII, No. 4, Summer, 1963.

Ritchie, Andrew C., *Sculpture of the Twentieth Century,* New York: The Museum of Modern Art, 1953.

Ritchie, Andrew C., editor, *German Art of the Twentieth Century,* New York: The Museum of Modern Art, 1959.

Rodin, Auguste, *On Art and Artists,* New York: Philosophical Library, 1957.

Schmalenbach, Werner, *African Art,* New York: Macmillan, 1954.

Seuphor, Michel, *The Sculpture of This Century,* New York: Braziller, 1960.

Architecture

Andrews, Wayne, *Architecture, Ambition and Americans,* New York: Harper, 1955.

Boyd, Robin, *Kenzo Tange,* New York: Braziller, 1962.

Burchard, John, and Albert Bush-Brown, *The Architecture of America,* Boston: Little, Brown, 1961.

Conrads, Ulrich, and Hans Sperlich, *The Architecture of Fantasy: Utopian Building and Planning in Modern Times,* New York: Praeger, 1962.

Drexler, Arthur, *Ludwig Mies van der Rohe,* New York: Braziller, 1960.

Fitch, James M., *American Building,* Boston: Houghton Mifflin, 1948.

Giedion, Sigfried, *Space, Time and Architecture,* Cambridge: Harvard University Press, 1954.

Hitchcock, Henry-Russell, and Philip Johnson, *The International Style: Architecture since 1922,* New York: Norton, 1932.

Hitchcock, Henry-Russell, *In the Nature of Materials: The Buildings of Frank Lloyd Wright, 1887–1941,* New York: Duell, Sloan and Pearce, 1942.

Le Corbusier (pseudonym of Charles E. Jeanneret-Gris) and Pierre Jeanneret, *Oeuvre Complète:*
  Vol. 1, 1929–1934, Zurich: Boesiger, 1935.

Vol. 2, 1934–1938, Zurich: Girsberger, 1939.

Vol. 3, 1938–1946, Zurich: Boesiger, 1946.

Vol. 4, 1946–1952, Zurich: Girsberger, 1953.

Le Corbusier, *New World of Space,* New York: Reynal and Hitchcock, 1948.

Neutra, Richard, *Survival through Design,* New York: Oxford University Press, 1954.

Rasmussen, Stien Eiler, *Experiencing Architecture,* Cambridge: Massachusetts Institute of Technology Press, 1959.

Richards, J. M., *An Introduction to Modern Architecture,* Baltimore: Penguin Books, 1948.

Rudofsky, Bernard, *Architecture Without Architects: An Introduction to Non-Pedigreed Architecture,* New York: The Museum of Modern Art, 1964.

Salvadori, Mario, and Robert Heller, *Structure in Architecture,* Englewood Cliffs: Prentice-Hall, 1963.

Scott, Geoffrey, *The Architecture of Humanism: A Study in the History of Taste,* London: Constable and Company, 1914.

Torroja, Eduardo, *Philosophy of Structures,* Berkeley and Los Angeles: University of California Press, 1958.

City Planning

Goodman, Paul and Percival, *Communitas: Means of Livelihood and Ways of Life,* New York: Vintage Books, 1960.

Gropius, Walter, *Rebuilding Our Communities,* Chicago: Theobald, 1945.

Jacobs, Jane, *The Death and Life of Great American Cities,* New York: Random House, 1961.

Larkin, Oliver W., *Art and Life in America,* New York: Rinehart, 1949.

Le Corbusier, *Concerning Town Planning,* tr. by Clive Entwistle, New Haven: Yale University Press, 1948.

Lynch, Kevin, *The Image of the City,* Cambridge: The Technology Press and Harvard University Press, 1960.

Meyerson, Martin, and Associates, *Face of the Metropolis,* New York: Random House, 1963.

Mumford, Lewis, *The City in History,* New York: Harcourt, Brace, 1961.

Sert, José Luis, *Can Our Cities Survive?* Cambridge: Harvard University Press, 1942.

Sitte, Camillo, *The Art of Building Cities,* New York: Reinhold, 1945.

Tunnard, Christopher, and Boris Pushkarev, *Man-Made America: Chaos or Control; An Inquiry into Selected Problems of Design in the Urbanized Landscape,* New Haven: Yale University Press, 1963.

Wright, Frank Lloyd, *The Living City,* New York: Horizon Press, 1958.

Zucker, Paul, *Town and Square,* New York: Columbia University Press, 1959.

The Crafts and Industrial Design

Banham, Reyner, *Theory and Design in the First Machine Age,* New York: Praeger, 1960.

Daniel, Greta, *Useful Objects Today,* New York: The Museum of Modern Art, 1954.

Ditzel, Ninna and Jorgen, *Danske Stole* (Danish Chairs), Copenhagen: Høst and Sons Forlag, 1954.

Drexler, Arthur, "The Disappearing Object," in *Saturday Review,* May 23, 1964.

Drexler, Arthur, and Greta Daniel, *Introduction to Twentieth Century Design,* New York: The Museum of Modern Art, 1959.

Giedion, Sigfried, *Mechanization Takes Command,* New York: Oxford, 1948.

Gropius, Walter, and Bayer Herbert, *Bauhaus, 1919–1928,* New York: The Museum of Modern Art, 1938.

Hatje, Gerd, *New Furniture,* New York: Praeger, n.d.

Kouwenhoven, John A., *Made in America: the Arts in Modern Civilization,* New York: Doubleday, 1949.

Morris, William, *Collected Works,* vol. XXIII, *Hopes and Fears for Art,* London: Longmans Green, 1914.

Mumford, Lewis, *Technics and Civilization,* New York: Harcourt, Brace, 1934.

Pevsner, Nikolaus, *Pioneers of Modern Design from William Morris to Walter Gropius,* New York: The Museum of Modern Art, 1949.

Read, Herbert, *Art and Industry,*

London: Faber and Faber, 1934.

Rosenthal, Rudolph, and Helena L. Ratzka, *The Story of Modern Applied Art,* New York: Harper, 1948.

Art Criticism

Boas, George, *A Primer for Critics,* Baltimore: Johns Hopkins Press, 1937.

Canaday, John, *Embattled Critic,* New York: Farrar, Straus and Cudahy, 1962.

Feldman, Edmund B., "Works of Art as Humanistic Inquiries," in *The School Review,* Vol. 72, No. 3, 1964.

Greenberg, Clement, "How Art Writing Earns its Bad Name," in *Encounter,* XIX:6.

Greene, Theodore M., *The Arts and the Art of Criticism,* Princeton: Princeton University Press, 1947.

Heyl, Bernard C., "The Critic's Reasons," in *Journal of Aesthetics and Art Criticism,* Vol. XVI, No. 2, December, 1957.

Jacobs, Jay, "What Should a Critic Be?" in *Art in America,* No. 1, 1965.

Kaplan, Abraham, "Referential Meaning in the Arts," in *Journal of Aesthetics and Art Criticism,* Vol. XII, No. 4, June, 1954.

Lynes, Russell, *The Tastemakers,* New York: Harper, 1954.

Neumeyer, Alfred, *The Search for Meaning in Modern Art,* Englewood Cliffs: Prentice-Hall, 1964.

Panofsky, Erwin, *Studies in Iconology,* New York: Oxford University Press, 1939.

Pepper, Stephen C., *The Basis of Criticism in the Arts,* Cambridge: Harvard University Press, 1949.

Rader, Melvin, *A Modern Book of Esthetics,* New York: Holt, Rinehart and Winston, 1960.

Rosenberg, Harold, *The Anxious Object,* New York: Horizon Press, 1964.

Stolnitz, Jerome, *Aesthetics and Philosophy of Art Criticism: A Critical Introduction,* Boston: Houghton Mifflin, 1960.

Venturi, Lionello, *History of Art Criticism,* New York: Dutton, 1936.

Vivas, Eliseo, and Murray Krieger, *The Problems of Aesthetics,* New York: Holt, Rinehart and Winston, 1960.

INDEX OF NAMES AND WORKS

Page numbers in italics indicate black-and-white illustrations; page numbers in bold face indicate color illustrations.

A

Aalto, Alvar, 129, 130, 132, 270
   Armchair, 82
   Experiment with bentwood, 270
   Lounge chair, 129
Abramovitz, Max (see Harrison & Abramovitz)
Abu Kassim, Baharuddin bin, 436
   National Mosque, Kuala Lumpur, 436, 437
Adrian, Barbara
   Bed of Stones, 14
Agam (Yaacov Gipstein)
   Double Metamorphosis II, 343
Albers, Josef, 228, 248, 343, 450
   Aquarium, 228
Albright, Ivan, 22, 149, 150, 152, 374
   Into the World There Came a Soul Called Ida, 150, 374
   Self Portrait (1935), 22
   That which I should have done I did not do, 298
Ammann & Whitney
   Hangar, Miami airport, 264
Anderson, John, 355–356
   Wall Piece, 355
Antellami, Benedetto
   King David, San Donnino Cathedral, 377
Anuszkiewicz, Richard, 344
Archipenko, Alexander, 363
Aristotle, 324
Arman (Fernandez), 375–376
   Chopin's Waterloo, 376
   Little Hands, 375, 376
Arp, Jean, 12, 68, 171–172, 212, 235–236, 237, 240, 270, 333, 361, 386
   Human Concretion, 171
   Madame Torso with Wavy Hat, 237, 238
   Olympia, 264
   The Star, 235, 236
   Torse Gerbe, 12
Aspdin, Joseph, 413
Austin, Darrel, 188–189
   The Black Beast, 188

B

Bacon, Francis, 35, 192, 195–196, 198, 374
   Screaming Man, 195, 196, 198, 375
Bacon, Peggy, 60
   The Patroness, 60
Barlach, Ernst, 46–47, 159
   Man Drawing Sword, 158
   Veiled Beggar Woman, 47
Baskin, Leonard, 361
   St. Thomas Aquinas, 357
   Seated Man with Owl, 361
Bass, Saul, 68
   Poster for Pabco Paint Company, 68
Baziotes, William, 175, 254
   Pompeii, 174, 175
Beckett, Welton, and Associates
   First State Bank, Clear Lake City, Texas, 422
Beckmann, Max, 301, 490–491
   Self Portrait in a Tuxedo, 490
Bell, Clive, 458
Benton, Thomas Hart, 453–454
   Arts of the West, 454
Berenson, Bernard, 458
Berg, Max, 430
   Centennial Hall, Breslau, 430
Bergman, Ingmar, 207–208
   Still from The Magician, 208
Bernini, Gianlorenzo, 310, 360, 395
   Ecstasy of St. Theresa, 310, 360, 395
   St. Peter's colonnade, 430
Bertoia, Harry, 179
   Screen, Manufacturers Hanover Trust Company, 179
Bigelow, M. S.
   Fashion drawing, 273
Bischoff, Elmer, 195
Bloc, André
   Sculpture Habitacle No. 2, 379
Bloom, Hyman, 23
   Corpse of an Elderly Female, 23
Boccioni, Umberto, 28–29, 33, 271, 362
   Unique Forms of Continuity in Space, 29, 271

Bogardus, James, 407
Bohrod, Aaron, 50–51
   Grotto, 378
   Landscape Near Chicago, 50, 51
Bonet, Kurchan, Ferrarihardoy
   Lounge chair, 126
Bonnard, Pierre, 177, 178
   The Breakfast Room, 177
Bontecou, Lee, 367–368
   Untitled relief, 368
Bosa, Louis, 50
   My Family Reunion, 50
Bosch, Hieronymus, 216, 376
   Hell (detail of The Garden of Delights), 215, 216
Botticelli, Sandro, 193, 487
Bouché, René, 150–151
   Elsa Maxwell, 150
Brancusi, Constantin, 172, 230, 236, 361
   Fish, 236
   Torso of a Young Man, 172
Brandt, Marianne
   Teapot, 122
Braque, Georges, 31–32, 64, 65, 160, 168–169, 177–178, 250, 261, 265, 300, 301, 302, 333, 337
   Man with a Guitar, 168
   The Round Table, 31, 261
   Woman with a Mandolin, 177
Breton, André, 199
Breuer, Marcel, 75, 79, 81, 126–127, 128, 129, 436
   Armchair, 126, 127
   Begrisch Hall, 421
Brockhurst, Gerald, 19
   Adolescence, 19
Bronzino (Agnolo di Cosimo di Mariano), 490–491
   Portrait of a Young Man, 490
Brownell, Baker, 93n
Bruegel, Pieter (the Elder)
   Tower of Babel, 404
Bullough, Edward, 284, 285, 286–287
Bunshaft, Gordon, 436
Burchard, John, 404n
Burchfield, Charles, 8
   An April Mood, 8, 9

Burri, Alberto, 23
Sacco B., 23
Bush-Brown, Albert, *404n*

C

Calder, Alexander, 33–34, 229, 386–387, 389, 393
The Hostess, 229, 230
Spring Blossoms, 32, 33, 387
Candela, Felix, 201–202, 306, 434, 438
Band shell, Santa Fé, Mexico, *438*
Housing development entrance, Tequexquitergo, Mexico, *438*
Los Manantiales Restaurant, Xochimilco, 201, *202*
Capp, Al
Panels from *Li'l Abner,* Ugly Woman Contest, *56*
Caravaggio, 211, 244
The Calling of St. Matthew, **244**
Cassatt, Mary, 11
La Toilette, 10, 11
Cellini, Benvenuto, 63, 366
The Salt Cellar of Francis I, 63, 366
Cennini, Cennino, 312, 319
César (Baldaccini), 327–328, 345, 371, 372
Portrait of Patrick Waldberg, 327
Sculpture Picture, 371, 372
Cézanne, Paul, 39–40, 199, 239, 251, 253, 260–261, 265, 282, 300, 319, 323, 330
The Cardplayers, 239
Mont Sainte Victoire Seen from Bibemus Quarry (near Aix), 260
Self Portrait (c.1879), 323
Chagall, Marc, 12, 16, 174, 199–200, 206, 253, 266
Birthday, 12, **13**
Flying over the Town, 199, 200
Chamberlain, John, 371, 372
Essex, 371, 372
Chaplin, Charlie, 198, 387, 483
Chardin, Jean-Baptiste Siméon, 342, 383
Chirico, Giorgio de (*see* de Chirico, Giorgio)
Christo (Javacheff), 374, 375
The Wheelbarrow, 375
Cocteau, Jean, 207
Stills from *Beauty and the Beast, 207*
Stills from *Blood of a Poet, 207*
Conner, Bruce, 374–375
Child, 374, 375
Constable, John, 248
Corbino, Jon, 321
Stampeding Bulls, **320,** *321*
Corneille (Cornelis van Beverloo), 229
Drawing in Color, 229
Cornell, Joseph, 383–384
Blériot, 383
Habitat for a Shooting Gallery, 383
Soap Bubble Set, 383
Couelle, Jacques
Houses, Castellaras, France, *435*

Courbet, Gustave, 342
Couzijn, Wessel
Sculpture for Unilever building, *349*
Cremean, Robert
Swinging Woman, 355

D

Daedalus, 385
Dali, Salvador, 174, 210–211, 227
The Persistence of Memory, 227
Soft Construction with Boiled Beans: Premonition of Civil War, 210, *211*
Darius, 116
Daumier, Honoré
Connoisseurs, 332
David, Jacques Louis, 180, 322
Davies, Arthur B., 45
da Vinci, Leonardo (*see* Leonardo da Vinci)
Davis, Stuart, 34, 270
Composition No. 5, 233
Report from Rockport, 34
Dean, Abner, 232
de Chirico, Giorgio, 174, 473
Deeter-Richey-Sippel
Circular dormitories, University of Pittsburgh, *413*
Degas, Edgar, 147, 177, 178, 356
The Glass of Absinthe, 146, 147
Statuette: Developpé en avant, 356
de Kooning, Willem, 35, 59–60, 164, 301, 303, 313, 329, 369, 373, 491
Merritt Parkway, 329
Woman, I, 303
Woman, II, 59, 210, 324, 373
Woman, IV, 303
Woman, VI, 303 (detail, *313*)
Delacroix, Eugène, 39, 190, 319–321, 330
Entrance of the Crusaders into Constantinople, 190
Liberty Leading the People, 39, 40
The Lion Hunt, **320**
A Mounted Arab Attacking a Panther, 322
Sketch for *The Lion Hunt, 320*
de la Fresnaye, Roger (*see* la Fresnaye, Roger de)
de La Tour, Georges (*see* La Tour, Georges de)
Delaunay, Robert, 170
Eiffel Tower, 170
della Porta, Giacomo
St. Peter's dome, *430*
dell'Arca, Niccolo
The Lamentation, 354
della Robbia, Luca, 352
Madonna and Angels, 352
Delvaux, Paul, 174
Demuth, Charles, 170
My Egypt, 170
Derain, André, 251, 253
London Bridge, **249,** 251
de Rivera, José, 33, 300
Construction "Blue and Black," 32, 33, *300*

Homage to the World of Minkowski, 387
de Saint Phalle, Niki (*see* Saint Phalle, Niki de)
de Vasarely, Victor
Kalota, 343
de Vries, Adrien
Mercury and Psyche, 360
Dewey, John, 287, 290–291, 292
Diebenkorn, Richard, 195, 301
Dietrick, W. H. (*see* Nowicki & Dietrick)
Diller, Burgoyne, 226
Dine, James, 339, 340
"Santa Claus in Cellophane," from *The Shining Bed, 341*
Dix, Otto, 142, 143
Lens Bombed, 461
My Parents, 142, 143
Doesburg, Theo van (*see* van Doesburg, Theo)
Dolce, Robert
Today Show billboards, *67*
Dove, Arthur G.
The Critic, 449
Drexler, Arthur, 205–206
Dreyfuss, Russell, 134
Duble, Lu, 195
Cain, 194, 195
Dubuffet, Jean, 35, 240, 328, 330, 334–335, 342, 344
Corps de Dame—paysage, sanguine et grenat, 334
The Maestro, 334
My Cart, My Garden, 335
Person in Red Costume, 460
Duchamp, Marcel, 67, 217, 271, 328, 333, 370, 382–383
Boîte-en-valise, 382
The Bride, 217
Nude Descending a Staircase, No. 2, 271
Duchamp-Villon, Raymond, 169
The Horse, 169
Dutert & Contamin, 410
Halle des Machines, 410

E

Eakins, Thomas, 24, 147–148, 271
The Agnew Clinic, 24, 147, **148**
The Gross Clinic, **148**
Man Pole Vaulting, 271
Eames, Charles, 130–131, 132, 134, 348
Dining chair, *130*
Lounge chair, 130, *131*
Ehrenzweig, Anton, 344
Eiffel, Gustave, 408, 410–411, 413, 434
Eiffel Tower, *410*
Eiffel Tower (joint), *412*
Einstein, Albert, 169
El Greco, 198, 244–245, 313, 318, 323
Agony in the Garden, **244,** *313,* 323
Eliot, T. S., 391
Emery, Lin, 390
Homage to Amercreo, 390
Ensor, James, 200

Epstein, Jacob, 11, 158–159, 165, 354, 471
 Head of Joseph Conrad, 158
 Madonna and Child, 10, 11, 165, 354
 Mother and Child, 171
Epstein & Sons, 110
 Sara Lee Administration Building, *110*
Ernst, Max, 208, 325–327, 328, 333, 334, 338
 The Eye of Silence, 325
 Swamp Angel, 326
Etherington, F. C.
 Central Technical School, Toronto, *437*

F

Fabriano, Gentile da (*see* Gentile da Fabriano)
Fairfield and Dubois, 437
 Central Technical School, Toronto, *437*
Feininger, Lyonel, 154, 166–167, 170, 450
 Church of the Minorites (II), 166
 The Steamer "Odin," II, 154
Ferber, Herbert, 261–262, 300
 "and the bush was not consumed," 261
 Homage to Piranesi, 300
Fitzgerald, James
 Fountain Sculpture, 388
Flanders, Walter, 118
Ford, Henry, 118–119, 392
Fragonard, Jean Honoré, 315, 492
 The Meeting, 315
Freire, Segundo, 64
 Carnival poster, *64*
Fresnaye, Roger de la (*see* la Fresnaye, Roger de)
Freud, Sigmund, 184, 210
Freyssinet, Eugène, 417, 427, 434, 438
 Orly airport hangar, *427*
 Pius X Basilica, Lourdes, 438, *439*
Friberg, Bernt, 121
Fry, Roger, 458
Fujiwara, Tsuneji, 65
 Cosmetics poster, 65, *66*
Fuller, R. Buckminster, 75, 426, 432, 433
 Geodesic Dome over New York City (proposed), *75*
 Monohex Dome, Cinerama Theater, Los Angeles, *432*

G

Gabo, Naum, 362, 363, 364–365, 386, 395, 450
 Blue Construction in Space, 386
 Linear Construction #1, 363
 Monument for a Physics Observatory, 364
 Realist Manifesto (book), 386
Gainsborough, Thomas, 250
 Blue Boy, 250
Galbraith, J. K., 313–314
Galileo, 263
Gallo, Frank, 352–353
 Swimmer, 352, 353
Gaudí, Antonio, 202, 236, 378
 Casa Milá, 236, *237*
 Casa Milá (garret), *378*

Gauguin, Paul, 187–188, 191, 246
 The Spirit of the Dead Watching, 187, 246
Gaynor, J. P., 408
 The Haughwout Building, *408*
Gentile da Fabriano
 The Adoration of the Magi, **317**
Géricault, Théodore, 20, 22, 190
 Madwoman, 20
 The Raft of the Medusa, 190
Getlein, Frank, 452
Ghirlandaio, Domenico, 22
 An Old Man and His Grandson, 22
Giacometti, Alberto, 6–7, 192, 275, 301, 354
 Large Nude, 6, 7
 Man Pointing, 6, 7
Giedion, Siegfried, 378
Glackens, William, 45
Glanzman, Martin, 196
 See Hockey at the Garden, 196, 197
Glarner, Fritz
 Tondo No. 54, 324
Goethe, 240
Goldberg, Rube, 389, 393
Gombrich, E. H., 161
Gonzalez, Julio, 230, 231, 364–365, 368, 395
 Maternity, 230, 395
 Woman Combing Her Hair, 364
Gorin, Jean
 Composition No. 9 (1934), 264
Gorky, Arshile, 454
 Waterfall, 454
Goto, Joseph, 230
 Organic Form Number 1, 230
Gottlieb, Adolph, 48, 179, 238, 254
 Blast II, 48, 238, 254, 265
Goya, Francisco, 48, 194
 Disasters of War: And They Are Wild Beasts, 48
 Disasters of War: It Will Be the Same, 375
Graves, Robert, 385
Greco, El (*see* El Greco)
Greenberg, Clement, 357
Gris, Juan, 8, 64, 160, 168, 337
 Portrait of Max Jacob, 8
Gromaire, Marcel, 172
 Nu bras levé sur fond gris et or, 172
Grooms, Red, 340
Groos, Karl, 282, 295
Gropius, Walter, 75, 79, 81, 120, 122, 413, 419, 434, 436
 Bauhaus, Dessau, 419, *420*
 Pan Am building, *274,* 413
Gropper, William, 192
 Gourmet, 60
 The Senate, 192, 193
Grosz, George, 7–8, 16
 Couple, 16
 The Poet Max Hermann-Neisse, 7, 8
 Street Scene, 339
Gruen, Victor, 75, 104 (*see also* Victor Gruen Associates)
Guarnerius, 114
Guglielmi, Louis
 Terror in Brooklyn, **53**
Guimard, Hector, 78, 79, 128, 408
 Entrance gate, Paris subway station, 78, *79*
 Side table, *128*
Gutenberg, 116–117

H

Hadrian, 430, 431
 Pantheon, *429,* 430, 431
Hals, Frans, 4–5, 45
 Governors of the Old Men's Almshouse, Haarlem, 322 (detail, *322*)
Hanke, Ted, 66–67
 Film illustration, *Oil Men Call This a Christmas Tree, 66*
Hare, David, 33–34
 Juggler, 33
Harnett, William M., 155
 Old Models, 155
Harrison, Wallace K., 105, 276 (*see also* Harrison & Abramovitz)
 Rockefeller Center, *106*
 United Nations headquarters, *402*
Harrison & Abramovitz, 436
 Assembly Hall, University of Illinois, 436, *437*
Hartley, Marsden
 Smelt Brook Falls, 262
Helmholtz, H. von, 248
Henri, Robert, 45, 453
Hess, Thomas, 452
Hicks, Edward, 206
 Peaceable Kingdom, 206
Hoeydonck, Paul van (*see* van Hoeydonck, Paul)
Hofer, Carl, 12, 16
 Early Hour, 12, 14
Hofmann, Hans, 315, 338
 Number 21 (1962), 315
Holbein, Hans, 157
Holmes, Oliver Wendell, 176*n*
Homer, Winslow, 187
 Northeaster, 187
Hopper, Edward, 51, 103, 149–150
 Gas, 103
 House by the Railroad, 51
 Nighthawks, **149**
Howard, Ebenezer, 90–91
 Garden City plans, *90*
Howells & Hood, 303
 Chicago Tribune Building, *302,* 303
 Daily News Building, *302,* 303
Hunt, Richard
 Icarus, 385

I

Indiana, Robert, 336, 338
 The Beware-Danger American Dream #4, 338
Ingres, Jean August Dominique, 319, 322, 485
 Madame Moitessier Seated, 322
 Venus Anadyomene, **485**

J

Jacobs, Jane, 112
Jawlensky, Alexei von, 251–252
 Still Life with Blue Can, **249,** 251
Jeanneret-Gris, Charles-Édouard (*see* Le Corbusier)
Jefferson, Thomas, 62, 91, 117
 Monticello, 62
Johns, Jasper, 336
Johnson, Philip, 81, 300, 331, 435, 488
 Dumbarton Oaks wing, *435*
 Glass house, *81, 300,* 488

Juhl, Finn, 131–132
    Leather-and-teak armchair, *132*
    Teak armchair, *131*
Justinian, 430, 431
    Hagia Sophia, 430–431 (interior, *431*)

K

Kage, Wilhelm, 121
Kahn, Ely J., 111
    Municipal Asphalt Plant, *111*
Kandinsky, Wassily, 180, 251, 253–254, 275, 300, 459
    All Saint's Day, **252,** 253
    Composition No. 2 (1910), **252,** 253
    Concerning the Spiritual in Art (book), 180
    Landscape with Houses, **252,** 253
    Study for Composition No. 7, 459
Kane, John, 153–154
    Self Portrait (1929), *153*
Kant, Immanuel, 284
Kaprow, Allan, 340–341, 342, 392
    A Service for the Dead, 341
Kazan, Elia, 46
    Stills from *America, America,* 46
Kelly, Ellsworth
    Aubade, 237
Kepes, Gyorgy, 259n
Kienholz, Edward, 372–374
    The Beanery, 340
    John Doe, 372, *373*
    The Widow, 373
Kiesler, Frederick, 378
    Endless House, 378
Kingman, Dong, 51
    The 'El' and Snow, 51, **52**
Kirby, Michael, 342n
Kirk, Wallace, McKinley
    Church of the Good Shepherd, *406*
Klee, Paul, 68, 228–229, 232–233, 238–239, 241, 304, 328
    And I Shall Say, 232
    Family Walk, 228
    Flight from Oneself, 228, 229, 239
    The Great Dome, 238
    Self Portrait (1939), *240,* 241
    Senecio, 68
Kline, Franz, 51, 53
    Third Avenue, 51, *52*
Koch, John, 14
    Siesta, 14
Koffka, Kurt, 293, 294
Köhler, W., 295
Kohn, Gabriel
    Nantucket, 355
Kokko, Bruce W.
    Paint Can with Brush, 393
Kokoschka, Oskar, 12, 16, 197–198, 244
    Self Portrait (1913), *198*
    The Tempest, or *The Wind's Bride,* 12, **13**
Kollwitz, Käthe, 17, 18
    Death and the Mother, 17
Kooning, Willem de (*see* de Kooning, Willem)

Kramer, Hilton, 452
Krieger, Murray, 278n

L

Labrouste, Henri, 408, 434
    Bibliothèque Nationale, 408
    Bibliothèque Sainte Geneviève, reading room (interior), 408, *409*
Lachaise, Gaston, 11, 16
    Standing Woman (1912–27), *11*
    Standing Woman (1932), *11*
la Fresnaye, Roger de, 14–16, 215
    Conjugal Life, 14, *15*
    The Conquest of the Air, 215
Laning, Edward
    The Role of the Immigrant in the Industrial Development of America (details of mural), *466*
Laroye, Samuel
    Ceremonial mask, *38*
Lassaw, Ibram, 300, 306
    Sirius, 300
La Tour, Georges de, 244
    La Madeleine, **244**
Lawrence, Jacob, 49–50
    Pool Parlor, 49
Lawson, Ernest, 45
le Blanc, 117, 119
Lebrun, Rico, 196–197
    Migration to Nowhere, 196, *197*
Le Corbusier (Charles-Édouard Jeanneret-gris), 26, 73, 79, 81–86, 88, 93–97, 128–129, 236, 272, 282, 306, 326, 331, 403, 415, 420, 433, 434, 435
    Armchair, *82, 128*
    Chaise longue, *129*
    Chapel at Ronchamp, *26, 85, 236,* 435
    High Court Building, Chandigarh, *84*
    Modulor, *95, 272*
    Unités d'Habitation, 81, 82, 85, 86, 95, 433
    Villa Savoye, *81, 83*
    Villa Shodan, *83*
    Ville Radieuse, 93, 93–97
    Wooden formwork, Chandigarh, *84*
Lee, Vernon, 295
Léger, Fernand, 64, 67, 157, 168, 232, 369
    Big Julie (La Grande Julie), 232, 369
    Three Women, 64, *65*
Lehmbruck, Wilhelm, 4, 151–152, 192, 275
    Young Man Seated, 151, *152*
Leland, Henry, 118
Leonardo da Vinci, 57, 159, 184, 234, 241, 243, 312, 385, 393
    Caricature of an Ugly Old Person, 57
    Studio del corpo humano, 164
    Study for *Adoration of the Magi, 317*
Leonhardt, Fritz, 437

Stuggart TV Tower, *437*
Levine, Jack, 58–59, 60, 193, 313
    The Feast of Pure Reason, 58, *59*
    Welcome Home, 193
Lewis, Sinclair, 372
Lichtenstein, Roy, 336, 337, 338
    The Kiss, 337
Lindberg, Stig, 121
Lippold, Richard, 178–179, 261, 395
    Variation Number 7: Full Moon, 178, 261
Lipps, Theodor, 283, 284, 292, 295, 344
Lipton, Seymour, 26, 483
    Archangel, 357
    Cerberus, 483
    Menorah, 26
Loewy, Raymond, 134
Louis XIV, 116
Lovell, S. Maynard
    Wentbridge Viaduct, *416*
Low, David, 57–58
    Cartoon, *The Angels of Peace Descend on Belgium, 58*
    Cartoon, *Rendezvous,* 57, *58*
Lucchesi, Bruno, 369
    Seated Woman #2, 386
    Woman on a Bicycle, 370
Luks, George, 45
Lustig, Alvin, 64–65
    Cover design for *Fortune* magazine, 64, *65*
Lye, Len, 388
    Fountain, 388
Lytle, Richard, 321
    The Possessed, **320,** 321

M

MacDonald-Wright, Stanton, 251
Maillart, Robert, 72, 413–414, 417, 434
    Schwandbach Bridge, *414*
Maillol, Aristide, 11, 158, 164, 270, 359, 361, 471
    Desire, 10, 11
Malevich, Kasimir, 241, 275
    Eight Red Rectangles, 270
    Suprematist Composition: White on White, 240, 241
Mallary, Robert, 370
    The Juggler, 370
Malraux, André, 488
Manet, Édouard, 15, 45, 246
    The Dead Christ with Angels, **160**
    Le Déjeuner sur l'Herbe, 15, 246
    Olympia, 246
Manship, Paul
    Prometheus, 106
Mantegna, Andrea
    The Lamentation, **160**
Manzù, Giacomo, 151, 152
    Girl in Chair, 151, *152*
Marc, Franz, 299
    Blue Horses, 299
Margoulies, Berta, 44–45
    Mine Disaster, 44
Marin, John, 199, 270
    Sun, Isles, and Sea, 199

Marini, Marino, 298–299
  Horse and Rider, 298
Marisol (Escobar), 218
  The Generals, 218
Mason, John, 372
  Relief panel, Wilshire-Flower Tish-
    man Building, *372*
Mathieu, Georges, 315, 492–493, 494
  La Mort d'Attila, 315
  Painting (1952), **492**
Mathsson, Bruno, 129–130, 132
  Armchair, *129*
Matisse, Henri, 178, 231–232, 251,
    252, 253, 254, 301, 343, 344
  Lady in Blue, 178
  Nude (face partly showing), 231,
    232
Matta (Sebastian Antonio Matta
    Echaurren), 215–216, 274
  The Disasters of Mysticism, 274,
    275
  Here Sir Fire, Eat!, 215
Mattson, Henry E., 187
  Wings of the Morning, 187
McKim, Mead, and White, 112
  Pennsylvania Station (interior), *112*
Mencken, H. L., 372
Michelangelo, 62, 191, 310, 312, 350,
    351, 353, 359, 374, 398, 464–
    465
  David, 191
  Isaiah (from the Sistine Chapel
    ceiling), *310*
  Last Judgment, 191
  Pietà, 464, 465
  The Rebellious Slave, 374
  St. Peter's, Rome, 62, 398, 410,
    429, *430*
  Sistine Chapel ceiling, 310
  Studies for the *Libyan Sibyl, 316*
  Unfinished slave, from tomb of
    Pope Julius II, *350*
Michelucci, Giovanni, 435
  Church of the Autostrada, *435*
Mies van der Rohe, Ludwig, 75, 78–
    81, 86, 88, 126, 127, 129, 170–
    171, 226, 331, 379, 412, 413,
    434, 435, 436, 450, 457–458,
    493
  Armchair, 126, *127*
  Barcelona chair, *82,* 126
  Circular glass skyscraper (model),
    413
  Crown Hall, *80,* 110, *412*
  Farnsworth House, *80*
  Seagram Building, *166,* 170, 413,
    458
  Tugendhat House, *79*
Milonadis, Konstantin
  Flower Garden, 389
Minguzzi, Luciano
  Woman Jumping Rope, 386
Miró, Joan, 68, 173–175, 237–238,
    240, 267, 301, 386
  Composition (1933), *68*
  Harlequinade, 237, 238
  Maternity, 267
  Personnages Rythmiques, 173, *174,*
    175
Modigliani, Amedeo, 11, 16, 65–66,
    172, 192, 193, 270, 275
  Anna Zborowska (detail), 66
  Reclining Nude, 11, **12**
Mogensen, Borge, 132
  Oak-and-leather armchair, *132*

Moholy-Nagy, Laszlo, 122, 386, 395
Molière, 220, 233
Mondrian, Piet, 54, 79, 127, 164, 168,
    170, 171, 184, 185, 226, 244,
    282, 301, 344, 379, 450, 457,
    459
  Broadway Boogie Woogie, 54, *55*
  *Composition with Red, Yellow and
    Blue, 168*
  Flowering Trees, 170
  Painting I (1926), *459*
Monet, Claude, 145, 146, 177, 290,
    292, 319, 329–330
  Cathedral (in Sunshine), 145
  Cathedral (in the Fog), 145
  Haystacks in Setting Sun, 292
  Haystacks in Snow, 292
  Old St. Lazare Station, Paris, 290
  Two Haystacks, 292
  Water Lilies, 146, *328–329,* 330
    (detail, *329*)
Monier, Jacques, 413
Moore, Henry, 28, 172–173, 185–186,
    240, 270, 361
  Falling Warrior, 185, *186*
  Family Group, 172, *173*
  Reclining Nude (1937), *360*
  Sculpture for UNESCO headquarters,
    28, 348
Morandi, Riccardo, 434, 438
  Turin Exhibition Hall, 438, *439*
Morisseau, André
  Royan marketplace, *414,* 436
Morris, William, 72, 120, 122
Mourgue, Olivier
  Chairs, *132*
Mu Ch'i
  Six Persimmons, 268
Mumford, Lewis, 104, 393
Munch, Edvard, 4, 18, 19, 22, 40, 192,
    194, 195, 244
  The Dead Mother, 18
  Puberty, 19
  The Scream, 40, 194, *195*
Muthesius, Dr. Hermann, 121, 122
Muybridge, Eadweard, 271

N

Nagare, Masayuki
  Wall of the Japan Pavilion, New
    York World's Fair (1964), *403*
Nakian, Reuben
  Voyage to Crete, 351
Naramore, Bain, Brady, & Johanson
  IBM Building, Seattle, *436*
Nelson, George, 134
Nervi, Pier Luigi, 72, 306, 409, 434,
    435, 438
  Burgo Paper Mill, *409*
  Little Sports Palace, *175, 440*
  Turin Exhibition Hall, 438, *439*
Neuschatz, Perry (Gary Call, asso-
    ciate)
  Convention hall, Phoenix, *417*
Neutra, Richard, 79, 88, 99, 101, 436
Nevelson, Louise, 301, 365, 380–381,
    383
  Dawn's Wedding Feast, 381
  Royal Tide I, 380, *381*
  Totality Dark, 381
Newcomen, Thomas, 117
Newman, Barnett, 179
Nicholson, Ben, 301–302
  Still Life, 301
Niemeyer, Oscar, 83, 84

President's residence, Brasília, *84*
Nietzsche, Friedrich Wilhelm, 164
Nolde, Emil, 246–247
  Prophet, 246, *247*
Nowicki, Mathew (*see* Nowicki &
    Dietrick)
Nowicki & Dietrick, 111–112
  North Carolina State Fair Arena,
    111

O

O'Keefe, Georgia, 270
Oldenburg, Claes, 336, 340, 370–371,
    372, 496
  Dual Hamburgers, 496
  The Stove, 370
Oppenheim, Meret
  Object (fur-covered cup, saucer, and
    spoon), *210*
Ordoñez, Joaquin Alvares, 201
  Los Manantiales Restaurant,
    Xochimilco, 201, *202*
Orozco, José Clemente, 40, 41, 42, 169
  Gods of the Modern World, 41
  The Mechanical Horse, 169
Orwell, George, 391
Oster, Gerald
  Conic Sections II, 342
Osthaus, Karl, 121

P

Pani, Mano
  Band shell, Santa Fé, Mexico, *438*
Panofsky, Erwin, 272n
Paolozzi, Eduardo, 35, 298, 390
  Japanese War God, 298
Paxton, Joseph, 72, 408, 410, 434
  Crystal Palace, 409–410, *410*
Pei, I. M., 436
Pepper, Stephen C., 287, 290–291
Peterdi, Gabor, 368
  The Black Horne, 369
Peto, John, 155
Pevsner, Antoine, 362, 363, 365, 395
  Bird in Flight, 111
  Construction in the Egg, 264, *364*
  Developable Column, 364, *365*
  Torso, 363
Picasso, Pablo, 11, 19, 20–21, 22, 47–
    48, 64, 65, 157, 160, 164, 168,
    172, 177, 189, 194, 212–213,
    225, 227–228, 230, 234, 250,
    265, 275, 301, 304, 333, 337,
    364, 368–369, 454, 471, 473–
    477, 483–486, 493–494)
  Bottle of Suze, 65
  Les Demoiselles d'Avignon, 471,
    473–477, *474,* 483–486, **484**
    (details, *474, 475, 476, 477,
    485*)
  Design, color stencil, *64*
  Diaghilev and Selisburg, 227
  The Frugal Repast, 21
  Girl before a Mirror, 19
  Goat Skull and Bottle, 368, *369*
  Guernica, 47, 48, 189, 194, 213, 234
    (details, *225, 234*)
  Minotauromachy, 212, *213,* 368
  Seated Bather, 275, 368, *369*
  Shepherd Holding a Lamb, 10, 11
Pickering, H. Douglas, 240
  Pomegranate, 240
Plato, 166, 169, 458–459

Poleo, Hector, 42
    The Andean Family, 42
Pollock, Jackson, 29–30, 229, 301, 306,
    327, 338, 360, 454
    Deposition, 454
    Number 1 (1948), *29* (detail, *229*)
Polyclitus
    Spear Bearer, 350
Pope Julius II, 430
Poussin, Nicolas, 457
    *Landscape with the Burial of
    Phocion, 457*
Prendergast, Maurice, 45
Puccini, Giacomo, 21
Puvis de Chavannes, Pierre C., 289,
    290
    *A Vision of Antiquity—Symbol of
    Form, 289*

R

Raphael, 312, 483
    The Three Graces, 483, **484**
Rauschenberg, Robert, 330, 336–338,
    339, 491
    Canyon, 337
    Odalisque, 337
Redon, Odilon, 200
Reinhardt, Ad, 180
Rembrandt van Rijn, 23, 148, 193,
    245, 313, 318
    The Anatomy Lesson of Dr. Tulp,
    148
    Man with a Magnifying Glass,
    245 (detail, **245**)
    Night Watch, 318
    Old Woman Cutting Her Nails, **313**
    Slaughtered Ox, 23
Renoir, Auguste, 177, 289, 290
    Le Moulin de la Galette, 289
Renouf, Edward
    Chow, 361
Resnais, Alain
    Stills from *Last Year at Marienbad,*
    272
Richardson, H. H., 408
Richier, Germaine, 185, 186
    The Bat, 185
Riesman, David, 267*n*, 303
Rietveld, Gerrit, 127
    Armchair, 127
Riley, Bridget
    Blaze I, 343
    Current, 254
Rivera, Diego, 40, 41–42, 465–466
    Agrarian Leader Zapata, 465
    Night of the Poor, 41, 42
    Night of the Rich, 41, 42
    Two Women, 466
Rivera, José de (*see* de Rivera, José)
Robbia, Luca della (*see* della Robbia,
    Luca)
Rodin, Auguste, 11, 156–157, 158, 164,
    165, 242, 349, 353, 354, 356,
    359, 360, 471
    Balzac, 356, 357
    The Burghers of Calais, 157, *349*
    Head of Eustache de St. Pierre
    (detail from *The Burghers of
    Calais*), *157, 159*

The Kiss, 10, 11, *242*
*St. John the Baptist Preaching, 165,
    359*
Roebling, John, 72, 408–409
    Brooklyn Bridge, 408, *409*
Rosell, Guilhermo, & Manuel La Rosa
    Housing development entrance,
    Tequexquitergo, Mexico, *438*
Rosenberg, Harold, 321, 452
Rosenquist, James, 336
Rossellini, Roberto
    Stills from *Open City, 58*
Rossen, Robert
    Still from *The Hustler, 49*
Rosso, Medardo, 158, 356–357
    The Age of Gold (L'Età d'Oro), 158
    The Bookmaker, 356
Roszak, Theodore J., 189–190, 231
    Sea Sentinel, 235
    Spectre of Kitty Hawk, 189, 231
Rothko, Mark, 179, 254, 330, 343
    Earth and Green, **253,** 254
Rouault, Georges, 24, 26–28, 247, 301,
    370
    Christ and the Apostles, 24, 26, *27*
    Dura Lex Sed Lex (Harsh Law, but
    Law), *247*
    La Loge, 334
    Three Clowns, 24, *25*
Rousseau, Henri, 213–214, 250
    The Dream, 213, *250*
Rubens, Peter Paul, 313, 318, 319,
    321, 483, 491
    The Judgment of Paris, 483, **484**
    (detail, *313*)
    Lion Hunt, 321
Rubenstein, Lewis
    Good Friday, 242
Rudolph, Paul, 85, 110, 300, 435
    Art and Architecture Building, Yale
    University, *84,* 85, 110, *300*
    Endo Pharmaceutical Center, *110,*
    111
Rush, William, 374
    The Schuylkill Chained, 374
Ruskin, John, 120, 410
Russell, Morgan, 251
Ryder, Albert Pinkham, 17
    *Death on a Pale Horse (The Race
    Track), 17*

S

Saarinen, Eero, 110, 112, 130, 270,
    409, 426–427
    Armchair, 130
    The David S. Ingalls Hockey Rink,
    Yale University, *426*
    Dulles Airport (interior), *409*
    Gateway Arch, 427
    General Motors, Administration
    Building, 110, *111,* 112
    Kresge Auditorium, MIT, *427*
    TWA Terminal, Kennedy Interna-
    tional Airport, *111, 270*
Saarinen, Eliel, 110, 112
    General Motors Administration
    Building, 110, *111,* 112
Saint Phalle, Niki de, 327, 328, 338

Painting with a rifle, 327
Samaras, Lucas, 379
    Room, 379
Schmalenbach, Werner, 384*n*
Schmidt, Clarence, 340
    Residence, 340
Schmidt, Julius, 390
    Untitled iron sculpture, 390
Schweikher, Paul, 412
    Fine Arts Center, Maryville College,
    412
Schwitters, Kurt, 333, 338–339, 340,
    342, 344, 365, 378
    Cathedral of Erotic Misery, 339
    For Kate, 337
    Merzbau, 338, *339*
Scully, Vincent, 472–473, 474
Searle, Ronald, 66
    Lemon Hart advertising design, *66*
Secunda, Arthur, 389–390
    Music Machine, 389
Segal, George, 9, 342, 353
    The Dinner Table, 9
    Girl in Doorway, 380
Seley, Jason, 217–218, 365
    Masculine Presence, 217, *218*
Selz, Peter, 455
Seurat, Georges, 244, 288, 289, 290,
    299, 343, 481–482
    *Sunday Afternoon on the Island of
    La Grande Jatte,* 288, 299,
    481, 482 (detail, *481*)
Seuss, Dr., 238
Severini, Gino, 271–272
    *Dynamic Hieroglyphic of the Bal
    Tabarin, 271*
Shahn, Ben, 18–19, 22, 153, 159, 196–
    197, 319
    Handball, **153**
    Liberation, 196, *197*
    The Passion of Sacco and Vanzetti,
    18, 22
Shakespeare, William, 288
Sheeler, Charles, 67, 144, 154–155, 170
    City Interior, 144
    Upper Deck, 154
Shinn, Everett, 45
Siqueiros, David Alfaro, 40, 270
    Echo of a Scream, 40, *41*
    New Democracy (detail of mural),
    465
Skidmore, Owings & Merrill, 62, 109,
    331
    Beinecke Rare Book and Manu-
    script Library, Yale University,
    472
    B.M.A. Tower, Kansas City, *420*
    Chase Manhattan Plaza, 109, *110*
    City College of New York (plans),
    109
    Lever House, 109, *110,* 413, 416
Sloan, John, 45
    McSorley's Bar, 45
Smith, David, 231, 243, 368, 395
    The Banquet, 231
    Drawing 1959–8, 242
    Royal Bird, 231
Smith & Williams
    Church in California City, *400*

Soutine, Chaim, 20, 22, 144, 151, 182, 185, 186, 192, 244, 301, 313
  The Madwoman, 20, **313**
  Side of Beef, 185
Soyer, Isaac, 43–44
  Employment Agency, 43, *44*
Spencer, Stanley, 24
  Christ Preaching at Cookham Regatta: Series VI: Four Girls Listening, 24, *25*
Stanislavsky, Konstantin, 285
Stankiewicz, Richard, 211–212, 306, 368, 369
  Europa on a Cycle, 368, *369*
  Secretary, 211, *212*
Steig, William, 232
  No One Is Exactly Like Anyone Else, *232*
Steinberg, Saul, 229
Stella, Joseph, 53–54, 272
  Battle of Light, Coney Island, 53, *54*, 272
Stieglitz, Alfred, 45–46
  The Steerage, 45, *46*
Stone, Edward Durrell, 200–202, 435, 436
  Beckman Auditorium, *436*
  U. S. Pavilion, Brussels World's Fair, 200, *201*
Stradivarius, 114
Strasberg, Lee, 285
Strauss, Joseph B.
  Golden Gate Bridge, *411*
Sullivan, Louis, 123, 434

T

Takis (Vassilakis)
  Signal Rocket, *389*
Tamayo, Rufino, 188–189
  Animals, *188*
Tange, Kenzo, 85
  Imabari City Hall, *85*
  Kurashiki City Hall (interior), *85*
  Peace Museum, Hiroshima, 85
  Tokyo City Hall, 85
Tanguy, Yves, 174, 215, 216–217
  Infinite Divisibility, 215, *216*, *217*
Tapies, Antonio, 330
  Painting (1962), *326*
Tatlin, Vladmir, 362
Tchelitchew, Pavel, 208
  Hide and Seek, 208, *209* (detail, *209*)
Teniers, David
  The Picture Gallery of Archduke Leopold Wilhelm, *332*
Thiebaud, Wayne
  Pies and Cakes, *336*
  Seven Jellied Apples, *268*
Thompson, William
  Archangel, *352*
Thonet, Gebruder, 126, 348
  Rocking chair, 126, *127*
Tinguely, Jean, 344, 368, 376, 391–392, 393
  Artist at work, *392*
  Homage to New York, 376, *391*, 392
  Méta-Mécanique, *392*, 393
  Piano before its incorporation into *Homage to New York*, 376
Tintoretto, 244
Titian, 244, 312, 318, 319
Tobey, Mark, 54, 301, 493
  Broadway, 54, *55*

Written Over the Plains, *492*
Tomlin, Bradley Walker, 179, 180, 270, 493
  No. 10, *179*, 180
Tooker, George, 43
  Government Bureau, 43
  The Subway, **52**
Torroja, Eduardo, 409, 418, 434, 437–438
  Grandstand, La Zarzuela Racecourse, Madrid, *438*
  Tordera Bridge (joint), *412*
Toulouse-Lautrec, Henri de, 67, 147, 191–192
  À la Mie, *192*
  Maxime Dethomas, **241**
  Monsieur Boileau at the Café, 146, 147
  Moulin Rouge—La Gouloue, 67
Tovaglia, Pino, 64
  Railway poster, 64, *65*
Trova, Ernst, 390–391
  Landscape #1, *391*
  Study Falling Man, 390, *391*
Turner, Joseph Mallord William, 145, 248
  Steamer in a Snowstorm, **145**

U

Upjohn, Richard
  Trinity Church, *274*
Utzon, Joern
  Sydney Opera House (model), *268*

V

van der Velde, Henri, 121
van Doesburg, Theo, 239, 339
  Composition: The Cardplayers, *239*
van Eyck, Jan, 308
  A Man in a Red Turban, **317**
van Gogh, Vincent, 24, 26, 28, 167, 182, 184–185, 192, 301, 319, 323
  The Ravine, *323*
  The Starry Night, 24, *26*, 167
van Hoeydonck, Paul
  The Couple, *353*
  Space-Boys, *353*
Vasarely, Victor de (*see* de Vasarely, Victor)
Velázquez, Diego, 45
Venturi, Lionello, 304
Victor Gruen Associates, 104
  Cherry Hill Shopping Center, 104, *105*
  Midtown Plaza, 104, *105*
  Southdale Shopping Center, 104
Vitruvius, 76
Vivas, Eliseo, 278n
Vlaminck, Maurice, 251
  La Nationale, *191*
von Eckardt, Wolf, 402n
Voulkos, Peter, 362, 372, 393
  Gallas Rock, 372, *393*

W

Warhol, Andy, 269, 336, 337, 338
  Brillo Boxes, *269*
  Marilyn Monroe, *336*
Washington, A.
  Brooklyn Bridge, *409*
Watt, James, 117
Watteau, Jean Antoine, 492

Embarkation for Cythera, **492**
Weber, Max, 198–199
  Hassidic Dance, 198, *199*
Wegner, Hans, 78, 131, 132
  Armchair, 78, *131*
Wesselmann, Tom, 336
  Still Life No. 15, *336*
Westermann, H. C., 356, 384
  The Big Change, *356*
  Memorial to the Idea of Man, If He Was an Idea, *384*
  Nouveau Rat Trap, *61*
White, Stanford
  Washington Square Arch, 37, *38*
Whitehead, A. N., 41
Whitman, Robert, 340
  The American Moon, *341*
Whitman, Walt, 340
Whitney, Eli, 117–118, *119*
Wilde, Oscar, 149, 290
Williams, Hiram, 195
  Guilty Men, *196*
Wimberly, Whisenand, Allison & Tong
  Waikiki branch, Bank of Hawaii (model), *434*
Wölfflin, Heinrich, 243, 296–298, 299, 300, 301, 302–304, 319
Womack, J. C.
  Elysian Viaduct, Los Angeles, *416*
Wood, Grant, 142–143, 373
  American Gothic, 142, *143*, 373
Wright, Frank Lloyd, 75, 76–78, 79, 83, 85, 86, 88, 91–93, 96, 100, 109, 123, 128, 176, 202, 270, 331, 415, 418, 434, 438, 457
  Armchair, *128*
  Broadacre City plan, 91–93, *92*
  Hanna House, 78
  Johnson Wax Administration and Research Center, *82*, 83, *109*, 438
  The Kalita Humphreys Theater, Dallas, *421*
  Kaufmann House, "Fallingwater," *76*, 415
  Office armchair, *128*
  Robie House, 76
  The Solomon R. Guggenheim Museum, 176, *270*, *331*, 415
  Sturges House, 83
  Taliesin East, 77, 78
Wright, Russell, 134
Wyeth, Andrew, 141–142, 149, 153, 159, 316, 319
  Christina's World, *141*, 153, **160**
Wyman, George Herbert, 408
  Bradbury Building (interior), *408*

Y

Yamasaki, Minoru, 111, 202, 435, 436
  IBM Building, Seattle, *436*
  St. Louis Airport Terminal, *111*
Yvaral
  Acceleration Number 19, Series B, *343*

Z

Zachai, Dorian
  Complacent Man, *394*
Zerbe, Karl, 22
  Aging Harlequin, *22*
Zeuxis, 163

A

Absolute clarity, 302–303
Abstract art, 32 (*see also* Abstraction)
Abstract Expressionism, 210, 253, 321, 328, 337: work of Pollock, 29–30
Abstraction: in design, 64; of female form in sculpture, 12; and purely aesthetic goals, 32–33; and satire, 60–61
Action painting, 321, 329
Adolescence, expressions of, 19
Advertising and art, 3, 61–69
Aesthetic effect, 498
Aesthetic expression, 30–35, 65
Aesthetic order, 176–180: painting and, 177–178; sculpture and, 178–179
Aesthetic pleasure, 33
Aesthetics, 279–304: aesthetic experience, 33, 280; aesthetic frame, 284–285; aesthetic structure vs. visual form, 278–281; closure, 291–296; *defined,* 281; empathy, 281–283; funding, 287–291; fusion, 287–291; and Gestalt psychology, 291–296; psychic distance, 284–287; Wölfflin's categories, 296–304
African art, 16, 38, 474, 475
Aging process, as depicted in art, 22–23
Air-conditioning, 75
Analogous color, 249
Analytical Cubism, 168
Anthropomorphism, 8
Apartment houses (*see also* Domestic architecture): Le Corbusier's solutions, 81–82, 85–86; special problems of, 87–88
Apollonian tendencies in art, 164
Arches, 424–427: centering, 424, 426; keystone, 424; spandrel, 425; and vaulting, 427; voussoirs, 424
Architects (*see also individual architects in Index of Names*): constructors vs. sculptors, 434–440
Architecture, 396–440 (*see also* Architects; City planning; *and specific styles, e.g.,* Gothic architecture): apartment houses, 87–88; the arch, 424–427; balance in, 263; biomorphic order in, 175–176; brick, 403–405; the cantilever, 421–422; cast iron, 407–411; concrete construction, 81–85, 413–417; criticism of, 488–489; the dome, 429–432; domestic (*see* Do-

mestic architecture); industrial and commercial, 108–112; intellectual order in, 170–171; interior decoration, 77–79, 87–88; International style, 75–76, 78–80; joyful, 200–202; landmark preservation, 94; Le Corbusier's career and influence, 81–86; Mies' career and influence, 78–81, 170–171; modern materials, 405–417; Mondrian and, 79; organic shapes in, 236–237; and painting, 330–331; post-and-lintel, 418–421; prefabricated materials, 405–407; prestressed concrete, 416–417; proportion, 273–276; reinforced concrete, 413–416; rhythm, 268, 269–270; shell structures, 432–433; steel, 411–413; stone, 399, 401–403; structural devices, 417–433; traditional materials of, 398–405; the truss, 424; use of glass, 74–75; the vault, 427–429; wood, 400–401; Wright's career and influence, 76–78, 109, 176
Art (*see also* Architecture; Criticism; Style; Visual Elements; *specific periods, e.g.,* Renaissance; *and specific styles, e.g.,* Art Nouveau): aesthetics, 279–304; advertising, 61–69; Apollonian strain in, 164; and communication, 6, 63–64; and design, 61–69, 257–277; Dionysiac strain in, 164, 167; and economic forces, 313–314; emotion and, 182–183; and engineering, 72, 169–170; grammar of, 222–255; as language, 4, 6; and literature, 6; mathematics and, 164, 167, 272–273; meaning of, 3; perception and, 296–304; personality and, 164, 170; Platonism and, 166, 169; and recognition, 31; social values of, 2–3; and society, 21; as "theatre," 327–328; themes of, 4; and ugliness, 57
Artistic intent, 498
Artistic perception (*see* Perception)
Artists (*see also* Style; *and individual artists in Index of Names*): as detached observers, 144–148; as objective observers, 140–144; as selective eyes, 149–153; social role, 39
Art Nouveau, 78–79, 270, 408: nature of, 79; re-examination of, 455
"Ash Can School" of painting, 45, 151

Assemblage, 212, 333–335: sculpture and, 365–377
Asymmetrical balance, 263–267
A-tectonic form, 300
Automobiles: appeal of, 100–101; sport models, 101–102

B

Balance: asymmetrical, 263–267; by color, 264–265; by contrast, 266; design and, 263–267; hidden, 263; by interest, 265–266; symmetrical, 263, 264; by weight, 264–265
Baroque treatment of light, 243–246
Bauhaus, 83, 362–363: and industrial design, 122–123
Bilateral symmetry, 263
Biomorphic order, 171–176: in architecture, 175–176; organic shape, 235–238; in painting, 175; Surrealism and, 174
Box sculpture, 377, 380–384
Brick in architecture, 403–405
Bridges, 408–409, 411–412, 413–414
Brise-soleil, 83
Broadacre City, 91–93: principles of organization, 93
Bronze (*see* Metal sculpture)
Brooklyn Bridge, 408–409
Brushwork in direct painting technique, 319–323

C

Camp, 379
Cantilever, 126, 263, 421–422, 438
Caricature, 57, 192–193
Cartoons, 57–58, 66, 229, 232–233
Carving, 350–351
Casein paints, 319
Casting, 349, 351–354
Cast iron, 407–411
Chairs, 83, 125–134 (*see also names of specific designers in Index of Names, e.g.,* Le Corbusier): design and production factors, 133
Chiaroscuro, 240–247
Children: art of, 140, 461; and fantasy, 204–206; and myths, 207
Cinema, 62 (*see also specific directors in Index of Names, e.g.* Ingmar Bergman): as art form, 202; myths and, 207–208; rhythm in, 272

Cities (*see also* City planning): garden type, 90–91; problems of, 89

City planning, 72, 89–113: civic centers, 103–108; fantasy in, 206; garden cities, 90–91; greenbelts, 90–91; of Gruen, Victor, 104–105; and highways, 100–103; of Howard, Ebenezer, 90–91; and industry, 108–112; landmark preservation, 94; of Le Corbusier, 93–96; malls, 103–108; and mass production, 96; plazas, 103–108; problems of, 112–113; residential grouping, 97–100; Rockefeller Center, 105–107; of Wright, 91–93

Civic centers, 103–108

Classicism (*see* Formal order)

Clay in sculpture, 351, 353–354

Closed form, 300–301

Closure, in aesthetics, 291–296

Coffers, 431

Collage, 333 (*see also* Assemblage): and happenings, 338–340; technique, 65

Collective art, 62

Color, 247–254: analogous, 249; balance and, 264–265; complementary, 249; cool, 249–250; as device of objective accuracy, 159; hue, 248; of Impressionists, 248; intensity, 248–249; language of, 250–254; and large-scale painting, 329–330; local, 249; terminology of, 248–250; theory, 247–248; tonality, 250; value, 248; warm, 249–250

Combine art, 337–338

Commercial art (*see* Advertising)

Communication, art as, 6, 63–64

Community planning (*see* City planning)

Complementary color, 249

Concrete: in architecture, 413–417; prestressed, 416–417; reinforced, 413–416

Conoisseurs, 487

Constructivism, 348, 362–365, 386

Constructors, architects as, 434–440

Contraposto, 191

Craftmanship, and criticism, 494–498

Crafts: appeal of, 115; and change, 114–115; and industrial design, 113–134; and industrialization, 115–116; and mass production, 114; quality, 115; and sculpture, 393–394

Criticism, 444–467: artistic intent vs. aesthetic effect, 498; and craftmanship, 494–498; critical sensibility, 450; description, 470–473; example of, 473–477; expressivism, 460–462; formal analysis, 473–477; formalism, 457–460; historical comparison, 488–491; instrumentalism, 463–467; interpretation, 477–486; journalistic, 452–453; judgment, 486–498; of *Les Demoiselles d'Avignon,* 471, 473–477, 483–486; Marxist, 465–466; methods, 469–498; mimetic theory, 482–483; operations, 469–498; of originality, 491–494; pedagogical, 453–454; popular, 455–456; purposes, 444–448; scholarly, 454–455; of *Sunday Afternoon on the Island of La Grande Jatte,* 481–482; of technique, 494–498; tools of, 448–451; types, 451–456

Crystal Palace, 409–410

Cubism, 14, 34, 160, 166, 168–170, 177, 199, 244, 252: and Constructivism, 362–363; effect on design, 64–65; effect on sculpture, 29, 169; role of Braque, 29–31

D

Dadaism, 333, 338–339

Darkness, use in art, 240–247: in Baroque art, 243–246; connotations of, 242; in modern art, 246–247

Death: artistic expressions of, 16–19; attitudes toward, 16–19; and magic, 17–18

Decalcomania, 326–327

Decoration (*see* Interior decoration)

Description, in criticism, 470–473

Design (*see also* City planning; Domestic architecture; *and* Industrial design): balance, 263–267; *defined,* 256–257; principles, 258; proportion, 272–276; rhythm, 267–272; as structural element, 257–277, 280; unity, 259–262

de Stijl group, 339, 344, 362

Dictatorship and formal order, 181

Dionysiac tendencies in art, 164, 167

Direct painting, 316, 319–324: brushwork, 319–323; Cézanne's technique, 323; importance of Delacroix, 319–321; van Gogh's technique, 323

Distant stimuli, 291–292, 293, 294, 295

Distortion in art, 191–194

Domes (*see also* Geodesic domes): in architecture, 429–432; coffers, 431; pendentives, 430–431; squinches, 430–431

Domestic architecture, 73–89 (*see also* Apartment houses): furnishings of, 73, 74, 77, 78, 79, 88; interactions of families and homes, 73; interior decoration, 77–79, 87–88; labor-saving devices, 73; Le Corbusier's work and influence, 81–86; Mies' work and influence, 78–81; modern, 86–89; principles of, 86–89; and technology, 73–76; use of air-conditioning, 75; Wright's work and influence, 76–78

Dominance, in design, 260

Dreams: expressions in art, 209–214; Surrealists' interest in, 210–211

E

Éclaboussage, 327

Eclecticism, 200

Egg tempera (*see* Tempera painting)

Egyptian architecture, 399–400

Egyptian art, 16

"Eight, The," 45

Electronic Revolution, 72

Emotion, as style of art, 182–186: anxiety, 194–198; contrast with intellectual style, 184–185; despair, 194–198; joyful art, 198–203; Romanticism, 186–190; theory of emotional perception, 184; use of distortion, 191–194

Empathy, 281–283

Encaustic painting, 319

Engineering and art, 72, 169–170, 408–412, 413–414, 437–438

Environments (*see* Happenings)

Expressionism, 20, 197–198, 210: Abstract, 210, 253, 321, 328, 337; German, 47; relation to Romanticism, 20

Expressivism, as type of criticism, 460–462

F

Fantasy, as style of art, 204–207 (*see also specific forms, e.g.,* Surrealism): dreams, 209–214; fantasy vs. reality, 206; hallucinations, 209–214; illusionism, 216–218; myths, 207–209; scientific, 214–216

Fauves, 251–253

Female form, treatments of, 11–12, 200 (*see also* Human form)

Ferroconcrete (*see* Reinforced concrete)

Film (*see* Cinema)

Focus, as device of objective accuracy, 157–159

Formal analysis, in criticism, 473–477

Formalism, as type of criticism, 457–460

Formal order, as style of art, 162–181: aesthetic, 176–180; in architecture, 170–171, 175–176; biomorphic, 171–176; Cubism, 168–169; cultural uses of, 180–181; in Greek art, 162–164; intellectual, 168–171; kinds of, 167–181; permanence vs. transience, 165–167; and religion, 167

Formgefühl, 362

Fresco painting, 309, 319

Frottage, 325–326

Function, in industrial design, 123–125

Funded perception, 280

Funding, aesthetic concept, 287–291

Furniture (*see* Household furnishings)

Fusion, aesthetic concept, 287–291

Futurism, 28, 272, 362–363, 386

G

Garden cities, 90–91

Geodesic domes, 432–433

Geometric shapes, 234

Gestalt psychology, 184, 273: aesthetics, 291–296

Golden Section, 272–273

Gothic architecture, 402–403: arches, 425–427; vaults, 428–429

Gothic style, 8, 47, 151–152, 258

Graffiti, 334

Grammar of art (*see* Visual elements)

Graphic art, 61–69

Grattage, 326

Greek art, 39: and formal order, 162–167; human form, 162–164; and mathematics, 164, 167

Greenbelt, 90–91

Grottoes, 378–379

H

Hallucinations, artistic expressions of, 209–214

Handicraft (*see* Crafts)

Happenings, 338–342: and collage, 338–340; future of, 341–342; nature of, 339–340

Highways, 100–103

Homes (*see* Domestic architecture)

Household furnishings, 73, 74, 77, 78, 79, 88 (*see also* Chairs; *and* Industrial design): modern, 74, 77, 83; traditional, 74; Wright and, 77–78

Houses (*see* Domestic architecture)

Hue, 248

Human form in art, 11–16, 162–164: and biomorphic order, 171–174; and geometrical shapes, 239; in Greek art, 162–164; and line, 225–227; and proportion, 273

Humanitarian expressions in art, 43–48

Humor, 33 (*see also* Cartoons; Joyful Art; *and* Satire)

I

Ideological expression in art, 39–48

Illness, depictions in art, 20–24

Illumination: Baroque use of, 243–246; and objective accuracy, 156–157

Illusionism, 216–218: in sculpture, 217–218; and Surrealism, 216–217; use of perspective, 159–161

Image, *defined,* 222

Imitation of nature (*see* Objective accuracy)

Impressionism, 145–147, 151, 177, 251, 302–303, 323, 329, 386: and color, 248

Indirect painting, 316–324: brushwork, 321–322

Industrial design, 119–123 (*see also* Mass production): and Bauhaus, 122–123; chairs as case study, 125–134; crafts, 113–134; and function, 123–125; planned obsolescence, 124–125

Industrial Revolution, 72, 120

Industry: art and, 3; and city planning, 108–112

Information, conveyed through art, 61–69

Intellectual order, as style of art, 168–171

Intensity of color, 248–249

Interior decoration, 77–79, 87–88 (*see also* Household furnishings)

International style of architecture, 75–76, 78–80

Interpretation, as stage in criticism, 477–486: forming an hypothesis, 480–482

Instrumentalism, as critical theory, 463–467

Iron (*see also* Steel): cast, 407–411

Isomorphism, 292–295, 321

J

"Jo" blocks, 118

Johansson blocks, 118

Joyful art, 198–203

Judgment, in criticism, 486–498

K

Keystone, 424

Kinetic sculpture, 385–393: artificially driven, 388; examples of, 390–393; naturally driven, 387–388; types of motion, 388–390

Kirchkoff's Law, 294

L

Landmark preservation, 94

Landscape painting, 8, 50–54

Latin American art, 40–42

Law of Prägnanz, 291, 293, 294, 295

Light, use in art, 240–247: in Baroque art, 243–246; connotations of, 240, 242; in Impressionism, 145–146; in modern art, 54, 246–247; in sculpture, 156–157

Line, 224–233 (*see also* Shape): connotations of 226–227; *defined,* 224; in painting, 227–229, 231–233; in sculpture, 229–231, 359–360; types of, 225–227; uses of, 227–233

Linear mode, 298–299

Literature and art, 6

Local color, 249

Love, depictions in art, 11–16, 21

M

Magic, and death, 17–18

Magic realism, 155

Malls, in city planning, 103–108

Marble, use in sculpture, 350–351

Marriage, depictions in art, 12–16

Mass production: accuracy, 116; assembly line, 118; and city planning, 96; and crafts, 114; duplication, 116; Ford, Henry, 118–119; in gunsmithing, 117–118; Gutenberg, 116–117; interchangeability, 116; le Blanc, 117; origin of, 116–119; principles of, 116–119; and quality, 115; specialization, 116, 118; of steam engine, 117; and war, 116; in watchmaking, 117; Watt, 117; Whitney, 117–118

Material, *defined,* 306

Maternity, depictions in art, 11, 16, 19

Mathematics and art, 164, 167, 272–273

Mediterranean style, 8

Medium, *defined,* 306

Mental illness, artistic expressions of, 20

Metal sculpture, 349–350, 352, 354

Mexican art, 40–42

Mimetic theory of criticism, 482–483

Mobiles, 33, 386–387

Modeling in sculpture, 348–350

Modulor, 95, 272

Monolithic sculpture, 358–362

Monuments, 349: aesthetic response to, 37–38

Morbidity in art, 16–24

Mortality (*see* Death)

Motion, as artistic device, 28, 29

Motion pictures (*see* Cinema)

Multiplicity, as aesthetic category, 301–302

Music and painting, 251, 266

Myths, artistic expression of, 207–209

N

Naturalism, 138 (*see also* Objective accuracy)

Niches, 377–378, 380

Nonobjective art (*see* Abstract art)

O

Objective accuracy: attitude of the artist, 144–152; devices of, 156–161; and emotional detachment, 144–148; focus, 157–159; illusion of reality, 138–139; imitation of reality, 140–144; and Impressionism, 145–147; individual varieties, 153–156; and selection of detail, 149–152; *trompe-l'oeil,* 141, 155–156; use of color, 159; use of illumination, 156–157; use of perspective, 159–161

Oil painting: advantages of, 308–310; discovery of, 308

Op art, 248, 254, 343–344: rhythm in, 269, 271

Open form, 300–301: in sculpture, 358–362

Optical art (*see* Op art)

Order (*see* Formal order)

Organic shapes, 235–240 (*see also* Biomorphic order): in architecture, 236–237; in painting, 237–239; in sculpture, 236

Originality, evaluation of, 491–494

Ornament (*see* Interior decoration)

P

Painterly mode, 298–299

Painting, 308–345: action, 321; and aesthetic order, 177–178; as architecture, 330; "Ash Can School," 45; and assemblage, 333–335; biomorphic order in, 173–175; brushwork, 319–323; caricature, 7–8; chiaroscuro, 240–247; color, 247–254; decalcomania, 326–327; direct technique, 319–324; durability of, 311–316; *éclaboussage,* 327; and economic forces, 313–314; *frottage,* 325–326; *grattage,* 326; illumination in, 243–246; indirect technique, 316–324; landscape painting, 8, 50–54; large-scale, 328–332; light in, 240–247; line in, 227–229, 231–233; oil painting, 308–310; organic shapes in, 237–239; permanence of, 311–316; portraiture, 7–8, 490–491; Surrealist, 210–211; technique, 309–333; as "theatre," 327–328; varnish, 318–319

Paleolithic art (*see* Prehistoric art)

Pendentives, 430–431

Perception: aesthetic, 292; *defined,* 280; phases of, 297–304; Wölfflin's categories, 296–304

Permanence of art, 313–316

Personal functions of art, 4–35: aesthetic expression, 30–35; expressions of death, 16–19; expressions of illness, 19–24; expressions of love, sex, and marriage, 11–16; expressions of spiritual concern, 24–30; psychological expression, 6–9

Personality (*see also* Emotion): and art, 164, 170, 173

Perspective, 159–161

Photographic realism, 139, 241

Photography, 45–46, 66–67, 271, 461

Physical functions of art, 70–134: community design, 89–100, 103–108; crafts, 113–116; *defined,* 70; design of dwellings, 73–89; design of industrial and commercial buildings, 108–112; highway design, 100–103; industrial design, 119–134

Pilotis, 82–83, 420

Planar mode, 299–300

Planning (*see* City planning)

Plastics in sculpture, 348, 352–354, 363, 365

Platonism, 166, 169, 458–459

Plazas in city planning, 103–108

Plywood, 129, 130, 356, 400–401

Political expression in art, 39–48: satire, 55–59

Polymer tempera, 319

Pop art, 61, 335–338: rhythm in, 269; sculpture, 352–353, 370

Portraiture, 7–8, 150, 490–491

Post-and-lintel contruction, 418–421

Pottery, and sculpture, 393–394

Prägnanz, Law of (*see* Law of Prägnanz)

Prehistoric art, 16, 140, 399

Prehistoric industry, 116

Prestressed concrete, 416–417

Propaganda in art, 38

Proportion, 163–164, 272–276: importance of human figure, 273–274

Proximal stimuli, 292, 293, 294, 295

Psychic distance, 284–287

Psychological expression in art, 6–10, 141–144, 150–152, 153–154, 490–491

R

Realism (*see* Objective accuracy)

Recessional mode, 299–300

Reinforced concrete, 413–416

Relative clarity, 302–303

Religious art, 25–26, 167, 463–464: distinguished from spiritual art, 24

Renaissance, 72: architecture, 425; art technique, 316–319

Repoussoir, 160

Residential grouping, 97–100

Revolutionary art, 39–42

Rhythm in design, 267–272: alternating, 269; *defined,* 267; flowing, 270–271; progressive, 269–270; repetitive, 268–269; varieties of, 268

Roads (*see* Highways)

Romanesque architecture, 428

Romanticism: and aesthetic perception, 290; and emotion, 186–190; nature of, 187–190; relation to Expressionism, 20

S

Satire, 55–61: and political expression, 55–59

Scientific fantasy, 214–216

Sculpture, 348–395: abstraction in, 12; and aesthetic order, 178–179; African, 16, 38; assemblage, 365–377; and biomorphic order, 171–173; box sculpture, 377, 380–384; bronze, 349–350, 352, 354; carving, 350–351; casting, 349, 351–354; clay, 351, 353–354; constructivist, 362–365; and crafts, 393–394; Egyptian, 16; evolution of, 358–362; focus in, 157–159; grottoes, 378–379; and illusionism, 217–218; kinetic, 385–393; line in, 229–231, 359–360; marble, 350–351; mobiles, 33, 386–387; modeling, 348–350; monolithic vs. open-form, 358–362; niches, 377–378, 380; organic shapes in, 236; and painting, 310; plastics, 348, 352–354; and pottery, 393–394; and psychological expression, 6–7, 9; replica technique in, 8; as social criticism, 390–393; as social expression, 47; spiritual, 28; and style of objective accuracy, 151–152; Surrealist, 211–212; terra cotta, 352; as "theatre," 327–328; use of light, 156–159, 242–243; wax, 356–357; wood, 354–356

Sex in art, 11–16

Shape, 233–240 (*see also* Line): geometric, 234, 238–239; relation to line, 233–234; organic, 235–240

Shell structures, 432–433

Silhouette, 241

Skyscrapers: design, 413; Le Corbusier's influence, 93–94; and post-and-lintel construction, 420

Social description, 49–54

Social functions of art, 36–69: art as education, 42; humanitarian expressions, 43–48; political and ideological expressions, 39–48; satire, 55–61; social description, 49–54; social response to art, 36–38

Social protest through art, 18–19, 22

Society and art, 2–3, 21

Spandrel, 425

Spiritual concern in art, 24–30 (*see also* Religious art): *defined,* 24; in sculpture, 28

Squinches, 431

Stained glass, 258

Steam engine, 117

Steel, 411–413

Stone, 339, 401–403

Streets (*see* Highways)

Structure of art, 220–221 (*see also* Aesthetics; Design; *and* Visual elements)

Style (*see also individual artists, e.g.,* Albright; *and specific forms, e.g.,* Objective accuracy): cultural power factors and, 164; of emotion, 182–

203; of fantasy, 204–218; of formal order, 162–181; general characteristics, 136–137; and imitation of reality, 140–144; Impressionism, 145–147; of objective accuracy, 140–161; and personality, 164, 170, 173

Subordination in design, 260

Surrealism, 43, 266, 267, 363: biomorphic order and, 174; Chagall, 199; Dali, 210–211; and fantasy, 210–211; and Freudian psychology, 210; illusionism, 216–217; use of perspective, 160; and scientific fantasy, 215; and *trompe l'oeil,* 155

Symmetrical balance, 263

Synchromism, 251

Synthetic Cubism, 252

T

Technique: criticism of, 494–498; *defined,* 306; painting, 309–333

Tectonic form, 300

Television, art in, 67–68

Tempera painting, 312, 317–319

Terra cotta, 352

Theatre: art as, 327–328; Happenings, 341–342

Tonality in color, 250

Town planning (*see* City planning)

Transportation (*see* Highways)

Trompe l'oeil, 144, 155–156: and Surrealism, 155

Trusses, 422–424

U

Unity: aesthetic category, 301–302; and coherence, 260–261; and design, 259–262; dominance, 260; subordination, 260

Utopias as fantasy, 206–207

V

Value of color, 248

Varnish, 318–319

Vaults, 427–429

Ville Radieuse, principles of organization, 93–94, 96

Visual elements, 224–255: color, 247–254; light and dark, 240–247; line, 224–233; shape, 233–240

Visual form, *defined,* 280

Voussoirs, 424

W

War: depicted in art, 47–48, 194, 196–197; and mass production, 116; World War II, 23, 57–58

Wax sculpture, 356–357

"Wild Beasts" (*see* Fauves)

Wood: architecture, 400–401; sculpture, 354–356

Z

Ziggurats, 404